CONNECTIONISM IN PERSPECTIVE

sgaico

swiss group for artificial intelligence and cognitive science

special interest group of the swiss informaticians society

CONNECTIONISM IN PERSPECTIVE

Edited by

Rolf PFEIFER

Computer Science Department
University of Zurich
Switzerland

Zoltan SCHRETER

Sociology Department
(Unit for Conflict Research)
University of Zurich
Switzerland

Françoise FOGELMAN-SOULIÉ

Ecole des Hautes Etudes en Informatique
Laboratoire d'Intelligence Artificielle
Université de Paris V
France

Luc STEELS

Free University of Brussels
AI Lab
Belgium

1989

NORTH-HOLLAND
AMSTERDAM · NEW YORK · OXFORD · TOKYO

ELSEVIER SCIENCE PUBLISHERS B.V.
Sara Burgerhartstraat 25
P.O. Box 211, 1000 AE Amsterdam, The Netherlands

Distributors for the United States and Canada:

ELSEVIER SCIENCE PUBLISHING COMPANY INC.
655 Avenue of the Americas
New York, N.Y. 10010, U.S.A.

ISBN: 0 444 88061 5

Printed in the Netherlands

TABLE OF CONTENTS

PREFACE

The papers in this volume are based on an international conference on "Connectionism in Perspective" which was held at the University of Zurich, Switzerland, 11-13 October 1989. The conference was preceded by a series of tutorials on 10 October. It was jointly organized by the Swiss Group for Artificial Intelligence and Cognitive Science (SGAICO), the Computer Science Department of the University of Zurich, and the Gottlieb Duttweiler Institute. The goal was to promote "Connectionism" in Switzerland, to provide the possibility for interested researchers with no prior exposure to "Connectionism" to get acquainted with it, and to stimulate those already active in the field. An important goal was to not only present the most recent research results, but to criticially evaluate the achievements of "Connectionism" with respect to other disciplines involved in the study of intelligent systems, i.e. *to put "Connectionism" into perspective.* The response we had shows that the idea was appreciated by the research community. Another goal was to demonstrate trends and research programs, which is also reflected in this book.

I would like to take the opportunity to thank a number of people and institutions who made this conference (and this book) possible: Sanjeev Ahuja of Swiss Life (Rentenanstalt), Thomas Bernold of GDI, Françoise Fogelman-Soulié of the University of Paris V, Bernardo Huberman of XEROX PARC, Zoltan Schreter of the University of Zurich, and Luc Steels of the Free University of Brussels for serving on the program committee; Tony Bell, Roland Hübscher, Zoltan Schreter, and Gabi Vogl (all University of Zurich) for their involvement with local organization; all the people involved in running the conference — it is impossible to name them all, assistants, university employees, students, and so forth. I would like to give special thanks to Swiss Life (Rentenanstalt) for very generously supporting the conference, thereby confirming their commitment to basic research and signalling their willingness not only to collaborate with pertinent research institutions, but to make an active contribution. Additional sponsors of the conference were SGAICO, the Swiss National Science Foundation, the City and the Canton of Zurich, and Siemens-Albis AG, Zurich. Last, but not least, I would like to thank all the speakers and contributers for taking part in this event.

The production of this book was only possible because a number of people went through an enormous amount of work, like reviewing, proof-reading, formating, and urging authors to keep their deadlines and furnish the material we asked for in time. I would like to thank the members of the program committe and in particular Tony Bell for reviewing the papers. Special thanks go to Zoltan Schreter who was involved from the very beginning to the final production of the book and who invested an enormous amount of work, and to Roland Hübscher who was heavily involved in the production of the book. Without his efforts and his mastery of Latex we would have never succeeded. I would also like to thank Thomas Rothenfluh and Anne Egli for helping with the preparation of the final manuscript.

Zürich, 6 May 1989 Rolf Pfeifer

CONNECTIONISM IN PERSPECTIVE
R. Pfeifer, Z. Schreter, F. Fogelman-Soulié, L. Steels (Eds.)

Putting Connectionism into Perspective

Rolf Pfeifer[1], Zoltan Schreter[2], Françoise Fogelman-Soulié[3], & Luc Steels[4]
[1]Computer Science Department, University of Zurich, Switzerland
[2]Psychology Department, University of Zurich, Switzerland
[3]EHEI, LIA, Université de Paris V, France
[4]VUB, AI-Lab, Brussels, Belgium

1 INTRODUCTION

For the last couple of years we have been witnesses of an intriguing development in AI and Psychology: Connectionism — doing computation with neural-like networks — experiences a re-awakening.

Connectionism has a long history. Already in the 1940's, McCulloch and Pitts developed ideas about how to implement logical functions with the help of networks of simple units. In the 1950's and beginning of the 1960's connectionism was one of the two main frameworks for doing Artificial Intelligence(AI) research.[1] The other framework was the "symbolic" one. But by the end of the 1960's connectionism had lost most of its institutional support. In the 1970's and the beginning of the 1980's it was considered by many people as a blind alley in AI, only of interest as a curiosity in the history of science. This is indicated by AI textbooks. For example, neither Winston (1984) nor Charniak & McDermott (1985) — two well-known textbooks on AI — contain the words "connectionism", "neural networks" or "perceptron" in their index, or connectionist publications of the authors Frank Rosenblatt, Geoffrey Hinton, Jerome Feldman, Terrence Sejnowski or David Rumelhart in their bibliography.

One of the reasons for the decline of connectionism was presumably the growing availability and power of computers. The symbolic programs were better adapted to them than the connectionist ones: the parallel networks could use the sequential computers only very inefficiently and in very unnatural ways. A second reason for the dominance of symbolicism was that many earlier cognitive theories, particularly from linguistics and logic, have a natural mapping into symbols and symbol manipulation. A third reason was the increasing number of impressive performance programs, starting with game playing, like Samuel's checkers program (Samuel, 1959), and simulations of problem solving (Newell & Simon, 1972), leading to natural language understanding systems (Winograd, 1972) and expert systems such as MYCIN. These programs were written without any attempt to

[1] Interestingly enough, Marvin Minsky—one of the most famous representatives of symbolic Artificial Intelligence and co-author of *Perceptrons*, the book that has played a considerable role in the later extinction of connectionist research—was actually one of the first computer scientists to try to implement connectionist-type architectures and learning at the beginning of the 50's.

simulate the functioning of the human brain directly. A further reason for the failure of connectionism in the first part of its history have been the over-optimistic views of some of its representatives about the capabilities of the network models. The book *Perceptrons* published by Minsky and Papert in 1969 was probably not the catastrophic event for connectionism as it is sometimes described. Its brilliant analyses of the capabilities and limitations of the connectionist networks of the time — mainly two-layered perceptrons — were more like the last nails closing the coffin of connectionism.

Connectionism started to regain momentum around 1981. In that year the book *Parallel Models of Associative Memory* by Geoffrey Hinton and James Anderson as editors, and the first part of the article by James McClelland and David Rumelhart on their "Interactive Activation Model" of word perception appeared (McClelland & Rumelhart, 1981). In 1982 the paper by John Hopfield (Hopfield, 1982) arose a wide interest among physicists: it provided a model which, although not new (work by Little (1974) has already pointed in that direction), established an interesting connection between models in statistical mechanics and models for neural networks.

In 1986, after the appearance of the book *Parallel Distributed Processing*[2] by David Rumelhart and others (Rumelhart et al., 1986) the excitement about connectionism became so great that some people even talk about a paradigm shift in Cognitive Science (see the discussion later in this paper).

Now, why is there so much interest in connectionism again? The answer has to do with the hopes and promises generated by this new approach and proclaimed by its proponents. One of the major reasons for having a conference on "Connectionism in Perspective", and consequently this volume, is to evaluate to what extent these hopes and promises are justified, what some of the new problems are which are introduced by it, and in what ways other approaches or disciplines may have contributions to the study of intelligent systems.

2 HOPES AND PROMISES OF CONNECTIONISM — AND SOME OF ITS PROBLEMS

There is clearly a trend in current Computer Science towards parallel computation. In AI, in particular, it became clear during the 70's that intelligence is based on huge amounts of knowledge. Accessing such knowledge in an AI system—for example during visual recognition in real-time interaction with the environment—would necessitate immense amounts of computation done in a very short time. Connectionist networks with their inherent parallelism might be a good way to implement parallel algorithms and architectures, giving, perhaps, more efficient answers to the speed problem in AI.

In addition to inherent parallelism, properties like graceful degradation, learning, generalization and adaptability, associative and content-addressable memories, rule-like behaviors without explicitely coded rules and schema-like representations as emergent properties, as well as their neuron-like flavor, are typically mentioned when talking about the virtues of connectionism. Structured representations, variable binding, constituency, cross-

[2] Walter Schneider writes about this book: "The sales of the *Parallel Distributed Processing* books have been phenomenal. The books literally sold out (6.000 copies) before they went to press. One wonders if psychology has ever before had a two-volume advanced textbook sell-out."(Schneider, 1987, p. 77)

talk, sequential processing, reasoning, and explainability of behavior are characteristics typically mentioned when talking about problems of connectionism. In order to study these issues systematically, a framework based on Don Norman's "Twelve Issues for Cognitive Science" (Norman, 1980) is used.

Norman is a cognitive psychologist. Because of his frustration with the dominance of the computer metaphor and with the neglect of natural intelligence in Cognitive Science, he proposed a set of issues for the study of intelligent systems, the famous "Twelve Issues": belief systems, consciousness, development, emotion, interaction, language, learning, memory, perception, performance, skill, and thought. For our purposes we modified the framework somewhat and arrived at four broad issues: (1) Knowledge representation and memory, (2) Perception and action, (3) Learning, and (4) Problem solving and reasoning.

Of course, intelligent systems have not only been studied by connectionism, AI and psychology, but also by neuroscience, and by the theory of complex dynamical systems. The basic idea of this volume is to have researchers from these various disciplines discuss the four issues from their perspective. Not only should they report their most recent research, but also put it "into perspective". In other words, they should deal with the relations of their own discipline with connectionism, the contribution of connectionist models to their field and vice versa. They should take issue with the hopes and promises of the connectionist approach, discuss its potential as a computational paradigm — alone, or in combination with other approaches.

2.1 Knowledge Representation and Memory

In contrast to traditional AI and Cognitive Science systems, connectionist models are often considered to be very good for realizing *associative memory* and *content-addressable-memory*. Associative memory means that pairs of items are associated with each other, so that presenting one of the items results in the elicitation of the other. In a content addressable memory several items are associated, so that the presentation of one item — part of the "content" — elicits all the other items — the full "content".

Also, while traditional AI programs typically rely on the von Neumann type computer as hardware (Hillis, 1985), connectionist models are *inherently parallel*. In this respect they are similar to human and animal brains and can — in principle — overcome the famous "100-step-constraint" (Feldman & Ballard, 1982). This constraint can be described as follows: neurons, the basic elements of brains, react much slower than the basic elements of computers — maximally a few 100 times a second. However, the brain is capable of recognizing visual scenes or understanding natural language within around 500 milliseconds — a performance inconceivable for today's computers. If one assumes that a huge number of basic operations are necessary to execute such complex tasks, the assumption of massively parallel operations in the brain is unavoidable. Such parallelism would result in a high fault tolerance and a "graceful degradation" of performance of connectionist memory systems — if they were implemented in hardware. Most current connectionist systems are implemented as simulations on traditional computers, but there is a tendency toward parallel implementations. One such implementation is described in the paper by **Genthner, Hauser, Horner, Lange & Männer**.

In connectionist associative/content-addressable memory models the items are represented by nodes — or collections of nodes — and the associations between them are represented by the connections between the nodes. Many current connectionist models can be seen as realization of such memories. Also, many of the papers in this book — like those by **Le Cun**, **Thorpe & Pouget**, **Bounds**, **Alpaydin & Marchal**, **Herz**, **Linden & Kindermann**, **Linster**, **Schmidhuber**, **Wettler & Rapp** and **de Bollivier & Fogelman-Soulié** — deal with different aspects of connectionist associative memory models.

Although associative memory is certainly an important feature of natural memory systems, it is not the only one. There is, in particular, much *structuredness* in human memory, which is not easily described by a connectionist associative memory system. How could, for example, part-whole relationships or constituency be described in a connectionist model? These and other questions have been thoroughly discussed in a recent paper by Jerry Fodor and Zenon Pylyshyn (Fodor & Pylyshyn, 1988). They conclude that many of the important features of human knowledge representation cannot be adequately described in connectionist models. At most, connectionist models can be used to *implement* symbolicist models of cognition.

A paper dealing with Fodor and Pylyshyn's criticism is the one by **Smolensky**. Smolensky argues against Fodor and Pylyshyn's thesis that realistic knowledge representation in connectionist models is only possible as an implementation of classical architectures in connectionist terms. He shows that connectionist models can very well represent structured knowledge and shows a particular connectionist-type mechanism — tensor product representation — for achieving this. Another perspective on connectionist knowledge representation is taken by **Feldman**. Using partly similar arguments as Fodor and Pylyshyn, he criticises two positions that can be taken in connectionist knowledge representation — the extreme "distributionist" and the extreme "localist". However, his conclusion is different from that of Fodor and Pylyshyn. He thinks that an intermediate type of representation could enable connectionist systems to realistically model human memories.

Language has always been strongly related to the debate on knowledge representation. Two papers dealing with issues related to language from a connectionist perspective are those by **Allen & Riecken**, who discuss problems of reference in questions about "objects" in a microworld and by **Wettler & Rapp**, who present a connectionist system that simulates the lexical aspects of query formation in information retrieval.

2.2 Perception and Action

Another promise of connectionism is that it might lead to better models of perception — particularly "low-level" perception. One important feature of connectionist perceptual systems is that noise in their inputs cause a *"graceful degradation"* of performance — i.e., they are noise-tolerant to a high degree. Another feature is the ability of connectionist systems to *generalize*, i.e., use stored knowledge to understand or categorize inputs never experienced before. An approach which is exploiting and improving this latter capacity in a particular type of connectionist model is described in the paper by **Le Cun** on generalization and network design strategies.

This volume contains several papers in which the feasibility of using connectionist systems to model human and animal perception is shown. **Thorpe & Pouget** demonstrate how a network can account for orientation coding by the visual cortex. **Martinetz, Ritter & Schulten**'s paper deals with the simulation of the bat's auditory cortex by a particular kind of connectionist model — the self-organizing topological map. **Herz** shows how a Hopfield-type network can deal with spatio-temporal object recognition.

On the critical side, **Thorpe & Imbert** demonstrate some psychological and physiological constraints on the human brain architecture. In particular, they show that much high-level perception must be achieved in the brain by networks containing feedforward connections only. This makes the physiological validity of a class of network models for human pattern recognition, which rely on recurrent connections (like the "Interactive Activation Model"; McClelland & Rumelhart, 1981), questionable. In a second section they describe biological constraints on learning mechanisms in the brain. **Peters, Frauenfelder & Wittenburg** describe limitations of the psychological validity of a connectionist model — TRACE — for auditory word perception. One other critical paper is that by **Chen.** Using data from psychological experiments, he shows that one type of argument against Minsky and Papert's *Perceptrons* — "Not only perceptrons have problems with recognizing (e.g.) connectedness, but people as well" — might not be valid. That is, people seem to be really better at such tasks than perceptrons with one modifiable connection layer.

Other fields with high hopes for connectionism are robotics and sensory-motor integration. Connectionist networks are expected to smoothly map perception into action, to learn these mappings through experience, to exhibit noise tolerant perception, and to generalize appropriately. **Morasso, Mussa Ivaldi, Vercelli & Zaccaria** 's paper describes a framework for motor plan representation. Although the nodes in their network are more complex than nodes in usual connectionist networks, their system has still the "flavor" of a connectionist model: it is highly parallel, without a central interpreter. One difficult task for a free-moving robot is finding its way in a complex environment. **Prassler** describes a connectionist approach to such path-finding tasks.

One interesting realization of sensory-motor integration in a connectionist system is described in the paper by **Kuperstein & Rubinstein.** Their system is based on the sensory-motor learning theory by Piaget. The connectionist network constitutes the "nervous system" of a robot which learns how to grasp objects put in front of it, without any information about the geometry of the physical sensory-motor system.

One intriguing question for connectionism is the following: What is actually "neural" in connectionist models? What do, for example, the nodes and connections represent? Not many people think that they describe neurons and synapses, but then *what* do they describe? For **Reeke, Sporns & Edelman** the structure and the components of most connectionist models are far too simple to represent anything interesting in real brains. Their network model, called DARWIN III, realizes sensory-motor integration and learning in a way that is an implementation of the evolutionary, "selectionist" theory of the authors on such processes in real nervous systems. Consequently, it is a highly complex structure containing many different types of nodes.

On the application side, connectionist systems for perceptual pattern recognition and categorization — e.g. in vision and auditory perception — have potentially a great importance. **Wellekens** applies a connectionist framework to speech recognition. **Bridle** is also concerned with speech processing. He reviews knowledge intensive approaches, hidden markov models and connectionist models and compares their virtues. Among the three approaches, hidden markov models seem to perform currently the best. Bridle comes, however, to the conclusion that "hybrid" sytems, containing elements of hidden markov models and of connectionist ones might be the best final solution. **Vercauteren, Vingerhoeds, Lee & Boullart** are also concerned with auditory pattern recognition. They describe a complex expert system for the diagnosis of automobile engine malfunctioning, which contains two neural network modules. The system learns to recognise and to discriminate the noise patterns of properly and improperly functioning engine parts. Another application is the system of **Alpaydin & Marchal**, SNARK. It is a system for optical character recognition and is based on the results of experiments with several types of connectionist networks. **De Bollivier & Fogelman-Soulié** describe several projects for building connectionist systems for signal, speech and image processing. They show that very good results can be achieved, for example in the case of speech processing, even with multiple speakers.

2.3 Learning

Consider the following description of what intelligence is, found in the *Encyclopedia of Artificial Intelligence* : "The key concept of ... most ... definitions regards adaptation of the individual to the demands of the environment."(Shapiro, 1987)

In spite of the importance of adaptation and learning for intelligent systems, "Machine Learning" does not seem to have played a correspondingly central role in AI. It is just one subfield among others, and many traditional AI programs are built by direct programming, instead of by learning. In contrast, connectionist models are not only supposed to be very well suited for learning from experience, but, in fact, adaptability and learning are a necessity in connectionist systems. It is normally impossible to determine all the weights in a network in an a priori manner, especially if there are many connections. This is why most connectionist models contain learning algorithms.

Naturally, a learning rule can enable the network to learn only those things which the network in principle has the capability to do. For example, there are many interesting possible mappings between an input and an output layer of nodes which a network containing only one layer of modifiable connections simply cannot achieve. One of the major achievements of connectionism in the 80's has been the discovery of learning rules — like the "backpropagation" rule — which are applicable in networks with multiple layers of modifiable connections.

Linster's paper shows how a two-layer network can build up — using backpropagation — a hierarchical representation for rhythm patterns. It also demonstrates the ability of such networks to generalize: a network that has learned to analyze rhythm in Mozart's music, can do the same successfully with regard to the music of other composers of the same period — but not for jazz.

One problem with such learning rules is speed. They often need the presentation of the inputs hundreds of times. Although this seems to be an inherent problem of adjusting systems with such a high number of parameters, there are remedies, and the papers of **Le Cun** and of **Schmidhuber** ("Accelerated Learning in Back-Propagation Nets") describe methods for speeding up backpropagation learning in multi-layer networks. **Linden & Kindermann**'s paper deals with improvements of the backpropagation algorithm, too. These authors propose to extend backpropagation to symmetric weights which would make the network trainable on constraint satisfaction tasks.

Connectionist learning can also be improved using ideas from various other fields. **Mühlenbein & Kindermann** try to unite models of evolution with connectionist models. They extend the scope of connectionist learning — which deals with individual networks — to whole populations of networks. They study so-called genetic neural networks and apply them to a number of problems which are known to be very hard not only for traditional systems but also for "plain" connectionist networks. **Schmidhuber** ("The Neural Bucket Brigade") describes how a particular learning rule for classifier systems — the "bucket brigade" algorithm — can be incorporated into a connectionist framework.

Another problem has already been pointed out: the questionable physiological validity of some connectionist assumptions. For example, the backpropagation learning rule has been frequently criticized as physiologically implausible. But there are other learning rules which seem to be more physiologically realistic. The article by **Granger, Ambros-Ingerson, Whitson, Staubli & Lynch** describes a network simulation of the rabbit olfactory cortex, in which the use of a competitive-type learning rule resulted in hierarchical concept (odor) representations of a particularly interesting type: concepts from different levels of the hierarchy can be recalled depending on the temporal relationships of the recall operations (sniffs).

One other criticism against connectionist learning concerns the fact that such learning in most cases means just building associative memories. But, as already pointed out earlier, more complex — structured — memory representations are important as well. "Machine Learning" has dealt with learning such representations in traditional AI systems for a long time. One of the representatives of this research field, **Kodratoff**, describes his views on the virtues of machine learning as opposed to connectionist learning. He argues that one of the most important features of traditional AI is that its programs can be explained in natural ways, whereas connectionist models — which essentially only manipulate numbers — cannot be explained adequately. Certainly, the capability for explanation is a challange for future research on connectionist systems. **Smolensky**'s paper is relevant to the issue of learning structured representations as well. He shows how such representations can be built up in a particular type of connectionist network.

2.4 Problem Solving and Reasoning

Problem solving and reasoning are the traditional domains of symbolic Artificial Intelligence. Prototypical examples are, of course, expert systems. Although there are a few examples of connectionist systems in which traditional types of reasoning are implemented (see **Kurfess & Reich** for a discussion in this volume), reasoning is still a very much unexplored field for connectionism. On the other hand, some critics, such as Dreyfus & Dreyfus (1986) have argued that certain types of problem solving do not involve many sequential inferences. Instead, the perception of a problem situation is followed immediately by the recall of a solution to the problem. In their opinion, expert problem solving functions in such a one-shot manner. This kind of associative problem solving can be easily implemented in connectionist networks. Also, one promise of connectionism is that it might help in overcoming the well-known "Feigenbaum-bottleneck" — or knowledge acquisition bottleneck — for expert systems. One paper exploring these possibilities of connectionist modelling is that by **Bounds.** He compares connectionist and traditional expert systems and gives an outline of the advantages and limitations of both approaches. In another paper, **Ahuja & Soh** describe their approach to learning and doing diagnostic reasoning based on an interactive-type connectionist network with recurrent connections.

The problems of connectionist reasoning and expert systems are described by **Steels** from an AI perspective. He points out that, in contrast to the above opinion of Dreyfus & Dreyfus (1986), although problem solving through classification is one type of expert reasoning, other types of reasoning based on more complex problem solving methods also occur. In his view, there are two different types of problem solving: behavior-based (like locomotion, perception and speech) and knowledge-based (like configuring a computer system, medical diagnosis and common sense reasoning). The latter — in contrast to the former — involves volition, deliberation and choice. The natural domain of connectionism is behavior-based problem solving, while traditional methods seem to be much better at knowledge-based problem solving. **Rosenbloom** argues in his paper — also from an AI perspective — that connectionism has a long way to go if it is to achieve only a fraction of the capabilities of traditional goal-oriented systems — but he sees no in-principle barriers for connectionism to get there eventually. He ends with a speculation on what a connectionist learning and problem solving model would look like. **Serra** and **Compiano, Montanari, Serra & Simonini** take a comparative view, too. They contrast the connectionist approach to reasoning and to expert systems with the approach of another type of parallel complex dynamical models, classifier systems.

If both connectionist and traditional AI systems have advantages — as, for example, Steels points out — then why should it not be possible to build models which contain both connectionist and traditional modules, using each of them for the tasks they are best suited for? This "hybrid systems" approach is taken by **Hendler**. The diagnostic expert system of **Vercauteren, Vingerhoeds, Lee & Boullart** — mentioned above — also contains interacting symbolic and neural network modules.

Given all this new research on connectionism — and the many new questions, problems and methods generated by it — the question naturally arises whether connectionism can be considered a new paradigm for AI and Cognitive Science.

3 CONNECTIONISM: IS IT A NEW PARADIGM?

Walter Schneider, an eminent cognitive psychologist who is well-known for his work on information processing psychology, suggests that connectionism may be the largest paradigm shift that most psychologists will see during their careers (Schneider, 1987).

In his view, connectionism qualifies as a paradigm shift in psychology because the following features of a paradigm shift, as defined by Kuhn, are present in the current situtation: (1) A loosening of rules for "normal" research, i.e., an eclectic use of different types of models (like production systems, semantic networks, box models); (2) anomalies, i.e., chronic difficulties in normal science to deal with certain research problems (like the problem of learning from experience and the problem of obviously rule-following behavior without the ability to specify the rules); (3) the emergence of a new point of view (like connectionism) which provides the hope to go forward; (4) a "large but never complete overlap between the problems that can be solved by the old and the new paradigm."(Kuhn, 1970, p.85)

According to Schneider there are additional points in favor of this view, namely the exposure of new issues by connectionist research and its substantial social and political impact. Some new issues are: the hidden units problem and learning rules (e.g., how many layers should a particular network have and what learning rule should be used?), the problem of the use of teachers in learning (error-correcting vs. self-organized learning), and the problem of how to sequence the learning process (in what order should the examples be presented?).

Even if connectionism is a new paradigm for *Psychology* (which has an overlap with Cognitive Science), it does not mean that it is a new paradigm for *Artificial Intelligence* (which is part of Cognitive Science). Margaret Boden, a psychologist and philosopher, and a well-known analyst of developments in AI, argued in her opening lecture at the conference that, although connectionism is an important development, it is not a new paradigm for AI. According to Kuhn, an important feature of paradigms has to do with *incommensurability:* somebody working in one paradigm is not just giving different answers to the questions than someone working in another, but the two are asking utterly different questions. The degree of incommensurability is such that people from different paradigms cannot even communicate. But in the case of connectionism and GOFAI ("Good Old Fashioned AI"), Boden argues, the situation is different: They both have their origins in the seminal contributions by John von Neumann *and* McCulloch and Pitts. Moreover, they both see the mind as a representational and computational system, and there is no doubt that they can communicate, compare each other's results, even combine each other's approaches (and make "hybrid systems", like e.g., **Hendler**; see also the paper by **Steels** in this volume).

Perhaps it is not so important to decide whether connectionism is a new paradigm or not. It is probably better to leave the decision about this question to future historians of science who will look at the current developments from a different perspective. The future of connectionism will depend on its ability to realize the hopes and promises of its advocates and to give good solutions to the notorious problems that "GOFAI" has struggled with so long.

The results already achieved give rise to hopes that connectionist techniques could eventually lead to important breakthroughs in a variety of applications, ranging from image and speech recognition to sophisticated engineering tasks. In the US, DARPA has founded a study which was aimed at gathering facts and figures for the evaluation of the technological potential of the neural network field. As a result, DARPA will provide $33 million over the next 28 months for financing connectionist projects. DARPA will be followed by other granting agencies in the US as well as in Europe (ESPRIT, BRAIN) and in Japan. Not surprisingly, this massive financial support is paralleled by rapid developments in the research community: new scientific journals (like Neural Networks, Connection Science and Neural Computation) are established and annual conferences (like the IEEE International Conference on Neural Networks or the Meeting of the International Neural Network Society) are organized attracting thousands of participants. New teams are popping up everywhere, in universities, research centers and companies. The work of some of these teams is described in the papers by **Chadwick**, **de Bollivier & Fogelman-Soulié** and **Personnaz**,

Johannet & Dreyfus. Additional work in progress is described by **Brauer, Freksa & the AI/Cognition Group, Dorffner, Gehm, Hernández, Krasznai, Rihs-Middel** and **Van Loocke.** In order to promote connectionist/neural network research in Switzerland the neuro-informatics initiative (described in the paper of **Hepp**) was launched jointly by the University of Zürich and the Swiss Federal Institute of Technology (ETH-Z). We also hope that the present volume represents a contribution to this effect.

REFERENCES

Charniak, E. & McDermott, D. (1985). *Introduction to Artificial Intelligence.* Reading, MA: Addison-Wesley.

Dreyfus, H.L. & Dreyfus, S.E. (1986). *Mind over machine.* New York: The Free Press.

Feldman, J.A. & Ballard, D. (1982). Connectionist models and their properties. *Cognitive Science,* **6**, 205 - 254.

Fodor, J.A., & Pylyshyn, Z.W. (1988). Connectionism and cognitive architecture: A critical analysis. *Cognition,* **28**, 3-71.

Hillis, D. (1985). *The Connection Machine.* Cambridge, MA: The MIT Press.

Hinton, G. E. & Anderson, J. A. (1981). *Parallel models of associative memory.* Hillsdale, NJ: Lawrence Erlbaum.

Hopfield, J.J. (1982). Neural networks and physical systems with emergent collective computational abilities. *Proc. Nat. Acad. Sci. USA,* **79**, 2554-2558.

Kuhn, T.S. (1970).*The structure of scientific revolutions.* Chicago: University of Chicago Press.

Little, W.A. (1974). The existence of persistent states in the brain. *Math. Biosci.,* **19**, 101-120.

McClelland, J.L., & Rumelhart, D.E. (1981). An interactive model of context effects in letter perception: Part 1. An account of basic findings. *Psychological Review,* **88**, 375-407.

McClelland, J.L., Rumelhart, D.E., and the PDP Research Group (1986). *Parallel Distributed Processing.Volume 2: Psychological and Biological Models.* Cambridge, MA: MIT-Press.

Minsky, M., & Papert, S. (1969). *Perceptrons.* Cambridge, MA: The MIT Press.

Newell, A. & Simon, H. (1972). *Human Problem Solving.* Englewood Cliffs, NJ: Prentice-Hall.

Norman, D. (1980). Twelve issues for Cognitive Science. *Cognitive Science,* **4**, 1-32

Rumelhart, D.E., McClelland, J.L. and the PDP Research Group (1986). *Parallel Distributed Processing.Volume 1: Foundations.* Cambridge, MA: MIT-Press.

Samuel, A.L. (1959). Some studies in machine learning using the game of checkers. *IBM Journal of Research and Development,* **3**, 386 - 407.

Schneider, W. (1987). Connectionism: Is it a paradigm shift for psychology? *Behavior Research Methods, Instruments & Computers,* **19**, (2), 73 - 83.

Shapiro, S.C.(Ed.) (1987). *Encyclopedia of Artificial Intelligence.* New York: Wiley.

Winograd, T. (1972). *Understanding natural language*. New York: Academic Press.

Winston, P.H. (1984). *Artificial Intelligence*. Reading, MA: Addison-Wesley.

KNOWLEDGE REPRESENTATION AND MEMORY

CONNECTIONISM IN PERSPECTIVE
R. Pfeifer, Z. Schreter, F. Fogelman-Soulié, L. Steels (Eds.)

Connectionism and Constituent Structure

Paul Smolensky

Department of Computer Science & Institute of Cognitive Science
University of Colorado at Boulder

Abstract—*In their paper, "Connectionism and Cognitive Architecture," Fodor and Pylyshyn (1988) argue that connectionism cannot offer a cognitive architecture that is both viable and different from the Classical language of thought architecture: if it differs from the Classical architecture it is because it reinstantiates simple associationism, and is therefore not a viable candidate; if it is viable, it is because it implements the Classical view and therefore does not offer a new cognitive architecture—just a new implementation of the old one. It is my purpose here to expose the false dichotomy in this argument, to show that the space of connectionist cognitive architectures is much richer than this simple dichotomy presumes, and that in this space is a large region of architectures that are implementations neither of a Classical architecture nor of a simple associationist architecture; these architectures provide structured mental representations and structure-sensitive processes in a truly non-Classical way.*

Keywords—Connectionism, symbolic and subsymbolic knowledge representation, variable binding, tensor product representation, language of thought, constituency structure

This rebuttal of Fodor and Pylyshyn's argument [see abstract] will take the following form. In Section 1, I make a number of general remarks about connectionism, Fodor and Pylyshyn's argumentation, and the abuse of the term "implementation." In Section 2, I focus on the crux of their argument, which turns on the compositional structure of mental states. I develop in some detail the argument that, unlike simple associationist models, connectionist models using *distributed representations* can embody compositionality at the same time as providing a new cognitive architecture that is not an implementation of a Classical language of thought. In Section 3, I bring together the more technical discussion of Section 2 back in contact with the more general issues raised in Section 1. I argue that the debate surrounding compositionality illustrates the general point that by finding new formal instantiations of basic computation notions in the category of continuous mathematics, connectionism can open up genuinely new and powerful accounts of computation and cognition that go well beyond the limited progress that can be afforded by the kind of implementationalist strategy that Fodor and Pylyshyn advocate.

1 GENERAL REMARKS

1.1 In-principle arguments

It is worth stating up front that, in my opinion, the highly general, *negative*, in-principle arguments one finds on the issue of cognitive architecture—like that of Fodor & Pylyshyn (1988; henceforth, F&P)—are stimulating and useful but quite inconclusive; this is as true of anti-Classical arguments as it is of anti-connectionist arguments. On the other hand, *positive* in-principle arguments can serve the valuable role of showing how to conceive of previously inconceivable accounts; they serve as programmatic statements of research agenda. It was in this spirit, for example, that Smolensky (1988a) was written; it was intended not as an in-principle attack on the Classical view but as a positive in-principle argument for a fairly comprehensive connectionist framework for cognitive science.

This issue of negative vs. positive in-principle arguments bears strongly on Section Four of F&P, which proceeds basically on the following plan:

(1) a. Collect many positive arguments for connectionism.
b. Present them as negative in-principle arguments against the Classical account.
c. Show that, as negative arguments, they don't hold up.

It is interesting to note the shift from an offensive to a defensive posture here. Whereas arguments from advocates of the Classical view used to be of the form, "the trouble with connectionism is that it can't do X," increasingly we now hear arguments of the form "well, Classical architectures can do X too." In Section Four, F&P offer us about a dozen defensive arguments of just this form, where X ranges from graceful degradation and massive parallelism to inexplicit rules and soft constraint satisfaction.

The moral seems to be that arguments of the form "formalism Y can't do X" are sometimes provocative but, at least when Y is a general, powerful formalism like symbolic or connectionist computation, such arguments are almost virtually sure to fail. Arguments standing a chance of surviving that concern such features as massive parallelism, soft constraints, and neural plausibility, must be positive arguments that connectionism achieves these particularly well, not negative arguments that the symbolic approach can't achieve them at all.

1.2 The argument structure

In their offensive attack, F&P follow an argument structure frequently used in attacks on connectionism:

(2) a. Propose a simplistic representation and process.
b. Claim this is what connectionism advocates.
c. Point out the inadequacies of the proposal.
d. Claim that any improvement requires abandoning connectionist commitments, and turns the proposal into a "Classical account" or an "implementation" of one.

This argument can be made rather cheaply through three tricks:

(3) a. Make the proposed representation and process as simple-minded as possible.
b. Bloat the territory covered by the term "Classical account" as much as possible.
c. Bloat the relations covered by the term "implementation" as much as possible.

Each of these tricks are used in good measure by F&P, as by other critics of connectionism, and in this response I will have to call them on all three accounts.

For F&P, the straw man required for step (2a) is provided, of course, by simple associationism. In order to expose F&P's trivialization of the real issue, I will argue

(4) a. that the true commitment of connectionism is not to simple associationism, but to something else that can be clearly distinguished from that to which the Classical view is committed;
b. that this less simple-minded view of connectionism provides for ways of instantiating the compositional structure of mental states; and
c. that these connectionist instantiations of compositionality do not all reduce to "an implementation of the Classical view," and in fact offer a new candidate for the cognitive architecture.

1.3 The true commitment of connectionism: PTC version

In this paper I adopt a view of connectionism that was presented and discussed at some length in Smolensky (1988a,b), a view I call PTC (for the Proper Treatment of Connectionism). Oversimplifying a bit, according to PTC, the true commitment of connectionism is to a very general formalism for describing mental representations and mental processes. The Classical view is of course committed to the hypothesis that mental representations are elements of a *symbol system*, and that mental processes consist of symbol manipulation operations. PTC is committed to the hypothesis that mental representations are *vectors* partially specifying the state of a dynamical system (the activities of units in a connectionist network), and that mental processes are specified by the differential equations governing the evolution of that dynamical system.

The main point is this: under the influence of the Classical view, computation and cognition have been studied almost exclusively under the umbrella of discrete mathematics; the connectionist approach, on the other hand, brings the study of computation and cognition squarely in contact with the other half of mathematics—continuous mathematics. The true commitment, according to PTC, is to uncovering the insights this other half of mathematics can provide us into the nature of computation and cognition.

On this account, simple associationism is a particularly impoverished and impotent corner of the connectionist universe. It may well be that the attraction a number of people feel to connectionism is an attraction to neo-associationism; but it is nonetheless a serious mistake to presume connectionism to be committed to simple associationist principles. To equate connectionism with simple associationism is no more appropriate than equating Classical symbolic theory with Aristotelean logic. (The temptation Fodor may provide his readers notwithstanding, I don't recommend the second identification any more than the first.)

In fact, the comparison with Aristotle is not wholly inappropriate. Our current understanding of the power of connectionist computation might well be compared with Aristotle's understanding of symbolic computation; before connectionism can take really serious shots at cognitive modeling, we probably have at least as far to go in developing connectionist computation as symbolic computation had to go between Aristotle and Turing. In giving up symbolic computation to undertake connectionist modeling, we connectionists have taken out an enormous loan, on which we are still paying nearly all interest: solving the basic problems we have created for ourselves rather than solving the problems of cognition. In my view, the loan is worth taking out for the goal of understanding how symbolic computation, or approximations to it, can emerge from numerical computation in a class of dynamical systems sharing the most general characteristics of neural computation.

Under this characterization of the commitments of the Classical and connectionist approach, to claim, as F&P explicitly do, that any cognitive architecture that incorporates structured mental representations and processes sensitive to that structure is a Classical Architecture, is to bloat the notion of "Classical Architecture" to an unacceptable degree—in accord with (3b).

1.4 Implementation vs. refinement

The bottom line of F&P can be paraphrased as follows. "*Standard* connectionism is just simple associationism wrapped in new jargon, and as such, is fatally flawed. Connectionists should pursue instead a *nonstandard* connectionism, embracing the principles of compositionality and structure-sensitive processing: they should accept the Classical view and should design their nets to be implementations of Classical architectures." Behind this moral is the assumption that connectionist models with compositionally structured representations must necessarily be implementations of a Classical architecture; it will be my major purpose to show that this is false. The connectionist systems I will advocate hypothesize models that are not an *implementation* but rather a *refinement* of the Classical symbolic approach; these connectionist models hypothesize a truly different cognitive architecture, to which the Classical architecture is a scientifically important approximation. The reader may suspect that I will be splitting hairs and that the difference between "implementation" and "refinement" will be of no philosophical significance. But in fact the new cognitive architecture I will hypothesize lacks the most crucial property of Fodor & Pylyshyn's Classical architecture: mental representations and mental processes are not supported by the same formal entities—there are no "symbols" that can do both jobs.[1] The new cognitive architecture is fundamentally two-level: formal, algorithmic specification of processing mechanisms, on the one hand, and semantic interpretation, on the other, must be done at two different levels of description.

Bloating "implementation"

There is a sense of "implementation" that cognitive science has inherited from computer science, and I propose that we use it. If there is an account of a computational system at one level and an account at a lower level, then the lower one is an *implementation* of the higher one if and only if the higher description is a complete, precise, algorithmic account of the behavior of that system. It is *not* sufficient that the higher-level account provide some sort of rough summary of the interactions at the lower level. It is *not* sufficient that the lower-level account involves some of the same basic ideas of how the problem is to

[1] This point is brought out nicely in Cummins and Schwarz (1987), Schwarz (1987), and Cummins (1988).

be solved (for example, a decomposition of the problem into subproblems). Such weak usages of "implementation" abound in the literature, particularly in the numerous attempts to dismiss connectionism as "mere implementation"—following (3c). But in its correct usage, *implementation* requires that the higher-level account provide an exact, precise, algorithmic account of the system's behavior.

It's important to see that, unless this definition of implementation is adopted, it is impossible to legitimately argue to F&P's ultimate conclusion: as long as connectionists are doing implementation, they're not going to provide a new cognitive architecture. If it is shown only that connectionism "implements" the Classical Architecture under a looser definition of the term, then the conclusion that follows is that the Classical account provides a rough, higher-level approximation to the connectionist account, or involves some of the same basic ideas about how information is represented and processed. This is a *much weaker* conclusion than what F&P are after. They want the conclusion that only true implementation will license: since the Classical account provides a complete, precise, algorithmic account of the cognitive system, there is nothing to be gained by going to the lower level account, as long as the phenomena of interest can be seen at the higher level; and, of course, it is exactly those phenomena that the Classicist will count as "truly cognitive." To account for intrinsically lower-level phenomena—in which category the Classicist will certainly include neural phenomena and may also include certain perceptual/motor phenomena—the Classicist will acknowledge the need to condescend to a lower level account; but within the domain of "pure cognition," Classicists won't need to get their hands so dirty. These are the sorts of conclusions that Classicists have pushed for decades on the basis of analogies to higher- and lower-level computer languages. But of course these languages, by *design*, satisfy the *correct* definition of implementation; none of these conclusions follow from weaker definitions, and none follow from the connectionist position I defend here. Far from the conclusion that "*nothing* can be gained from going to the lower level account," there is *plenty* to be gained: completeness, precision, and algorithmic accounts of processing, none of which are in general available at the higher level, according to PTC.

Since F&P's conclusions cannot be licensed under any definition of "implementation" weaker than the correct one, it is that one I will use. I will show that distributed connectionism can, without implementing the Classical architecture, meet the basic demands F&P have outlined for a cognitive architecture. To repeat, then:

(5) X is implemented by Y if and only if X provides a complete, precise algorithmic higher-level account of the system described at a lower level by Y.

Alternatively, in place of the word "algorithmic" I often use "formal" to avoid the discrete, sequential connotations the former term can carry.

A two-level cognitive architecture

To see how the distributed connectionist architecture differs fundamentally from the Classical one—fails to provide an "implementation" using the correct definition of the term—I will now sketch how the connectionist architecture is intrinsically split over two levels of description. We'll consider the purest case: distributed connectionist models having the following two properties:

(6) a. Interpretation can be assigned to large-scale activity patterns but not to individual units;

b. The dynamics governing the interaction of individual units is sufficiently complex that the algorithm defining the interactions of individual units cannot be translated into a tractably-specified algorithm for the interaction of whole patterns.[2]

As a result of these two properties, we can see that there are two levels of analysis with very different characteristics. At the lower level, where the state variables are the activities of individual units, the processing is described by a complete, precise, and formal algorithm, but semantic interpretation cannot be done. At the higher level, where the system's state is described in terms of the presence of certain large-scale patterns, semantic interpretation can be done, but now complete, precise algorithms for the processing cannot be stated. As I have characterized this in Smolensky (1988a), the *syntax* or processing algorithm strictly resides at the lower level, while the semantics strictly resides at the upper level. Since both the "syntax" and the *semantics* are essential to the cognitive architecture, we have an intrinsically split-level cognitive architecture here: There is no account of the architecture in which the same elements carry both the syntax and the semantics. Thus we have a fundamentally new candidate for the cognitive architecture which is simply *not* an implementation of the Classical one.

Note that the conclusions of this section depend crucially on the assumption (6a) that connectionist representations are *distributed* (when viewed at the level of individual units, the level at which processing algorithms can be identified (6b)). Thus, while F&P and others may attempt to give the impression that the issue of local vs. distributed representations is a little technical squabble between connectionists of no philosophical consequence, I believe this to be profound mistake. Distributed representations, when combined with (6b), entail that in the connectionist cognitive architecture, mental representations bear a fundamentally different relation to mental processes than is true in the Classical account. I will return to this crucial point in Section 3.

1.5 Summary

As indicated in Sections 1.3 and 1.4, I am arguing that what the Classical/connectionist debate should really be about is

(7) a. whether mental representations and processes are to be formally described by symbol systems, within the category of discrete mathematics; and

b. whether in the cognitive architecture the semantics of mental representation and the algorithms of mental processes both derive from the same formal entities and reside at a single level of description.

If this is correct, then any attempt to cast the connectionist position as either being defined by a commitment to simple associationism or as "merely implementing" the Classical Architecture must rely on oversimplifying the true commitment of connectionism, or to bloating either the terms "Classical Architecture" or "implementation" to a truly misleading and unacceptable degree. F&P have made all three of these moves.

[2]The complexity criterion here is very low: the interactions should be more complex than purely linear. A lengthy and hopefully accessible discussion may be found in Smolensky, 1986.

2 COMPOSITIONALITY AND DISTRIBUTED CONNECTIONIST REPRESENTATIONS

In this section I consider the crux of F&P's argument, and argue that distributed connectionist architectures, without implementing the Classical architecture, can nontheless provide structured mental representations and mental processes sensitive to that structure.

2.1 The ultralocal case

Here is a quick summary of what I take to be the central argument of F&P.

(8) a. Thoughts have composite structure.

By this they mean things like: the thought that *John loves the girl* is not atomic; it's a composite mental state built out of thoughts about *John, loves*, and *the girl*.

(8) b. Mental processes are sensitive to this composite structure.

For example, from any thought of the form p & q—regardless of what p and q are—we can deduce p.

F&P elevate (8) to the status of defining the Classical View of Cognition, and claim that this is what is being challenged by connectionism. I am arguing that this is wrong, but for now we continue with F&P's argument.

Having identified claims (8) as definitive of the Classical View, F&P go on to argue that there are compelling arguments for these claims.[3] According to these arguments, mental states have the properties of productivity, systematicity, compositionality, and inferential coherence. Without going into all these arguments, let me simply state that for present purposes I'm willing to accept that they are convincing enough to justify the conclusion that (8) must be taken quite seriously.

Now for F&P's analysis of connectionism. They assert that in (standard) connectionism, all representations are atomic; mental states have no composite structure, violating (8a). Furthermore, they assert, (standard) connectionist processing is association which is sensitive only to *statistics*, not to *structure*—in violation of (8b). Therefore, they conclude, (standard) connectionism is maximally non-Classical: it violates both the defining principles. Therefore connectionism is defeated by the compelling arguments in favor of the Classical View.

What makes F&P say that connectionist representations are atomic? The second figure of their paper (p. 16) says it all—it is rendered here as Figure 1. This network is supposed to illustrate the standard connectionist account of the inference from A & B to A and to B. It is true that Ballard and Hayes wrote a paper (Ballard & Hayes, 1984; also Ballard, 1986) about using connectionist networks to do automated resolution theorem proving in which networks like this appear. However it is a serious mistake to view this as the paradigmatic connectionist account for anything like human inferences of this sort. This kind of *ultralocal* connectionist representation, in which entire propositions are represented by individual nodes, is far from typical of connectionist models, and certainly not to be taken as *definitive* of the connectionist approach.

[3] They admit up front that these arguments are a rerun updated for the 80's, a colorized version of a film that was shown in black and white some time ago—where the color comes mainly from replacing everywhere the word "behaviorism" by "connectionism."

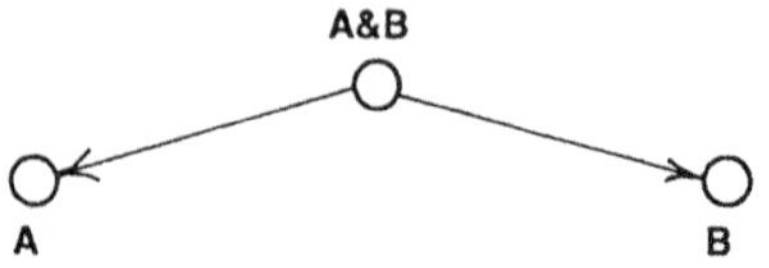

Figure 1: Fodor & Pylyshyn's network

A central claim in my response to F&P is that any critique of the connectionist approach must consider the consequences of using distributed representations, in which the representation of high level conceptual entities such as propositions are distributed over many nodes, and the same nodes simultaneously participate in the representation of many entities. Their response, in Section 2.1.3, (p. 19) is as follows. The distributed/local representation issue concerns (they assume) whether each of the nodes in Figure 1 refers to something complicated and lower level (the distributed case) or not (the local case). But, they claim, this issue is irrelevant, because it pertains to a *between-level* issue, and the compositionality of mental states is a *within-level* issue.

My response is that they are correct that compositionality is a within-level issue, and correct that the distributed/local distinction is a between-level issue. Their argument presumes that because of this difference, one issue cannot influence the other. But that is a fallacy. It assumes that the between-level relation in distributed representations can not have any consequences on the within-level structure of the relationships between the representations of A & B and the representation of A. And that's simply false. There are profound implications of distributed representations for compositionality; these are the subject of all of Section 2 of this paper. In particular, it will turn out that Figure 1 is exactly as relevant to a distributed connectionist account of inference as it is to a symbolic account. In the ultralocal case, Figure 1 is relevant and their critique stands; in the distributed case, Figure 1 is a bogus characterization of the connectionist account and their critique completely misses its target. It will further turn out that a valid analysis of the actual distributed case, based on suggestions of Pylyshyn himself, leads to quite the opposite conclusion: connectionist models using distributed representations describe mental states with a relevant kind of (within-level) constituent structure. The rather weak sense of constituent structure in generic distributed representations, identified in Section 2.2, will be made much stronger in explicitly designed distributed representations, discussed in Section 2.3, in which constituents can fill varying structural roles.

2.2 The distributed (weakly compositional) case

For now, the goal is to show that generic connectionist models using distributed representations ascribe to mental states the kind of compositional structure demanded by (8a), contrary to F&P's conclusion based on the ultralocal network of Figure 1.

The *coffee* story

My argument consists primarily in carrying out an analysis that was suggested by Zenon Pylyshyn himself at the 1984 Cognitive Science Meeting in Boulder. A sort of debate about connectionism was held between Geoffrey Hinton and David Rumelhart on the one hand, and Zenon Pylyshyn and Kurt VanLehn on the other. While pursuing the nature of connectionist representations, Pylyshyn asked Rumelhart: "Look, can you guys represent a cup of coffee in these networks?" Rumelhart's reply was "Sure" so Pylyshyn continued: "And can you represent a cup without coffee in it?" Waiting for the trap to close, Rumelhart said "Yes," at which point Pylyshyn pounced: "Ah-hah, well, the difference between the two is just the representation of *coffee*—you've just built a representation of *cup with coffee* by combining a representation of *cup* with a representation of *coffee*."

I propose to carry out exactly the construction suggested by Pylyshyn, and see what conclusions it leads us to. We'll take a *distributed* representation of *cup with coffee* and subtract from it a distributed representation of *cup without coffee* and we'll call what's left "the connectionist representation of *coffee*."

To generate these distributed representations I will use a set of "microfeatures" (Hinton, McClelland, & Rumelhart, 1986) that are not very micro—but that's always what happens in examples that are cooked up to be intuitively understandable in a nontechnical exposition. These microfeatures are shown in Figure 2.

Units	Microfeatures
●	upright container
●	hot liquid
○	glass contacting wood
●	porcelain curved surface
●	burnt odor
●	brown liquid contacting porcelain
○	oblong silver object
●	finger-sized handle
●	brown liquid with curved sides and bottom

Figure 2: Representation of *cup with coffee*

Figure 2 shows a distributed representation of *cup with coffee*: a pattern of activity in which those units that are active (black) are those that correspond to microfeatures present in the description of a cup containing coffee. Obviously, this is a crude, nearly sensory-level representation, but, again, that helps make the example more intuitive—it's not essential.

Given the representation of *cup with coffee* displayed in Figure 2, Pylyshyn suggests we subtract the representation of *cup without coffee*. The representation of *cup without coffee* is shown in Figure 3, and Figure 4 shows the result of subtracting it from the representation of *cup with coffee*.

Units	Microfeatures
●	upright container
○	hot liquid
○	glass contacting wood
●	porcelain curved surface
○	burnt odor
○	brown liquid contacting porcelain
○	oblong silver object
●	finger-sized handle
○	brown liquid with curved sides and bottom

Figure 3: Representation of *cup without coffee*

Units	Microfeatures
○	upright container
●	hot liquid
○	glass contacting wood
○	porcelain curved surface
●	burnt odor
●	brown liquid contacting porcelain
○	oblong silver object
○	finger-sized handle
●	brown liquid with curved sides and bottom

Figure 4: "Representation of *coffee*"

So what does this procedure produce as "the connectionist representation of coffee"? Reading off from Figure 4, we have a burnt odor and hot brown liquid with curved sides and bottom surfaces contacting porcelain. This is indeed a representation of coffee, but in a very particular context: the context provided by cup.

What does this mean for Pylyshyn's conclusion that "the connectionist representation of *cup with coffee* is just the representation of *cup without coffee* combined with the representation of coffee"? What is involved in combining the representations of Figures 3 and 4 back together to form that of Figure 2? We assemble the representation of *cup with coffee* from a representation of a *cup*, and a representation of *coffee*, but it's a rather strange combination. There's also the representation of the *interaction* of the cup with coffee—like *brown liquid contacting porcelain.* Thus the composite representation is built from coffee *extracted* from the situation *cup with coffee*, together with *cup* extracted from the situation *cup with coffee*, together with their interaction.

So the compositional structure is there, but it's there in an *approximate* sense. It's *not* equivalent to taking a context-independent representation of *coffee* and a context-independent representation of *cup*—and certainly not equivalent to taking a context-independent representation of the relationship in or *with*—and sticking them all together in a symbolic structure, concatenating them together to form the kind of syntactic compositional structures like `with(cup,coffee)` that F&P want connectionist nets to implement.

To draw this point out further, let's reconsider the representation of *coffee* once the cup has been subtracted off. This, suggests Pylyshyn, is the connectionist representation of *coffee*. But as we have already observed, this is really a representation of *coffee* in the particular context of being inside a cup. According to Pylyshyn's formula, to get the connectionist representation of *coffee* it should have been in principle possible to take the connectionist representation of *can with coffee* and subtract from it the connectionist representation of *can without coffee*. What would happen if we actually did this? We would get a representation of ground brown burnt smelling granules stacked in a cylindrical shape, together with granules contacting tin. This is the connectionist representation of *coffee* we get by starting with *can with coffee* instead of *cup with coffee*. Or we could start with the representation of *tree with coffee* and subtract off *tree without coffee*. We would get a connectionist representation for *coffee* which would be a representation of brown beans in a funny shape hanging suspended in mid-air. Or again we could start with *man with coffee* and get still another connectionist representation of *coffee*: one quite similar to the entire representation of *cup with coffee* from which we extracted our first representation of *coffee*.

The point is that the representation of *coffee* that we get out of the construction starting with *cup with coffee* leads to a different representation of *coffee* than we get out of other constructions that have equivalent a priori status. That means that if you want to talk about the connectionist representation of *coffee* in this distributed scheme, you have to talk about a *family of distributed activity patterns*. What knits together all these particular representations of *coffee* is nothing other than a type of family resemblance.

Morals of the *coffee* story

The first moral I want to draw out of this *coffee* story is this: unlike the ultralocal case of Figure 1, with distributed representations, complex representations are composed of representations of constituents. The constituency relation here is a *within-level* relation, as F&P require: the pattern or *vector* representing *cup with coffee* is composed of a *vector* that can be identified as a distributed representation of *cup without coffee* together with a *vector* that can be identified as a particular distributed representation of *coffee*. In characterizing the constituent vectors of the vector representing the composite, we are *not* concerned with the fact that the vector representing *cup with coffee* is a vector comprised of the activity of individual microfeature units. The *between-level* relation between the vector and its individual numerical elements is *not* the constituency relation, and so section 2.1.4 (p. 19–28) of F&P is irrelevant—it addresses a mistake that is not being made.

The second moral is that the constituency relation among distributed representations is one that is important for the analysis of connectionist models, and for explaining their behavior, but it is *not* a part of the information processing mechanism within the connectionist model. In order to process the vector representing *cup with coffee*, the network does not have to decompose it into constituents. For processing, it is the *between-level* relation, not the within-level relation, that matters. The processing of the vector representing *cup with coffee* is determined by the individual numerical activities that make up the vector: it is over these lower-level activities that the processes are defined. Thus the fact that there is considerable arbitrariness in the way the constituents of *cup with coffee* are defined introduces no ambiguities in the way the network processes that representation—the ambiguities exist only for us who analyze the model and try to explain its behavior. Any particular definition of constituency that gives us explanatory leverage is a valid definition of constituency; lack of uniqueness is not a problem.

This leads directly to the third moral: the decomposition of composite states into their constituents is not precise and uniquely defined. The notion of constituency is important but attempts to formalize it are likely to crucially involve *approximation*. As discussed at some length in Smolensky (1988a), this is the typical case: notions from symbolic computation provide important tools for constructing higher-level accounts of the behavior of connectionist models using distributed representation—but these notions provide approximate, not precise, accounts.

Which leads to the fourth moral: while connectionist networks using distributed representations *do* describe mental states with the type of constituency required by (8a), they do *not* provide an implementation—correctly defined—of a symbolic language of thought. The context-dependency of the constituents, the interactions that must be accommodated when they are combined, the inability to uniquely, precisely identify constituents, the imperative to take seriously the notion that the representation of *coffee* is a collection of vectors knit together by family resemblance—all these entail that the relation between connectionist constituency and syntactic symbolic constituency is *not* one of implementation. In particular, it would be absurd to claim that even if the connectionist story is correct then that would have no implications for the cognitive architecture, that it would merely fill in lower-level details without important implications for the higher-level account.

These conclusions all address compositional representation (8a) without explicitly addressing structure-sensitive processing (8b). Addressing structure-sensitivity to the depth necessary to grapple with real cognitive modeling is far beyond the scope of this paper; to a considerable extent, it is beyond the scope of current connectionism. However, let me simply state the fundamental hypothesis of PTC that weaves the statistical sensitivity characteristic of connectionist processing together with the notion of structure sensitivity: *the mind is a statistics-sensitive engine operating on structure-sensitive (numerical) representations*. The previous arguments have shown that distributed representations do possess constituency relations, and that, properly analyzed, these representations can be seen to encode structure. Extending this to grapple with the complexity of the kinds of rich structures implicated in complex cognitive processes is the topic of the next section. Here it suffices to observe that once we have complex structured information represented in distributed numerical patterns, statistics-sensitive processes can proceed to analyze the statistical regularities in a fully structure-sensitive way. Whether such processes can provide structure-sensitivity that is adequate to cope with the demands of linguistic and inferential processing is sure to be unknown for some time yet.

The conclusion, then, is that distributed models *can* satisfy (8). Whether (8) can be satisfied to the depth required by the full demands of cognitive modeling is of course an open empirical question—just as it is for the symbolic approach to satisfying (8). At the same time, distributed connectionist models do not amount to an implementation of the symbolic instantiations of (8) that F&P are committed to.

Before summing up, I'd like to return to Figure 1. In what sense can Figure 1 be said to describe the relation between the distributed representation of $A\&B$ and the distributed representations of A and B? It was the intent of the *coffee* story to show that the distributed representations of the constituents are, in an approximate but explanation-relevant sense, part of the representation of the composite. Thus, in the distributed case, the relation between the node of Figure 1 labeled $A\&B$ and the others is one kind of whole/part relation. An inference mechanism that takes as input the vector representing $A\&B$ and produces as output the vector representing A is a mechanism that extracts a part from a whole. And in this sense it is no different from a symbolic inference mechanism that takes the syntactic structure `A & B` and extracts from it the syntactic constituent `A`. The connectionist mechanisms for doing this are of course quite different than the symbolic mechanisms, and the approximate nature of the whole/part relation gives the connectionist computation different overall characteristics: we don't have simply a new implementation of the old computation.

It is clear that, just as Figure 1 offers a crude summary of the symbolic process of passing from `A & B` to `A`, a summary that uses the labels to encode hidden internal structures within the nodes, *exactly the same is true of the distributed connectionist case.* In the distributed connectionist case—*just as in the symbolic case*—the links in Figure 1 are crude summaries of complex processes and not simple-minded causal channels that pass activity from the top node to the lower nodes. Such a simple causal story applies only to the ultralocal connectionist case, which is the only legitimate target of F&P's attack.

Let me be clear: there is no serious distributed connectionist model, as far as I know, of the kind of formal inference F&P have in mind here. Many proponents of connectionism would be content to claim that formal inference is a specially trained, poorly practiced skill that is far from central to cognition, and that therefore we can afford to put off worrying about providing a connectionist model of it for a long time. I prefer to say that, at root, the F&P argument concerns an important and central issue: the constituent structure of mental states; formal inference is just one setting in which to see the importance of that constituent structure. So the preceding discussion of the constituent structure of distributed representations does address the heart of their critique, even if a well-developed connectionist account of formal inference remains unavailable.

2.3 The distributed (strongly compositional) case

But, one might well argue, the sense in which the vector encoding the distributed representation of *cup with coffee* has constituent vectors representing *cup* and *coffee* is too weak to serve all the uses of constituent structure—in particular, too weak to support formal inference—because the vector representing cup cannot fill multiple structural roles. A true constituent can move around and fill any of a number of different roles in different structures. Can *this* be done with vectors encoding distributed representations, and be done in a way that doesn't amount to simply implementing symbolic syntactic constituency? The purpose of this section is to describe research showing that the answer is affirmative.

A large class of connectionist representations, which I call *tensor product representations,* is defined and analyzed in Smolensky (1987a), and applied in Dolan & Smolensky (1988). We generate various members of this class by variously specifying several parameters in a highly general method for creating connectionist representations of structured information. The resulting parametric variation in the representations is very broad, encompassing very simple representations such as the case of Figure 1, as well as representations that are close to true implementations of a syntactic language of thought. This class of representations covers the spectrum from fully distributed representations to ultralocal ones, and includes representations with a full sense of constituency, where role-independent constituents are assigned to roles in a structure and the representation of the structure is built up systematically from the representation of the constituents.

The problem that motivates this work is mapping complex structures such as parse trees into vectors of activity in connectionist networks, in such a way that the constituent structure is available for connectionist processing. A general formal framework for stating this problem is to assume that there is a set of discrete structures S (like parse trees) and a vector space V—a space of activity states of a connectionist network. A connectionist representation is a mapping from S to V; the theorist's job is to identify such mappings having various desirable properties. Tensor product representations can provide many of these properties.

A particular tensor product representation is constructed in two steps.

(9) a. Specify a decompositional process whereby the discrete structures are explicitly broken down as a set of constituents, each filling a particular role in the structure as a whole. This step has nothing to do with connectionism per se, it just amounts to being specific about the kind of constituent structure we want to represent.

b. Specify two connectionist representations: one for the structural roles and another for their fillers (the constituents). Thus, for every filler, we assign a vector in the state space of some network for representing fillers; similarly, we assign to every role a vector in the state space of some network for representing roles.

These two steps indicate the "parameters" in the general tensor product representational scheme that must be specified to individuate a particular representation. Once these are parameters are specified, two very simple operations from the theory of vector spaces are used to generate the representation of a particular discrete structure. The representation of the whole is built from the representation of its constituent parts by the operation of *superposition* which is simply *vector addition*: the vector representing the whole is the sum of the vectors representing the parts. Step (9a) above specifies exactly what constituents are involved in this process. The vector representing a given constituent is actually a role-sensitive representation: a representation of that constituent *in the role it plays in the whole*. This vector is built by taking a particular vector product of the vector that represents the constituent independent of any role, and the vector representing the role in the structure that is filled by the constituent. Step (9b) specifies a set of vectors that represent individual structural roles and another set of vectors that represent individual fillers for those roles (constituents) independently of any role. The product operation here is a vector operation called the *tensor product* that takes two vectors and produces a new vector; if the two vectors consist of n and m activity values, then their tensor product is a vector of nm activity values, each one being a different product (using ordinary numerical multiplication) of two activity values, one from each of the original vectors.[4]

[4]The tensor product is closely related to what is called the *outer product* in matrix algebra (not to be

The tensor product provides a general solution to a problem that has been nagging the distributed connectionist representational world for a long time, the so-called *variable binding problem*: How can we take an activity pattern representing a variable and another pattern representing a value and generate a connectionist representation of their binding that has the right computational properties? The simplicity of the tensor product makes it possible to show it does in fact satisfy the computational demands of (distributed) connectionist variable binding. The tensor product technique is a generalization of specific tricks (especially, *conjunctive coding*: Hinton, McClelland, & Rumelhart, 1986; McClelland & Kawamoto, 1986; Smolensky, forthcoming a) that have been used to solve this problem in particular instances in the past.

The tensor product representation of constituent structure considerably strengthens the notion of constituency brought out in the previous section through the *coffee story*. There we saw that the whole/part relation between *cup with coffee* and *coffee* is mirrored in a whole/part relation between their respective representations: the latter relation was not the whole/part relation between molecular symbolic structures and their atomic constituents, as in a symbolic language of thought, but rather the relation between a sum vector w and the component vectors that add up to it: $\mathbf{w} = \mathbf{c}_1 + \mathbf{c}_2 + \cdots$. The same is true here generally with respect to tensor product representations, but now in addition we can identify the representations of each constituent as a role-*dependent* representation built in a systematic way (through tensor product variable binding) from a role-*independent* representation of the filler and a filler-independent representation of its role.

Among the computational properties required of the variable binding mechanism is the possibility of *unbinding*: from the role-dependent representation of some constituent we must be able to extract the role-independent representation of that constituent. Similarly, given the vector representing a symbolic structure as a whole, it should be possible to extract the role-independent representation of the filler of any given role in the structure. Under a wide variety of conditions, this is possible with the tensor product representation, although when so many roles are simultaneously filled that the capacity of the representing network is exceeded, corruptions, confusions, and errors can be introduced during unbinding. The conditions under which error-free unbinding can be performed, and characterization of the errors occurring when these conditions are violated, can be computed (Smolensky, 1987a). Thus, for example, if we have a tensor product representation for $P\&Q$, and we wish to extract the first element P as part of a deductive process, then as long as the representing network is not trivially small, we can easily do so without error, using very simple (linear) connectionist processes.

So, returning to F&P's critique, let's see what the tensor product representational scheme can do for us in terms of the simple Aristotelean inference problems they talk about.

Using the tensor product technique, it is possible to define a family of representations

confused with the physicists' cross product of three-dimensional vectors, which is sometimes also called the "outer product"). If $\mathbf{u}$ and $\mathbf{v}$ are two column-vectors, $[N \times 1]$ and $[M \times 1]$ respectively, their outer product is the $[N \times M]$ matrix $\mathbf{u}\mathbf{v}^T$, where $\mathbf{v}^T$ is the $[1 \times M]$ row-vector transpose of $\mathbf{v}$. If the NM numbers in this $[N \times M]$ matrix are considered as the elements of vector (rather than a matrix) then this vector is the tensor product of $\mathbf{u}$ and $\mathbf{v}$. In order for the connectionist representational scheme we are considering to be able to handle recursive decompositions of structures, the product operation we use must be extensible to products of arbitrarily many vectors; with the tensor product, this is nonproblematic, whereas the utility of matrix algebra is essentially limited to outer products of two vectors.

of tree structures. We can consider a simple tree for $P\&Q$ consisting of & at the top, P as its left child, and Q as its right child; and we can view the roles as positions in the tree, the simplest kind of role decomposition. The tensor product representation of that tree structure is a vector $\mathbf{F}(P\&Q)$ which is related to the vectors representing the constituents, $\mathbf{F}(P)$ and $\mathbf{F}(Q)$, by a function $B_\&$ that is particular to constructing conjunctions:

$$\mathbf{F}(P\&Q) = B_\&[\mathbf{F}(P), \mathbf{F}(Q)]$$

The function $B_\&$ is defined by

$$B_\&(\mathbf{u}, \mathbf{v}) = \mathbf{c}_\& + \tau_0\mathbf{u} + \tau_1\mathbf{v}$$

where $\mathbf{c}_\&$ is a constant vector and τ_0 and τ_1 are linear operators (the most natural vector operators) that vary depending on how the parameters individuating the tensor product representation are chosen.

I have descended to this level of detail and used this notation because in footnote 9 (p. 14) of F&P, exactly this property is chosen to define $\mathbf{F}$ as a "physical instantiation mapping of combinatorial structure." In this sense the tensor product representation meets F&P's formal requirements for a representation of combinatorial structure.

But have we merely provided an implementation then of a symbolic language of thought? In general, the answer is "no." Depending on how we have chosen to set the parameters in specifying the tensor product representation (which determines the properties of τ_0 and τ_1), we can fail to have any of the following properties holding (Smolensky, 1987a):

(10) a. *Uniqueness with respect to roles or fillers.* If we're not careful, even though the above equation is satisfied, we can end up with $P\&Q$ having the same representation as $Q\&P$, or other more subtle ambiguities about what fills various roles in the structure.

b. *Unbounded depth.* We may avoid the first problem (10a) for sufficiently small structures, but when representing sufficiently large or deep structures, these problems may appear. Unless the vector space in which we do our representation is infinite-dimensional (corresponding to a network with infinitely many units), we cannot solve (10a) for unbounded depth. (Of course, the same is true of Turing/von Neumann machines if they are only allowed bounded resources; but whereas the capacity limit in the symbolic case is a hard one, the tensor product representation allows for graceful degradation as resources are saturated.)

c. *Nonconfusability in memory.* Even when problem (10a) is avoided, when we have representations with uniquely determined filler/role bindings, it can easily happen that we cannot simultaneously store many such structures in a connectionist memory without getting intrusions of undesired memories during the retrieval of a given memory.

d. *Processing independence.* This is in a sense a generalization of the preceding point, concerning processing constraints that may arise even when problem (10a) is avoided. In simple associative processing, for example, we may find that we can associate two vectors representing symbolic structures with what we like, but then find ourselves unable to associate the representation of a third structure with what we like, because its associate is constrained by the other two.

With all these properties potentially failing to hold, it doesn't sound to me like we're dealing with an implementation of a symbolic language of thought. But at this point somebody's going to want to say, "Well, you've just got a lousy implementation of a symbolic language of thought." But it's not that simple. We may have lost some (superficially desirable, at least) features of a symbolic language of thought, but we've gained some (superficially desirable, at least) features of connectionist processing in return.

(11) a. *Massive parallelism.* Since we have a vector that represents an entire tree at once, we can feed it into the usual connectionist massively parallel processes. We don't have to chunk around taking the `car` of the `cdr` of the `cdr` of the `car` to get to one of the multitude of pieces of information we need for a given process: It's all there at once, all accessible in parallel.[5]

b. *Content-addressable memory.* This is the usual distributed connectionist story, but now it applies to structured information.

c. *Statistical inference.* F&P are among the first to attack connectionism for basing its processing mechanisms on statistical inference. One more reason for them to deny that the connectionist framework I am discussing truly constitutes an implementation of their preferred architecture. Yet their arguments against statistical processing are much less compelling than their arguments for structure-sensitive processing. We are now in a position to go after both, in a unified framework, dissolving a long-standing tension arising from a failure to see how to formally unify structure-sensitive and statistical processing. Rather than having to model the mind as either a structure cruncher or a number cruncher, we can now see it as a number cruncher in which the numbers crunched are in fact representing complex structures.[6]

d. *Statistical learning.* Since structure can now be brought fully into the world of connectionist learning research, we can move from declarations of dogma to actual empirical results about what structurally-rich representations and processes can and cannot be acquired from experience through statistically based learning. We can now foresee a time when it will be too late to put your money down on the fate of the "poverty of the stimulus" dogma.

---

[5]See Dolan & Smolensky (1988) for an actual distributed connectionist model, TPPS, that uses the tensor product to represent a symbolic structure and operate on it with massive parallelism. The system is an exercise in applying the tensor product representation to put on a somewhat more general and simple mathematical footing Touretzky & Hinton's (1985) Boltzmann machine implementation of a distributed connectionist production system, DCPS. Each production in TPPS does pattern matching against the whole symbolic structure in working memory in parallel, and does all parts of its action in parallel. Since it is an implementation of a traditional production system, however, productions are fired one at a time, although conflict resolution is done in parallel.

[6]Like connectionist networks, traditional computers were originally viewed exclusively as number processors. Newell and Simon are credited with teaching us that traditional computers could also be used as powerful structure processors. I am essentially trying to make the same point about connectionist networks.

The bottom line is that the parametric variation in tensor product representations extends from simple ultralocal representations of the sort F&P correctly dismiss towards—I hesitate to say all the way up to, but quite close to—a true implementation of a symbolic language of thought. If you want such an implementation, you have to go to a limit that includes the following characteristics:

(12) a. *Orthogonality.* The angle between the vectors representing different roles needs to go to 90 degrees, and similarly for vectors representing the fillers, to eliminate non-uniqueness and minimize interference in memory.

b. *Infinite-dimensional representations.* Otherwise, we can't represent unboundedly deep structures without confusion.

c. *Simple operations.* If we happen to want an implementation of sequential algorithms, then in processing these representations we insist that the vector equivalent of the primitive symbolic operations like `car`, `cdr`, and `cons` are all that can be done in one time step: We don't avail ourselves of the massively parallel operations that otherwise would be available to us.

I have talked so far mostly about representations and little about processing. If we are interested, as F&P are, in inferences such as that from $P\&Q$ to P, it turns out that with tensor product representations, this operation can be achieved by a simple linear transformation upon these representational vectors, the kind of transformation most natural in this category of representations.[7] Not only can this structure-sensitive process be achieved by connectionist mechanisms on connectionist representations, but it can be achieved through the simplest of all connectionist operations: linear mapping. All in an architecture that differs fundamentally from the Classical one; we have not implemented a symbolic language of thought.

3 CONNECTIONISM AND IMPLEMENTATIONALISM

In this final section I'd like to bring together the arguments of the first two sections, showing how the debate over constituent structure relates to larger issues such as the import of rejecting implementationalism and of viewing the commitment of connectionism as being the development of accounts of computation and cognition that exploit insights from vector space theory and other branches of continuous mathematics.

The constituency argument can be summarized as follows. We've got F&P's principles of structure (8), and we've got a symbolic instantiation of these in a language of thought using syntactic constituency. According to F&P, what connectionists should do is take that symbolic language of thought as a higher level description and then produce a connectionist implementation. The syntactic operations of the symbolic language of thought then provide an exact formal higher level account of mental representations and processes.

By contrast, I have argued that the distributed view of connectionist compositionality allows us to instantiate the same basic principles (8) *without* going through a symbolic language of thought. By going straight to distributed connectionist models we get new formal instantiations of compositionality principles.

[7]This is true provided the parameter values defining the representation satisfy the very weak constraint that the simplest possible confusions are avoided (such as confusing $P\&Q$ with $Q\&P$ or with P or Q).

Thus the PTC position is that distributed representations provide a description of mental states with semantically interpretable constituents, but that there is no complete, precise formal account of the construction of composites or of mental processes in general that can be stated solely in terms of context-independent semantically interpretable constituents. On this account, there *is* a language of thought—but only approximately; the language of thought by itself does not provide a basis for an exact formal account of mental structure or processes—it cannot by itself support a precise formal account of the cognitive architecture.

The PTC research agenda consists in taking fundamental cognitive notions such as compositionality and finding new ways to instantiate them in formal principles based on the continuous mathematics of dynamical systems. Examples of other such principles are provided by memory and inference. The concept of memory retrieval is reformalized in terms of the continuous evolution of a dynamical system towards a point attractor whose position in the state space is the memory; we naturally get content-addressed memory instead of location-addressed memory. Memory storage becomes modification of the dynamics of the system so that its attractors are located where the memories are supposed to be; thus the principles of memory storage are even more unlike their symbolic counterparts than those of memory retrieval. When reformalizing inference principles, the continuous formalism leads naturally to principles of statistical inference rather than logical inference. In each case, a single underlying cognitive notion is formalized in the connectionist and symbolic frameworks in mathematically quite different ways.

This PTC research strategy is to be contrasted with an implementational view of connectionism such as that which F&P advocate: connectionists should take the symbolic formalizations of the fundamental cognitive notions and find ways of implementing *them* in connectionist networks.

As a final note, I would point out that the view of constituency presented here is a perfectly natural outcome of adopting the new formal perspective of computation in dynamical systems. For centuries, an important technique for understanding and explaining the behavior of certain dynamical systems has been to view the total state vector as a superposition of constituent vectors: the behavior of the whole is explained with reference to the behavior of the parts. The tensor product technique for building the vectors for the parts out of a vector representing the constituent independent of its role in the whole, and another vector representing the role independent of the constituent that fills it, is also familiar in dynamical systems theory. For this is exactly how, in quantum theory, the state vector for an atom is built from state vectors for the constituent particles and vectors describing the spatial distribution of those particles in the atom.

4 SUMMARY

Shifting attention away from the refutation of F&P's argument, let me try to summarize what I take to be the positive contributions of the argument presented in this paper.

(13) a. As F&P plead, it *is* crucial for connectionism to separate itself from simplistic associationist psychology.

b. Connectionism should accept (not deny) the importance of a number of computational principles fundamental to traditional cognitive science, such as those relating to structure that F&P emphasize, which go beyond the computational repertoire of simple traditional connectionist networks.

c. The computational repertoire of connectionism should be extended by finding ways of directly, naturally, and powerfully realizing these computational principles within the continuous mathematics of dynamical systems (not indirectly, as F&P advocate, by implementing the discrete symbolic formalization of these principles in connectionist networks).

d. The resulting connectionist cognitive models aim to refine the account of cognition provided by symbolic models: the symbolic models provide a scientifically important higher-level approximate account of the connectionist model.

e. Just as a set of symbolic structures offers a domain for modeling structured mental representation and processing, so do sets of vectors, once the appropriate notions are recognized in the new mathematical category. Thus distributed (but not localist) connectionist representations provide a computational arena for structure processing.

f. The tensor product representation is a general technique for creating vectorial (distributed) representations of structures; these representations are built up systematically by binding role-independent vectors representing constituents to vectors representing their roles in the structure as a whole, and superimposing the vectors representing these bindings.

g. Superposition and tensor products provide simple, natural, but powerful means to instantiate within continuous mathematics the basic computational ingredients needed for representing and processing structured mental states.

h. The resulting connectionist model of mental processing is characterized by context-sensitive constituents, approximately (but not exactly) compositional semantics, massively parallel structure-sensitive processing, statistical inference and statistical learning with structured representations.

i. This connectionist cognitive architecture is intrinsically two-level: semantic interpretation is carried out at the level of patterns of activity while the complete, precise, and formal account of mental processing must be carried out at the level of individual activity values and connections.

j. Thus, mental representations are carried by activity vectors while mental processes are carried by activity values: Mental representation and mental processes reside at two different levels of analysis.

Acknowledgements

I have benefited greatly from personal conversations with Jerry Fodor and Zenon Pylyshyn, and with Rob Cummins, Geoff Hinton, Terry Horgan, Jay McClelland, Alan Prince, Georges Rey, Dave Rumelhart, Georg Schwarz, and David Touretzky. I thank Horgan, John Tienson, and the *Southern Journal of Philosophy* for permission to include a portion of Smolensky (1987b) here. Thanks also to Rey, Barry Loewer, and Blackwell's for permission to include some of the material to appear in Smolensky (forthcoming b). Smolensky (1988c) expands upon some of the topics discussed here. Finally, thanks to Rolf Pfeifer for the invitation to participate in the stimulating "Connectionism in Perspective" meeting, and for his help and gratious cooperation in preparing this contribution.

This work has been supported by NSF grants IRI-8609599 and ECE-8617947 to the author, by a grant to the author from the Sloan Foundation's computational neuroscience program, and by the Optical Connectionist Machine Program of the NSF Engineering Research Center for Optoelectronic Computing Systems at the University of Colorado at Boulder.

REFERENCES

Anderson, J.A. & Mozer, M.C. (1981). Categorization and selective neurons. In G. E. Hinton and J. A. Anderson, (eds.), *Parallel models of associative memory*. Hillsdale, NJ: Erlbaum.

Ballard, D. (1986). Parallel logical inference and energy minimization. Technical Report TR142. Computer Science Department, University of Rochester.

Ballard, D. & Hayes, P.J. (1984). Parallel logical inference. *Proceedings of the Sixth Annual Conference of the Cognitive Science Society*. Rochester, N.Y.

Cognitive Science. (1985). Special issue on connectionist models and their applications. 9 (1).

Cummins, R. (1988). *Meaning and mental representation*. Cambridge, MA: MIT Press/Bradford Books.

Cummins, R., & Schwarz, G. (1987). Radical Connectionism. *Southern Journal of Philosophy*, XXVI (Supplement), 43–61.

Dolan, C. & Smolensky, P. (1988). Implementing a connectionist production system using tensor products. In D. Touretzky, G. E. Hinton, & T. J. Sejnowski (Eds.), *Proceedings of the Connectionist Models Summer School*, 1988. Palo Alto, CA: Morgan Kaufmann.

Feldman, J.A. & Ballard, D.H. (1982). Connectionist models and their properties. *Cognitive Science*, **6**, 205–254.

Fodor, J. A. & Pylyshyn, Z. W. (1988). Connectionism and cognitive architecture: A critical analysis. *Cognition*, **28**, 3–71.

Hinton, G.E., McClelland, J.L., & Rumelhart, D.E. (1986). Distributed representations. In J. L. McClelland, D. E. Rumelhart, & the PDP Research Group, *Parallel distributed processing: Explorations in the microstructure of cognition. Volume 2: Psychological and biological models*. Cambridge, MA: MIT Press/Bradford Books.

McClelland, J.L. & Kawamoto, A.H. (1986). Mechanisms of sentence processing: Assigning roles to constituents. In J. L. McClelland, D. E. Rumelhart, & the PDP Research Group, *Parallel distributed processing: Explorations in the microstructure of cognition. Volume 2: Psychological and biological models*. Cambridge, MA: MIT Press/Bradford Books.

McClelland, J.L., Rumelhart, D.E., & the PDP Research Group, (1986). *Parallel distributed processing: Explorations in the microstructure of cognition. Volume 2: Psychological and biological models*. Cambridge, MA: MIT Press/Bradford Books.

Rumelhart, D.E., McClelland, J.L., & the PDP Research Group. (1986). *Parallel distributed processing: Explorations in the microstructure of cognition. Volume 1: Foundations*. Cambridge, MA: MIT Press/Bradford Books.

Schwarz, G. (1987). Explaining cognition as computation. Masters Thesis, Department of Philosophy, University of Colorado at Boulder.

Smolensky, P. (1986). Neural and conceptual interpretations of parallel distributed processing models. In J. L. McClelland, D. E. Rumelhart, & the PDP Research Group, *Parallel distributed processing: Explorations in the microstructure of cognition. Volume 2: Psychological and biological models.* Cambridge, MA: MIT Press/Bradford Books.

Smolensky, P. (1987a). On variable binding and the representation of symbolic structures in connectionist systems. Technical Report CU-CS-355-87. Department of Computer Science, University of Colorado at Boulder. (Revised version to appear in Artificial Intelligence.)

Smolensky, P. (1987b). The constituent structure of connectionist mental states: A reply to Fodor and Pylyshyn. *Southern Journal of Philosophy*, XXVI (Supplement), 137–163.

Smolensky, P. (1988a). On the proper treatment of connectionism. *The Behavioral and Brain Sciences*, **11**, 1–23.

Smolensky, P. (1988b). Putting together connectionism-again. *The Behavioral and Brain Sciences*, **11**, 59–74.

Smolensky, P. (1988c). Connectionism, constituency, and the language of thought. Technical Report CU-CS-416-88. Department of Computer Science, University of Colorado at Boulder.

Smolensky, P. (forthcoming a). *Lectures on connectionist cognitive modeling*. Hillsdale, NJ: Erlbaum.

Smolensky, P. (forthcoming b). Connectionism, constituency, and the language of thought. In B. Loewer & G. Rey (eds.), *Fodor and his critics*. Blackwell's.

Touretzky, D.S. & Hinton, G.E. (1985). Symbols among the neurons: Details of a connectionist inference architecture. In *Proceedings of the International Joint Conference on Artificial Intelligence*, 238–243.

CONNECTIONISM IN PERSPECTIVE
R. Pfeifer, Z. Schreter, F. Fogelman-Soulié, L. Steels (Eds.)

Connectionist Representation of Concepts

Jerome A. Feldman
Computer Science Department
University of Rochester

Abstract—*One of the most attractive features of connectionist systems is their potential to support models that combine constraints from different disciplines. The method of converging constraints is paradigmatic for Cognitive Science and connectionist models are having some of their greatest impact in this new discipline. The methodology can help constrain speculation about neural representation and computation even without detailed anatomical and physiological knowledge. Some proposed solutions to classical questions can be precluded on first order computational grounds. This seems to be the case for one of the most basic questions about mental activities: how does conceptual memory work?*

Recent advances in the behavioral, biological and computational sciences may yield a major improvement in our understanding of the neural coding of memory. Taken together, these developments are leading to a theoretical neuroscience that can integrate and inform experimental work. The use of connectionist computational models is likely to be central to these efforts. Connectionist systems allow us to combine directly results from various disciplines and evaluate alternative models of conceptual knowledge.

Keywords—Connectionist models, conceptual memory, converging constraints, punctate or compact models, diffuse or holographic models, structureless approach, structured connectionist systems, evidence-combining simple units, generalization, learning

One of the most attractive features of connectionist systems is their potential to support models that combine constraints from different disciplines. The method of converging constraints is paradigmatic for Cognitive Science and connectionist models are having some of their greatest impact in this new discipline. The methodology can help constrain speculation about neural representation and computation even without detailed anatomical and physiological knowledge. Some proposed solutions to classical questions can be precluded on first order computational grounds. This seems to be the case for one of the most basic questions about mental activity—how does conceptual memory work?

The nature of the neural substrate of memory is of compelling scientific interest and considerable practical importance. There are obvious applications in neurology, but it goes well beyond that. Our understanding of how human minds incorporate and process information has a marked influence on many aspects of social intercourse including formal and informal education, psychotherapy, public information and inter-personal communication (Minsky, 1987; Roediger, 1980). Implicit assumptions about neural encoding can have a profound influence on experimental research in many fields.

Recent advances in the behavioral, biological and computational sciences may yield a major improvement in our understanding of the neural coding of memory. Neurobiology is making remarkable strides in elucidating the structure of the nervous system and the details of its functioning. The behavioral sciences are developing deep structural models of mental operations and employing increasingly sophisticated experimental and simulation techniques to refine them. Computer science has produced powerful devices and principles of representation and computation that are supporting the study of how the complex structural theories of the behavioral scientists could be carried out by the information processing mechanisms revealed by neurobiology. Taken together, these developments are leading to a theoretical neuroscience that can integrate and inform experimental work. The use of connectionist computational models is likely to be central to these efforts. Figure 1 depicts one example of a connectionist model that captures and predicts a large number of regularities in behavioral studies of reading (Rumelhart & McClelland, 1981). It is simply a hierarchy of excitatory and inhibitory (circle-tipped) links among units representing letter-features, letters, and words. Among the success of this model is an elegant explanation of the word superiority effect previously considered to be paradoxical. It turns out that subjects can more reliably recognize a letter, for example, "A," in the context of a word, for example "TAKE," than in isolation. The model suggests that word superiority is due to feedback links from words to letters that provide additional activation for letters presented in the context of words; the same mechanism accounts for other behavioral data discussed below. We will also return to the fact that the model uses exactly one unit to represent each item of interest. Connectionist systems like Figure 1 allow us to combine directly results from various disciplines and evaluate alternative models of conceptual knowledge.

For concreteness, let us suppose that the problem is to describe how the neurons of a human brain could represent and exploit the information in a standard encyclopedia. The representation of such knowledge must include the concepts (e.g. people, places, events) involved as well as how they relate to one another. Formal models follow our intuition in assuming that the totality of knowledge can be captured as a (large) collection of relations among primitive concepts. The literature contains a wide range of notions on the nature of concepts and their neural representation. The simplest view restricts consideration to very concrete nouns such as "horse" or "chair," ignoring more complex concepts such as "game," "yesterday," "active" or "love." Even in this quite restricted context, the representation of concepts has proven to be a deep problem for philosophers, linguists and psychologists. The related fields of artificial intelligence and cognitive psychology have provided considerable detail on how people use concepts and the kinds of information processing required (Smith & Medin, 1981). As a minimum, any representation must support the answering of questions about concepts and about their relations. One simple kind of question concerns the structure of the object itself, for example, how many legs has some chair. Theories that treat concepts as unstructured collections of attributes will need to provide additional mechanisms for answering even these simple questions.

The range of possible representations of concepts in the brain is constrained by a combination of computational considerations and neurobiological findings. Neurons with

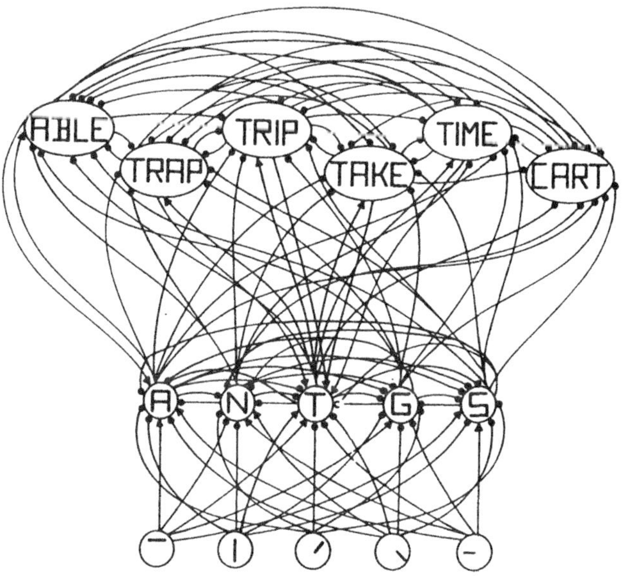

Figure 1: Reading model after McClelland and Rumelhart (1981). Units representing letter features (bottom), letters and words form a hierarchical excitation-inhibition network. Feedback links from word nodes to letter nodes facilitate identification of a letter in the context of a word.

about a 5 millisecond firing rate support our ability to solve non-trivial perception and conceptual problems in about 500 milliseconds. This remarkable performance in just 100 sequential time steps contrasts with conventional computers which require millions of time steps. Other pertinent facts include the relatively small number of neurons (about 10^{11} or one-hundred billion), the large number of connections between neurons (about 10^4 per unit), and the low rate of information transfer. It may seem that 10^{11} is not a small number, but when one considers the 10^6 input fibres from each eye, a computer scientist immediately detects a major constraint. For example, having a separate neuron to test for a possible line between any pair of points in the retina would require more neurons (10^{6^2}) than there are in the cortex. The information rate between individual neurons at a firing rate of 100 spikes per second is about five bits or enough to encode one letter of the alphabet. Thus, if complex messages are being conveyed, it is not by individual neurons. Much of the computational power of the brain derives from its great connectivity and a challenge to connectionist theory is to explain how this power is realized.

When one combines the constraints from biology, computation and psychology, the range of plausible encodings of conceptual knowledge is relatively small. Two simple theories embody the extreme ends of the range of possible answers. The most compact representation possible would be to have a unique unit dedicated to each concept. If we assume that a unit corresponds to one neuron then this punctate model is the "grandmother cell" or "pontifical cell" theory. The other extreme would be to have each concept representated as a pattern of activity in all of the units in the system. This is known as the "holographic" model of memory and is the most highly distributed theory that we will consider. In addition to the pure theory based on optical holograms, we will call holographic any model that has all the units in a system encoding each concept (Golden 1986; Ackley et al., 1985; Willshaw, 1981); most of these are matrix formulations.

We should first dispense with an abstract argument that equates the punctate and hologram models. It is true, in a sense, that an encoding having one active unit per concept is a pattern of activity in the mass. But this identification is too abstract to be meaningful. Another proposed way to identify holographic and punctate representations comes from linear algebra and the idea of alternate coordinate axes for a vector space. If, as in many models, the output of a unit is the (thresholded) linear combination of its inputs, one can view this unit as a (very large) vector, v, whose coordinates are the outputs of each predecessor unit. There is, in principle, another set of bases for the vector space for which this vector, v, is an axis and can therefore be represented by one non-zero coordinate. This argument fails for three reasons. Even for strictly linear input combinations, the output threshold destroys the applicability of linear algebra and there is no biologically plausible way to eliminate nonlinearity. In addition, no single transform would work unless the set of concepts were independent and therefore small. More importantly, the computational properties of the two representations are radically different.

The extreme opposite models of neural representation lead to radically different views of many aspects of Cognitive Science. Table 1 presents a number of contrasting terms that arise, respectively, from the punctate and fully distributed views of neural coding. While the two extreme models have traditionally been seen as fundamentally incompatible, the method of converging constraints applied to either extreme yields essentially the same answer. From this perspective, the two styles of model can be seen as arising from different research strategies. To greatly oversimplify the discussion of the rest of the chapter: punctate models have focussed on structural issues while diffuse models have concentrated on error tolerance and generalization.

Contrasting Terms

punctuate	diffuse
local	highly distributed
grandmother neuron	hologram, spin-glass
disjoint codes	homogeneous code
detector	filter
labelled line	pattern of activity
active memory	passive memory
reduction	emergence
hierarchy	complete connectivity
recruiting	adapting
general computation	correlation

Table 1

COMPACT MODELS

The extreme compact representation position is to assume each concept is represented by exactly one neuron. This view received considerable support from single unit recording research, which found that units in sensory areas responded best to a relatively narrow class of stimuli (Hubel & Wiesel, 1979). The punctate encoding is also called "labelled lines" emphasizing the fact that, in this encoding, each axon will be conveying a specific message when it is active. The most influential expression of this position was Horace Barlow's "neuron doctrine" (Barlow, 1972). His five dogmas are:

> The following five brief statements are intended to define which aspect of the brain's activity is important for understanding its main function, to suggest the way that single neurons represent what is going on around us, and to say how this is related to our subjective experience. The statements are dogmatic and incautious because it is important that they should be clear and testable.
>
> *First dogma*
>
> A description of that activity of a single nerve cell which is transmitted to and influences other nerve cells, and of a nerve cell's response to such influences from other cells, is a complete enough description for functional understanding of the nervous system. There is nothing else 'looking at' or controlling this activity, which must therefore provide a basis for understanding how the brain controls behaviour.
>
> *Second dogma*
>
> At progressively higher levels in sensory pathways information about the physical stimulus is carried by progressively fewer active neurons. The sensory system is organized to achieve as complete a representation as possible with the minimum number of active neurons. (cf. Figure 4)
>
> *Third dogma*
>
> Trigger features of neurons are matched to the redundant features of sensory stimulation in order to achieve greater completeness and economy of representation. This selective responsiveness is determined by the sensory stimulation to which neurons have been exposed, as well as by genetic factors operating during development.
>
> *Fourth dogma*
>
> Just as physical stimuli directly cause receptors to initiate neural activity, so the active high-level neurons directly and simply cause the elements of our perception.
>
> *Fifth dogma*
>
> The frequency of neural impulses codes subjective certainty: A high impulse frequency in a given neuron corresponds to a high degree of confidence that the cause of the percept is present in the external world.

Figure 2 (after Shastri (Shastri & Feldman, 1986)) provides one example of how a punctate system might encode and exploit conceptual knowledge. The memory network is a category-based hierarchy with each concept and property-name represented by a rectangular unit. The triangular nodes stand for intermediate units which become active when two of their three input lines are active. Suppose the system has a routine that retrieves its knowledge of food tastes as an aid to ordering wine, such as that cartooned in the lower half of the figure. If activation is spread simultaneously to the "main course" of the meal and to the desired property "has-taste," exactly one triangular evidence node, b1, will receive two active inputs leading to the activation of the concept "salty." This is the required answer, but for technical reasons an intervening clean-up network is needed to actually use the result. Figure 2b shows an activation record of the "potentials of units" in the network responding to the query. One interesting feature of the model is that the same memory network is able to categorize a salty, pink food as ham—the triangular evidence nodes work in both directions.

While oversimplified, Figure 2 does convey much of the flavor of punctate (and other compact) connectionist models and their appeal to some scientists and rejection by others. The main point is that everything is quite explicit; the concepts, properties and even the rules of operation are simple and direct. This makes it relatively easy to express and test specific models either at the neural level or more abstractly as in our example. No one believes that the brain uses exactly the structure of Figure 2, but any highly compact concept representation could behave in essentially the same way. Notice that even in this extreme case many units (representing features and components) will be active for each concept. A great deal of interesting work is being done with such models, but there are also a variety of arguments why the neural encoding must be more complex.

The first point is that a large number of neurons ($\sim 10^5$) die each day and these are distributed throughout the brain. If each concept were represented by exactly one neuron, one would expect to lose at least some concepts (at random) each day. This argument is often taken to be conclusive evidence against any compact model, but a slight variant of the punctate view is stable under the death of individual units. Suppose that instead of one unit per concept, the system dedicated three or five, distributed somewhat physically. All of the theories and experiments would look the same as in the single unit case, but the redundancy would solve the problem of neuron death. While the number of neurons dying is large, the fraction is quite small ($\sim 10^{-6}$) so the probability of losing two of the representatives of a concept in a lifetime is quite low.

Another argument used against compact models of neural representation arises from bulk activity experiments, which show that single small stimulus can give rise to activity in a significant fraction of the total population. There are several reasons why this fact does not preclude compact representations. For one thing, the "simplicity" of a stimulus looks different from various encoding schemes. A small dot, in a Fourier encoding, activates receptors for all spatial frequencies. In a parameter-space encoding (Ballard, 1986), a single feature provides evidence for many higher-level features and these may be suppressed slower than when more information is present (cf. Figure 1). Finally, there appears to be some non-specific evoked potentials (Barber, 1980) which activate an entire structure on any input.

While the cell-death and bulk activities arguments against punctate representation are easily answered, one can see that there really could not be enough neurons to have one for each concept of interest. One example arises in early vision. It is well known that the visual system is sensitive to at least the following local stimulus properties: orientation, intensity, hue, depth, motion direction and size. A system that could resolve 10 values

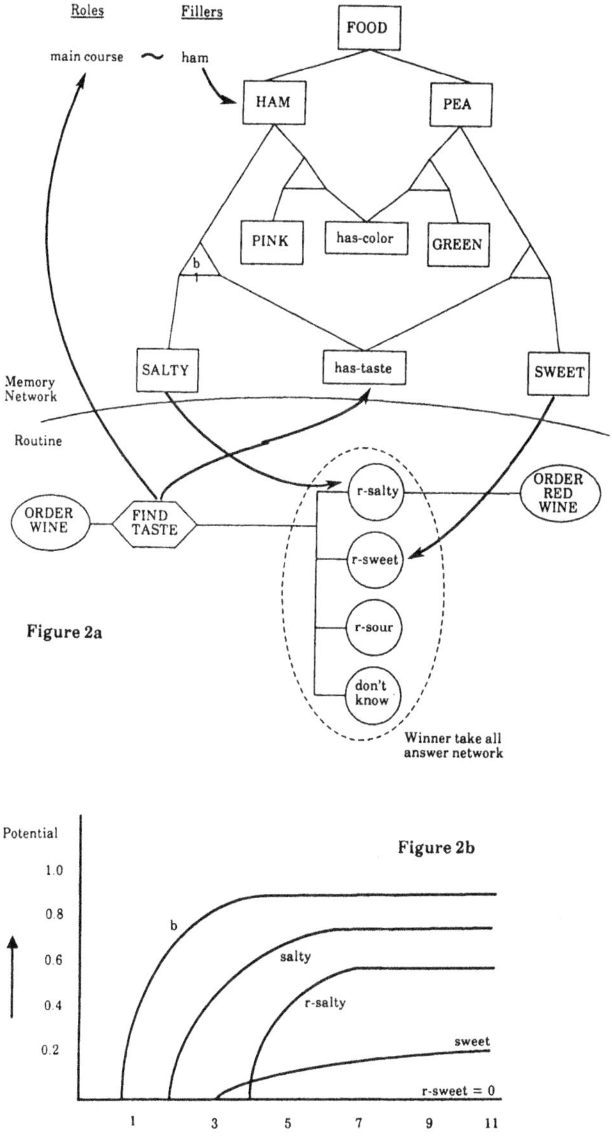

Figure 2: A connectionist retrieval system after Shastri (Shastri & Feldman, 1986). Figure 2a is a network fragment whose behavior is described in the text, 2b depicts the time course of activation in selected units.

for each of the six dimensions would require 10^6 units to represent all combinations of values. But there are about 10^6 separate points at the narrowest (retinal ganglion) level that must be represented so the total requirement would be 10^{12}, which is too many.

Experimentalists have also been reframing their view of the activity of single units. For some time, the idea of a neuron as a "detector" of one event type has been declining but no alternative term has yet evolved. The notion of a "filter" is the diffuse equivalent (all units filter all signals) and equally misleading. Although no new word has been established, experimentalists now view sensory neurons as having responsivity of different coarseness to a variety of stimulus dimensions. Studies in single unit neurophysiology are finding effects of stimuli beyond the classical receptive field (Allman et al., 1985) as seems inevitable in an interacting system of units. A proposed revision of Barlow's dogmas that takes these developments into account is given in the Appendix.

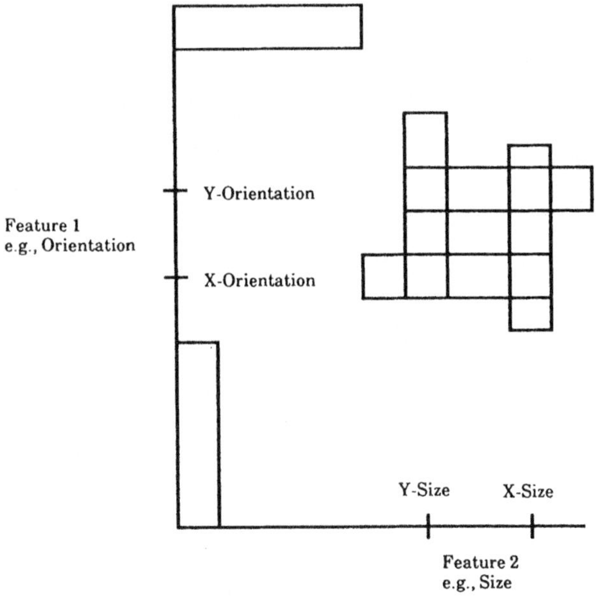

Figure 3: Coarse-Fine coding. Both computational and biological considerations suggest overlapping representations. When two stimuli that are too close appear together, confusing (ghost) activation can result.

There is a concise computational account that both helps organize the experimental data and contributes to our goal of constraining the possible models of neural encoding. The basic idea is depicted in Figure 3 for the case of two stimulus dimensions. Suppose (as appears to be the case in the brain) that units respond non-uniformly to various stimulus dimensions. For example, the vertical rectangle in the lower left depicts the responsiveness of a cell that is five times more sensitive to size than to orientation and the horizontal rectangle the opposite. The nice point is that the joint activity of two such cells can code the stimulus space as finely as the finest dimension of either (cf. the crossed rectangles), while requiring significantly fewer units. This computational mechanism goes by the name "coarse-fine" coding and appears to characterize a good deal of neural computation. In general, given K stimulus dimensions, each with a desired resolution of N values, the punctate encoding requires N^K units. A coarse-fine encoding with the coarse dimensions D requires a total of

$$T = K \cdot N \left(\frac{N}{D}\right)^{K-1}$$

units. This is because there will be K separate covers of the K-dimensional space, but each will be covered coarsely and this requires (N/D) units in all dimensions but one, which has N units. This formula still grows exponentially, but is significantly smaller for the cases of interest. For example, our early vision example had $K = 6$ and $N = 10$. With $D = 5$, this yields 1920 units per point instead of the 1,000,000 for the pure punctate encoding. An additional saving arises from having the converging inputs each go to a separate site (dendritic subtree).

The critical point in the construction is the overlap of receptive fields, not their as-symmetric shape. Essentially the same arguments can be made for symmetric overlapping fields and this is known as coarse-coding (Hinton et al., 1986). Computational ideas of this kind have been known for some time to provide a nice account of hyper-acuity, the ability of people to resolve details finer than the spacing of their receptors. In both coarse and coarse-fine coding there is a price to be paid for saving all these units. If two stimuli that overlap occur simultaneously, the system will be unable to resolve them. In Figure 3, one stimulus is encoded by the two rectangles containing X and the other by the two rectangles containing Y. The intersections labelled X and Y encode the desired information, but the "ghosts" labelled G would be equally active. One of these expresses the conjunction of Y-size and X-orientation and the other the converse. This is an instance of "cross-talk" in neural encodings. Cross-talk is the fundamental problem of shared encodings and appears to be a critical limiting factor on distributed models.

The coarse-fine coding examples used overlapping encodings, but were based on the minimum possible number of cells to cover some feature space. Suppose instead we allowed for redundancy in the coverage, say three separate tesselations of the space. In terms of Figure 3, a second covering could be similar bars at 45° and 315° to the axes. We could still use separate receiving sites for each desired stimulus, but the computation would be not just a logical AND. In fact, a thresholded sum of activity might be quite plausible as the sites way of computing the likelihood of its combination being present. This would combine the error tolerance and information reduction ideas in a simple and plausible way. Edelman has come to essentially the same kind of model through a very different route, starting from his expertise in immunology (Edelman, 1981).

HOLOGRAPHIC MODELS

Holographic models have been fervently supported by biologists, psychologists and theoreticians. There is no comparable fervor for compact models. In fact, several researchers advocate fully distributed models while employing punctate ones, (Hopfield & Tank, 1985; Hopfield, 1982) sometimes in the same paper (Hinton, 1986). One major contributing factor in the popularity of this view was the early work of Karl Lashley who found that for a variety of tasks, the deficit exhibited by lesioned rats was best explained by the total amount of cortex removed—the "law of mass action." Lashley summarized his view of memory representation in the classic 1950 paper "In Search of the Engram." The following quotation continues to motivate much current work (Lashley, 1950):

> It is difficult to interpret such findings, but I think that they point to the conclusions that the associative connections or memory traces of the conditioned reflex do not extend across the cortex as well-defined arcs or paths. Such arcs are either diffused through all parts of the cortex, pass by relay through lower centres, or do not exist. [Lashley, 1950, p. 461]

Recent work (Thompson, 1986) has established that conditioned reflexes are supported by remarkably compact cerebellar structures, but the general idea of holographic memory continues to attract attention. Since all of the primary sensory and motor areas have been found to have specialized structure, the holographic hypothesis is currently restricted to "higher" brain areas whose functional organization is not yet understood. Another historical source of motivation for diffuse models was the landmark 1949 book, *The Organization of Behavior*, by Donald Hebb (Hebb, 1949). Hebb introduced the notion of cell assemblies, but was (appropriately for the time) vague about how they actually encode knowledge. Hebb definitely envisioned a dynamic pattern of activity, but there are two interpretations of this. The most literal would be to assume concepts are purely dynamic and are not tied to any particular tissue; this idea has been pursued a bit (von der Malsburg, 1985) but without much success and the experimental data is not encouraging. A more general notion of dynamic activity of cell assemblies is inherent in all current connectionist theories; the compact-diffuse question is about what fraction of a system is involved in representing a concept.

Holographic models are theoretically attractive because of two properties: fault-tolerance and generalization. The brain clearly has these properties and it is easy to see informally why holographic models do also. If all of the units of a large system are involved in coding one concept, the failure of some of them can be tolerated. Furthermore, two concepts that share much of their activity patterns will tend to behave similarly. An excellent compendium of holographic-style models can be found in (Hinton & Anderson, 1981). More recently, there has been a flurry of interest in spin-glasses as holographic memory models in the theoretical physics community (Hopfield, 1982).

The purest holographic model is, unsurprisingly, the optical hologram itself. A nice presentation can be found in (Willshaw, 1981) where it is also shown that that the purely linear hologram is undesirable on both computational and biological grounds. The models typically studied are large rectangular matrices representing all the possible connections between m input units and n output units, which need not be distinct. The most common case, and one of the easiest to consider, is where each unit compares the sum of its weighted inputs to its threshold and emits 1 if the sum of inputs is greater and 0 otherwise. A concept is represented as a binary vector over all the input lines. Each element of the vector may be uninterpreted or can be thought of as the presence or absence of a microfeature characterizing the concept.

If the input and output are identified, the matrix becomes a pattern completion machine. The basic idea is simple and derives from the mathematical notion of correlation. The correlation of a binary vector, u, with another, v, is:

$$\sum_{j=1}^{n} u_j v_j$$

and this is obviously maximized when $u = v$. In a well distributed set of vectors, an input distorted by modest noise or omission will correlate best with the appropriate complete vector. This is the basic source of error resistance and generalization in holographic-style models. What makes them interesting is that a connection matrix with the appropriate weights can be learned with a simple, local procedure. For the auto-associative, pattern completion case, the learning procedure should yield weights such that each output unit is most likely to be active when the corresponding input is active. The natural local weight-change rule is to increase the weight between two units when they both are active (output = 1). This is essentially Hebb's rule (Hebb, 1949) and can be interpreted as increasing the weight of units whose firing is correlated.

The resulting matrix can be shown to be optimal in some cases (orthogonal vectors) and is a good estimator in many others (Kohonen, 1984). Thus a simple and biologically plausible local learning rule yields a matrix which reliably finds the best match to an input pattern under some distortion conditions (but not others). The binary, linear auto-associator is the simplest of wide variety of essentially similar models. Many variations have been tried on all aspects of the model (Hinton & Anderson, 1981). The more refined models use a variant of Hebb's rule which allows feedback from some external result to affect the weight change process (Kohonen, 1984; Barto et al., 1981). The shortcomings of the methodology do not lie in the learning rules, which demonstrate that essentially anything that can be represented as a linear threshold matrix can be learned by correlation. While something like associative matrices may occur in nature (Lynch, 1986), the representation is much too weak to support human concept memory.

The basic problems with any holographic representational scheme are cross-talk, communication, invariance and the inability to capture structure. Essentially the same problems have prevented the development of holographic computer memories or recognition systems despite considerable effort. Consider the problem of representing a concept like "grandmother" as a pattern of activity in all the units in some memory network. Notice what would happen if two (or more) concepts were presented at the same time, e.g., grandmother at the White House. The encodings for the two concepts would overlap and the system would get garbled. This is a massive instance of the cross-talk problem of Figure 3. We can reduce the probability of cross-talk by having fewer units active for each pattern. If one assumes that the cross-talk is randomly distributed, Willshaw (1981) has shown that the system will be reliable (even for single entries) only if the number of units active for each pattern is proportional to the logarithm of the number of units in the diffuse memory. This means that a network of 1,000,000 units should use an encoding with about 20 active units per concept—this is interestingly close to the number for a redundant, coarse-coded compact approach as derived in the previous section.

A related problem with diffuse representations is that only one concept at a time could be transmitted between subsystems. The sequential nature of diffuse representations is particularly troublesome when we consider how information about a complex scene could be transferred from vision to other systems such as language and motor control. There appears to be no alternative to assuming that, at least for simultaneous communication, representation of concepts must be largely disjoint and thus compact.

The same communication problem arises within the concept memory itself if one tried to build a knowledge structure like Figure 2 with a diffuse representation. If a concept like "salty" were represented only by a large pattern, the links for this entire pattern would have to go to all the places that related to saltiness—and be treated correctly at each of these. If a concept encoded by N units needed to be linked to M other concepts, a total of $M * N$ links would be needed. The more distributed the representation, the more serious this problem becomes. Again, any serious reduction in this wiring requirement constitutes a compact representation. And, as in the inter-modal case, unless these representations were largely disjoint, concept processing would have to be sequential to avoid cross-talk. This eliminates the massively parallel processing that is required by the 100-step constraint.

Moreover, no one has suggested how to represent any but the simplest concepts in the holographic style. For example, the problem of all the different historical views of ones grandmother is as difficult for the hologram as for the punctate model. In fact, it is far from obvious how to make the same distributed pattern active for alternative views of a chair. All concepts in any holographic structure that have been proposed are totally without internal structure. There is an idea of associating the components of a representation with microfeatures (Anderson & Mozer, 1981) but these are still unstructured. Nor do any of the holographic proposals provide a way of answering even simple questions like the color of grandmother's hair. The only suggestion on how to encode structured knowledge in a holographic system is to encode each proposition (e.g. Dave likes candy) as a separate "memory" (Touretzky & Hinton, 1985). One can build up arbitrary structures in this way, but at the cost of losing all the advantages that led to connectionist models in the first place. There may be some technical advantages to exploring such models, but they have nothing to do with human concept memory—for example, they violate the 100-step constraint by many orders of magnitude.

The biological evidence against anything vaguely like a holographic model is equally compelling. This is only fair, since the holographic hypothesis denies any relevance to neuroanatomy and physiology. Since intricate specificity and detailed visuotopic, tonotopic, etc. maps have been discovered everywhere in the brain in which they have been sought, the only hope for the hologram is for some higher association areas. Even there, the anatomical structure has been found to be much like the sensory areas (Goldman-Rakic & Schwartz, 1982) and nothing like the connection of each input to each output required by matrix models.

Another argument for highly distributed representations derives from the large number of input fibers ($\sim 10^4$) to cortical neurons. If all of these fibers participate actively then, *ipso facto*, the representation is diffuse. While there has been no definitive study on the number of pre-synaptic events required for neural firing, estimates gleaned from papers and conversations run from one event to a few dozen (Shepard, 1986). No one has suggested that several thousand synapses must fire at once for an action potential. Also, we can see from Figure 4 that many of the connections could represent alternative ways of activating the same concept (e.g. from different points in space). Another way of looking at this is that the thousand-fold connectivity is capturing an "OR" of activation conditions rather than an "AND." Finally, as we discuss below, learning in a connectionist system requires the potential for many more connections than are ever made functional. The most striking physiological demonstration of this principle is in neural reorganization studies (Merzenich et al., 1984).

THE MIDDLE GROUND AND BEYOND

A variety of findings have all converged on the idea that concepts are represented by overlapping activity among a modest number of units and that the structure within and across these groups can not be uniform or arbitrary. The fact that both the punctate and holographic approaches yield essentially the same result is also reflected in current research on neural representation.

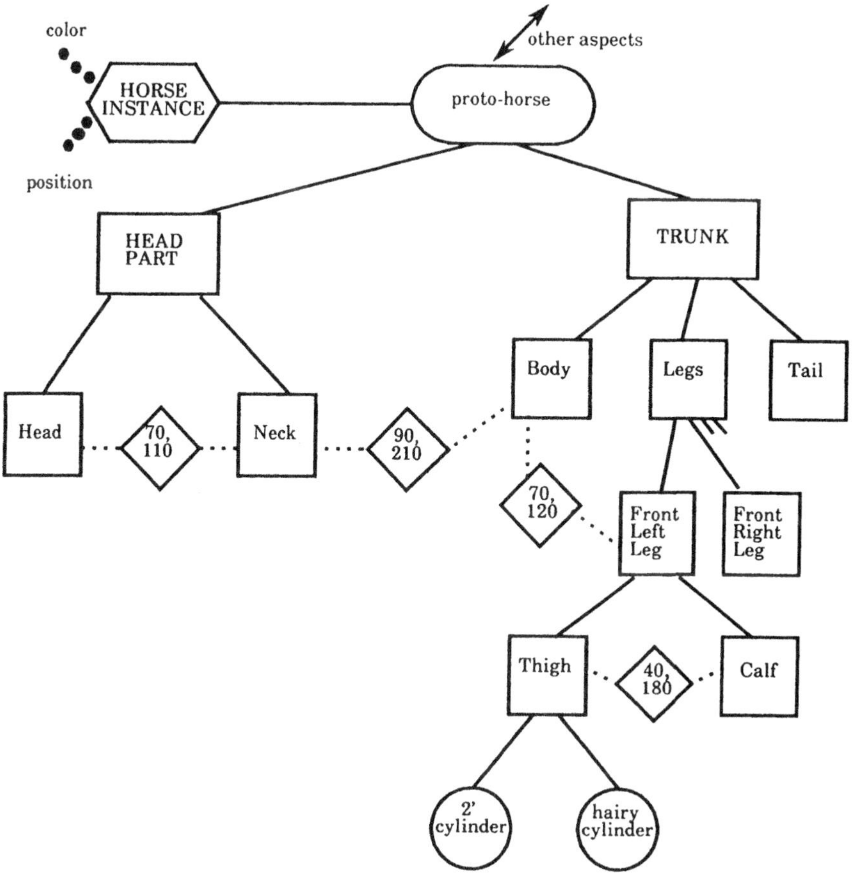

Figure 4: Simplified hierarchical model of the appereance of horses after (Feldman, 1985). Spreading activation selects the concept best matching the visual features. Circular junctions depict gated inputs.

Consider the punctate model of the appearance of horses shown in Figure 4 (Feldman, 1985). At the lowest level are feature pairs, which are assumed to be derived by early vision networks. The remaining structure is organized as a hierarchy (cf. Table 1 and dogma 2) where activation propagates towards the top pontifical cell which is active when a horse is recognized. Even in this unrealistically punctate version, the recognition of a horse is a "pattern of activation" in many of these units. Since the connections are bi-directional, mentioning the name of a horse will cause (some) activation in all the nodes comprising visual and other descriptions of horses. Notice that it makes no sense to talk about the activation of a single concept in such structure—activation automatically spreads to encompass a sub-network. Notice furthermore that this structure will recognize a horse even when some features are missing or distorted if the other features plus context are sufficiently strong. This captures the error tolerance and some of the generalization ability that were most attractive about correlation matrices. Computer experiments of moderate complexity along these lines have been successfully carried out (Cooper & Hollbach, 1987; Sabbah, 1985). The main current versions of holographic correlation theory use microfeatures essentially identical to the bottom row of Figure 4. The difference is that a holographic model would not have the hierarchical structure but would represent horse exclusively by the pattern of activity of the feature-pair units. The previous section has suggested that feature vectors without the hierarchical structure of Figure 4 will not support the requirements of conceptual memory. In fact, pure feature representations have no way at all to represent particular concepts such as a horse named *Secretariat*. Nevertheless, some very interesting work has been done by suppressing structure and focussing on the properties of feature vectors.

There are two important problems that have been effectively studied using the structureless approach —generalization and learning. Recall that the reading model of Figure 1 helped explain why people can recognize a letter better in context than in isolation. The model actually did much more than this; it turns out the model (and the subjects) also recognize letters better in the context of pronounceable non-words, but not generally in unpronounceable non-words. Since there are no units representing non-words, the network exhibits an important generalization ability. What happens is that pronounceable letter combinations moderately activate units representing similar words and the combined effect of these word-units produces the enhancement. From the perspective of diffuse modelling one can view this as a "distributed representation" of non-words by the network. But there are many aspects of the non-words (size, pronunciation, etc.) which are not represented and it is more accurate to say that the system *behaves for this task* as if it had explicit representations of nonwords. System ("emergent") properties of neural networks have fascinated many investigators (Rumelhart & McClelland, 1986) and remain one of the major motivations for studying diffuse models. Correlation-based learning schemes, like those discussed above, can be used to generate systems that capture important generalizations including some of the ones discussed above. Golden (1988) discusses the relationship between the two styles of model for the reading task.

There is no inherent conflict between structured, compact models such as Figure 4 and generalization but a model that is *strictly* hierarchical will be weak at generalization. In the horse example, one might want to capture the generalization that animals with hair are mammals. We could link horse to mammal, but this is of no direct use in classifying novel hairy animals. The point is that if all uses of a concept were forced to go through some focus, the system would be unable to yield many crucial generalizations. There are systematic relationships among properties that are best captured directly. The relations between syntactic and case roles, between pronunciation and morphology and between hairiness and mammalhood are systematic and most compactly encoded by circumventing particular instances of words or mammals. There is an interesting duality here. If one knew enough hairy mammals, it is likely that activation of "hairy" would lead (indirectly) to the activation of "mammal." One could view this as all the individual mammals constituting a distributed representation of the hair-mammal relations. A great deal of generalization to totally new examples probably takes this form, but our conceptual memory also has the ability to represent much richer evidential relations among concepts (Shastri & Feldman, 1986).

LEARNING

The preceding discussion has explored the ways in which conceptual knowledge might be represented in neural networks, suppressing the critical problem of learning. It is clear that evolution provides humans with an enormous amount of pre-wired structure, which develops a great deal more through interaction with the environment, and that this continues throughout life. This presents a severe methodological problem for computational learning research.

The basic difficulty is that we know human learning is based on an elaborate existing structure, but we know very little about the exact nature of this structure, particularly in the area of conceptual knowledge. Any study of learning either assumes some existing structure (at the risk of trivializing the learning aspects) or assumes no existing structure and is restricted to quite simple problems. The correlation matrix models of memory have presented an attractive research vehicle. The total initial connectivity and linear threshold rule are a minimal *a priori* structure, and the correlation method of updating is an easily analyzed learning rule.

These correlation matrices employ a diffuse encoding and the appeal of the two ideas is strongly interrelated. But the ideas of correlation, feedback and weight change are not restricted to diffuse representations, linear threshold rules or complete connectivity matrices. In fact, complete connectivity is not biologically plausible and the other assumptions are similarly problematical.

It has been known for some time that any effective learning rule must include an input from the ultimate result of the computation; Hebbs correlation rule has no way to punish a connection that leads to a disaster. In a network that directly links inputs and outputs, like a matrix model or a 1-layer perceptron (Fogelman-Soulie et al., in press), it is easy to punish the offending links. For a system with more structure and indirect links, it has not been obvious how to assess credit and blame. Recent developments in learning theory, while not totally solving this problem, have facilitated the study of learning in much richer structures (Rumelhart et al., 1986; Parker, 1985).

The development of back-propagation learning techniques (Rumelhart et al., 1986) has had a complex effect on theories of representation. Although no one has suggested that animal learning works the same way, several studies have used the results of back-propagation experiments to pursue the compact-diffuse issue. Scalleter and Zee (1988) establish conditions under which punctate representation is optimal while Rosenberg and Blelloch's results (Rosenberg & Blelloch, 1988) yield a somewhat more distributed representation. The fundamental structure requirements described in this chapter are independent of whether the information is pre-specified or learned and suggest that if learning systems ever reach the complexity of Figure 2, they will have compact representations.

Learning in structured connectionist systems has been studied directly. A major problem in this formulation is "recruiting" the compact representation for new concepts (Fanty, 1987; Feldman, 1982; Wickelgren, 1979). It is all very well to show the advantages of representational schemes like Figures 1, 2 and 4, but how could they arise? This question is far from settled, but there are some encouraging preliminary results. The central question is how a system that grows essentially no new connections could recruit compact groups of units to capture new concepts and relations. One relevant result concerns the probability of finding compact groups that link nodes in a random graph (Feldman, 1982). It turns out that, for biologically reasonable parameters, the probability of a compact cluster ($\sim$ 20 units) is quite high. The brain is not random, except perhaps very locally, but that increases the probability of recruiting compact concept representations. Current work on learning in more structured networks (Hinton, 1986; Fanty, 1987) is examining this more closely.

In summary, connectionist studies of pure generalization and learning minimize the pre-existing structure and tend to study diffuse models. This has turned out to be very valuable and will continue to be. Like the studies of overall convergence, e.g., (Cohen & Grossberg, 1983; Hopfield, 1982; Wilson & Cowan, 1972), these are best done assuming no particular structure of the network. But the structure exists and only compact representations can capture it.

Structured networks of evidence-combining simple units have a number of attractive computational properties. Error resistance, context dependence, and the ability to assimilate conflicting information are natural properties of such systems. A reasonable degree of generalization follows from these properties. Simple weight-change rules can enable these systems to improve their performance significantly. The collective behavior of such systems can produce powerful computations not easily anticipated, as is true of any complex circuit. While certain concepts are represented explicitly, the system is not restricted to dealing only with those. A properly structured network can behave, in certain situations, as if it had concepts and relations implicitly represented. An explicit, compact representation of concepts is required when they have disjunction or internal structure or when they participate in relations or are communicated among sub-systems. In addition, the nature of any emergent system properties depends heavily on which concepts are explicitly represented and the detailed structure of the presentation.

From this perspective, connectionist concept representation presents no paradigmatic conflict or unapproachable mystery but a deep and fascinating set of scientific questions. The issues discussed in this paper arose from considering only the simplest concepts and properties. Human conceptual memory extends to much richer concepts, to relations among them, and to knowledge of space, time, and intensionality. All of these issues have been studied seriously in several disciplines and an imposing collection of problems has been elucidated (Brachman & Levesque, 1985). The hope of connectionist research is that explicit consideration of the computational mechanisms used by the brain will help clarify how it does its marvelous work.

APPENDIX

Interim Neuron Doctrine

The following five brief statements are intended to define which aspect of the brain's activity is important for understanding its main function, to suggest the way that single neurons represent what is going on around us, and to say how this is related to our subjective experience. The statements are dogmatic and incautious because it is important that they should be clear and testable.

First dogma

A description of that activity of a single nerve cell which is transmitted to and influences other nerve cells, and of a nerve cell's response to such influences from other cells, is a complete enough description for functional understanding of the nervous system. There is nothing else "looking at" or controlling this activity, which must therefore provide a basis for understanding how the brain controls behaviour. **Since significant behaviors involve many individual nerve cells, functional understanding of the nervous system will require scientific languages for characterizing the behavior of networks of neurons.**

Second dogma

Efficient coding of information is a central problem of the sensory system. At progressively higher levels in the sensory pathways information about the physical stimulus is more abstract and is represented by progressively fewer active neurons.

Third dogma

Trigger features of neurons are matched to the redundant features of sensory stimulation in order to achieve greater completeness and economy of representation. This selective responsiveness is determined by the sensory stimulation to which neurons have been exposed, as well as by genetic factors operating during development.

Fourth dogma

Just as physical stimuli directly cause receptors to initiate neural activity, so the active **networks of intermediate and** high-level neurons directly and simply cause the elements of our perceptions.

Fifth dogma

Frequency coding is the primary basis of neural communication. Sensory neurons respond with high frequency discharge to external stimuli which fit into a narrow range of possibilities; the higher the discharge the more narrow the range of possible causes.

Zeroth dogma

Intelligent behavior and its neural realization are incredibly complex. A functional understanding of this will require organizational principles from the behavioral and computational sciences as well as biology.

REFERENCES

Ackley, D.H., Hinton, G.E., & Sejnowski, T.J. (1988). A learning algorithm for Boltzmann machines. *Cognitive Science*, **9**:1, 147–169, January-March 1985; also in D. Waltz & J.A. Feldman (eds.), (1988), *Connectionist Models and Their Implications: Readings from Cognitive Science*. Ablex Publishing Corp., 285–308.

Allman, J., Miezen, F., & McGuiness, E. (1985). Stimulus specific responses from beyond the classical receptive field: Neurophysiological mechanisms for local-global comparisons in visual neurons. *Annual Review of Neuroscience*, **8**, 407–430.

Amari, S., & Arbib, M.A. (1982). *Competition and Cooperation in Neural Networks*. Vol. 45 of Lecture Notes in Biomathematics, S. Levin (ed.), Springer-Verlag.

Anderson, J.A., & Hinton, G.E. (1981). Models of information processing in the brain. In G.E. Hinton & J.A. Anderson (eds.), *Parallel Models of Associative Memory*, Hillsdale NJ: Lawrence Erlbaum.

Anderson, J.A., & Mozer, M.C. (1981). Categorization and selective neurons. In G.E. Hinton & J.A. Anderson (eds.), *Parallel Models of Associative Memory*, Hillsdale NJ: Lawrence Erlbaum.

Ballard, D.H. (1986a). Cortical connections and parallel processing: Structure and function. *The Behavioral and Brain Sciences*,**9**:1, 67–120.

Barber, C. (1980). *Evoked Potentials*. Baltimore: University Park Press.

Barlow, H.B. (1972). Single units and sensation: A neuron doctrine for perceptual psychology? *Perception*, **1**, 371–392.

Barto, A.G., Sutton, R.S., & Brouwer, P.S. (1981). Associative search network: A reinforcement learning associative memory. *Biological Cybernetics*, **40**, 201–211.

Barto, A.G., & Anandan, P. (1984). Pattern recognizing stochastic learning automata. Tech. Report 84-30, Computer and Information Science, Univ. Massachusetts at Amherst.

Brachman, R.J., & Levesque, H.J. (1985). *Readings in Knowledge Representation*. Palo Alto, CA: Morgan-Kaufman Publishers.

Cohen, M.A., & Grossberg, S. (1983). Absolute stability of global pattern formation and parallel memory storage by competitive neural networks. *IEEE Transactions: Systems, Man and Cybernetics*, **13**, 815–825.

Cooper, P.R., & Hollbach, S.C. (1987). Parallel recognition of objects comprised of pure structure. *Proceedings DARPA Image Understanding Workshop*, Los Angeles, CA.

Desimone, R., Schein, S.J., Moran, J., & Ungerleider, L.G. (1985). Contour, color, and shape analysis beyond the striate cortex. *Vision Research*, **25**, 441–452.

Edelman, G.M. (1981). Group selection as the basis for higher brain function in The Organization of Cerebral Cortex. F.O. Schmitt, F.G. Worden, G. Adelman, & S.G. Dennis (eds.), MIT Press, Cambridge, MA.

Fanty, M.A. (1987). Learning in structured connectionist networks. Forthcoming Ph.D. dissertation, Computer Science Dept., Univ. Rochester.

Feldman, J.A. (1985). Four frames suffice: A provisional model of vision and space. *The Behavioral and Brain Sciences*, **8,** 265–289.

Feldman, J.A. (1982). Dynamic connections in neural networks. *Biological Cybernetics*, **46,** 27–39.

Feldman, J.A., & Ballard, D.H. (1982). Connectionist models and their properties. *Cognitive Science*, **6,** 205–254.

Fogelman-Soulie, F., Gallinari, P., LeCun, Y., & Thiria, S. Automata networks and artificial intelligence. In F. Fogelman-Soulie, Y. Robert, & M. Tchuente (eds.), *Automata Networks in Computer Science, Theory and Applications*, Manchester University Press, to appear.

Golden, R.M. (1986). A developmental neural model of visual word perception. *Cognitive Science*,**10**:3, 241–276; also in D. Waltz & J.A. Feldman (eds.) (1988), *Connectionist Models and Their Implications: Readings from Cognitive Science*, Ablex Publishing Corp., 119–154.

Goldman-Rakic, P.S., & Schwartz, M.L. (1982). Interdigitation of contralateral and ipsilateral columnar projections to frontal association cortex in primates. *Science*, **216,** 755–757.

Hebb, D.O. (1949). *The Organization of Behavior*. New York: John Wiley.

Hinton, G.E. (1986). Learning distributed representations of concepts. *Proceedings, 8th Annual Conf. of Cognitive Science Society*, Amherst MA.

Hinton, G.E. (1981). Implementing semantic networks in parallel hardware, in *Parallel Models of Associative Memory*. G.E. Hinton, & J.A. Anderson (eds.), Hillsdale, NJ: Lawrence Erlbaum Assoc.

Hinton, G.E., & Anderson, J.A. (eds) (1981). *Parallel Models of Associative Memory*. Hillsdale, NJ: Lawrence Erlbaum Assoc.

Hinton, G.E., McClelland, J.L. & Rumelhart, D.E. (1986). Distributed representations. In D.E. Rumelhart & J.L. McClelland (eds.), *Parallel Distributed Processing, Explorations in the Microstructure of Cognition, Vol.1: Foundations*, Bradford Books/MIT Press.

Hopfield, J.J. (1982). Neural networks and physical systems with emergent collective computational abilities. *Proceedings of the National Academy of Sciences of the United States of America*, **79,** 2554–2558.

Hopfield, J.J., & Tank, D.W. (1985). Neural computation in optimization problems. *Biological Cybernetics*.

Hubel, D.H., & Wiesel, T.N. (1979). Brain mechanisms of vision. *Scientific American*,**241**:3, 150–162.

Kohonen, T. (1984). *Self-Organization and Associative Memory*. Springer Series in Information Sciences, 8, Springer Verlag.

Lashley, K. (1959). In search of the engram. In Symposia of the Society for Experimental Biology, No. 4, *Physiological Mechanisms in Animal Behavior*, New York: Academic Press, 454–483.

Lashley, K.S. (1929). *Brain Mechanisms and Intelligence.* Chicago: University of Chicago Press.

Lynch, G. (1986). *The Neurobiology of Learning and Memory.* Cambridge, MA: MIT Press.

McClelland, J.L., & Rumelhart, D.E. (1986). *Parallel Distributed Processing: Explorations in the Microstructure of Cognition. Vol 2: Applications.* Cambridge, Mass: Bradford Books/ MIT Press.

McClelland, J.L., & Rumelhart, D.E. (1981). An interactive activation model of the effect of context on language learning (Part I). *Psychological Review*,**88,** 375–401.

Merzenich, M.M., Nelson, R.J., Stryker, M.P., Cynader, M.S., Schoppmann, A., & Zook, J.M. (1984). Somatosensory cortical map changes following digit amputation in adult monkeys. *The Journal of Comparative Neurology*, **224,** 591–605.

Minsky, M. (1987). New York: Simon and Schuster.

Minsky, M., & Papert, S. (1972). *Perceptrons.* Second edition, Cambridge, MA: MIT Press.

Mishkin, M. (1987). The anatomy of memory. *Scientific American*, June.

Newell, A. (1983). Intellectual issues in the history of artificial intelligence. In F. Machlup & U. Mansfield (eds.), *The Study of Information: Interdisciplinary Messages*, New York: John Wiley & Sons, Inc.

Palm, G. (1980). On associative memory. *Biological Cybernetics*, **36,** 19–31.

Parker, D.B. (1985). Learning-Logic. TR-47, Center for Computational Research in Economics and Management Science, MIT.

Phillips, C.G., Zeki, S., & Barlow, H.B. (1984). Localization of function in the cerebral cortex, *Brain*, **107,** 328–361.

Pribram, K.H., Nuwer, M. & Baron, R. (1974). The holographic hypothesis of memory structure in brain function and perception,. In R.C. Atkinson, D.H. Krantz, R.C. Luce, & P. Suppes (eds.), *Contemporary Developments in Mathematical Psychology*, San Francisco: Freeman, W.H.

Roediger, H.L. III, (1980). Memory metaphors in cognitive psychology. *Memory and Cognition*,**8**:1, 231–246.

Rosenberg, C. R., & Blelloch, G. (1988). An implementation of network learning on the connection machine. In D.A. Waltz & J.A. Feldman (eds.) *Connectionist Models and Their Implications: Readings from Cognitive Science*, Ablex Publishing Corp.

Rumelhart, D.E., & McClelland, J.L. (1986). *Parallel Distributed Processing: Explorations in the Microstructure of Cognition. Vol 1: Foundations.* Cambridge, Mass: Bradford Books/ MIT Press.

Rumelhart, D.E., & McClelland, J.L. (1981). An interactive activation model of the effect of context in language learning (Part 2) *Psychological Review*, **89,** 60–94.

Rumelhart, D.E., Hinton, G.E., & Williams, R.J. (1986). Learning internal representations by error propagation. In D.E. Rumelhart & J.L. McClelland (eds.), *Parallel Distributed Processing, Explorations in the Microstructure of Cognition,.Vol.1: Foundations*, Cambridge, Mass: Bradford Books/MIT Press.

Sabbah, D. (1985). Computing with connections in visual recognition of Origami objects. *Cognitive Science*, **9**, 25–50.

Scalletar, R. & Zee, A. (1988). Emergence of grandmother memory in feed foward networks: Learning with noise and forgetfulnes. In J.L. McClelland & D.E. Rumelhart (eds.) *Parallel Distributed Processing, Explorations in the Microstructure of Cognition, Vol. 2: Applications*, Bradford Books/MIT Press.

Sejnowski, T.J. (1986). Open questions about computation in cerebral cortex. In J.L. McClelland & D.E. Rumelhart (eds.), *Parallel Distributed Processing: Explorations in the Microstructure of Cognition, Vol. 2: Applications*, Cambridge, Mass: Bradford Books/ MIT Press.

Shastri, L. (1985). Evidential reasoning in semantic networks: A formal theory and its parallel implementation. Ph.D. thesis and TR166, Computer Science Dept., Univ. Rochester.

Shastri, L., & Feldman, J.A. (1986). Neural nets, routines and semantic networks. In N. Sharkey (ed.), *Advances in Cognitive Science*, Chichesster, UK: Ellis Horwood Publishers.

Shaw, G.L., Silverman, D.J., & Pearson, J.C. (1985). Model of cortical organization embodying a basis for a theory of information processing and memory recall. *Proceedings of the National Academy of Sciences of the United States of America*, **82**, 2364–2368.

Shepard, G. (1986). *The Neurobiology of Learning and Memory.* G. Lynch (ed.), Cambridge, MA: MIT Press.

Smith, E.E., & Medin, D.L. (1981). *Categories and Concepts.* Cambridge, MA: Harvard University Press.

Thompson, R.F. (1986). The neurobiology of learning and memory. *Science*, **233**, 941–947.

Touretzky, D.S., & Hinton, G.E. (1985). Symbols among neurons: Details of a connectionist inference architecture. *Proceedings, IJCAI*, Los Angeles, CA, 238–243.

van Heerden, P.J. (1963). A new optical method of storing and retrieving information. *Applied Optics*, **2**, 387–392.

von der Malsburg, C. (1985). Nervous structures with dynamical links. *Berichte der Bunsen-Gesellschaft fur Physikalische Chemie*, in press.

Wickelgren, W.A. (1979). Chunking and consolidation: A theoretical synthesis of semantic networks, configuring in conditioning, S-R versus cognitive learning, normal forgetting the amnesic syndrome, and the hippocampal arousal system. *Psychological Review*, **86**, 44–60.

Willshaw, D. (1981). Holography, associative memory, and inductive generalization. In G.E. Hinton, & J.A. Anderson (eds.), *Parallel Models of Associative Memory*, Hillsdale, NJ: Lawrence Erlbaum.

Wilson, H.R., & Cowan, J.D. (1972). Excitatory and inhibitory interactions in localized populations of model neurons. *Biophysical Journal*, **12**, 1–24.

PERCEPTION AND ACTION

Implementation of an Adaptive Neural Controller for Sensory-Motor Coordination

Michael Kuperstein and Jorge Rubinstein
Neurogen Laboratories Inc., 325 Harvard St. suite 202
Brookline, MA. 02146 USA

Abstract - *We present a theory and prototype of a neural controller called INFANT that learns sensory-motor coordination from its own experience. INFANT adapts to unforeseen changes in the geometry of the physical motor system and to the location, orientation, shape and size of objects. It can learn to accurately grasp an elongated object without any information about the geometry of the physical sensory-motor system. This new neural controller relies on the self-consistency between sensory and motor signals to achieve unsupervised learning. It is designed to be generalized for coordinating any number of sensory inputs with limbs of any number of joints. INFANT is implemented with an image processor, stereo cameras and a five degree-of freedom robot arm. Its average grasping accuracy after learning is 3% of the arm's length in position and 6 degrees in orientation.*

Keywords - neural networks, adaptive sensory-motor coordination, robotics.

1. INTRODUCTION

The human brain develops accurate sensory-motor coordination in the face of many unforeseen changes in the dimensions of the body, strength of the muscles and placements of the sensory organs. This is accomplished for the most part without a teacher. A simple version of this skill has now been implemented in a robot control system. We present a new theory and implementation that suggest how at least one type of adaptive sensory-motor coordination might be developed and maintained by animals as well as robot controllers. The theory relies on the self-consistency between sensory and motor signals to achieve unsupervised learning. The self-consistency hypothesis is an extension of results from developmental studies in coordination behavior. Studies in the kitten (Held and Hine, 1963) show that visually guided behavior develops only when changes in visual stimulation are systematically related to self-produced movement. The hypothesis is also consistent with the motor theory of speech perception (Liberman et. al., 1967; Williams and Nottebohm, 1985).

The new theory also relies on the topography of neural units in a network. Topography is the ordered contiguous representation of inputs or outputs across a surface with possible overlap of neighboring representations. Topographic mappings have been found in most sensory and motor brain structures (Kandel and Schwartz, 1985).

This study combines the constraints of self-consistency and topography for adaptively coordinating a multijoint arm to reach an elongated object arbitrarily positioned in space, as viewed by two cameras. The architectures of neural networks in this study consist of arrays of simple identical computational elements, called neurons, where each neuron can modify the relationship between its inputs and its output by some rule. The power of these neural networks comes from a combination of the geometry used for the connections, the operations used for the interaction between neurons and the learning rules.

2. ADAPTIVE CONTROL

We define adaptive control to mean one that can learn and maintain accurate performance even after unpredictable changes are made in either the geometrical, mechanical or sensing parameters or from partial internal damage. Learning must be achieved without a teacher. Changes in a motor plant after wear include :

1. Transformation of sensor signals to actuator movement.
2. Link lengths.
3. Signal noise.
4. Potential internal processor faults .

To be useful, an autonomous controller must operate in real time, learn and maintain its own calibration and be expandable to accommodate many robot joints. Currently, autonomous robots are controlled by either direct program control, teaching pendants, inverse kinematics or classical adaptive control techniques. None of the first three methods are adaptive. As for classical adaptive control techniques, they require a model of the robot plant and actuators, which may be difficult to obtain beforehand. Also, multijoint inverse kinematic methods are computationally intensive which slow down the control process considerably .

The specific problem that this study addresses is controlling a robot to reach objects in space. This is laid physically as a 5-degree of freedom arm being guided by stereo cameras to reach an elongated object (figure 1).

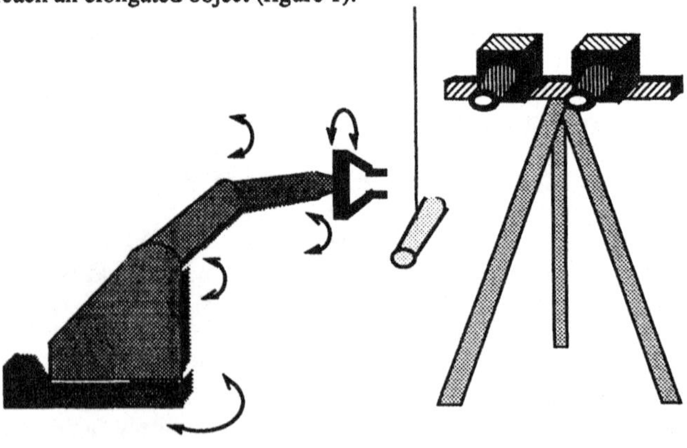

Figure 1. Schematic of the 5-degree of freedom arm and stereo camera system.

3. NEURAL CONTROLLER CONSTRAINTS

The design of the neural network that adaptively controls the motor plant has a number of constraints.

1. The Neural Controller design must not contain information about the plant or actuator characteristics. By being independent of any plant, it can be generically applied to all plants.

2. The neural network has to learn the association between the stereo image of a an object and the pattern of motor signals to all the joints.

3. The neural network computation must be parallel so that is can be generalized to many joints without increasing processing time.

The specific problem of reaching an elongated object in space has another constraint: Since an object can be at any location in 3D space and at any orientation, the controller must have some way of processing 3D information from stereo views of the object.

These constraints were first used in a previous study to create a 3D computer simulation of a neural network controller (Kuperstein, 1987, 1988a, 1988b). The current implementation is an extension of that simulation. The Neural Controller is based on newly discovered distributive neural representations and computations. The following sections will discuss the design of the Neural Controller in increasing levels of detail.

4. NEURAL CONTROLLER SYSTEM

The Neural Controller is designed to learn self-consistency between sensory and motor signals without supervision. In general it operates in two phases in a process called a circular reaction, shown in figure 2. The current use of circular reaction is an extension of one of J. Piaget's developmental stages (1952). In the first phase, sensory-motor relations are learned via correlations between input and output signals. In the second phase, the system uses the learned correlations to evoke the correct posture that manipulates a sensed object.

The block diagram in figure 2 shows the major modules that embody the Neural Controller During learning in the first phase, a random generator first produces random postures of the multijoint arm in space, while the gripper holds an object such as a cylinder. Then the stereo cameras snap the image of the arm holding the object. These images are transformed into neural input maps. The signals coming from the input maps are modulated by a set of weight signals to produce target signals. The weights constitute the global association between all possible images of an object and the arm motor signals.

The target map outputs are compared with the random outputs that generated the arm posture to produce error signals. These error signals are then used to update the weight signals which improves the reaching performance.

During performance in the second phase, the object is located somewhere free in space. The sequence of transformations from the stereo cameras to the target map is reiterated as in the learning phase. The resulting target map outputs then drive the arm actuators. Because of the learned associations between the object images and the arm

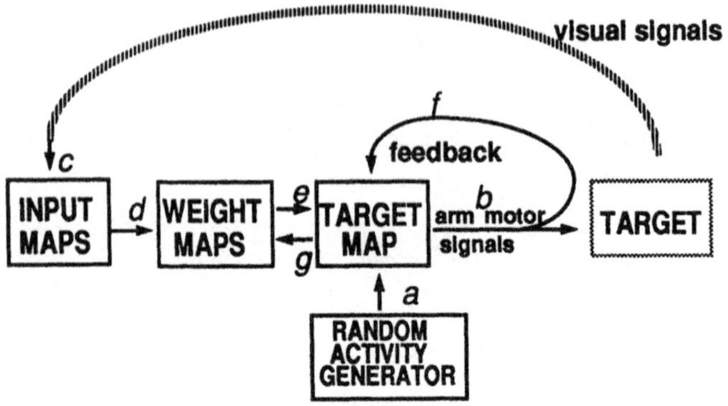

Figure 2. The circular reaction. Self-produced motor signals that manipulate an object target are correlated with target sensation signals. The sequence for training is *a, b, c, d, (e+f), g*. Correlated learning is done in step *g*. After the correlation is achieved, target sensation signals alone can evoke the associated motor signals to accurately manipulate the target. The sequence for performance is *c, d, e, b*.

motor signals, the hand will superimpose on the object.

The control performance process is achieved without feedback and without knowledge of the spatial relations of the mechanical system.

5. SELF CONSISTENT SENSORY-MOTOR LEARNING

The inputs to the Neural Controller are camera images and the outputs are arm signals. Stationary stereo cameras register images composed of light intensity I_{ij}, i=1,2...I, j=1,2...J. while arm signals a_m (m=1..M) activate four joint angles of the arm (see figure 1): the base, the shoulder, the elbow, and gripper roll. The gripper is controlled by conventional methods. The Neural Controller has no a priori knowledge of spatial relations of the mechanical system.

On learning trial n, the arm signals are first randomly generated in user coordinates, which range from 0 to 1, and are transformed into joint angles for the arm. These joint angles in turn are transformed in the required stepping motor steps of each joint. In this simplest case, the joint angle of the limbs are computed to be linearly proportional to the user coordinates. However, any one of many monotonic functions of user coordinates can be chosen with similar results. Random activation of the arm joints leads to an arm posture with the two fingered hand initially holding a cylinder.

Then, the stereo cameras register two views of the arm holding the cylinder. Each image is first processed for novel contrast in the scene as compared against the background. This allows the controller to be insensitive to potentially distracting background objects. Next, the novel contrast view is processed for the cartesian location of the center of highest visual contrast or peak location. Visual contrast is determined by a combination of a high spatial contrast convolution followed by a low spatial smearing.

The peak locations identify the target to be grasped. These locations are first transformed into neural input maps. All the neural input maps have the same format. They are composed of linear arrays of discrete values across one parameter dimension.

There are six neural input maps for gaze, g_{pqn} (p=1,2; q=1,2,3; n = 1,2...N) which represent the x position and y position for each camera and the x position disparity and y position disparity for each camera. Disparity is defined as a monotonic function of the difference between the peak locations at each camera. The gaze maps are generated as unimodal distributions of activity. Any one of a large family of transformations can be chosen without affecting the results. The main criterion for these transformations is that the positions of unimodal distribution peaks vary monotonically with a parameter dimension which in this case is the Cartesian location or Cartesian disparity. For this implementation we used an inverse parabola function where x_{pq} is the gaze position or disparity parameter, n is the map index and α and β are normalization constants.

$$g_{pqn} = \max [\, 0, \ \alpha \,(1 - (x_{pq} - n)^2/\beta) \,] \qquad (1)$$

There are two benefits to choosing a unimodal distribution that results in overlapping activation of neighboring neural elements: 1. The system can effectively average out signal noise and 2. the system provides accurate interpolation for reaching objects that have never been encountered during learning.

Each camera receives a two-dimensional visual projection of the cylinder target in space. Each image V_q is processed for visual contrast orientation. There are twelve neural visual maps v_{rqn} (r=1..4; q=1,2,3; n=1,2...N) which represent 4 graded contrast orientations (0°, 45°, 90°, 135°) for the left camera, right camera and the orientation disparity between cameras. To get a visual neural map, a measure of normalized orientation, d_{rq} is first computed. This measure is achieved by convolving an image neighborhood around the center of contrast location from each camera with an orientation kernel k_r. In this convolution, q is the left or right camera and r is the orientation direction.

$$d_{rq} = V_q * k_r \qquad (2)$$

The kernel matrices, k_r, have the same nonpositive coefficients everywhere except along one string in one of the four orientations, r. The coefficients in that string are all the same positive number. Other orientation-response functions can be used with similar results.

Next the measures of contrast orientations are normalized to each other, so that the orientation measures will be insensitive to different lighting conditions:

$$d'_{rq} = d_{rq} \,/ \textstyle\sum_{rq} (d_{rq}) \qquad (3)$$

Note, that since the measure of orientation is sampled for only a small neighborhood around the contrast center of the object, this measure is insensitive to object size.

The orientation measure is then used to generate the visual neural maps (the same as the gaze maps) where δ and λ are constants.

$$v_{rqn} = \max [0, \ \delta (1 - (d'_{rq} - n)^2/\lambda)] \tag{4}$$

After the neural maps are computed, they can be used to generate arm signals, a'_m through their respective weight maps. Each gaze and visual neural map is connected with a weight map for each joint, m = 1..4 . The modifiable target weights in these maps act as associative gates between sensation and posture. In this equation $w_{pqn<m>}$ are the modifiable weights from all input map elements to all joints.

$$a'_m = \Sigma_{pqn} (g_{pqn} \, w_{pqn<m>}) + \Sigma_{rqn} (v_{rqn} \, w_{rqn<m>}) \tag{5}$$

Note that weight values can be negative. All weights are initialized to 0.

The model develops self-consistency and improves its performance by modifying the target weights. The weights are changed by a learning rule during each trial, which develops the correlation between topographic sensory signals and topographic motor signals across all trials. The learning rule minimizes the difference between the actual (random) and computed motor signals. Thus, the differences or errors ε_m are

$$\varepsilon_m = a_m - a'_m \tag{6}$$

Minimizing these differences while allowing global convergence requires changing all active target weights by a small amount. In this equation **k** is the learning trial number and σ is the learning rate.

$$w_{(k+1)pqn<m>} = w_{(k)pqn<m>} + \sigma \, \varepsilon_m \, g_{pqn} \tag{7}$$

$$w_{(k+1)rqn<m>} = w_{(k)rqn<m>} + \sigma \, \varepsilon_m \, v_{rqn} \tag{8}$$

The learning rule states that the target weights corresponding to those sensory inputs that are active, are changed by an increment that depends on the component of an error in the respective joint. This component specific learning occurs back in the weight maps. With this incremental learning rule, the computed motor signals for all targets converge towards the actual motor signals in successive trials, thereby minimizing ε_m .

When learning has converged, accurate performance can begin. The object is located somewhere free in space. The sequence of transformations from the stereo cameras to the target map is reiterated as in the learning phase (equations 1 - 5). The resulting target map outputs, a'_m then drive the arm actuators. Because of the learned associations between the object images and the arm motor signals, the hand will superimpose on the object.

During the learning phase, similar object orientations can be reached by two extremely different wrist roll angular positions. For example, a vertical orientation of a cylinder can be reached by a 0 degree wrist roll or 180 degree wrist roll. This presents a problem in trying to determine which angular wrist position should be used when the cylinder is vertical.

The approach we took was to introduce the concept of multiple virtual joints that make up a single physical joint. The purpose of virtual joints is to distinguish which one of multiple, different behaviors is most appropriate for a similar presentation of an object. The idea is that the controller first associates different behaviors with overlapping ranges of object presentation. Then for a single object presentation, the learned behaviors compete for being most appropriate.

Virtual and physical joints both have weight maps associated with them. While the weight maps for physical joints are always updated during learning, the weight maps of virtual joints are updated only for the corresponding subrange of a joint postures. For example, one virtual joint corresponds to the range of wrist roll from 0 to 90 degrees and the second virtual joint corresponds to the range of wrist roll from 90 to 180 degrees.

During performance, the neural controller makes a decision about which of the multiple virtual joints and associated weight maps are most appropriate to the orientation of the object. Neural weight maps of all virtual joints are concurrently activated by the same object. Then all virtual joints produce computed arm signals. How can the controller distinguish an appropriate arm signal from an inappropriate arm signal? It can not distinguish on the level of activity alone since appropriate and inappropriate behaviors can both generate a large or small arm signal. Our solution is to incorporate antagonistic arm signals for all virtual joints whose sum is a constant. Then appropriately learned behaviors will generate antagonistic arm signals that sum to that constant while inappropriate behaviors will generate a low level of activity smaller than the constant.

6. SENSORY ERROR LEARNING

Additional learning can occur to fine tune and maintain accurate grasping performance in the face of unexpected changes in the geometry of the physical plant. This learning is based on errors derived from visual feedback after an attempted grasp. This sensory based scheme was rejected as a method for learning fundamental sensory-motor coordination. To learn a motor position using sensory based errors would require a priori knowledge of the correspondence between sensory errors and motor errors. Our self-consistent learning scheme avoids this requirement and thus allows motor learning from any relation between the cameras and the arm. However, once a global association between sensation and posture is learned, it can be used to define the correspondence between sensory errors and motor errors. This section describes this secondary sensory-based learning.

In an attempt to grasp the target, for example a ball, the gripper may miss the target. In this case, the mismatch between the position of the ball and the gripper is the source of an error. Our sensory based learning scheme requires the object and the gripper to be treated as two distinct sensory inputs with separate neural input map representations. These are mapped into different computed arm postures using the same current weight maps. The computed arm posture for the gripper, a''_m is determined by the following equation where g'_{pqn} is the input neural map for the gripper.

$$a''_m = \Sigma_{pqn} (g'_{pqn} \, w_{pqn<m>}) \qquad (9)$$

The differences between the computed arm postures are the motor errors, ε'_m, used to update the current weight maps:

$$\varepsilon'_m = a'_m - a''_m \tag{10}$$

This error is used to update the neural weights similar to equations 7,8. The weights are updated in a region centered around the peak of the object's input neural map, g_{pqn}. In this equation ϕ is a learning rate.

$$w_{(k+1)pqn<m>} = w_{(k)pqn<m>} + \phi\, \varepsilon'_m\, g_{pqn} \tag{11}$$

The updated weights represent an improved correspondence between the where the object is seen with where the gripper should move. This sensory-based learning scheme can be repeated in a sequence of improved reaching performances up to a specified accuracy.

7. NEURAL CONTROLLER IMPLEMENTATION

The neural network controller is implemented on an industrial robot arm and commercial image processing system. The implementation of the Neural Controller was achieved by developing software that embodies the Neural Controller processing into an image processor. Equations and procedures for the INFANT were translated into a sequence of image processing commands and robot commands from both the image processing software and robot control software. During implementation it was determined that processing weight maps values required at least 16 bits of resolution in order to provide sufficient dynamic range for accurate learning. Figure 3 shows an example of the gaze and visual input maps for one trial. Each map has a population of 640 neural elements. The location of the peak of the inverted parabola along the neural map dimension is proportional to the size of the input parameter.

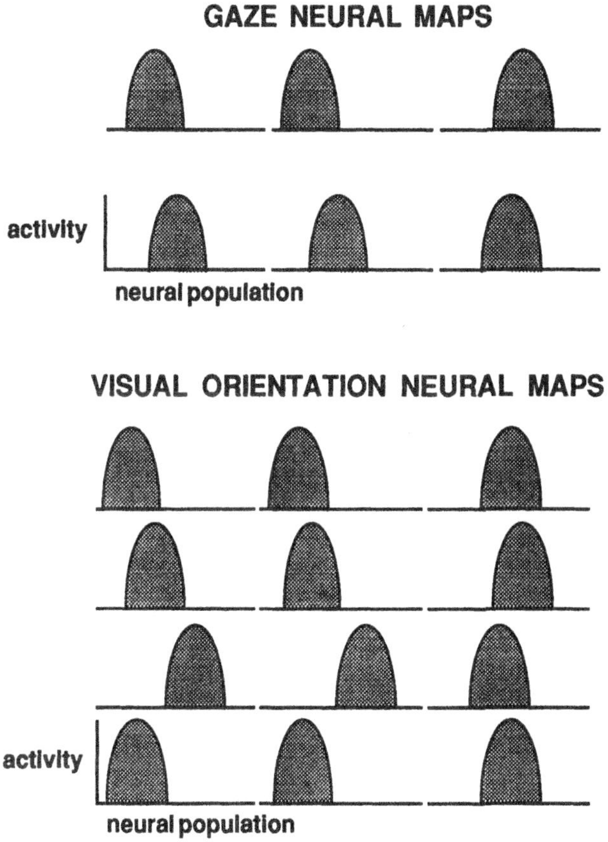

Figure 3. Gaze and visual neural maps for one trial. Each map has a population of 640 neural elements. The location of the peak of the parabola along the neural map dimension is proportional to the size of the input parameter. For the gaze neural maps, the columns represent (from left to right) the left camera, the right camera and the gaze disparity. Top row is for x positions and the bottom row is for y position. For the visual orientation neural maps, the columns represent (from left to right) the left camera, the right camera and the orientation disparity. The rows represent (from top to bottom) 0, 45, 90, 135 degrees of orientation sensitivity.

Figure 4 shows the neural weight maps after learning that associate the gaze neural maps to each of the first 3 joints.

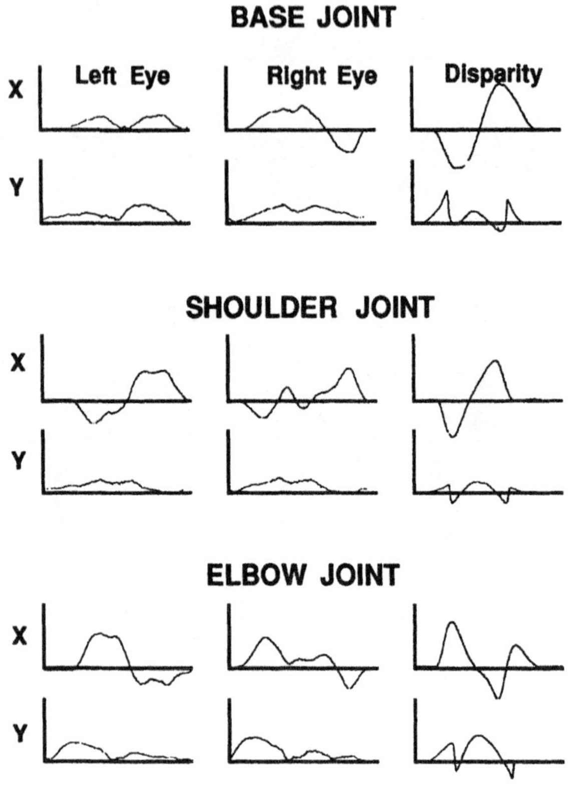

Figure 4. Gaze neural weights after learning for three joints. Vertical axes represent amplitude of weights in relative units. Horizontal axes represent discrete neural elements across a population.

Figure 5 shows the neural weight maps after learning that associate the visual neural maps to the gripper wrist joint.

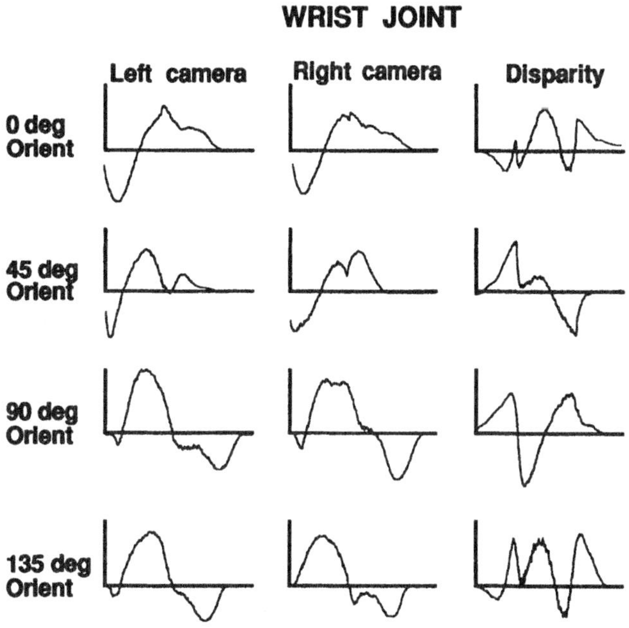

Figure 5. Visual neural weights after learning for the wrist joint. Vertical axes represent amplitude of weights in relative units. Horizontal axes represent discrete neural elements across a population.

8. NEURAL CONTROLLER PERFORMANCE

The Neural Controller was able to accurately reach a cylinder that was arbitrarily positioned anywhere in space within arm's reach. It could not only reach the cylinder that it was trained on, but could also accurately reach many other elongated objects including cylinders of different diameters, lengths and visual contrasts, as well as a piece of paper that was rolled into an irregular elongated form.

During one learning set, the image processor experienced a bit fault (bit 5 of 16) which affected every weight map value. Despite this extreme hardware fault, the reaching performance was not significantly affected.

Performance accuracy was measured for reaching a cylinder target. The accuracy reached an asymptote after about 1,200 learning trials. The average cartesian distance between the intended reach and the actual reach was 3 % of the length of the arm. The average angular deviation between intended gripper wrist orientation and the actual cylinder orientation was 6 degrees.

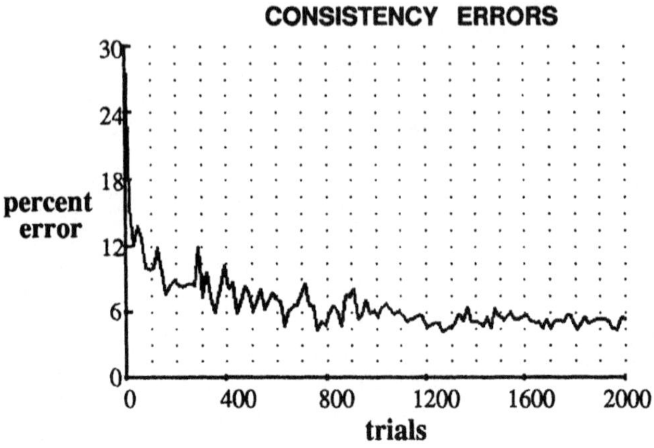

Figure 6. Converge of consistency

Figure 6 shows the consistency errors across learning trials. The consistency error is determined by the following equation where m = 1,2...M.

$$(100 / M) \Sigma_m | \varepsilon_m | \tag{12}$$

Random performance would result in 50% consistency error while the final consistency error of 5% corresponds to the final average distance and orientation errors that were objectively measured.

Whole learning runs were done with different arm and camera positions and a range of neural parameters including neural map width, error rate normalization constants. The Neural Controller showed very similar error convergence for a large range of parameter choices.

9. CONCLUSIONS

A Neural Controller has been implemented to achieve adaptive hand-eye coordination in reaching an elongated object in space. There are four key conclusions from this study:

1. The Neural Controller learns about space by associating how the arm moves with what the cameras see. It does not use any knowledge of the geometry of the mechanical system and there are no inverse computations nor control transfer functions.

2. Learning is achieved without any external source of error correction. This allows the controller to be completely independent of supervision. The learning for one elongated object transfers to any elongated object. Moreover, no calibration for binocular parallax is required.

3. The implementation is fault tolerant to hardware errors.

4. The Neural Controller adapts to unforeseen changes in the geometry of the motor plant.

The algorithmic flow of control is both feedforward and parallel during performance, which makes it fast. After each reach, internal feedback is used to improve subsequent performance through learning.

When implemented in custom hardware, this system will coordinate a multi-joint robot arm to adaptively reach targets in three dimensions in real time. The system will self-organize and maintain motor calibrations starting with only loosely defined relationships. The system will tolerate internal noise, partial control system damage and changes in the geometric, mechanical and sensing parameters of the robot as they occur during wear. This adaptability replaces the need for operator calibration.

The this study has resulted in sufficient understanding of the boundary conditions and the range of parameter choices for implementing a neural robot. Using this knowledge, in phase II of this project, we can design and build an adaptive dynamic Neural Controller for reaching moving objects with multi-joint robots.

The neural network controller in this study has a number of application benefits. The controller will deal effectively in novel environments because of its ability to deal with unforeseen changes in the mechanical plant and actuators. Its adaptability will allow continuous self-calibration and its generic design will allow it to be implemented in many different robots. This will greatly reduce tooling costs and setup time.

10. ACKNOWLEDGEMENT

The authors thank the National Science Foundation and the Air Force Office of Scientific Research for their financial support of this research (Contract #8896210).

11. REFERENCES

Held, R. and Hine , A.(1963) Movement-produced stimulation in the development of visually guided behavior , *J. Comp. Physiol. Psych.* **56**, 872 .

Kandel, E.R. and Schwartz, J.H. (1985) *Principles of Neural Science* (Elsevier Science Publishing).

Kuperstein M. (1987) Adaptive Visual-Motor Coordination in Multijoint Robots using Parallel Architecture *Proc. IEEE Internat. Conf. Automat. Robotics*, March, Raleigh, N.C. 1595-1602

Kuperstein M. (1988a) An adaptive neural model for mapping invariant target position. *Behav. Neurosci.* **102**(1):148-162

Kuperstein M. (1988b) Neural Network Model for Adaptive Hand-Eye Coordination for Single Postures *Science*.**239**:1308-1311

Liberman, A.M., Cooper, F.S., Shankweiler, D.P. & Studdert-Kennedy, M. (1967) Perception of the speech code, *Psychol. Rev.* **74**, 431.

Piaget, J. (1952), *The Origins of Intelligence in Children*, translated by M.Cook, (International University Press, New York.

Williams, H. and Nottebohm, F. (1985), Auditory responses in avian vocal motor neurons: A motor theory for song perception in birds. *Science* **229**, 279.

CONNECTIONISM IN PERSPECTIVE
R. Pfeifer, Z. Schreter, F. Fogelman-Soulié, L. Steels (Eds.)

Biological Constraints on Connectionist Modelling

Simon J. Thorpe and Michel Imbert
Institut des Neurosciences, Departement des Neurosciences de la Vision
Université Pierre et Marie Curie, 9, Quai St. Bernard
75005, Paris, FRANCE.

Abstract—*Many researchers interested in connectionist models accept that such models are "neurally inspired" but do not worry too much about whether their models are biologically realistic. While such a position may be perfectly justifiable, the present paper attempts to illustrate how biological information can be used to constrain connectionist models. Two particular areas are discussed. The first section deals with visual information processing in the primate and human visual system. It is argued that the speed with which visual information is processed imposes major constraints on the architecture and operation of the visual system. In particular, it seems that a great deal of processing must depend on a single bottom-up pass. The second section deals with biological aspects of learning algorithms. It is argued that although there is good evidence for certain coactivation related synaptic modification schemes, other learning mechanisms, including back-propagation, are not currently supported by experimental data.*

Keywords—Vision, learning algorithms, back-propagation, Hebb, parallel processing, multi-layer architectures, feedback, coding, context, temporal constraints.

1. INTRODUCTION

Connectionist models can be used in two rather different ways. The aim of the first approach is the development of artificial intelligent systems. If this is the aim then biological realism is not really an important design factor - one can take the view that although "neurally-inspired", the actual architectures and learning algorithms used can be fundamentally different from those used in real brains - the only real criterion for progress is "Does is work?" Alternatively, connectionist models can be specifically used to further our understanding of how real nervous systems function. Obviously, in such a case, a high priority should be placed on making the model as biologically reasonable as possible. This sort of direct modelisation of neural systems was previously rather rare, but a number of examples have appeared in the literature in the last year or so (see for example, Lehky and Sejnowski (1988), Zipser and Anderson (1988), Sejnowski, Koch and Churchland (1988), Thorpe and Pouget (this volume)).

In principle, there is no reason why these two different ways of using connectionist modelling could not be used relatively independently. Nevertheless, it would be unfortunate if applications-oriented research workers were ignorant of the progress being made in understanding the function of real brains. After all, the human brain is the product of millions of years of trial and error - the solutions adopted as a result of intense natural selection may not be the only way of solving problems, but at least they work! On the other hand, researchers working on biological systems can benefit from the insights obtained by those involved in artificial intelligence research.

Biological data can potentially provide useful information about a number of different computational issues. One important area is coding. Connectionist coding schemes can be distributed, local or something in between (Hinton and Anderson, 1981; Smolensky, 1988; Rumelhart and McClelland, 1986; Feldman, 1985), and biological data may well help in defining those situations in which it may be advantageous to use one or other. Another important area concerns the precision with which such values as synaptic weight strengths should be coded. Current hardware implementations of neural networks use 1, 2, 4, 8 or even 16 bit precision. Biological data could help those involved in designing such systems to decide what level of precision to use. However, in this chapter, we would like to concentrate on two other areas in which biological constraints may be important. The first area concerns the way in which information is processed by the visual system. There are currently a large number of suggestions as to how visual information is handled, involving various degrees of "bottom-up" and "top-down" processing, mechanisms akin to relaxation and so on. It will be argued that the speed with which visual information is processed, together with information about the anatomical organization of the visual system and the activity of neurons in the visual system, provide heavy constraints on the types of models which are biologically feasible.

The second topic concerns the sorts of learning algorithms used by nervous systems. Various possibilities have been proposed, including variations on Hebbian plasticity, the Perceptron learning algorithm, back-propagation and the Boltzmann algorithm. Neurophysiological, psychological and theoretical reasons will be presented for thinking that not all such mechanisms are likely to be implemented in biological "wet-ware".

Before discussing these two problems in detail, it may be worth first characterizing in a bit more detail the sorts of selection pressures that were at work during the evolution of the human brain. Natural selection has probably favoured those variations which improve the animals ability to generate appropriate behavioural responses to environmental situations. However, not all such solutions are likely to be selected. One particularly important factor is speed. If we consider two animals - both of which have visual systems capable of detecting the presence of a predator - but one of which can reach a decision a few milliseconds faster than the other, even such a small difference will be rapidly amplified in the survival rates of their respective offspring. This speed constraint will have been particularly important, given the relatively slow nature of information transmission by individual neurons.

A second factor which will have been of vital importance is size. Again, let us consider two animals, both of which can detect the presence of a predator. Let us assume that both have visual systems that can come to a decision after the same amount of processing time. However, suppose that one can solve the problem with a visual system containing 1,000,000 neurons, whereas the other needs 10% more. It has to be remembered that 10% more neurons means that the animal has to provide 10% more energy for the metabolic requirements of this extra tissue, and there will also be a cost related to the extra weight that must be carried. Thus all other things being equal, the 1 million neuron solution will have a significant advantage. Calculations have shown that even minute differences in reproductive success can result in significant selection over a large number of generations (Dawkins, 1987).

Clearly, the constraints that apply when designing an artificial vision system are not usually so tight. An increase of 1% in the time taken to reach a decision would not be considered significant for most engineering applications, and if 10% more components were used, this would increase the price slightly, but at least in the absence of competition from Taiwanese clones, such extravagance can usually be tolerated!

2. PROCESSING

Jerry Feldman has pointed out a major biological constraint on information processing by animals and humans (Feldman and Ballard, 1982; Feldman, 1985a, Feldman, 1985b. Sophisticated behavioural responses can often be generated only a few hundred msec after a change in the environment. Since neurons can only generate spikes at about one every 5 msec, even when firing maximally, Feldman concluded that this puts a limit of roughly 100 computational steps between input and output. In this section, we would like to see what happens if we limit the discussion to the sensory processing component.

2.1 Information processing by the brain

The human brain has specialized structures for processing information from various sensory modalities - vision, audition, touch, smell and taste. For each of these modalities, we can present a sensory stimulus and ask how long it takes for it to be processed. In general, processing will be taken as meaning the time taken for the stimulus to be identified. In a number of respects, the question is easier to pose in the case of vision. Presenting olfactory and gustatory stimuli at a precise moment is difficult, and so measuring latencies is problematic. In the case of audition, much auditory information is by its very nature temporally structured and so presenting an auditory stimulus such as a word obviously takes a certain time - so here again measuring processing time becomes difficult. Touch is also often used in a dynamic way - we often explore an object actively in order to identify it by touch. However, in the case of vision, it is relatively easy to present even complex visual patterns at a precise point in time and see how long processing takes.

This is the principle reason why we will restrict our discussion of sensory processing to the visual modality. However, it is also the case that vision has for various reasons been more intensively studied in the past. The primary question that we will address concerns the time taken by the visual system to process an image. Both Human Experimental Psychology and Neurophysiology provide data relevant to this issue.

2.2 Psychological data on visual processing time

Visual identification is so easy for humans that we often fail to realize just what a difficult task it is. Imagine flicking through a magazine full of photos. Even if the photos are of widely varying objects and scenes, we usually have no trouble in identifying what they are. How long does this identification process take? A variety of different approaches have been used in Psychology, and these will be briefly reviewed in this section (see also Riddoch and Humphreys, 1988; Humphreys and Quinlan, 1988). Other neurophysiological evidence will be discussed in the next section.

Naming time. Perhaps the most obvious source of information is simply to measure the time it takes people to name a picture of an object or scene. This approach goes back more than 100 years to the studies of James McKeen Cattell (1886a,b), whose findings have been expanded on by more recent studies (e.g. Oldfield, 1966; Potter and Faulconer, 1975; Intraub, 1979; Carr et al, 1982; Henderson et al, 1987). Typically, it takes about 750 msec to name an object. However, the time taken depends on the object in question - an apple, for example, can be named in 600 msec (Intraub, 1979), whereas less familiar objects, such as a xylophone can take as long as 1200 msec (Oldfield, 1966). The problem with such an approach is that we measure not only the time taken by the visual processing, but also the time needed to find the right word to describe the object and the time taken to generate the verbal response. We still need to know what proportion of the naming time is taken up by the visual processing per se.

Minimum presentation time. Another possibility is to measure the minimum presentation time required for an object to be identified correctly. Such studies have shown that in most cases, a presentation lasting 10 to 15 msec is sufficient (Oldfield, 1965; Intraub, 1979). However, this is only the case if the picture is followed by a blank field. If the presentation is followed by the presentation of a complex visual mask, the time required increases to 100 to 120 msec, but even in this case, it is difficult to be sure that visual processing does not continue after this time.

Rapid serial visual presentation. In 1975, Molly Potter, working at M.I.T., introduced an new technique for studying visual processing (Potter, 1975; Potter, 1976). She presented sequences of 16 colour images, with a presentation time varying between 113 and 333 msec per image. Subjects were instructed to press a button as soon as they saw a particular image (e.g. "A boat on a beach"), which could be situated anywhere in the sequence. The results showed that even with the shortest presentation times, the subjects were able to find more than 60% of the targets, leading Potter to conclude that even with presentations of only 113 msec, a great deal of visual processing was possible.

More recently, Helene Intraub has used variations on Potter's technique (Intraub, 1980, 1981). Instead of verbally specifying the target ("a baby reaching for a rattle"), the target was either specified by giving a category ("press when you see an animal") or a negative category ("press when you see something that you don't find in a house"). With presentation times of 114 msec per image, performance was somewhat lower than in Potter's original experiments, but the subjects still managed to find 46% of the targets when the category was specified and 35% when a negative category was used.

There is, however, a complication in the interpretation of such experiments. The fact the subjects are looking for a particular visual target means that in some way the visual system could be primed to look for particular visual features. What would happen if the subject had no contextual information about the type of image that was going to be presented?

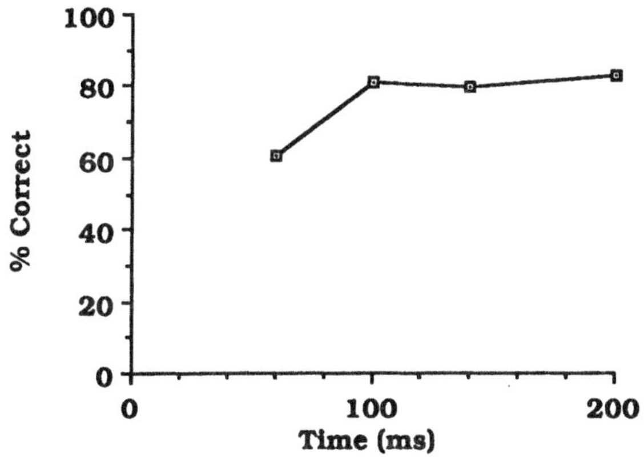

Figure 1: The influence of exposure time on the ability of subjects to identify complex images. A pair of images was presented, and the subject required to identify both. The probability that the subject could correctly identify the first image is plotted as a function of presentation time for those trials on which the second image was also correctly identified. (Thorpe, 1988, and in preparation).

Identification of rapidly presented images. To try and answer this question, we have recently developed an experimental paradigm designed to test the performance of the visual system under conditions in which the effect of context is reduced to a minimum (Thorpe, 1988). We have digitized a large stock of pictures (faces of famous people, paintings, everyday objects, advertising logos, cartoon characters etc), chosen to be a varied as possible, but at the same time being well-known to the majority of people. Using an image processing system, we can present a pair of such images, one immediately after the other to naive subjects. Their task is to name both the images ("Charlie Chaplin", "Concorde", "The Eiffel Tower", etc.). The duration of the images was varied systematically (60, 100, 140 or 200 msec), and the effect on the percentage of images that could be successfully identified determined. Identification of both the first and second images was remarkably robust, averaging 80%, but perhaps the most interesting observation came from looking at the ability of subjects to identify the first image, but taking into account only those trials on which they successfully identified the second. The results of this analysis are illustrated in Figure 1.

It can be seen that reducing the presentation time from 200 to 100 msec had no significant effect on identification, which remained constant at around 80%. Only when presentation time was reduced to 60 msec was there any real effect on performance, and even then, the effect was by no means catastrophic - 60% correct is still a remarkably good level of performance, given the complexity of the visual processing needed to identify the images in question.

Thus, even when the subjects had no advance information about the type of image to be presented, and when they had to process another similar image immediately afterwards, 100 msec presentation times are sufficient for accurate identification of real everyday images.

2.3 The number of identifiable objects and scenes

This level of performance is particularly impressive, especially when one bears in mind the number of such objects and scenes that can be identified in this way by the average human subject. Although some images and scenes need considerable time to be interpreted, a great many objects and scenes can be identified very rapidly and without effort. Is it possible to say how many? Clearly, this figure should include familiar objects ("can-opener", "telephone", "hair-dryer" etc), animals and plants ("tiger", "carnation", "spider" etc.), geographical locations ("The empire state building", "Big Ben" etc.), signs ("MacDonalds", "Mercedes" etc), as well as faces ("Ronald Reagan", "Michael Jackson", etc.). Biederman (1987) estimated that we can name approximately 30,000 different objects. This estimate was based on a sample of the entries in Webster's dictionary, in which he counted the number of words that corresponded to objects which could be easily identified visually. Thus he counted penguin and ostrich, since they were clearly distinguishable, but not garden warbler, which, at least for him, was not sufficiently different from other types of bird.

Nevertheless, the value of 30,000 visually identifiable objects proposed by Biederman is certainly an underestimate, for two reasons in particular. Firstly, if instead of counting entries in a dictionary, you use a large encyclopedia, you will count not only simple words such as "chair", "hammer" and "ostrich", but also specific terms such as "Eiffel tower", "Mona Lisa" and "Adolf Hitler", which are also easy for most people to identify. Using the Encyclopedia Britannica, we have made such an estimation and found a value of 50,000 to 60,000 visually identifiable entries.

The second point is that even this value does not include all the objects and images that are part of the personal repertoire of every one of us, such as the faces of our family and friends, the school we attended when we were young, the sofa in our living room and so on. It is even harder to get a clear idea of the size of this number but it seems likely that the total number of objects and scenes that can be identified rapidly is well in excess of 100,000.

So psychological data leads us to the conclusion that with only 100 msec of presentation time, the human visual system can probably access any one of upwards of 100,000 different internal representations. But there are other neurophysiological arguments in support of the idea that visual information processing is a very rapid process.

2.4 Neurophysiological data on processing time

In the last two decades, a number of researchers have started to analyze the visual response properties of individual neurons in different parts of the brain of awake behaving monkeys. Such studies have revealed that some neurons with quite complicated response properties can respond with remarkably short response latencies following the presentation of a visual stimulus.

Visual responses selective for food. In 1976, Edmund Rolls and his collaborators reported the existence of a population of neurons in a region known as the lateral hypothalamus which became active when the animal was looking at food (e.g. a piece of banana, a peanut, a syringe filled with glucose solution etc) (Rolls, Burton and Mora, 1976). Similar neurons have also been reported in the sheep (Kendrick and Baldwin, 1986). One of the remarkable features of these neurons is that they can respond to any visual stimulus that the animal associated with food, including initially neutral stimuli such as a white square, if such a stimulus came to signal that food was available. The latency at which such neurons became active was found to be around 150 msec (Rolls, Sanghera and Roper-Hall, 1979), and since in order to show such properties, the visual analysis of the stimulus must have been complete, the visual processing time must be less than 150 msec.

More recently, Thorpe, Rolls and Maddison (1983) described neurones in another brain region, namely the orbitofrontal cortex, which also had selective visual responses to food, but with even shorter latencies (around 120 msec). Interestingly, other neurons in the same area also showed selective gustatory responses, and a few neurons responded to both the sight and taste of particular foods. But the main point of relevance here is that highly processed visual information gets to the frontal lobe only 120 msec after the presentation of the stimulus.

Visual responses selective for faces. Other studies by Edmund Rolls, Dave Perrett and their colleagues have described a population of neurons in a part of the temporal lobe known as the superior temporal sulcus which have visual responses that are selective for faces and face features (Perrett, Rolls and Caan, 1982; Rolls, 1986; Perrett, Mistlin and Chitty, 1987). Similar neurons have also been reported in the temporal lobe of the sheep (Kendrick and Baldwin, 1987). The existence of such neurons implies a high level of visual processing, especially when one bears in mind the observation that some of these neurons can respond to a large range of sizes, colours and so on. Nevertheless, the latency with which such cells respond is typically in the range 100 to 140 msec.

Visual responses to familiar objects. Finally, the same group reported a population of neurons in the anterior thalamus which showed highly characteristic responses during the performance of a visual recognition memory task (Rolls, Perrett, Caan and Wilson, 1982). These neurons had the remarkable property of responding selectively to familiar visual stimuli. If a novel visual stimulus (for instance a Coca-Cola bottle) was presented to the monkey, there was no response on the first presentation. However, if the same object was presented a second time, there was a large response from the neuron, even if the first and second presentations were separated in time by as much as 1 to 2 hours. Furthermore, these visual responses could be obtained with any visual stimulus - thus the same neuron could respond to faces, bunches of keys, pens and so on - the only essential characteristic was that the object should have been seen by the monkey shortly before.

The shortness of the latency of some of these neurons was particularly remarkable - 130 msec in one case. Given that the neurons were able to respond to any visual stimulus, as long as it was familiar, this would imply that most visual processing can be achieved in this time.

Selective evoked potentials in humans. Aled Jeffreys, working at Keele University in the U.K., has recently reported the existence of selective visual evoked responses in humans to faces, and other complex meaningful stimuli (Jeffreys, 1988). These potentials, which can be recorded from electrodes attached to the subject's scalp, apparently only occur to stimuli that the subject himself considers as "face-like". A variety of controls indicate that the potentials cannot be accounted for in terms of simple image characteristics such as contour, contrast and so on. The important point as far as the present argument is concerned is that such potentials have peaks at 150 to 180 msec, thus confirming the results of single unit studies in awake behaving animals.

2.5 Interim conclusion - Visual processing time

We have reviewed a variety of experimental results which relate to the speed with which visual processing is achieved. Data from psychological experiments indicate that the human visual system can handle images presented at a rate of about one every 100 msec or so. Even with such short presentation times, it would appear that human subjects can identify well in excess of 100,000 different objects and scenes. Although such experiments do not rule out the possibility that visual processing can continue even when the image is no longer present on the retina, neurophysiological data obtained by recording the activity of single cells in awake behaving monkeys, and by recording visual evoked potentials in humans show that nevertheless, in 100 to 150 msec a great deal of visual information processing has been achieved, and that for many images, processing may even be complete.

What does such information tell us about the way in which information is processed by the visual system? Before coming to any firm conclusions, we will first briefly review some of the salient features of the visual system (Imbert, 1988).

2.6 Visual system anatomy

The pattern of light falling on the retina is sampled by approximately 100 million photoreceptors - the rods and cones. The pattern of activity of these photoreceptors is processed in the retina via a network of bipolar, amacrine and horizontal cells before being transmitted to the brain by approximately 1 million ganglion cells whose axons form the optic nerve. Clearly, the retina must be performing some sort of sophisticated data compression algorithm in order to get through the information bottle-neck of the optic nerve, since, on average, there is only one optic nerve fibre for every 100 photoreceptors, although this ratio varies dramatically across the retina - indeed the ratio is more like one-to-one in the fovea - the part used for the most fine detailed analysis of the image.

The first structure in the central nervous system to receive the visual information arriving from the retina is the lateral geniculate nucleus, which also contains approximately 1 million cells. These cells in turn project to the first cortical visual area, the striate cortex, also known as area 17 or V1. Here we see a massive expansion in the number of neurons available for processing the visual input - there are something like 500 million neurons in V1 alone.

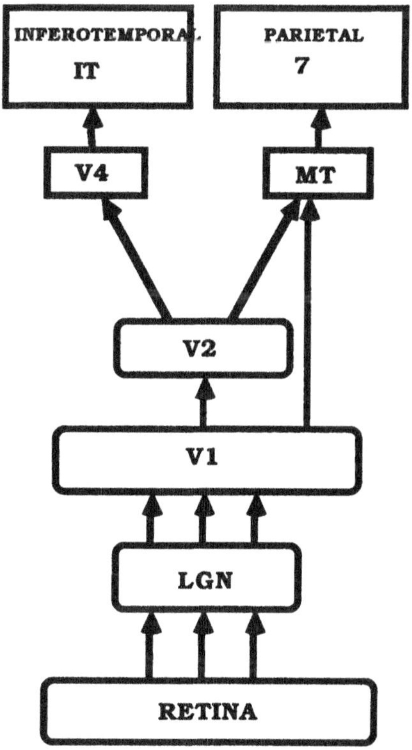

Figure 2 : Schematic diagram of the organization of the primate visual system.

In addition to V1, it now appears that there are a large number of other cortical areas that are also involved in visual processing, but that, at least in the primate, most visual information has first to pass via V1. These other areas include V2, V3, MT, V4 and Inferotemporal cortex. Knowledge about the anatomical organization of these different extra-striate visual areas is advancing rapidly (For reviews see DeYoe and Van Essen, 1988; Martin, 1988; Maunsell and Newsome, 1987; Van Essen and Maunsell, 1983; Zeki and Shipp, 1988), and it is now generally accepted that different cortical visual areas are to some extent specialized for particular aspects of visual processing. For example, neurons in MT (Mid-temporal cortex) are known to be particularly sensitive to stimulus movement (Hildreth and Koch, 1987) and lesions to this area and an adjacent area known as MST have been reported to result in selective deficits in motion perception and pursuit eye movements (Newsome and Wurtz, 1988). In contrast, neurons in V4 have been shown by Zeki to be particularly important in colour processing (Zeki, 1980), an idea that would appear to be born out by the effects of lesions (Wild et al, 1986; but see Heywood and Cowey, 1988).

At a more global level, Mishkin and his co-workers have argued that a distinction can be made between two major cortical processing streams (Mishkin, Ungerleider and Macko, 1983). The first one, involving more ventral structures and leading ultimately to the inferotemporal cortex, is involved in the identification of visual objects. The second, involving the more dorsal areas and the parietal cortex, is suggested to be more important in analyzing the spatial configuration of visual space. Clearly, from the point of view of how visual identification occurs, it is the ventral path to the temporal lobe which is the most relevant. In a previous section we mentioned the face-selective neurons described by Perrett, Rolls and others in the superior temporal sulcus (part of the temporal lobe), whose visual responses have latencies which are typically in the range 100 to 140 msec. We can ask the question what is the shortest anatomical path by which such neurons can be activated? It would appear that in order to reach this part of inferotemporal cortex, the visual information would have to go through at least 3 intermediate cortical areas, namely V1, V2 and V4. This is because there is apparently no direct projection from V1 to V4, nor from V2 to IT (see figure 2).

A second question to ask concerns the number of synaptic stages that have to be negotiated in each cortical area. Although a definitive answer to such a question is not yet available, it does seem clear that more than one synaptic stage is involved, since the neurons that receive inputs from the preceding stage are not those which project to the next cortical area. In fact, the cortex is organized as a sandwich of horizontal layers - numbered I to VI, although subdivisions are often found. For example, in the striate cortex, layer IV has three main subdivisions, IVA, IVB, and IVC, and IVC is in turn subdivided into IVCa and IVCb. We know that most of the fibres arriving from the lateral geniculate nucleus synapse in IVCa but that the neurons which project from striate cortex to V2 and MT are found in layers III and V. Do the neurons in IVCa project directly to these output neurons? As yet, the answer is not clear - interneurons may well be necessary (Lund, 1988), but in any case, it is obvious that at least two synapses must be traversed at each cortical stage.

So, what is the minimum number of synaptic stages that have to be passed in order to get from the photoreceptors of the retina to the face-selective neurons in the temporal lobe? The answer would appear to be at least 10 - one synapse between the photoreceptors and the bipolar cells of the retina, one between the bipolar cells and the ganglion cells, one between the ganglion cells and cells in the lateral geniculate nucleus, one between geniculate cells and cells in layer IV of striate cortex, one or two between these cells and the striate cortex output cells, another 2 or 3 in V2, another 2 or 3 in V4 and at least one between the V4 output cells and the first neurons in inferotemporal cortex.

Thus, even taking the shortest known anatomical pathway involves at least 10 synaptic stages to get from photoreceptor to temporal lobe. Of course, somebody may discover a short-cut - a direct projection from the lateral geniculate nucleus to the temporal lobe for example, but for the moment, such a possibility seems completely at odds with current anatomical knowledge.

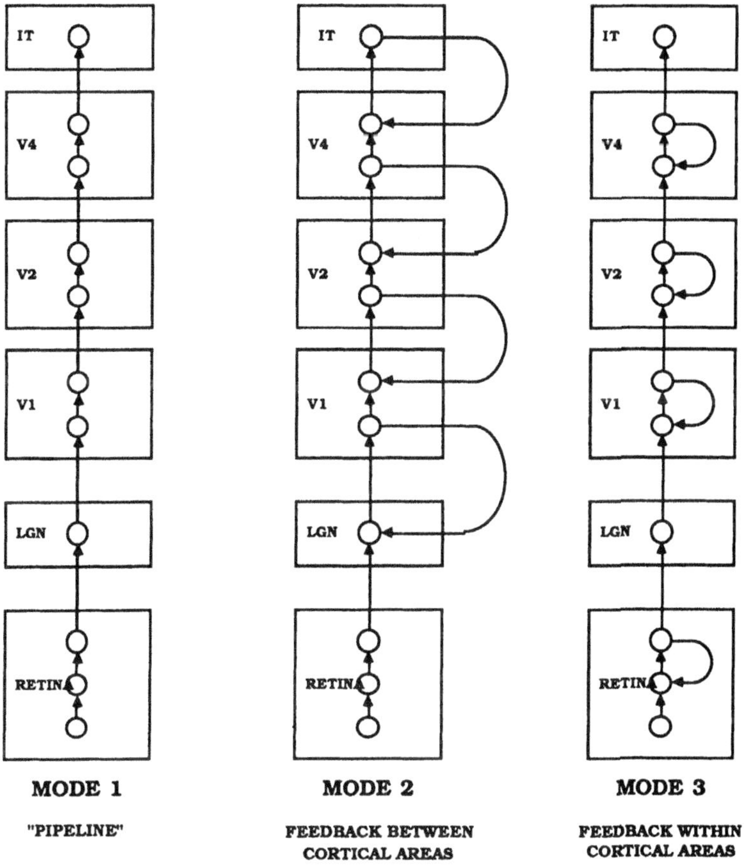

Figure 3 : Three different ways in which information may flow in the visual system.

2.7 Feed-forward and feed-back pathways.

For the moment, we have only considered the feed-forward connections which would allow information to get from the retina to the temporal lobe. In fact, recent anatomical findings stress the numerical importance of feedback pathways in the visual system. For example, there are apparently virtually the same number of fibres from V1 to the the lateral geniculate as there are running in the "normal" feedforward direction. Similar findings have been reported for the connections between cortical areas - in general, wherever there is a feed-forward projection from one area to another, one can find a substantial reciprocal backward projection. Interestingly, it appears that cells in different layers are involved in making these forward and backward projections - and this probably is highly significant in terms of cortical information processing (Zeki and Shipp, 1988).

To what extent are these feedback pathways used in normal visual processing? In principle, one can imagine the visual system being used in a variety of different ways. Let us consider the anatomical pathway from the retina to the temporal lobe, in which at least 10 synaptic stages are involved. The simplest possibility is that the information flow is exclusively feedforward - in which case the visual system can be considered as a sort of "pipeline" processor (see Figure 3, left). Alternatively, the flow of information could involve numerous feedback loops between cortical areas (Figure 3 centre). or loops within a particular cortical area (see Figure 3, right).

Which of these different schemes actually applies during normal visual processing? To what extent can visual processing be achieved using only feedforward pathways? Are feedback loops always used? The next two sections will briefly discuss two ways in which we are currently trying to get a handle on these important questions.

2.8 Neurophysiological approaches

One way to approach the problem is to record the activity of single neurons in the visual system, present a visual pattern, and determine how the neuronal response changes as a function of time. Various types of information can be obtained using such an approach. The first thing one can learn is the latency at which neurons in different structures start to become activated after the presentation of the visual stimulus. We have already mentioned the work of Rolls and his collaborators who have shown that in the awake behaving monkey, neurons in the temporal lobe typically have response latencies of around 100 to 140 msec. Preliminary work in our own laboratory indicates that in V1, latencies are often in the range 60 to 70 msec. Such data gives some sort of feel for the sequence in which visual structures are activated.

But the temporal analysis of information processing by neurons in the visual system need not be limited to simply measuring latencies. Yves Trotter, Simona Celebrini and ourselves have recently been looking at whether the response properties of neurons in visual cortex vary in the 100 msec or so following the presentation of a visual stimulus (manuscript in preparation). We have been interested in one of the characteristic properties of neurons in the visual cortex, namely, their selectivity to stimulus orientation. Is this property already present as soon as such neurons start to respond, or is orientation selectivity something that changes as a function of time? Some models in which feedback loops are used to progressively increase orientation selectivity would require that at the moment they start to fire following the presentation of a stimulus, the neurons should be relatively non-selective.

Although we have only recently started these investigations, the results already look promising. By analysing orientation selectivity in 10 msec time slices, starting from the moment that the neuron starts to respond, we have found that at least for some neurons, orientation selectivity is already present at the moment the neuron starts to respond, and remains virtually constant during the following 50 to 100 msec. In other words, such neurons appear to code the same information when they start responding at around 60 msec as they do 50 or 100 msec later. This would imply that at least for the stimuli used, feedback loops and processes related to relaxation do not seem to play a vital role. However, it could be that the grating stimuli used in our experiments are too simple - perhaps the situation would be different with more natural complex stimuli. Furthermore, it should be pointed out that this result is somewhat controversial - Dinse and Best (1988) and Shevelev (1987) have both reported changes in orientation preference as a function of time, although their experiments are based on recordings from anaesthetised cats, whereas our own data was obtained from awake behaving primates. On the other hand, Edmund Rolls and his collaborators (personal communication) have recently been looking for temporal changes in the selectivity functions of face-selective neurons in the temporal lobe of the awake monkey, and their results are in agreement with our own. It appears that in general, at the moment the neurons start to respond (around 100 msec) they already show the same pattern of selectivity as they will later on.

Clearly more work is required on this important question, but these preliminary results indicate that at least some neurons in the visual system are not influenced by subsequent processing and seem not to be modulated by "top-down" influences.

2.10 Temporal constraints

In addition to evidence provided by direct neurophysiological analysis, there is also a logical argument that considerable visual processing must be achieved without extensive use of feedback loops. The argument is as follows. In an earlier section we pointed out that anatomically, a minimum of 10 synaptic stages are involved in getting from the photoreceptors of the retina to the visual areas of the temporal lobe. Given that neurons in the temporal lobe have visual responses with latencies of the order of 100 msec, it is therefore inevitable that at least 10 synaptic stages must have been negotiated in this time - that is to say, an average of 10 msec per synapse. In fact, synaptic transmission can be considerably faster than this - synaptic delay is normally considered to be about 1 msec, and thus in the case of neurons which are relatively close to each other, and where axonal conduction time is not too long, it is theoretically possible for a nervous message to get through as many as 50 synapses in 100 msec. However, V1 and the temporal lobe are not close together. In the primate, there is a distance of some 20 to 30 mm to cover, and the distance is even greater in humans. Recent estimates put the conduction speed of intracortical fibres at around 1 m/sec (Bullier et al, 1988) which presumably slows the arrival of spikes in the temporal lobe by a further 20 to 30 msec. Thus it would seem that the number of synaptic integration steps is at least 10 (the anatomical minimum) and considerably less than 50 (the neurophysiological maximum).

To realize the significance of this observation, we will have to take into account neurophysiological data on the firing rate of neurons in the visual system. Neurons normally communicate by sending a string of action potentials along their axons - information is generally thought to be transmitted by varying the interval between successive spikes. In general, firing rate varies between zero and around 100 spikes per second (i.e. one spike every 10 msec), although for a fraction of a second, some neurons can be seen to generate spikes every 5 or so msec.

The inevitable conclusion is that since the visual information must pass through a minimum of 10 synaptic stages in 100 msec, and that neurons at each stage cannot generate more than 1 or at most 2 spikes in 10 msec, each stage must respond on the basis of 0, 1 or at most 2 spikes in the neurons of the previous stage. It should be remembered that this calculation is based on the assumption that the visual information takes the shortest known anatomical pathway from the retina to the temporal lobe. If visual information processing involves the use of feedback loops, the temporal constraints would be even more severe, and each cell in the processing sequence would be effectively reduced to signalling binary values (i.e. 0 or 1).

Of course, we have to remember that an individual neuron does not only receive information from a single neuron in the preceding layer. There may be 1000 or more inputs converging on any particular neuron, and although the "decision" as to whether or not to generate a spike may be based on the presence or absence of a spike in each of the input axons, considerable subtlety can be obtained by combining the information from a large number of different neurons.

Nevertheless, this conclusion has a number of important implications for the way in which information is processed by the visual system. These different points will be discussed separately.

Analogue coding by individual neurons. It is commonly felt that the firing rate of individual neurons can be used to code analogue values such as intensity - the higher the firing rate, the higher the intensity. While this may well be the case, in the particular case of rapid analysis of information by the visual system, the fact that each stage of neuronal processing has to respond on the basis of the presence or absence of activity in the neurons of the preceding stage means that firing rate as such cannot be used to code analogue values with any real precision. However, as will be argued later, it could be used to code such analogue parameters as contrast or the probability that a particular feature is present.

Feedback loops. If neuron A projects to neuron B which in turn can influence neuron A, and if neuron A has a maximum firing rate of one spike every 5 msec, it is clear that each iteration of such a feedback loop must take at least 5 msec. Furthermore, if the firing rate was more typical (for example, 50 spikes per second), each loop would take 20 msec. Given that a great deal of visual processing can be accomplished in 100 msec, and a minimum of 10 synaptic stages are involved, the opportunity for the extensive use of feedback loops must be severely limited. However, one way in which feedback might be used is on a purely local basis. In the retina, for example, it is known that neuronal communication is achieved without the use of action potentials - signals are transmitted by the use of graded potentials. Feedback loops between adjacent neurons could be achieved using such graded potentials without suffering from the temporal constraints involved in spike generation (Koch et al, 1986). However, such a mechanism would clearly be restricted to a very local scale and could not be implemented in the case of geniculo-cortico-geniculate loops or for feedback between different cortical areas.

Relaxation. A number of connectionist models have proposed that visual processing involves a process related to relaxation, in which the system settles down to a minimum energy state compatible with the input configuration. Often, such models assume 50 or so cycles in which the activation levels of each processing element are allowed to influence each other. Without denying that such mechanisms may be of considerable importance, particularly in longer timecourse cognitive processes, it would appear that normal visual processing has to be achieved with a smaller number of processing cycles.

Iteration. Many machine vision algorithms for contour finding, erosion, skeletonisation etc. rely on large numbers of iterations of particular algorithms. The temporal constraints on visual system functioning imply that if something equivalent occurs in the human brain, the number of iterations must be reduced to an absolute minimum, perhaps by the use of parallel processing algorithms. This is in itself an argument that machine visual algorithms must be "parallelisable".

Top-down influences and the role of context. It is widely assumed that one of the main reasons for why the human visual system is so much better than currently available machine vision systems is that humans can make use of context. That is to say, the knowledge that one is in a restaurant makes it easier to identify the pepper-mill on the table. This ability to use context is certainly important. However, the high level of performance of subjects in our visual identification task (see section 2.2), despite the fact that the subjects had no advance information about the type of image with which they were to be presented indicates that even in the absence of contextual cues, the human visual system is capable of functioning remarkably well.

In this respect, it is important to realize that context can work in a variety of ways. Imagine an experiment in which you are presented with an unknown picture which you have to identify. Let us suppose that the picture is of a car on a motorway. The motorway provides a "within-picture" context which may help with the identification of the car. However, the fact that such contextual help is not essential is clear from the fact that you could also identify the same car against a plain white background. On the other hand, there is good evidence that an inappropriate context can severely impair visual identification (Palmer, 1975) - a drawing of a car in a living room is particularly difficult to identify. However, showing that an inappropriate context can make identification difficult does not mean that context is necessary for visual processing. Nevertheless, there is a clear distinction between this type of "within-picture" context, and the sort of context that would be provided if the picture of a car came in a series of pictures of different means of transport (train, aeroplane, bicycle etc.). This sort of continuous updating of the context on the basis of previous stimuli may well be important, but is not relevant to the question of the flow of information which occurs during the processing of a particular image by the visual system.

Temporal coding. A final implication of these temporal constraints on visual processing concerns the possibility of various types of temporal coding schemes in the visual system. While traditional views of neural coding have generally assumed that information is primarily encoded by the firing rate of neurons, a number of authors have recently proposed that information is encoded in the temporal sequence of activity of individual neurons. For example, Lestienne and Strehler (1988, Strehler and Lestienne, 1986) have proposed that the temporal organization of triplets of spikes in individual neurons may itself carry information important for visual processing. Thus if a neuron emits three spikes with interspike intervals of 10 msec and 20 msec, this could have a different "meaning" to three spikes generated with intervals of 20 msec and 10 msec. One problem with such a model is that a delay of 30 msec would be introduced before a neuron at the next stage would be able to decode such information. Given that at minimum of 10 synaptic stages have to be negotiated in 100 msec, it is clear that there is insufficient time to use such a code at each stage, although it is perhaps possible that one or two processing stages might use such information.

Similar arguments apply to the model proposed by Richmond and coworkers (Richmond et al, 1987a,b,c) who proposed that the temporal sequence of activity in inferotemporal cortex neurons contains information about the stimulus. While this may well be the case, their suggestion that changes in activity over a period of 100 to 200 msec could be used to code information could certainly not be used at each stage of visual processing - if each of 10 processing stages had to wait for 100 msec to process the information encoded by the neurons of the previous level, visual processing would take more than 1 second.

Finally, von der Malsburg and Bienenstock (1986, Bienenstock and von der Malsburg, 1987) have suggested that information is carried in the degree of correlation between neurons. They estimate that 100 or 200 msec are needed for the degree of correlation between two neurons to be determined. While such a mechanism could be used in a simple 2 layer network composed of a "retinal" input layer and a "cortical" output layer, the fact that visual processing involves a minimum of 10 processing stages makes it difficult to see how such a mechanisms could allow the activation of highly selective temporal lobe neurons with such short latencies.

Thus it would appear that this examination of the anatomical, neurophysiological and psychological constraints on visual processing has wide ranging implications for the way information is processed by the visual system. In the next two sections we would like to deal with two specific points. The first concerns alternative ways of coding analogue values which avoid the serious temporal constraints that arise if firing rate is used as a code. The second concerns possible alternative roles for the anatomically widespread feedback connections found in the visual system.

2.11 Alternative ways of coding analogue information

In the last section it was argued that the temporal constraints associated with visual information processing in humans make it unlikely that the firing rate of neurons could be used to code analogue values. While it is true that in principle, neuronal firing rate can be used to code analogue values with arbitrary levels of precision, the fact that in the visual system each processing stage has only about 10 msec of computation time means that a great deal of processing has to be done on the basis of only one spike in each of the neurons of the preceding layer. Nevertheless, there are other ways of increasing analogue precision. One way is to take advantage of the massively parallel nature of visual processing. Imagine a neuron which receives inputs from 100 different neurons at the preceding stage, and that the probability that neurons in the preceding layer fire in response to a stimulus varies with stimulus intensity. Clearly the proportion of the 100 input neurons which are active will be a monotonic function of stimulus intensity - and this could be used to code as many as 100 different analogue values. Such a scheme seems quite plausible in real brains but has the fairly obvious disadvantage of using large numbers of units.

However, there is another way of encoding analogue information which may be of great importance. It is known that the time taken for a neuron to reach its firing threshold depends on the intensity of the stimulus. Thus a neuron which responds with a latency of 4 msec to an intense stimulus might take 10 msec or more in the case of a weak stimulus. Such properties are well known phenomena that result from the temporal summation properties of neurons. Imagine that an image is presented at time T_0. Certain parts of the image may contain contours with high contrast, whereas in other regions the contrast may be low. As a result, the first spikes to leave the retina would be those in the high contrast regions, whereas the first spikes would have longer latencies in the low contrast regions.

Thus information is presumably contained in the relative arrival times of action potentials coming from different sources. How might higher level neurons make use of such information? It is known that neurons in the auditory system are sensitive to differences in the arrival time of auditory stimuli at the two ears of around 1 msec (Knudsen et al, 1987), and recent work on the electric fish has shown that neurons can be sensitive to information in the microsecond range (Kawasaki et al, 1988). Poggio and Koch (1986) have proposed that sophisticated processing may occur in the dendritic trees of neurons. For example, imagine a dendrite on which two synapses make contact, an inhibitory terminal and an excitatory one, and that the inhibitory terminal is the closest to the cell body. If the excitatory signal arrives first, it would propagate along the dendrite without difficulty. However, if the inhibitory input arrives first, it could "veto" the passage of the second excitatory input. As a result, the cell itself could be sensitive to the relative arrival times of the two inputs, responding only when they arrive in a particular order. In Poggio and Koch's description, such synaptic "veto" mechanisms were suggested to be involved in the calculation of stimulus motion. However, it seems reasonable to suggest that equivalent circuits could be used to pick up on analogue information contained in spike arrival times.

Furthermore, spike arrival times do not have to be thought of as only dependent on such attributes as stimulus contrast and intensity. More generally, firing rate has often been thought of as a code for the probability that a particular feature is present (Barlow, 1972). The same could be true in the case of spike arrival times. If we consider a neuron in V2 receiving information from a variety of orientation-tuned neurons in V1, one can imagine that if spikes from the vertically-tuned neurons arrived first, this could provide additional information about stimulus orientation.

2.12 What do feedback circuits do?

In section 2.10 it was argued that a great of visual information processing must be achieved without the need for feedback pathways. However, this fails to account for one very obvious fact, namely that such pathways do exist, and are even numerically very important. In this section, we would like put forward a few suggestions of the other possible roles for feedback pathways.

Context. Although in the last section it was argued that the visual system can process visual information even in the absence of context, there is no doubt that contextual information can influence visual information processing. A large number of experiments have investigated "priming" effects in vision. For example, it is well established that the time taken by subjects to judge whether a presented letter string is a word or not (i.e. a lexical decision task) can be reduced if another semantically related word is presented just beforehand. Such effects may be due to top-down preactivation of the appropriate visual processing elements.

Imagery. A possibly related process is that of visual imagery. Recent experiments have shown that visual processing in the occipital lobe can be influenced if the subject imagines the presence of a stimulus in a particular part of the visual field (Farah et al, 1988). It is possible that such effects are mediated by descending pathways to the visual cortex from higher order areas such as the temporal lobe.

Attention. When a subject focuses his attention on a particular part of the visual field, his ability to detect a stimulus presented in that region is improved (Posner, and Presti, 1987). This attention-related sensory enhancement is quite possibly related to the enhancement of the responsiveness of single neurons in awake primates described by Wurtz and his collaborators (Wurtz, Goldberg and Robinson, 1980). Such excitability changes could well be mediated by descending influences from higher order areas.

Ambiguous stimuli. There are numerous situations in which the interpretation of a particular visual pattern is ambiguous. A classic case is the Necker cube, which can be seen in one of two different configurations. Such ambiguous figures can often be flipped from one state to the other under voluntary control - perhaps this could reflect another case of top-down influences on perception.

Conflicting stimuli. If different images are presented to the two eyes which cannot be fused, one typically experiences a phenomenon known as binocular rivalry. For example, if the left eye sees the world through a red filter and the right eye through a green one, each particular part of the visual field is either seen as red or green, but not both. It is possible that corticogeniculate pathways may be involved in suppressing one or other eye's input in such rivalrous situations.

Learning. Considerable attention has recently been paid to the possibility of learning in neural networks using the Back-propagation learning algorithm (Rumelhart, Hinton and Williams, 1986). Although as we will see in a later section, there is some doubt as to whether such an algorithm is implemented in real brains, if it were to be implemented, then feedback pathways could be involved. The algorithm requires that an error signal from output neurons be back-propagated to neurons in preceding levels. In principle, this could be achieved by either sending signals backwards along the originally activated axons, or alternatively, by using topographically precise reverse projections from the output layer to units in the hidden layers.

Thus, even if it is the case that in normal visual processing, feedback loops are only used sparingly, there is no shortage of candidate roles for the large number of feedback pathways which have been found anatomically.

2.13 Processing - Final conclusions.

Current connectionist models are only fairly loosely constrained by biological data. However, if we restrict ourselves to a particular domain, namely visual information processing, biological constraints can be used to specify in considerably greater detail the main features of a connectionist visual system designed to simulate the capacities of the human visual system. These constraints can be summarized as follows.

A. The visual system is arranged as a massively parallel multilayer feedforward net with at least 10 processing layers.

B. Considerable visual analysis is possible with a single forward pass through the network.

C. In many situations, each unit can only emit 1 spike before the units in the next layer have to respond.

D. Firing rate per se cannot be used during visual processing to code analogue values with any real precision.

E. Coding of analogue values could however be achieved by making use of the arrival times of spikes from different sources - the earliest arriving signals could be given priority.

F. Sophisticated dendritic processing could mean that each unit could be doing more than simply calculating the sum of all the input activations - logical "and", "and not" functions could well make the system highly non-linear.

G. Although feedback pathways between different layers are present, there may not be time to use them during normal visual processing. They could however play a role in the effects of context, imagery, attention, resolution of ambiguous stimuli and learning.

H. The use of iterative loops is kept to an absolute minimum and perhaps even eliminated by the use of massive parallelism.

3. LEARNING

3.1 Introduction - Different learning algorithms.

One of the main reasons for the current explosion of interest in connectionist modelling is that such systems can self-organize. This ability depends on the implementation within the network of some sort of learning algorithm. Currently, there are a number of learning rules available, including variations of the Hebb learning rule, the Perceptron learning rule, Back-propagation and the Boltzmann learning algorithm. (For reviews, see Sejnowski, 1988; Arbib, 1988; Soucek and Soucek, 1988).

As was the case with processing, one can take one of two positions. One possibility is to say that we do not mind whether the algorithm we use is biologically realistic - the only important criterion is whether it works or not. Alternatively we can take the view that it is important to try to understand the only truly intelligent system we have that we are sure can actually work - namely, real biological brains.

In this section, we would like to look at some of the evidence relating to the biological plausibility of some of these different rules. It will be argued that whereas there is considerable reason to believe that something like Hebbian learning occurs in the brain, there is currently little clear evidence for certain other learning mechanisms, and in particular Back-propagation.

3.2 Hebbian learning rules.

In his classic book, "The Organization of Behavior", published in 1949, the Canadian psychologist Donald Hebb proposed the following neurophysiolgical postulate :

"When an axon of cell A is near enough to excite a cell B and repeatedly or persistently takes part in firing it, some growth process or metabolic change takes place in one or both cells such that A's efficiency, as one of the cells firing B, is increased" (page 62)

This suggestion, which has since become known as Hebb's postulate, has been widely used in theoretical analyses of neural function. In fact, several variants have been suggested, but they all have the basic feature that the connection strength between two neurons depends on the degree of coactivation of the two neurons. In the most elementary form there is an increase in connectivity if a synaptic terminal and its post-synaptic target cell are active simultaneously. There is now a considerable amount of neurophysiological evidence favouring the existence of such synaptic modification mechanisms. For example, Frégnac, Shultz, Thorpe and Bienenstock (1988) were able to modify the response properties of neurons in the cat visual cortex using an experimental protocol which artificially changed the degree of coactivation between pre- and post-synaptic elements. Visual cortical neurons typically show orientation selectivity, responding best to certain orientations. In their experiments, Frégnac and coworkers first determined the orientation selectivity of a cortical neuron, and then used a conditioning procedure in which two orientations were repeatedly presented - the preferred orientation, and a second orientation to which the neuron responded, but not as strongly. During this conditioning, every time the preferred orientation was presented, the activity of the neuron was artificially suppressed by passing current through the recording electrode. By contrast, every time the non-preferred orientation was presented, the neurons activity was artificially increased. Subsequently, it was found that many neurons changed their orientation preference in favour of the orientation associated with high levels of neuronal activity. Thus, such evidence supports the basic premise of Hebb's postulate, namely the idea that synapses that are active at the same time as the post-synaptic neuron can become strengthened. Other support can be found in the experiments of Baranyi and Feher (1981) who were able to increase the strength of synaptic inputs to cat motor cortex neurons by artificially activating the neuron every time the synapse was active, and in a number of studies of synaptic plasticity in the hippocampus (e.g. Kelso et al, 1986).

These experiments support the original proposition made by Hebb, namely that synaptic efficiency increases when the pre and post-synaptic elements are active at the same time. However, there are other variations on the basic Hebb rule. One possibility is that synapses which are inactive when the cell is active become less effective in driving the cell (see Sejnowski, 1977), and Singer (1987) has recently argued for such a mechanism.

A fundamentally different suggestion is to propose that synaptic modification can occur even when the post-synaptic element is inactive. Until recently, the idea that changes can occur in the absence of neuronal activity has been only a theoretical possibility. However, Reiter and Stryker (1988) have provided experimental evidence which implies that such a process does indeed occur. It has been known since the early 1960s that if a kitten is subjected to monocular deprivation, the eye that has normal visual experience comes to dominate visually responsive cells in the visual cortex. This phenomenon can be readily explained on the basis of Hebb-like mechanisms - only synapses driven by the exposed eye can be reinforced because only they can be activated visually. Reiter and Stryker used a variant on this technique in which during the period of monocular deprivation, the activity of visual cortical neurons was locally suppressed by directly infusing an inhibitory substance into the cortex. Subsequently, they found that the eye that had been occluded was actually better at driving the cortical cells than the eye which had received normal visual experience. This seemingly counter-intuitive result is actually consistent with a particular type of coactivation based modifiability - when there is no post-synaptic activity, inactive synapses have an advantage, but as yet it is unclear whether this is because the inactive synapses become more effective, or whether the active synapses become less effective.

Thus, there is now a considerable body of experimental data in support of the idea that the degree of coactivation between pre and post-synaptic elements can lead to modifications in synaptic weight. Such correlation based learning rules have been widely used in a variety of theoretical studies, including matrix memory models (Amari, 1977; Kohonen, 1977, 1984; Palm, 1982), reinforcement learning (Sutton and Barto, 1981), competitive learning (Fukushima, 1975; Fukushima and Miyaki, 1982; Grossberg, 1982; Rumelhart and Zipser, 1985, von der Malsburg, 1973), the formation of higher level response properties in multilayer networks (Linsker, 1986a,b,c) and Hopfield nets (Hopfield, 1982).

3.3 Error correction rules

Another common type of learning algorithm uses an error signal to modify synaptic weights. This involves a calculation of the difference between the desired output of a unit and its actual state. The resulting error signal is then used to control the amount of synaptic weight change. For example, in the Perceptron model developed by Frank Rosenblatt and his colleagues (Rosenblatt, 1962), if an output unit is active when it should have been inactive, active inputs are decreased in weight, while inactive inputs are increased in weight. Conversely, if the output unit is inactive when it should have been active, active synaptic inputs are increased in weight whilst those which are inactive become less effective. The net effect is to minimize errors. Similar mechanisms underlie the Widrow-Hoff rule, and the recently developed Back-propagation algorithm (although in the latter case, the error signals in the output units can be used to adjust weights on intermediate "hidden" units).

While there is no doubt that such error-correction rules have considerable power, the question needs to raised as to whether or not such mechanisms actually occur in real nervous systems, and in particular in the human brain. As far as we are aware there is as yet no direct neurophysiological evidence for such mechanisms, although it has to be said that there have probably not been any experiments specifically designed to test such a notion.

Nevertheless, there are certain theoretical arguments that indicate that at least compared with the coactivation related synaptic learning rules discussed in the previous section, error correction mechanisms may be relatively difficult to implement in real neurons. There is now good reason to think that coactivation based modification can be achieved on a purely local basis, and indeed considerable progress has recently been made on the cellular processes that could underlie such modifiability (Artola and Singer, 1987, Cotman et al, 1988). When neural networks with error correction are simulated on a computer, the question of how to calculate the error signal is minimized - you just subtract one floating point value from another. However, in a real neural net the problem is not so trivial and may well require a minimum circuit of three neurons - one neuron would signal the desired activity level, another would signal the actual activity level generated by the network, and a third neuron would be required to signal the difference between these two levels of activation. While potentially the anatomical substrate for such circuits exists in the brain, it certainly involves a greater level of complexity compared with local coactivation based modification.

3.4 Back-propagation

One particular kind of error-correction rule has received a great deal of attention in the last few years. This is the Back-propagation algorithm discussed in detail by Rumelhart, Hinton and Williams (1986). This algorithm can be used to modify weights in multi-layer networks, something which earlier error-correction rules like the Perceptron learning rule were unable to do. Indeed, this gets round one of the major criticisms made by Marvin Minsky and Seymour Papert in their classic book on Perceptrons published in 1969. They proved that a single layer Perceptron was unable to solve certain types of pattern classification problem, such as the parity problem (respond if an odd number of inputs are active), and problems involving "exclusive-or" (XOR) rules (respond if one or other but not both of a pair of inputs are active). At the time it was felt that such limitations would prevent neural networks forming the basis of a truly intelligent artificial system, and this led to the great majority of researchers in artificial intelligence turning to symbol manipulation paradigms during the 1970s. The development of the back-propagation algorithm has changed all that, because now it is possible to train multi-layer Perceptron like networks to solve previously intractable pattern classification problems, and in the last few years we have witnessed a veritable explosion of interest in neural networks.

However, is it really the case that an intelligent system must be able to train layers of hidden units in order to be worthy of the label "intelligent". What evidence is there for this type of learning in humans? Recently, Thorpe, O'Regan and Pouget (1988) tried to examine this question by looking at the ability of humans to solve pattern classification problems of the type that single layer Perceptrons are unable to solve. The subject was presented with a series of random configurations of high or low intensity squares arranged in a 4 by 4 array on the screen of a computer terminal. At the center of the array was a fixation point, which the subject was instructed to fixate. New configurations were presented at a rate of 5 per second, accompanied by a beep if the pattern fulfilled some particular rule. Various boolean rules were used, including "simple" rules (beep if a particular square was on), "and" rules (beep if particular pair of elements are both on) and "Xor" rules (beep if one or other of a pair of squares is on, but not both). Varying numbers of training patterns were presented (10, 20, 30, 40, 60, 100, 160 or more) after which the subject had to indicate which of the 16 squares were relevant. For each type of problem ("simple", "and" and "Xor") and for each training sequence length, the entire procedure was repeated 100 times in order to calculate the percentage of runs on which the subject correctly identified the relevant squares.

It was found that "simple" and "and" rules could be solved rapidly - often the solution could be found after only 40-60 training patterns. However, in the case of "XOR" rules, there was no evidence for learning even after 4000 training examples had been presented. By contrast, a three-layer neural network using back-propagation, while relatively slow at solving equivalent "simple" and "and" problems, was consistently able to solve the problems involving "Xor" relationships. Although it would certainly be premature to conclude that humans are unable to solve any problems involving "XOR" relations, it would appear that at least in this particular case, there is as yet no reason to believe that they can. What are the implications of such findings?

The first point would seem to be that the ability to solve problems such as Xor, parity and so on should not necessarily be thought of as the hallmark of an intelligent system. Human beings evolved cognitive capacities that were useful to them in the evolutionary struggle for survival. For this, one can well imagine that the ability to rapidly spot correlations between events in the outside world (i.e. conjunctions) could be of great importance. It is therefore perhaps not so surprising that humans seem to be remarkably good at detecting correlations between the presence of a particular square in a visual array and the presentation of a beep. By contrast, it is really quite difficult to think of a natural situation in which the ability to solve an exclusive or problem would confer and advantage. In general, if two cues both signal that food is about to arrive, when the two are present at the same time, the food is even more likely to appear!

Even if natural events involving Xor relations do occur, one could well argue that if at least 2000 training sessions are required in order to find the underlying rule (as was the case for the network in our simulation), the advantage for an individual who possessed the means for solving such problems relative to his less sophisticated competitor would be only marginal - how often is he going to get 2000 chances to observe the relevant events? If, however, the number of relevant features is small, and new patterns are presented only relatively infrequently, then it may be possible to solve the problem by sequential reasoning - but this is hardly what is thought to occur in a back-propagation programmed neural network.

But there is a second reason to think that an ability to solve Xor type problems would be difficult to evolve. Currently, the back-propagation algorithm would appear to be the best tool we have for solving Xor problems with neuron-like networks. Is back-propagation feasible neurophysiologically? In the previous section we have already pointed out that the calculation of error signals in real nervous systems may not be as easy as it appears when doing neural network simulations on a digital computer. However, in addition to this, back-propagation requires that this error signal be sent back to neurons at lower levels in the processing sequence. With a computer simulation, it is trivial to "propagate" the resulting error value to the input units - but how could this be done in a real nervous system? Retrograde transport of chemical substances along axons is known to exist but it is generally a rather slow process and would be unlikely to have the temporal resolution necessary for processing the 2000 training trials that would be necessary. Another possibility, namely that the error signal could be sent along separate feedback pathways, would require a topographic precision that would be difficult to imagine in a real nervous system. All of these considerations make the evolution of a new neurophysiological mechanism capable of supporting the back-propagation algorithm unlikely.

3.5 Learning - Final Conclusions

We have argued that whereas in the case of Hebb-like coactivation based synaptic weight changes there is now reasonably good experimental evidence that such mechanisms actually occur in real brains, there is as yet little evidence that either error-correction learning rules or back-propagation are implemented in biological neural networks.

However, it is important to stress that even if the human brain turns out to be a highly intelligent system that manages without back-propagation, this should not be taken as an argument for reducing the current intense research effort into the development of such tools. There is no reason why researchers working on artificial neuron-like systems should be subject to the same constraints that have applied during the evolution of the human nervous system. Firstly, in an artificial nervous system, the calculation of error and its propagation pose no particular problems. Secondly, whereas under natural conditions, animals are unlikely to experience the several thousands of training trials necessary to resolve complex problems, the presentation of large numbers of examples to modern digital computers can be done very rapidly.

On the other hand, if humans do achieve a high level of intelligence without using back-propagation, this could be seen as an argument for investing a significant research effort into simpler mechanisms. Coactivation-based synaptic modification has been used in a large number of theoretical studies, and it seems unlikely that we have done more than scratch the surface of the full potential of such mechanisms for the development of intelligent artificial systems.

4. PERSPECTIVES

In the introduction, we pointed out that connectionist modelling can be used in two fairly distinct ways. One approach is aimed at the development of sophisticated artificial intelligence, the other is aimed at understanding how real brains work, and in particular the mechanisms underlying the functioning of the human brain. It was suggested that computer scientists and engineers endeavoring to design and construct artificial systems could in principle use "neurally-inspired" connectionist architectures without worrying too much about whether or not they are biologically realistic. While this is true, we feel strongly that greater information flow between researchers in these different fields will be of great benefit.

In this article, we have reviewed two particular areas of research, namely information processing by the human and primate visual system, and learning algorithms in biological systems. There can be little doubt that the performance of the human brain on tasks such as visual object identification and pattern classification is highly impressive. And yet the evidence suggests that the underlying mechanisms may not be completely intractable.

The human brain has the great advantage of being a compact connectionist system which really works - all of us have in our possession a highly perfected system which has had virtually all the "bugs" removed by millions of years of natural selection. The processing architectures and learning algorithms have been thoroughly tried and tested. Connectionist modelling, lying as it does between the natural and the artificial, is the perfect domain for demonstrating that genuine interdisciplinary co-operation can reap enormous benefits.

5. REFERENCES

Amari, S. (1977) Neural theory of association and concept formation. *Biological Cybernetics*, **26**, 175-185.

Arbib, M.A. (1988) *Brains, machines and mathematics*, 2nd edition. New York : Springer-Verlag.

Artola, A. and Singer, W. (1987) Long-term potentiation and NMDA receptors in the visual cortex. *Nature*, **330**, 649.

Baranyi A. and Féher O. (1981) *Nature*, **290**, 413-415.

Barlow, H.B. (1972) Single units and sensation : A neuron doctrine for perceptual psychology. *Perception*, **1**, 371-394.

Bienenstock E. and von der Malsburg C. (1987) A neural network for invariant pattern recognition. *Europhysics Letters*, **4**, 121-126.

Biederman, I. (1987) Recognition by components : A theory of human image understanding. *Psychological Review*, **94**, 115-147.

Bullier, J., McCourt, M.E. and Henry, G.H. (1988) Physiological studies on the feedback connection to the striate cortex from cortical areas 18 and 19 in the cat. *Experimental Brain Research*, **70**, 90-98.

Carr, T.H., McCauley, C., Sperber, R.D., and Parmelee, C.M. (1982) Words, pictures and priming : On semantic activation, conscious identification and the automaticity of information processing. *Journal of Experimental Psychology: Human Perception and Performance*, **8**, 757-777.

Cattell, J.M. (1886a) The time it takes to see and name objects. *Mind*, **11**, 63-65.

Cattell, J.M. (1886b) The time taken up by cerebral operations. *Mind*, **11**, 277-292.

Cotman, C.W., Monaghan, D.T. and Ganong, A.H. (1988) Excitatory amino acid neurotransmission : NMDA receptors and Hebb-type synaptic plasticity. *Annual Review of Neuroscience*, **11**, 61-80.

Dawkins, R. (1986) *The blind watch-maker*. London : Longmans.

DeYoe, E.A. and Van Essen, D.C. (1988) Concurrent processing streams in monkey visual cortex. *Trends in Neurosciences*, **11**, 219.

Dinse, H. and Best, J. (1988) Paper presented at the First European Conference on Neural Networks, Paris.

Farah, M.J., Péronnet, F., Gonon, M.A. and Giard, M.H. (1988) Electrophysiological evidence for a shared representation medium for visual images and visual percepts. *Journal of Experimental Psychology : General*, **117**, 248-257.

Feldman, J.A. (1985a) Connectionist models and parallelism in high level vision. In A. Rosenfeld (ed.), *Human and Machine Vision II*. (pp 86-108). Orlando : Academic Press.

Feldman, J.A. (1985b) Four frames suffice : A provisional model of vision and space. *Behavioral and Brain Sciences*, **8**, 265-289.

Feldman, J.A. and Ballard, D.H. (1982) Connectionist models and their properties. *Cognitive Science*, **6**, 205-254.

Frégnac, Y., Shultz, D., Thorpe, S. and Bienenstock, E. (1988) A cellular analogue of visual cortical plasticity. *Nature*, **333**, 367-370.

Fukushima, K. (1975) Cognitron : A self-organizing multilayered neural network. *Biological Cybernetics*, **20**, 121-136.

Fukushima, K. and Miyaki, S. (1982) Neocognitron : A new algorithm for pattern recognition tolerant of deformations and shifts in position. *Pattern Recognition*, **15**, 455-469.

Grossberg, S. (1982) *Studies of Mind and Brain*. Reidel.

Hebb D.O. (1949) *Organization of Behavior*. New York : Wiley.

Henderson, J.M., Pollatsek, A. and Rayner, K. (1987) Effects of foveal priming and extra-foveal preview on object identification. *Journal of Experimental Psychology: Human Perception and Performance*, **13**, 449-463.

Heywood, C.A. and Cowey, A. (1988) On the role of cortical area V4 in the discrimination of hue and pattern in macaque monkeys. *Journal of Neuroscience*, **7**, 2601-2617.

Hildreth, E.C. and Koch, C. (1987) The analysis of visual motion : From computational theory to neuronal mechanisms. *Annual Review of Neuroscience*, **10**, 477-534.

Hopfield J. (1982) Neural networks and physical systems with emergent collective computational properties. *Proceedings of the National Academy of Science*, **79**, 2554-2558.

Hinton, G.E. and Anderson, J.A. (1981) *Parallel models of associative memory*. Hillsdale : Lawrence Erlbaum.

Humphreys, G.W. and Quinlan, P.T. (1988) Normal and pathological processes in visual object constancy. In G.W. Humphreys and M.J. Riddoch (Eds.) *Visual object recognition : A cognitive neuropsychological approach*. (pp. 43-105) Hillsdale: Lawrence Erlbaum.

Imbert, M. (1988) La vision naturalle : Le traitement neuronal de l'information visuelle. *Intellectica*, **5**, 3-31.

Intraub, H. (1979) The role of explicit naming in pictorial encoding. *Journal of Experimental Psychology: Human Learning and Memory*, **5**, 78-87.

Intraub, H. (1980) Presentation rate and the representation of briefly glimpsed pictures in memory. *Journal of Experimental Psychology: Human Learning and Memory*, **6**, 604-610.

Intraub, H. (1981) Rapid conceptual identification of sequential presented pictures. *Journal of Experimental Psychology : Human Perception and Performance*, **7**, 604-610.

Jeffreys, A. (1988) A human scalp-potential sensitive to faces. *Perception*, **17**, A31.

Kawasaki, M., Rose, G. and Heiligenberg, W. (1988) Temporal hyperacuity in single neurons of electric fish. *Nature*, **336**, 173-176.

Kelso, S.R., Ganong, A.H. and Brown, T.J. (1986) Hebbian synapses in hippocampus, *Proceedings of the National Academy of Science*, **83**, 5326-5330.

Kendrick, K.M. and Baldwin, B.A. (1986) The activity of neurons in the lateral hypothalamus and zona incerta of the sheep responding to the sight or approach of food is modified by learning and reflects food preference. *Brain Research*, **375**, 320-328.

Kendrick, K.M. and Baldwin, B.A. (1987) Cells in the temporal lobe of the sheep can respond preferentially to the sight of faces. *Science*, **236**, 448.

Knudsen, E.I., du Lac, S. and Esterley, S.D. (1987) Computational maps in the brain. *Annual Review of Neuroscience*, **10**, 41-66.

Koch, C., Marroquin, J. and Yuille, A. (1986) Analogue "neuronal" networks in early vision. *Proceedings of the National Academy of Science*, **83**, 4263-4267.

Kohonen, T. (1977) *Associative memory : A system-theoretical approach*. Berlin: Springer-Verlag.

Kohonen, T. (1984) *Self-organization and associative memory*. Berlin: Springer-Verlag.

Lehky, S.R. and Sejnowski, T.J. (1988) Network model of shape-from-shading : neural function arises from both receptive and projective fields. *Nature*, **333**, 452-454.

Lestienne, R. and Strehler, B.L. (1988) Differences between visual cortical cells in triplet and ghost doublet informational symbols relationships. *Biological Cybernetics*, **59**, 337-352.

Linsker, R. (1986a) From basic network principles to neural architecture : Emergence of spatial opponent cells. *Proceedings of the National Academy of Science*, **83**, 7508-7512.

Linsker, R. (1986b) From basic network principles to neural architecture : Emergence of orientation selective cells. *Proceedings of the National Academy of Science*, **83**, 8390-8394.

Linsker, R. (1986a) From basic network principles to neural architecture : Emergence of orientation columns. *Proceedings of the National Academy of Science*, **83**, 8779-8783.

Lund, J.S. (1988) Anatomical organization of macaque monkey striate cortex. *Annual Review of Neuroscience*, **11**, 253-288.

Martin, K.A.C. (1988) From enzymes to perception: A bridge too far? *Trends in Neurosciences*, **11**, 380-387.

Maunsell, J.H.R. and Newsome, W.T. (1987) Visual processing in monkey extrastriate cortex. *Annual Review of Neuroscience*, **10**, 363-402.

Minsky, M. and Papert S. (1969) *Perceptrons*. MIT Press.

Minsky M. and Papert S. (1988) *Perceptrons*. Expanded Edition. MIT Press.

Mishkin, M., Ungerleider, L.G. and Macko, K.A. (1983) Object vision and spatial vision : Two cortical pathways. *Trends in Neurosciences,*. **6**, 414-416.

Newsome, W.T. and Wurtz R.H. (1988) Probing visual cortical function with discrete chemical lesions. *Trends in Neurosciences*, **11**, 394-399.

Oldfield, R.C. (1966) Things, words and the brain. *Quarterly Journal of Experimental Psychology*, **18**, 340-353.

Oldfield, R.C. and Wingfield, A. (1965) Response latencies in naming objects. *Quarterly Journal of Experimental Psychology*, **17**, 273-281.

Palm, G. (1982) *Neural Assemblies*. Berlin : Springer-Verlag.

Palmer, S.E. (1975) The effect of contextual scenes on the identification of objects. *Memory and Cognition*, **3**, 519-526.

Perrett D.I., Rolls E.T. and Caan W.C. (1982) Visual neurons responsive to faces in the monkey temporal cortex. *Experimental Brain Research*, **47**, 329-342.

Perrett, D.I., Mistlin, A.J. and Chitty A.J. (1987) Visual neurons responsive to faces. *Trends in Neurosciences*, **10**, 358.

Poggio, T. and Koch, C. (1986) Synapses that compute motion. *Scientific American*, **256**, 46-71.

Posner, M.I. and Presti, D.E. (1987) Selective attention and cognitive control. *Trends in Neurosciences,* **10**, 13.

Potter, M.C. (1975) Meaning in visual search. *Science*, **187**, 965-966.

Potter, M.C. (1976) Short-term conceptual memory for pictures. *Journal of Experimental Psychology : Human Learning and Memory*, **2**, 509-522.

Potter, M.C. and Faulconer, B.A. (1975) Time to understand pictures and words. *Nature*, **253**, 437-438.

Reiter, H.O. and Stryker, M.P. (1988) Neural plasticity without post-synaptic action potentials : Less active inputs become dominant when kitten visual cortical cells are pharmacologically inhibited. *Proceedings of the National Academy of Science*, **85**, 3623-3627.

Richmond, B.J. Optican, L.M. Podell, M, and Spitzer H. (1987a) Temporal encoding of two-dimensional patterns by single units in primate inferior temporal cortex. I. Response characteristics. *Journal of Neurophysiology*, **57**, 132-146.

Richmond, B.J. and Optican, L.M. (1987b) Temporal encoding of two-dimensional patterns by single units in primate inferior temporal cortex. II. Quantification of response waveform. *Journal of Neurophysiology*, **57**, 147-161.

Richmond, B.J. and Sato, T. (1987c) Temporal encoding of two-dimensional patterns by single units in primate inferior temporal cortex. III. Information theoretic analysis. *Journal of Neurophysiology*, **57**, 161-178.

Riddoch, M.J. and Humphreys, G.W. (1988) Picture naming. In G.W. Humphreys and M.J. Riddoch (Eds.) *Visual Object Processing : A Cognitive Neuropsychological approach*. (pp107-143).

Rolls, E.T. (1986) Information representation, processing and storage in the brain : analysis at the single unit level. In J.P. Changeux and M. Konishi (Eds.), *Neural and molecular mechanisms of learning*. Berlin : Springer-Verlag.

Rolls E.T., Burton M. and Mora F. (1976) Hypothalamic neuronal responses associated with the sight of food. *Brain Research*, **111**, 53-66.

Rolls E.T., Perrett D.I., Caan W.C. and Wilson F.A.W. (1982) Neuronal responses related to visual recognition. *Brain*, **105**, 611-646.

Rolls E.T., Sanghera M. and Roper-Hall A. (1979) The latency of activation of neurones in the lateral hypothalamus and substantia innominata during feeding in the monkey. *Brain Research*, **164**, 121-135.

Rosenblatt F. (1962) *Principles of Neurodynamics*. Spartan Books.

Rumelhart D., Hinton G. and Williams D. (1986) Learning internal representations by error propagations. In Rumelhart and McClelland (Eds.)Vol 1. (pp 318-362).

Rumelhart, D.E. and McClelland J. (1986) *Parallel Distributed Processing : Explorations in the microstructure of cognition*. MIT Press/Bradford Books.

Rumelhart, D.E. and Zipser D. (1985) Feature discovery by competitive learning. *Cognitive Science*, **9**, 75-112.

Sejnowski, T.J. (1977) Storing covariance with nonlinearly interacting neurons. *Journal of Mathematical Biology*, **4**, 303-321.

Sejnowski, T.J. (1988) Neural network learning algorithms. In R. Eckmiller and C. von der Malsburg (eds.) *Neural computing*. (pp 291-300).

Sejnowski, T.J., Koch, C. and Churchland, P.S. (1988) Computational Neuroscience, *Science*, **241**, 1299-1306.

Shevelev, I.A. (1987) Temporal processing of orientation signals in the visual cortex. *Perception*, **16**, 263-264.

Singer W. (1987) Activity dependent self-organization of synaptic connections as a substrate of learning. In J.P. Changeux and M. Konishi (eds.) *The neural and molecular bases of learning*. (pp. 301-336).

Smolensky, P. (1988) On the proper treatment of connectionism. *Behavioural and Brain Sciences*, **11**, 1-76.

Soucek, B. and Soucek, M. (1988) *Neural and massively parallel computers*. New York : Wiley.

Strehler, B.L. and Lestienne, R. (1986) Evidence on precise time-coded symbols and memory of patterns in monkey cortical neuronal spike trains. *Proceedings of the National Academy of Science*, **83**, 9812-9816.

Sutton, R.S. and Barto, A.G. (1981) Toward a modern theory of adaptive networks : Expectation and prediction. *Psychological Review*, **88**, 135-170.

Thorpe, S.J. (1988) Identification of rapidly presented images by the human visual system. *Perception*, **17**, A77.

Thorpe, S.J. and Pouget, A. (1989) Coding of orientation by the visual cortex : Neural network modelling. In Pfeifer, R., Schreter, Z., Fogelman, F.and Steels, L. (eds.): *Connectionism in Perspective*. Amsterdam: Elsevier.

Thorpe, S.J., O'Regan, J.K and Pouget, A. (1988) Humans fail on XOR pattern recognition problems. *Proceedings of the First European conference on Neural Networks*.

Thorpe, S.J., Rolls, E.T. and Maddison, S. (1983) The orbitofrontal cortex : Neuronal activity in the behaving monkey. *Experimental Brain Research*, **49**, 93-115.

Van Essen, D.C. and Maunsell, J.H.R. (1983) Hierachical organization and functional streams in visual cortex. *Trends in Neurosciences*, **6**, 370-375.

von der Malsburg, C. (1973) Self-organizing of orientation sensitive cells in the striate cortex. *Kybernetik*, **14**, 85-100.

von der Malsburg, C. and Bienenstock, E. (1986) A neural network for the retrieval of superimposed connection patterns. In F. Fogelman, F. Weisbuch and E. Bienenstock (Eds.) *Disordered systems and biological organization*. Berlin : Springer-Verlag.

Wild, H.M, Butler, S.R., Carden, D., and Kulikowski, J.J. (1986) Primate cortical area V4 important for colour constancy but not wavelength discrimination. *Nature*, **313**, 133-134.

Wurtz, R.H., Goldberg, M.E. and Robinson, D.L. (1980) Behavioral modulation of visual responses in the monkey : stimulus selection for attention and movement. *Progress in Psychobiology and Physiological Psychology*, **9**, 43-83.

Zeki, S. (1980) The representation of colour in the cerebral cortex. *Nature*, **284,** 412-418.

Zeki S. and Shipp S. (1988) The functional logic of cortical connections. *Nature*, **335**, 311-316.

Zipser, D. and Anderson R.A. (1988) A back-propagation programmed network that simulates response properties of a subset of posterior parietal neurons. *Nature*, **331**, 679-684.

CONNECTIONISM IN PERSPECTIVE
R. Pfeifer, Z. Schreter, F. Fogelman-Soulié, L. Steels (Eds.)
Elsevier Science Publishers B.V. (North-Holland), 1989

Connectionist Approaches to Artificial Perception and Temporal Processing: A Speech Pattern Processing Perspective*

John S. Bridle

Royal Signals and Radar Establishment
Malvern UK

Abstract—*Automatic speech recognition (ASR) is an archetypal problem in Artificial Perception. We review three styles of approach to ASR: the "classic" Strong Knowledge approach (using Artificial Intelligence Techniques), the Stochastic Model paradigm and the New Connectionist onslaught.*

Keywords— Artificial perception, pattern processing, speech recognition, connectionism, neural networks, stochastic models

1 INTRODUCTION: PERCEPTION

Perception is the mysterious, largely automatic process by which raw sensory data is turned into useful interpretations. In lower animals (and much of the time in humans) perception is intimately linked with action. Artificial Perception (AP) can be defined as the goal of building artificial systems that could exhibit a degree of robustness and flexibilty, in responding to real-world data, that we normally associate with animals (including humans). AP research is thus a branch of Artificial Intelligence research (where AI is similarly defined as a goal, rather than a set of techniques

In some cases the interpretations of the world that perception produces are available to conscious inspection. Occasionally we are aware of a kind of reasoning (about the data) which seems to be involved in interpretation. Helmholtz suggested that the processes of perception were of the same kind as those consciously-accessible reasonings. An alternative view is that all pre-conscious perception is of a quite different nature: for instance more like the settling into an equilibrium state of a large network which instantiates the constraints which relate the sensory data and its possible interpretations (Hinton, 1980). It may well be that conscious, symbolic reasoning is used merely as a justification for a conclusion which has been reached by a process of "deep perception" more often than we realise.

Smolensky dramatises our ignorance of the representations, processes and mechanisms which mediate between sensory data and conscious thought as a "conceptual abyss", and suggests (Smolensky, 1987) that the symbolic level of description of our minds is best seen as an approximation to the much richer *sub*-symbolic level at which the computation actually takes place. The most visible products of AI research are based on a symbolic mode, appropriate, perhaps, to emulating conscious thought processes. (The main exceptions are in the field of computer vision, where numerical methods are dominant for the early stages.)

By the above definition, Artificial Perception is a branch of engineering, and its products can be judged by results independently of any relationship to theories of the operation of biological systems. However, the argument that "Nature's way is best" has a great deal of force in speech processing, because it is reasonable to assume that the speech code has evolved to make maximum use of the available (and co-evolving) processes of perception.

Artificial Perception has to deal with several hard problems simultaneously. They include Continuity, Uncertainty and Complexity. These problems are the special domains of Signal Processing, Statistics and Computer Science respectively.

2 SPEECH RECOGNITION

Automatic Speech Recognition (ASR) is a problem in Artificial Perception: the input is a continuous, undifferentiated, flowing pattern of sound (no symbols!) but the desired output is symbolic (words-label, meanings, or text).

Speech is essentially a function of time, and any serious attempt at ASR has to deal with time in a principled way. Normal, natural speech recognition is performed (apparently effortlessly) by our brains, without the need for conscious thought (Marslen-Wilson, 1979).

Speech can be described at many levels, ranging from the shape of waveforms to the meaning of whole sentences. Speech science is largely concerned with identifying useful levels of description (Repp, 1981) and relating descriptions at different levels. Speech technology typically deals with methods for moving between levels automatically.

The automatic speech recognition systems available today are based on a simple two-stage process. First the unknown speech signal is converted to a *pattern* which makes explicit the changing spectrum shape caused by the changing shape of the speaker's mouth and ignores details caused by e.g. the pitch of the voice. Then this pattern is compared with reference patterns ('models'), one or more for each word, stored in the system's memory, and a decision is made about the most likely word or sequence of words.

The specifications for speech synthesis, and the desired output of Automatic Speech Recognition, are symbolic. There has been some success in synthesising intelligible speech from symbolic specifications, including conventional text, but all practical, working automatic speech-recognition systems avoid bridging the signal-to-symbol gulf, and leap from sound patterns to the identification of whole words or phrases. (Although several impressive research systems have a meaningful sub-word representation, decisions are always delayed until whole phrases have been analysed.)

We review three styles of approach to ASR which have each been in fashion (at least once) in the past 20 years. The Strong Knowledge approach starts with the assumption that what speech experts (phoneticians) know about speech is relevant and applicable to ASR. In the Stochastic Model and Connectionist approaches, most of the speech knowledge comes from automatic analysis of speech in terms of the models and networks to be used in recognition ("the speech speaks for itself").

3 STRONG KNOWLEDGE APPROACHES

The Strong Knowledge approach starts with the assumption that what speech experts (mainly phoneticians) know about speech is relevant and applicable to ASR. It is clear that a much better performance should be possible, if only we could build into ASR machines more of the rich and useful-looking knowledge about the structure of speech that seems to exist in the domains of phonetics, psychology, physiology and linguistics. The technology is normally that of mainstream applied Artificial Intelligence (*i.e.* somewhere between the simulation of conscious reasoning and the use of high-level symbolic programming techniques). However, some SK approaches to ASR have also incorporated techniques from statistical pattern recognition (Cole, 1984) and combinatorial search algorithms.

The problems are of two kinds: the suitabilty and adequacy of the speech knowledge, and the suitability of the "knowledge engineering" techniques.

The relationship between acoustic pattern and meaning is very complicated. We suspect that it would be useful to describe the relationship via several intermediate concepts such as words. Speech Science provides several other useful-looking intermediate concepts, such as formant and phoneme. Unfortunately, when we come to apply such ideas we typically find them lacking in the kind of precise definition that we need in order to translate directly into computationally–useful form.

There have been many attempts to use strong speech knowledge and AI techniques to ASR. One of the biggest was the ARPA Speech Understanding Systems (SUS) project, in the early 1970's (Klatt, 1977). The emphasis was on the use of "higher level" knowledge (syntactic, semantic and pragmatic) to make up for the ambiguities of the acoustic signal. (There is no doubt that some form of reasoning is needed in systems which are to maintain a useful dialogue in a human-like way.) One of the most interesting system architectures was that of Hearsay. The basic idea was that the recognition process was divided up into separate but interacting "knowledge sources", for example acoustic, phonetic, syntactic and semantic. The knowledge sources communicated using a "blackboard". Although the Hearsay blackboard architecture is now one of the standard examples in introductions to Expert Systems, the original speech recognition system did not perform particularly well. It can be argued that the blackboard architecture idea has served as stimulus to connectionist approaches to speech and language processing (Arbib, 1987).

The only ARPA SUS system that met all the original specifications was called Harpy. It worked in a quite different way, with two quite separate phases. In the first phase (model building) all the grammatical, lexical and phonological knowledge was "compiled" into a single huge network-type structure, which was a compact way of specifying all possible valid utterances in the task domain. In the second phase (recognition) the utterance to be recognised was compared with the whole network to find the path for which the acoustic expectations were closest to the input. Because of the restricted form of the network it was possible to use a powerful and near-optimal search technique, which is the same as that used in the stochastic model paradigm described below. Indeed, Harpy was the result of combining speech knowledge techniques from Hearsay with the stochastic model representation and search methods developed for the Dragon (Baker, 1975) speech recognition system.

The current big US government attempt to push back the frontiers of automatic speech recognition was also founded on an assumption that better speech knowledge needed to be used, and that techniques were available to exploit it. This DARPA speech programme has also seen a swing to stochastic-model based techniques and a (relatively) crude interpretation of current phonetic knowledge, (although significant advances have been made in techniques for incorporating speech knowledge and training in the details). In the U.K. the Alvey Programme's big ASR demonstrator project has similarly swung towards stochastic model based methods, both at the acoustic-phonetic level and the grammatical level.

It is not clear whether the relative failure of the knowledge intensive methods has been because the knowledge or the techniques were not up to the job, or because the approach was not pursued far enough.

4 STOCHASTIC MODELS

In Strong Algorithms approaches to ASR the emphasis is on the ability, of the techniques used, to solve well-defined mathematical problems which, it is hoped, are relevant to speech processing. Powerful mathematical techniques are typically used for finding optimal "decodings" of speech patterns, in the sense of minimising an "energy" or maximising a likelihood. One particularly powerful set of algorithms derives from treating the speech data as if it were the output of a *stochastic* system.

A *stochastic system* is one that evolves in time or space according to probabilistic laws (Cox & Millar, 1965). In a *Stochastic Model* (SM) approach the patterns are treated as if they are outputs of a stochastic system. Information about the classes of patterns is encoded as the structure of such "laws" and the probabilities that govern their operation. The word *model* is used for this representation of a hypothetical generator of data. It should not be confused with a "connectionist model", which is likely to be a computational embodiment of a theory of perception. In an SM approach the "perception" is done by an an algorithm designed to suit the form of the model. It is necessary to choose the form of the models as a careful compromise between availability of good algorithms and faithfulness to the nature of speech patterns. The Stochastic Model approach makes no claims to be relevant to human speech recognition, but does have principled ways of dealing with uncertainty and temporal structure.

A stochastic word model contains enough information to produce, with appropriate probabilities, many different "pronunciations" of a single word. (The variations in the spectrum and timescales would be realistic if the model were a very good one, but current stochastic models do not make good synthesisers.) Alternatively, the same information can be used to compute the probability with which the model would generate any particular pattern. Speech recognition decisions are made by choosing the stochastic word model which is "most likely" to produce the unknown speech pattern.

The best established type of stochastic word model has a mathematical form known variously as a "probabilistic finite state automaton", a "hidden Markov model" (HMM) or a "stochastic regular grammar". In a simple type of hidden Markov model the hypothetical pattern generating machine has an internal state which is not directly observed. A word model might have between 4 and 20 states. The machine proceeds through a sequence of these states, changing state every hundredth of a second (perhaps to repeat a state). The state sequence is a first-order Markov Chain, which means that the influence of past states on the current state can be expressed in terms of the dependence on the immediately past state alone. (The *state transition matrix.*) The observable acoustic data at each time depends directly on only the state at that time. (The *output distributions.*) The output distributions may be discrete or continuous with parameters (*e.g.* multi-variate Gaussian) depending on the amount and type of pre-processing of the data. Variability of timescale and of structure is expressed in the state transition matrix, and variability of the spectrum shape is expressed in the output distributions (Levinson, Rabiner & Sohndi, 1983; Levinson, 1984; Russell & Moore, 1985).

Recognition of an unknown word pattern can be done by computing the probability with which each model model would generate the given pattern. The most likely word is then chosen, or the word probabilities are passed on to higher levels of analysis. This recognition computation involves a probability-weighted sum over all state sequences (altenatively the probability of the best state sequence is computed). Because of the simple (Markovian) structure of dependencies between states, it is possible to compute such sums (and maxima) without a combinatorial explosion.

This approach can be extended to deal with sequences of words (Bridle, Brown, & Chamberlain, 1983). It is possible to take the integration of levels of representation of speech even further, and include models of language and phonetics. This amounts to probabilities for transitions between complete word models, and for transitions between "phonetic segment" units within a word. Using this approach, some success has been reported for the "decoding" of sentences dictated from real documents (Bahl, Cole, Jelinek, Mercer, Nadas, Nakamoo, & Pitcheny, 1983), and recently speaker-independent connected-word sentence recognition (Lee, 1988).

An HMM recognition algorithm is designed to find the best explanation of the input in terms of the model. It tracks scores for all plausible current states of the generator and throws away explanations which lead to a current state for which there is a better explaination (Bellman's Dynamic Programming (Bellman & Dreyfus, 1962)), It may also throw away explainations which lead to a current state much worse than the best current state (score pruning, producing a Beam Search method (Lowerre, 1976)). (It is important to keep many hypotheses in hand, particularly when the current input is ambiguious.)

Model building is of crucial importance. Essentially it is a matter of estimating the conditional probabilities and the parameters of the output distributions. Elegant methods are available for "tuning" an initial word model using many examples of each word (Levinson et al., 1983; Baum, 1972).

To build a set of word models for a speaker-independent isolated digit recogniser, we would need examples of the words from many speakers (say 100) recorded under conditions relevant to our intended application. Using any one of several acoustic analysis techniques the waveforms would be converted to one vector of say 10 numbers 100 times per second. We might further reduce this representation (using "vector quantisation") to one integer 100 times per second. We would choose the number of states and other aspects of the models, perhaps by experiment using part of the data. Initial settings of the parameters of the models might be set by dividing the timescale of each word pattern equally between a sequence of states. The re-estimation method needs time proportional to number of states per word times total amount of training data, and space proportional to number of states per word times total length of training data for a word.

The art of applying the SM approach is to choose a class of models which is realistic enough to be likely to be able to capture the distinctions (between speech sounds or words for instance) and yet have a structure which makes it ammenable to algorithms for building the detail of the models based on examples, and for interpreting particular unknown patterns. Future systems will need to exploit the regularities descrided by phonetics, to allow the construction of high-performance systems with large vocabularies, and their adaptation to the characteristics of each new user.

5 CONNECTIONIST APPROACHES

Whereas the Strong Knowledge approach starts with the prior information which should be used, and the Stochastic Model approach starts by assuming a form for the generator of the data, Connectionist (or PDP or "Neural Network") approaches start with an idea of the *types of process* to be used to transform the data into answers.

Connectionist or NN approaches can claim some legitimacy by reference to new (or renewed) theories of cognitive processing. The actual mechanisms used are simpler than those of the SM method, but the mathematical theory (of what can be learnt or computed for instance) is more difficult, particularly for structures which have been proposed for dealing with temporal processing.

Some will be interested in the potential for connectionist methods to be relevant as models of perception, or for their potential compatibility with future methods of fabrication, be that electronic or something more exotic. For a comprehensive review of neural network approaches to speech recognition, see (Lippmann, 1989).

One of the dreams for connectionist approaches to speech is a network whose inputs accept the speech data as it arrives, it would have an internal state which contains all necessary information about the past input, and the output would be as accurate and early as possible. The training of networks with their own dynamics is particularly difficult, especially when we are unable to specify what the internal state should be. The Trace Model was constructed to have an appropriate kind of dynamics. Almeida (Almeida, 1987) and Rohwer (Rohwer & Forrest, 1987; Rohwer & Renals, 1988) are developing methods for training the fixed points of continuous-valued recurrent non-linear synchronous networks. There is work (e.g. (Coolen & Ruijgrok, 1988; Sompolinsky & Kanter, 1986)) on the theory of the dynamics of systems composed of large numbers of binary "neurons" with time delays and assymetrical connections. Watrous (1988) limits his recurrent connections to self-loops on hidden and output units, but even so the general theory of such recursive non-linear filters is formida ble.

Waibel et.al. (Waibel, Hanazawa, Hinton, Shikano, & Lang, 1989) use an arrangement which can be thought of either as the replication of smaller networks across the time-window (a time-spread network (Bridle& Moore, 1984)) or as a single small network with internal delay lines (a Time-Delay Neural Network, TDNN). There are no recurrent links (except for simple ones at the output), so training (using Backpropagation) is no great problem. We may think of the hidden layers of a TDNN as a finite-impulse-response non-linear filter, as distinct from a recursive filter in the case of recurrent networks. Reported results on consonant discrimination are encouraging, and better than those of a HMM system on the same data.

Kohonen has constructed and demonstrated large vocabulary isolated word (Kohonen et al., 1984) and unrestricted vocabulary continuous speech transcription (Kohonen, 1988) systems which are inspired by neural network ideas, but implemented as algorithms more suitable for current programmed digital signal processor and CPU chips. (Omohundro (Omohundro, 1987) has pointed out that most of the desirable properties of neural network type systems can often be achieved much more efficiently using appropriate algorithms.)

Kohonen's *phonotopic map* technique can be thought of as an unsupervised adaptive quantiser constrained to put its reference points in a non-linear low-dimensional sub-space. His *learning vector quantiser* technique used for initial labelling combines the advantages of the classic nearest-neighbour method and discriminant training. The *redundant hash addressing* used for subsequent lexical access processing in the isolated-word system is related to hash coding and perhaps also to some learning networks such as WISARD (Aleksander, Thomas, & Bowden, 1984).

One of the conceptually simplest approaches is to treat a whole time-frequency-amplitude array (resulting from initial acoustic analysis) as the input to a network, and require a (word) label as output. For example, the performance that Peeling et.al. (Peeling, Moore, & Tomlinson, 1986; Peeling & Moore, 1988) report on small-vocabulary isolated word recognition tasks approach those of the best HMM techniques available on the same data. The problem of invariance to temporal position was dealt with simply by training the network with the patterns at random positions in a fixed time-window. This approach does not seem to be applicable to connected word recognition.

If we were to apply this technique to the multi-speaker isolated digit data discussed above we must choose the type of neural units, the structure of the network, the learning rule and the order of presentation of training data. A typical choice might be semi-linear logistic units, with one hidden layer of say 50 such units, and of course ten output units (one for each class). The total number of weights (assuming a one-second input array of 100 10-dimensional vectors) is $(100 * 10 + 1) * 50 + (50 + 1) * 10 = 505510$, where the odd 1s are for the biasses. The amount of computation for a forward pass is dominated by a multiply and an add for each weight. During training twice this amount of computation is needed for every pattern presentation, to compute contributions to the derivatives of the error with respect to each weight. We might arrange to present one example of each of the ten classes before updating the weights. The amount of computer time needed to train such a system is typically more than an order of magnitude greater than for an HMM method, but the amount of computation for recognition only is typically less than for the HMM. TDNN methods can be trained significantly faster than fully connected networks.

Among other types of networks which have been applied to speech we must mention an interesting class based not on correlations with weight vectors (dot-product) but on distances from reference points. *Radial Basis Function* theory (Powell, 1985) was developed for multi-dimensional interpolation, and was shown by Broomhead and Lowe (1988) to be suitable for many of the jobs that feed-forward networks are used for. The advantage is that it is not difficult to find useful positions for the reference points which define the first, non-linear, transformation. If this is followed by a linear output transformation then the weights can be found by methods which are fast and straightforward. The reference points can be adapted using methods based on back-propagation. Related methods include potential functions (Aizerman, Braverman, & Rozonoer, 1964), Kernel methods (Hand, 1882) and the modified Kanerva network (Prager & Fallside).

6 COMPARISONS, PROSPECTS AND IMPLICATIONS

There is no doubt that the Stochastic model based methods work best at present, but current systems are generally far inferior to humans even in situations where the usefulness of higher-level processing is minimal. Stochastic model based methods offer principled ways of dealing with uncertainty and with temporal structure, plus powerful algorithms for decoding (recognition) and for model building (learning). There is no clear limit to development of SM methods for speech, and the recognition algorithms are not difficult to map on to parallel hardware. However, there seems to be a culture gap between the type of mathematics underlying SMs and most speech scientists: the number of individuals who appreciate both fields is quite small.

The connectionist (neural network) approach offers a different viewpoint, and a language for thought and communication. It is a way of making contact with many ideas which may not have been applied to speech before. The training methods for neural network classifiers are based on improving discrimination between classes, whereas SM methods usually model each class separately (Niles, Silverman, Tajchman, & Bush, 1989). (But see (Bahl, Brown, de Souza, & Mercer, 1988).) It seems that speech scientists find it easier to see how to use neural networks than stochastic models, so we can expect to see NN approaches with a good basis in appreciation of the subtleties of speech. For examples of NN methods applied in a knowledge-intensive way, see (Howard & Huckvale, 1988; Bengio, Cardin, de Mori, & Merlo, 1989).

I predict that the next generation of ASR systems will be based on a combination of connectionist and SM theory and techniques, with mainstream speech knowledge probably used in a rather soft way to decide the structure. This can be done in a small way already, if NNs are treated as a way of parameterising a set of more or less high-order correlations, which can be used as an alternative to the usual discrete or continuous output distributions (Bourlard & Wellekens, 1989). I feel that much more should be possible by mimicking in neural networks the type of computations which take place in a SM based speech recognition system, where the state of the recogniser is a vector of scores for alternative states of the (hypothetical) generator at the current time, plus information needed to recover the best interpretation (traceback pointers).

A successful marriage of domain knowledge, stochastic model based methods and connectionist methods will be part of a revolution in Artificial Intelligence, both in the importance given to perceptual pattern processing and in the types of processing paradigms.

REFERENCES

Aizerman, M. A., Braverman, E. M. & Rozonoer, L. I. (1964). On the method of potential functions. *Automatika i Telemekhanika*, **26**, 2086–2088.

Aleksander, I., Thomas, W. V., & Bowden, P. A. (1984). WISARD - A radical step forward in image recognition. *Sensor Review,* 120–124.

Almeida (1987). A learning rule for asynchronous perceptrons with feedback in a combinatorial environment. *Proc. IEEE Int. Conf. Neural Networks*, San Diego.

Arbib, M. A. (1987). *Brains, Machines, and Mathematics* (2nd ed.). Springer-Verlag.

Bahl, L. R., Brown, P. F., de Souza, P. V., & Mercer, R. L. (1988). A New algorithm for the estimation of HMM parameters. *Proc. IEEE ICASSP*, 493–496.

Bahl, L., Cole, A., Jelinek, F., Mercer, R., Nadas, R., Nakamoo, D., & Pitcheny, M. (1983). Recognition of isolated-word sentences from a 5000-word vocabulary office correspondence task. *Proc. IEEE Int. Conf. on Acoustics Speech and Signal Processing*, Boston.

Baker, J. K. (1975). The Dragon system: an overview. *IEEE Trans. ASSP*, **23,** 24–29.

Baum, L. E. (1972). An inequality and associated maximisation technique in statistical estimation for probabilistic functions of a Markov process. *Inequalities,* **3,** 1–8.

Bellman, R, & Dreyfus, S. (1962). *Applied dynamic programming.* Princeton University Press.

Bengio, Y., Cardin, R., de Mori, R., & Merlo, E. (1989). Programmable execution of multi-layered networks for automatic speech recognition. *Comm. ACM,* **32,** 195–199.

Bourlard, H. & Wellekens, C. J. (1989). Links between Markov models and multilayer perceptrons. *Computer, Speech and Language.*

Bridle, J. S. & Moore, R. K. (1984). Boltzmann machines for speech pattern processing. *Proc. Inst. Acoust.*, 1–8.

Bridle, J. S., Brown, M. D., & Chamberlain, R. M. (1983). Continuous connected speech recognition using whole-word templates. *The Radio and Electronic Engineer*, **53,** 167–175.

Broomhead, D. & Lowe, D. (1988). *Multi-variable interpolation and adaptive networks* (RSRE memo 4148). Royal Signals and Radar Est.

Cole, R. A., et.al. (1984). Performing fine phonetic distinctions: templates vs features, in Perkell, J. & Klatt, D. H. (Eds.), *Symposium on invariance and variability of speech processes*. Hillsdale, NJ: Erlbaum.

Coolen, A. C. C., & Ruijgrok, T. W. (1988). *Phys. Rev. A,* **38.**

Cox, D. R., & Millar, H. D. (1965). *The Theory of stochastic processes* (pp. 721–741).Methuen.

Hand (1882). *Kernel discriminant analysis.* Research Studies Press.

Hinton, G. E. (1980). Inferring the meaning of direct perception. *The Behavioral and Brain Sciences*, **3,** 387–388.

Howard, I. S., & Huckvale, M. A. (1988). Acoustic-phonetic attribute determination using Multi-layer Perceptrons. *IEE Colloquium Digest.*

Klatt, D. H. (1977). Review of the ARPA speech understanding project. *J. Acoust. Soc. Amer.*, **62,** 1345–1366.

Kohonen, T. (1988). The "Neural" phonetic typewriter. *IEEE Computer.*

Kohonen, T., et.al. (1984). On-line Recognition of spoken words from a large vocabulary. *Information Sciences*, **33,** 3–30.

Lee, K-F (1988). On Large-vocabulary speaker-independent continuous speech recognition. *Speech Communication*, **7,** 375–379.

Levinson, S. E. (1984). A Unified theory of composite pattern analysis for automatic speech recognition, in Fallside F. & Woods, W. (Eds.), *Computer Speech Processing*. Prentice Hall.

Levinson, S. E., Rabiner, L. R., & Sohndi, M. M. (1983). An Introduction to the application of the theory of probabilistic functions of a Markov process to automatic speech recognition. *Bell Syst. Tech. J.*, **62,** 1035–1074.

Lippmann, R. P. (1989). Review of neural networks for speech recognition. *Neural Network Computation*, **1**.

Lowerre, B. T. (1976). *The HARPY speech recognition system.* Ph.D. thesis, Carnegie-Mellon University, Dept. of Computer Science.

Marslen-Wilson, W. D. (1979). Speech understanding as a psychological process, in *Spoken language generation and understanding* (pp. 39–67), Proc. NATO ASI, Series C. Reidel.

Niles, L., Silverman, H., Tajchman, G., & Bush, M. (1989). How limited training data can allow a neural network to out-perform an 'optimal' classifier. *Proc. ICASSP.*

Omohundro, S. M. (1987). Efficient algorithms with neural network behaviour, *Complex Systems*, **1,** 273–347.

Peeling, S. M., & Moore, R. K. (1988). Isolated digit recognition experimants using the multi-layer perceptron. *Speech Communication,* **7,** 403–409.

Peeling, S. M., Moore, R. K., & Tomlinson, M. J. (1986). The multi–layer perceptron as a tool for speech pattern processing research. *Proc. Inst. Acoustics Conf. on Speech and Hearing*, Windermere.

Powell, M. D. J. (1985). Radial basis functions for multi-variate interpolation: a review. *IMA Conf. on algorithms for the approximation of functions and data*, Shrivenham.

Prager, R. W., & Fallside, F. *Modified Kanerva model for automatic speech recognition.* Submitted to Computer Speech and Language.

Repp, B. H. (1981). On levels of description in speech research. *J. Acoust. Soc. Amer.*, **69,** 1462–1464.

Rohwer, R. & Renals, S. (1988). Training recurrent networks. *Proc. N'Euro-88*, Paris.

Rohwer, R., & B. Forrest, B. (1987). Training time-dependencies in neural networks. *Proc. First Intl. Conf. on Neural Networks*, IEEE.

Rumelhart, D. E., Hinton, G. E., & Williams, R. J. (1985). *Learning Internal Representations by Error Propagation* (ICS Report 8506). University of California, San Diego.

Russell, M. J., & Moore, R. K. (1985). Explicit modelling of state occupancy in hidden Markov models for automatic speech recognition. *IEEE ICASSP-85.*

Smolensky, P. (1987). Connectionist AI, symbolic AI and the Brain. *Artificial Intelligence Review*, **1,** 95–109.

Sompolinsky, H., & Kanter, I. (1986). Temporal Association in assymetrical neural networks. *Physical Review Letters*, **57,** 2861–2864.

Waibel, A., Hanazawa, T., Hinton, G., Shikano, K., & Lang, K. (1989). Phoneme recognition using time-delay neural networks. *IEEE Trans. ASSP.*

Watrous, R. L. (1988). Connectionist speech recognition using the Temporal Flow model. *Proc. IEEE Workshop on Speech Recognition*, Harriman NY.

CONNECTIONISM IN PERSPECTIVE
R. Pfeifer, Z. Schreter, F. Fogelman-Soulié, L. Steels (Eds.)

Speech Recognition Using Connectionist Methods

Christian J. Wellekens
Philips Research Laboratory Brussels, Av. Em. Van Becelaere 2, Box 8
B-1170 Brussels, Belgium.
Phone: (+32) 2 6742275, E-mail: wlk@prlb2.uucp

Abstract–*The difficulties of speech recognition are analyzed. Classical approaches are described and their weak points are brought out: non discriminant training, difficulty to incorporate contextual information, insufficient flexibility of the architecture.*
A recurrent multilayer perceptron is shown to be able to advantageously replace the classical Markov models and to circumvent their drawbacks.
However, dynamic programming remains the basic tool for connected speech recognition.
Connectionist methods raise strong expectations in recognition and research must be devoted in parallel to this new field as well as to the more classical Markov models. Moreover, speech recognition constitutes a large scale application which will lead to a better understanding of the connectionist mechanisms themselves.

Keywords—Speech recognition, connectionism, multilayer perceptrons, Markov models, Boltzmann machine, neural networks, discrimination, classifiers, dynamic programming.

1. INTRODUCTION

Speech recognition is only a part of speech understanding which is a much more ambitious task: while recognition only provides a sequence of words satisfying a given syntax, understanding requires the transformation of such a sequence into a semantic representation which can enrich a data base or which can immediately activate a process such as robot, textprocessing, baggage sorting, air flight reservations, data base query ... Achieving speech understanding implies the combination of several knowledge sources as phonetics, lexical properties, syntax, semantics and even pragmatics. The latter one restricts the search for a recognized sentence to the domain of interest and is crucial for the disambiguation of the anaphoras. The quality of the phonetic or lexical recognition could be significantly improved by the cooperation of all levels which restricts the search domain. The implementation of such interactions is particularly difficult and research goes on to solve the problem by using Artificial Intelligence methods such as blackboards and knowledge sources as in the early

HEARSAY system. Most of the high level techniques developed for natural language processing rely on error-free low level inputs. As a consequence, the understanding is often split in two steps: recognition and natural language processing. The rôle of recognition which extends from the acoustic data acquisition to the syntactical level is to provide the most reliable input as possible to the higher levels.

2. MODELS OF SPEECH UNITS

The simplest method occurring in the mind of an engineer for solving the problem of speech recognition is to identify typical features of the signals to be classified and then to try and detect these features in a recognition phase. Each word is then identified by its acoustic signature. The early methods of speech recognition were based on such a pattern recognition approach but formed the weak link of ambitious projects such as HEARSAY. The first step requires indeed expert knowledge in phonetics. However,the utterance of a speech signal differs so strongly from one speaker to another and its variability even for the same speaker is so important that it is a tremendous work to specify the characteristic features of a speech unit such as a word, a syllable and a fortiori a phoneme, particularly when embedded in a discourse. Moreover, industrial production tends to avoid the need of human expertise each time a different application must be designed.

The representation of the speech signal is obtained by a preprocessing that achieves some data compression.Spectral or cepstral analysis are applied to sliding windows of the time signal. The extracted parameters form an *acoustic vector* associated with each time slot. Linear predictive coding is also commonly used but requires a special metric, known as the Itakura distance, contrary to the other representations which are compatible with an Euclidean metric.

A supplementary data compression may be obtained by vector quantization. Each acoustic vector is replaced by the nearest prototype. Prototypes are computed by a clustering algorithm such as K-MEANS on a large acoustic vector data base.

2.1 Template Models

In small vocabulary applications, the word could be selected as the basic unit for speech recognition. Typical records of words, named templates, are memorized and uttered signals are compared with them. Variability of speechproduction is taken into account by storing several templates per word uttered by the same speaker (for speaker dependent recognition) or by different speakers (for the multispeaker mode).

For large vocabulary applications, smaller sub-units must be used in order to limit their number. The smallest sub-unit set able to cover an unlimited vocabulary is the phoneme set but phonemes are highly coarticulated so that they cannot be easily and accurately excised out of a continuous text.

A significant improvement for the recognition was the *Dynamic Time Warping* (DTW) (Vintsyuk, 1968; Sakoe & Chiba, 1978). This algorithm based on the dynamic programming principles achieves the optimal matching between an acoustic vector sequence and the stored models. The nonlinear distortions of the time axis between a reference template and an actual utterance are smoothed out.

To cope with the high variability of the speech signals, reference templates have been replaced by statistical models.

2.2 Hidden Markov Models

Stochastic models of speech units (Jelinek, 1976) able to be automatically trained on a speech data base have been developed. A *Hidden Markov Model (HMM)* is constituted by a set of states connected together by transition edges. A probability density (named local probability) to produce an acoustic vector is associated with each transition. The probability to produce an acoustic vector sequence with a model, often known as score, is the sum of the cumulated probabilities corresponding to each path in this model from a given initial state to a final one (Bahl et al., 1983; Bourlard et al., 1985). A usual simplification is to reduce this sum to its dominant term. Under this assumption, the score of the best path can be easily computed by using a dynamic programming algorithm similar to the *DTW* and known as the *Viterbi* algorithm. The *Viterbi* algorithm achieves the optimal matching between an acoustic vector sequence and the states of the model. It also plays an essential role in connected speech recognition: indeed, the determination of the best path with possible discontinuities at the boundaries of the word models simultaneously provides the segmentation and the labeling of words (Bridle et al., 1982; Sakoe, 1978, Myers & Rabiner, 1981; Ney, 1984).

The parameters of the models are estimated by training. Known sentences are matched against the corresponding chain of models and the parameters are tuned to maximize the global probability over the complete training data set. Such an "embedded training" avoids the tedious a priori phonetic segmentation and the coarticulation effects are incorporated by the stochastic nature of the representation (Bourlard et al., 1985). *HMM* 's, coupled with the *Viterbi* algorithm, are particularly well suited for modeling the sequential nature of speech.

Hidden Markov models led to a breakthrough in the recognition score improvement. However, during the last two years, any supplementary progress is obtained only at the price of an excessively increased complexity (Aubert et al., 1988). The main difficulties lie in the lack of discrimination between models of different speech units and in the ignorance of the contextual speech information.

To make the models context-sensitive, two solutions are possible: either the data structure can be modified by replacing each acoustic vector by a larger one containing also its left and right neighbours (Furui, 1986; Marcus, 1981) or a new probability density can be defined which depends on the neighbours (Wellekens, 1987). In both cases, the number of parameters of the densities becomes so large that a meaningful training would require an unrealistic amount of data. Moreover, in the second case, any modification of the contextual window width would require an explicit reformulation.

The most commonly used learning criterion, known as the *Maximum Likelihood Estimation* (Bahl et al., 1983; Bourlard et al., 1985) maximizes the global probability of the model associated with the training set (Baum-Welch algorithm) but does not simultaneously minimize the probabilities associated with all other models and which could yield false recognitions. The score of the correct path differs very slightly from that of the second candidate: no discrimination occurs. Alternative criteria have been proposed as the *Maximum Mutual Information* (Bahl et al., 1986) but they are difficult to work out and often at the price of simplifying hypotheses (Brown, 1987). Another approach is a modification of the *HMM*'s by the definition of discriminant local probabilities (Bourlard & Wellekens, 1988b) which allow Bayes classification of the acoustic vectors (Fukunaga, 1972). Such discriminant *HMM*'s are closely related to connectionist networks as *Multilayer Perceptrons (MLP)* as will be shown in section 4.

3. CONNECTIONIST REPRESENTATIONS

These drawbacks are easily circumvented by using connectionist machines such as *Boltzmann machines* or *Multilayer Perceptrons*. Just like the *HMM*'s, connectionist machines are trained on examples. The explicit formulation of the characteristics of the processed information is not required but its main features are automatically captured and stored in a distributed and hidden way in the parameters of the machines. This property is essential when the underlying structure of the signals is not available as for example in speech recognition or in vision: indeed, it is impossible to explicit the rules used by a listener or an observer to come to a decision on the signal.

Another advantage of these machines is their *generalization* property which is closely related to their non-linear characteristics. It plays an important role as it is impossible in a training data base to include all possible speech events. Moreover, the hidden units of these machines allow the construction of an internal representation of the speech. This self-organization is useful as important hidden features of the internal structure of speech can be so captured during the training phase.

The particular architecture of the connectionist networks make them suitable for parallel computation so that the use of dedicated hardware will be a step towards real time speech recognition.

3.1 Boltzmann machines

Boltzmann machines (Hinton et al., 1984) form a particular family of connectionist machines which provide a solution by running to an equilibrium point which corresponds to the minimum of an energy function. In the context of speech applications, "solution" means recognition of a phoneme, a word or a sentence.

Boltzmann machines are constituted by a very large number of elementary computational units with binary states. If some units are specialized to constitute an input and an output field (visible units), they can be used as recognizers: the input units are clamped to represent a stimulus the identification of which is displayed on the output field. The remaining units are the hidden units.*Boltzmann machines* are said to be "stochastic" since the output of a unit is "on" or "off" according to a probability depending on the weighted sum of the outputs of the other units and of a control parameter known as the "temperature". The energy minimization is performed by a *simulated annealing* algorithm (Kirkpatrick et al., 1982; Aarts & Korst, 1988). While in a simple descent algorithm, a unit will change its state only if it results in a decrease of the energy, a temporary increase of the energy is statistically accepted in a simulated annealing process: the higher the temperature, the more probable are the upward energy jumps. If the temperature is slowly decreased, a global minimum of the energy is eventually reached.

The weights, known as *synaptic weights*, are bidirectional and symmetrical; their values are determined by the training phase. A Kullback-Leibler criterion is minimized which tends to equalize, for a given input field, the probabilities to observe an equilibrium point with an output field clamped on desired states on the one hand and with free outputs on the other hand. During this training, an internal representation of the input/output mapping is automatically built on the hidden units.

A huge amount of CPU time is required as well for the training as for the dynamic energy minimization. That may be acceptable for the training phase since it is performed off-line but a real-time convergence to the solution is compulsory in the recognition phase.

Although *Boltzmann machines* exhibit attractive features for simulating human recognition processes, the required optimizations constitute a major hindrance to practical implementations.

3.2 Multilayer Perceptrons

The architecture of *multilayer perceptrons (MLP)* is much simpler (Rumelhart et al., 1986). Units are organized into layers; the last one is the output field and the other layers are *hidden* for the outside world. The input of a unit is the weighted sum of the output activations of the units of the preceding layer. The synaptic weights are thus unidirectional and for that reason, no iterative process is required in the recognition phase.Thus real time applications can be considered in particular by using a hardware implementation taking full advantage of the parallel structure. This property justifies the fact that *MLP*'s presently stand in the focus of the connectionist research in speech recognition.

The training of *MLP's* is based on the gradient minimization of a criterion: the one most commonly used is the least mean squared error between the desired and the actually observed outputs. This minimization is cleverly programmed as an *error back propagation* (Rumelhart al., 1986). A forward computation provides the activations of the output layer and the differences with the desired outputs are computed. Then in a backward computational wave, corrections are applied to the weights. However, just like for the *Boltzmann machine* (although it is based on a different algorithm), the training is very time consuming since it requires a very large number of iteration cycles during which a large data base is forwarded in the input field with the corresponding desired activations on the output units.

Multilayer perceptrons have been used as discriminant nonlinear classifiers (Lippmann, 1987). They are able to classify data having nonlinear separating curves or even forming non connected sets in the feature space.

A particular application in speech recognition is the representation of the whole set of phonemes of a lexicon by a *single MLP* with one hidden layer (Bourlard & Wellekens, 1987, 1988a). Since this machine is globally trained on the whole data set contrary to what happens for *HMM* models which are separately trained class by class, it can provide simultaneous information on the probability that the input is a member of a class and on the probability that it does not belong to the others. In other words, discrimination can be easily enforced.

The input field may include contextual information in the same spirit as the famous NETtalk network (Sejnowski & Rosenberg, 1987) which learns and memorizes in its synaptic weights the English language pronunciation rules which are indeed fundamentally context-dependent.

In this particular configuration, each letter of a written word is supplied to the input field surrounded by several left and right neighbouring letters (or silences). The associated output is the phoneme that must be associated in a normal English pronunciation. The input field has thus the structure of a shift register. During the training, the synaptic weights are iteratively updated. After a large number of iteration cycles, NETtalk is able to deliver the correct phonetic labeling of any written word. In an impressive demonstration by Sejnowski, this machine activates a speech synthesizer showing that it has thus learned to read aloud.

In a speech recognition application, the letters are replaced by acoustic vectors and still more variability appears in the input/output mapping: in our case between the acoustic input and the phonemic labeling. However, it must be noticed that, even with quantized acoustic vector inputs, the number of possible different stimuli increases exponentially with the width of the contextual window: it is thus impossible to estimate the local probabilities by counting as in a *HMM* due to the excessive size of the data set that would be required for a meaningful training. The generalization property plays here a key role: indeed, during the training, the synaptic weights have been tuned in order to generate at the outputs of the hidden units linear combinations of cross-products between the inputs. Activations at the output layer are obtained by recombining these cross-products (Bourlard & Wellekens, 1987,1988a). Thus, a stimulus never observed in the input field, will preferably activate an output corresponding to an input that possesses in common as many cross-products as possible. On the contrary, with a discrete *HMM*, the activation would be zero or artificially fixed at a lower bound.

4. RECURRENT AND CONTEXT-SENSITIVE MLP

But classification is a static application. For speech recognition, a weakness of the connectionist structures is the difficulty to cope with the sequential nature of the speech signal or signal dynamics. Addition of *feedback loops* provides a solution to this shortcoming.

For instance, Prager, Harrison and Fallside (Prager et al., 1986) have described a *Boltzmann machine* supplied with a feedback loop that, at the thermal equilibrium, brings the decisions taken at the preceding instant in the input field. Unfortunately, this attractive principle suffers from the drawbacks of the *Boltzmann machines,* i.e. excessive CPU requirements even in the recognition phase.

The same principle has been applied to *MLP's*. Several applications for isolated word recognition have been proposed in the literature but most of them are restricted to low size lexicons and thus still remain at the level of research experiments.

In this section, a recurrent and context-sensitive *MLP* is described that can be used as local probability generator (Bourlard & Wellekens, 1988b).

The input signal is a quantized acoustic vector sequence. Part of the inputs of the *MLP* represents a current prototype vector. The output field contains a number of units equal to the number of phonemes in the lexicon and it is fed back as such or after recoding to form the second part of the input field.

Such a recurrent architecture allows the simulation of some useful properties of the discriminant hidden Markov models. In the discriminant *HMM*'s, the local probability is defined as the probability to be on state (say q_k) under the condition that the current observed vector is y_i and that the precedingly visited state was q_m. The estimators of these local probabilities are precisely the *optimal* output activations of the recurrent *MLP* (Bourlard & Wellekens, 1988b). The optimal activations do not depend on the internal topology of the machine but are immediately related to the data base statistics. They are actually the observed outputs of the *MLP* provided the machine contains enough parameters. This condition is generally not satisfied by nonlinear classifiers without hidden layers (Bourlard & Wellekens, 1986).

The input field can also be extended to the neighbouring vectors to take the context into account as explained in the preceding section.

The training of this recurrent machine is totally supervised. Indeed, the data base is constituted by prototype vectors and associated phonemes so that even the correct feedback can be supplied to the input.

As such, this machine performs phonemic labeling. To solve more realistic tasks as large lexicon connected speech recognition, it is useful to resort to the Dynamic Time Warping procedure.

5. CONNECTED SPEECH RECOGNITION

Since the outputs of the recurrent context sensitive *MLP* are equivalent to the local probabilities of a discriminant hidden Markov model, classical recognition packages based on the Viterbi algorithm accept their activations as local probabilities. The *multilayer perceptron* plays thus here the role of a local contribution generator able to force discrimination between phonemes and to include wide contextual acoustic information.

A large tableau is built (Bourlard et al., 1985). Its column index represents the time. The rows are associated with states and are ordered to form state sequences that correspond to words. A one level *Viterbi* algorithm (Bridle et al., 1982; Ney, 1984) is used to find in the tableau the best path between the beginning of a word model at the first instant to the end of a word model at the last instant. Constraints are applied that forbid path discontinuities inside a word. This path provides the word segmentation and the word labeling of the utterance.

Transition probabilities as in the *HMM* are no longer required in the *DTW* tableau itself since they have been learned by the *MLP* which provides dynamical and context-sensitive contributions.

6. CONCLUSIONS

Speech recognition still requires a huge amount of research before reaching a high level application field such as natural language recognition with large vocabulary, without speaker constraints and in a noisy environment. Meanwhile, less ambitious applications, based on classical techniques as *HMM's* have been commercialized.

Connectionist methods must be considered as one alternative technique towards achievement of more difficult tasks. Results obtained up to now do not transcend the level of preliminary studies. Thanks to the flexibility of their architecture which allows an easy incorporation of contextual sensitivity and of recursion, the use of discriminant criteria and the generalization ability, *MLP's* constitute extremely promising tools. Nevertheless, research is going on to improve *HMM* performances, viz. discrimination, state occupation duration, model topology and nature of the local probability densities.

Connectionist models have not yet proved any definitive superiority versus classical models but become everyday more challenging and raise expectations for increased speech recognition scores. Conversely, their use in recognition allows a better understanding of the connectionist mechanisms by applying their principles on a real industrial task.

REFERENCES

Aarts E.H.L., & Korst J.H.M. (1988). *Simulated Annealing and Boltzmann Machines*, Wiley, (to appear)

Aubert X., Bourlard H., Kamp Y., & Wellekens C.J. (1988). Improved Hidden Markov Models for Speech Recognition. *Philips Journal of Research*, vol.43, nos 3/4, 224-245.

Bahl L.R., Jelinek F,.& Mercer R.L.(1983). A Maximum Likelihood Approach to Continuous Speech Recognition, *IEEE Transactions on Pattern Analysis and Machine Intelligence*, vol. PAMI-5, no 2, 179-190.

Bahl L.R., Brown P.F., de Souza P.V., & Mercer R.L. (1986). Maximum Mutual Information Estimation of Hidden Markov Model Parameters for Speech Recognition, *Proceedings of the International Conference on Acoustics, Speech and Signal Processing*, 49-52, Tokyo.

Bourlard H., Kamp Y., Ney H., & Wellekens C.J. (1985). Speaker-Dependent Connected Speech Recognition via Dynamic Programming and Statistical Methods, in M.R. Schroeder (Ed.), *Speech and Speaker Recognition*, Zurich: Karger.

Bourlard H., & Wellekens C.J. (1986). Discriminant Functions for Connected Speech Recognition, in I.T. Young, J. Biemond, R.P.W. Duin & J.J. Gerbrands, (Eds.), *Proceedings of the European Signal Processing Conference*, 507-510,The Hague (The Netherlands).

Bourlard H., & Wellekens C.J. (1987). Multilayer Perceptrons and Automatic Speech Recognition, *Proceedings of the First International Conference on Neural Networks*, IV, 407-416, San Diego, CA.

Bourlard H., & Wellekens C.J. (1988a). Speech Pattern Discrimination and Multilayer Perceptrons, *Computer, Speech and Language*, vol.3, 1-19.

Bourlard H., & Wellekens C.J. (1988b). Links between Markov Models and Multilayer Perceptrons, *Proceedings of the Neural Information Processing Systems Conference 1988, Denver, CO*, to appear.

Bridle J.S., Brown M.D., & Chamberlain R.M. (1982). An algorithm for connected word recognition, *Proceedings of the International Conference on Acoustics, Speech and Signal Processing*, 899-902, Paris.

Brown P. (1987).*The Acoustic-Modeling Problem in Automatic Speech Recognition*, Ph.D. thesis, Computer Science Department, Carnegie-Mellon University.

Furui S. (1986). Speaker Independent Isolated Word Recognizer Using Dynamic Features of Speech Spectrum, *IEEE Transactions on Acoustics, Speech and Signal Processing*, vol. ASSP-34, 52-59.

Fukunaga, K. (1972). *Introduction to Statistical Pattern Recognition*, Academic Press, NY.

Hinton G.E., Sejnowski T.J., & Ackley D.H. (1984). Boltzmann Machines: Constraint Satisfaction Networks that Learn, *Technical Report CMU-CS-84-119*, Carnegie Mellon University.

Jelinek F. (1976). Continuous Recognition by Statistical Methods, *Proceedings IEEE*, vol.64, no.4, 532-555.

Kirkpatrick S., Gelatt C.D. jr., & Vecchi M.P. (1982). Optimization by Simulated Annealing, *IBM Research Report RC 9355*.

Lippmann R.P. (1987). An Introduction to Computing with Neural Nets, *IEEE Magazine on Acoustics, Speech and Signal Processing*, vol. 4, 4-22.

Marcus S.M. (1981). ERIS-context sensitive coding in speech perception, *Journal of Phonetics* , 9, 197-220.

Myers C.S., & Rabiner L.R. (1981). Connected Digit Recognition Using a Level-Building DTW Algorithm, *IEEE Transactions on Acoustics, Speech and Signal Processing*, vol. ASSP-29, 351-363.

Ney H. (1984). The use of a one-stage dynamic programming algorithm for connected word recognition. *IEEE Transactions on Acoustics, Speech and Signal Processing*, vol. ASSP-32, 263-271.

Prager R.W., Harrison T.D., & Fallside F. (1986). Boltzmann machines for speech recognition, *Computer, Speech and Language*, vol.1, 3-27.

Rumelhart D.E., Hinton G.E., & Williams R.J. (1986). Learning Internal Representations by Error Propagation, in D.E.Rumelhart & J.L. McClelland, (Eds.), *Parallel Distributed Processing. Exploration in the Microstructure of Cognition, vol.1: Foundations*, MIT Press.

Sakoe H., & Chiba S. (1978). Dynamic programming algorithm optimization for spoken word recognition, *IEEE Transactions on Acoustics, Speech and Signal Processing*, vol. ASSP-26, 43-49.

Sakoe H. (1979). Two-Level DP Matching. A Dynamic Programming-Based Pattern Matching Algorithm for Connected Word Recognition, *IEEE Transactions on Acoustics, Speech and Signal Processing*, vol. ASSP-27, 588-595.

Sejnowski T.J., & Rosenberg C.R. (1987). Parallel Networks that Learn to Pronounce English Text, *Complex Systems*, vol.1, 145-168.

Vintsyuk K. (1968). Speech Discrimination by Dynamic Programming, *Kibernetika (Cybernetics)*, 4, 81-88.

Wellekens C.J. (1987). Explicit Time Correlation in Hidden Markov Models for Speech Recognition, *Proceedings of the International Conference on Acoustics, Speech and Signal Processing*, 10.7.1-10.7.3, Dallas, TX.

Synthetic Neural Modelling: Comparisons of Population and Connectionist Approaches

George N. Reeke, Jr., Olaf Sporns, and Gerald M. Edelman
The Rockefeller University and The Neurosciences Institute
New York, New York 10021

Abstract–*Using an approach called synthetic neural modelling, we are constructing automata of a new kind in which the environment, the phenotype, and the nervous system are integrated into a single computer model. The simulated neurons of the automata organize into competing groups as described by the theory of neuronal group selection. Selection acts upon preexisting diversity to strengthen the responses of groups contributing to behaviors having adaptive value for the organism. Current work focuses on Darwin III, a sessile "creature" with an eye and a multi-jointed arm; its nervous system consists of some 50,000 cells of about 50 different kinds connected by about 620,000 synaptic junctions. Darwin III can be trained to track moving objects with its eye, to reach out and touch objects with its arm, to categorize objects according to combinations of visual and tactile cues, and to respond in a positive or negative way to such objects depending on previous experience with similar objects.*

The selectionist view of nervous system function underlying these automata is contrasted with the computational paradigm that provides the basis for connectionist models. This contrast brings out certain aspects in which connectionist models neglect important properties of the real world, suggesting reasons why they are unlikely to capture the essential features of biological perception and behavior.

Keywords—Neural darwinism, synthetic neural modelling, pattern recognition, selection, automata, visual tracking, reach, categorization

INTRODUCTION

In the ongoing series of studies described here, we are mainly concerned with the problem of understanding the origins and mechanisms of adaptive behavior in animals. We accept without discussion a materialist philosophical position and accordingly seek answers that can be expressed in terms of the activity of neuronal cells connected together to form networks in the brain. As will be seen, our examination of the basic requirements for adaptive behavior to emerge from brain activity leads us to reject the common assumption that such capabilities are based on symbolic computation and instead to adopt an alternative *Weltanschauung* based on population thinking and an extension of the concept of Darwinian selection to the somatic time frame and the setting of the nervous system. While this view of the biological solution does not necessarily entail a corresponding stance towards the construction of useful artifacts with some of the cognitive properties of animal nervous systems, we will suggest that the fundamental nature of category and information in the world dictates an approach using selectional mechanisms.

A number of difficulties have so far prevented problems of cognition and behavior from yielding to the reductionist methods that have served so well in the physical sciences, including the mechanical and chemical aspects of biological organisms. Three of these difficulties might be cited as primary contributors to the current state of ignorance concerning the basic principles that underlie intelligent behavior:

The first problem is that behavior always has an essentially unpredictable component that defies all attempts to describe it in terms of deterministic laws. In fact, people value this indeterminism very highly. While philosophers have long debated whether its nature is consistent with the concept of "free will", the phenomenon is in any case real enough to give serious challenge to any deterministic theory of information processing in the brain.

The second difficulty is a corresponding indeterminism in the objects and events in the world which an animal must recognize and to which it must respond. The very term "adaptation" suggests the highly individual, subjective, and context-dependent nature of the categorizations that every animal must make in order to impose its own unique order on the ever-changing kaleidoscope of signals reaching it through its senses. All attempts at rule-based descriptions of this process, for example, the "production systems" of artificial intelligence research, fail to capture the essential ability of the nervous system to generalize and respond appropriately to novelty.

The third difficulty stems from the complexity of the nervous system itself. Its multiple levels of function make it extremely unlikely that we can ever observe simultaneously the activity of all or even a small portion of the cells contributing to any one behavioral act. This basic observational constraint has encouraged the fragmentation of the brain sciences and the proliferation of hypotheses based on alternative modes of understanding which are nonexperimental and inherently unreliable.

One of the most misleading of these alternative modes of understanding is analogy. In the study of behavior by analogy, the nervous system is typically compared to physical systems that are simpler and better understood, such as spin glasses, cellular automata, and, most often, computers. The spin glass analogy leads to a view of neural networks as energy minimizers operating by a relaxation process. In contrast (because all computational manipulations of symbols have essentially equal energetic cost) the computer analogy leads to the attribution to the nervous system of the properties of formal symbol-processing systems (Turing machines), such as coded representations and their manipulation by algorithms. However, it is widely disregarded that scientific analogies like this one can have no more than suggestive value.

The dominant paradigm today for understanding adaptive behavior—the symbol processing paradigm—arises fundamentally from the computer analogy (see Pylyshyn, 1984, for a careful discussion of the arguments). This paradigm is so widely accepted that most workers in the field do not question that the brain generates behavior by carrying out computations that are no different in principle from those carried out by computers. If this view is correct, then the basic problem of behavior has already been solved and all that is needed now is to investigate the specific mechanisms of specific behavioral processes in order to fill in the details of how each particular type of computation is carried out.

In questioning this dominant paradigm, we emphasize the importance of considering all aspects of the solution nature has arrived at to the problem of generating adaptive behavior, including its evolution, its development in individuals, and the physiology of the elementary processes involved (what the proponents of symbolic processing would call the "functional architecture" of the system). Consideration of all these aspects strongly suggests that symbol processing on an elementary neuronal level could hardly arise by known evolutionary processes, would be most difficult to transfer from one generation to the next by known genetic or social mechanisms, and could not be carried out very reliably with neuronal machinery of the kind known to exist in real animals. (The fact that individuals embedded in a speech community can exchange messages with symbolic content must be separated from considerations involving neuronal interactions within these individual's brains.)

In attempting to find an alternative paradigm that is consistent with all these extra-behavioral constraints, we will emphasize the idiosyncratic nature of the solution as it is found in each individual, which results from the critical importance of that individual's history of interaction with the environment. This uniqueness of individual experience, and the unique way of categorizing the world that must result from it in each individual, leads directly to the postulate that selective events in the nervous system constitute the fundamental mechanism of adaptive behavior.

THE SYNTHETIC NEURAL MODELLING APPROACH

A bottom-up experimental approach to understanding adaptive behavior gives some hope of avoiding the difficult theoretical problems we have alluded to. Indeed, the classical neurosciences have always pursued just such an approach. In this way, a great deal of information has been gathered about the workings of the neural machinery in the absence of a theoretical framework to describe their function. Nonetheless, this approach too has limits. These limits are becoming increasingly manifest as our detailed knowledge of the nervous system continues to increase with no obvious end in sight and no clear connection between anatomy, physiology, and function yet apparent.

What is needed to make this connection is the very thing that the bottom-up approach has tried so hard to avoid—namely, a theory. In the face of the complexity of the nervous system and the evident failure of an explanation of its function to "fall out" of the experimental data, it seems clear that only a theory that can be combined with detailed modelling to generate testable predictions can have much chance of showing how the well-understood components of the nervous system work together in complex networks to give high-level function.

In order to test such a theory, all of the levels of explanation brought together in the theory must also be brought together in a single model for testing. These levels include the environment, which provides the sensory signals that the nervous system must deal with, the phenotype of a particular creature, which provides the apparatus for expressing behavior, and the nervous system itself, where the behavior is generated. To omit any of these components is to invite inconsistent assumptions into the model.

In accord with these ideas, we present both a theory that permits neuronal activity to be related to behavior, and a method of modelling that permits this theory to be tested in realistic situations that include the triad of environment, phenotype, and nervous system. The particular theory we shall explore is the theory of neuronal group selection (TNGS). This theory incorporates not just a mechanism for "computation" in the nervous system, but a view of the nature of the categories in the world that the nervous system must deal with, the way the system evolved to handle its task, and the way the developmental process brings this evolutionary plan to idiosyncratic fruition in each individual (Edelman, 1987).

The TNGS postulates that two kinds of selection events, generally operating at different stages of the life cycle, but overlapping at early phases, play critical roles in the development of the nervous system. During embryogenesis, patterns of synaptic connectivity are shaped by selection among competing neuronal cells and their processes. This competition is played out through the basic developmental processes of cell adhesion, movement, growth, division, and death; the criteria for success are internal and genetically specified. Later, during postnatal experience, the mechanism of selection shifts to differential modification of synaptic strengths, usually without further changes in connectivity. This stage of selection defines the perceptual categories, the significance of neuronal signals, and the behavioral strategies of the animal; the ultimate criterion of success is nothing less than the survival of the organism. The result is different in each individual, just as the history of encounter with the environment, and thus the order of selective events, is different in each individual.

In order for selection to operate in the nervous system, each functional unit (group of cells) must be exposed (either directly or through intermediate relays) to a sufficient sample of the afferent sensory signals to permit it to respond selectively to different perceptual categories in the environment, and each unit must be able to contribute, through its output signals, to some aspect of the behavior of the organism. Finally, the units must have the capacity to change their responses according to the relative success or failure of behaviors to which they contribute. These conditions are met by a system in which the functional units are small collections of neurons (called groups) that are sufficiently complex to respond distinctively to relevant patterns of excitation arriving at their inputs. Groups are arranged in collections (called repertoires), within which competition occurs for access to common signalling pathways, both incoming and outgoing. Connections within and among groups are strengthened or weakened according to the organism's global evaluation of its recent behavior. Such evaluation is the function of "value schemes" (which are related to "drives"). Value schemes must be so simple that we can suppose them to be innate. Therefore, they can only embody criteria for the relative success of behavior, but *not* specific programs for *how* behavior is to be carried out. Value schemes, as well as the general interconnections of groups and of repertoires, may be assumed to be under evolutionary control, which assures that the neuronal equipment of any particular organism is appropriate to generate the degree of behavioral diversity necessary for its survival.

A selective system can have no *a priori* information about the particular stimuli that might be encountered, other than boundary conditions implicit in the genetic rules for the construction of the recognizing elements. In order to be assured of some response to any stimulus, the system must be equipped with units having specificities covering the entire range of possible stimuli. The number of units required increases with the number of potential stimuli as well as with the degree of specificity required in each recognition act. Given the indefinite nature of the boundaries between categories in the world, the only possible strategy is to construct units with arbitrary but overlapping specificities. The overlap provides assurance of coverage of the range, as well as functional redundancy permitting the system to continue operating when some of its units fail. We call this important property *degeneracy*, to suggest the presence of multiple, structurally different but functionally interreplaceable units.

Besides being able to recognize relevant stimuli and categories in the environment, the nervous system must be able to associate stimuli according to their temporal and spatial correlations, as well as, in higher animals, various abstract properties. Association requires comparison, and hence memory. In order for comparison and association to take place, recognition events relating to different times and places must come together in common loci in the nervous system. In the TNGS, this conjunction is brought about by *reentry,* the dynamic connection of outputs from one repertoire into inputs of other repertoires and back again at the same or prior levels of the hierarchy. Often, reentry involves mappings of responses between different sensory pathways. Memory is then the enhanced ability to produce categorical responses that were selected in response to prior occurrences of the same or similar stimuli; associations are developed through the same kinds of synaptic modification mechanisms, operating in loci of reentry, as are used to stabilize memories of initial categorical responses. Reentry is likely to be a key element in the development of consciousness, one essential component of which is the constant comparison of ongoing reality with anticipation.

THE "DARWIN" SERIES OF SELECTIVE NEURAL NETWORK MODELS

In order to test these ideas, we have constructed a series of computer models that embody the principles of neuronal group selection in simple but realistic nervous systems that are embedded in specific "creatures" living in a specific "environment." Our hope is that these models can serve not only to check the consistency of the TNGS, but also to focus experimental questions for further investigation. As an incidental feature, they may also provide a way for ideas developed in the study of the nervous system to be applied to the development of robots, artificial intelligence systems, and non-von Neumann computers. We shall now digress to present a brief summary of our work with these models in order to provide necessary background for our main theme of the contrast between the biological and the computational approaches to understanding adaptive behavior.

The immediate goal of our modelling studies is to demonstrate that automata can be constructed according to the principles of the TNGS that have, in a crude form, some of the behavioral capabilities of animals, without the use of *a priori* definitions of categories, codes, or information-processing algorithms. We examine, in a single system of interconnected neuronal repertoires, sensory acts involving recognition and classification, motor acts, such as visual saccades, reaching, and touch-exploration, and the combination of both in a behaving automaton in which the effects of selection on *output* can influence the perceptual categorizations of the system through the rearrangement of the environment produced by the creature's own actions.

These goals are complex, and we began with a system, Darwin I, which was designed to consider only the actual process of recognition and some factors relating to the statistics of recognition in a selective system (Edelman, 1981). In Darwin I, recognition was based on the degree of match (by a Hamming measure) between complementary bit strings designated as stimuli and as recognizers; selective amplification was accomplished by literal duplication of successful recognizing elements in a repertoire. This model demonstrated the fundamental role of thresholding in the recognition process, and showed how the existence of different thresholds for recognition and for amplification could lead to generalization, and thus to improvements in performance toward novel stimuli. The introduction of errors in the replication process provided a particularly effective mechanism for generalization.

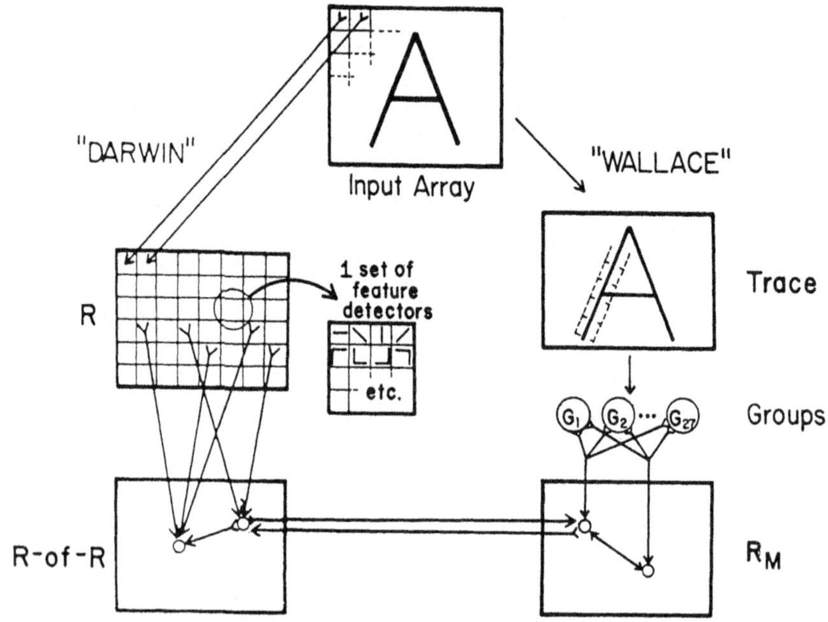

Figure 1: Simplified plan of construction for Darwin II. Boxes represent repertoires, circles represent neuronal groups, and arrows represent synaptic connections. Darwin II has two sets of neuronal repertoires forming a classification couple: at the left, "Darwin", which is designed to respond to combinations of local features defining an individual stimulus object; at the right, "Wallace", which is designed to respond to modes of correlation of features defining the class characteristics of an object. Each set of repertoires has a primary sensory repertoire ("R", or "recognizer", for Darwin; "Trace" for Wallace) and a higher level repertoire that responds to combinations of active groups in the primary repertoires ("R-of-R" and "R_M", respectively. The inset to the right of the R repertoire is an expanded view of one of the topographically mapped subrepertoires, showing individual units that respond to oriented line segments and angles (Reprinted from Reeke and Edelman (1984) with permission.)

A more advanced model, Darwin II, introduced recognition units with properties like those of neuronal groups, connected in networks to explore aspects of the recognition process leading to categorization, generalization, and associative memory (Edelman & Reeke, 1982; Reeke & Edelman, 1984). Darwin II has two parallel series of repertoires, one constructed to respond uniquely to combinations of local features that define *individual* stimuli, while the other responds to correlations of features that define possible *class properties* of stimuli (Fig. 1). Categorization in this system takes the form of common patterns of response to related stimuli. By reentrant interactions, the two subsystems are able to associate individual stimuli (first subsystem) that are members of the same class (second subsystem), and to generalize to class members not previously encountered while retaining the individuality of response to each. While it demonstrated these crucial aspects of the recognition process, Darwin II did not have means to interact actively with the environment, and responses had to be assessed by statistical analysis of the activity patterns in its neuronal groups.

A more recent model, Darwin III, is an automaton with both senses and responses, the behavior of which can be evaluated by an observer. (In this respect Darwin III is like an artificial animal whose behavior can be observed; unlike a real experimental animal, its complete internal states can also be monitored.) Like Darwin I and Darwin II, Darwin III is constructed according to rules derived from the TNGS. It takes the form of a set of interconnected repertoires of neuronal groups, simulated at the level of single cells. The connections, initial connection strengths, and rules for cell responses and synaptic modifications are specified by the experimenter for each repertoire, but no prior information about particular stimuli, and no algorithms for operation of the network, are specified. Responses are determined solely by what the components actually do, and not by any built-in rules of performance at the system level.

GENERAL DESCRIPTION OF DARWIN III

The simulation code that implements Darwin III permits the construction of very general neural network systems (Reeke & Edelman, 1987). Any number of repertoires can be established, with cells of one or more kinds arranged in layers within each repertoire. These cells may be allowed to form groups as a result of their competitive interactions (Finkel & Edelman, 1985), or, for convenience, the group structure may be specified *a priori*. Each cell may have connections selected from three generic types: specific (constructed according to some specific rule, e.g. to form a topographic mapping), geometric (constructed according to a given density vs distance relationship, often to provide lateral inhibition), or modulatory (receiving input proportional to the overall level of activity in some region). There are a variety of possible rules for synaptic amplification, but only specific connections may be plastic.

Darwin III repertoires have access to three sensory modalities: vision, touch, and kinesthesia. On the motor side, there may be one or two eyes with lateral and vertical orbital motions, and one or more arms with multiple joints, each controlled by motor neurons in some specified repertoire.

Every cell in Darwin III has a single-valued activity state determined by a "response function". This function has terms corresponding to synaptic inputs, Gaussian noise, decay of previous activity, depression and refractory periods, and long-term potentiation (LTP). The relative magnitudes of these terms can be varied parametrically. The mathematical details will be presented elsewhere (Reeke et al., in preparation).

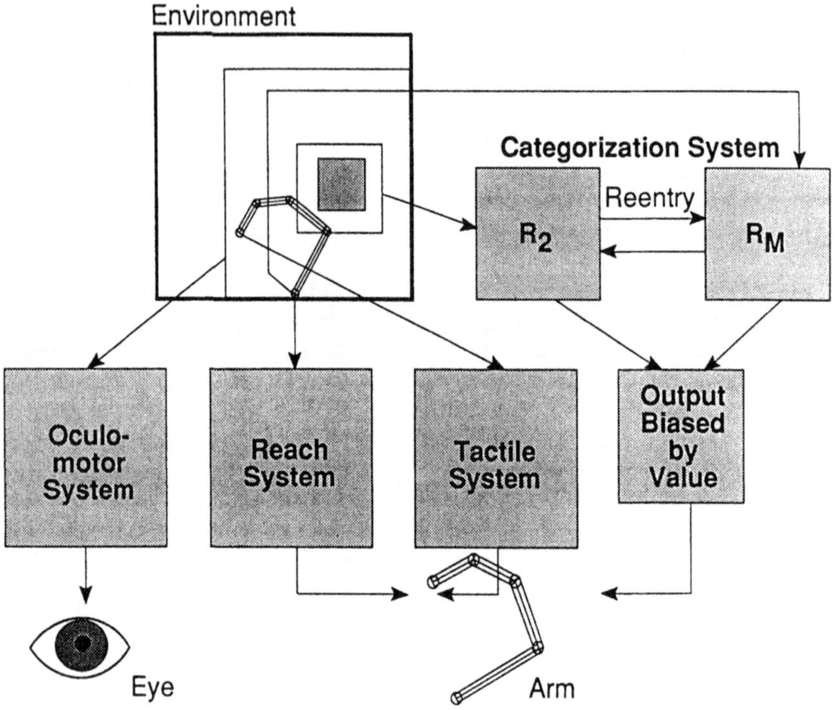

Figure 2: Schematic diagram of the subsystems of Darwin III. Objects (stippled square on the right of the "Environment" box) move within an "environment", a portion of which is viewed by the eye (large square: limits of peripheral vision; small square: central vision). Movements of the eye and the four-jointed arm (bottom) are controlled by the oculomotor and reach systems, respectively. The distal arm digit contains touch sensors used by the tactile system to trace the edges of objects. The categorization system receives sensory inputs from the central part of the visual field and from kinesthetic joint receptors signalling arm movements as tracing of object edges occurs. These inputs connect to a higher-order visual center, R_2, and to an area correlating motion signals over time, R_M. R_2 and R_M are reciprocally connected to form a classification couple. Correlation of firing patterns in these repertoires via reentry leads to classification of objects and eventually yields an output biased by value which can activate reflex movements of the arm.

Rules for synaptic modification contain features reflecting the complex properties of real neurons: in addition to depending on local activity, changes in connection strengths also may be made to depend heterosynaptically on inputs from nearby synapses. These are usually connected to cells in a specialized repertoire, the activity of which reflects the organism's evaluation of its recent behavior according to a particular "value scheme". Synaptic changes may be applied as either increases or decreases according to whether pre- and post-synaptic activity levels are above or below certain thresholds. These synaptic rules constitute a simplified version of a set of rules derived from a careful evaluation of the available physiological data and shown to give rise to group properties in model neuronal networks (Finkel & Edelman, 1985; Pearson et al., 1987). The simplifications, which are made in Darwin III for reasons of computational economy, preserve the functionally critical heterosynaptic and potentiation/depression effects included in the detailed rules, but omit the separation of the synaptic change into separate pre- and post-synaptic components with different localizations and different time courses.

In its present version (Fig. 2), Darwin III consists of four neuronal subsystems: (a) a saccade and fine-tracking oculomotor system, (b) a reaching system using a single arm, (c) a touch-exploration system using a different set of "muscles" in the same arm, and (d) a reentrant categorizing system. These systems have been combined to form an automaton able to use its sensorimotor apparatus in an adaptive way for autonomous behavior and categorization.

NEURONAL SUBSYSTEMS OF DARWIN III

The simplest part of Darwin III is its oculomotor subsystem. This set of repertoires is designed to let us study selective mechanisms in a simple motor control system. The system acquires the ability, after training, to move the eye toward objects in its visual field and to track moving objects. Because it tracks only one of several objects that may be present, based on criteria of saliency such as size, brightness, or central location, it provides a simple "attentional" mechanism for the automaton as a whole. Because our main interest is to understand how such a system can develop without precisely prespecified circuitry, we have omitted the complications of multiple visual pathways and separate control mechanisms for visual saccades and fine tracking movements that are found in real visual systems.

Visual signals impinge on a retina-like visual repertoire containing excitatory and inhibitory cells (Fig. 3). The excitatory cells are mapped topographically to a second repertoire of similar construction that loosely represents the superior colliculus. Excitatory cells in this repertoire are densely connected to ocular motor neurons, which in turn innervate the simulated muscles that move the eye in its orbit. Initial connection strengths are assigned at random, so that eye motions are at first uncorrelated to visual stimulation.

An innate value scheme imposes a global constraint on the selection of eye movements: only those motions are selected which bring visual stimuli into the foveal part of the retina. All that is needed to accomplish this is a value repertoire containing cells connected densely to the fovea and more sparsely to the periphery. The responses of these cells provide a heterosynaptic component which modulates the modification of connections from the "colliculus" to the motor neurons. Connections which are active in a short time interval before foveation occurs are thus selected and strengthened. Note that this selection is strictly *a posteriori*. Motion initially can occur only because of spontaneous activity in the motor neurons; what is selected are populations of connections that favor the reoccurrence of motions that happen to give foveation. There is no *a priori* analysis indicating which connections may have adaptive value in this regard, and no error signal is computed and "back-propagated" into the network.

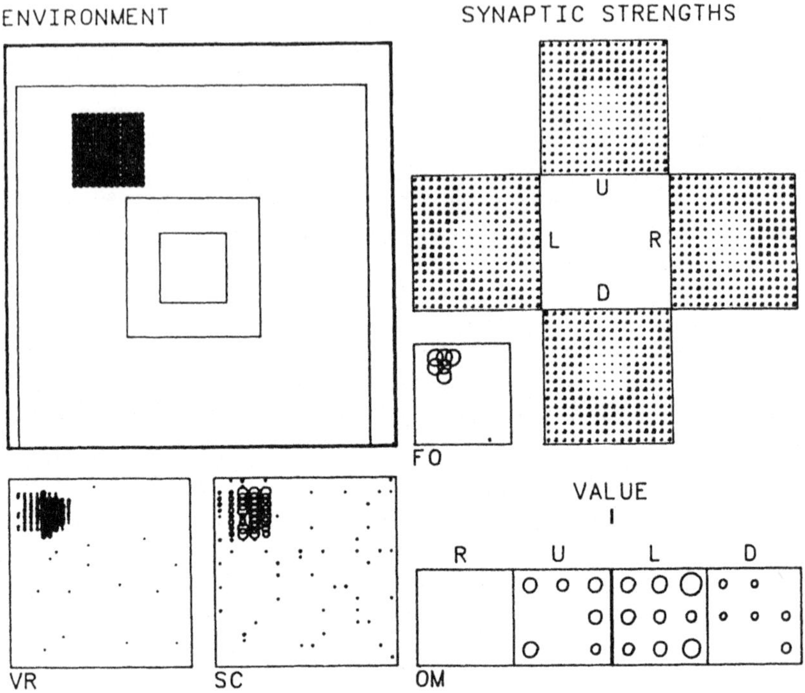

Figure 3: Display of Darwin III's environment and the neural repertoires of the oculomotor system. The object is represented by the dark square at the upper left of the environment. Darwin III's visual field is indicated by the three squares centered on each other within the environment; the outer and the two inner squares delineate the outer boundaries of the visual field, and the perifoveal and foveal regions, respectively. Circles within the boxes labelled VR, SC, FO, and OM correspond to responses of units in the neuronal repertoires of the system. VR receives topographically mapped connections from the visual field, which moves as the eye moves. Its excitatory units map onto another repertoire, SC, which in turn connects to four collections of neurons that move the eye (OM). A repertoire of value-sensitive units (FO) receives dense connections from the center of the foveal region of the visual field. It responds vigorously to bright stimuli in the fovea and less vigorously (as shown) to stimuli in the periphery. The map of the excitatory connections from SC to OM is displayed for the motor neurons that move the eye to the right, up, left, and down, respectively (R,U,L,D). A unit in OM receives connections from all positions in SC, and the black dots in the connection strength plot are proportional to the average strengths of the connections that arrive at all OM cells associated with one direction of movement from the position in SC corresponding to the position of the black dot. Initially these connections have random strengths, and consequently movements elicited by sensory stimulation appear to be uncoordinated. After selective amplification under the influence of the global heterosynaptic input from FO, the maps show a characteristic pattern with a central hole and a shallow gradient across the array. The asymmetric distribution of connections across SC guides the eye towards the stimulus, and once the eye is centered, only small corrective movements are made. Notice that at the moment shown motor units in OM for left- and upward motion are active, corresponding to a movement towards the target which is about to occur.

The system only repeats what works for it. In a standard training protocol, an object is presented at changing locations in the input array and eye motions occur. The improvement of the system is measured by the ability quickly to foveate on a stimulus after its onset. Initially, there is no systematic eye motion, but after some 150 presentations of an object at different locations for 16 cycles each, the eye quickly centers on any stimulus that illuminates any part of the peripheral field.

The inhibitory cells previously mentioned come into play when single large objects or multiple objects are encountered. Competition between objects, or between different parts of large objects, occurs through mutual inhibition of their visual responses. The inhibition is of the shunting type, which tends to give an "all-or-nothing" response, with the winner being an object that is favored because of greater size, brightness, or proximity to the fovea, where the inhibitory connections are stronger. The system thus displays a simple form of attention, tending to favor objects that might be of greater interest to an animal—objects that are larger or more directly ahead.

Experiments of this kind show how selection based on value can shape the development of a sensorimotor system in which successful behavior requires little more than guidance in a particular direction through a topographic mapping. In the next example, there is no such simple relationship between sensory signals and appropriate outputs; a full analysis of the reaching problem is still a formidable problem for robotics engineering.

The basic idea of the Darwin III reaching system is to use both vision and kinesthesia to guide selection of smooth grasping movements from a prior repertoire of spontaneous gestural motions of the arm. A neuronal repertoire representing "motor cortex" (MC) initiates gestures, and the neural activity is fed via an intermediate repertoire, representing brainstem nuclei or an additional motor cortical layer, to the motor neurons that move arm muscles (Fig. 4). Gestures emanating from these systems are filtered by a cerebellum-like structure, here simplified to just "granule cells" (GR) and "Purkinje cells" (PK). GR inputs come from both kinesthesia (which senses the angular positions of the various joints in the arm) and target vision. As a result, the firing of GR units corresponds to combinations of joint positions, i.e. particular conformations of the arm, and positions of the target. The system has the task of associating these arm positions with appropriate and inappropriate gestures through modification of synaptic connections, primarily those between units in GR and PK. PK units then act directly to inhibit inappropriate gestures at the motor cortical level (cerebellar and thalamic nuclei are omitted here).

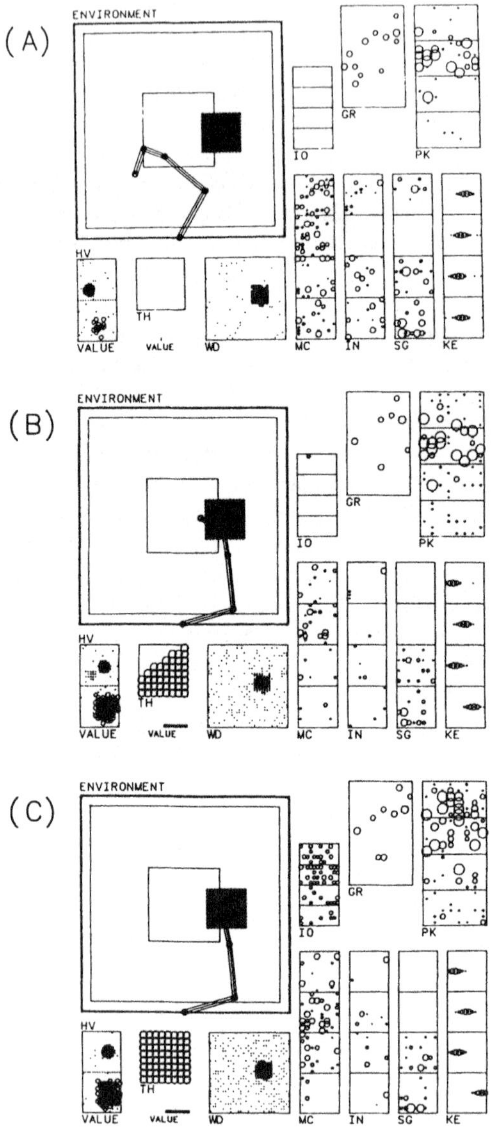

Figure 4: Display of Darwin III's four-jointed reaching system on three consecutive cycles (A), (B), and (C). In addition to object and visual field (as in Fig. 3) the environment display contains a four-jointed arm, anchored at the bottom edge. In the version shown here, a visual repertoire WD reports the position of the target object to MC and GR, networks representing motor cortex and granule cells of the cerebellum, respectively. In addition to this visual input, MC and GR receive sub-threshold inputs from KE, a kinesthetic network that reports the positions of the four joints. Notice how the activity in KE varies systematically with changing

arm position. The pattern of activity in MC is transmitted to IO, which sends a number of strong excitatory connections to a repertoire, PK, representing Purkinje cells. Units in IO only fire if positive value occurred in the previous cycle (as happens in (C)); value thus acts as a modulatory signal that allows activity in MC to be transmitted via IO to PK ("gating"). There is also a great number of initially weak connections between GR and PK; these connections as well as descending inhibitory fibers from PK terminating on IN are modifiable. The PK inhibitory fibers act to select signals for appropriate motor gestures that are generated in MC and transmitted to the motor neurons, SG, through IN. Thus it is the pattern of active units in IN that determines which path the arm will describe. The IN activity pattern in (A) determines that the arm will move towards the target and is the result of a combination of excitatory influences from MC as well as the inhibitory action of PK units. At this stage, after training has been completed, PK units are activated by strengthened connections from GR and the IO network is superfluous. Upon impact on the target ((B) and (C)), touch-sensitive neurons in a sensory sheet tied to the tip of the arm, TH, are activated and guide the subsequent tracing of the edges of the object (not shown). A value-sensitive network (VALUE) receives topographically mapped inputs from both the target visual area WD as well as from a repertoire sensitive to the position of the hand (HV). VALUE fires more vigorously when the hand approaches the target (compare (A) with (B)); the global output of VALUE is used to modulate activity in IO and the amplification of connections between WD and MC. The connections between GR and PK, as well as those between IO and PK, are modified without the participation of value but modification can only occur if the IO network is active and fires PK units. In the example shown, the inhibitory action of PK units results in the second joint's becoming frozen while the first joint is flexed (A). On impact gross arm motion is inhibited (B), and an additional motion of the third and fourth joint establishes full contact (C).

Nothing in these circuits prejudices the arm to move in a coordinated way, or even in a particular direction, before training occurs. Instead, motions are selected from spontaneous movements when these are successful in getting the arm closer to the object. Success is evaluated by a simple value repertoire in which signals from a visual area responsive to the creature's own hand and signals from another visual area responsive to stimulus objects are combined in a common map such that the activity of the value repertoire increases when the two visual responses map near a common location. Activity in the value repertoire is carried to MC, where it influences the extent of synaptic modification as described earlier, as well as to the "inferior olive" (IO), where it gates activity emanating from the MC network to units in PK. Connections whose activation leads to an increase in the value response, representing motion of the arm closer to the object, are selectively favored. As in the case with saccades, no calculation is required to identify the most effective connections; unlike the case with saccades, there are degenerate solutions to the problem corresponding to different positions of the joints that give the same final hand position.

Training of Darwin III's reaching system leads to significant increases in performance (Fig. 5). The system finally works as a gestural module, several of which could be combined in a map to accomplish reaching movements over a wide range of space. Another reaching model not described here uses plastic neuronal maps similar to the ones discussed for the oculomotor system and gives a similar result using a two-jointed arm. The gestural content of the arm motions in this latter model is not as rich but performance on a variety of positions in space is superior. That mapped representations of space are necessary for models of arm posture has also been shown by Kuperstein (1988), who relies on an unbiological form of error feedback in an abstract network to achieve his otherwise impressive results. Our construction of two complementary reaching models shows how the concept of synthetic neural modelling helps to compare models as to their properties and biological value.

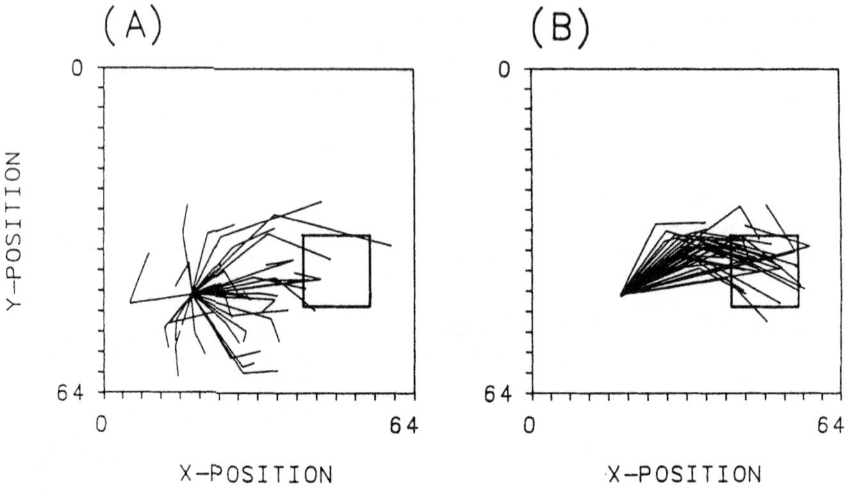

Figure 5: Traces of paths taken by the distal tip of the four-jointed arm before (A) and after (B) 180 training cycles. Training proceeded as follows: for each of 30 trials, the arm was placed in a standard position with the tip at the point where the trajectories diverge (lower left). It was then allowed to move for 6 cycles, and synaptic changes occurred depending upon the success of the movements relative to a target object whose position is shown by the square at the right. After training (B), movements which reached the object on a direct path have been selected.

We have also used the arm of Darwin III to study possible neural mechanisms of exploratory behavior. For the present, we have examined only a limited mode in which the arm is guided by the sense of touch in the single distal digit. The arm assumes a canonical straightened posture by reflex during such exploration to facilitate the tracing of objects (see Fig. 6). Exploratory motions are generated initially in random directions by spontaneous neural activity in the relevant motor repertoires. A scheme that assigns positive value to the presence of touch signals of an intermediate pressure level on the digit is used to modify the random activity when it begins to lose touch with the object being palpated. The system at present has no place memory, but is able to detect repetition in the patterns of motion sensed via kinesthesia. The continuing presence of novel motor patterns during exploration inhibits categorical response to the current stimulus (discussed below), permitting exploration to be completed before attention passes on to another object. Touch-exploration is complementary to reaching in that different mechanisms are required to generate and control fine, non-ballistic and coarse, ballistic motions of the arm.

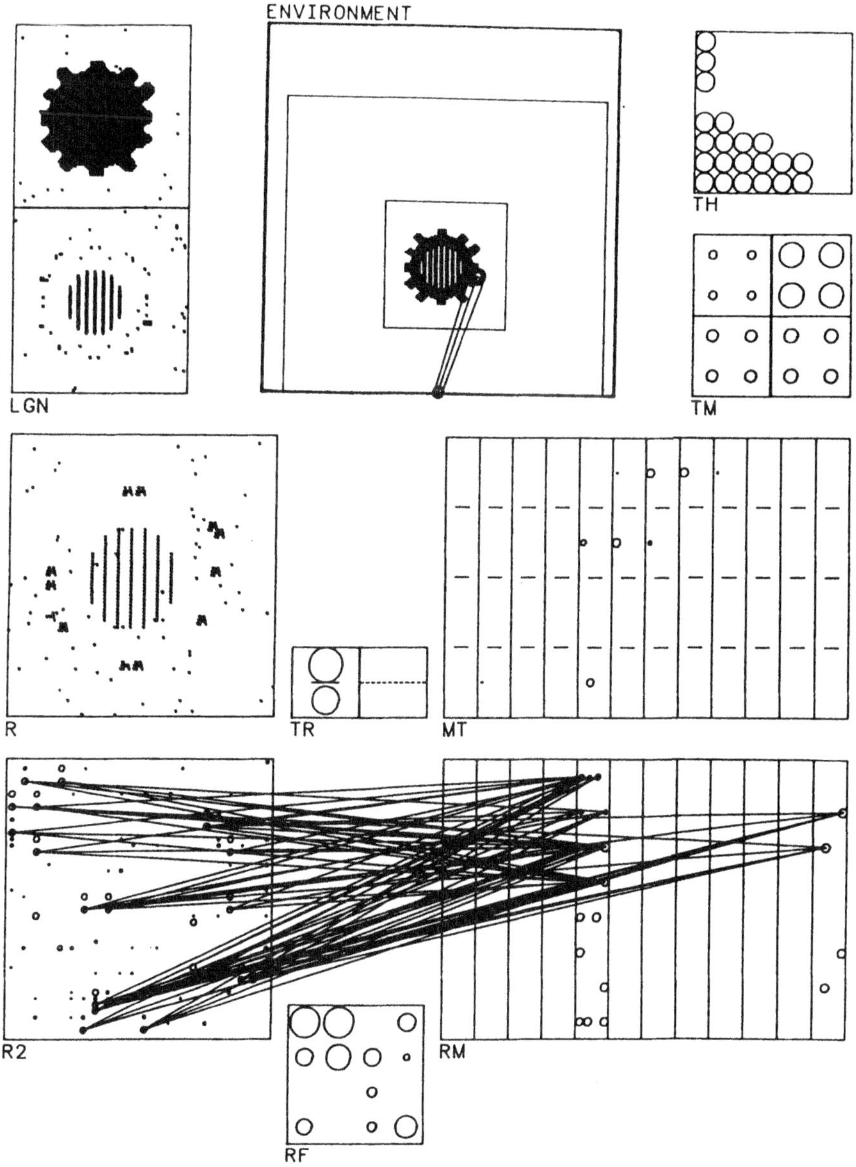

Figure 6: Classification of an object by Darwin III. A single cycle is shown, recorded after Darwin III has had time visually and tactually to explore the object. Darwin III's arm is in the canonical trace position; all joints except the shoulder are stiffened and tracing proceeds as the touch-sensitive receptors at the tip of the arm (TH) guide motion of the shoulder joint through motor units in TM. Units analogous to on- and off-center cells in the LGN connect to an array

of feature detectors (R), selective for oriented lines. The topographic pattern of features in R is transformed into a nonmapped representation in R_2. The pattern of activation in R_2 is unique for individual stimuli or stimuli at different positions. These characteristics make R and R_2 analogous to the "Darwin" part of Darwin II (see Fig. 1). Repertoire M_T receives inputs from kinesthetic units reporting the motions of the shoulder joint in tracing, and thus correlates tactual features of an object over time. R_M is a higher order representation of patterns of activity in M_T. M_T and R_M correspond to the "Wallace" part of Darwin II (see Fig. 1). R_2 and R_M are connected densely by reciprocal connections that can be triggered to correlate the patterns of activity in the two networks (see text). Triggering of reentrant activity occurs when repertoire TR becomes active upon the completion of tracing. TR has a high level of spontaneous activity which is inhibited by units in M_T. TR thus acts as a sort of inverse "novelty detector" that becomes active only when new features cease to be registered in M_T. If a positive correlation occurs (shown here as active connections between R_2 and R_M), a large subpopulation of these reciprocal connections fires and units triggering a reflex motion of the arm are activated (RF). (There are 27,840 reentrant connections in this version of Darwin III, and only the most active ones are displayed in the figure.)

The final and most complex part of Darwin III is the neural machinery for categorization. Categorization is an absolutely critical ability for animals, as it is needed to provide discrimination as a basis for purely consummatory functions as well as for all forms of learning, as discussed in the Introduction. To deal with non-trivial categorizations, a recognition system must be responsive to stimulus features of more than one kind. Coupled subsystems responsive to different sensory modalities (or submodalities) constitute particularly good examples; we have called such systems "classification couples" (Edelman, 1987). In Darwin III, we have chosen to combine vision and touch in a reentrant classification system related to the one already discussed in connection with Darwin II (Fig. 1).

For an animal in a natural environment, apparently arbitrary combinations of features may be indicative of certain categories having ethological value, for example, "good to eat". Classification does not exist as an abstract skill to be tested by psychologists; rather its value is manifested only when it is coupled to appropriate behaviors having survival value for the organism. Because there can be in general no simple computable function relating perceptual category to behavior, an association network capable of arbitrary couplings must be interposed between the perceptual and motor systems.

These and other considerations, including simplicity, led to the design of the coupled categorization-response system in Darwin III (Fig. 6). Since category formation in some form must exist prior to learning, we have made use of relatively impoverished low-level sensory networks capable of distinguishing just two categories to construct the first version of this system. The categories are "rough-striped" objects (bad for this species) and all others (good). The result of a "rough-striped" categorization is one of the simplest possible behaviors, a reflex—in this case a "swat" at the noxious object with the arm, performed with the usual result of removing the stimulus from the creature's vicinity.

The visual component of the classification couple consists of three repertoires. Receiving connections from LGN on- and off-units, a repertoire analogous to V1 (R) is responsive to oriented line segments. A higher-level repertoire (R_2) contains cells that are connected to local clusters of groups in R responding to the same or different orientations. The responses of R_2

signal the presence of stimuli of particular visual classes, for example, those with stripes or other visual textures.

The touch component consists of a repertoire which comprises cells responsive to two broad classes of stimulus shapes—smooth and rough. The inputs to these cells come from kinesthetic receptors in the touch-exploration motor system, and not from touch itself, because the intent is to categorize on the basis of gross shape as revealed by tracing, rather than on the basis of tactile textures. The latter could equally well have been used. Smooth-sensitive cells combine kinesthetic inputs corresponding to some angle of tracing with other excitatory inputs corresponding to the same angle but with some time delay. Other trace directions provide inhibitory inputs. These cells thus respond most strongly when tracing continues in a single direction and are inhibited when the direction of trace changes. Conversely, rough-sensitive cells combine excitatory time-delayed inputs from cells with different orientation from the prompt input, and inhibitory inputs from cells with the same orientation. These cells thus respond most strongly when the direction of tracing changes and are inhibited when it remains the same.

The basis for associations between the visual and touch-sensitive systems is a set of reentrant connections in both directions between higher-order visual cells and rough or smooth touch cells. The firing thresholds of these connections are lowered by continued correlated stimulation from an object with an appropriate combination of visual and tactile characteristics, in a process similar to the "long-term potentiation" (LTP) effect observed in the nervous system (for a recent review see Nicoll et al., 1988). A "triggering" repertoire gives a "completion" response when visual inspection and tracing of a stimulus object reveals no more novel features.

Firing in the triggering repertoire, which indicates completion of the examination of a stimulus but is indifferent as to category, is coupled back to the two sensory repertoires, where it reexcites only those cells that were previously stimulated enough both to sensitize them by LTP and to strengthen their reentrant connections from their opposite numbers in the other modality. The category-specific combined output enters an ethological-value association area that in turn couples it to a motor center that generates the swat reflex.

As a result of all these connections, stimuli are subjected to both visual and tactile examination, which is terminated as soon as novel features cease to be found. When this happens, a pattern is evoked in the reentrant categorization area that is characteristic of the particular class to which the object belongs. This pattern, if it is one that is recognized by the ethological value system, evokes the swat reflex to remove the stimulus. Stimuli not recognized as noxious are left undisturbed. The value scheme that selects rough-striped objects for rejection is here built in as an evolutionary imperative, but present work is aimed at selective formation of category-response associations based on experience with past stimuli. In order for responses to go beyond mere instinct in such cases, there obviously must be an ability to evaluate consequences of behavioral acts. The results obtained so far (Fig. 7) give us reasonable confidence that we can model the formation of categories from complex stimuli with conjunctively or disjunctively related features as well as the classification of individual stimuli according to these categories.

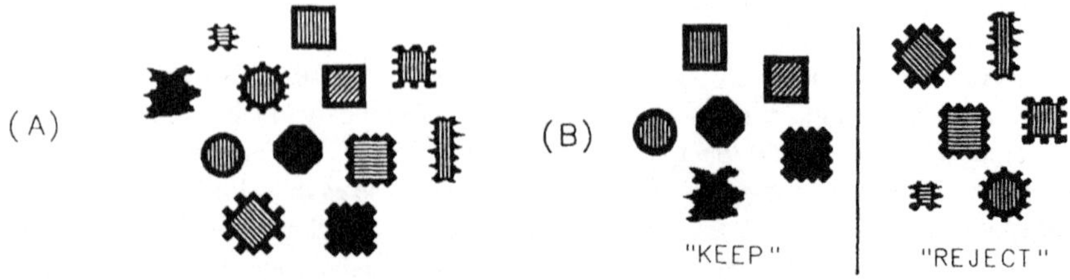

Figure 7. Result of a classification experiment with Darwin III. (A) shows a collection of objects presented to Darwin III's categorization system in random order, one at a time, four times each. Darwin III evaluated the objects visually and tactually, and a maximal time of 50 cycles per object was allowed. Tracing started at different positions on the objects (usually close to the center) and the activity of the reflex output network (RF, see Fig. 6) was recorded. If the correlation of visual and tactile features performed by Darwin III elicited a rejection response, the object was gripped and removed from the vicinity of the automaton. An activation of the rejection response at any time within the 50 cycle time interval was counted as a negative response ("reject" object), and a new object was entered. If no response occurred within the 50 cycle time limit, the trial was ended, counted as a positive response ("keep" object), and a new object was entered. (B) shows how the objects were classified: those on the left side of the boundary were rejected with a probability of less than 5% (once in 24 trials), while those on the right side were rejected with a probability of 80% (19 in 24 trials).

DARWIN III—THE COMPLETE AUTOMATON

With Darwin III, we have succeeded in modelling the behavior of an entire organism from units defined at the neuronal level. This model allows us heuristically to bridge the oft-cited gap between the neuronal and psychological levels of description of mental functions, and provides an excellent experimental domain for testing a wide variety of ideas at all three levels.

Results to date indicate how selection based on value schemes simple enough to be innate without straining credulity can "bootstrap" an organism to states in which it can make more elaborate categorical discriminations. The same principle shapes the development of sensorimotor systems without prespecification of movement parameters. These results may be compared with those obtained from "connectionist" models, a class of essentially computational models that also claim to address questions of brain function.

A CONTRASTING APPROACH—CONNECTIONISM, ITS ORIGINS AND CURRENT PARADIGMS

Connectionist models trace their origins to the conceptual models of neurons as binary threshold units introduced by McCulloch and Pitts (1943). In the McCulloch and Pitts formulation neurons are simple logical switches very much analogous to the binary units of digital computers, which were being developed at about the same time. Interconnected, these units form "neural nets" carrying out symbolic logical operations. McCulloch and Pitts proved that for every computable function a logical circuit consisting of binary neurons could be constructed that would carry out that function. A neural net could therefore serve as an implementation of a Turing machine, an argument that encouraged the view of animal nervous systems as computational systems. Computers, however, are very much unlike biological brains with their highly variable units and connections, a discrepancy of which von Neumann (1958) was well aware. Not only are neuronal connections geometrically imprecise, but their strength can vary with experience. A learning machine constructed as a neural network and learning according to theorems of statistical separability was proposed by Frank Rosenblatt (Rosenblatt, 1958). He called such systems "perceptrons" and considered both single and multilayer versions (a fact that was forgotten by many of his critics).

A simple (or "alpha") perceptron consists of two layers of units, associators and response units. The connections between these units have weights that can be adjusted during a learning process. Simple perceptrons can successfully solve problems that require no more than linear classification of patterns. More precisely, if two sets of patterns can be separated by a hyperplane in a multidimensional feature space, then a perceptron will converge in a finite number of learning steps to a set of weights that can carry out this separation (Rosenblatt, 1962a, 1962b). During learning, every response the system produces is compared to the desired response for the given input as determined by an outside agent. When an incorrect response occurs incremental changes of weights are made. Similar error correction procedures, all belonging to the class of optimization methods, have been described by Widrow and Hoff (1960), Selfridge (Selfridge, 1959; Selfridge & Minsky, 1961), and many others.

One effect of these early studies of neural-like systems was to focus attention on some of the characteristic features of neural networks such as distributed storage, reliability under fluctuation and damage, and learning through synaptic modification. Learning was considered a form of self-organization and some theorems of statistical pattern recognition were implemented into "neural" models and tested experimentally. Unfortunately, the lack of a cogent biological theory led to an unfruitful confounding of learning with optimization. Although Rosenblatt's work on perceptrons promised to overcome the more obvious shortcomings of the previous approaches to brain theory (see his introduction in Rosenblatt, 1958), specifically by replacing symbolic logic by probabilistic formulations, the perceptron studies did not succeed in producing really autonomous, self-organizing behavior. Admittedly, it was possible to reproduce psychological learning curves using these devices, and even mathematically to predict responses from structural parameters of the network. However, the human programmer or instructor was never removed. In order to work predictably well the models used learning algorithms that require the objects of the world to be divided into unambiguously defined categories which are known to some outside intelligence acting on the network. In reality, however, categories are not just lists of weighted properties of objects nor are they independent of contextual influence, as brilliantly shown in the studies of Bongard (Bongard, 1970).

Despite these limitations, many of the paradigms created in the early days of neural networks are still in use today, albeit with some modifications. "Connectionism" is intimately tied to the language and concepts of cognitive science and much of the recent discussion on the merits of connectionism is cast in cognitive terms (Stilling et al., 1987; Smolensky, 1988). Unlike artificial intelligence, connectionism does not accept symbolic structures as the primary, undecomposable units of cognition. Instead, a "subsymbolic" level is often invoked. In a connectionist scheme knowledge is represented as a meshwork of links of variable weight between elementary units that themselves have little computational power. As Feldman and Ballard (1982) put it, "neurons do not transmit large amounts of symbolic information. Instead they compute by being appropriately connected..." (Feldman & Ballard, 1982, p.208). In the formulation of Feldman and Ballard, the firing of individual units represents simple and preassigned concepts that form combinations by communicating through the network. A model of word recognition (McClelland & Rumelhart, 1981), with units and connections standing for local hypotheses of increasing complexity, provides a specific example of this scheme for using a network to represent knowledge about the world. Much of the performance of these systems depends on the exact wiring of the connections and their resistance against external (statistical) influences. This localist variety of connectionism still has close ties to paradigms of classical AI (in which the corresponding operation is list construction), differing mainly in its emphasis on parallel hardware. Some difficulties with these paradigms have been discussed recently by Reeke and Edelman (1988).

Phenomenologically, the notion of spatially delocalized (distributed) representations (reviewed in Hinton & Anderson, 1981) seems to be more realistic and appealing. A few years ago, a group of cognitive psychologists and neuroscientists, calling themselves the PDP research group (PDP standing for "Parallel Distributed Processing", Rumelhart & McClelland, 1986; McClelland & Rumelhart, 1986), put forth a theoretical concept that is mainly based on the themes of distributed memory and parallel computation. While details differ, a typical PDP network configuration is three-layered: input and output units connected to the outside are supplemented by "hidden" units that form an intermediate layer. In models that can be trained to perform a task the synaptic weights between the different layers are changed according to a learning procedure. Connectivities are often complete (every node in the source layer is connected to every node in the target layer) and symmetrical for reasons discussed later.

PDP claims to have introduced a number of theoretical innovations that distinguish it from earlier models of neural circuits: the use of hidden units in intermediate layers, the introduction of learning algorithms for multilayer networks, and the interpretation of neural computation as a relaxation process in a densely connected matrix of cells. Intermediate layers can serve as detectors of higher-order relationships among combinations of input units and allow the use of contextual information. Experiments have shown that very simple networks consisting of three layers can solve second-order problems like the exclusive OR function or symmetry detection (Sejnowski et al., 1986) that cannot be solved by simple perceptrons (Minsky & Papert, 1969). Nonlinearities in the input-output relations of the elementary units produce an additional effect: now nonlinear discriminant functions separating classes in pattern hyperspace are allowed and more complex classifications are possible. An extension to multilayer feed-forward nets of the Widrow-Hoff rule has been formulated, the so-called generalized delta rule (Rumelhart & McClelland, 1986, p.326; Rumelhart et al., 1986). Error correction proceeds stepwise from the output layer towards earlier layers of the networks, thus errors are "back-propagated" through the system. As with all learning algorithms of this type, back-propagation can only succeed if the exact desired output vector of the system is known in advance and purposeful microscopic synaptic changes are made. Feedforward-feedback networks with symmetric inter-layer connections can be treated as well, but no intrinsic connections within layers are allowed.

PDP looks upon the brain as a giant parallel processing device that computes solutions to problems as they are encountered. Much of the appeal of PDP models comes from the possibility of constructing networks that, for a given input, will, by adjusting activities and weights, settle into stable states corresponding to the solution of a problem. In fact, PDP claims that "relaxation is the dominant mode of computation" in the brain (Rumelhart & McClelland, 1986, p.135). Computation proceeds by iteratively seeking to satisfy a large number of weak local constraints between units representing hypotheses or local features. Independent of learning, fixed-parameter networks like those introduced by Hopfield (1982) (following upon earlier work by Little & Shaw, 1975) compute by minimizing an energy function that guides the dynamics of the system. Other models use modification of synaptic weights according to a learning algorithm to minimize an error function defining the distance between the actual and desired outputs. Learning rules can operate on probabilistic formulations of unit firing, as in the case of Boltzmann machines (see below). As the complexity of the networks and the computational task increases, the topography of the "computational landscape" traced out by the energy function can become very involved. Local search algorithms invariably converge on sets of synaptic weights that produce globally non-optimal responses that represent local optima in weight space. To avoid such local optima, a strategy to find the global optimum must be found. An example of a semilocal strategy widely used in the design of neural networks is simulated annealing (Kirkpatrick et al., 1983). With such procedures, networks eventually reach a state of minimal energy corresponding to maximal global consistency for a given input. This input has to be clamped for a sufficiently long time to allow the network to reach equilibrium. Like all relaxation procedures, simulated annealing relies on the existence of bidirectional symmetry in the connections between elementary units (Ackley et al., 1985), as other connectivities lead potentially to time-dependent asymptotic behavior of the system in the form of limit cycles or even chaos (Choi & Huberman, 1983).

Relaxation networks of this type are generally known as Boltzmann machines because of their relationship to systems of interacting particles in statistical physics. Boltzmann machines have been successfully used to solve problems like encoding (Ackley et al., 1985), symmetry detection (Sejnowski, Kienker & Hinton, 1986), figure-ground discrimination (Kienker et al., 1987) and pronunciation of written text (Sejnowski & Rosenberg, 1987). As one example, a network that recognizes and classifies written T's and C's (Sejnowski et al., 1986) consists of an input layer that is completely and symmetrically connected to an intermediate layer of hidden units. These units are connected in turn to two output units corresponding to the two possible answers. After every presentation of a stimulus the network is allowed to reach equilibrium by using a simulated annealing schedule and weights are updated. After completion of the learning program the network correctly classifies T's and C's independent of position on the input array. This kind of problem cannot be solved by simple perceptrons without the use of intermediary layers (Minsky & Papert, 1988). The size of the input array and the number of hidden units both critically affect the shape of the learning curve, especially the time required for the network to reach a reasonable level of performance. Convergence is generally very slow (Jeffrey & Rosner, 1986). In the case of T's and C's, a network of 100 input and 24 hidden units needs a million presentations to reach a 75% success level (random performance is 50%). That error minimization procedures can indeed be very costly, especially when global solutions are required, is illustrated also by a model of figure-ground discrimination in early visual perception (Kienker et al., 1987). A network of edge and figure units receives a double input: contrast-boundaries (edges) from the visual image and an attentional focus biasing the figure-ground distinction. The network reaches its final state through a combined random updating and annealing algorithm, converging reliably and relatively fast for simple figures. However, a very slow annealing schedule is needed for more complicated visual images.

One of the most widely publicized models is NETTalk, a network designed to transcribe written text into phonemes (Sejnowski & Rosenberg, 1987). It replaces the look-up-table storage of other text-to-speech systems by a distributed and thus presumably more efficient representational scheme using hidden units. Input units look at a written text sample through a window holding several (viz. seven) letters at once. They connect to hidden units that store contextual information as learning proceeds and in turn connect to output units representing phonemes. The back-propagation algorithm is used to minimize discrepancies between a text sample and a transcription of this text into phonemes. Learning curves show significant improvements on the training texts and generalization to new words to a certain degree. The relation of this abstract model to human reading or speech performance, as with other connectionist models, remains unclear (Pinker & Prince, 1988; Prince & Pinker, 1988). An almost identical network architecture has been used by Qian and Sejnowski (1988) to predict basic secondary structural features of proteins from primary sequence data. Although these authors demonstrate the applicability of neural networks to a wide problem domain by this example, they find only marginal improvements in prediction accuracy over "non-neural" empirical methods, which are themselves inadequate as predictors of the actual three-dimensional structures of proteins (Kabsch & Sander, 1983).

CONNECTIONISM IN PERSPECTIVE

Any concept of neural modelling like connectionism that offers new ways to solve computational problems and furthermore claims that these new ways throw light on modes of "biological computation" faces major challenges in both areas:

The first challenge relates to the purely computational advantages of these models: How does their reliability, effectiveness, and range of application compare with that of programs running in serial, general-purpose computers? Neural networks are often described as examples of new strategies of computation. There is in fact evidence—and some examples have been discussed in the previous section—that simple "neural net" models can have interesting properties when used to solve computational problems: simplicity of design, speed of computation, generalization across different examples of the same problem, reliability in the presence of fluctuations or damage, etc. However, very little is known of the scaling properties of these models. Minsky and Papert (1988) observed that PDP has been most successful with "toy" problems of very small size. There are indications that the convergence speed of learning algorithms like back-propagation as well as that of relaxation in "taught" networks scales unfavorably as problems and networks grow larger. Tens of thousands of iterations are needed to "learn" very simple problems like symmetry detection in an array of six cells. In Minsky and Papert's words, "most observers would lose interest", given such lengthy learning procedures, especially since algorithms for solving the same problems on general purpose computers exist. Efforts to improve on the speed of learning algorithms are under way (e.g. Moody & Darken, 1988), but the fitness of such algorithms when confronted with complex tasks in a real world situation remains to be shown.

In addition, many connectionist models are strongly based on notions of fixed (albeit distributed) representations, implicitly or explicitly fixed input-output relationships, and content-addressable replicative memory (Hinton & Anderson, 1981). There is often only a difference in emphasis between these connectionist models and AI strategies based on fixed knowledge representations. The task of finding a representation and an effective procedure in AI is the task of the programmer; his replacement in connectionism is the electrician and teacher optimizing synaptic weight matrices under instruction using an algorithm.

As biologists we are concerned mainly with the second area of challenge: whether or not connectionist models can really explain how the brain works. Are "neural net" models in accord with known facts of anatomy and physiology, and could such structures have evolved and be built up in embryonic development? The literature on neural networks is full of biological terminology and analogies to brain processes. Nonetheless, almost all connectionist neural modelling so far has exclusively used principles that we look upon as being foreign to biology, namely information processing and computation (Reeke & Edelman, 1988). Conclusive evidence that computation on a symbolic or subsymbolic level actually occurs inside the brain is lacking. Furthermore, we challenge the notion that the world contains structured information that can be sensed and processed by effective procedures implemented in neural structures. The ability of animals to survive in a world full of novelty and surprise seems to rule out the notion that a nervous system could have evolved that is instructive and rule-driven at its most fundamental level. No instructive design principles are known that would ensure adaptive responses to the great number of possible situations within the physical limits of an actual biological structure. For the same reason a neural model employing exclusively instructive procedures of training and operation will always be severely limited in its performance and would have no chance of survival in a real world. On the other hand, response to novelty and amplification of adaptive responses are characteristic properties of selective systems. The synthetic neural modelling approach we have outlined shows how these problems can be solved with selectional mechanisms and how a different interpretation of neural structure and function leads to a re-interpretation of the concept of information. Other, nonselectionist approaches (Carpenter & Grossberg, 1988) also address some of the issues we have discussed.

Technically, recent connectionist models have not introduced major innovations. Neurons are still often treated as binary (nonlinear) threshold elements having no internal dynamics of any interest. Connectivities are usually complete and symmetrical. Learning is algorithmic and under the control of an external teacher. Many theoretical features of PDP models like the spin glass analogy (the "computation as relaxation" concept with its use of simulated annealing) have further obscured rather than clarified biological issues. This is because PDP models are widely being taken as brain models despite the disclaimers of their authors, and despite the fact that they have properties significantly different from those of real neuronal networks. In the words of PDP's proponents, "we have not focused on neural modelling but rather we have focused on neurally inspired modelling of cognitive processes" (Rumelhart & McClelland, 1986, p.130), and these are of course governed by rules and representations.

The biologically implausible aspects of PDP mechanisms include annealing schedules, back-propagation of errors, relaxation to stable states under constant input, generally symmetrical relations between neurons, and systematic connectivities. All of these aspects are cornerstones of connectionist methodology but none of them correlates well with any known neurobiological facts. Special-purpose networks of the Hopfield type (Hopfield & Tank, 1985) exhibit an almost complete neglect of biology, in addition to being unreliable and slow (Wilson & Pawley, 1988). Engineering takes the place of evolution and performance depends crucially on connections specified by the programmer for the task. It is hard to see what exactly is the ingredient that transforms these telephone-switchboard circuits into "neural" networks.

In summary, connectionist models stand in striking contrast to the way real biological systems work. In fixed synaptic weight (Hopfield) networks, wiring of the appropriate connections takes the place of programming a conventional computer. In modifiable networks learning can only proceed properly upon lengthy presentations of an extensive sample or even the complete set of correct input-output pairs by an omniscient agent. Categorization is understood simply as statistical matching to templates of "prototypes" and is thus not understood at all. Connectionist networks are generally designed to capture explicit regularities in the environment and thus rely on a more or less explicit representation of information. Different PDP models use almost identical architectures to handle very different problems, from logical functions (exclusive OR) to pronunciation of text. As much as this commonality may appeal to one's sense of order, the evidence is that there is no one solution used by the brain for all kinds of problems.

CONCLUSIONS AND PROSPECTS

The characteristics of connectionist models just discussed suggest that they will be most likely to perform well when input-output relationships are straightforward and known in advance. The time and resources to construct very densely connected networks and to expose them to long training sessions will be required. These efforts will often be justified when compared to the even larger ones needed to program explicit behavioral rules in AI-style "production systems." On the other hand, connectionist systems are not likely to be useful when categories are more complex and not given in advance, or when responses based on past experience are needed to survive in the face of novel stimuli and situations.

These problems are just the kind that have been most difficult to solve with present computational techniques. Connectionism shares with AI the underlying assumption that adaptive behavior is the result of computational processes; thus it is no surprise that the areas of weakness of the two approaches are so much alike. To overcome these limitations, we believe it will be necessary to adopt a radically different strategy that abandons the computational metaphor in favor of an approach more solidly grounded in biological reality. We have briefly described several models based on the theory of neuronal group selection that in fact perform well on a variety of tasks without any of the implausible assumptions of more conventional "connectionist" models. We conclude that Darwin's principle of natural selection provides the soundest basis for formulating a theory of the nervous system that accounts for its evolution, development, and function in the real world.

ACKNOWLEDGEMENTS

This research has been supported in part by the John D. and Catherine T. MacArthur Foundation, the Lucille P. Markey Charitable Trust, The Pew Charitable Trusts, the von Ameringen Foundation, the IBM Corporation, and the Office of Naval Research. O.S. is a Fellow of the Lucille P. Markey Charitable Trust. Part of the research was conducted using the Cornell National Supercomputer Facility, a resource of the Center for Theory and Simulations in Science and Engineering at Cornell University, which receives funding from the National Science Foundation and the IBM Corporation, with additional support from New York State and members of the Corporate Research Institute.

REFERENCES

Ackley, D.H., Hinton, G.E. & Sejnowski, T.J. (1985). A learning algorithm for Boltzmann machines. *Cognitive Science*, **9**, 147-169.

Bongard, M. (1970). Pattern recognition. New York, Washington: Spartan Books.

Carpenter, G.A. & Grossberg, S. (1988). The ART of adaptive pattern recognition by a self-organizing neural network. *Computer*, **21**, #3, 77-88.

Choi, M.Y. & Huberman, B.A. (1983). Dynamic behavior of nonlinear networks. *Physical Review A*, **28**, 1204-1206.

Edelman, G.M. (1978). Group selection and phasic re-entrant signalling: A theory of higher brain function. In G.M. Edelman and V.B. Mountcastle, (Eds.), *The Mindful Brain* (pp. 51-100), Cambridge: MIT Press.

Edelman, G.M. (1981). Group selection as the basis for higher brain function. In F.O. Schmitt et al. (Eds.), *Organization of the Cerebral Cortex* (pp. 535-563). Cambridge: MIT Press.

Edelman, G.M. (1987). Neural Darwinism. New York: Basic Books.

Edelman, G.M. & Reeke, G.N.,Jr. (1982). Selective networks capable of representative transformations, limited generalizations, and associative memory. *Proc. Natl. Acad. Sci. USA*, **79**, 2091-2095.

Feldman, J.A. & Ballard, D.H. (1982). Connectionist models and their properties. *Cognitive Science*, **6**, 205-254.

Finkel, L.H. & Edelman, G.M. (1985). Interaction of synaptic modification rules within populations of neurons. *Proc. Natl. Acad. Sci. USA*, **82**, 1291-1295.

Hinton, G.E. & Anderson, J.A. (1981). Parallel models of associative memory. Hillsdale: Erlbaum.

Hopfield, J.J. (1982). Neural networks and physical systems with emergent collective computational abilities. *Proc. Natl. Acad. Sci. USA*, **79**, 2554-2558.

Hopfield, J.J. & Tank, D.W. (1985). "Neural" computation of decisions in optimization problems. *Biological Cybernetics*, **52**, 141-152.

Jeffrey, W. & Rosner, R. (1986). Optimization algorithms: Simulated annealing and neural network processing. *The Astrophysical Journal*, **310**, 473-481.

Kabsch, W. & Sander, C. (1983). How good are predictions of protein secondary structure? *FEBS Letters*, **155**, 179-182.

Kienker, P.K., Sejnowski, T.J., Hinton, G.E. & Schumacher, L.E. (1986). Separating figure from ground with a parallel network. *Perception*, **15**, 197-216.

Kirkpatrick, S., Gelatt, C.D.,Jr., & Vecchi, M.P. (1983). Optimization by simulated annealing. *Science*, **220**, 671-680.

Kuperstein, M. (1988). Neural model of adaptive hand-eye coordination for single postures. *Science*, **239**, 1308-1311.

Little, W.A. & Shaw, G.L. (1975). A statistical theory of short and long term memory. *Behavioral Biology*, **14**, 115-133.

McClelland, J.L., Rumelhart, D.E., and the PDP Research Group (1986). *Parallel Distributed Processing. Explorations in the microstructure of cognition. Volume 2: Psychological and biological models*. Cambridge, London: MIT Press.

McClelland, J.L., & Rumelhart, D.E. (1981). An interactive activation model of context effects in letter perception: Part 1. An account of basic findings. *Psychological Review*, **88**, 375-407.

McCulloch, W.S. & Pitts, W. (1943). A logical calculus of the ideas immanent in nervous activity. *Bulletin of Mathematical Biophysics*, **5**, 115-133.

Minsky, M.L. & Selfridge, O.G. (1961). Learning in random nets. In Cherry (Ed.), *Information theory*.

Minsky, M.L. & Papert, S.A. (1969). *Perceptrons*. Cambridge: MIT Press.

Minsky, M.L. & Papert, S.A. (1988). *Perceptrons*. 2nd Edition, Cambridge: MIT Press.

Moody, J. & Darken, C. (1988). Speedy alternatives to back propagation. *Neural Networks*, **1**, Supplement 1, 202.

von Neumann, J. (1958). *The computer and the brain*. New Haven: Yale University Press.

Nicoll, R.A., Kauer, J.A. & Malenka, R.C. (1988). The current excitement in long-term potentiation. *Neuron*, **1**, 97-103.

Pearson, J.C., Finkel, L.H. & Edelman, G.M. (1987). Plasticity in the organization of adult cortical maps: A computer model based on neuronal group selection. *Journal of Neuroscience*, **7**, 4209-4223.

Pinker, S. & Prince, A. (1988). On language and connectionism: Analysis of a parallel distributed processing model of language acquisition. *Cognition*, **28**, 73-193.

Prince, A. & Pinker, S. (1988). Rules and connections in human language. *Trends in Neurosciences*, **11**, 195-202.

Pylyshyn, Z.W. (1984). *Computation and Cognition: Toward a Foundation for Cognitive Science*. Cambridge: MIT Press.

Qian, N., & Sejnowski, T.J. (1988). Predicting the secondary structure of globular proteins using neural network models. *Journal of Molecular Biology*, **202**, 865-884.

Reeke, G.N., Jr. & Edelman, G.M. (1984). Selective networks and recognition automata. *Annals of the New York Academy of Sciences*, **426**, 181-201.

Reeke, G.N., Jr. & Edelman, G.M. (1987). Selective neural networks and their implications for recognition automata. *International Journal of Supercomputer* Applications, **1**, 44-69.

Reeke, G.N., Jr. & Edelman, G.M. (1988). Real brains and artificial intelligence. *Daedalus*, **117**, 143-173.

Rosenblatt, F. (1958). The perceptron: a probabilistic model for information storage and organization in the brain. *Psychological Reviw*, **65**, 386- 408.

Rosenblatt, F. (1962a). Strategic approaches to the study of brain models. In H. von Foerster & G.W. Zopf (Eds.), *Principles of self-organization* (pp. 385-402). Pergamon Press.

Rosenblatt, F. (1962b). *Principles of neurodynamics: Perceptrons and the theory of brain mechanisms*. Washington: Spartan Books.

Rumelhart, D.E., McClelland, J.L., and the PDP Research Group (1986). *Parallel Distributed Processing. Explorations in the microstructure of cognition. Volume 1: Foundations*. Cambridge, London: MIT Press.

Rumelhart, D.E., Hinton, G.E. & Williams, R.J. (1986). Learning representations by back-propagating errors. *Nature*, **323**, 533-536.

Sejnowski, T.J. & Rosenberg, C.R. (1987). Parallel networks that learn to pronounce English text. *Complex Systems*, **1**, 145-168.

Sejnowski, T.J., Kienker, P.K. & Hinton, G.E. (1986). Learning symmetry groups with hidden units: beyond the perceptron. *Physica*, **22D**, 260-275.

Selfridge, O.G. (1959). Pandemonium: A paradigm for learning. In *Mechanization of thought processes*. Volume I. London: Her Majesty's Stationery Office.

Smolensky, P. (1988). On the proper treatment of connectionism. *Behavioral and Brain Sciences*, **11**, 1-74.

Stilling, N.A., Feinstein, M.H., Garfield, J.L., Rissland, E.L., Rosenbaum, D.A., Weisler, S.E. & Baker-Ward, L. (1987). *Cognitive science*. Cambridge: MIT Press.

Widrow, G. & Hoff, M.E. (1960). Adaptive switching circuits. *Institute of Radio Engineers, Western Electronic Show and Convention, Convention Record*, Part 4, 96-104.

Wilson, G.V. & Pawley, G.S. (1988). On the stability of the travelling salesman problem algorithm of Hopfield and Tank. *Biological Cybernetics*, **58**, 63-70.

LEARNING

CONNECTIONISM IN PERSPECTIVE
R. Pfeifer, Z. Schreter, F. Fogelman-Soulié, L. Steels (Eds.)

Generalization and Network Design Strategies

Yann le Cun *
Department of Computer Science, University of Toronto
Toronto, Ontario, M5S 1A4, CANADA

Abstract— *An interesting property of connectionist systems is their ability to learn from examples. Although most recent work in the field concentrates on reducing learning times, the most important feature of a learning machine is its generalization performance. It is usually accepted that good generalization performance on real-world problems cannot be achieved unless some a priori knowledge about the task is built into the system. Back-Propagation networks provide a way of specifying such knowledge by imposing constraints both on the architecture of the network and on its weights. In general, such constraints can be considered as particular transformations of the parameter space.*

Building a constrained network for image recognition appears to be a feasible task. We describe a small handwritten digit recognition problem and show that, even though the problem is linearly separable, single layer networks exhibit poor generalization performance. Multilayer constrained networks perform very well on this task when organized in a hierarchical structure with shift invariant feature detectors.

These results confirm the idea that minimizing the number of free parameters in the network enhances generalization.

Keywords—Learning-algorithms, multy-layer connectionist networks, Back-Propagation, generalization, speed of learning, digit-recognition

1 INTRODUCTION

Connectionist architectures have drawn considerable attention in recent years because of their interesting learning abilities. Among the numerous learning algorithms that have been proposed for complex connectionist networks, Back-Propagation (BP) is probably the most widespread. BP was proposed in (Rumelhart et al., 1986), but had been developed before by several independent groups in different contexts and for different purposes (Bryson & Ho, 1969; Werbos, 1974; le Cun, 1985; Parker, 1985; le Cun, 1986). Reference (Bryson & Ho, 1969) was in the framework of optimal control and system identification, and one could argue that the basic idea behind BP had been used in optimal control long before its application to machine learning was considered (le Cun, 1988).

Two performance measures should be considered when testing a learning algorithm: learning speed and generalization performance. Generalization is the main property that

*Present address: Room 4G-332, AT&T Bell Laboratories, Crawfords Corner Rd, Holmdel, NJ 07733.

should be sought; it determines the amount of data needed to train the system such that a correct response is produced when presented with patterns outside of the training set. We will see that learning speed and generalization are closely related.

Although various successful applications of BP have been described in the literature, the conditions under which good generalization performance can be obtained are not understood. Considering BP as a general learning rule that can be used as a black box for a wide variety of problems is, of course, wishful thinking. Although some moderate sized problems can be solved using unstructured networks, we cannot expect an unstructured network to generalize correctly on every problem. The main point of this paper is to show that good generalization performance *can* be obtained if some *a priori* knowledge about the task is built into the network. Although in the general case specifying such knowledge may be difficult, it appears feasible on some highly regular tasks such as image and speech recognition.

Tailoring the network architecture to the task can be thought of as a way of reducing the size of the space of possible functions that the network can generate, without overly reducing its computational power. Theoretical studies (Denker et al., 1987) (Patarnello & Carnevali, 1987) have shown that the likelihood of correct generalization depends on the size of the hypothesis space (total number of networks being considered), the size of the solution space (set of networks that give good generalization), and the number of training examples. If the hypothesis space is too large and/or the number of traning examples is too small, then there will be a vast number of networks which are consistent with the training data, only a small proportion of which will lie in the true solution space, so poor generalization is to be expected. Conversely, if good generalization is required, when the generality of the architecture is increased, the number of training examples must also be increased. Specifically, the required number of examples scales like the logarithm of the number of functions that the network architecture can implement.

An illuminating analogy can be drawn between BP learning and curve fitting. When using a curve model (say a polynomial) with lots of parameters compared to the number of points, the fitted curve will closely model the training data but will not be likely to accurately represent new data. On the other hand, if the number of parameters in the model is small, the model will not necessarily represent the training data but will be more likely to capture the regularity of the data and extrapolate (or interpolate) correctly. When the data is not too noisy, the optimal choice is the minimum size model that represents the data.

A common-sense rule inspired by this analogy tells us to minimize the number of free parameters in the network to increase the likelihood of correct generalization. But this must be done without reducing the size of the network to the point where it can no longer compute the desired function. A good compromise becomes possible when some knowledge about the task is available, but the price to pay is an increased effort in the design of the architecture.

2 WEIGHT SPACE TRANSFORMATION

Reducing the number of free parameters in a network does not necessarily imply reducing the size of the network. Such techniques as weight sharing, described in (Rumelhart et al., 1986) for the so-called T-C problem, can be used to reduce the number of free parameters while preserving the size of the network and specifying some symmetries that the problem may have.

In fact, three main techniques can be used to build a reduced size network.

The first technique is problem-independent and consists of dynamically deleting "useless" connections during training. This can be done by adding a term in the cost function that penalizes big networks with many parameters. Several authors have described such schemes, usually implemented as a non-proportional weight decay (Rumelhart, personnal communication 1988), (Chauvin, 1989; Hanson & Pratt, 1989), or using "gating coefficients" (Mozer & Smolensky, 1989). Generalization performance has been reported to increase significantly on small problems. Two drawbacks of this technique are that it requires a fine tuning of the "pruning" coefficient to avoid catastrophic effects, and also that the convergence is significantly slowed down.

2.1 Weight Sharing

The second technique is weight sharing. Weight sharing consists in having several connections (links) be controlled by a single parameter (weight). Weight sharing can be interpreted as imposing equality constraints among the connection strengths. An interesting feature of weight sharing is that it can be implemented with very little computational overhead. Weight sharing is a very general paradigm that can be used to describe so-called Time Delay Neural Networks used for speech recognition (Waibel et al., 1988; Bottou, 1988), time-unfolded recurrent networks, or shift-invariant feature extractors. The experimental results presented in this paper make extensive use of weight sharing.

2.2 General Weight Space Transformations

The third technique, which really is a generalization of weight sharing, is called weight-space transformation (WST) (le Cun, 1988). WST is based on the fact that the search performed by the learning procedure need not be done in the space of connection strengths, but can be done in any parameter space that is suitable for the task. This can be achieved provided that the connections strengths can be computed from the parameters through a given transformation, and provided that the Jacobian matrix of this transformation is known, so that we are able to compute the partials of the cost function with respect to the parameters. The gradient of the cost function with respect to the parameters is then just the product of the Jacobian matrix of the transformation by the gradient with respect to the connection strengths. The situation is depicted in Figure 1.

2.2.1 WST to improve learning speed

Several types of WST can be defined, not only for reducing the size of the parameter space, but also for speeding up the learning.

Although the following example is quite difficult to implement in practice, it gives an idea about how WST can accelerate learning. Let us assume that the cost function C minimized by the learning procedure is purely quadratic with regard to the connection strengths W. In other words, C is of the form

$$C(W) = \frac{1}{2}W^T HW + J^T W + K$$

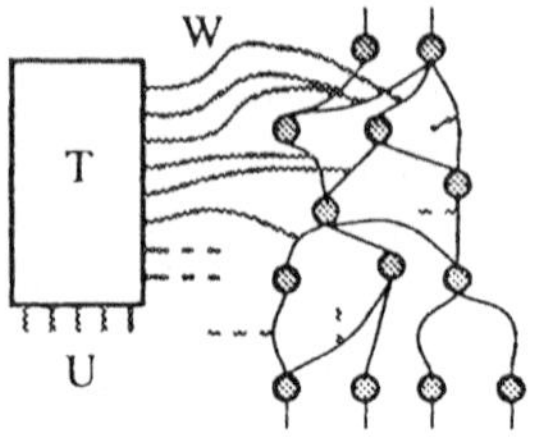

Figure 1: Weight Space Transformation.

where W is the vector of connection strengths, H the Hessian matrix (the matrix of second derivatives) which will be assumed positive definite. Then the surfaces of equal cost are hyperparaboloids centered around the optimal solution. Performing steepest descent in this space will be inefficient if the eigenvalues of H have wide variations. In this case the paraboloids of equal cost are very elongated forming a steep ravine. The learning time is known to depend heavily on the ratio of the largest to the smallest eigenvalue. The larger this ratio, the more elongated the paraboloids, and the slower the convergence. Let us denote Λ the diagonalized version of H, and Q the unitary matrix formed by the (orthonormal) eigenvectors of H, we have $H = Q^T \Lambda Q$. Now, let Σ be the diagonal matrix whose elements are the square root of the elements of Λ, then H can be rewritten as $H = Q^T \Sigma \Sigma Q$. We can now rewrite the expression for $C(W)$ in the following way

$$C(W) = \frac{1}{2} W^T Q^T \Sigma \Sigma Q W + (J')^T \Sigma Q W + K$$

Using the notation $U = \Sigma Q W$ we obtain

$$C(U) = \frac{1}{2} U^T U + (J')^T U + K$$

In the space of U, the steepest descent search will be trivial since the Hessian matrix is equal to the identity and the surfaces of equal cost are hyper-spheres. The steepest descent direction points in the direction of the solution and *is* the shortest path to the solution. Perfect learning can be achieved in one single iteration if Q and Σ are known accurately. The transformation for obtaining the connection strengths W from the parameters U is simply

$$W = Q^T \Sigma^{-1} U$$

During learning, the path followed by U in U space is a straight line, as well as the path followed by W in W space. This algorithm is known as Newton's algorithm, but is usually expressed directly in W space. Performing steepest descent in U space is equivalent to using Newton's algorithm in W space.

Of course in practice this kind of WST is unrealistic since the size of the Hessian matrix is huge (number of connections squared), and since it is quite expensive to estimate and diagonalize. Moreover, the cost function is usually *not* quadratic in connection space,

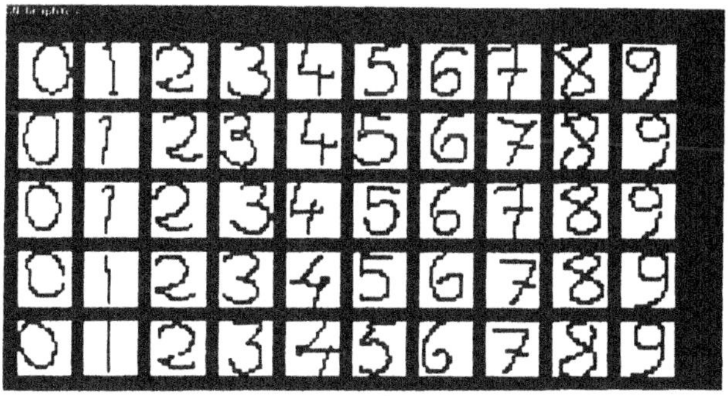

Figure 2: Some examples of input patterns.

which may cause the Hessian matrix to be non positive, non definite, and may cause it to vary with W. Nevertheless, some approximations can be made which make these ideas implementable (le Cun, 1987; Becker & le Cun, 1988).

2.2.2 WST and generalization

The WST just described is an example of *problem-independent* WST, Other kinds of WST which are *problem-dependent* can be devised. Building such transformation requires a fair amount of knowledge about the problem as well as a reasonable guess about what an optimal network solution for this problem could be. Finding WST that improve generalization usually amounts to reducing the size of the parameter space. In the following sections we describe an example where simple WST such as weight sharing have been used to improve generalization.

3 AN EXAMPLE: A SMALL DIGIT RECOGNITION PROBLEM

The following experimental results are presented to illustrate the strategies that can be used to design a network for a particular problem. The problem described here is in no way a real world application but is sufficient for our purpose. The intermediate size of the database makes the problem non-trivial, but also allows for extensive tests of learning speed and generalization performance.

3.1 Description of the Problem

The database is composed of 480 examples of numerals represented as 16 pixels by 16 pixels binary images. 12 examples of each of the 10 digits were hand-drawn by a single person on a 16 by 13 bitmap using a mouse. Each image was then used to generate 4 examples by putting the original image in 4 consecutive horizontal positions on a 16 by 16 bitmap. The training set was then formed by choosing 32 examples of each class at random among the complete set of 480 images. the remaining 16 examples of each class were used as the test set. Thus, the training set contained 320 images, and the test set contained 160 images. Some of the training examples are represented in Figure 2.

3.2 Experimental Setup

All simulations were performed using the BP simulator SN (Bottou & le Cun, 1988).

Each unit in the network computes a dot product between its input vector and its weight vector. This weighted sum, denoted a_i for unit i, is then passed through a sigmoid squashing function to produce the state of unit i, denoted by x_i:

$$x_i = f(a_i)$$

The squashing function is a scaled hyperbolic tangent:

$$f(a) = A \tanh Sa$$

where A is the amplitude of the function and S determines its slope at the origin, and f is an odd function, with horizontal asymptotes $+A$ and $-A$.

Symmetric functions are believed to yield faster convergence, although the learning can become extremely slow if the weights are too small. The cause of this problem is that the origin of weight space is a stable point for the learning dynamics, and, although it is a saddle point, it is attractive in almost all directions. For our simulations, we use $A = 1.7159$ and $S = \frac{2}{3}$. With this choice of parameters, the equalities $f(1) = 1$ and $f(-1) = -1$ are satisfied. The rationale behind this is that the overall gain of the squashing transformation is around 1 in normal operating conditions, and the interpretation of the state of the network is simplified. Moreover, the absolute value of the second derivative of f is a maximum at $+1$ and -1, which improves the convergence at the end of the learning session.

Before training, the weights are initialized with random values using a uniform distribution between $-2.4/F_i$ and $2.4/F_i$ where F_i is the number of inputs (fan-in) of the unit which the connection belongs to.[1] The reason for dividing by the fan-in is that we would like the initial standard deviation of the weighted sums to be in the same range for each unit, and to fall within the normal operating region of the sigmoid. If the initial weights are too small, the gradients are very small and the learning is slow, if they are too large, the sigmoids are saturated and the gradient is also very small. The variance of the weighted sum scales like the square root of the number of inputs when the inputs are independent, and it scales linearly with the number of inputs if the inputs are highly correlated. We chose to assume the second hypothesis since some units receive highly correlated signals.

The output cost function is the usual mean squared error:

$$C = \frac{1}{P} \sum_p \sum_o \frac{1}{2} (D_{op} - X_{op})^2$$

where P is the number of patterns, D_{op} is the desired state for output unit o when pattern p is presented on the input. X_{op} is the state of output unit o when pattern p is presented. It is worth pointing out that the target values for the output units are well within the range of the sigmoid. This prevents the weights from growing indefinitely and prevents the output units from operating in the flat spot of the sigmoid. Additionally, since the second derivative of the sigmoid is maximum near the target values, the depth of the solution bowl is maximized and the convergence speed during the final phase of the learning process is improved.

[1] Since several connections share a weight this rule could be difficult to apply, but in our case, all connections sharing a same weight belong to units with identical fan-ins.

During each learning experiment, the patterns were presented in a constant order, and the training set was repeated 30 times. The weights were updated after each presentation of a single pattern according to the so-called stochastic gradient or "on-line" procedure. Each learning experiment was performed 10 times with different initial conditions. All experiments were done both using standard gradient descent and a special version of Newton's algorithm that uses a positive, diagonal approximation of the Hessian matrix (le Cun, 1987; Becker & le Cun, 1988). The details of this pseudo-Newton algorithm will be described in an other paper.

In this paper, we only report the results obtained through the pseudo-Newton algorithm since they were consistently better than the one obtained through standard gradient descent. The input layer of all networks were 16 by 16 binary images, and their output layer was composed of 10 units, one per class. An output configuration was considered correct if the most-activated unit corresponded to the correct class.

In the following, when talking about layered networks, we will refer to the number of layers of modifiable weights. Thus, a network with one hidden layer is referred to as a two-layer network.

3.3 Net-1: A Single Layer Network

The simplest network that can be tested on this problem is a single layer, fully connected network with 10 sigmoid output units (2570 weights including the biases). Such a network has successfully learned the training set, which means that the problem is linearly separable. But, even though the training set can be learned perfectly, the generalization performance is disappointing: between 80% and 72% depending on when the learning is stopped (see curve 1 in Figure 3). Interestingly, the performance on the test set reaches a maximum quite early during training and goes down afterwards. This over-training phenomenon has been reported by many authors. The analysis of this phenomenon is outside the scope of this paper. When observing the weight vectors of the output units, it becomes obvious that the network can do nothing but develop a set of matched filters tuned to match an "average pattern" formed by superimposing all the training examples. Despite its relatively large number of parameters, such a system cannot possibly generalize correctly except in trivial situations, and certainly not when the input patterns are slightly translated. The classification is essentially based on the computation of a weighted overlap between the input pattern and the "average prototype".

3.4 Net-2: A Two-Layer, Fully Connected Network

The second step is to insert a hidden layer between the input and the output. The network has 12 hidden units, fully connected both to the input and the output. There is a total of 3240 weights including the biases. Predictably, this network can also learn perfectly the training set in a few epochs[2] (between 7 and 15). The generalization performance is better than with the previous network and reaches 87% after only 6 epochs (see Figure 3). A very slight over-learning effect is also observed, but its amplitude is much smaller than with the previous network. It is interesting to note that the standard deviation on the generalization performance is significantly larger than with the first network. This an

[2]The word epoch is used to designate an entire pass through the training set, which in our case is equivalent to 320 pattern presentations.

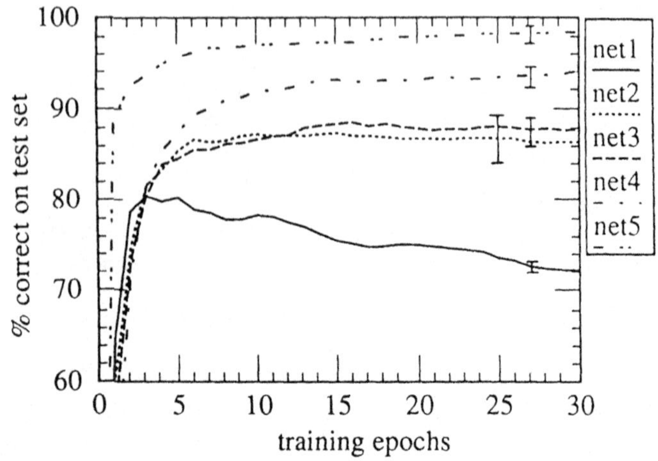

Figure 3: Generalization performance vs training time for 5 network architectures. Net-1: single layer; Net-2: 12 hidden units fully connected; Net-3: 2 hidden layers locally connected; Net-4: 2 hidden layers, locally connected with constraints; Net-5: 2 hidden layers, local connections, two levels of constraints.

indication that the network is largely underdetermined, and the number of solutions that are consistent with the training set is large. Unfortunately, these various solutions do not give equivalent results on the test set, thereby explaining the large variations in generalization performance.

From this result, it is quite clear that this network is too big (or has too many degrees of freedom).

3.5 Net-3: A Locally Connected, 3-Layer Network

Since reducing the size of the network will also reduce its generality, some knowledge about the task will be necessary in order to preserve the network's ability to solve the problem. A simple solution to our over-parameterization problem can be found if we remember that the network should recognize images. Classical work in visual pattern recognition have demonstrated the advantage of extracting local features and combining them to form higher order features. We can easily build this knowledge into the network by forcing the hidden units to only combine local sources of information. The architecture comprises two hidden layers named H1 and H2. The first hidden layer, H1, is a 2-dimensional array of size 8 by 8. Each unit in H1 takes its inputs from 9 units on the input plane situated in a 3 by 3 square neighborhood. For units in layer H1 that are one unit apart, their receptive fields (in the input layer) are two pixels apart. Thus, the receptive fields of two neighbouring hidden units overlap by one row or one column. Because of this two-to-one undersampling in

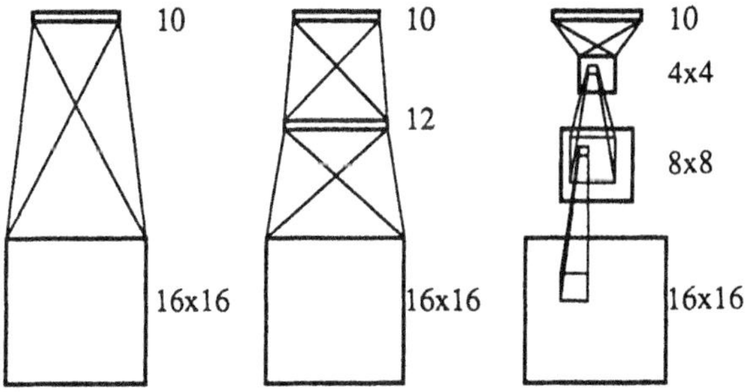

Figure 4: Three network architectures: Net-1, Net-2 and Net-3

each direction, the information is compacted by a factor of 4 going from the input to H1.

Layer H2 is a 4 by 4 plane, thus, a similar two-to-one undersampling occurs going from layer H1 to H2, but the receptive fields are now 5 by 5. H2 is fully connected to the 10 output units. The network has 1226 connections (see Figure 4).

The performance is slightly better than with Net-2: 88.5%, but is obtained at a considerably lower computational cost since Net-3 is almost 3 times smaller than Net-2. Also note that the standard deviation on the performance of Net-3 is smaller than for Net-2. This is thought to mean that the hypothesis space for Net-3 (the space of possible functions it can implement) is much smaller than for Net-2.

3.6 Net-4: A Constrained Network

One of the major problems of image recognition, even as simple as the one we consider in this work, is that distinctive features of an object can appear at various locations on the input image. Therefore it seems useful to have a set of feature detectors that can detect a particular instance of a feature anywhere on the input plane. Since the *precise* location of a feature is not relevant to the classification, we can afford to loose some position information in the process. Nevertheless, an *approximate* position information must be preserved in order to allow for the next levels to detect higher order features.

Detection of features at any location on the input can be easily done using weight sharing. The first hidden layer can be composed of several planes that we will call *feature maps*. All units in a plane share the same set of weights, thereby detecting the same feature at different locations. Since the exact position of the feature is not important, the feature maps need not be as large as the input. An interesting side effect of this technique is that it reduces the number of free weights in the network by a large amount.

The architecture of Net-4 is very similar to Net-3 and also has two hidden layers. The first hidden layer is composed of two 8 by 8 feature maps. Each unit in a feature map takes input from a 3 by 3 neighborhood on the input plane. For units in a feature map that are one unit apart, their receptive fields in the input layer are two pixels apart. Thus, as with Net-3 the input image is *undersampled*. The main difference from Net-3 is that all units in a feature map share the same set of 9 weights (but each of them has an independent bias). The undersampling technique serves two purposes. The first is to keep the size of the

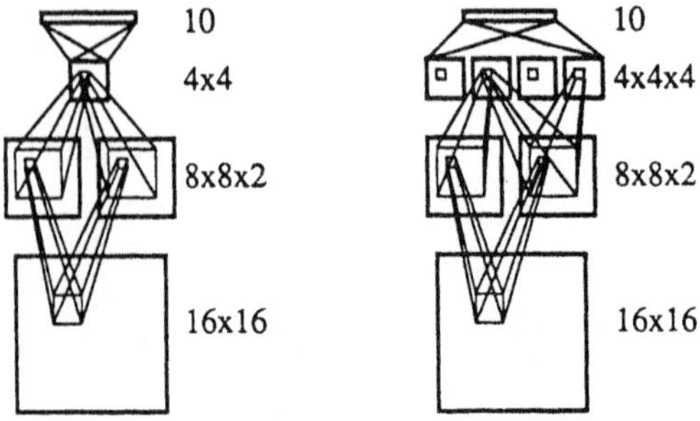

Figure 5: Two network architectures with shared weights: Net-4 and Net-5

network within reasonable limits. The second is to ensure that some location information is discarded during the feature detection.

Even though the feature detectors are shift invariant, the operation they collectively perform is not. When the input image is shifted, the output of the feature maps is also shifted, but is otherwise left almost unchanged. Because of the two-to-one undersampling, when the shift of the input is small, the output of the feature maps is *not* shifted, but merely slightly distorted.

As in the previous network, the second hidden layer is a 4 by 4 plane with 5 by 5 local receptive fields and no weight sharing. The output is fully connected to the second hidden layer and has, of course, 10 units. The network has 2266 connections but only 1132 (free) weights (see Figure 5).

The generalization performance of this network jumps to 94%, indicating that built-in shift invariant features are quite useful for this task. This result also indicates that, despite the very small number of independent weights, the computational power of the network is increased.

3.7 Net-5: A Network with Hierarchical Feature Extractors

The same idea can be pushed further, leading to a hierarchical structure where several levels of constrained feature maps.

The architecture of Net-5 is very similar to the one of Net-4, except that the second hidden layer H2 has been replaced by four feature maps each of which is a 4 by 4 plane. Units in these feature maps have 5 by 5 receptive fields in the first hidden layer. Again, all units in a feature map share the same set of 25 weights and have independent biases. And again, the two-to-one undersampling occurs between the first and the second hidden layer.

The network has 5194 connections but only 1060 free parameters, the smallest number of all networks described in this paper (see Figure 5).

The generalization performance is 98.4% (100% generalization was obtained during two of the ten runs) and increases extremely quickly at the beginning of learning. This suggests that using several levels of constrained feature maps is a big help for shift invariance.

network architecture	links	weights	performance
single layer network	2570	2570	80 %
two layer network	3240	3240	87 %
locally connected	1226	1226	88.5 %
constrained network	2266	1132	94 %
constrained network 2	5194	1060	98.4 %

Table 1: Generalization performance for 5 network architectures. Net-1: single layer; Net-2: 12 hidden units fully connected; Net-3: 2 hidden layers locally connected; Net-4: 2 hidden layers, locally connected with constraints; Net-5: 2 hidden layers, local connections, two levels of constraints. Performance on training set is 100% for all networks.

4 DISCUSSION

The results are summarized on Table 1.

As expected, the generalization performance goes up as the number of free parameters in the network goes down and as the amount of built-in knowledge goes up. A noticeable exception to this rule is the result given by the single-layer network and the two-layer, fully connected network. Even though the two layer net has more parameters, the generalization performance is significantly better. One explanation could be that the one-layer network cannot classify the whole set (training plus testing) correctly, but experiments show that it can. We see two other possible explanations. The first one is that some knowledge is implicitly put in by inserting a hidden layer: we tell the system that the problem is not first order. The second one is that the efficiency of the learning procedure (as defined in (Denker et al., 1987)) is better with a two layer net than with a one layer net, meaning that more information is extracted from each example with the former. This is highly speculative and should be investigated further.

4.1 Tradeoff Between Speed, Generality and Generalization

Computer scientists know that storage space, computation time and generality of the code can be exchanged when designing a program to solve a particular problem. For example, a program that computes a trigonometric function can use a series expansion, or a lookup table. the latter uses more memory than the former but is faster. Using properties of trigonometric functions, the same code (or table) can be used to compute several functions, but usually results in some loss in efficiency.

The same kind of exchange exists for learning machines. It is trivial to design a machine that learns very quickly, does not generalize, and requires an enormous amount of hardware. In fact this learning machine has already been built and is called a Random Access Memory. On the other hand, a back-propagation network[3] takes longer to train but is expected to generalize. Unfortunately, as shown in (Denker et al., 1987), generalization can be obtained only at the price of generality.

[3]unless it is designed to emulate a RAM

4.2 On-Line Update vs Batch Update

All simulations described in this paper were performed using the so-called "on-line" or "stochastic" version of back-propagation where the weights are updated after each pattern, as opposed to the "batch" version where the weights are updated after the gradient have been accumulated over the whole training set. Experiment show that stochastic update is far superior to batch update when there is some redundancy in the data. In fact stochastic update *must* be better when a certain level of generalization is expected. Let us take an example where the training database is composed of two copies of the same subset. Then accumulating the gradient over the whole set would cause redundant computations to be performed. Stochastic gradient does not have this problem. This idea can be generalized to training sets where there exists no precise repetition of the same pattern but where some redundancy is present.

4.3 Conclusion

We showed an example where constraining the network architecture improves both learning speed and generalization performance dramatically. This is really not surprising but it is more easily said than done. However, we have demonstrated that it *can* be done in at least one case, image recognition, using a hierarchy of shift invariant local feature detectors. These techniques can be easily (and have been) extended to other domains such as speech recognition.

Complex software tools with advanced user interfaces for network description and simulation control are required in order to solve a real application. Several network structures must be tried before an acceptable one is found and a quick feedback on the peformance is critical.

We are just beginning to collect the tools and to understand the principles which can help us to *design* a network for a particular task. Designing a network for a real problem will require a significant amount of engineering, which the availability of powerful learning algorithms will hopefully keep to a bare minimum.

Acknowledgments

This work has been supported by a grant from the Fyssen foundation, and a grant from the Sloan foundation to Geoffrey Hinton. The author wishes to thank Geoff Hinton, Mike Mozer, Sue Becker and Steve Nowlan for helpful discussions, and John Denker and Larry Jackel for useful comments. The Neural Network simulator SN is the result of a collaboration between Leon-Yves Bottou and the author.

REFERENCES

Becker, S. & le Cun, Y. (1988). Improving the convergence of back-propagation learning with second-order methods. Technical Report CRG-TR-88-5, University of Toronto Connectionist Research Group.

Bottou, L.-Y. (1988). Master's thesis, EHEI, Universite de Paris 5.

Bottou, L.-Y. & le Cun, Y. (1988). Sn: a simulator for connectionist models. In *Proceedings of NeuroNimes 88*, Nimes, France.

Bryson, A. & Ho, Y. (1969). *Applied Optimal Control.* Blaisdell Publishing Co.

Chauvin, Y. (1989). A back-propagation algorithm with optimal use of hidden units. In D. Touretzky, (ed.), *Advances in Neural Information Processing Systems.* Morgan Kaufmann.

Denker, J., Schwartz, D., Wittner, B., Solla, S., Howard, R., Jackel, L., & Hopfield, J. (1987). Large automatic learning, rule extraction and generalization. *Complex Systems*, **1**, 877–922.

Hanson, S. J. & Pratt, L. Y. (1989). Some comparisons of constraints for minimal network construction with back-propagation. In D. Touretzky, (ed.), *Advances in Neural Information Processing Systems.* Los Altos, CA: Morgan Kaufmann.

le Cun, Y. (1985). A learning scheme for asymmetric threshold networks. In *Proceedings of Cognitiva 85*, pp. 599–604, Paris, France.

le Cun, Y. (1986). Learning processes in an asymmetric threshold network. In E. Bienenstock, F. Fogelman-Soulie, & G. Weisbuch, (eds.), *Disordered systems and biological organization*, pp. 233–240, Les Houches, France. Springer-Verlag.

le Cun, Y. (1987). *Modeles Connexionnistes de l'Apprentissage.* PhD thesis, Universite Pierre et Marie Curie, Paris, France.

le Cun, Y. (1988). A theoretical framework for back-propagation. In D. Touretzky, G. Hinton, & T. Sejnowski, (eds.), *Proceedings of the 1988 Connectionist Models Summer School*, pages 21–28, CMU, Pittsburgh, Pa., Los Altos: Morgan Kaufmann.

Mozer, M. C. & Smolensky, P. (1989). Skeletonization: A technique for trimming the fat from a network via relevance assessment. In D. Touretzky, (ed.), *Advances in Neural Information Processing Systems.* Los Altos, CA: Morgan Kaufmann.

Parker, D. B. (1985). Learning-logic. Technical report, TR-47, Sloan School of Management, MIT, Cambridge, Mass.

Patarnello, S. & Carnevali, P. (1987). Learning networks of neurons with boolean logic. *Europhysics Letters*, **4**, 503–508.

Rumelhart, D. E., Hinton, G. E., & Williams, R. J. (1986). Learning internal representations by error propagation. In D.E. Rumelhart & J.L. McClelland, (eds.), *Parallel distributed processing: Explorations in the microstructure of cognition*, volume I. Cambridge, MA: Bradford Books.

Waibel, A., Hanazawa, T., Hinton, G., Shikano, K., & Lang, K. (1988). Phoneme recognition using time-delay neural networks. *IEEE Transactions on Acoustics, Speech and Signal Processing.*

Werbos, P. (1974). *Beyond Regression.* Phd thesis, Harvard University.

CONNECTIONISM IN PERSPECTIVE
R. Pfeifer, Z. Schreter, F. Fogelman-Soulié, L. Steels (Eds.)

Enlarging Symbols to More Than Numbers or Artificial Intelligence Is The Science of Explanations

Yves Kodratoff

CNRS & Université Paris Sud, LRI, Bldg 490, 91405 Orsay, France
George Mason University, AI Center, Fairfax, Virginia 22030, USA

Abstract—*Numbers are almost the only kind of symbols that have been taken into account so far by Science. The birth and extraordinary quick growth of Artificial Intelligence show that we are now needing symbols conveying more precise information than simple numbers. We analyze this phenomenon, and show that the need for explanations is the information required by modern applications of Science. As long as Connectionism will keep its roots in the realm of purely numeric representation of the external world, its links with AI will stay purely fortuitous.*

Keywords—Explanation, explanation-based learning, symbols vs. numbers

1. INTRODUCTION

The analysis of the differences between numerical and symbolic approaches, Artificial Intelligence (AI) being prototypical of the last one, relies on the definition which is given of AI. In the introduction of this paper we shall first present some of the acknowledged features of AI, within its own micro-world, and then we shall develop our own personal view that AI is a science the topic of which is the definition, analysis, measurement, and comparison of explanations relative to an automatically executed reasoning session, and provided in the user's language (see Kodratoff, 1986, 1988).

The AI approach to Machine Learning (ML) carries the same kind of misunderstandings as AI does. This is why, even though this paper is devoted to ML rather than to AI in general, we shall speak of AI as well as of ML in this introduction.

The first and main misunderstanding about AI comes from its name, from which one tends to believe that everything that is both intelligent and artificial belongs to AI. Actually, as any other science did, AI built its own definition progressively through its own more significant results, and became a doctrinal corpus that contains technologies, methodologies, and addresses a specific topic, all of which are concerned with the intelligent and the artificial, in a specific way, to be more precisely defined. Let us stress at once that other sub-fields of Computer Science create systems that are artificial and intelligent, and nevertheless do not claim belonging to AI. For instance, Data Analysis, finding a new significant clustering shows intelligent behavior. Another instance is provided by compilers that behave most often intelligently without any hint to AI.

These very simple examples show that the definition of the Handbook of AI of Barr & Feigenbaum (1981) ("AI is the part of computer science concerned with designing intelligent computer systems, that is systems that exhibit the characteristics we associate with intelligence in human behavior - understanding language, learning, reasoning, solving problems, and so on") is presently obsolete, and needs refinement.

1.1. What is not AI, and what is AI

We present here five features characterizing AI, that make the AI approach to ML original. When they are used in a very strict way, that is to say when all of them are requested to be fulfilled, one defines something like the core of AI. A softer definition of AI, that will include all the existing AI systems, will be to request that some of the features given below are partly fulfilled.

Firstly, as opposed to the "intelligent machine" definition of Barr and Feigenbaum (1981), AI refuses to work with intelligent black boxes. For instance, Roger Schank (1986) points out that the chess playing machines presently available on the market are out of AI[1] even though they start being real good players. The reasons why they play so well are available to their designers only, not to their users, and therefore they cannot be considered as AI. We do not claim here that temporary stoppage of communication is impossible in AI, we rather point out that a definitive loss of any communication abilities is contrary to the spirit of AI. AI systems are open to their users who must understand them.

Secondly, AI tends to avoid using implicit knowledge. A clear illustration of this assertion is the marked preference AI shows for declarative knowledge representation, in which knowledge and the way to use it are clearly differentiated. On the contrary, AI tends to avoid procedural representations where knowledge and its use are merged. For instance, AI favored the birth of rather strongly declarative languages like LISP and PROLOG. An other well-known example is the one of Expert Systems. An Expert System is nothing but a kind of decision tree, except that the tree has been flattened in a declarative form by writing out each rule that lead to a decision, without telling in advance in which order they must be called. This generates the so-called "conflict resolution" problem, which is the price that must be paid to declarativity. In an AI system, knowledge should be stated explicitly, preferably in a declarative way; as little as possible should procedural knowledge be expressed in a programming language. Similarly, fancy ad hoc codings are very much in opposition with the spirit of AI.

Thirdly, as opposed to what the early workers believed, a system cannot pass the above tests without already carrying a huge amount of preliminary knowledge. This is illustrated by the importance given to knowledge bases in AI. Knowledge is a kind of data: We do not speak of data bases because our bases have to be declarative and understandable by their users. An AI system is supposed to make heavy use of background knowledge, provided by the user in a knowledge base.

---

[1] Attributing these chess machines to AI would be somewhat dishonest with Operation Research where this marked success comes from.

Fourthly, in accordance with the need for user understandability, an AI system has to speak its user's language, instead of speaking a (actually non-existing) "language of AI". This feature contrasts AI well with other sciences the first worry of which is the creation of their own jargon, to be imposed on their user as part of his/her scientific formation. For instance, statistics does describe interesting natural phenomena, and does it in terms of "mean squares distances" etc., which is its own language, instead of expressing the knowledge in its user's language, as AI attempts to do.

1.2. What AI is only partly

It happens quite often that AI is defined as a subset of itself. We shall not attempt to present all the reductions proposed, but give some of the most common ones.

AI reduces to Expert Systems. Expert Systems are certainly the most well-known success of the AI approach to knowledge processing, but it never has been the main stream of ongoing AI research at any time. There is even now a tendency to exclude Expert System from the international congresses' programmes as a specific topic. People working on the topic are requested to find other key-words to characterize their work.

AI reduces to LISP (or PROLOG, or object-oriented languages). Declarative programming languages seldom originated from within the AI community itself. The role of this community is rather to adopt, and modify them to its needs, to make them famous in the end. It is quite funny to see that these languages, born from theoreticians, have been also "definitively" criticized by other theoreticians who have shown how improper those languages where. It is quite true that LISP semantics is not completely justified, that PROLOG unification has a terrible flaw, but all those critics are important from the theoretical point of view only. The success of LISP and PROLOG is explained by their adequacy to handle AI needs.

AI reduces to Pattern Recognition (or intelligent robotics, or games, or automatic translation etc.). AI is born from the need --shown by some research fields, such as pattern recognition, robotics etc. -- for declarative components, and for large knowledge bases, understandable to the user. It is therefore quite natural to confuse these fields with AI. They are still privileged application fields, but they are different from AI itself.

AI reduces to the finding of cognitive models. Form its start, AI has been interested in building operational models of human intelligence. It is even typical of AI, as opposed to most other sciences, to accept explicit anthropomorphic models. It is nevertheless ridiculous to believe that any AI model has to be a faithful representation of what is happening in our brains. Anyhow, natural intelligence still shows much of the properties given above as being not AI.

1.3. Application fields of AI

The reader already understood that no application domain is really typical of AI, that the way to work on it is the real feature characterizing AI. Nevertheless, experience shows that some fields are favoring the AI approach. Here are some of them, taken from several recent international congresses. Natural language understanding, perception, robotics, machines for

AI, languages for AI, cognitive modelling, intelligent tutoring, games, automatic programming.

Natural language understanding is quite typical since there has always been a mother science, linguistics, the specialists of which often reject AI because of its alleged lack of rigor. Actually, linguistics attempts to characterize the properties of natural language, while AI addresses a different problem. AI tries to characterize how natural language is a good communication means between two systems (one of them possibly human). It will therefore always look at subsets of natural language, avoiding the complexity of its full use, but digging out the problem of mutual understanding.

1.4. AI methodologies

Each of the above fields uses tools, methodologies stemming from AI, that are independent of the specific field. The acknowledged main methodological topics of research for AI have always been knowledge representation (semantic nets are an example of this trend), and reasoning, including all deductive techniques and theorem proving in classic and modal logics. Progress in ML, i.e. discovery and inductive reasoning techniques, lead ML to become another acknowledged methodology of AI. We think that the next one will be collaborative agents, i.e., the AI approach to parallelism.

1.5. AI topic

There is no consensus at present on what the topic of AI really is, which is not such a shame for an emerging science. We would say that most of the AI community tends to follow the Handbook of AI definition already cited as obsolete.

Our own personal definition, viz. that AI is concerned with the definition, analysis, measurement, and comparison of explanations relative to an automatically executed reasoning session, and provided in the user's language, is far from being accepted by all our colleagues. Our main argument follows from the observation that explicability fulfills the needs expressed above.

1 - the concern for understandability is perfectly fulfilled by a system capable of providing itself and its user with explanations,

2 - a huge amount of background knowledge is anyhow necessary to be able to find relevant explanations.

Moreover, the recent history of AI illustrates well the importance that AI specialists attribute to explanations. For instance,

1 - recent progress in ML is partly due to the recognition of the importance of explanations to control the learning process,

2 - improving the inference ability of Expert Systems finds little interest in the research community which is, on the contrary, fascinated by the problem of improving their explanatory ability.

To conclude, we claim that AI is a science essentially characterized by its approach to problems, and by a specific topic of interest. It bases its reasoning methods on the use large declarative background knowledge bases, that must be open to their user. Its topics are the definition, the measurement, and the use of explanations.

2. AN ILLUSTRATION OF THE DILEMMA: NUMBERS VERSUS EXPLICABILITY

Before going into more detail on the way explanations of high quality can be automatically provided, let us insist on the difference - and a kind of opposition - between numbers and explicability. Expert Systems are a very good example of such an opposition.

In most cases, especially diagnosis cases, the human expert is not 100% sure of the validity of the rules s/he is using. Therefore, for the sake of efficiency, coefficients of some kind, like the famous belief coefficients of MYCIN (Shortliffe, 1976), are attached to each rule. While reasoning proceeds, the coefficients are combined in order to express the confidence one grants to the final conclusion. The existence of uncertain rules implies the possible existence of contradictions, hence the impossibility of explanations, see Duval & Kodratoff (1986), when numeric combinations are performed.

Let us give an example of this claim, expressed in Edinburgh's PROLOG notation, on an ad hoc medical basis. The beliefs are given in word form as expressions in brackets at the head of the clause.

Consider a basis stating that vomitings imply sometimes gall bladder problems, that vomitings often imply digestive problems, that fever and digestive problems generally imply appendicitis. One will introduce potential contradiction each time some state is recognized as impossible. For instance, when adding to the basis that, typically, appendicitis does not occur with gall bladder problems. All this provides the (not saturated) coherent uncertain data basis:

[*sometimes*]	gall-bladder-problems	:-	vomitings
[*often*]	digestive-problems	:-	vomitings
[*generally*]	appendicitis	:-	fever, digestive-problems
[*typically*]		:-	gall-bladder-problems, appendicitis

If one is concerned by a patient who actually has fever together with vomitings, one introduces a contradiction in the data basis since

[*certain*]	fever	:-	
[*certain*]	vomitings	:-	
[*sometimes*]	gall-bladder-problems	:-	vomitings
[*often*]	digestive-problems	:-	vomitings
[*generally*]	appendicitis	:-	fever, digestive-problems
[*typically*]		:-	gall-bladder-problems, appendicitis

leads to the empty clause as shown below by the sequence of resolution steps:

:- vomitings, appendicitis
:- appendicitis
:- fever, digestive-problems
:- digestive-problems
:- vomitings

The problem with this data basis is that one can prove A and ¬A from it. For instance, if one asks if the patient has appendicitis, one will get an empty clause by adding

:- appendicitis

to the basis (that proves that there is appendicitis with a modulation *[generally, [certain,[often, certain]]]*), but also by adding

appendicitis :-

and that proves that there is no appendicitis with a modulation *[typically, [sometimes, certain]]*.

When these modulations are expressed by numbers, the relevant problem becomes to express by combinations of numbers the following properties.

1- associate a reasonable number with each of the qualifiers (this is easily performed),
2- find combination laws for sequences, like *[sometimes, certain]*,
3- find combination laws for sequences of sequences, like *[generally, [certain,[...]]]*,
4- find combination laws for positive evidence and negative evidence.

Once all these combination laws have been chosen, the computations will be performed very quickly, and the final result will be stored with little memory, thus achieving an efficiency goal.

On the contrary, unless all the combination laws are reversible operations (which is unlikely), once the operations have been performed, it will be impossible to track back the way a particular result was obtained. Besides, it will be often the case that the semantics of the domain will be difficult to fit with the semantics of number combinations. For instance, suppose that the domain is such that linear reasoning (corresponding to simple sequences of modulations) are preferred to branching reasoning (corresponding to sequences of the form [...[...[...]]]). The system will therefore need to compute a kind of "branching index", and use it in its computations. The more complex the numerical representation, the less it will have any explanative value.

On the contrary, more complex representations, using strings of symbols may better convey the semantics of the domain. For instance, in the above appendicitis example, the two strings of symbols we obtained may be interpreted as follows. Choose to believe first, that there is appendicitis (because all evidence in favor of it is strong, while one branch of the reasoning against it is a bit weak), but beware that at the first sign of weakness in new data confirming appendicitis, both hypotheses become equivalent, and the whole reasoning should be done again with the new evidence included. Including such a procedural interpretation of strings of symbols is heavily domain dependent, and should be part of the information requested from human experts.

3. EXPLANATION-BASED LEARNING IN STRONG THEORY DOMAINS

3.1. EBG: An intuitive presentation

EBG is given a complete theory of the domain in which the learning takes place and a training instance of the concept to be learned. Since the system knows the complete theory, it knows a definition of the concept to be learned. The goal of the learning process is to learn a new "better" definition of this concept. To achieve this goal, EBG works as follows. Using its knowledge of the domain theory, it proves that the training instance is actually an instance of the learned concept. The proof trace is then pruned by using an operationality criterion that tells which are the operators that must be left out. Notice the importance of this criterion on which relies all the efficiency of the process. The pruned proof trace is then generalized into an explanation structure, which contains the parts of the original clauses that have been used. A variablized version of the training instance is then regressed, as explained in Waldinger (1977), through the explanation structure. The result of this regression is a new, more operational definition of the concept.

3.2. EBL and the refinement of strong theories

For the management of incomplete theories, the central idea is to complete the failure proofs by an abduction mechanism of the same kind as the one of Duval & Kodratoff (1989). This abduction process is guided by analogical reasoning about explanations and enables the discovery of new rules that refine the domain theory. We illustrate this limitation with the following example drawn from DeJong & Mooney (1986). In this example, our aim is learning a definition of the concept of suicide, Kill(x,x). The domain theory TH0 contains the following rules.

KILL(a,b)	:-	HATE(a,b), POSSESS(a,c), WEAPON(c).
HATE(w,w)	:-	DEPRESSED(w).
POSSESS(u,v)	:-	BUY(u,v).
WEAPON(z)	:-	SHOT-GUN(z).
WEAPON(z)	:-	PISTOL(z).

The training instance is a suicide, described by the following facts.

DEPRESSED(JOHN)	:-	
BUY(JOHN,OBJ1)	:-	
SHOT-GUN(OBJ1)	:-	
	:-	KILL(JOHN, JOHN)

This training instance leads us to learn the following rule for suicide.

KILL(x,x)	:-	DEPRESSED(x), BUY(x,c), SHOT-GUN(c).

3.2.1. Abduction guided by analogical reasoning about explanations

3.2.1.1. Analogical reasoning

First, let us briefly recall what is analogical reasoning (for more details, see e.g. Chouraqui, 1985, Davies & Russel, 1987, or Kodratoff, 1988). Let us suppose that we dispose of a piece of information, called the source S and that this information can be put into the form of a doublet (A, B) in which B depends causally on A. Let us suppose now that another piece of information, called the target T, can be put into the same form (A', B') with the requirement that there exists some resemblance between A and A'.

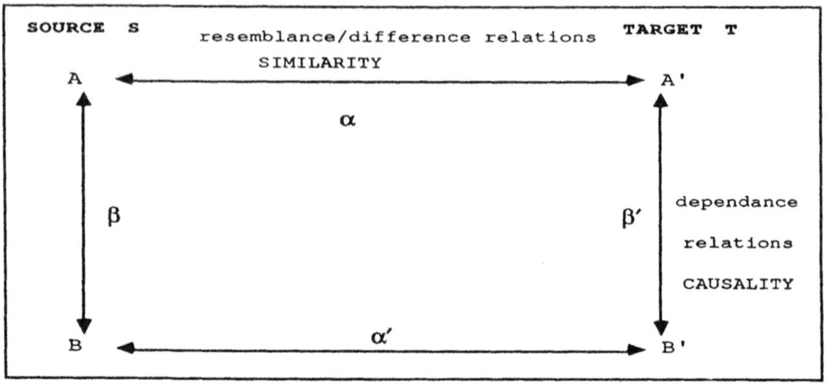

This scheme can be used in different ways to define analogical reasoning. In all cases, we consider that we know more or less precisely A, B, A', α and β and that we try to invent B' or to justify its plausibility.

We apply this paradigm in a situation where S and T are two explanation structures of a given concept C. This method will be called *analogical reasoning between explanation structures*. More precisely, the source S is a generalized proof for the concept C. We suppose that this precedent for analogy is given, and do not consider the problem of memory retrieval of a correct source. Yet, we shall see further that several matchings with this precedent are possible and that heuristics must be computed to select a good matching.

Let us suppose that we study the concept C of suicide and that we know the following generalized proof structure, that will be the source in our analogical process.

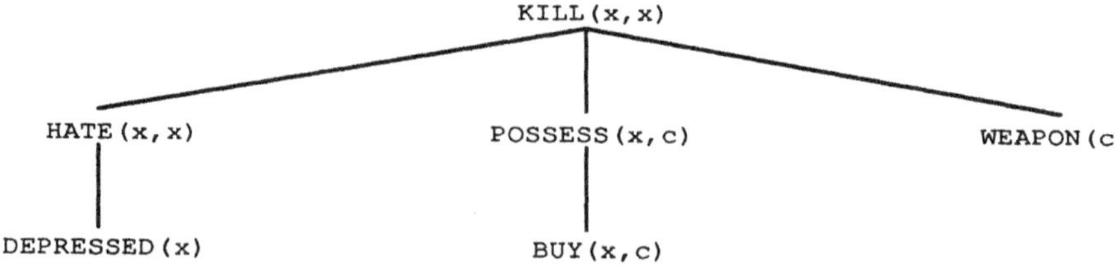

In this section, we consider the case where the system is provided with an example E of concept C which is not recognized by the theory; it means that the PROLOG solver fails to prove that example E verifies the definition of concept C. The target T of our analogy schema is a proof tree that insures that E is an example of concept C. This proof is in fact unknown since our solver fails to recognize example E. Yet the trace of this proof failure may contain some sub-goals of the generalized explanation S that are true for example E. These common features between S and E are called a partial explanation. Let us call A the partial explanation extracted from the source S, and A' the partial explanation applied to the description of example E. We insist on the point that finding such a partial explanation is an essential step of our methodology since the analogy would fail without it. According to the previous notation, the analogical inference enables to construct B' by analogy to B; B is the complementary part of sub-structure A in the general explanation (source S) and B' is a set of relations that completes the proof (target T) that E is an instance of concept C .

To illustrate these definitions, let us examine a very simple example; we consider a suicide instance described by the following facts.

DEPRESSED(MARY)	:-
BUY(MARY,OBJ3)	:-
SLEEPING-PILLS(OBJ3)	:-
PRICE(OBJ3, 20)	:-

This instance, E, is not recognized by the theory. The failure comes from the fact that our definition of KILL(x,x) always involves a weapon, and none of the objects that Mary owns is recognized as a weapon. Yet it is not a hopeless failure. As suggested by Hall (1986) in a different context, it is possible to learn by failing to explain. Since we have confidence in the relevance of the example, this failure can help us to discover lacking information that will strengthen our domain theory.

One of the requirements to apply analogical reasoning is that some sub-structures of the source S and the target T must be similar. Our system examines traces of proof failures in order to find a common partial explanation between the generalized proof S and the studied instance E. Intuitively, a partial explanation between S and the example E means that Mary's situation matches partially the general suicide circumstances.

For the above example, only one partial explanation is found. It corresponds to the sub-structure:

Partial explanation

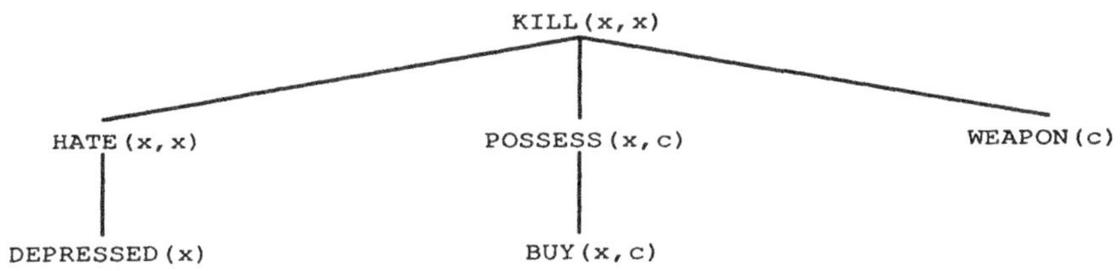

It is similar to a sub-structure of the generalized proof S:

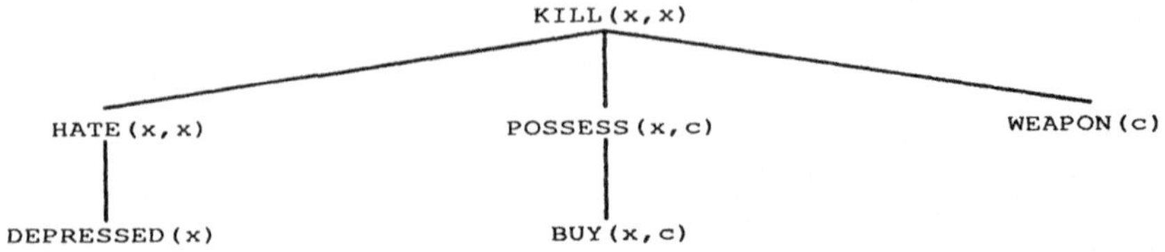

Once we have found this partial explanation, we look for the information that must be added to the theory to complete this partial proof. This process is an abduction mechanism: since we consider that example E is an instance of concept C, we generate hypotheses that enable a complete recognition of this example. This abduction process may provide multiple solutions. We decide to give more confidence to the explanation that is the most analogous to the general proof structure S. This choice means that we search which minimal changes to the theory are necessary for recognition of new examples. Of course, our system cannot discover a new and original explanation in order to explain a quite different example. In such a case, it would be necessary to use empirical learning based on the study of many examples.

3.2.1.2. Abduction

Let us see now what hypotheses we can generate by comparison of the general proof S and the partial explanation A'. We have seen that Mary's suicide presents some similarities with the known suicide schema but Mary possesses no weapon. We can consider two reasons that justify the explanation failure.

First hypothesis: Mary possesses an object that is in fact a weapon, but our knowledge about weapons is not sufficient to identify this object. In this case the rule

KILL(x,x) :- DEPRESSED(x), BUY(x,c), WEAPON(c).

is considered as correct and the unknown property WEAPON(OBJ3) is the cause that explains Mary's suicide. From the analogy point of view, this hypothesis corresponds to the case where α (similarity relation between source and target) is the identity relation: the same explanation as in the source S is applied to the target T and leads to assert a new property about OBJ3. This process is the only one considered in other work about abduction such as Cox & Pietrzykowski (1986), but we want to propose another possibility that considers rule refinement rather than fact assertion.

Second hypothesis: To explain the failure about Mary's suicide, we may consider that the rule

KILL(x,x) :- DEPRESSED(x), BUY(x,c), WEAPON(c).

is too restrictive since no weapons are used in the present case. So we propose to refine this rule by introducing another object class that will replace WEAPON. To guide this hypothesis generation, we rely on the analogical precedent S. We consider all the properties involved in

Mary's suicide description and we apply syntactic and semantic constraints that enable to choose the predicate which is the most analogous to WEAPON.

In the general explanation, WEAPON(c) is a property of an object possessed by the person that kills oneself. We must respect this dependence, so we consider the predicates that involve OBJ3, the only object that Mary owns. Moreover, we search a predicate of the same kind as WEAPON, that is to say a predicate that indicates an object type.

Let us recall that Mary's suicide is described by the following facts:

DEPRESSED(MARY) :-
BUY(MARY,OBJ3) :-
SLEEPING-PILLS(OBJ3) :-
PRICE(OBJ3, 20) :-

The property PRICE(OBJ3,20) is a binary predicate that expresses an attribute relation and is not retained as a possible candidate for the proof completion. But SLEEPING-PILLS(OBJ3) is a plausible hypothesis since Mary possesses OBJ3 and SLEEPING-PILLS is a predicate of the same type as WEAPON. So we can propose two hypotheses that give the following completed proofs:

First completion:

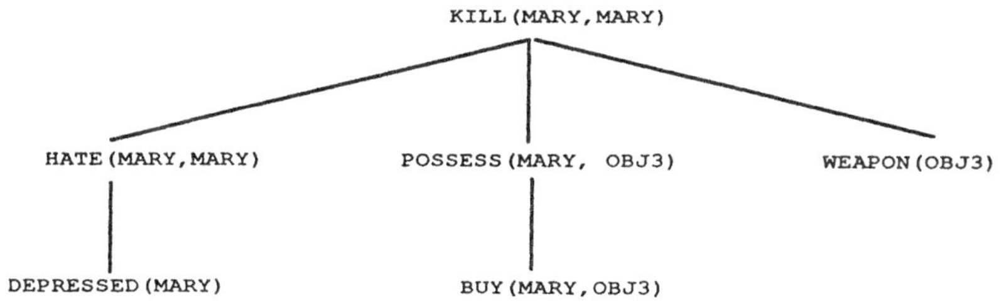

Second completion:

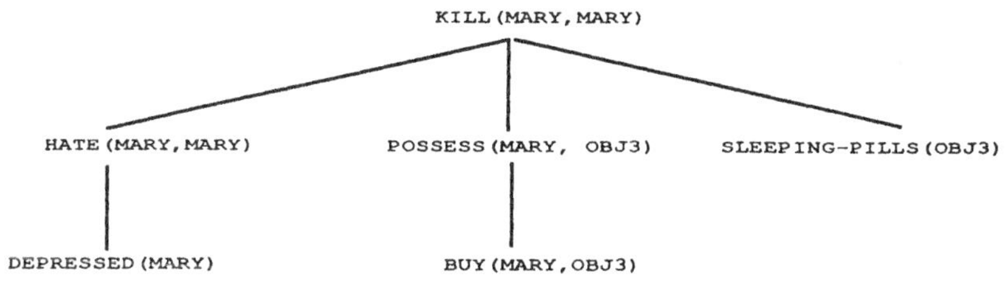

We do not discuss here the problem of choosing the best completion, which is linked to the one of limiting the number of possible such completions in realistic cases where the number of predicates satisfying our weak selection conditions may become very large. Obviously, a non-toy system should combine this abductive process with some selection measurement to direct its working. Nevertheless, one should point out that this task cannot be realized without considering other knowledge or other examples, and that, precisely, this information will be available in realistic cases. For instance, in our example, confidence in the first completion is enforced if OBJ3 shares a lot of weapon properties. The second completion is preferred if, for instance, other similar examples involving sleeping-pills or drugs are encountered, or if some knowledge about chemical products (one of the possible generalizations of "sleeping-pill" that brings in the idea of danger) restricts their use as weapons to war-like situations.

4. EXPLANATION-BASED LEARNING IN SOFT THEORY DOMAINS

Three different approaches have extracted explanations from soft deep theories (by soft, we mean : "from which no formal proof can be drawn"). One is illustrated by the system PROTOS of Bareiss et al. (1989), the other one by the system DISCIPLE of Kodratoff & Tecuci (1987a, 1987b), and the third one by Schank's (1987) theory of XPs.

4.1. Definition of an explanation for PROTOS

In PROTOS, the production rules are associated to elementary explanations, that describe what kind of relation exists between the antecedent and the consequent of each production rule. There are six such elementary explanations. Among them, one finds the classical ISA (generality relationship), and PART-OF (part to whole mappings), but also ENABLES, telling that a feature enables the function of an object (e.g., wings enable flight). An explanation is a combination of such elementary explanations as given by a path in the relationship frame among objects.

4.2. Definition of an explanation for DISCIPLE

DISCIPLE is an interactive Learning Apprentice System for weak theory fields. In DISCIPLE, the learning process starts with an example of a problem solving step as, for instance, the following rule:

Example1

ATTACH sectors ON chassis-membrane-assembly

$\vdash$

APPLY mowicoll ON sectors
PRESS sectors ON chassis-membrane-assembly

where A $\vdash$ B means: "in order to achieve action A, perform actions B". This is interpreted as an example of a general rule indicating a way of performing the ATTACH action:

General Rule1
ATTACH x ON y
$\vdash$
APPLY z ON x
PRESS x ON y

We have to learn when it is valid to perform an ATTACH operation as a sequence of APPLY and PRESS. In order to achieve this goal, the system over-generalizes the examples (by transforming Example1 into General Rule1, for instance) and applies this over-generalization to the data basis of the user in order to find instances of the over-generalization. These instances are proposed to the user as tentative rules. When the user validates such a system-produced rule, we say that the system is provided with a positive example of its over-generalization. When the user rejects such a rule, we speak of a negative example.

An explanation in DISCIPLE is a set of conditions that authorizes the application of a general rule. For instance, the conditions of such a rule, say General Rule2, are an explanation of General Rule1. It is always obtained as the generalization of the particular proofs of the example rules provided to the system.

4.3. Pre-stored explanations : Schank's XPs

Roger Schank (1987) recently proposed his own vision of ML and AI, of which creativity is the central theme. Nevertheless, in this theory, the essential creative information is constituted by a set of Explanation Patterns (XPs). These XPs are pre-stored explanations that can be applied in a variety of situations, i.e. scripts for an explanation.

5. CONCLUSIONS

5.1. Explanations in AI and ML

We present here a non-exhaustive collection of different types of explanations that can be obtained in domains having a strong and complete theory (EBG), a strong but incomplete theory, and a soft one in which no formal proofs can be drawn. Our purpose is to show that all kinds of background knowledge have been studied as possible explanation generators.

The number and extent of the efforts under way in AI to build systems providing explanations to their users is really impressive. This illustrates our claim that AI is the science of explanations, without proving it. Anyhow, such claims are usually proven several decades after the fact, and their proofs are done by followers, not by creators of the facts. We nevertheless felt compelled to state it because of the extraordinary confusion that takes place about AI in the countries where it is poorly developed. It allows to make the limits of AI a bit more precise and argue about them.

5.2. Connectionist learning in the view of AI and ML

5.2.1. Casual versus expert knowledge

Expert knowledge can be defined by the fact that there exists a well-known body of knowledge in the field, which means that an expert of the field is able to explain to an other expert the reason of his/her choices. When the field is formalized enough, the possible disagreements between experts are on the reasons rather than on the choices themselves. This allows to make the difference between expert knowledge, and casual knowledge that does not fulfill the above conditions. Typically mathematics is expert knowledge, bicycle riding casual knowledge. Notice that in our definition, we take as granted that the knowledge is efficient (even though it is casual, a bicycle rider usually succeeds in performing the task), while in practice much expert knowledge -- economics is a good example of it -- is not 100% efficient, and this is not required to accept it as expert knowledge.

5.2.2. Connectionist versus AI learning

Any activity we are able to perform unconsciously once it has been learned, for instance the learning of bicycle riding, is out of the range of AI learning which concentrates on learning methods that make use of explicit background knowledge, rather than implicit one. The visible difference between AI learning and non-AI learning will therefore be in the ability to provide explanations about the learned knowledge. Since it deals with explicit knowledge, AI learning is able to give explanations, while the non-AI one is not able to do so.

In other words, one can always use rote learning to "teach" a computer to ride a bicycle by programming it to do so. The program will contain the knowledge implicit to bicycle riding. This example is typical of the problems met when including implicit knowledge in a program: the methods developed by the AI approach to ML tend to consider that declarative (and explicative, and easy-to-modify, and understandable to the user) knowledge is explicit knowledge. On the contrary, implicit knowledge is the one which is contained in procedures as pre-programmed by the creator of the system. This implicit knowledge is not easily understandable, it cannot provide explanations, it is hard to modify, i.e. it fulfills none of the conditions to belong to AI.

The connectionist approach to learning is intended to deal with such hard problems as learning casual knowledge, and represents it implicitly by the connection coefficients that link the cells of the connectionist net. From all the above, it seems to us that connectionism addresses a problem which is too difficult to be tackled with AI techniques. On the one hand it is therefore totally alien to AI. On the other hand, since real-life problems do not care about the above distinction between casual and expert knowledge, since they tend to mix them up, we can validly claim that any real-life problem should be addressed by the AI and the connectionist approaches in a complementary way.

5.2.3. Explicit and modular versus implicit and distributed

As a conclusion let us state that the AI approach deals with concepts that can be explicitly described, and that can be isolated as individual viable modules of knowledge. On the contrary, Connectionism deals with implicit concepts, the definition of which can be distributed over several sites.

We mean that this approach chooses a distributed representation of the (implicit) background knowledge by way of the structure of the connectionist net. The coefficients computed during the learning phase are a representation of distributed acquired knowledge. It happens from time to time that the connectionist net itself rejects a distributed representation of knowledge when some of its coefficients become approximately equal to 1. In that case, one is able to find a symbolic interpretation of the cell that tends towards 1.

The usefulness and efficiency of the connectionist approach have been often shown. We think that we still poorly understand the concept of distributed knowledge representation, especially its semantics, i.e. how are we to understand what is going on during the learning of a connectionist net? The answer to this question seems to us one the challenges for ML research in the years to come.

REFERENCES

Barr A., Feigenbaum E. A., (1981) The Handbook of Artificial Intelligence, Volume 1. Los Altos: William Kaufmann.

Bareiss E. R., Porter B. W., Kibler, D. & Wier C. C. (1989). Protos: An Exemplar-Based Learning Apprentice. To appear in Y. Kodratoff, R.S. Michalski (Eds.). *Machine Learning: An Artificial Intelligence Approach,* Volume 3. Los Altos: Morgan Kaufmann.

Chouraqui E., (1985). Construction of a model for reasoning by analogy. In: L. Steels & J.A. Campbell (Eds.). *Progress in Artificial Intelligence.* London: Ellis Horwood, 169-183.

Cox P.T., & Pietrzykowski T. (1986). Causes for events: Their computation and applications. *Proceedings of the eighth International Conference on Automated Deduction.* Oxford.

Davies T. R., & Russell S. T., (1987). A logical approach to reasoning by analogy. *Proceedings of IJCAI 87,* Milan. Los Altos, Ca: Morgan Kaufmann, 264-269.

DeJong G. (1981). "Generalizations based on explanations", *Proc. 7th IJCAI,* 1981, 67-69.

DeJong G., & Mooney R. Explanation-based learning: An alternative view. *Machine Learning,* **1** , 145-176.

Duval B., & Kodratoff Y. (1986). Automated deduction in an uncertain and inconsistent data basis. *Proc. ECAI-86,* Brighton, 101-108.

Duval B., & Kodratoff Y. (1989). A tool for the management of incomplete theories: Reasoning about explanations. To appear in: P. Brazdil (Ed.). *Machine learning, meta-reasoning, logic.* London: Pitman.

Hall R. J. (1986). Learning by failing to explain. *Proceedings of AAAI -86*. Philadelphia. Los Altos, Ca: Morgan Kaufmann. 568-572.

Kedar-Cabelli S. T., & McCarty L. T. (1987). Explanation-based generalization as resolution theorem proving. *Proceedings of the Fourth International Machine Learning Workshop*. Irvine. 383-389.

Kodratoff Y., Ganascia J.G., Clavieras B., Bollinger T., & Tecuci G. (1984). Careful generalization for concept learning, *Proc. ECAI-1984*, Pisa. 483-492. Also in: T. O'Shea (Ed). *Advances in Artificial Intelligence*. Amsterdam: North-Holland, 229-238.

Kodratoff Y. & Tecuci G. (1987a). DISCIPLE1: Interactive apprentice system in weak theory fields. *Proceedings of the 10th International Joint Conference on Artificial Intelligence*, Milan. Los Altos, Ca.: Morgan Kaufmann, 271-273.

Kodratoff Y. & Tecuci G. (1987b). Techniques of design and DISCIPLE learning apprentice. *International Journal of Expert Systems: Research and Applications*, **1**, no.1, 39-66.

Kodratoff Y. (1988). Introduction to machine learning. London: Pitman.

Mitchell T., Keller R., & Kedar-Cabelli S. (1986). Explanation-based generalization: A unifying view. *Machine Learning* ,**1**, 47-80.

Puget J.-F., (1987). Apprentissage de plans à partir de preuves. *Proceedings of AFCET 87*. Antibes. November 87.

Schank R. C. (1986). Unpublished set of talks made during the winter 1986, at University Paris 7.

Schank R. C. (1987). Explanation patterns: Understanding mechanically and creatively. Ablex.

Shortliffe E. H. (1986). Computer-based medical consultations: MYCIN. New York: Elsevier.

de Siqueira J.L. & Puget J.-F. (1988). Explanation-based generalization of failures, *Proc. ECAI-88*. Pitman, 339-344.

Waldinger R., (1977). Achieving several goals simultaneously. In: E. Elcock and D. Michie (Eds.). *Machine Intelligence, 8*. London: Ellis Horwood. A comprehensive presentation can also be found in: Nilsson, N.J. Principles of artificial intelligence. Palo Alto: Tioga, (section 7.4, 287-297).

CONNECTIONISM IN PERSPECTIVE
R. Pfeifer, Z. Schreter, F. Fogelman-Soulié, L. Steels (Eds.)
Elsevier Science Publishers B.V. (North-Holland), 1989

The Dynamics of Evolution and Learning — Towards Genetic Neural Networks

H. Mühlenbein & J. Kindermann
German National Research Center for Computer Science
Postfach 1240, D-5205 St. Augustin 1

Abstract—*In this paper we outline a minimal model for learning of a system in a changing environment. The model consists of a genotype which expresses itself as a phenotype. We discuss the power of "genotype learning" and "phenotype learning" as well as using both methods together in a system. The power of genotype learning will be shown with our parallel genetic algorithm. This algorithm is the fastest heuristic for solving big combinatorial optimization problems. It shows a superlinear speedup with parallel processors. Genotype learning and phenotype learning will be discussed with the example of a famous game – the iterated prisoner's dilemma. The interaction of evolution and learning is discussed with an architecture which combines genetics with neural networks. This architecture is called Pandemonium. It is based on evolutionary epistomology.*

Keywords—Parallel genetic algorithm, genetic neural networks, evolution, prisoners dilemma

1 INTRODUCTION

Neural networks are proposed for at least two, may be opposing reasons - as a model to explain how part of the brain works and as a new paradigm for parallel processing. In this paper we focus on the second, the engineering approach. This gives us freedom to discuss neural networks from a performance point of view. Our method is top down compared to the usual bottom up approach in neural networks. It is based on evolutionary principles.

In (Mühlenbein, 1988) we have outlined a minimal model for learning of a system in a changing environment. The goal of the system is to maximize a measure of success in the long-term. In order to achieve the long-term goal, the system has to change on at least two time scales.

On the fast time scale, each system adapts to a given environment. On the slow time scale an ensemble of such systems adapt to changes in the environment. The environment employs selection on the ensemble. The poor performing systems are eliminated and the rest creates new systems, which are slightly different.

In biological terms our model consists of genotypes which express themselves as phenotypes which act in an environment.

In this paper we discuss within this model the questions

- What is the power of "genotype learning" ?
- What is the power of "phenotype learning" ?
- What is the power of using both methods together ?

The main emphasis we will put on the first question. There are two reasons for this. First, in our proposed top down approach we have to start with genotype learning. Second, we have very successfully applied genotype learning to difficult optimization problems.

The outline of the paper is as follows. In chapter 2 we argue that learning is inevitably connected to a change in the behavior of the observed system. We state some facts about genotype (inherited) and phenotype (learned) behavior. In chapter 3, experiments with genetic artificial neural networks (GANN's) are discussed. The central problem to be solved is: How do the genes specify the neural network ? In chapter 4 we return to our top down approach. We present models describing the dynamics of genotype - phenotype evolution. These models have been proposed in theoretical biology. They are the foundation for the evolutionary algorithms presented in chapter 5.

In chapter 6 we present our parallel genetic algorithm. We demonstrate the power of this algorithm by giving results for a combinatorial optimization problem. The algorithm has found one of the best solutions for a big traveling salesman problem. It has a superlinear speedup on multiprocessor systems. In chapter 7 we compare genotype learning with phenotype learning. Our example is the iterated prisoner's dilemma. In chapter 8 we sketch Pandemonium II. With Pandemonium II we want to investigate our third question. Pandemonium II consists of vehicles which are simulated on a parallel processor. The vehicles have higher level genes for strategies and neural networks for learning.

2 LEARNING AND INHERITANCE

Learning can be defined as any change in the knowledge structure of a system that allows it to behave differently on later repetitions of some given type of task. Learning occurs therefore at least on two levels — a macroscopic one where the behavior of the system can be observed, and a microscopic one where the internal structure of the system is modified. The problem is how to correlate these two!

Many results are now available on the macroscopic level, explaining the behavior of higher animals. It is now recognized that inheritance and learning are both fundamental in determining the behavior. The contributions of these elements are inextricably intertwined in most behavior patterns. Inheritance is now regarded as determining the limits within which a particular behavior can be modified, while learning of the individual determines, within these limits, the precise character of the behavior pattern.

In some cases the limits imposed by inheritance leave no room for modification by experience, while in other cases the inherited limits may be so wide that learning plays a major part in determining behavior. It is outside the scope of this paper, to discuss this topic in greater detail — the most thorough study has been done by Lorenz (1973). We only want to note that the microscopic mechanism for "coding" inherited or learned behavior is believed to be the same.

Regardless of debates about general definitions, researchers agree that neuronal activity is fundamental for this mechanism. It induces transient and permanent changes at many different levels within the nervous system. One can view these levels as a hierarchy of increasing complexity. At the most basic level, molecular changes occur within single neurons. Next there is communication among neurons at synapses. Higher still are circuits of interconnected neurons. And at the top is activity within whole assemblies of interconnected neurons, which might control patterns of behavior (see figure 1). Much data is

```
          neuron
     neuron + synapses
    circuits of neurons
   assemblies of neurons
   ---------------------
   ---------------------
         behavior
  innate          learned
```

Figure 1: Relation between microstructure (nervous system) and macrostructure

available for the first two levels, but up till now it was impossible to correlate this data with changes in the higher levels and with changes in the behavior.

We believe that this bottom - up approach should be complemented by a **'historical-evolutionary' approach**. In this approach we

- try to understand the formation of the network during individual development
- try to understand the genetic evolution of a species of networks within generations.

The answers to these questions need less information than to understand the existing nervous system by analyzing its different parts. In numbers: Less than 250.000 genes code our nervous system which has more than 10^{14} elements. Furthermore, evolution has invented the nervous system. We conjecture that it is impossible to understand nervous systems without understanding their construction and evolution.

We investigate this problem with genetic artificial neural networks (ANN). The minimal framework is as follows: Genetic ANN's are controlled by "genes" and change in a population according to evolutionary principles.

3 GENES AND NEURAL NETWORKS

Genetic neural networks consist of the following components

- genes that specify classes of networks
- a procedure for constructing a phenotype (a set of networks) from the genotype
- a fitness function that measures how well a phenotype performs
- a nondeterministic procedure for mutating a genotype

These components are described more formally in the next chapter. Here we discuss the problem: How do genes construct the network? At first we look at the nervous system of mammals.

It appears impossible that the genes specify the exact structure of the nervous system; rather it is much likely that they determine patterns of growth more or less open to the modifying effects of experience. To require that individual links are coded for in the genes would mean that the genetic code is in the size of the network!

What is the best architecture for an intelligent nervous system?

In a first approximation, one may assume that neural networks are analogous to computers constructed by wiring up many simple units. There are two conflicting points of view concerning the higher level functions of the networks

- higher functions are emergent properties of flat highly connected networks
- higher functions result from specific substructures and connections genetically determined

A discussion of this problem can be found in (Gierer, 1988) from a biological point of view.

This problem has been recently investigated also with ANN's by Dolan (Dolan & Dyer, 1987). He states: "By starting with an architecture that meets the minimum requirements for performance in a domain, mutation and selection are the evolutionary forces which can yield the most functional structure.

Mutation at the link level (of the network) is too slow to be operated on an evolutionary time scale. It is better to assume a basic level of architectural organization and then mutate at that level".

Mutation on this level needs genes that code higher structures. It is interesting to note that Lorenz (1973) has argued in the same direction for the evolution of higher animals. Evolution at a particular time works in his opinion with a hierarchy of subsystems which have been invented by the evolution before.

Dolan investigates his postulate with a simulation experiment. He obtains the following result.

The most fit functional network structure is dependent on the environment. In a fixed environment there is a clear disadvantage for large flat network organizations. Using a severe selection process would weed these phenotypes out of the gene pool. However, if the environment were to change radically, then these architectures would have an advantage because they are capable of mutating quickly into large hierarchical architectures. Furthermore, in the model of Dolan, flat architectures have a higher band-width for the number of patterns they can learn.

A simpler model has been investigated by Merril and Port (Merril & Port, 1988). In their model the genes code an architecture which is in the middle between a flat and a structured network. Each node of their network is assigned three real parameters which control its behavior in a link decision procedure. They call their architecture "fractally configured networks".

In this architecture the number of genes is still proportional to the number of nodes. To reduce the number of genes, the network therefore was divided up into cliques. The genes now code the cliques, the parameters of individual nodes in a clique are computed by interpolation.

These investigations are first steps in looking for the minimal requirements that evolution of artificial neural networks can take place. We freely admit that nobody knows how genes code the nervous system of living beings. In addition, we have only some preliminary ideas how genes could code the connection of artificial neural networks. We therefore propose as a first step genetic neural networks, where the genes do not code links of a network but higher level functions, like behavioral strategies and the functional character of the neural networks of the individuals.

This top-down approach has to be contrasted to the bottom-up approach formulated by Grossberg (1982, pp. 69) "This is the method of minimal anatomies. Giving specific psychological postulates, we derive the minimal network of embedding field type that realizes these postulates ... In this way, a hierarchy of networks is derived, corresponding to ever more sophisticated postulates".

I believe that such a hierarchy cannot be built without taking genetic and developmental factors into account. There is general agreement that genetics, environment and learning determines the construction and the higher level functions of the nervous system. All three elements work by selection based on sophisticated trial and error. Extensive information processing capabilities of neural networks are possible with a very low contribution of genetically determined network characteristics, if time and memory would be unlimited resources for the individual. However, within the real lifespan of the individual organism efficient results are not obtained by the minimal requirements for information processing, but by optimizing the relative contributions of the above three modes of learning

- genotype learning
- learning during development
- phenotype learning

Genetically specified a priori conditions for the neural network taking into account features which vary rarely provides the organism with a clear head start compared with a "tabula rasa" neural network (Gierer, 1988). We will describe an artificial system which combines the above three modes of learning in chapter 8. The system is called Pandemonium II. In order to understand this system, we will discuss the complex interaction between genotype and phenotype more formally in the next chapters. We will abstract from the internal organization of the phenotype. A phenotype is characterized just by a set of traits or phenes.

4 FORMALIZATION OF THE EVOLUTIONARY STRATEGY

Evolution works with populations of individuals. We assume that the individuals are characterized by n genes (denoted by $g_1, \ldots, g_n$) and m traits (phenes, denoted by $f_1, \ldots f_m$). The genes define the genotype g and the phenes the phenotype p.

To my knowledge, Waddington (1974) was the first to stress the importance of the relationship between genotype and phenotype. "The population will inhibit a heterogeneous environment. We have a multidimensional space of 'epigenetic environments'. The phenotype is the product of the genotype and the environment. The phenotype is then acted on by a heterogeneous 'selective environment'! Note that this multidimensional selective environment is not the same as the epigenetic environment space ... Now, fitness is the 'product' of the phenotype space and the selective environment space. Usually it is taken as one-dimensional, a simple matter of 'how many offspring are contributed to the next generation!"

We will try to formalize this model which can be called a **system theory of evolution**. Figure 2 shows this relationship. The genes define the genotype space GS, the phenes the

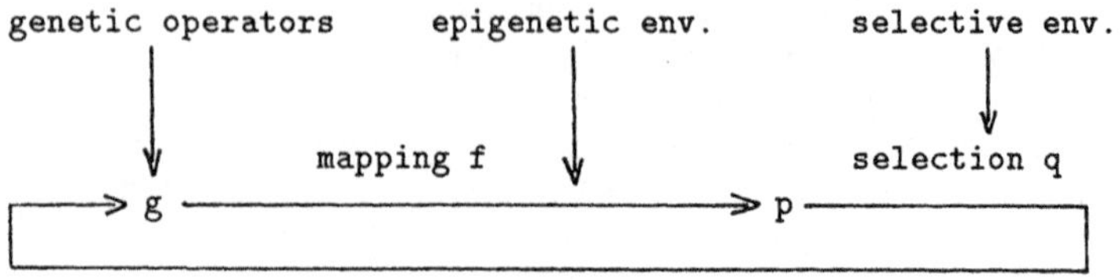

Figure 2: Major components of evolution

phenotypes space PS.

$$GS = \{g = (a_1, \ldots, a_n), a_i \in A_i\} \tag{1}$$

$$PS = \{p = (p_1, \ldots, p_m), p_i \in I\!R\} \tag{2}$$

The possible values of gene g_i are called alleles. In Mendelian genetics each gene is assumed to have a finite number of alleles.

Further we are given a set of epigenetic environments.

$$EP = \{EP_1, \ldots, EP_k\}$$

and a mapping function $f : GS \times EP \rightarrow PS$

$$p = f(g, EP) \tag{3}$$

The mapping function models the fact, that a phenotype develops by an interaction of the genes and the environment. The mapping process is highly nonlinear. The ultimate phenotypic characters bear anything but a simple one-to-one relationship to the original gene products. This interaction is shown in figure 3.

Last, we need a quality function q which gives the quality of a phenotype in a particular selective environment ES_i

$$q(p, ES_i, t) \rightarrow I\!R^+ \tag{4}$$

The quality defines the fitness and is used for Darwinian selection.

Research so far has concentrated on three special cases of the general model

- Mendelian genetics
- genetic ecology
- evolutionary games

In Mendelian genetics, the genotype is modeled in detail, whereas phenotype and environment are almost neglected. In genetic ecology the opposite is true. Evolutionary game theory is a model derived from sociobiology. Here the genes express themselves as strategies.

Each of the models leads to nonlinear dynamic systems. An investigation of the general model seems to be outside the scope of mathematical analysis. We will discuss the three submodels in greater detail.

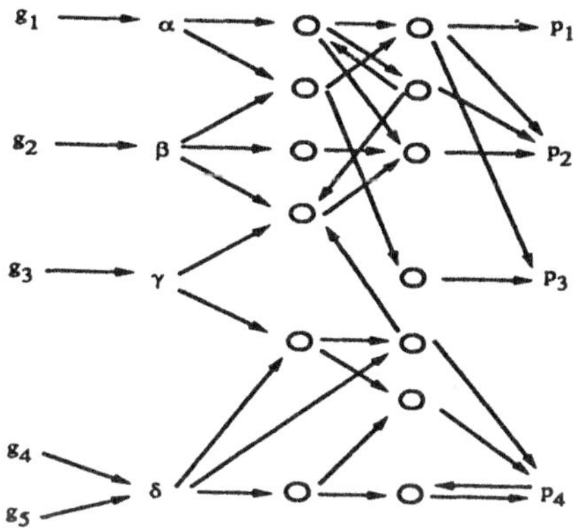

Figure 3: Gene-phene interaction (without environmental factors)

4.1 The selection model of Mendelian genetics

For simplicity we consider just one gene with n alleles $a_1, \ldots, a_n$.

A diploid genotype is characterized by a tuple (a_i, a_j). We define $p_{i,j}$ as the frequency of the genotype (a_i, a_j) in the total population. We equate genotype with phenotype. The quality function assigns each phenotype a value

$$q(a_i, a_j)_i = q_{i,j}$$

$q_{i,j}$ is interpreted as birthrate minus deathrate. Let $p'_{i,j}$ be the frequency of phenotype (a_i, a_j) in the next generation. Darwinian selection then adjusts the distribution of the phenotypes according to the **selection equation**

$$p'_{i,j} = p_{i,j} \frac{q_{i,j}}{\overline{Q}} \tag{5}$$

$$\overline{Q} = \sum_{i,j} q_{i,j} p_{i,j} \tag{6}$$

$\overline{Q}$ is the average fitness of the population. Let p_i be the frequency of allele a_i in the population. If we assume the Hardy-Weinberg equation

$$p_{i,j} = p_i p_j$$

then we obtain from (5) a selection equation in GS

$$p'_i = p_i Q_i / \overline{Q} \tag{7}$$

$$Q_i = \sum_j q_{i,j} p_j \tag{8}$$

The discrete selection equation can be approximated by a continuous equation

$$\frac{dp_i}{dt} = p_i (Q_i - \overline{Q}) / \overline{Q} \tag{9}$$

The flows and stationary points of this equation are identical to those of the replicator equation (if $q_{i,j} = q_{j,i}$)

$$\frac{dp_i}{dt} = p_i(Q_i - \overline{Q}) \tag{10}$$

This equation has been investigated in detail by Hofbauer and Sigmund (1984). It is easily shown that

$$\frac{d\overline{Q}}{dt} = 2\left(E\left(Q^2\right) - \overline{Q}^2\right) = 2Var(Q) \geq 0 \tag{11}$$

This result is called Fisher's fundamental theorem. It states that the mean fitness increases proportional to the variance of the fitness.

So far mainly the continuous selection equation has been analyzed. Losert and Akin (1983) have investigated discrete versus continuous time in the dynamics. Only with the symmetry assumption there is an agreement between both dynamics! The relation between discrete versus continuous time dynamics has to be investigated further — as well for genotype learning as for neural networks. Our understanding is that the continuous time is an approximation of the discrete time and not vice versa!

The above model does not incorporate 'genetic' operators. It is assumed that every genotype is expressed in the population and evaluated as a phenotype. This is highly unrealistic. In nature, only a fraction of all possible genotypes are realized. It is the task of the genetic operators to explore the genotype space with a relatively small number of individuals. These operators are the source of genetic variability in a population. The most important operators are mutation and recombination. Figure 4 shows haploid recombination, where the genes of two parents mix Recombination works if genes are connected

```
o o o o o o o o                           o o x x o o o o
                     haploid              o x x o o x x o
                     recombination                .
x x x x x x x x                                   .
```

Figure 4: Haploid recombination

on a string (chromosome). What are the combined effects of selection and recombination on a population? This question has been analyzed with a simple model. We consider two genes, each of which has two alleles. We then have four genotypes

$$s_1 = A_1B_1 \qquad s_2 = A_1B_2 \qquad s_3 = A_2B_1 \qquad s_4 = A_2B_2$$

Let x_i be the frequency of gene string s_i in the population, $0 \leq r \leq 1$ be the probability of a recombination. We then obtain the following equation for the evolution of frequencies (see (Hofbauer & Sigmund, 1984)).

$$x_i' = (x_iQ_i - brD)/\overline{Q} \qquad i = 1,4 \tag{12}$$

$$x_i' = (x_iQ_i + brD)/\overline{Q} \qquad i = 2,3 \tag{13}$$

$$D = x_1x_4 - x_2x_3 \tag{14}$$

The above equation models the selection process with genetic recombination. The constant b is not relevant for our discussion. With $r = 0$, we obtain the selection equation 7. If there is no selection, i.e. $Q_i = \overline{Q}$, we get for the next generation

$$D' = (1 - r)D$$

With $r > 0$ the frequencies converge to $D = 0$. D is a measure for the coupling of the genes, because

$$D = x_1 - (x_1 + x_3)(x_1 + x_2)$$

can be written as follows

$$D = prob(A_1 B_1) - prob(B_1) prob(A_1)$$

$D = 0$ is called the equilibrum of the coupling of the genes. The dynamics of equations (12) and (13) has been investigated by Akin (1979). It can be shown that the mean fitness $\overline{Q}$ does not necessarily increase along the trajectories.

It is still an open question, whether there exists another "fitness function" which is a Lyapunov function of (12) and (13), i.e. is minimized by (12) and (13).

This example shows that the interaction of two forces (selection and recombination) leads already to very complicated problems for the mathematical analysis.

The extension of the above model to n genes is mathematically difficult (see (Akin, 1979)). The model is biologically unrealistic because a fixed recombination rate between all the possible genotypes is assumed and a simple fitness function is used.

Genetic recombination is now in the center of biological discussion. Why are almost all higher animals using recombination ? Recombination is a constant 'stirring' of the gene pool, resulting in a greater diversity among the offsprings of an individual. But recombination needs two sexes, a costly process in terms of the energy expended in the synthesis of sex organs, in the finding of a mate and frequently also in the care for the young.

Asexual reproduction, on the other hand, allows for more rapid production of offsprings and the advantages of this proliferation may outweight the advantages of recombination in each generation.

The big question therefore is: which evolution method is faster in adapting to changes in an environment — recombination with a small number of offsprings, or asexual reproduction with point mutation and a large number of offsprings?

It should be noted that the above question is also central to evolutionary algorithms which are used for optimization problems. This will be discussed in chapter 5.

4.2 Models in ecological genetics

In these models it is assumed that a phene is inherited by the action of a large number of gene loci. At each locus, two alleles segregate, one of which tends to increase, the other to decrease the value of the phene.

The phenotypic value of an individual is expressed as follows

$$P_{i,j} = \mu + G_i + E_{i,j} + (GE)_{i,j} \tag{15}$$

μ is the general mean of the phene, G_i is the effect of the i-th genotype, $E_{i,j}$ is the effect of the environment on the j-th individual with genotype i. GE is the genotype×environment interaction.

For the mathematical analysis normal distributions of the different components are assumed. One can easily show that the complex relation of the components prevent the direct access of the population to some "optimum phenotype". This relationship constrains the selection. Important constraints are the absence of genetic variation, the correlation of genes and nonlinear mappings from genotype to phenotype. It is outside the scope of this paper to specify some of the proposed models mathematically (see (Loeschke, 1987) for a recent survey).

An interesting investigation by computer simulation has been done by Kerszberg (1988). In his model genotype and phenotype are represented as bit strings. He considers the effects of several nonlinear mapping functions. With nonlinear mapping functions different genotypes can be mapped into the same or very similar phenotype. This effect is called canalization. Canalization will be discussed in section 6.1.

4.3 Models in evolutionary game theory

In these models, each individual can adapt a number N of strategies (or genes). Let be p_i the frequency of individuals adapting strategy i in successive generations.

Let $E_{i,j}$ be the payoff to an individual adapting strategy i against an opponent adapting strategy j. (We may equate strategy i with a gene, coding it). The quality of individuals adapting strategy i is

$$Q_i = \sum_j p_j E(i,j)$$

The mean fitness of the population is

$$\overline{Q} = \sum_i p_i Q_i$$

It is supposed that individuals reproduce their kind asexually, in numbers proportional to their fitness. This can be described by the familiar selection equation (7)

$$p_i' = p_i \frac{Q_i}{\overline{Q}} \tag{16}$$

In evolutionary game theory the attractors of the dynamics are looked for. These attractors are called evolutionarily stable strategies (ESS). ESS are characterized by $Q_i = Q_j$ for $p_i, p_j \neq 0$ (see (Maynard Smith, 1982)).

The above model can be extended, incorporating for instance a separation between phenotype and genotype.

5 EVOLUTIONARY ALGORITHMS

In evolutionary algorithms the models of chapter 4 are applied to artificial problems. We are given an optimization problem and try to find a population of artificial individuals converging to the optimum. The algorithms developed so far can be divided into three classes

- algorithms using differential equations
- algorithms using simple mutation/selection dynamics; 'Darwinian algorithms'
- algorithms incorporating complex genetic operators; 'genetic algorithms'

The first class is based on the replicator equation (10). Applications are given in (Mühlenbein, Gorges-Schleuter, & Kramer, 1988). The second class has been developed by Rechenberg (1986) and Schwefel (1981) and (1987). These algorithms have been mainly used for the optimization of continuous functions. They are based on quantitative genetics.

Genetic algorithms have been proposed by Holland (1975). They are based on Mendelian genetics.

We will discuss the last two classes in more detail.

5.1 Darwinian algorithms

The different modes of the Darwinian algorithms can be described as follows (Rechenberg, 1986)

$$(\mu/\rho, \lambda) \qquad (\mu/\rho + \lambda) \tag{17}$$

μ is the number of parents of a generation, λ the number of children. The integer ρ is referred to as the "mixing" number. If two parents mix their genes, we have $\rho = 2$.

The selection is done in the following way: Only the μ best of the individuals are allowed to produce offsprings. A comma indicates that parents are not included in the selection, a plus that parents are included.

An important component of the algorithm is the fact, that the range of mutations (the 'stepsize') is not fixed, but inherited. It will be adapted by the evolution process itself.

We will explain the $(1, \lambda)$ strategy in greater detail. We are looking for

$$x^* = \max_{x \in B} Q(x) \qquad \text{where } B \subset I\!R^n \tag{18}$$

Evolutionary algorithm

STEP 0: Create initial population

STEP 1: Create offsprings by mutation

$$\begin{aligned} s'_1 &= s g_1 \\ x'_1 &= x + s'_1 Z_1 \\ &\vdots \\ s'_\lambda &= s g_\lambda \\ x'_\lambda &= x + s'_\lambda Z_\lambda \end{aligned}$$

STEP 3: Selection

$$Q(x) = \max_{1 \le i \le \lambda} \{Q(x')\}$$

Continue with step 1.

In this algorithm the random vectors Z_i have normally distributed components, the g_is are obtained from log-normally distributed numbers. The algorithm therefore creates λ offsprings in the neighborhood of the parent. The neighborhood is inherited and adapted by the evolution process. In the language of chapter three: Each individual has $(n + 1)$ genes, where the first gene controls the other.

The model can be extended to $2n$ genes, where the range of mutation is controlled individually for each direction in the n-dimensional space. Another extension, the evolution of linear correlations between the mutations is discussed in (Schwefel, 1987). It is interesting to note that Rechenberg's idea of adaptation of the mutation range is now discussed in biology (Wagner, 1985).

5.2 Genetic algorithms

Genetic algorithms are based on the discrete Mendelian genetic model. A genetic algorithm consists of five components

- a chromosomal representation of solutions to the given problem
- an initial population of solutions
- a quality function that plays the role of the environment
- a selection procedure giving the individuals which may produce offsprings
- a genetic operator e.g. mutations, recombination
- parameters that control the algorithms itself (e.g. probability of mutations)

A recent survey of genetic algorithms and their applications can be found in (Davis, 1987).

In this paper we only want to mention some of the problems connected with the selection procedure.

In classical genetic algorithms, selection is done according to the natural selection equation (7).

One of the major problems of (7) is the scaling of the quality function: If the difference of the qualities of very good individuals and very poor ones is small, the selection will take many generations before descendants of the good individuals outnumber those of the poor ones in the population. This can easily be shown. Let $p_{i,n}$ denote the frequency of phenotype i in the n-th generation. Equation 7 then gives

$$\frac{p_{i,n}}{p_{j,n}} = \frac{p_{i,0}}{p_{j,0}} \left(\frac{Q_i}{Q_j}\right)^n \tag{19}$$

If $Q_i < Q_j$, then we have $p_i \to 0$, where the speed of convergence depends on Q_i/Q_j.

The second problem is the performance on multi-modal fitness functions with many local minima. Natural selection tends to eventually cluster all of its individuals about one local maxima. This is the effect of the finite size of the population. Goldberg (Goldberg & Richardson, 1987) has therefore suggested to modify the quality function for the selection process. The new selection quality is defined as old quality divided by the number of individuals in some neighborhood in phenotype space PS. With this selection procedure, individuals are spread apart in PS.

The third problem we see is more fundamental. The natural selection equation depends on the global average of the fitness of the population. Who is calculating this average in nature?

Selection in nature is done locally in the environment the individuals are living. The natural selection equation abstracts from the environment. This abstraction leads to the danger of a tautology. Natural selection is responsible for 'survival of the fittest', but the fittest are defined as the ones which survive. We will discuss a new selection procedure which takes the environment factor into account in more detail in chapter 6.

6 PARALLEL GENETIC ALGORITHM FOR COMBINATORIAL OPTIMIZATION

Parallel genetic algorithms have been designed to run effectively on parallel computers. Each individual of a population is simulated on a separate processor and therefore acts in parallel to other individuals. Parallel genetic algorithms have been applied very successfully to a number of combinatorial problems (see (Mühlenbein, Gorges-Schleuter, & Kramer, 1987; Muhlenbein, Gorges-Schleuter, & Kramer, 1988) for first applications).

The basic algorithm can be described as follows

Parallel Genetic Algorithm

GE1: Give the problem to N individuals with different starting configurations

GE2: Each individual computes a local maximum

GE3: Selection — choose a partner for mating in the 'neighborhood'

GE4: Create new offspring with recombination and mutation

continue with GE2

The two major differences to classical genetic algorithms are

- selection is done locally in a neighborhood
- each individual (phenotype) does hill climbing

Parallel genetic algorithms therefore use genotype learning and phenotype learning. Furthermore, individuals are living in an environment. Mating and selection is done in this environment, e.g. a 2-D grid. The neighborhood of an individual is not connected to a metric in genotype or phenotype space. Local hill climbing of the phenotype has the following effect. Recombination is now done in the space of genotypes representing a local fitness maxima. In this space there is a strong correlation between the different parts of the genotypes. It can be shown that recombination is especially efficient in such spaces (Mühlenbein, Gorges-Schleuter, & Kramer, 1988).

Parallel genetic algorithms are a major departure from genetic algorithms. In genetic algorithms individuals are passive. They are being acted on. Evolution is seen as selection of 'optimal behavior'. In contrast parallel genetic algorithms are driven from within. Our simulations suggest that the mechanism for generating and maintaining variability will be an important part of the evolutionary process. Parallel genetic algorithms lead to much greater diversity than is possible with the usual genetic algorithms. Evolution is driven by self-organizing forces within the system itself!

Parallel genetic algorithms confirm research in biology where it is conjectured that evolution with small isolated groups of individuals and migration is faster than in large populations with random mating. We will demonstrate this with a specific optimization problem.

6.1 A parallel genetic algorithm for the Travelling Salesman Problem

The Travelling Salesman Problem (TSP) is defined as follows: given a set of n cities, find the shortest tour that visits each city exactly once. The TSP is NP-hard and therefore probably does not have any polynomial time algorithmic solution. The TSP is the most important benchmark problem for testing new heuristics in combinatorial optimization. It has been recently attacked by simulated annealing, simulated tunneling, neural networks, replicator equation and genetic algorithms. It is outside the scope of this paper to discuss the different heuristics in more detail. Our parallel genetic algorithm outperformed the other algorithms in a competition for far. In this algorithm, the chromosomal representation is simple

$$\text{chromosome} = \text{tour}$$

"Gene" g_i on position i of the chromosome has the alleles $city_1, \ldots, city_n$. A phenotype $p = (p_1, \ldots, p_n)$ is just the string represented by the chromosome. The quality of p is defined as

$$q(p) = \sum_i d(p_{i+1}, p_i) \tag{20}$$

where d is the distance between two cities.

Only a small fraction of all chromosomes give a valid phenotype. A valid phenotype is characterized by the constraint that each city occurs exactly once on the chromosome.

The mapping function genotype-phenotype therefore has a canalization effect.

After an offspring has been created, it does local hill climbing. This is achieved by a new heuristic which takes only $\mathcal{O}(n)$ time.

New offsprings are created with recombination and mutation. A simple recombination between two chromosomes will produce an invalid tour most of the time. Our recombination operator avoids this. It is similar to the PMX crossover operator from Goldberg and Lingle. A discussion of crossover operators for the TSP can be found in (Oliver, Smith, & Holland, 1987).

An example is shown in figure 5. The selection is done as follows. Each individual has a neighborhood consisting of other individuals. After having done hill climbing, it chooses locally a partner for mating in this neighborhood. The neighborhood is connected to the topology of the multiprocessor used. We have made experiments with different neighborhoods.

The neighborhood influences the way selection is done. An in depth discussion of the art of selection is outside the scope of this paper. A good introduction into this topic can be found in Falconer's book (Falconer, 1981). He discusses selection from the breeders point of view.

The next figures show results obtained with a MEGAFRAME SUPERCLUSTER (Kübler, 1988). A SUPERCLUSTER consists of 64 transputers. We consider a TSP with 532 cities.

```
A B C D E F                          b B C D f e      invalid
             haploid
             Recombination
b c d a f e                          a B C D f e      valid
```

Figure 5: Recombination in the TSP

This TSP has been defined by Padberg (Padberg & Rinaldi, 1987). The optimal tour length is 27686. Figure 6 shows a solution, which we have computed. The tour length obtained (27702) is the best tour length which has been found by a heuristic!

Figure 6: Tour obtained by parallel genetic algorithm

Table 1 shows the influence of the population size on the speed of convergence. In this table the real time needed to achieve a tour length of 5200 for Grotschel's problem with 442 cities (Muhlenbein, Gorges-Schleuter, & Kramer, 1988) is given. The table shows a

processor	time
16	5000
32	1500
64	600

Table 1: Time needed for path length of 5200

remarkable "superlinear" speedup of the parallel genetic algorithm. The time needed to get the same quality of solution on a 64 processor system is not 1/4 but less than 1/8 of the time on a 16 processor system. The power of parallel genetic algorithms therefore shows up with parallel multiprocessors.

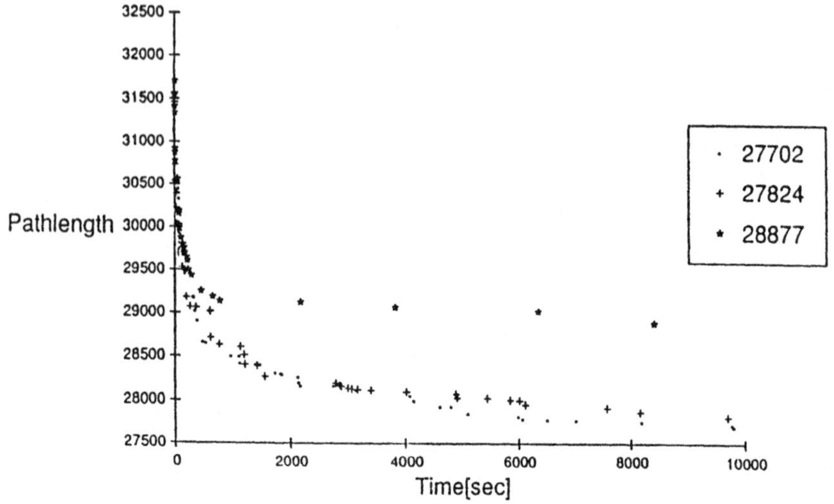

Figure 7: Progress for three different selection procedures

Figure 7 shows the influence of the selection procedure on the quality of the solution and the progress. We compare three neighborhoods. The first one is virtual and consists of the global best individual only, the second one consists of seven neighbors and the global best individual. In the third neighborhood we have the seven neighbors only. The quality of the solutions are $28877, 27824, 27702$.

The third selection procedure has always given the best results. This shows that we have to balance carefully in the selection procedure. There is an inherent tradeoff between exploitation and exploring, i.e. between exploiting what already works best and exploring possibilities that might eventually evolve into something even better.

7 GENOTYPE LEARNING AND PHENOTYPE LEARNING

Learning shapes behavior within generations, while genetic evolution operates between generations. The question now arises: Are both methods equally powerful? Can the efficiency of these methods be compared? The first question was addressed by Harley (Harley, 1981). He used the framework of evolutionary game theory to show that genotype learning and phenotype learning by a certain learning rule can lead to the same equilibrium. We believe that the above questions need further research. Harley's learning rule cannot be applied because it does not specify how a newborn individual should start.

We investigated the above problem with an specific example, the iterated prisoners dilemma. This game is played by a population where genes specify the strategies and learning is done by Darwinian selection. The second population uses only neural networks and reinforcement learning. We will describe both populations in more detail.

7.1 Genotype learning for the Iterated Prisoner's Dilemma

The Prisoner's Dilemma is very popular in researching the evolution of cooperation. In this game, two individuals can either cooperate or defect. Defection yields a higher payoff than cooperation. But if both players defect, both do worse than if both had cooperated. A typical payoff matrix is shown in figure 8. Axelrod (1987).investigated the set of strategies

	C	D
C	(R,R)	(S,T)
D	(T,S)	(P,P)

Figure 8: Payoff matrix ($T > R > P > S$, e.g.,$T = 5, R = 3, P = 1, S = 0$)

that are deterministic and use the payoffs of the three previous moves to make a choice in the current move. The payoffs may have four different values, so we have $4 \times 4 \times 4 = 64$ different possibilities. Axelrod's evolutionary game consists of a population of individuals where each individual is defined by a set of 64 strategies. These strategies can be seen as being coded by 64 genes. Each gene has only two alleles, so we have 2^{64} different genotypes.

The program simulating the evolution of this population works now like a genetic algorithm discussed in 5.2.

The most interesting aspect of this application is the fact that the fitness of an individual cannot be specified in a closed mathematical form. The fitness of the phenotype is the result of the payoffs received in playing against other individuals. Two cases can be distinguished. In the static case, our phenotypes play against a fixed set of representative strategies. In the dynamic case, the individuals play against each other.

In the latter case, adaptation must be done in the face of a moving target. Moreover, the selection process is frequency dependent, which means that the effectiveness of a strategy depends upon which strategies are being used by the other members of the population. Axelrod (1987) states: "The evolving social environment first led to a pattern of decreased cooperation and decreased effectiveness, followed by a complete reversal." As individuals who cooperate with each other do well, they spread in the population, resulting in more and more cooperation.

We have to mention that the behavior of the above phenotype is totally inherited. The phenotype has no provision for learning. The next section will describe the opposite — individuals use only phenotype learning for this game.

7.2 Phenotype learning for the prisoners dilemma

For comparison we use the same model as Axelrod. A strategy is defined as a mapping of the results of the last three moves (the 'history') to 0,1. Here, 0 means "defect" and 1 means "cooperate". Each phenotype thus has a strategy which uses 64 components.

The evaluation of strategies is done by a multilayer feedforward network. Each network-"player" has an "action" network which produces the decision for defect or cooperation and an "evaluation" network which judges on the performance of the player in the preceding moves. Figure 9 shows the components of the simulation system. Each player receives an input and a reinforcement signal from the environment. The reinforcement signal indicates how well the performance of the player has been in the past. It may depend

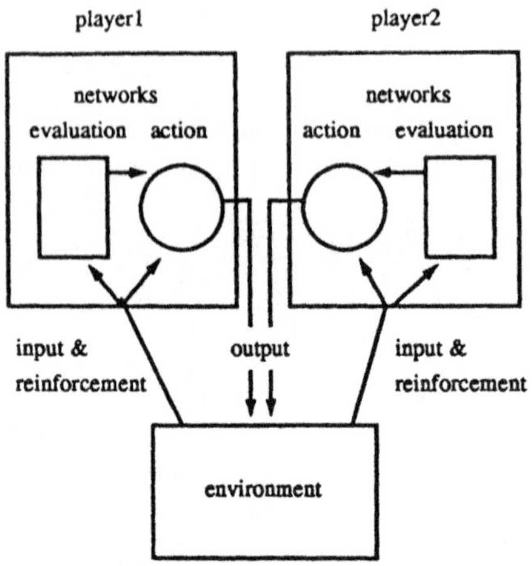

Figure 9: components of the simulation system

on more moves than the most recent one. The learning algorithm changes the weights according to the goal to obtain maximal reinforcement for future moves. The weights thus encode the reactions of the player on each of the 64 possible situations. This means that a set of network weights represents one strategy in terms of Axelrod.

Both the action network and the evaluation network have three layers. The input layer is connected to both the hidden and the output layer. There are 6 units in the input layer, 5 units in the hidden layer and one unit in the output layer. The network topology is shown in figure 10. In the network the activation values travel along the straight lines. An intersection of two lines represents a weighted connection between two units. The input of unit j in the hidden or output layer is the usual weighted sum

$$net_j = \sum_i w_{ij} x_i$$

with activation x_i of predecessor unit i and connection weights w_{ij}. The output function of units in the hidden layer is the well known sigmoidal function. In addition there are some special features of the action and evaluation network.

- Action network: the output unit has nondeterministic behavior. This is achieved by adding a random variable η to its netinput:

  $$net = \sum_i w_i x_i + \eta$$

  The output function of the output unit is

  $$g(net) = \left\{ \begin{array}{ll} 1 & \text{if } net > 0 \\ 0 & \text{otherwise} \end{array} \right\}$$

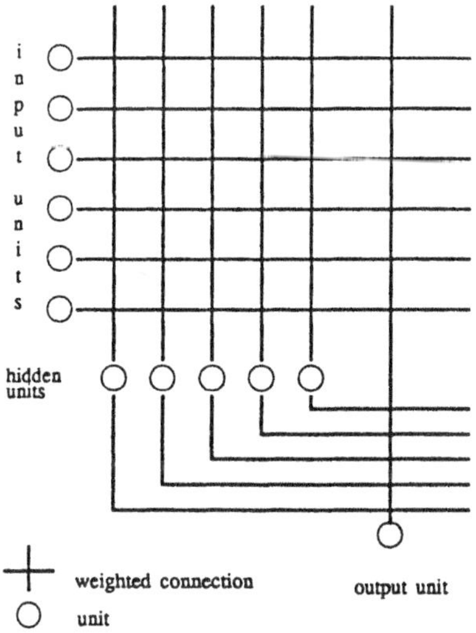

Figure 10: topology of the action and evaluation networks

- Evaluation network: the output function of the output unit is the identity.

  The learning algorithm needs a comparison between outputs of the evaluation network in two successive time steps. The functions of this network therefore have to be doubly time-indexed. For simplicity this is not shown in the formulas.

The coding scheme is shown in table 2. This defines 64 different possible input patterns. The network is capable to represent each of 2^{64} different strategies by mapping the 64

unit	denotes
1	own payoff for move $n-2$
2	opponent's payoff for move $n-2$
3	own payoff for move $n-1$
4	opponent's payoff for move $n-1$
5	own payoff for move n
6	opponent's payoff for move n

Table 2: input coding

different input patterns to $\{0, 1\}$, because it has internal units with variable **thresholds**. It is thus able to develop different internal representations for each of the input patterns. This means that the network is able to distinguish between all possible input patterns and therefore each of the 2^{64} strategies could be encoded in a special set of weights for the action network.

The learning algorithm is described in detail in (Kindermann & Muhlenbein, 1989). It uses a form of reinforcement learning, the Adaptive Heuristic Critic (AHC) algorithm (Anderson, 1986; Sutton, 1988) for adaptation. This algorithm does not need training examples like backpropagation (Werbos, 1974; Rumelhart, Hinton, & Williams). It only requires a scalar value, the reinforcement signal. This reinforcement signal is produced by the environment of the network as a reaction on its output.

The external reinforcement signal r for the nth move is computed from the current score of the player and the last three payoffs by the following formula:

$$r = \frac{\sum_{i=1}^{n} p_i}{n} + \frac{\sum_{j=n-2}^{n} p_j}{3} - \frac{\sum_{i=1}^{n} p_i}{n} * \frac{\sum_{j=n-2}^{n} p_j}{3} - \theta$$

where p_k is the payoff for move k and $0 < \theta < 1$. This formula takes into account both the overall performance of a player and his most recent payoffs. If at least one of these is high the reinforcement signal will be high.

7.3 Preliminary experiments

Several simulations with varying parameters were run starting with "dumb" networks. The nets were initially set to random weights from the interval $[-0.1, 0.1]$. The action networks therefore had nondeterministic output behavior. We performed simulations with two different operation modes.

- Mode 1: a network plays against a fixed strategy. We used constant-defect, constant-cooperation, mixed, and "tit-for-tat" strategies as test cases. The latter means that the opponent alway takes the decision which the network made in the preceding move.
- Mode 2: two networks play against each other.

In general the behavior of the networks was dependent on their internal parameters. They did not develop strategies with very distinct elements like those of Axelrod's simulations. Rather there always was the tendency to uniformly answer every input with either "defect" or "cooperate". Within these limits however the network behavior was reasonable. The networks responded with "defect" to the constant-defect strategy of mode 1 in every run of the simulations. In the other cases both "defect" and "cooperate" strategies were adopted, depending on the internal parameters. In mode 2 in most cases the stable "defect" attractor was reached by both networks. In some cases they both also stuck to cooperation. The cases where one of the networks was constantly winning (the "T/S" situation) turned out not to be stable. The loosing network always turned to defect quickly, moving the game to a stable situation of mutual defect.

Another interesting aspect is that the evaluation networks developed a distinct rating of those 64 possible combinations of preceding decisions which are represented by the input patterns. The rating resembles closely what humans would judge to be a good or poor performance. Two examples of such ratings are shown in figure 11. The inputs are drawn on the horizontal axis. The input patterns are ordered in a special way. They are sorted lexicographically, comparing them from left to right, i.e. input "PRR" comes in front of "PSR". This has the effect that there are subsets of inputs with a common **rightmost** letter. This letter is given in the figure for every such subset.

The first graph is generated from a network which played against another network and developed a strategy of constant defect. Patterns with high payoff in the most recent move are rated better. Clearly the network considers a defeat in the last move to be the worst thing.

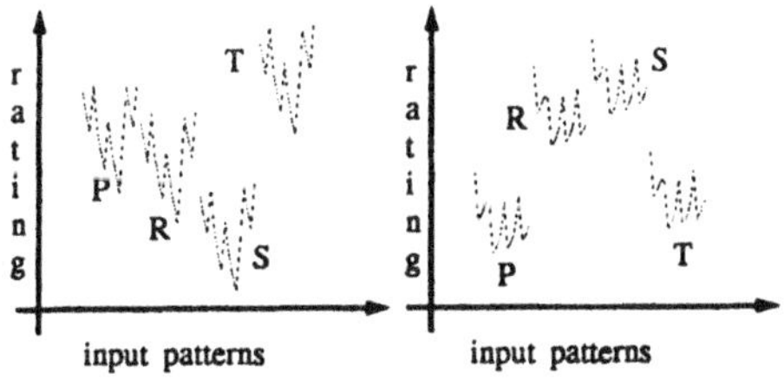

Figure 11: Ratings of the 64 input patterns by different evaluation networks

The second graph shows the rating of a network which played against a fixed, "friendly" strategy. The fixed strategy only defects after receiving an "S" (which means "T" for the network) in the last move or a combination of "SP" or "PP" in the two last moves. It cooperates in all other situations. This behavior in turn leads the network to generate a low rating for "P" "T" payoffs, because its opponent always will defect in the following move. Nevertheless the network stuck to constant defect because of a high value of the θ threshold in the reinforcement signal. In test runs with low θ the net turned to constant cooperation.

The two examples show that the rating depends on the strategy of the opponent.

A comparison of phenotype vs. genotype learning shows the following. Genotype learning explores the space of all strategies more broadly. Because of the recombination operator, it always tries new strategies.

Phenotype learning adapts strongly to the strategy the opponent is playing. It needs a carefully tuned set of a priori parameters.

We will now test phenotype learning with with a population of neural networks in a tournament.

So far our research confirms the statements of chapter 3 — genotype and phenotype learning seem to be equally powerful, but genetically specified a priori conditions give individuals a head start in solving complex problems.

We are also investigating the combination of genetic algorithms and reinforcement learning with a second task domain. This is described in the next chapter.

8 PANDEMONIUM REVISITED

We are now investigating the interaction of genetics and neural networks with an artificial vehicle. The vehicle exists in an environment consisting of other objects which are known as moving particles, obstacles and other vehicles. The first version of the vehicles has to solve two tasks

- The vehicle is required to move from point A to a point B in a busy environment. The vehicle must do this as quickly as possible without colliding with other objects
- The vehicle should try to find a way through a maze. With this task, the "intelligence" of the vehicle may be easily evaluated.

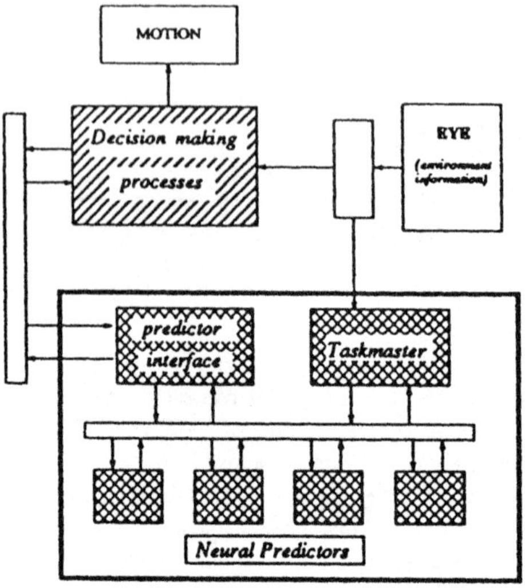

Figure 12: The general structure of Pandemonium II

The overall architecture is given in figure 12. The different neural nets predict the motion of a particle. They are feed-forward networks with one layer of hidden units. The job of the taskmaster is to be the supervisor of the neural nets. The task master compares the actual motions with the predicted motions. It delegates the motion to be predicted to the neural net which was the closest to the actual motion. This is done by backpropagation.

We hope that with this kind of selection the different neural nets will specialize on different types of perceptions, e.g. recognition of motion with constant velocity, constant acceleration, etc.

The predictor interface is responsible for the immediate response. It picks the prediction which has the greatest 'conviction'. Out of all the nets and out of all the output units (neurons), the one with the highest activation is chosen.

In the decision making process higher level strategies are employed. These are controlled by genes (like in evolutionary game theory).

In the first implementation, the low level mechanism of the genes (i.e. the neural nets doing the decision making process) are not modeled. At first we seek to isolate and confirm the usefulness of a set of strategies specific enough to be successful in reasonable situations, but also general enough to be successful in various types of environments and tasks. The idea is then gradually to replace each of the 'macro' components by lower-level modules, which may eventually be interpreted as neural networks.

Pandemonium II therefore combines the three most important learning strategies

- genotype learning (Genes)
- developmental learning (network competition)
- individual learning (network)

At this stage of development genes do not yet specify the structure of the neural networks.

This top-down approach has to be contrasted with the 'bottom-up' approach: a flat (totally connected, random weights, unspecified unit functions) net is taken. In this 'neural soup' one waits for intelligent behavior to evolve.

A detailed description of Pandemonium is contained in (Smieja, 1988).

The architecture of our vehicle resembles the Pandemonium proposed in 1959 by Selfridge (1959). His Pandemonium consists of a hierarchy of subdemons which shout to a decision demon. Selfridge states: "The second kind of adaptive change that we wish to incorporate into our pandemonium is subdemon selection. Subdemon selection generates new subdemons for trial and eliminates inefficient ones. This is really a natural selection on the subdemons. ... It is perfectly reasonable to conceive of this taking place on a broader scale. We might have a crowd of Pandemoniums and employ natural selection on the crowd of them".

Selfridge was not able to carry out bigger computer experiments with his architecture. We will do these experiments with our architecture.

The Pandemonium architectures have much in common with the neuronal group selection advocated by Edelman (1987). Both architectures employ selection on different levels. Edelman's artificial vehicle DARWIN III uses somatic selection so far. Somatic selection is done during the prenatal and postnatal development of each individual. Selection within a crowd of DARWIN III's is not yet being considered.

9 CONCLUSION

In the paper we have discussed the interaction genotype–phenotype. This interaction can only be investigated by computer simulations. In the future, more complex and realistic simulations are possible. These simulations will provide a different scientific perspective on biological evolution. Instead of having to rely on observations or mathematical models only, we will be able to approach the dynamics of evolution by experiments. We can begin to investigate alternative ways genetics might have evolved and see from these experiments which properties of our biological heritage are arbitrary and which not. The reconstruction of possible evolution paths from lower to higher complex systems will yield important results for our understanding of the living beings.

This research may at last unite the "hard" and the "soft" sciences. Instead of simply asking how a system "works", evolutionary modeling is concerned with the question how the system got to be as it is and how it may evolve in the future.

Our simulations confirm the "New Biology" which regards evolution as an optimistic force driven from within the living beings. This has to be contrasted to the view that evolution is just selection of the fittest in a hostile environment.

REFERENCES

Akin, E. (1979). The Geometry of Population Genetics. *Lecture Notes in Biomathematics.* New York: Springer-Verlag.

Anderson, W.A. (1986). *Learning and Problem Solving with Multilayer Networks.* Technical Report COINS Technical Report 86-50, Dept. of Computer and Information Science, Univ. of Massachusetts, Amherst (MA).

Axelrod, R. (1987). The Evolution of Strategies in the Iterated Prisoner's Dilemma. In Davis.

Davis (1987). *Genetic Algorithms and Simulated Annealing*. Los Altos: Morgan Kaufman Publ.

Dolan C.P., & Dyer M.G. (1987). Towards the Evolution of Symbols. In Grefenstette (pp. 123–130).

Edelman, G.M. (1987). *Neural Darwinism*. New York: Basic Books.

Falconer, D.S. (1981). *Introduction to Quantitative Genetics*. 2nd edn. London: Longman.

Gierer A. (1988) Spatial Organization and Genetic Information in Brain Development. In *Biol. Cybern.* **59** (pp. 13–21).

Goldberg P.E., & Richardson J. (1987). Genetic Algorithms with Sharing for Multimodal Function Optimization. In Grefenstette.

Grefenstette. (1987). Genetic Algorithms and their Applications. *Proceedings of the Second Conference on Genetic Algorithms and their Applications*. Hillsdale: Lawrence Erlbaum Associates.

Grossberg, S. (1982). *Studies of Mind and Brain*. D. Reidel Dordrecht.

Harley, C.B. (1981). Learning the evolutionary stable strategy. *J. Theor. Biol.* 89 (pp. 611–633).

Hofbauer J., & Sigmund K. (1984). *Evolutionstheorie und dynamische Systeme*. Berlin: Paul Parey.

Holland, J.H. (1975). Adaptation in Natural and Artificial Systems. Ann Arbor: University of Michigan Press.

Kerszberg, M. (1988). Developmental Canalization can Enhance Species Survival. Julich: Internal Report KFA.

Kindermann J., & Muhlenbein, H. (1989). Neural Networks for the Iterated Prisoner's Dilemma. GMD, in preparation.

Kübler, F.D. (1988). MEGAFRAME SUPERCLUSTER Series. Aachen: Parsytec.

Loeschke V. (Ed.) (1987). *Genetic Constraints on Adaptive Evolution*. Springer, Berlin.

Lorenz, K. (1973). *Die Ruckseite des Spiegels*. Piper, Munchen.

Losert V., & Akin E. (1983). Dynamics of games and Genes: Discrete versus Continuous Time. *J. Math. Biol.* 17 (pp. 241–251).

Maynard Smith J. (1982). Evolution and the Theory of Games. Cambridge University Press.

Merril J.W.L., & Port R.F. (1988). Fractally Configured Neural. Networks Rep. 249. Bloomington: Indiana University.

Mühlenbein H., Gorges-Schleuter M., & Kramer O. (1987). New solutions of the mapping problem of parallel systems - the evolution approach. *Parallel Computing* **4** (pp. 269–279).

Mühlenbein H., Gorges-Schleuter M., & Kramer O. (1988). Evolution Algorithms in Combinatorial Optimization. *Parallel Computing* **7** (pp. 65–85).

Mühlenbein, H. (1988). Adaptation in Open Systems: Learning and Evolution. In J. Kindermann, C. Lischka (Eds.), Workshop Konnektionismus, GMD.

Oliver I.M., Smith D.J., & Holland J.R.C. (1987). A Study of Permutation Crossover Operators on the Traveling Salesman Problem. In Grefenstette (pp. 224–230).

Padberg M.W., & Rinaldi G. (1987). Optimization of a 532-City Symmetric Traveling Salesman Problem by Branch and Cut. *Oper. Res. Lett.* 6 (pp. 1–7).

Rechenberg I. (1986). Evolution Strategy and Human Decision Making. In Willumeit (Ed.) *Human decision making and manual control*. Amsterdam: North-Holland.

Rumelhart, D.E., Hinton, G.E., & Williams, R.J., (1986). *Learning Internal Representations by Error Propagation*. In Rumelhart, D. E. & McClelland, J. L., editors, Parallel Distributed Processing. Vol. I + II, MIT Press.

Schwefel H.-P. (1981). Numerical Optimization of Computer Models. Chichester: Wiley.

Schwefel H.-P. (1987). Collective Phenomena in Evolutionary Systems. In *Problems of Constancy and Change*, Vol. II. Budapest: Int. Society for General System Res.

Selfridge O.G. (1959). Pandemonium: A paradigm for learning. In *Mechanization of Thought Processes*. Her Majesty's Stationary Office (pp. 511–531).

Smieja F. J. (1988). *Evolution of Intelligent Systems in a Changing Environment*, Int. Report, GMD

Sutton, R., (1988). Learning to predict by the methods of temporal differences. *Machine Learning*, 3:9–44.

Waddington C.H. (1974). A catastrophic theory of evolution. *Annals of the New York Academy of Sciences* 231 (pp. 32–42).

Wagner G.P. (1985). Uber die populationsgenetischen Grundlagen einer Systemtheorie der Evolution. In *Evolution, Ordnung und Erkenntnis*, J.A. Ott (Ed.). Berlin: Paul Parey.

Werbos, P.J., (1974). *Beyond Reasoning: New Tools for Prediction and Analysis in the Behavioral Sciences*.

CONNECTIONISM IN PERSPECTIVE
R. Pfeifer, Z. Schreter, F. Fogelman-Soulié, L. Steels (Eds.)

Clustering Computations of Brain Network Simulations*

Richard Granger, José Ambros-Ingerson,
James W. Whitson Jr., Ursula Staubli, and Gary Lynch

Center for the Neurobiology of Learning and Memory, and
Computer Science Department, University of California, Irvine, CA. 92717

Abstract—*A neural network model based on the biological details of a sensory cortical structure is presented. It is shown that the model exhibits behavior distinguishing it from other network approaches: the net repeatedly samples cues, learning over trials to provide distinct hierarchical levels of information on each of a sequence of responses to a cue. The sequence of responses provides first coarse-coded category or cluster information followed by successive approximations to a unique identifier for a cue. Thus an apparently complex behavior that might have been thought as a higher cognitive, symbolic function, i.e., learning a hierarchical organization of arbitrary cues, is performed by a primary sensory cortical network, suggesting that this function might be a building block underlying other cognitive abilities.*

Keywords—Biological modeling, perceptual learning, olfactory cortex, unsupervised learning, hierarchical clustering

1 INTRODUCTION TO THE PROBLEM AND APPROACH

The fields of artificial intelligence and cognitive science address questions of learning and memory from various different perspectives; yet although much of this work tends to focus on relatively high-level cognitive abilities, such as learning to play games, plan, problem-solving and even (occasionally) learning language, there are a number of lower-level issues of learning and memory processes that presumably underlie some of these higher capabilities. One such ability, learning associations, has been focused on somewhat by the machine learning community under the rubric of 'learning from examples', or empirical learning techniques, and has become a central issue in the connectionist or neural network community. Another low-level ability, that of learning representations, has barely been addressed in either community, and yet may be fundamental to the operation of other mechanisms including that of learning associations. A solution to the representation-learning task is almost universally assumed in the AI literature as a precondition for other learning algorithms; that is, it is presumed that the learner has some internal language for the representation of objects, and some rules for composing and manipulating representations of novel objects. A simple and widely-used assumption is that the internal

*This research was supported in part by the Office of Naval Research under grants N00014-87-K-0838 and N00014-89-J-1255, the National Science Foundation under grant IST-85-12419, and by a grant from the J. Howard Pew Trust.

representation of objects is a straightforward Boolean combination of the constituent features of an object (e.g., and[color(yellow),shape(elliptical)]); the next step up from Boolean feature representations is representation of structures (e.g., above[house,roof] distinguished from above[roof,house]). A problem is that any learning system interacting with even a moderately real world will have thousands or hundreds of thousands of potential features for every state or object it takes as input; yet dealing with 100K-feature representations of objects poses quite difficult problems of storage and transmission, let alone appropriate generalization, discrimination and categorization of such cues. At least one of the major problems of complex objects is that they are rarely if ever apprehended the same way twice, and yet novel presentations are recognized; presumably representations must be able to be unique and discriminable, and yet represent the shared attributes of objects with overlapping features, to allow generalization across them.

Clustering methods categorize inputs by similarities and differences in such a way as to form useful inferential categories, by maximizing certain measures, such as inter-category distance, and minimizing others, such as intra-category distance among members of a single category. We have investigated a network mechanism based directly on the anatomical architecture and physiological function of sensory brain structures which are involved in the perception, learning, and recognition of complex stimuli. To process sensory data, sensory brain areas must preserve information about both the similarities and differences among learned cues: without the latter, acuity would be lost, whereas without the former, degraded versions of a cue would be erroneously thought to be distinct cues, and would not be recognized. Using biological parameters from olfactory cortex, we have designed a network that takes multiple samples of a cue, providing a sequence of distinct output responses to the cue. Our analyses have shown that each response encodes different information about the cue, such that initial responses coarsely code cluster information about categories of similar cues, and later responses provide successive approximations of unique encodings of each cue. Thus later responses can be viewed as enhancing the acuity of the network; even 90%-similar cues are differentiated to near-zero overlapping responses, enabling the network to distinguish among even very-similar cues. On the other hand, the initial responses are properly viewed as a partitioning mechanism, mapping quite-distinct input cues onto identical response patterns, or category indicators.

2 ARCHITECTURE OF THE CORTICAL MODEL

2.1 An asymmetric feedforward network

Our simulation of piriform cortex consists of the connectivity layer (layer I) and a cell layer (layer II) composed of excitatory and inhibitory cells arranged as in Figure 1. Both types of cells are connected sparsely, randomly and with uniform probability distribution to their inputs. Excitatory cells generate outputs that are connected to 'deeper' layers via feedforward collaterals, creating 'hybrid layers' of cells that receive both input and collateral lines. Deeper hybrid layers are increasingly dominated by collaterals, as the input lines diminish their probability of contact. Inhibitory cells are connected to excitatory cells only within a small radius, creating a local 'patch' of excitatory cells dominated by a single inhibitory cell; such patches behave in the simulation as modified 'winner-take-all' subnets, such that only a group of the most strongly activated cells within a patch

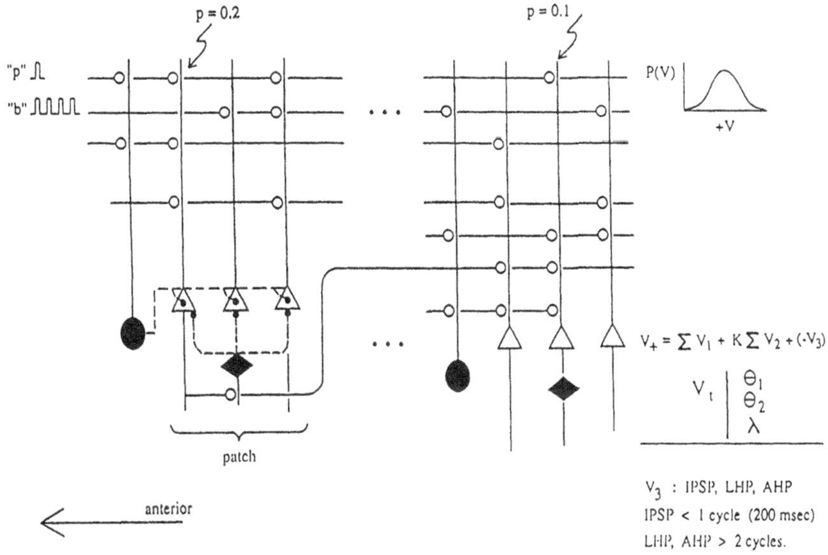

Figure 1: Schematic diagram of simulation of layers I and II piriform cortex. Lateral olfactory tract axons (LOT) from bulb arrive at the anterior portion of cortex (upper left) and synapse sparsely in layer Ia (top portion of diagram), becoming increasingly sparse posteriorly (right-hand side). Axon collaterals from cortical layer II cells (white triangles) flow predominantly from rostral (anterior) to caudal (posterior), left to right in the diagram (Schwob & Price, 1973). Inhibitory cells (black diamonds) organize layer II into patches with dense local connectivity; three types of inhibition are present: IPSPs, long hyperpolarization or LHP, and cell-specific afterhyperpolarization (AHP); see text for description. Synaptic transmission is probabilistic; there are distinct voltage thresholds for performance (spiking) and learning (NMDA receptor thresholds).

will respond to the inputs, while other cells within the patch will remain quiescent. This architectural organization resembles that of a set of 'competitive learning' architectures (Grossberg, 1976; von der Malsburg, 1973; Rumelhart & Zipser, 1986); Granger et al., (1988) compare these architectures with the anatomical one described here. The actual paleocortical anatomy that this model is derived from is described in (Schwob & Price 1978; Haberly 1977, 1985), and our derivation of the simplified model is described in (Lynch & Granger 1988; Granger et al., 1988).

2.2 Hypergeometric connectivity

Assuming that the probability distribution of input axons onto cell dendrites is roughly uniform (i.e., each cell dendrite receives approximately a fixed number of input connections) and the number of active input lines per input cue is also roughly uniform, the probabilities of particular numbers of connections being activated on a dendrite can be calculated via the hypergeometric distribution (Granger et al., 1988). Thus the connectivity alone can be viewed as 'recruiting' (strongly activating) certain cells given a certain spatial pattern of input activation; for a fixed firing threshold, only those cells receiving more activation than that threshold can fire: these correspond to the right-hand tail of the hypergeometric (past the threshold). We have found that the connectivity-based cell recruitment alone gives rise to initial broadly-tuned categorization or partitioning of the space of input cues: sufficiently similar cues (i.e., those sharing a large percentage of their activated input lines) will tend to recruit somewhat similar populations of output cells (Granger et al., 1987):

Restricting ourselves to rostral piriform, which is dominated by LOT axons, we may neglect the small number of collaterals. In the rostral region, the expected value of $\hat{d}$, the Hamming distance between responses for two input cues differing by $2d$ LOT lines (input Hamming distance of d) is:

$$E(\hat{d}) = \sum_{k=1}^{N_o} \left[\sum_{\substack{i \geq \theta \\ j < \theta}} S_i I(i,j) + \sum_{\substack{i < \theta \\ j \geq \theta}} S_i I(i,j) \right]$$

where N_o is the number of postsynaptic cells, each S_i is the probability that a cell will have precisely i active contacts from one of the two cues, and $I(i,j)$ is the probability that the number of contacts on the cell will increase (or decrease) from i to j with the change in d LOT lines; i.e., changing from the first cue to the second. Hence, the first term denotes the probability of a cell decreasing its number of active contacts from above to below some threshold, θ, such that that cell fired in response to one cue but not the other (and therefore is one of the cells that will contribute to the difference between responses to the two cues). Reciprocally, the second term is the probability that the cell increases its number of active synapses such that it is now over the threshold; this cell also will contribute to the difference in response. The value for each S_a (the probability of a active contacts on a cell) is the hypergeometric function referred to earlier:

$$S_a = p(a\ active\ synapses) = \frac{\binom{A}{a}\binom{N-A}{n-a}}{\binom{N}{n}}$$

where N is the number of LOT lines, A is the number of active (firing) LOT lines, n is the number of synapses per dendrite formed by the LOT, and a is the number of active such synapses.

The probability of a cell changing its number of contacts from a to $\hat{a}$ is:

$$I(a,\hat{a}) = \sum_{\substack{g-l= \\ a-\hat{a}}} \left[\frac{\binom{a}{l}\binom{A-a}{d-l}}{\binom{A}{d}} \frac{\binom{n-a}{g}\binom{N-A-(n-a)}{d-g}}{\binom{N-A}{d}} \right]$$

where N, n, A, and a are as above, l is the "loss" or reduction in the number of active synapses, and g is the gain or increase. Hence the left expression is the probability of losing l active synapses by changing d LOT lines, and the right-hand expression is the probability of gaining g active synapses. The product of the expressions are summed over all the ways of choosing l and g such that the net change $g - l$ is the desired difference $a - \hat{a}$.

Furthermore, we have shown that learning via a network learning rule derived from synaptic long-term potentiation (LTP) enhances this partitioning effect, decreasing noise in the response (Granger et al., 1988): this point will be returned to in the section on learning rules.

2.3 Winner-take-all subassemblies or patches

The piriform simulation assumes that the network is divided into coherent subnets in each of which a small number of inhibitory cells is densely and reciprocally connected to the excitatory cells within the subnet or patch. This assumption is based on the fact that there are roughly an order of magnitude more excitatory than inhibitory cells in the structure, that the latter are relatively evenly spaced, and that their axonal arborization is dense within a short (compared to excitatory-cell axons) fixed radius. We have suggested that these patches may serve to function as a form of winner-take-all network: only those cells that are most strongly activated within a subnet can overcome feedforward and feedback inhibition sufficiently to fire in response to an input. Such patches serve to normalize the size of the output response from the network, since the response size will then vary linearly with the number of patches. Without patches, the expected number of firing cells is bimodal. Assuming that probability of LOT contact reduces caudally, as new collaterals are added in, we may adopt a labelling scheme for axons and synaptic contacts in which some combination of LOT axons (x_k) and collateral axons (h_m) contact any particular layer II cell dendrite (h_n), each of which is itself the source of an additional collateral axon flowing to cells more caudal than itself. Then the cell firing function for layer II cell h_n is:

$$h_n = H\left(\sum_{m<n} h_m w_{nm} + \sum_{k\geq n} x_k w_{nk} - \theta\right)$$

where the x_k denote LOT axon activity of those axons still with nonzero probability of contact for layer II cell h_n, the h_m denote activity of layer II cells rostral of h_n, θ is the cell firing threshold, w_{nm} is the synaptic strength between axon m and dendrite n, and H is the Heaviside step function, equal to 1 or 0 according to whether its argument is positive or negative.

3 CORTICAL PERFORMANCE RULES

3.1 Multiple samples, multiple responses

An essential novel aspect of the network performance rule is that it takes multiple samples of its inputs, and produces distinct output responses on different samples. Inputs to the simulation consist of a fixed spatial pattern of activity (i.e., a set of active input lines), repeatedly activated at a constant frequency; these inputs are modeled after both recordings from awake animals (Freeman & Schneider, 1982) and stimulation experiments in which the input axons to piriform cortex were stimulated in short bursts repeated at the theta rhythm, in freely-moving animals learning an olfactory task (Staubli et al., 1985; Roman et al., 1987). It is assumed that there are distinct learning and performance 'modes' in the network, since it is known that cells can be repeatedly and persistently driven to fire without causing any synaptic changes (learning), and since two different dominant rhythms have been identified in animal recordings, possibly corresponding to learning (5 Hz) vs performance (40 Hz).

In response to these single (repeated) inputs, a sequence of distinct resposes is generated: after learning, each response contains different information about the input cue, with early cues being most broadly-tuned and later cues being fine-tuned to individual cues. Thus this network uses time in a novel way to produce response sequences that encode at least a two-level hierarchy of information about its inputs. Our analyses have shown that these effects arise in part from the anatomy and performance rules of the network, and are enhanced as a result of learning.

Figure 2 illustrates the results of the sequential cycling behavior of the network. After being trained on 10 cues that all share 75% of their input lines, the piriform cortical cell firing response is shown on the first and fourth cycles (sniffs) to each of the cues, for a 1000-cell network. The cortical responses to each cue are superimposed, and the size of each box corresponds to the number of cues to which that cell responded (cells that responded to 9 or 10 cues having the largest boxes and 1–2 cues the smallest). The first sniff responses superimpose very closely after learning, i.e., any cell that responded to any of the cues responded to all of them, meaning that the spatial patterns in response to each of the ten cues are nearly identical. In contrast, by the fourth sniff, there is almost no overlap among the ten spatial response patterns to the ten cues; each of the cues gives rise to a unique spatial pattern. What has been learned is a sequence of encodings of each of the ten cues, such that the first encoding, which is identical for all ten cues, denotes the similarity-based category of which they are all members, whereas the later encodings correspond to successive approximations of unique encodings of each individual cue.

3.2 Physiological inhibition modulating the network performance

The performance rules of the network are dominated by inhibition: in particular, three inhibitory mechanisms act in concert to mold the temporal response characteristics of the net to repeated stimuli. These performance rules are derived from the three inhibitory currents identified in both hippocampus (Larson & Lynch, 1986) and piriform cortex (Haberly, 1985): short inhibitory postsynaptic potentials (IPSPs), long hyperpolarizing currents (LHP) and extremely long afterhyperpolarization or AHP. The single excitatory cell response (short (10 msec) excitatory postsynaptic potentials or EPSPs) are ordinarily truncated by IPSPs and followed by a late hyperpolarization lasting on the order of half a second. The effect of these two currents is most dramatic in learning mode, and will be discussed in the following section (on the network learning rules). Cells that fire sufficiently strongly become afterhyperpolarized via a calcium-mediated potassium current in both hippocampus and piriform cortex (Tseng & Haberly, 1988). Afterhyperpolarized cells are refractory and cannot re-fire in response to a stimulus for approximately 1000 msec (1 sec): this corresponds to 25 input samples (sniffs) in 40 Hz 'performance mode' or 5 sniffs in 5 Hz 'learning mode'. Hence, cells that respond strongly enough to an input to enter

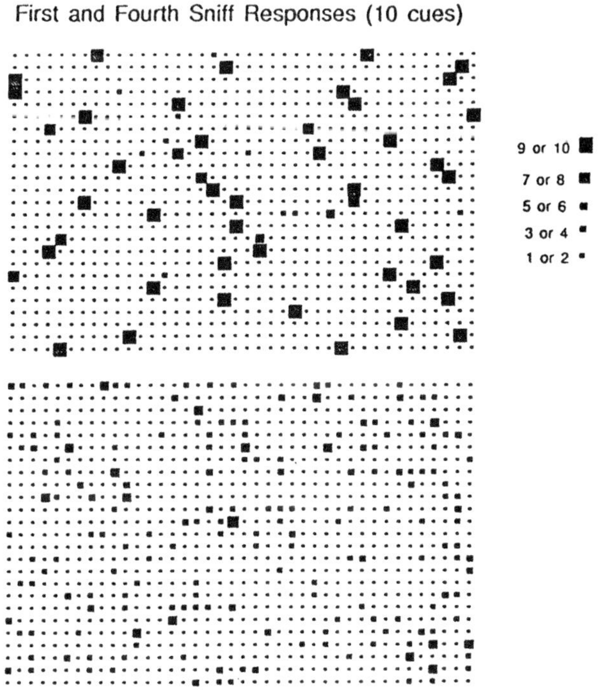

Figure 2: Depiction of first-sniff and fourth-sniff responses of piriform cortical simulation to ten similar learned cues. The ten cues overlap with each other by 70%, i.e., the vectors are roughly at angles of 45° (.79 radians) to each other. First and fourth-sniff responses to each of the ten cues in a 1000-cell piriform simulation are overlaid: the size of the box on a given cell indicates the number of cues (out of the ten total) that that cell responded to, on sniff 1 (top) and on sniff 4 (bottom). The first sniff responses overlay almost entirely onto each other; that is, each cell tended to respond either to all ten cues or to none of the cues. This means that these first-sniff responses to each of the ten cues were almost identical; i.e., the response simply denotes the fact that one of the ten members of this category was present, but not which one. In contrast, the fourth sniff responses were all quite distinct; few cells responded to more than one or two of the cues, indicating that each cue elicited a unique fourth-sniff response from the network.

this refractory period are eliminated from the network for the next 5-25 time steps: cells within the same patch that are next most strongly activated may have been suppressed by the winner-take-all operation of the patch in the presence of the strong responder, but now will respond in its stead. The result is a sequence of distinct spatial patterns of response to repeated input stimuli. Both empirical study of these response sequences in the computer simulation (Granger et al., 1987) and analytical study of a simplified tractable version of the network (Granger et al., 1988) indicate that, after learning, initial responses encode broadly-tuned categories or partitions of the input, and later responses encode successively finer-grained subpartitions, tending toward unique encodings of the input cues.

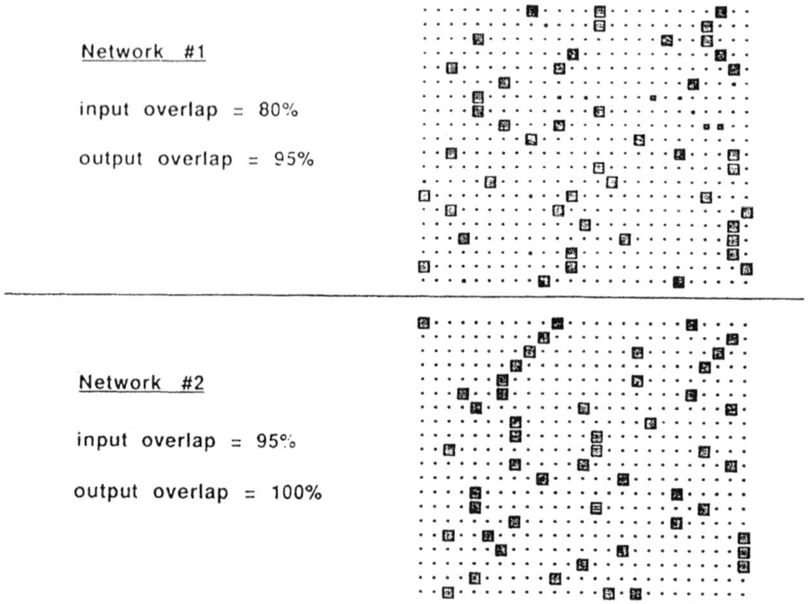

Figure 3: Example of relative partitioning operation of cortical simulation as a function of anterior-posterior distance from input. First-sniff responses of portions of the cortical network to ten different input vectors, after training, are superimposed as in the previous figure, such that the size of the box at a given cell indicates the number of vectors (out of the ten in this example) that that cell responded to; hence larger boxes on a given cell indicate the cell responded to more of the cues. The most anterior 400 cells in the cortical network, when trained on 400-cell input vectors overlapping by 80%, increased the overlap of these vectors to 90%; the next set of 400 cells in the network (immediately posterior to the first set) increased the overlap further, to 95%.

The graded feedforward architecture of the network yields a 'series circuit' of successively deeper hybrid layers, as schematized in Figure 3. Empirically, deeper layers in this net have been found to enhance both categorization and individuation: that is, deeper layers exhibit enhanced categorization on first responses, whereas those same deeper layers have enhanced individuation on later responses. Figure 3 illustrates an example of the enhancement of categorization on the first response cycle: a 1000-cell cortical network was divided into two 500-cell parts, corresponding roughly to rostral vs. caudal regions of piriform. Given a set of ten similar cues that overlap by 80%, the rostral or anterior network responds to each of these cues almost identically: the responses overlap with each other by 95%. By the next more caudal or posterior network, the responses have become completely identical, overlapping with each other by 100%.

3.3 Cortical network learning rules based on LTP

The learning rules employed in the net are derived from the synaptic physiology of long-term potentiation (LTP), which has been induced both *in vivo* in hippocampus (Staubli et al., 1987), and piriform (Staubli et al., 1985a,b; Roman et al., 1987) and *in vitro* in hippocampal slices (Larson & Lynch, 1986). As mentioned, the rules enhance both the partitioning and individuation (subpartitioning) effects of the network operation; in essence, learning moves sufficiently-close input vectors closer to each other on first responses (first sniffs) and separates them on subsequent responses.

Physiological rules underlying LTP that are applicable to a network learning rule have been outlined previously (Lynch & Granger, 1988); they include:

- distinct thresholds for performance (cell firing) and learning (LTP);
- requirement for rhythmic bursting to take advantage of inhibitory refractory periods;
- synaptic strength cannot increase beyond a fixed maximum ceiling;
- synaptic strength increases in quantal increments, and may be decreasable, though not past initial (naive) strength;

We have shown that learning via this LTP-derived learning rule enhances the first-sniff partitioning of input cues, eliminating noise: essentially, learning in small increments differentially increases the size of those synapses that are repeatedly stimulated by input features that are shared across similar members of a group of cues. The cells thus favored increase their probability of winning their winner-take-all patch, and become reliable responders to any member of the cue group (Granger et al., 1988).

The existence of distinct physiological requirements for learning and performance lead to the inclusion of distinct learning and performance modes in the simulation. Although changing the performance-mode values of synaptic weights is the very point of learning, the merit of changing learning-mode values of synaptic weights is not so clear. Empirical examination of this point in the simulation has indicated that partitioning performance is significantly better when it is assumed that previous learning episodes do not affect subsequent learning episodes, i.e., when synaptic weights remain constant in learning mode. Without this 'no-history' property, learning tends to generate strongly-potentiated 'attractor cells' that bias subsequent learning by their increased probability of being recruited. This gives rise to three undesirable properties:

- Individuation in the network after the first response is diminished, due to the increased tendency of the same cells to participate in representations of multiple cues;
- multiple learned categories overlap more with each other; and
- learned representations exhibit a strong 'order effect': i.e., they depend on what cues have been previously learned.

Incorporation of the 'no-history' rule reduces the appearance of these classes of problems in the simulation, yielding better individuation, partitioning and no order dependence in learning. There is physiological evidence for the no-history rule in hippocampal field CA1: the voltage induced in the postsynaptic target cell is typically measured as about 50% higher for potentiated synapses than naive synapses, when activated with single pulses of input stimulation. However, when activated in the theta-rhythm burst mode of stimulation which induces LTP, those synapses that have already been potentiated exhibit different rules for the summation of the voltage induced by burst inputs: the voltages do not sum, and as a result, the voltage contributed to the postsynaptic side by a burst is approximately the same regardless of whether the synapse is potentiated or naive, in contrast to the 50% difference in postsynaptic voltage contributed to the postsynaptic side by a single pulse on potentiated vs naive synapses.

4 OTHER NETWORKS, OTHER BEHAVIORS

A number of artificial "neural networks", using a variety of algorithms, share some basic computational characteristics with each other: in particular, they tend to optimize particular functions. The optimization problem can be translated into a large class of tasks, ranging from classic mathematical problems such as the traveling salesman problem (TSP) to related problems in classification. There is a relatively uniform set of characteristics of these problems: they take as input predefined sets of categories and sets of data to be placed into these categories (or, e.g., destinations and order-of-visit information, in the case of TSP). In addition to these performance capabilities, networks can have learning algorithms that enable them to discover regularities in the data as it is presented.

As a special case of these abilities, these networks can, under certain conditions, *discover* categories implicit in the data, rather than having the categories given to them. What is required for the discovery of categories is that second-order properties of the data be extracted and encoded. This cannot be accomplished in a densely-connected single-layer network, but it can be performed in either a sparsely-connected network (Keeler, 1987; Lynch et al., 1987; Granger et al., 1988a, 1988b; Lynch & Granger, 1988), or in a network (of any density) with multiple layers (Parker, 1985; Rumelhart et al., 1986). The *apparent* discovery of categories can be accomplished in an autoassociative network via careful preselection by the experimenter of those data that most prototypically define the intended categories (e.g., phonemes, letters of the alphabet: Anderson et al., 1977; Anderson & Mozer, 1981). If a simple network (e.g., dense, single-layer) is trained exclusively on such a data set, then in subsequent performance mode, novel inputs will be interpreted as 'degraded' versions of the learned cues, i.e., the net can generate the output corresponding to the learned cue that is most similar (minimum Hamming distance) to the novel input vector. However, if further learning occurs on any of the novel vectors, they will define new categories, just as the original learned inputs did, so that subsequent output responses will not reflect the originally-desired (and preselected) categories. Indeed, a new category will appear for all inputs on which sufficient learning occurs, so that if all inputs are learned, then each will give rise to its own response, until the capacity of the network is reached, at which point novel inputs will tend to give rise to previously-learned outputs, and further learning of unique encodings cannot occur.

Hence, the most common examples of categorization in the artificial neural network literature actually correspond to the learning of unique encodings of cues, up to the network's capacity limits, followed by a performance (non-learning) mode in which any novel cue is treated as a noisy variant of one of the trained exemplars; a category consists of the learned cue and its noisy variants. This noise-reduction ability is achieved by hand in such cases, by the experimenter preselecting those data that he or she wishes to form categories around ('prototypes'). The network is trained to criterion on those inputs alone, and then learning is terminated, and the network is then used exclusively as a performance mechanism (not a learning mechanism) from that point forward. The unique encodings generated by these networks have the interesting property that their Hamming distances are a monotonic function of the corresponding distances of their inputs. Kohonen (1984), Grossberg (1976, 1980), and others have made use of this fact to design hybrid mechanisms consisting of (at least) two modules: the first (which can be thought of as a 'novelty detector') tests each novel input for its similarity to those of already learned cues, and if the similarity is within some threshold (which can be set by adjustment of network parameters), then learning is prevented, and the input is interpreted by the second module (in performance mode) as a variant of the prototype that it is similar to; otherwise, the second module learns the novel cue as distinct from other learned cues. In this variant, the experimenter is preselecting the radius of similarity required for cues to be categorized together. It should be noted that the process of categorization around a central prototype or exemplar can be viewed either as a process of categorization of individual instances or as a 'noise reduction' or 'error reduction' process that effectively interprets a number of slightly-differing inputs as being simply the same cue but accompanied by noise. Learning *both* the individual identities of cues and their natural clusters or categories, as in the network described in this paper, amounts to learning a (two-level or deeper) *hierarchy* of information about each cue. In such a case, then a principled distinction can be made between noise reduction and categorization: the former can be considered to be performed (on the basis of acuity) in the set of representations of individual exemplars or instances, while the latter is being performed by the cluster representation. When only a single level of representation is learned, as in these other networks, then the two processes accomplish the same effect, as described above; noise reduction, by any method, amounts to a form of categorization at the single representational level.

5 CONCLUSIONS

The integrated action of the physiological mechanisms of layer II piriform cortex, as embedded in its anatomical structure, give rise to a coherent set of computational functions: with learning, layer II cells robustly generate particular temporal sequences of spatial cell firing patterns in response to particular olfactory inputs such that the first patterns in the sequence reflect similarity-based 'category membership' characteristics of the input (e.g., foods vs. non-foods; cheeses vs. fruits), while the later response patterns constitute unique encodings of individual cues (e.g., Jarlsberg, cheddar). Thus the hierarchical relationships among families of odors are preserved, and an object can be recognized as a unique odor, or a member of some category of odors that are similar to each other. These hierarchical encodings are learned rapidly and incrementally, and are sparsely coded, such that once learned, future learning offers little interference with extant learning, so that the encodings remain stable. It should be stressed that this form of encoding was not a starting hypothesis of this research; rather, these functions were discerned via observation of the behavior of a simulation that was fashioned to closely follow the physiological and anatomical characteristics of piriform cortex. But are hierarchical encoding and sequential readout fundamental properties of layer II cortex as suggested by the simulation? Are these properties that emerge due to learning in real cortical networks? The goal of the work reviewed here has been to predict the types of aggregate activities that appear when basic neurobiological properties are expressed in specific cortical circuitries. Success in the endeavor can be gauged by how useful, experimentally testable, and accurate the predictions prove to be. It is worth noting that the idea that organization of memories occurs hand in glove with the encoding of memory has received little attention in animal psychology, focusing as it has on associative learning. It is encouraging that the simulation has produced a behavioral hypothesis that emphasizes an aspect of learning that in fact has been largely ignored in the behavioral neurosciences; the organization of memory has been a major research theme in the cognitive sciences for a number of years.

The simulation and analytical work make predictions at two levels. First, it specifies how cells in layer II of piriform cortex should act during certain types of behavior. The model specifies sparse encoding which would mean that cells will not be broadly tuned. It also predicts that different groups of cells will fire on different sniffs, and that learning will profoundly affect what sensory characteristics the cells will respond to. As mentioned, the simulation also indicates that the anterior and posterior portions of the cortex will be quite different in their selectivity. Second, we can assume that the collective properties of the network will be evident in behavior. This follows from an unusual feature of olfactory cortex that has been discussed at length elsewhere (Lynch, 1986); namely, that it is but two synapses removed from the physical stimulus for smell, and serves as a relay to all higher brain structures involved in olfaction. Because of these properties, it is extremely likely that the cortex participates in and is crucial to all complex olfactory behavior. Accordingly, fundamental collective activities of the cortex should be detectable in behavior.

In all, the predictions of the model are testable. Chronic unit recordings are now being collected from layer II piriform cortex in rats engaged in sequential olfactory discriminations. Preliminary results indicate that coding is indeed extremely sparse and is markedly affected by learning in ways compatible with hypotheses based on the simulation and analysis. Work is also in progress to test the hypothesis that rats partition their olfactory world and use multiple sniffs to read out information in the manner predicted by the simulation. Finally, the purely computational aspects of the simulation are being actively pursued in more abstract versions of the model, to investigate the extent to which the hierarchical partitioning behavior can be applied to difficult clustering situations.

REFERENCES

Anderson, J.A., Silverstein, J.W., Ritz, S.A., & Jones, R.S. (1977). Distinctive features, categorical perception and probability learning. *Psychological Review*, **84,** 413–451.

Anderson, J.A., & Mozer, M. (1981). Categorization and selective neurons. In G.E. Hinton & J.A. Anderson (Eds.), *Parallel models of associative memory*, NJ: Erlbaum, pp.213–236.

Freeman, W.J., & Schneider, W. (1982). Changes in spatial patterns of rabbit olfactory EEG with conditioning to odors. *Psychophysiology*, **19,** 44–56.

Granger, R., Ambros-Ingerson, J., Henry, H., & Lynch, G. (1987). Partitioning of sensory data by a cortical network. *Proceedings of the IEEE Conference on Neural Information Processing Systems*, American Institute of Physics Publications.

Granger, R., Ambros-Ingerson, J., & Lynch, G. (1988). Derivation of encoding characteristics of layer II cerebral cortex. *Journal of Cognitive Neuroscience*, **1,** 61–87.

Grossberg, S. (1976). Adaptive pattern classification and universal recoding: Part I. *Biological Cybernetics*, **23,** 121–134.

Grossberg, S. (1980). How does the brain build a cognitive code? *Psychological Review*, **87,** 1–51.

Haberly, L.B., & J.L. Price (1977). The axonal projection of the mitral and tufted cells of the olfactory bulb in the rat. *Brain Research*, **129,** 152–157.

Haberly, L.B. (1985). Neuronal circuitry in olfactory cortex: Anatomy and functional implications. *Chemical Senses*, **10,** 219–238.

Kauer, J.S. (1987). Coding in the olfactory system. In T.E. Finger (ed.) *Neurobiology of Taste and Smell*, New York: Wiley, pp. 205–231.

Keeler, J.D. (1987). Capacity for patterns and sequences in Kanerva's SDM. RIACS TR #87.29, NASA Ames Research Center.

Kohonen, T. (1984). *Self-Organization and Associative Memory*. Berlin: Springer-Verlag.

Larson, J., & Lynch, G. (1986). Synaptic potentiation in hippocampus by patterned stimulation involves two events. *Science*, **232,** 985–988.

Larson, J., & Lynch, G. (1988). Role of N-Methyl-D-Aspartate receptors in the induction of synaptic potentiation by burst stimulation patterned after the hippocampal theta rhythm. *Brain Research*, **441,** 111–118.

Lynch, G., Granger, R., Baudry, M., & Larson, J. (1988). Cortical encoding of memory: Hypotheses derived from analysis and simulation of physiological learning rules in anatomical structures. In L. Nadel, L. Cooper, P. Culicover, R.M. Harnish (eds.), *Neural Connections, Mental Computations*, Cambridge: MIT Press (pp. 247–289).

Lynch, G. (1986). *Synapses, Circuits and the Beginnings of Memory*. Cambridge MIT Press.

Lynch, G., & Granger, R. (1988). Simulation and analysis of a cortical network. *The Psychology of Learning and Motivation*, Vol.22 (in press).

Parker, D.B. (1985). Learning-logic. MIT TR-47, Massachusetts Institute of Technology, Center for Computational Research in Economics and Management Science, Cambridge, Mass.

Roman, F., Staubli, U., & Lynch, G. (1987). Evidence for synaptic potentiation in a cortical network during learning. *Brain Research*, **418,** 221–226.

Rumelhart, D., Hinton, G., & Williams, R. (1986). Learning Internal Representations by Error Propagation. In D. Rumelhart & J. McClelland (eds.), *Parallel Distributed Processing*, Cambridge: MIT Press.

Rumelhart, D., & Zipser, D. (1986). Competitive Learning. In D.Rumelhart & J.McClelland (eds.), *Parallel Distributed Processing*, Cambridge: MIT Press.

Schwob, J.E., & Price, J.L. (1978). The cortical projection of the olfactory bulb: development in fetal and neonatal rats correlated with quantitative variation in adult rats. *Brain Research*, **151,** 369–374.

Staubli, U., Baudry, M., & Lynch, G. (1985a). Olfactory discrimination learning is blocked by leupeptin, a thiol-proteinase inhibitor. *Brain Research*, **337**, 333–336.

Staubli, U., Roman, F., & Lynch, G. (1985b). Selective changes in synaptic responses elicited in a cortical network by behaviorally relevant electrical stimulation. Society for Neuroscience Abstracts 837.

Staubli, U., & Lynch, G. (1987). Stable hippocampal long-term potentiation elicited by "theta" pattern stimulation. *Brain Research*, **435**, 227–234.

Tseng, G.F., & Haberly, L.B. (1988). Characterization of synaptically mediated fast and slow inhibitory processes in piriform cortex in an in vitro slice preparation. *Journal of Neurophysiology*, **59**, 1352–1376.

von der Malsburg, C. (1973). Self-organizing of orientation sensitive cells in the striate cortex. *Kybernetik*, **14**, 85–100.

PROBLEM SOLVING AND REASONING

Connectionist Problem Solving - An AI Perspective

Luc Steels

VUB AI Lab, Pleinlaan 2, 1050 Brussels, Belgium

Abstract—*The paper analyses connectionist problem solving from a knowledge-level perspective. The major conclusion is that connectionist problem solving can be viewed in terms of heuristic classification. This analysis makes it clear what contributions connectionism can make to implementation and knowledge acquisition of expert systems, but also what the limitations are.*

Keywords— Connectionism, behavior, problem solving.

1. INTRODUCTION

There are some AI researchers who dismiss connectionism as irrelevant for the study of intelligence and the construction of artificial intelligence. There are also connectionists who claim AI has failed to accomplish its goals and that connectionism is a way out. Both positions are of course equally silly. It is much more productive to see what connectionism can offer to AI and vice-versa, which is what I will try to do in this paper.

To clarify the discussion, a distinction is first made between knowledge-based tasks and behavior-based tasks, between symbolic and non-symbolic representations, and between problem solving through symbol manipulation vs. through dynamics. The rest of the paper analyses the kind of problem solving that is implicitly implemented in connectionist networks, more specifically spreading activation networks. It is claimed that this problem solving can be categorised in ways that are common in expert system research and that doing so makes it clear what the strengths and limitations are.

2. KNOWLEDGE VS. BEHAVIOR

It is useful to make a distinction between knowledge-based tasks and behavior-based tasks. Knowledge-based tasks involve volition, deliberation, choice, and reasoning. The problem solver is capable (at least to some extent) to articulate what knowledge he is using and how he is solving the problem. Typical examples of knowledge-based tasks are configuring a computer system, medical diagnosis, legal reasoning, and common sense reasoning. In contrast, behavior-based tasks do not involve volition, deliberation or problem solving. The agent is not able to make explicit how he is solving the problem. Typical examples are locomotion, perception, speech, but also acquired skills like (blind) typing, tying shoelaces, or playing tennis. Professional typists when asked cannot immediately give declarative descriptions of the keyboard although they exhibit behavior that implies 'knowing' something about the arrangement of the keys.[1] Skilled typing is therefore a clear case where behavior rather than knowledge seems to be at the heart of the task.

So far most of AI research has focused on knowledge based tasks. It is therefore no accident that it has been concentrating on theories, tools and techniques for knowledge representation and problem solving. The growing number of successful applications, particularly expert systems, show that the idea of using symbolic structures and symbol manipulation coupled to theories on heuristic problem solving and logical inference is a valid way to approach knowledge-based tasks.

The natural home for connectionism seems to be behavior. It is easy to see how a neural network could be designed that establishes a more or less direct relation between perception and action. Such a neural network would immediately solve many of the problems that are difficult for the symbolic paradigm, such as taking the dynamics of the world into account, adapting to changing circumstances, making a decision in a very short time (too short for interpreting the world into complex symbolic descriptions and manipulating these descriptions), and so on. On the other hand, it is already harder to see how a connectionist system could implement such features of knowledge-based problem solving as explanation, task verbalisation, declarative description of knowledge.

We can now take two positions:

(1) *All tasks executed by humans (including speech, locomotion, etc.) are knowledge-based.*

(2) *All tasks executed by humans (including legal reasoning, designing VLSI circuits, etc.) are behavior-based and thus can be modeled with neural networks.*

(1) is the extreme position of a 'traditional' AI scientist, although I suspect that it would be difficult to find anyone in AI adopting it. In any case, to validate this position it is not only necessary to demonstrate that expert systems can be built to deal with knowledge-based tasks, but also that a logical inference machine or some other knowledge-based reasoner can perform perception and action selection in real time. Even extreme proponents of the logical school such as Kowalski or Nilsson would probably hesitate to make this claim.

(2) is a position that at least some connectionists have taken quite explicitly. To show that this position is true the demonstration of a network that performs a perception or motor control task is not enough, instead connectionist solutions would have to be demonstrated for problems such as the design of computer systems based on a custom order which includes doing the necessary datagathering, interfacing with a database of more than 30,000 components, and giving explanations why a configuration is appropriate (see McDermott (1982) for a knowledge-based approach to this problem).

The truth, as often, probably lies in the middle. I take the position in this paper that it is useful to make a distinction between knowledge-based and behavior-based tasks and that each will require its own way of approaching it. If we want to understand the utility of connectionism or of traditional AI techniques we have to decide what we want to use it for. If somebody wants to build a vehicle to drive on the road and comes up with the car, one

[1] You can try this yourself (if you can type 'blindly'): What letter is under your right hand index finger on the middle bar?

should not complain that it does not fly! Of course, there may be tasks which have features of both and require a mixed approach. Maybe natural language is of this sort.

Part of the virtue of connectionism is that it has drawn attention again to the behavioral aspects of intelligence which after 1970 were not at the top of the mainstream AI agenda. It must be pointed out however that there is also growing work again on behavior in AI, see e.g. the work on locomotion (Raibert, 1986) or mobile robots (Brooks, 1988; Moravec, 1988). Comparison of this work to connectionist solutions is however beyond the scope of this paper.

There is a further question whether solving tasks using behavior deserves at all the label intelligence. If we consider a neural network such as that of a worm that regulates the connection between skin sensors and retraction behavior, it seems inappropriate to ascribe to this worm the property of intelligence, or even the property of feeling pain. On the other hand it may be possible that intelligence rests on a substrate of behaviors and therefore that intelligence as a whole can only be understood when this substrate is understood as well.

3. SYMBOLIC OR NON-SYMBOLIC?

A discussion which has already generated a lot of heat but little insight is concerned with the distinction between symbolic and non-symbolic. The claim often being made is that traditional AI is symbolic and connectionism is non-symbolic. This claim is unjustified. First of all, what do we mean by symbolic?

Symbolism involves two things:

1. A categorisation of the world. A category contains in the extreme case a single object.
2. The allocation of a physical object that will be used whenever we want to refer to the category.

This physical object could in principle be anything. AI technology has converged on the use of cells in computer memory as physical objects but this is a matter of implementation. The allocation is also arbitrary as long as it is consistent, i.e. if we decide that cell 012301010 corresponds to the category horse then this is okay, as long as we stick to it. The physical object need not be unique. It could just as well be a set of objects whose co-activation will be used to stand for the category. Finally, the category need not correspond to the categories we use. It is difficult to translate some concepts used by Hopi indians into their English language equivalents (see Lakoff's 'women, fire and dangerous things', 1987) but that does not mean that Hopi indians think non-symbolically. Given this analysis it is obvious that most of connectionism is as symbolic as any other work in AI. To call something a microfeature does not mean that it is no longer symbolic. A microfeature satisfies both (1) and (2). To say that we do not know what a node in a network stands for does not mean that this node has no symbolic function. As long as the node consistently categorises the world in a particular way, it behaves as a symbol. To say that there is no unique object corresponding to a symbol but a cloud of objects (as the distributed representations used in the Boltzmann machine (Hinton, Sejnowski and Ackley, 1984)), does not make any difference, it still satisfies the properties of symbols. Even systems that decompose symbols into smaller entities (called subsymbols in Smolensky, 1986) remain entirely symbolic as long as these entities perform a consistent categorisation. Indeed operations typically proposed in subsymbolic computation, e.g. if enough of the subsymbols are active the whole becomes active, can all be simulated by taking a traditional symbolic view.

Does all this mean that cognition is necessarily symbolic? I think not. The alternative to symbolic is analogical. A representation is analogical if what needs to be represented is kept implicit in the representation, i.e. there is a direct translation of the thing to be represented without prior categorisation. A typical example is a thermometer. If the temperature goes up, the liquid in the thermometer goes up. The thermometer does not assign categories (such as high, medium, or low). Another example is an image taken by a camera or sonar. Objects occur as blobs on the image. Relationships such as left-of are implicitly present in this representation, whereas a symbolic representation requires an interpretation of the world to represent the same information (fig 1).

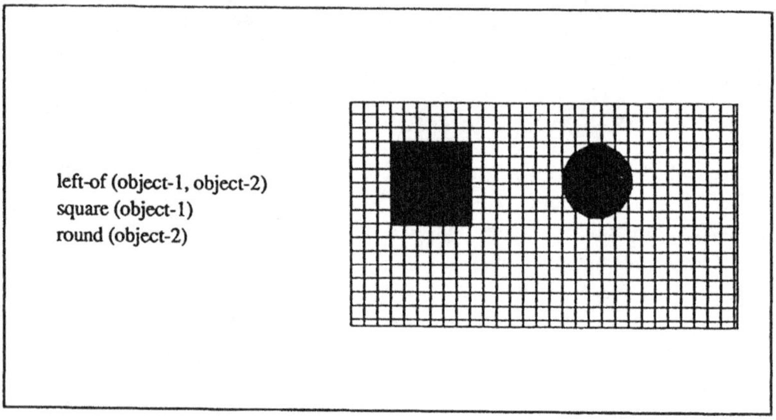

Fig 1: a. Symbolic representation. b. Analogical representation.

It is typical for analogical representations that they are continuous. In computer simulations there is necessarily a discretisation. For the temperature this will be a series of numbers which will have a finite precision. For images, a grid will be superimposed on the image and the grainsize of the grid will determine the precision. A representation is seldom completely analogical (otherwise it would be the world itself). Usually some parts are interpreted and others left implicit.

From this perspective we can ask the question what contributions connectionism has made to representation, symbolic or analogical. I see at least the following:

1. Category formation.

Most of traditional AI assumed as a working hypothesis that the categories are supplied by the designer of the program possibly in interaction with a human expert. Connectionist research has made two contributions:

a. It has proposed mechanisms how features present in analogical representations (e.g. output from sensors, camera's, etc.) can be converted into symbolic categories. This contribution is in the same line as the work on pattern recognition.

b. It has made some concrete proposals for how categories could be formed ab initio. Typical examples are the competitive learning scheme of Rumelhart and Zipser (1985), or the Kohonen feature map buildup (Kohonen, 1988).

2. Analogical representations

Some connectionist work has made important contributions to analogical representations. Specifically the Kohonen network (Kohonen, 1988) is capable to transform n-dimensional information (each dimension being an analogical representation of some environmental feature, e.g. sound pitch) into a 2-dimensional analogical representation known as a topographic feature map. The feature map is analogical because areas in the n-dimensional space are represented topographically as areas on the two-dimensional map. Thus a relation like 'close to' is implicitly available from the map. Topographic maps are not completely analogical because each area 'represents' a feature, i.e. categorisation, of the original information.

4. SYMBOL MANIPULATION VS. DYNAMICS

Analogical representations make it no longer possible to use logical inference or other forms of symbol manipulation as primary mechanism for decision making. The alternative to symbol manipulation is dynamics: the different continuous quantities of the representation are transformed in parallel based on dynamical laws. Even if the nodes in a network have symbolic functions, it is still possible to use dynamics as an alternative to symbol manipulation.

A first, very simple example would be a system with a thermometer that is linked to a valve. The higher the temperature the more the valve is opened:

$$t - k\alpha = 0$$

Where t is the temperature, k a constant, and α the degree to which the valve is opened. Note that there is no symbolic representation involved here, but nevertheless a useful relation is established between a sensor and an effector. Churchland (1986) hypothesised a similar direct association between the position of the eyes of a crab and the position of the legs needed to grab an object on which the eyes were focusing by a coordinate transformation on contiguous topographic maps (fig 2).

It is clear that neural networks have no problem implementing dynamical relations of this sort. Either a node can implement any desirable combination of the inputs to produce a new output. Or, the combination function can be assumed to be fixed in which case the dynamics can be varied by varying the weights or the threshold in a unit.

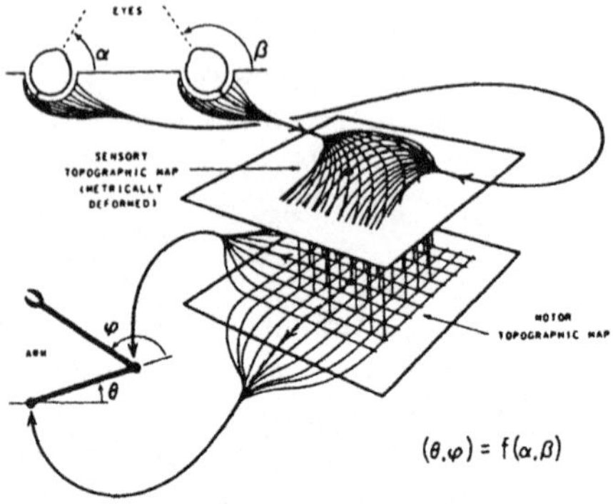

Fig 2. Direct relation between sensors and effectors in the crab.

A different example of dynamics is a gradient field established over an analogical representation of a terrain (see fig 3 from Payton, 1989). The gradient field goes around obstacles and thus indicates the direction in which a mobile vehicle may move. This technique has been successfully used to navigate mobile robots in a real world environment. Another example is the dynamics of an elastic which can be used over analogical representations to solve problems such as the traveling salesman or the recognition of contours of objects (De Mazeau, et.al, 1988).

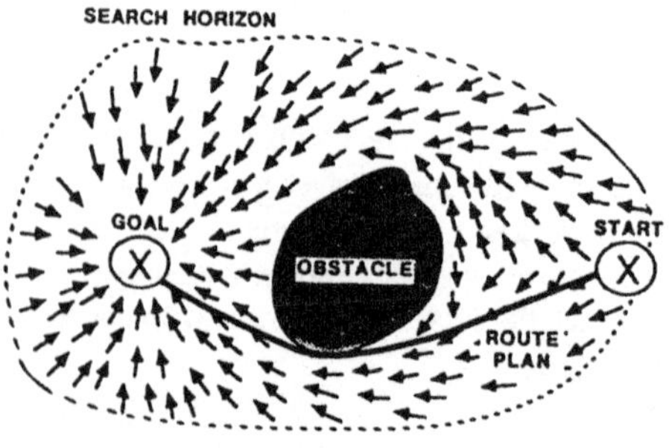

Fig 3. Gradient field for navigation.

The gradient field and the elastic are examples of analogous dynamics because the dynamics has a relationship to the problem that needs to be solved. I used similar techniques to handle planning of a robot arm and visual thinking (Steels, 1988). Connectionism mostly assumes a problem-independent dynamics, i.e. networks are designed to handle any relation between inputs and outputs.

5. CONNECTIONIST PROBLEM SOLVING

We have seen that nodes in connectionist networks (once they are one level up above the analogical representations) are in fact symbolic: they perform a consistent categorisation and constitute a physical object that is used to stand for this categorisation. This raises the next question: what kind of reasoning takes place inside the connectionist network itself. We have already one answer, namely that it is based on dynamics. But this answer only tells us more about computational processes. To answer the question more fully, we need to adopt a knowledge-level perspective, i.e. we have to look at the content of the knowledge and the kind of problem solving taking place, rather than the mechanisms used to implement it.

It is now common in knowledge-level theories of problem solving to make a distinction between the following aspects of a problem solving process (Chandrasekaran, 1983, McDermott, 1988, Steels, 1988b):

1. The task features
2. The problem solving method
3. The domain knowledge.

The task features characterise the conceptual and pragmatic aspects of a task. The conceptual aspects specify the nature of the task: Is it diagnosis, classification, interpretation, construction, design? The pragmatic aspects specify the environmental conditions and the epistemological problems that may occur in the task, such as what kind of observations are available, is the cost of observation important, are there time constraints, are there combinatorial explosions, are the concepts definable in terms of necessary and sufficient conditions or can they only be weakly defined, etc.

The problem solving method is the control strategy that will be used. It prescribes what problem solving actions are taken and in which order. One example is the following (useful for construction tasks):

Propose: Propose a partial solution to the problem.

Test: Test whether this solution satisfies the constraints.

Refine: Adapt the partial solution and reiterate until a complete solution has been reached.

Another example is the following (useful for classification tasks):

Differentiate: Find the most discriminating feature between the remaining list of classes.

Query: Make an observation or ask a question concerning this feature.

Eliminate: Eliminate the classes that do not have the feature and reiterate until only one class remains.

The domain knowledge contains facts and other information about the domain that is needed to drive the problem solving method. For example, to implement propose-test-refine, the domain knowledge should contain ways to propose partial solutions, constraints that need to be satisfied and mechanisms to test these constraints, as well as knowledge on how to adapt a partial solution based on a particular constraint violation.

At the moment research in expert systems concentrates on studying problem solving methods that occur in human expertise and on understanding the relation between task features and problem solving methods. There is an important underlying insight which maybe needs to be stressed: There is not one general inference method that will solve all problems and is used by humans to solve all problems, instead, there are many different methods each adapted to specific tasks. This insight has been learned after a few decades of experimentation in AI with general inference mechanisms which invariably proved to be too weak both from the viewpoints of effective problem solving as from the viewpoint of knowledge acquisition and system maintenance. Some researchers in connectionism (similar to some researchers coming from a logical paradigm) seem to assume that one general inference method will do. Because the evidence is so overwhelming against this position we will not pursue it here and will waste no time arguing about it.

Instead we will be interested in the question what kind of problem solving methods are implemented by connectionist systems and what kind of tasks these problem solving methods are good for. After this analysis, connectionist methods could be incorporated as problem solving methods alongside other known successful problem solving methods such as propose-test-refine. We will restrict our attention to 'standard' connectionism, i.e. based on spreading activation and using a learning method such as backpropagation. A similar analysis could be made for relaxation networks such as the Hopfield model.

It seems that the problem solving executed by a connectionist network can be seen as a special case of heuristic classification (Clancey, 1985). Heuristic classification contains three problem solving steps (fig 4):

- Abstraction of the data to classify the problem into a set of known categories (possibly one class)
- Association of the categories with a known (abstract) solution.
- Refinement of the solution to adapt it to the concrete case.

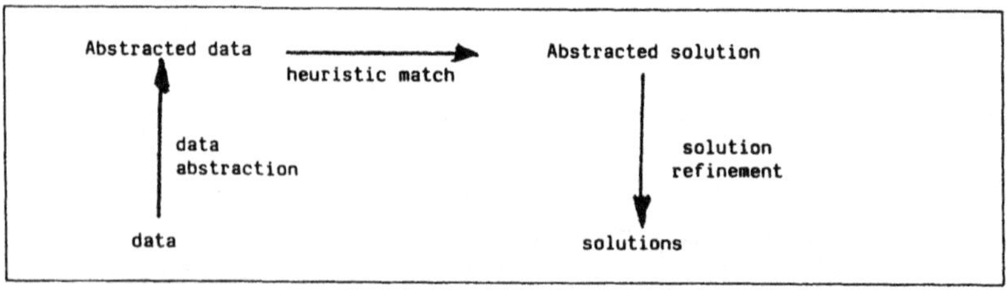

Fig 4. Heuristic classification problem solving method

Consider the following rule from the expert system MYCIN:

```
IF
  1. A complete blood count is available
  2. The white blood count is less than 2500
THEN
  The following bacteria might be
      causing infection:
           E.Coli (.75),
           Pseudomonas-aeruginosa (.5),
           Klebsiella-pneumoniae (.5)
```

This rule can be analysed in terms of the heuristic classification structure displayed in fig 5 (from Clancey, 1985, p. 295):

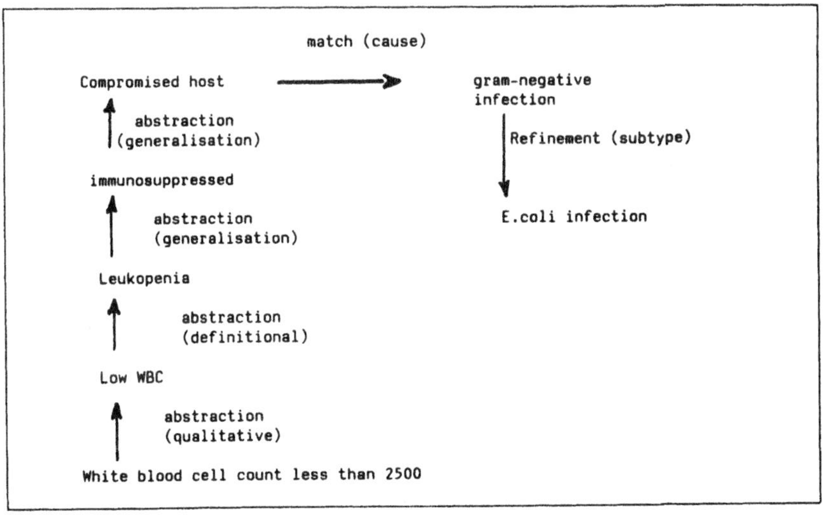

Fig 5. Heuristic classification underlying MYCIN rule

Fig 5 not only displays the problem solving steps but also what domain relation is used for each type of inference step. For example, abstraction makes here use of qualitative, definitional, and generalisation relations. Heuristic match is here based on a causal relation. Refinement is based on a subtype relation. Other applications may use different domain relations with the same roles or may further decompose some steps (such as heuristic match) into several intermediate steps. Note also that the MYCIN rule contains most of these steps only implicitly.

To see how connectionist systems implement heuristic classification, consider the well known example of the past tense system proposed by Rumelhart and McClelland (1986). This system starts from a phonological representation of a root form of an English verb decoded in the Wickelfeature representation, and outputs a phonological representation of the past tense. To do this task, it classifies the root into a number of categories using weighted evidence combination and then associates with the recognised class a solution (this is the heuristic match part of heuristic classification). There is no refinement of the solution in this case, although this could be implemented without any problem in a connectionist network. Relevant categories for the past-tense system are regular vs. irregular verbs, verbs with or without vowel change (e.g. bring/brought vs. talk/talked), verbs that change a final /d/ to /t/ (e.g. send/sent), etc.

There are variants of heuristic classification which remain closer to the cases. An extreme variant is memory-based reasoning which simply stores all the cases encountered in the past and categorises a new case in terms of its distance to stored cases (Stanfield and Waltz, 1985). Another variant is case-based reasoning which represents more abstract descriptions of specific cases. Case-based problem solvers still categorise the problem in terms of a set of known categories (i.e. cases), they associate a solution with the case so that the heuristic match step can take place, and refine the solution.

Case-based reasoning also occurs frequently in connectionist systems. Consider for example how Kuperstein (1989) solves the problem of sensory-motor coordination. Points in a sensory image are characterised in terms of a set of cases seen in the past. The Kuperstein system represents these categorisations as nodes in a network. Also the motorcontrol needed to reach these points is represented as nodes in the network. The system has associative relations between sensory categorisations and motorcontrol categorisations. When the arm needs to reach a certain target in the sensory image, the image is first classified. Then the solution heuristically associated with this classification is retrieved. And, because the match will never be entirely complete, there is some extrapolation being done which corresponds to a refinement of the solution.

So from a knowledge-level perspective, the differences between rule-based expert systems and connectionist problem solving, largely disappear. There are rule-based expert systems which use the same problem solving as found in connectionist systems. For example, MYCIN, a rule-based expert system for infectious diseases (Buchanan and Shortliffe, 1984), is entirely based on heuristic classification. It categorises the case in terms of clinical observations, the organism causing the infection, prior medication, etc. It associates a solution class, i.e. an appropriate therapy, which is possibly refined with additional patient data. SIZZLE, an expert system in computer sizing[1] (Offutt, 1988), uses case based reasoning similar to the Kuperstein sensory-motor controller: It categorizes a problem by comparing it to existing cases already encountered and associates with that a solution class. The solution class is extrapolated if the match was not entirely complete.

Heuristic classification is a problem solving method which has been discovered to underly a variety of expert systems, so in that sense a connectionist problem solver has high utility. However there are many other problem solving methods that are very common as well and absolutely necessary in other tasks. For example heuristic classification cannot be used in design tasks in which the set of solution classes cannot be enumerated in advance but needs to be constructed from smaller elements. Even for implementing heuristic classification, other problem solving methods may be more appropriate in some cases. Neural networks use weighted evidence combination for the classification part. The weights reflect statistical

[1] Computer sizing is the problem of determining what a computer installation should consist of based on the needs of the users, e.g. how many CPUs, disk drives, memory, terminals, etc.

regularitaries so that evidence combination is grounded in Bayesian inference. But other forms of evidence combination may be necessary or desirable. For example, MYCIN uses an uncertainty calculus (Buchanan and Shortliffe, 1984). The weights are based on the subjective belief of the expert which does not necessarily have any statistical relevance. The uncertainty calculus moreover collects evidence both for the positive and negative decision and only sums their result at the end. Classification can not only be done with weighted evidence combination but also with differentiation, association, or grouping and refinement. Statistically based weighted evidence combination is only useful in specific circumstances, such as

1. The cost of observation is not important. Otherwise it would be better to use differentiation, because one question can help you a lot to discriminate between different cases.
2. The features of the class do not necessarily all have to be present. If they do, weighing the evidence may lead to a false conclusion that the class is there.
3. The set of classes in which the object needs to be classified is known at the time classification has to take place.
4. The categorisations are based on statistical criteria.
5. The hierarchical structure imposed on the classes is only exploited in a bottom-up manner.

This analysis of the problem solving capabilities of neural networks leads us to the following conclusions:

1. Connectionist problem solvers implement specific problem solving methods, in particular heuristic classification and its variants. Although this problem solving method is common, it is by no means the only one possible and necessary. Connectionist problem solving therefore shows inherent limitations in terms of the task domains and the style of problem solving that can be supported.

2. The difference between connectionist problem solving and the problem solving used in expert systems based on heuristic classification is marginal. The difference is definitely not in the use of parallelism because both for rule-based implementations of weighted evidence combination and for case based reasoning parallel implementations are available. (See Stanfield and Waltz, 1986).

3. Moreover there are some clear disadvantages of using a connectionist implementation. For example, there are problems with extracting good explanations which is an essential feature of knowledge-based tasks, and communicating to the human expert using a shared conceptual vocabulary.

4. In expert systems research there is a tendency to represent the domain knowledge independent from the problem solving method and to represent the heuristic annotations (such as the weight of a particular piece of evidence) separate from the conceptual aspects of the domain (Steels, 1988). All this leads to systems which can adapt themselves to different characteristics of the task domain, have better explanations, allow easier maintenance, and so on. From this perspective, the compiled encoding of knowledge for immediate problem solving as is done with a connectionist implementation is a step backward.

But, our connectionist opponent will say, what about learning? Is this not the area where connectionism can offer solutions which go beyond current expert systems practice? Is there not supposed to be a knowledge acquisition bottleneck making it very difficult to extract knowledge from the expert? First of all, I believe that the knowledge acquisition bottleneck is overstated. Knowledge acquisition is indeed a problem for inexperienced knowledge engineers or for those who do not take a knowledge-level viewpoint in analysing expertise. But recent advances in knowledge acquisition tools show that interactions with the expert can to a large extent be automated. Nevertheless it is worthwile to look at connectionism as a source for aiding in knowledge acquisition which is what we will do very briefly in the next section.

6. LEARNING

In order to execute heuristic classification we have to learn the following things:

1. What are the categories in the domain?
2. What are the weights that can be used to decide on the presence of a category using weighted evidence combination?
3. What is the association between a category and a solution?
4. How can a solution be refined?

Connectionist learning proposes methods to accomplish all of these goals, which is very impressive indeed. It proceeds through statistical induction:

1. A series of cases is presented.
2. If there is no categorisation yet, new categorisations are postulated.
3. The weights needed to drive weighted evidence combination are continuously adapted until they classify the inputs received so far.
4. The associations are made stronger or weaker depending on whether they successfully predict a working solution.

But, there is again an important limitation. Research on learning has come to the same conclusion as research on problem solving: there is no unique mechanism that will be useful in all domains and for all tasks. Instead methods need to be selected that have the appropriate bias towards the task that needs to be executed (Van de Velde, 1988). It follows that we can ask the same question as before: what kind of task setting does connectionist learning assume?

We have already seen that connectionist problem solving assumes heuristic classification with statistically based weighted evidence combination. The approach is further limited to situations where (i) a sufficient amount of cases is available, and (ii) the weights are indeed related to the statistical properties of the cases presented. But both points may be unsatisfied. There may be domains where there simply is no database with enough cases to comfortably cover a wide spectrum of solutions. Second the appropriate weights may show no relation to the statistical properties of the input. The latter would be the case with decisions based on subjective beliefs, as used in MYCIN.

Connectionist learning is thus one point in a space of possible learning methods. This conclusion is both good and bad. It is good because the method can be used when we want to collect knowledge for the problem solving method of heuristic classification using weighted evidence combination with statistically based weights. It is bad because it means that connectionist learning is not the general purpose mechanism that will solve all learning problems in all possible task situations as some connectionist enthusiasts seem to think.

7. CONCLUSIONS

In this paper a distinction is made between behavior-based and knowledge-based tasks. The homeground for connectionism seems to be behavior and not knowledge-based problem solving. Nevertheless an analysis was made of the use of connectionism for problem solving. Following current practice in expert systems research, the problem solving methods supported by connectionist problem solving were analysed. This problem solving method appears to be a variant of heuristic classification with the classification part implemented through weighted evidence combination or case-based reasoning. When this analysis is made, both the strength and the weakness of connectionist problem solving become apparent. It becomes clear that the differences between expert systems and connectionist problem solving are relatively marginal as far as operation is concerned. The important difference is in the use of learning to build up the system in the first place.

8. ACKNOWLEDGEMENT

I am indebted to members of the VUB AI lab dynamics group (particularly Bernard Manderick and Jo Decuypers) for their help in understanding the new paradigms of computation through complex dynamics.

9. REFERENCES

Braitenberg, V. (1984) Vehicles. Experiments in synthetic psychology. Cambridge, Ma.: MIT Press.

Brooks, R. (1988) Intelligence without representation. Workshop on the foundations of Artificial Intelligence. Dedham, Ma.: Endicott House.

Buchanan, B. and Shortliffe T. (1984) The MYCIN experiments. New York: Addison-Wesley.

Chandrasekaran, B. (1983) Towards a Taxonomy of Problem Solving Types. *AI Magazine*, **4** (1) 9-17.

Churchland, P. (1986) Some Reductive Strategies in Cognitive Neurobiology. in *Mind* **95**, nr 379. 279-309.

Clancey, W.J. (1985). Heuristic classification. *Artificial Intelligence*, **27**, 289-350.

DeMazeau, et.al. (1988) Using an elastic for contour detection. Technical Report LIFIA Grenoble.

Hinton, G., Sejnowski, T., & Ackley D. (1984) Boltzmann Machines: Constraint satisfaction networks that learn. Tech. report CMU-CS-84-119. Carnegie Mellon University, Pittsburgh.

Hopfield, J., & Tank D. (1985) "Neural" computation of decisions in optimization problems. In *Biol. Cybern.* **52**, 141-152.

Kohonen, T. (1988) Self-organization and associative memory. Second edition. Springer series in information sciences. Heidelberg: Springer.

Kuperstein, M. (1989) Implementation of an Adaptive Neural Controller for Sensory-Motor Coordination. In. R. Pfeifer, Z.Schreter, F. Fogelman, and L. Steels (eds.) *Connectionism in Perspective*. Amsterdam: Elsevier.

Lakoff, G. (1987) Women, Fire, and Dangerous Things. Chicago: The University of Chicago press.

Marcus, S. (ed.) (1988) *Automating Knowledge Acquisition Tools*. Dordrecht: Kluwer.

Marcus, S. and McDermott J. (1988) VT: An expert system for elevator design. *AI Magazine*. 1988.

McDermott, J. (1988) A taxonomy of problem solving methods. In. S. Marcus, (ed.) *Automating Knowledge Acquisition Tools*. Dordrecht: Kluwer.

McDermott, J. (1982) R1: A rule-based configurer of computer systems. *Artificial Intelligence Journal*. **19**(1), 39-88.

Moravec, H. (1988) Artificial minds. Cambridge, MA: MIT Press.

Offutt, D. (1988) SIZZLE: A Knowledge-Acquisition Tool Specialised for the Sizing Task. 175-198. in S. Marcus, (ed).

Payton, D. W. (1989) Internalized plans: a representation for action resources. Hughes Artificial Intelligence Center, Calabasas, Ca.

Raibert, M. (1986) Legged robots that balance. Cambridge, MA: MIT Press.

Rumelhart, D. and D. Zipser (1985) Feature discovery by competitive learning. *Cognitive Science*, **9**, 75-112.

Rumelhart, D. and J. McClelland (1986) On Learning the Past Tenses of English Verbs. chapter 18, in Rumelhart and McClelland (1986).

Rumelhart, D. and McClelland J. (1986) Parallel distributed processing. Explorations in the Microstructures of Cognition. Cambridge Ma.: Bradford Books.

Smolensky, P. (1986) Information Processing in Dynamical Systems: Foundations of Harmony Theory. chapter 6. in Rumelhart, D. and J. McClelland (1986).

Stanfield, C. and Waltz D. (1986) Toward memory-based reasoning. *Communications of the ACM*, **29**, 1213-1229.

Steels, L. (1987) AI and complex dynamics. Proceedings of the IFIP workshop on concepts and techniques for knowledge-based systems. Mount Fuji, Japan.

Steels, L. (1988a) Steps towards common sense. In: *ECAI-88*, Munchen. London: Pitman.

Steels, L. (1988b) Components of expertise. VUB AI lab Memo 88-16.

Van de Velde, W. (1988) The quality of learning. In: *ECAI-88*, Munchen. London: Pitman.

Problem Solving and Reasoning: A Connectionist Perspective

James A. Hendler

University of Maryland, Institute for Advanced Computer Studies[1]
University of Maryland, College Park

Abstract—*Connectionism has recently seen a major resurgence of interest among researchers. The spectrum of connectionist approaches is quite large, ranging from structured models, in which individual network units carry meaning, through distributed models of weighted networks with learning algorithms. Very encouraging results, particularly in "low-level" perceptual and signal processing tasks, are being reported across the entire spectrum of these models. These models have had more limited success, however, in those"higher cognitive" areas where symbolic models have traditionally shown promise: expert reasoning, planning, and natural language processing.*

This paper discusses the problem of building systems which integrate such abilities. We present this issue from two approaches: the building of hybrid systems which integrate connectionist and symbolic components, and some steps towards providing symbolic reasoning from distributed merging structured and distributed connectionist techniques.

Keywords—Problem solving, reasoning, marker passing, hybrid system, structured (local) connectionist models

1. INTRODUCTION

Connectionism has recently seen a major resurgence of interest among researchers. The spectrum of connectionist approaches is quite large, ranging from structured models, in which individual network units carry meaning, through distributed models of weighted networks with learning algorithms. Very encouraging results, particularly in "low-level" perceptual and signal processing tasks, are being reported across the entire spectrum of these models. These models have had more limited success, however, in those "higher cognitive" areas where symbolic models have traditionally shown promise: expert reasoning, planning, and natural language processing.

---

[1]The author is also affiliated with the Systems Research Center and the Computer Science Dept. at the University of Maryland. Partial funding of this work was provided by the Office of Naval Research.

However, although connectionist techniques have had only limited success in such cognitive tasks, for a system to provide both "low-level" perceptual functionality as well as demonstrating high-level cognitive abilities, it must be able to capture the best features of each of the competing paradigms. There is a clear and present need for such systems as evidenced by applications such as:

- *Planning applications* where recognition of other agents' plans must be coupled to intelligent counteractions,

- *Natural language speech understanding programs* where speech processing, which has been most successful as a signal processing application, needs to be coupled with syntactic and semantic processing,

- *Automated manufacturing or testing applications* where visual perception needs to be coupled with expert reasoning, and

- *Expert image processing systems* where line or range detectors, radar signal classifiers, unknown perspective projections, quantitative image processors, etc. must be coupled to top-down knowledge sources such as maps and models of objects.

This paper discusses the problem of building systems which integrate such abilities. We present this issue from two approaches: the building of hybrid systems which integrate connectionist and symbolic components, and some steps towards providing symbolic reasoning from merging structured and distributed connectionist techniques.

2. THE HYBRID APPROACH

One approach to the integration of connectionist and symbolic techniques is the development of hybrid reasoning systems in which differing components can communicate in the solving of problems. In this section of the paper we will describe an approach to building such a system. We describe an experimental system which incorporates both back propagation learning and symbolic networks, and was designed for performing reasoning about perceptual similarities.

2.1 Perceptual Similarity

Many phenomena needing to be explained by the cognitive scientist have their roots in the perceptual similarities between various objects as viewed by the human cognitive apparatus. Some examples include:

Categorization, where humans can classify objects as better and worse examples of some category (for example, "sparrow" is consistently rated as a better "bird" than "turkey").

Priming, where the priming occurs for perceptually similar objects. An example of this is "rhyming priming" in which words which rhyme demonstrate priming effects.

Functional identification, in which objects which have perceptual features in common are used to perform functions associated with each other (for example, substituting a rock for a hammer due to a similarity in mass).

Traditional symbolic modeling, in the AI and cognitive psychology communities, has been unable to offer an explanation of these effects.

Connectionist approaches appear to have shed some light on a mechanism (or set thereof) which can be used to explain the recognition of perceptual similarities. In particular, distributed connectionist models can be trained so as to develop an internal representation that roughly corresponds to a set of non-symbolically-identifiable features which are used to determine such similarity over a set of inputs. Such features are often called microfeatures and are an important reason for the success of parallel distributed models (McClelland & Rumelhart, 1981).

Examples of the types of microfeatures learned by connectionist networks can be seen in examining a clustering analysis of the hidden network units of the NETTALK system (Sejnowski, 1986). NETTALK, a 3-layer network with an input layer, one hidden layer, and an output layer, was trained with letter strings and the corresponding phonemic encoding of the central letter of the string. A clustering analysis of the hidden unit weights developed during the running of the program indicated that certain input patterns caused greater activations of certain weights. An example would be a set of unit weights which was maximized when presented with most occurances of "A E I O and U." This set of weights would thus be said to encode what we call vowels, and thus we could refer to 'vowel' as a microfeature learned by the system. Other microfeatures discovered could not be as easily described. For example, in one run of the program a set of weights might be discovered which maximizes letters such as T and D when appearing near the end of words, but not at the front. This has no easily described symbolic label, it might most closely described as "letters whose pronunciation hardness changes in conjunction with nearness to a right hand space."

Connectionist models are usually associated with learning algorithms that enable them to create these microfeatures from a set of training examples. The networks can then produce output values for elements they were not trained on by, in essence, finding items with the most elements in common. This is particularly useful to networks which are trained as "classifiers," that is, the training set is used to get the network to have the behavior of differentiating a set of objects based on, for example, some sort of acoustic or other signals.

Unfortunately, while present connectionist models do allow this type of classification and recognition of perceptual similarity, they have not yet been made to perform the complex reasoning tasks that have been the forte of symbolic AI approaches. While such tasks as expert reasoning, natural language analysis and planning can be handled fairly easily (although primarily only in limited domains) by the rule-based approaches of symbolic AI systems, those neural network programs attempting these tasks have had limited success. Those connectionist systems which have been most successful in these traditional domains, structured connectionist systems (Feldman & Ballard, 1982), (Shastri, 1985), have not had the property of learning the types of microfeatures described earlier[2]

While it may not be inherently impossible for purely connectionist approaches to handle complex reasoning tasks someday, it will require significant breakthroughs for this to happen. Similarly, getting purely symbolic systems to handle the types of perceptual-similarity-based reasoning that connectionist networks perform well would require major advances in AI. In the remainder of this section, we present an approach in which a hybrid system, a semantic network merged with a back-propagation learning network, is used to provide complex reasoning about perceptual similarities.

2.2 The hybrid model

The hybrid model described in this paper is an extension of an earlier system described elsewhere (Hendler, 1987). The original system, called SCRAPS, used a marker-passing algorithm to find information of use to a planning system. In extending the SCRAPS model to do some simple similarity based reasoning we demonstrated that a massively parallel marker-passing algorithm, the "most connectionist" of many of the modern symbolic approaches, could be combined with a local connectionist model, the most "symbolic" of the connectionist approaches. This work focused on the embedding of a local connectionist-like network into a symbolic network, and used the marker-passing technique to provide "energy" into the lower level network. (Hendler, to appear) describes this model and presents an example in which merging these approaches enables us to deal with a task which neither approach, alone, has yet been able to solve.

Our recent work, however, has focused on a more powerful integration of the symbolic and connectionist techniques. A distributed network is trained on an encoding of objects corresponding to some of the nodes in a semantic associative network. Using the marker-passing technique a traditional symbolic reasoner is able to use the hidden nodes of the connectionist network as microfeatures for performing similarity-based reasoning.[3]

A diagram of the system is shown in Figure 1. The rectangle labeled 'semantic network' represents a small segment of the symbolic knowledge-base used by the program: nodes represent symbols while links represent relationships between them. The distributed network, contained in the lower rectangle of the figure, is a distributed network with a single layer of hidden units. The dark rectangle, labeled Microfeature Network, represents a section of the model in which the microfeatures learned by the distributed network are accessed by an activation spreading algorithm. It is this interaction which we will be discussing throughout the remainder of this section.

The system works by first training the distributed network as a classifier over the perceptual encoding of the items corresponding to the leaves of the semantic network. The classifier is trained using a version of the back propagation learning algorithm based on (Rumelhart & McClelland, 1987). The hidden unit layer develops a distributed internal representation (similar to the NETTALK encoding discussed in the introduction) in which the microfeatures serve to correlate the encodings to the objects.

---

[2]Local models will be discussed in more detail later in this paper.
[3]Where similarity is defined with regard to the encoding scheme used.

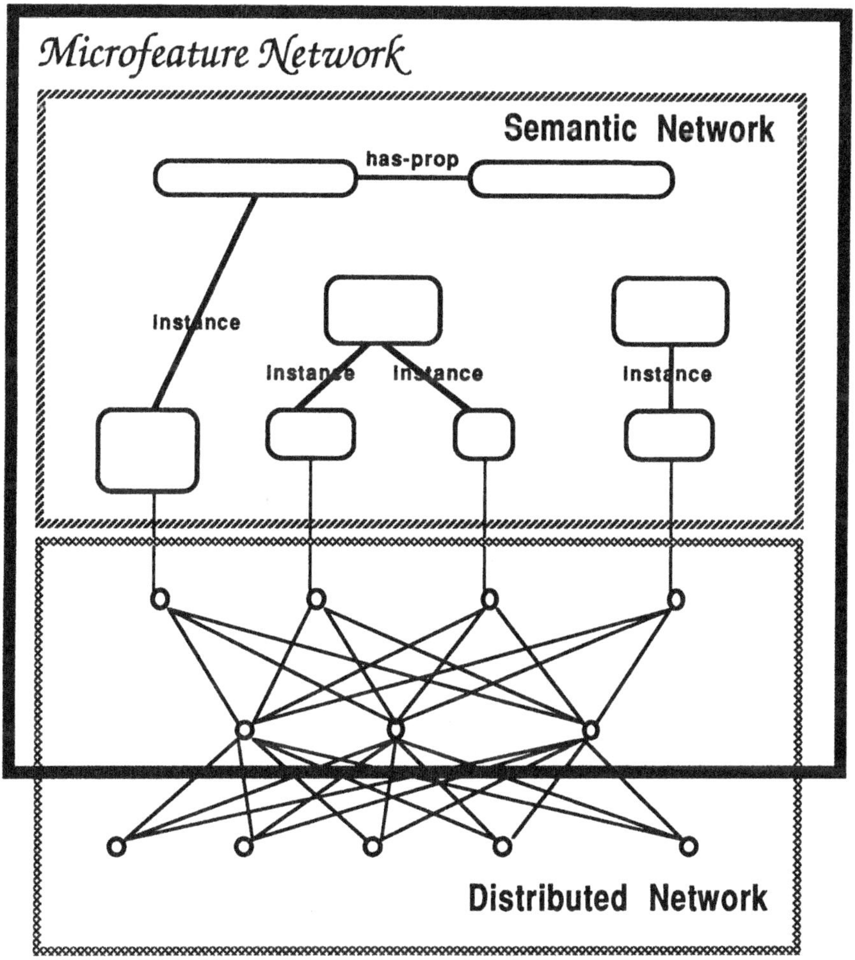

Figure 1: A hybrid network model

Once the training phase is completed, the links between the hidden and output units contain a weight space that can be used for performing the similarity-based reasoning. The mechanism used to provide the communication between the two networks is that of marker-passing. Essentially, symbolic activation spreads through the symbolic network. When a link to the distributed network is encountered, numeric activation, with strength corresponding to the activation energy of the symbolic marking, is passed into the distributed network. This energy propagates to the hidden units and then back to the output units. Those symbolic items most closely related, where closeness is now defined as similarity over the perceptual encoding, gain energy and are able to propagate symbolic information. Paths between activated items can now be found and evaluated by the symbolic mechanism. A detailed example of this mechanism and a description of the marker-passing algorithm are presented in the next section.

2.3 Details of the hybrid model

To understand the model in more depth, it is important to understand the basic marker-passing approach being used and how the energy levels that pass through the back-propagation network are computed. In this section we will first discuss these issues and then present some examples of the use of our model.

2.3.1 Marker-passing

One approach to certain AI tasks is that of using an activation spreading algorithm which passes symbolic information through a traditional associative network (one in which the arcs between nodes represent symbolic information rather than link strengths or the like). These "marker-passing algorithms" can pass very simple information (Fahlmann, 1979) or complex marks which include various amounts of control information for use in the marker-passing process (Charniak, 1986; Hendler, 1987; Quillian, 1966). Such systems have been shown to integrate gracefully with the standard AI technologies for natural language processing (Alterman, 1985; Norvig, 1986; Charniak, 1983, 1986; Hirst, 1986) and planning (Hendler, 1987). A detailed discussion of the various forms of these algorithms and their past use can be found in (Alterman, 1985).

The marker-passer used in our hybrid model is based on one first proposed in (Charniak, 1983) and later extended in (Hendler, 1987). This algorithm works by spreading activation, in the form of symbolic markers, throughout a knowledge base. When these markers encounter other markers an intersection is found. The paths meeting at this intersection are then returned to a path evaluation mechanism. This mechanism checks each path for information which can be used to help guide the natural language or planning component. If no such information is found, the path is ignored.

As an example consider the case of the use of this marker-passing approach in helping to identify a correct solution to a problem with several alternatives. For example, if we are attempting to plan

Trying to commit suicide while holding a gun

the system needs to choose between each of the possible ways of performing the suicide plan. The planning system would start by passing markers to each of the alternatives, these in turn mark their subplans, etc. While this goes on the system would also be passing markers starting with the frame gun. The path

SUICIDE -> to do SUICIDE(x) KILL (x,x) -> KILL -> method of KILL(y,x) is SHOOT(y,x) -> SHOOT -> precondition of SHOOT(y,x) is possess (y,GUN) -> GUN

is found by the marker-passer and is reported to the path evaluator. This path presents a potential solution to the task which has been posed, committing suicide and the path evaluator causes the problem solver to prefer the shoot plan for achieving the suicide goal. A similar path could be used by a natural language system in understanding the story[4]

Jack wanted to commit suicide. He picked up a gun.

Again, to summarize, the marker-passer works by spreading activation through a network starting from several initial nodes. When activation from one origin reaches activation spreading from another origin, a path is reported. This path is then examined by a path evaluation mechanism which determines whether the information reported is of use to the NLP or planning module. If it is appropriate actions are taken, if not the path is ignored.

One of the most important features in the design of a marker-passer is a mechanism which can limit the number of nodes marked and of paths returned. If too many paths are found by the marker-passer we lose efficiency since the evaluator must examine all those paths which are reported. If too few paths are reported the correct information can be missed. The marker-passer must be designed so as to constrain the number of paths reported.

The simplest form of such an attenuation mechanism can be built into the algorithm in the form of a length limitation. In a complex network all the nodes are connected to each other. Some of these paths are long and tortuous--they require that a large number of inferences hold true. If one holds the breadth of activation spreading to a set limit, these long paths can be avoided. Most marker-passing systems to date have used such a limitation. Another commonly used limitation is to check the outbranching of the nodes being marked. If the branchout goes above a certain number no marks propagate. This is to avoid very common nodes, such as Animal from marking all of their exemplars (Cat, Dog, ... Platypus, etc.).

The attenuation mechanism used by our marker-passer was designed to limit both the length and branchout of paths found without violating the locality constraints needed for massively parallel computing. This is done by using a numerical constant to represent activation strength, and by dividing this strength by each node's outbranching as marking proceeds. If we start at a highly branching node enough energy is available for it and all of its children to be marked. If, however, we hit such a promiscuous node late in processing, its children are not marked as the activation strength will have diminished based on the outbranching of the nodes in the path prior to the current node.

It turns out that designing the attenuation mechanism in this way has many desirable features. In particular it can be shown that this mechanism fits nicely into a massively parallel implementation of marker-passing where it can serve as a feedback mechanism between the marker-passer and the planning component of SCRAPS. Further, by using a computation based on the attenuation numbers reaching a node of intersection, a path strength can be efficiently computed for use by the path evaluator. Finally, it appears that such an attenuation mechanism accounts for certain cognitive findings better than either a length or promiscuity limitation. (For a discussion of all of these see (Hendler, 1987)).

2.3 Details of the hybrid model *(Continued)*

The hybrid mechanism works by using the activation strength of markers to provide the numeric activation necessary in the microfeature network. When a node connected to the back-propagation network is encountered, the activation strength of the symbolic mark is

[4]Based on Charniak, 1983.

used as activation energy over the distributed network's links. Since these are weighted links (with the weights learned by the back-propagation algorithm), the activation is divided by weight as it passes down the links and is recombined as it leaves the network (details of this process are provided in section 2.4). As other nodes of this network gain activation they start passing symbolic marks with activation strength based on the amount of energy reaching them through the network. Marking then proceeds as normal, paths are found, and the path evaluator is invoked as usual.

If the weight between two nodes in the distributed network is negative, this implies that there is no similarity between those nodes. That is, a negative link between a hidden unit an output unit implies that the microfeature which is encoded at that unit is not linked to the semantic node which the output unit is associated with. Positive links between an output node, a hidden unit, and another output node imply that the learned microfeature is shared by those units, and thus activation passes. Thus, if the activation finds an inhibitory link learned by the network no activation is spread over such a link. If a positive link is found activation can continue to propagate.

2.3.2 Using the hybrid system

In this example we describe how the hybrid system can be used to solve a simple (and, we admit, quite contrived) problem. Figure 2 shows a simple knowledge-base encoded as a semantic network. The facts represented include that **Rex** a **doberman** is known to chase the **mailman**, while **Spot**, a **tabby** cat, is seen to be **petted by** the **mailman**. We will now consider the hybrid system being used by a natural language component to fill in the blank in the sentence

Fido _______ the mailman.

where **Fido** is known to be a **poodle**. Since no direct connection can be found in the semantic system (we have not explicitely encoded, for example, that "dogs chase mailmen"), the system will have to use similarity based reasoning to decide if **Fido** is more like **Rex,** in which case we would assume that the blank would be filled with "chased," or if **Fido** is more like **Spot,** in which case the blank would correspond to "is petted by."

In testing our hybrid model we used a simplified encoding that was biased in one of two ways. In an 18-3-4 three-layer network each of the output nodes, corresponding to, **Rex**, **Fido**, etc., was associated with four input patterns. In one set of training exercises these inputs differed only in one set of features such that **Rex** and **Fido** shared the common set. In a second trial series only **Rex** and **Spot** shared these features. The other features were randomly assigned. (We should make it clear here that no actual significance should be associated with this particular encoding. That is, this example is not derived to show that a network could make the correct decision based on such simple inputs, but rather to have an example which shows the behavior of the hybrid system. As we will briefly discuss in the conclusion section, more realistic testing of the hybrid system is currently being undertaken.)

In each case the system was started by passing markers from **Fido** and from **mailman.** An initial activation energy was chosen to start marking[5] .When the marks from **Fido**

[5]The actual number is an empirically determined constant having to do with the average branchout in the network and the desired path lengths. Details can be found in (Hendler, 1987).

encountered the distributed network, they were propagated as described in the previous section. If the markers from the output nodes which shared activation continued through the semantic network to reach "mailman" a path was returned. If the activation proceeded through several nodes several paths would be returned.

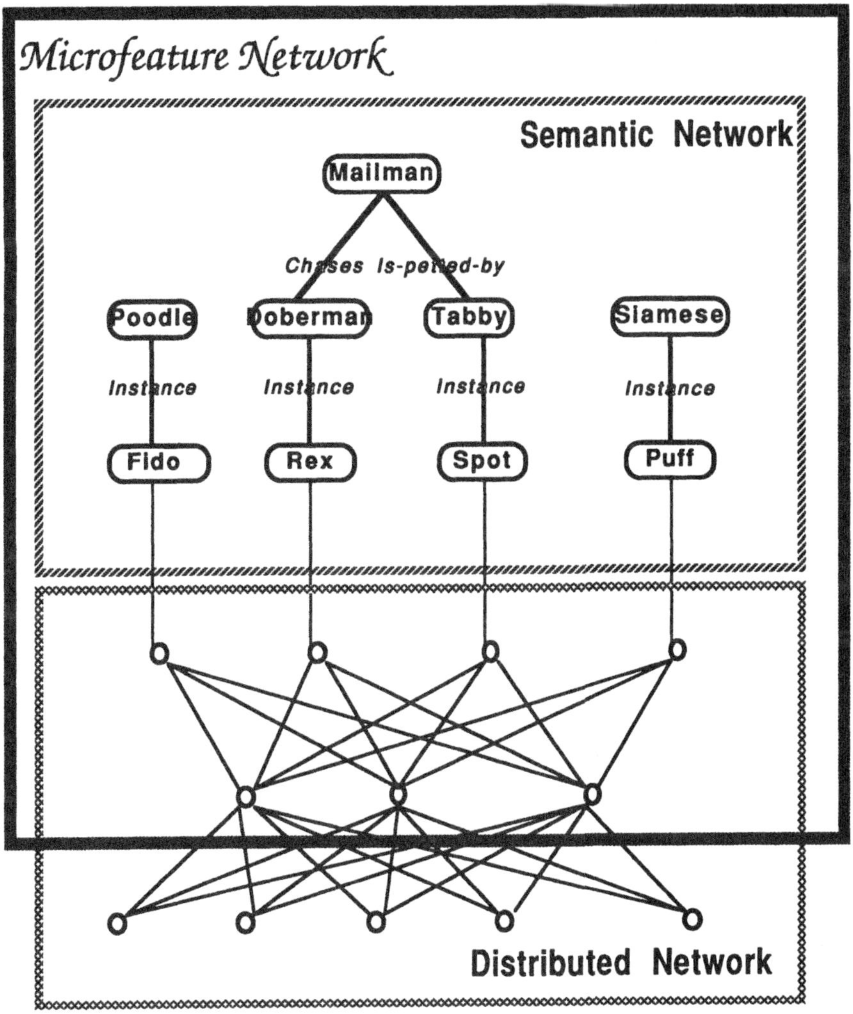

Figure 2: The hybrid model for the example above

In the first case, where **Fido** and **Rex** shared features, the activation spread from **Fido** to the hidden units and back to the output. As expected, only **Rex** was able to continue activation. This activation spread to **mailman**, and the path

Fido -> (Similar Fido Rex) -> Rex -> (Inst Rex Doberman) -> Doberman ->(Chases Doberman Mailman) -> Mailman

was found. In the second case the shared microfeature is between **Fido** and **Puff**, so the path

Fido -> (Similar Fido Puff) -> Puff -> (Inst Puff Tabby) -> Tabby -> (Pets Mailman Tabby) -> Mailman

is found instead.

2.4 Beyond the hybrid model

While it is clear that a model such as that described above adds power to a traditional symbolic model, haven't we violated the spirit of the title of this paper, that is, are we really presenting a connectionist perspective? After all, the bulk of the inferencing behavior is performed by the symbolic marker-passing of the symbolic system. Can't this be done completely within the connectionist framework? How do we probe, examine, and make inferences based on the internal representation developed by the back-prop or other learning algorithm? After all, it is the ability to create internal representations that differentiate modern distributed connectionist models from earlier models such as perceptrons.

While there are many possible answers to this question, and while this question focuses on the greatest failing of current connectionist models, we believe that the answer, at least in part, seems to lie within the activation spreading framework. The work described above extends the symbolic marker-passing algorithm to spread activation over a distributed network. Can we not look at stronger models of activation spreading, particularly those developed for making inferences with structured connectionist networks, and see if they can provide a mechanism to access these internal structures? In this section we describe some steps towards this end.

Input Pattern	Output Pattern
0 0 0 0 0 0	1 0 0 0 0 0 0 0
0 0 0 0 1 1	0 1 0 0 0 0 0 0
0 0 1 1 0 0	0 0 1 0 0 0 0 0
0 0 1 1 1 1	0 0 0 1 0 0 0 0
1 1 0 0 0 0	0 0 0 0 1 0 0 0
1 1 0 0 1 1	0 0 0 0 0 1 0 0
1 1 1 1 0 0	0 0 0 0 0 0 1 0
1 1 1 1 1 1	0 0 0 0 0 0 0 1

Table 1: Training Set

To make this point clearer, we will examine a particular example of the sort of activation spread described above. The particular network we will use in this example is a 6-3-8 node network trained by the back-propagation learning algorithm. The training set used is shown in table 1. The weights between the output nodes and hidden units which are learned by the network after learning to the 90% level for a typical run are shown in Figure 3.

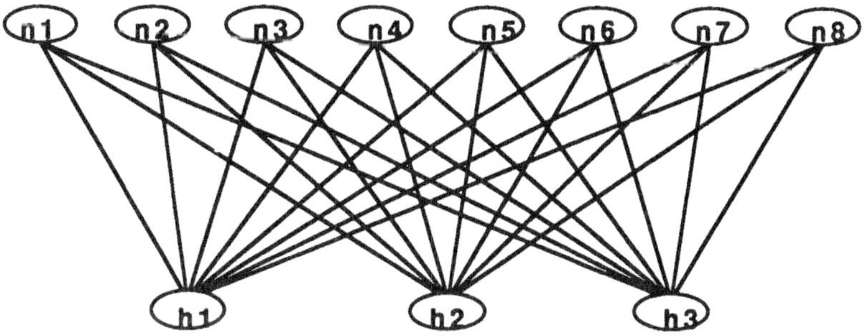

Weights

	h1	*h2*	*h3*
n1	-4.98	4.40	-2.82
n2	-6.99	-4.99	-2.23
n3	-6.11	3.49	0.30
n4	-6.37	-4.68	2.53
n5	4.36	3.73	-5.09
n6	4.38	-5.97	-3.67
n7	0.89	1.07	3.32
n8	3.88	-6.95	1.88

Figure 3: Weights learned

To understand how the activation spreads, let us examine what occurs when activation is started at node n1 with a weight of 1. This activation strength is divided by the outbranching of the node and then multiplied by the weight of each link to the hidden units. Thus activation flows from n1 to h1 with a strength of 1/3 x Weight(n1,h1). A similar computation is made to each of the other hidden units. This activation now spreads to each of the other output nodes in turn. Thus, n2 would gain activation of:

$$\left.\begin{array}{l} \mathit{Activation(h1)} \times \mathit{Weight(n2,h1)/8} + \\ \mathit{Activation(h2)} \times \mathit{Weight(n2,h2)/8} + \\ \mathit{Activation(h3)} \times \mathit{Weight(n2,h3)/8} \end{array}\right\} = \left\{\begin{array}{l} \mathit{Weight(n1,h1)/3} \times \mathit{Weight(n2,h1)/8} + \\ \mathit{Weight(n1,h2)/3} \times \mathit{Weight(n2,h2)/8} + \\ \mathit{Weight(n1,h3)/3} \times \mathit{Weight(n2,h3)/8} \end{array}\right.$$

or .80 from n1.

Table 2 shows a graph of the activation spread between the output units. The table, which is symmetric, can thus be read as showing the output at each of the other units when an activation strength of 1 is placed at the named node. Looking at the table we see that the highest activation occurs among nodes which share the most features of the input (i.e. same value and position) while the lowest is seen among those patterns sharing the fewest features (thus demonstrating the type of similarity-based activations described in the previous section).

	n1	*n2*	*n3*	*n4*	*n5*	*n6*	*n7*	*n8*
n1	•	.80	1.03	.17	.38	-1.57	-.38	-2.3
n2	.80	•	1.02	2.60	-1.57	.31	-.79	.14
n3	1.03	1.02	•	.97	-.63	-2.03	-.03	-1.97
n4	.17	2.60	.97	•	-2.42	-.38	-.09	.52
n5	.38	-1.57	-.63	-2.42	•	.64	-.38	-.77
n6	-1.57	.31	-2.03	-.38	.64	•	-.60	2.14
n7	-.38	-.79	-.03	-.09	-.38	-.60	•	.09
n8	-2.3	-.14	-1.97	.52	-.77	2.14	.09	•

Table 2: Activation spread in 6-3-8 network.

However, as well as having this property, which is crucial to the similarity based inferencing performed by the hybrid model, Table 2 can be seen as providing a matrix which specifies the weights between the output nodes if viewed as a structured network. That is, n1 is connected to n2 by a strength of +.80, to n3 by a strength of +1.03, etc. Thus, by using this technique distributed representations can be turned into connectivity weights for structured networks. When non-orthogonal weights are used, the same activation-spreading algorithm produces a structured network which can be used for more complex inferencing than can the distributed network alone.

We will demonstrate this by what is, again, a simple, contrived example. This example is motivated by Gary Cottrell's structured model for word sense disambiguation (Cottrell, 1985). Cottrell, using weights entered by hand, demonstrated that a structured connectionist network could distinguish both word-sense and case-slot assignments for ambiguous lexical items. Presented with the sentence "John threw the fight" the system would activate a node for one meaning of "throw," presented with "John threw the ball" it would come up with another. The nodes of Cottrell's network included words (John, Threw, etc.), word senses (John1, Propel, etc.) and case-slots (TAGT (agent of the throw), PAGT (agent of the Propel), etc.)

To duplicate Gary's network via training, we presented a 3-layer backprop network with a training set in which distributed patterns, very loosely corresponding to a "dictionary" of word encodings[6] were associated with a vector representing each of the individual nodes which would be represented in Cottrell's system, but with no structure. Thus, a typical element in the training set could be, for example, a 16 bit vector (representing a four word sentence, each word as a 4 bit pattern), associated with another 16 bit vector representing the nodes

Bob1 John1 propel threw fight1 ball1 pagt pobj tagt tobj bob john threw the fight ball1

For this example, the system was trained on the encodings of the four sentences

John threw the ball. John threw the fight.

Bob threw the ball. Bob threw the fight.

with the output set high for those objects in the second vector which were appropriately

[6]Which in any realistic system would some day be replaced by actual signal processing outputs or other representations of actual word pronunciation forms.

associated. Upon completion of the learning, the activation spreading algorithm was used to derive a table of connectivity weights between the output units as shown in Table 3.

***	-0.12	0.01	-0.01	-0.01	0.01	0.01	0.01	-0.01	-0.01	0.12	-0.12	-0.03	-0.03	-0.01	0.00
-0.12	***	-0.01	0.01	0.01	-0.01	-0.01	-0.01	0.01	0.01	-0.12	0.12	0.03	0.03	0.01	-0.01
0.01	-0.01	***	-0.04	-0.04	0.04	0.04	0.05	-0.05	-0.04	0.01	-0.01	-0.02	-0.02	-0.04	0.04
-0.01	0.01	-0.04	***	0.04	-0.04	-0.04	-0.05	0.05	0.04	-0.01	0.01	0.02	0.02	0.04	-0.04
-0.01	0.01	-0.04	0.04	***	-0.04	-0.05	-0.05	0.05	0.04	-0.01	0.01	0.02	0.02	0.04	-0.04
0.01	-0.01	0.04	-0.04	-0.04	***	0.05	0.05	-0.05	-0.04	0.01	-0.01	-0.02	-0.02	-0.04	0.04
0.01	-0.01	0.04	-0.04	-0.05	0.05	***	0.05	-0.05	-0.05	0.01	-0.00	-0.02	-0.02	-0.04	0.05
0.01	-0.01	0.05	-0.05	-0.05	0.05	0.05	***	-0.05	-0.05	0.01	-0.01	-0.02	-0.02	-0.04	0.05
-0.01	0.01	-0.05	0.05	0.05	-0.05	-0.05	-0.05	***	0.05	-0.01	0.01	0.02	0.03	0.04	-0.05
-0.01	0.01	-0.04	0.04	0.04	-0.04	-0.05	-0.05	0.05	***	-0.01	0.01	0.02	0.02	0.04	-0.05
0.12	-0.12	0.01	-0.01	-0.01	0.01	0.01	0.01	-0.01	-0.01	***	-0.12	-0.03	-0.03	-0.01	0.01
-0.12	0.12	-0.01	0.01	0.01	-0.01	-0.00	-0.01	0.01	0.01	-0.12	***	0.03	0.03	0.01	-0.00
-0.03	0.03	-0.02	0.02	0.02	-0.02	-0.02	-0.02	0.02	0.02	-0.03	0.03	***	0.20	0.02	-0.02
-0.03	0.03	-0.02	0.02	0.02	-0.02	-0.02	-0.02	0.03	0.02	-0.03	0.03	0.20	***	0.02	-0.02
-0.01	0.01	-0.04	0.04	0.04	-0.04	-0.04	-0.04	0.04	0.04	-0.01	0.01	0.02	0.02	***	-0.04
0.00	-0.01	0.04	-0.04	-0.04	0.04	0.05	0.05	-0.05	-0.05	0.01	-0.00	-0.02	-0.02	-0.04	***

Table 3: Connectivity weights

These weights were then transferred into a local connectionist simulator and a very simple activation spreading model was used to examine the results. When the simulator was run using the activation spreading over the learned weights, exactly the results produced by Cottrell's network are seen. Thus:

Activation from the nodes corresponding to John, throw, the, and fight cause a positive activation at the node for "Throw" and a negative activation at the node for "Propel".

Activation from John throw the ball spread positively to "Propel" and not to "throw".

Further, other effects which are also predicted by Cottrell's model are seen:

Activation at TAGT and TOBJ spreads positive activation to "Throw" and not to "Propel".

Activation at PAGT and POBJ causes a spread to Propel but not to "Throw". Etc.

We believe that results like this one may argue that structured networks are integrally linked to distributed networks in that distributed network learning techniques may provide a fundamental basis for explaining the cognitive development of structured networks. In particular, we see that inferential reasoning can be produced using purely connectionist models.

3. CONCLUDING REMARKS

What, therefore, has this paper had to say about reasoning and problem solving from a connectionist perspective? The first model discussed focuses on how connectionist models can be used by symbolic models to extend their reasoning power. In particular, we showed that a hybrid model can be developed for at least one kind of "perceptual reasoning": reasoning about perceived similarities. As described, the model contains both a semantic network and a distributed connectionist network in which the leaves of the semantic network are put in one-to-one correspondence with the output units of the distributed network. The distributed network was then trained to classify these nodes based on an input encoding. The weights learned in this training were used by a marker-passing component to recognize perceptual similarities.

It is important to realize that the microfeatures used in this model were distributed patterns. They may not correspond to single concepts, but rather as an ensemble they serve to correlate objects. However, it is equally important to note that this similarity is, as previously stated, similarity over the perceptual encoding Thus, if the encoding does not capture the appropriate similarities, inappropriate symbolic activations may result. As a rather extreme example of this, consider using "spelling" as the encoding. If the network were trained (in the manner of NETTALK), to associate letter strings to the objects. then Fido would be found to be most closely similar to Puff due to the shared feature "f." While this would not be incorrect, it would clearly not provide a useful encoding. This is a general problem for neural network-based computing. The general solution proposed is to use naturally occuring encodings, such as sonar signals, acoustic waves, pixel intensities, etc., as input to the networks.

In light of this, we are now working on extending this model to more realistic domains. In particular, we are examining an acoustic classification task in which a connectionist network is trained to classify various patterns. We are examining whether the hybrid network, using information about the similarities among signals, can perform a better job of recognition when the symbolic system predicts pattern classes.

For those not wishing to allow any symbolic reasoning at all, we have attempted to show that an alternative model, again using an activation spreading variant, can be used to take learned connectionist models and perform some limited forms of inferencing upon them. Further, we have argued that this technique may provide a computational model in which structured networks can be learned and that structured networks provide the inferencing capabilities missing in purely distributed models.

Before we can truly further this claim, significant work remains to be done. We must extend and explore such models, particularly examining whether these types of techniques can be extended to handle the complexity that can be found in real-world problems and serious cognitive models. In particular we should examine two crucial issues: First, will the technique described above work for realistic problems? In particular, can the inferencing be designed to impact on the recognition by the distributed network? If so, one could see, for example, a speech recognition program coupled to a system like Cottrell's natural language system, providing a handle for a text understanding system. Similarly such a technique might allow the integration of top-down and bottom-up processing for vision and other such signal processing tasks.

Secondly, we wish to see if more complex spreading activation models could be hooked to this type of model. Could networks such as those proposed by Shastri (Shastri, 1985), Diederich (Diederich, 1985), and Waltz and Pollack (Pollack, 1987; Waltz & Pollack, 1982), which provide complex inferencing, but also require more structure than simply weights between units, be abstracted out of the learned weights? Two particular areas currently being pursued by the author, for example, focus on active inhibition models for determining whether portions of the network can be suppressed to provide more complex inferencing and the learning of structures given temporally ordered information.

So, to end on a more philosophical note, we draw the following conclusion: reasoning in symbolic and connectionist systems have primarily focused on different, and orthogonal, reasoning interests. The building of systems allowing the integration of these reasoning powers must come from one of three approaches: a hybrid system, a connectionist system which can perform inferencing, or a symbolic system which can perform "low-level" reasoning. Steps towards the first two are described in this paper. The third, getting AI systems to bridge the gap to perceptual reasoning, is left as a challenge to those opposed to connectionist approaches.

4. REFERENCES

Alterman, R. (1985). A dictionary based on concept coherence *Artificial Intelligence*, **25**(2), 153-186.

Norvig, P. (1986). *Unified Theory of Inference for Text Understanding*, Doctoral Dissertation, Computer Science Department, University of California at Berkeley, (available as: Report No. UCB/CSD 87/339, Department of Computer Science, University of California Berkeley, Jan., 1987).

Charniak, E. (1983). Passing markers: A theory of contextual influence in language comprehension *Cognitive Science*, **7**(3), 171-190.

Charniak, E.C. (1986). A Neat Theory of Marker-Passing. *Proceedings of the 5th National Conference on Artificial Intelligence*, Philadelphia, Pa. 584-588.

Cottrell, G.W. (1985). *A Connectionist Approach to Word Sense Disambiguation* Doctoral Dissertation, Computer Science Department, University of Rochester.

Diederich, J. (1985). *Parallelverarbeitung in netzwerk-basierten Systemen.Strategien der Aktivationsausbreitung*, PhD Thesis, Dept. of Linguistics, University of Bielefeld.

Fahlman, S.E. (1979). *NETL: A System for Representing and Using Real World Knowledge*, Cambridge, Ma.: MIT Press.

Feldman, J.A. & Ballard, D.H. (1982). Connectionist models and their properties. *Cognitive Science*, **6**. 205-254.

Hendler, J.A. Marker-passing over microfeatures: A cautious step towards the subsymbolic. *Cognitive Science*, (to appear).

Hendler, J.A. (1988). Activation Spreading Inconsistencies: On the Need for hybrid symbolic/connectionist models, *Proceedings of the AAAI Symposium on Parallel Models of Intelligence.*

Hendler, J.A. (1987). *Integrating Marker-passing and Problem Solving: A spreading activation approach to improved choice in planning,* Hillsdale, N.J.: Erlbaum.

Hirst, G.J. (1986). *Semantic Interpretation and the Resolution of Ambiguity* Cambridge, Cambridge University Press, Cambridge, England.

McClelland, J.L., & Rumelhart, D.E. (1981). An interactive activation model of the effect of context in perception: Part I, An account of basic findings *Psychological Review,* **88**, 375-407.

Pollack, J.B. (1987). *On Connectionist Models of Natural Language* Processing. Doctoral Dissertation, Department of Computer Science, U. of Illinois.

Pollack, J.B., & Waltz, (1982). D.L Natural Language Processing using spreading activation and lateral inhibition *Proceedings of the Fourth International Conference of the Cognitive Science Society,* 50-53.

Quillian, M.R. (1966). *Semantic Memory,* Doctoral Dissertation, Carnegie Institute of Technology (Carnegie-Mellon University), 1966. Published as Report 2, Project 8668, Bolt, Baranek, and Newman Inc.

Rumelhart, D.E., & McClelland, J.L. (1987). *Parallel Distributed Processing,* Cambridge, Ma.: MIT Press.

Sejnowski, T. J., & Rosenberg, C. R. (1986). *NETTALK: A parallel network that learns to read aloud.* Johns Hopkins University, Electrical Engineering and Computer Science Technical Report JHU/EECS-86/0.

Shastri, L. (1985). *Evidential Reasoning in Semantic Networks: A formal theory and its parallel implementation.* Doctoral Dissertation, Computer Science Department, University of Rochester.

CONNECTIONISM IN PERSPECTIVE
R. Pfeifer, Z. Schreter, F. Fogelman-Soulié, L. Steels (Eds.)

A Symbolic Goal-oriented Perspective on Connectionism and Soar

Paul S. Rosenbloom
Information Sciences Institute
University of Southern California
Marina del Rey, California 90292-6695, USA

Abstract—*In this article we examine connectionism from the perspective of symbolic goal-oriented behavior. We present a functional analysis of the capabilities underlying symbolic-goal oriented behavior, map it onto Soar — a prototypical symbolic problem solver — and onto both basic and extended connectionist systems. This analysis reveals that connectionist systems have progressed only a fraction of the way towards general goal-oriented behavior, but that no fundamental roadblocks would appear to be in the way. We also speculate on how a hybrid connectionist Soar system might be constructed.*

Keywords—Connectionism, goals, hybrid systems, neural networks, problem solving, search, Soar, symbolic processing

The ability to set and achieve a wide range of goals is one of the principal hallmarks of intelligence. The goals faced by an intelligent system can range over a variety of external tasks, from solving simple puzzles, such as the Eight Puzzle, to accomplishing everyday tasks, such as getting home from work, to performing complex intellectual tasks, such as diagnosing medical diseases or configuring computers. They can also range over a variety of desired situations that are internal to the intelligent system itself; that is, to reflective processing. For example, one important type of internal goal is a goal to make a decision about what action to perform next.

The issue of goals, and of how they can be achieved, has been one of the major research foci of Artificial Intelligence (AI), and the understanding of how to construct systems that can accomplish a wide range of goals has been one of the major breakthroughs provided by the study of symbolic processing in AI. Soar — a symbolic architecture for intelligence that integrates together basic mechanisms for problem solving, use of knowledge, learning, and perceptual-motor behavior (Laird, Newell, & Rosenbloom, 1987) — is a prototypical example of a system constructed within this paradigm. Soar can work on the full range of goals mentioned above.

Connectionism[1], on the other hand, has not shared this focus on goals to any significant extent, choosing so far to concentrate primarily on issues of knowledge acquisition, storage and use. This article is based on the assumption that connectionist systems, if they are ever to be serious contenders for complete models of cognition, must eventually incorporate the ability to set and achieve the full range of goals faced by intelligent systems. Our primary purpose here is to analyze connectionist systems from the perspective of symbolic goal-oriented behavior. In the process we hope to provide a better understanding of what is needed, how far connectionist systems have come to date, and what is still left to be done. We also hope that this will further meaningful comparisons between connectionist and symbolic systems, by providing a functional framework within which both must fit, and which can therefore be mapped onto both types of systems. Our secondary purpose here is to begin the process of investigating a hybrid architecture — a connectionist Soar — by speculating about what such an architecture would look like, what issues would arise in constructing it, and what utility it might have.

The starting point for the analysis is a hierarchy of functional capabilities that has been abstracted out from the AI research on symbolic goal-oriented behavior (Section 1). We utilize a hierarchy that has been influenced by experience with Soar. Not all researchers will agree with all of the details of this hierarchy, but the main points should still hold true. Following the presentation of the functional hierarchy, it will be mapped onto the Soar system to concretely illustrate the abstract capabilities (Section 2), and to provide the basis for the later speculations on a connectionist Soar. In Section 3, we analyze connectionist systems with respect to the functional capabilities underlying symbolic goal-oriented behavior. In Section 4 we speculate about a potential synthesis of Soar and connectionism. Finally, in Section 5 we conclude with final remarks about connectionism and symbolic goal-oriented behavior.

1. FUNCTIONAL CAPABILITIES

Figure 1-1 shows a simplified functional hierarchy of the capabilities underlying symbolic goal-oriented behavior. In the figure, arrows represent functional dependencies between capabilities; for example, the performance of a sequence of task steps depends on being able to select and perform individual steps. Loops represent recursive uses of the functional hierarchy, allowing subcapabilities, such as the selection of task steps, to utilize the full power and flexibility of goal-oriented behavior. Terminals represent capabilities that, though clearly important, will not be focused on in detail here.

At the top of the hierarchy is a goal, which can be to reach one of a wide variety of desired internal and external situations. Satisfactory goal-oriented behavior requires that the goal be achieved, and that the system be able to detect that the goal has been achieved. Goal detection is necessary so that the system can behave differentially according to whether the

[1] As there is not yet a single universally accepted name for the broad study of neural (and neurally-inspired) network models, we will use connectionism as a stand-in generic name for the field.

goal has been achieved or not — for example, by ending the attempt to achieve it. We will not discuss goal detection in detail, but simply note that some form of it is required. Instead we focus on goal achievement, which can be accomplished in three distinct ways: by knowledge access, by performing a sequence of task steps, or by decomposing the goal into subgoals which then must themselves be achieved. In the remainder of this section we examine these three options, starting with knowledge access.

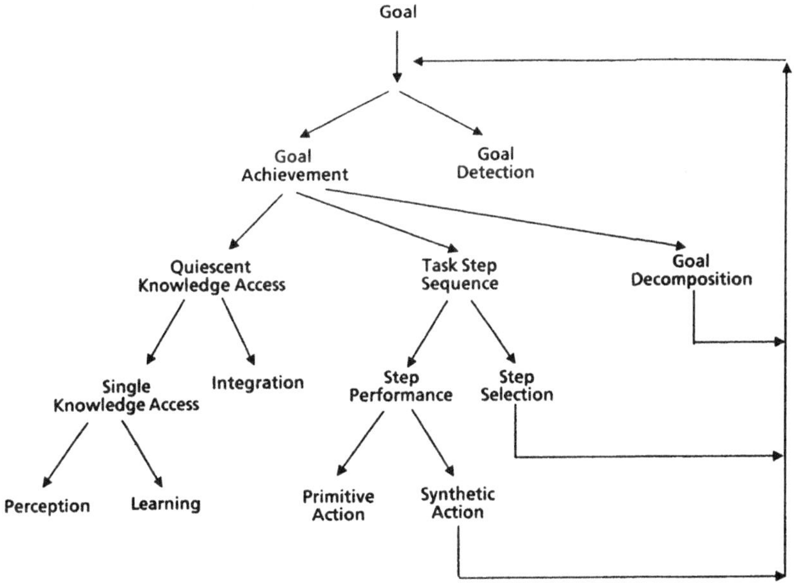

Figure 1-1: Simplified functional hierarchy for goal-oriented behavior.

1.1. Knowledge Access

Familiar internal goals — such as determining what move to make in Tic-Tac-Toe (for a system that has played the game repeatedly) — can be achieved directly by knowledge access. The goal must be internal because knowledge access does not directly affect the outside world. The goal must be familiar for the system to have been able to acquire previously the knowledge that achieves the goal. Consider, for instance, the internal goal of determining which Tic-Tac-Toe move is best for player O in Figure 1-2. An intelligent system that is familiar with Tic-Tac-Toe will have a variety of knowledge in its memory about which moves are better than which others in this situation. It might know that move 1 is better than move 9 because move 1 blocks two of X's one-in-a-rows and creates a two-in-a-row. Likewise it might know that move 6 is better than move 9 because move 6 blocks a two-in-a-row. If enough of this comparative knowledge can be retrieved from memory, along with knowledge about the relationships among the elements of comparative knowledge, the goal can be achieved directly by knowledge access. Even when knowledge access is insufficient by itself for the achievement of a goal, it can play a critical subrole via the recursive loops in the hierarchy.

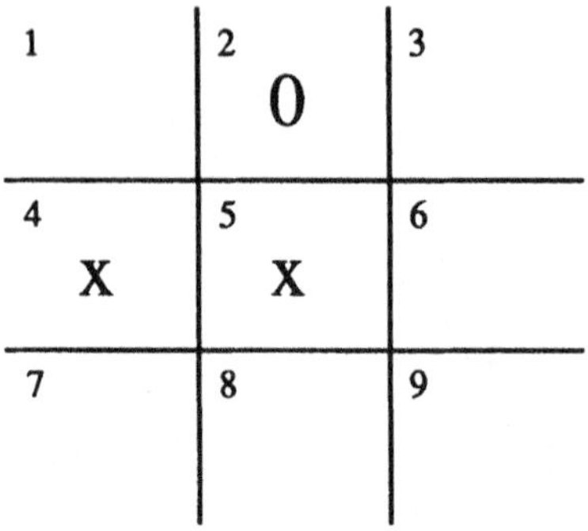

Figure 1-2: A Tic-Tac-Toe position

In an ideal world, all of the knowledge required to achieve a goal would be immediately available where and when it is required. However, the nature of the real world dictates otherwise. One problem with the real world is that any suitably large body of knowledge must be physically distributed over a region of space — the larger the body of knowledge, the larger the region of space.[2] Moreover, because of the variability in the range of goals that can arise, it is impossible to always guarantee that all of the knowledge required for any particular goal is proximally situated. Thus there is a need to transmit knowledge from distal regions of the system; that is, to access the distal memory in which the knowledge is located. What knowledge needs to be transmitted is a function of the current situation and the goal.

In Figure 1-1, knowledge access is partitioned into two distinguishable capabilities: single knowledge access and quiescent knowledge access. Single knowledge access consists of a single cycle of transmission of information from one part of the system to another — multiple parallel transmissions can all be considered as a single access. One effect of a single knowledge access is to augment the knowledge available about the current situation and goal. A second effect is to enable a second access that is based on the augmented situation and goal. Quiescent knowledge access involves repeated cycles of single knowledge access, continuing until no new knowledge about the situation or goal is accessed[3] . It also involves the integration of the independent pieces of retrieved knowledge into a coherent whole.

[2] The arguments in this paragraph are largely derived from Newell (1989).

[3] Another way of viewing this is that a single knowledge access is a single sample of what is known. The first sample allows a second, more informed sample to be made, and so on until the sampling process reaches quiescence. The sampling process could be either discrete or continuous.

Consider the example goal in Tic-Tac-Toe of selecting the right move to make in the position shown in Figure 1-2. The first cycle of transmission might access information about where there are one-in-a-rows, two-in-a-rows, etc. Based on this information, the second cycle would then access the comparative information about which moves are better than which other moves. The third cycle would then access the information about the relationships among the comparative information. Quiescence would then be reached. When this information is integrated together, it achieves the goal by determining that move 6 is the one to select. Quiescent knowledge access thus provides an approximation to the ideal situation, by allowing the relevant stored knowledge to be brought to bear on achieving the goal.

As described in this example, quiescence is purely a function of retrieval — when nothing more can be retrieved, quiescence is reached, and then integration occurs. It should be clear though that quiescence could equally well have been applied to the integration process, with retrieval and integration possibly being tightly interleaved. Under such circumstances, quiescence occurs when the results of the integration process are no longer changing.

Another problem with the real world is that in many cases the requisite knowledge will not already exist within the system's memory. Dealing with this problem requires perceptual and learning capabilities. Perception performs distal transmission of knowledge from outside of the system to the inside. It thus increases the knowledge that is immediately available for use, though only transiently (during the extent of the perceptual event). Learning results in an augmentation of the knowledge in the system's long-term memory, thus increasing what can be accessed for later goals. Both perception and learning need, and deserve, entire functional analyses of their own, but the important aspect here is how they support knowledge access, and thus goal-oriented behavior.

1.2. Task Step Sequence

The second way to achieve a goal is to perform a sequence of task steps. Each step in the sequence is a task-relevant action which modifies the current situation, yielding a new situation. The new situation may or may not have ever been previously experienced. In a game like Tic-Tac-Toe the task steps are the allowable moves — the placement of an X or an O in an empty position. In a task like computer configuration, the task steps are the configuration operations of putting two components, such as a box and a cabinet, together in an appropriate way. A sequence of task steps achieves a goal by starting with the initial situation and generating a sequence of intermediate situations, until ultimately the desired situation is reached.

Performance of task sequences is supported by two further capabilities: step performance, and step selection. Step performance consists of the execution of a single task-relevant action. The action can be a primitive one which directly alters the external or internal situation — for example, a primitive motor action — or it can be a synthetic one which is performed by a recursive use of the functional hierarchy. This recursive use of subgoals implies that, in addition to being able to perform the basic activities of goal achievement and detection, the system must also be able to suspend goals while their subgoals are being pursued, and to reactivate goals when their subgoals are achieved. The benefit of using subgoals for synthetic actions is the freedom it allows in the creation of task-relevant actions. Synthetic actions enable hierarchical action performance, with higher-level actions occurring via sequences of lower-level actions. They enable actions to be performed by knowledge access (at least for actions that need not directly affect the outside world). They also enable actions to be performed by the interpretation of declarative structures that describe the actions — that is, what is classically referred to as "rule-following behavior".

Step selection consists of determining which task-relevant actions should be performed in which situations. As with synthetic actions, step selection occurs via a recursive use of the functional hierarchy. Some decisions, such as the Tic-Tac-Toe one described earlier, can be made directly by quiescent knowledge access. Another example of using knowledge access for step selection occurs in following a deliberate plan, where a selection is made by accessing the portion of the plan relevant to the current situation.

When simple knowledge access is insufficient to make a selection, the system has three options: (1) it can make a possibly incorrect selection based on insufficient knowledge, while being prepared to recover if the choice does turn out to be wrong, (2) it can perform a sequence of actions that results in having sufficient knowledge to make the correct selection, or (3) it can attempt to decompose the problem into subgoals. The first two options intrinsically involve search (the third option is discussed in the following section). With the first option, search occurs in the process of trying options and recovering when they fail. With the second option, search occurs in the process of determining which option is correct; for example, by a lookahead search using a simulation of the task. Search arises not because it is the best way to achieve goals, but because of the uncertainty that arises from a lack of knowledge about what to do.

The necessity of performing effective search demands the ability to control the search. Consider, for example, the second option above, where the system attempts to perform a sequence of steps in service of determining what action to select. If the system is not to perform brute-force search, intelligent decisions must be made about which steps to select for this sequence. This, in turn, involves a second-level of recursion on the functional hierarchy, so that the search can be controlled by knowledge access — including knowledge about the weak methods (see, for example, Rich, 1983, Part 1) — or by further information-gathering search.

1.3. Goal Decomposition

Decomposing a goal into a set of independent subgoals is one of the principal ways to reduce complexity. Without goal decomposition, if there is a goal that requires a sequence of steps of length N for achievement, and if there are B potential task steps available at each point, then finding the sequence of task steps that achieves the goal requires a search of size B^N. However, if the goal can be decomposed into M independent subgoals, the cost of finding the desired sequence of task steps can be reduced to $M*B^{N/M}$. Not all goals can be decomposed into independent subgoals, but when they can, problem solving effort can be greatly reduced (see, for example, Korf, 1987).

2. AN EXAMPLE: SOAR

Soar is an attempt to bring together in one system as much of the basic functionality required for general intelligence as is currently possible. It is firmly rooted in the classic symbolic problem-solving tradition, and serves well as a prototype of state-of-the-art research on symbolic goal-oriented behavior. Our primary purposes here are to use Soar as an illustrative instantiation of the abstract functional hierarchy described in the previous section, and to provide the basis for speculations about what a combination of connectionism and Soar might look like (Section 4). However, by providing a somewhat non-standard analysis of Soar, it also provides new insight into the structure of Soar itself.

2.1. The Soar Architecture

Soar is based on formulating all symbolic goal-oriented behavior as search in problem spaces. The problem space determines the set of states and operators that can be used during the processing to attain a goal. The states represent situations. There is an initial state, representing the initial situation, and a set of desired states that represent the goal. An operator, when applied to a state in the problem space, yields another state in the problem space. The goal is achieved when a desired state is reached as the result of a sequence of operator applications starting from the initial state. Each goal defines a problem solving context ("context" for short) that contains, in addition to a goal, roles for a problem space, state, and an operator. The combination of a particular context and a particular role within the context is referred to as a "context slot", or just "slot".

Problem solving for a goal is driven by decisions that result in the selection of problem spaces, states, and operators for the appropriate roles in the context. Decisions are made by the retrieval and integration of preferences — special architecturally interpretable elements that describe the acceptability, desirability, and necessity of selecting particular problem spaces, states, and operators. Acceptability preferences determine which objects are candidates for selection. Desirability preferences establish a partial order on the set of candidates. Necessity preferences specify objects that must (or must not) be selected for the goal to be achieved.

All long-term knowledge is stored in a recognition-based memory — a production system. Each production is a cued-retrieval procedure that retrieves the contents of its actions when the pattern in its conditions is successfully matched. By sharing variables between conditions and actions, productions can retrieve information that is a function of what was matched. By having variables in actions that are not in conditions, new objects can be generated/retrieved.

Transient process state is contained in a working memory. This includes information retrieved from long-term memory (problem spaces, states, operators, etc.), results of decisions made by the architecture, information currently perceived from the external environment, and motor commands. Structurally, working memory consists of a set of objects and preferences about objects.

For each problem solving decision, an elaboration phase occurs in which long-term memory is accessed, retrieving into working memory new objects, new information about existing objects, and preferences. Elaboration proceeds in a sequence of synchronous cycles, during each of which all successfully matched productions are fired in parallel. When this process quiesces — that is, when no more productions can fire on a cycle — an architectural decision procedure is invoked that interpets the preferences in working memory according to their fixed semantics. If the preferences uniquely specify an object to be selected for a role in a context, then a decision can be made, and the specified object becomes the current value of the role. The whole process then repeats.

If the decision procedure is ever unable to make a selection — because the preferences in working memory are either incomplete or inconsistent — an impasse occurs in problem solving because the system does not know how to proceed. When an impasse occurs, a subgoal with an associated problem solving context is automatically generated for the task of resolving the impasse. The impasses, and thus their subgoals, vary from problems of selection (of problem spaces, states, and operators) to problems of generation (e.g., operator application). Given a subgoal, Soar can bring its full problem solving capability and knowledge to bear on resolving the impasse that caused the subgoal. When impasses occur within impasses — if, for example, there is insufficient knowledge about how to evaluate a competing alternative — then subgoals occur within subgoals, and a goal hierarchy results (which therefore defines a hierarchy of contexts). A subgoal terminates when its impasse (or some higher impasse) is resolved. Soar learns by acquiring new productions which summarize the processing that leads to results of subgoals, a process called chunking. The actions of the new productions are based on the results of the subgoal. The conditions are based on those working memory elements in supergoals that were relevant to the determination of the results. Chunking is a form of explanation-based learning (Rosenbloom & Laird, 1986).

Soar's perceptual-motor behavior is mediated through the state in the top context (Wiesmeyer, 1988). Each perceptual and motor system has its own field in the state. Perceptual systems behave by autonomously adding perceived information to their fields of the top state. This information is then available for examination by productions, until it is overwritten by later information arriving from the same system. Motor systems behave by autonomously executing commands that are placed (by the firing of productions) in their fields of the top state.

2.2. Mapping Symbolic Goal-Oriented Behavior onto Soar

Figure 2-1 shows the mapping of functional capabilities onto Soar (including capabilities mentioned in the text, but not explicitly in Figure 1-1). This mapping is relatively straightforward, as it should be, given that the hierarchy was strongly influenced by abstracting from the experience with Soar. However, the first step is a bit complicated: functional goals — that is, the kinds of goals that are included in the functional hierarchy — are mapped onto a combination of context slots and (Soar) goals.

In the traditional Soar view, goals only occur when an impasse occurs; that is, when a context slot cannot be filled by direct knowledge access. At that point there is a declarative structure in working memory that represents the goal of resolving the impasse. The non-standard mapping arises because in the functional hierarchy, knowledge access is considered one of the ways of achieving a goal, rather than a means of accomplishing things directly; that is, without requiring goal structures as intermediaries.

Symbolic Goal-Oriented Behavior	Soar
Goal	Determine value for context slot
Goal achievement	Determining value
Goal detection	Value determined (decision procedure)
Goal recursion	Impasse/goal/context creation
Goal suspension	Implicit (when can't make progress)
Goal reactivation	Automatic (when can make progress)
Goal decomposition	Decomposition into independent operators
Quiescent knowledge access	Elaboration phase
Integration	Preference combination (decision procedure)
Single knowledge access	Elaboration cycle
Perception	Input system
Learning	Chunking
Task step sequence	Operator sequence
Step performance	Operator application
Primitive action	Motor action
Synthetic action	Operator
Step selection	Operator selection
Search	Subgoal-based lookahead and reselection

Figure 2-1: Mapping of goal-oriented capabilities onto Soar.

Thus, in this mapping, the creation of a context slot is the act of creating a goal to have an appropriate value selected for that slot.[4] A problem-space slot is the goal of determining what problem space should be used in the context. A state slot is the goal of determining what the current state is in the context. An operator slot is the goal of determining what operator should be applied in the context. Consider, for example, what happens during medical diagnosis when a diagnose-illness operator is selected in a context. As a result of this selection, the state slot becomes the goal of selecting the state that results from applying the operator to the previous state; that is, the state slot is the goal of having a state representing the correct diagnosis.

An impasse provides a refinement of the goal defined by a context slot, incorporating additional information about the way in which quiescent knowledge access failed to accomplish the goal — whether there are no candidates remaining under consideration for selection or multiple candidates. The impasse also provides the new context that allows full recursive use of the functional hierarchy. Without this additional structure, only memory access could be used for the achievement of goals. With this additional structure, goal achievement can also be pursued by task step sequences and goal decomposition (as

[4] It is not clear whether this shift in view has any major implications for Soar, or even if it will necessarily prove a more useful way to describe Soar than existing ways. However, it is appropriate for this analysis, and it does have the side benefit of emphasizing the relationship of Soar to such slot-based architectures as Eurisko (Lenat, 1983) and Theo (Mitchell et al, 1989).

described below). The combination of context slots and impasses (with their associated goals and contexts) thus seems to provide the best mapping of the functional hierarchy onto Soar.

Goal detection occurs via the decision procedure — if the preferences available in working memory determine a unique object to be selected for a slot, then the goal is achieved. However, once a decision results in a change in the context hierarchy, the situation has changed, and each slot represents anew the goal of selecting the appropriate value given the (changed) situation.

Goal suspension occurs implicitly. Whenever nothing more can be done for a goal, it is effectively suspended. It is automatically reactivated whenever additional progress can be made on it. Reactivation usually occurs when a subgoal completes, providing the altered situation (or information) upon which the goal was waiting. However, goal reactivation can occur any time the required situation exists, whether as a direct result of subgoal completion or not.

2.2.1. Knowledge Access

Soar accesses its knowledge by the firing of productions. A single knowledge access consists of a single cycle of elaboration, during which all of the successfully matched productions fire in parallel. The result of a single access is the context-dependent augmentation of the local environment — the contents of working memory — with additional information.

A quiescent knowledge access consists of a single decision cycle — the combination of an elaboration phase followed by an application of the decision procedure. During the elaboration phase, single knowledge accesses are performed repeatedly until exhaustion (that is, until no more productions are able to fire). At exhaustion, all of the accessible knowledge about the goal and situation have been retrieved. Quiescence is purely a function of this retrieval process. Integration occurs immediately following quiescence, when the decision procedure interprets the set of preferences in working memory to determine what they jointly imply. This integration actually covers not just information retrieved by memory access, but all preferences in working memory, whether they are retrieved by memory access, or generated by perception, a sequence of task steps, or decomposed subgoals. Quiescent memory access occurs for each context slot in parallel, and is repeated each time a context slot is changed. It thus occurs for each functional goal.

Perception occurs in Soar by the autonomous input-driven creation of structures in working memory. Once in working memory, perceptual information acts just as if it were retrieved from memory (though it is possible to distinguish the two by their location in working memory).

Learning occurs by the chunking of Soar's experience. This places new productions in memory, which are then available for use during later goal-oriented behavior. Chunking learns both from the system's own behavior and from the outside world (Rosenbloom, Laird, & Newell, 1988).

2.2.2. Task Step Sequence

Problem space operators are the synthetic actions, and motor commands are the primitive actions. These two types of actions are closely coupled in Soar — motor commands (primitive actions) are generated by production firing (knowledge access) in service of applying operators (synthetic actions). This lets us focus on the selection and application of operators, while leaving motor commands in the background. In fact, most Soar operators actually bottom out in knowledge access anyway, rather than in primitive actions; or in other terms, operators tend to be synthetic actions which lead to subgoals that are achieved via knowledge access. Both operator selection and application, and thus step selection and performance, occur via a functional goal — an operator slot and a state slot, respectively (as discussed above). This enables Soar's full goal-oriented behavior to be available for both, allowing them to be performed by knowledge access, task step sequences, and decomposition. Search occurs when knowledge access is inadequate, usually as a lookahead search in service of determining which of several options is preferred. Backtracking on error can also occur by the reselection of objects (problem spaces, states, and operators) that were previously selected.

Soar has several other features that, though not mentioned explicitly in the functional hierarchy, are important to its production of goal-oriented behavior. One feature is that Soar embodies the notion of problem spaces — sets of states and operators. Problem spaces allow Soar to pursue goal achievement within an appropriately restricted context. This wasn't included as an essential capability in the functional hierarchy, but does appear to be implicated in effective goal-oriented behavior. The other feature is that Soar allows states to be selected, in addition to problem spaces and operators. This enables easy recovery from bad task step sequences by the reselection of previous states, and allows the use of search methods — such as best-first search — which require state selection.

2.2.3. Goal Decomposition

In Soar, a goal decomposition is indistinguishable from a task step sequence. This occurs because an operator is a deliberately generated structure whose selection leads to a subgoal to apply it. A goal can thus be decomposed by the generation, selection, and application of a set of operators which jointly accomplish the goal. The issue of how to automatically decompose goals into a set of independent operators has not been addressed in any great detail in Soar. However, if the knowledge about such decompositions are in Soar's memory, it can use them.

3. CONNECTIONISM

Now that the groundwork has been laid, it is time to examine connectionism, and its relationship to symbolic goal-oriented behavior. We start by reviewing basic connectionist architectures, then proceed to analyze how symbolic goal-oriented behavior maps onto this basic structure, and then look beyond the basic architecture to systems that embody additional high-level structure for goal-oriented behavior.

3.1. Basic Connectionist Architecture

A basic connectionist architecture – as described, for example, in Rumelhart, Hinton, & McClelland (1986) – consists of units and connections between units. Units have activations, and connections have weights (either positive or negative). During each unit of time, activation passes from each individual unit over connections to its neighbors as determined by an output function (a function of the unit's output and the connection's weight), and an activation rule (a function of the unit's input and current activation). In a simple linear system, the activation of a unit at time $t+1$ is the sum of the products of its neighbors' activations at time t and the weights of the connections to the neighbors, though many more sophisticated possibilities also exist.

Performance occurs by activating a set of input units, propagating activation through the network until it settles down, and then reading the results off as the activations of a set of output units. Learning occurs by experience-driven modification of connection weights.

At the level of detail at which this basic architecture is described, it abstracts away from many of the important distinctions among connectionist systems — single-level versus multi-level networks, feedforward versus feedback networks, supervised versus unsupervised learning, and local versus distributed representations. For most of goal-oriented behavior, these distinctions are not critical.

3.2. Mapping Symbolic Goal-Oriented Behavior onto Basic Connectionism

Figure 3-1 shows the mapping of the hierarchy of functional capabilities onto the basic connectionist architecture. The mapping is close to trivial, because the basic connectionist architecture provides only quiescent knowledge access. The structure and weights in the network embody the long-term knowledge in the system. The propagation of activation which occurs during a single time step corresponds to a single knowledge access — activation is a short-term reflection of the long-term structure of the system (and its input). Activation propagation transmits this information to distal parts of the network. Transmission occurs in parallel over the set of connections, but it still amounts to just a single knowledge access. Repeated propagation until the network has settled corresponds to quiescent knowledge access. This ensures that all relevant information has been transmitted to where it might be needed. It also performs knowledge integration during every cycle of propagation, by the addition and subtraction of activation, and possibly additional nonlinear transformations. Quiescence is a function of the integration process settling down, rather than purely the transmission (retrieval) process.

Perception occurs via the activation of special input units. This changes the short-term activation of the system, without changing its long-term structure. Learning occurs via the adjustment of connection weights, thus allowing the network to be more knowledgeable at later points in time.

Two main classes of capabilities are missing from the basic architecture. The first class includes the goal-centered capabilities: achievement, detection, recursion, suspension, reactivation, and decomposition. The second class includes the capabilities required for performing task step sequences. This includes step performance and selection, synthetic and primitive actions, and search. Without such capabilities, general goal-oriented behavior is impossible.

Symbolic Goal-Oriented Behavior	Basic Connectionism
Goal	
Goal achievement	
Goal detection	
Goal recursion	
Goal suspension	
Goal reactivation	
Goal decomposition	
Quiescent knowledge access	Activation passing until quiescence
Integration	Activation combination
Single knowledge access	One cycle of activation passing
Perception	Activation of input units
Learning	Adjustment of connection weights
Task step sequence	
Step performance	
Primitive action	
Synthetic action	
Step selection	
Search	

Figure 3-1: Mapping of goal-oriented capabilities onto basic connectionism.

3.3. Beyond the Basic Architecture

It should not be too surprising that the basic connectionist architecture does not by itself provide symbolic goal-oriented behavior, any more than would Soar with just its production memory (even when augmented a bit). As in Soar, additional structure is required. For goal-oriented behavior, it does not matter whether this structure is implemented in "symbolic matter" outside of the connectionist memory, or by a set of special-purpose connectionist memories that interact via hard-wired connections, or by structure (or weights) in a single connectionist memory — though, such considerations will certainly interact with other important issues, such as learning and simplicity. What does matter is the functionality provided.

Bits and pieces of the required structure can be found in some existing connectionist systems. One of the more straightforward approaches, taken from Rumelhart, Smolensky, McClelland, & Hinton (1986), is shown in Figure 3-2. This system, which is specialized to the domain of Tic-Tac-Toe, is able to select and execute a sequence of task steps. The task steps can be either primitive actions which result in actually playing the game, or synthetic actions which simulate the results of real actions. Distinct memories are used for step performance and selection.

Though this system does represent significant progress, much is still missing. One problem is that the system has no goals; or alternatively, it has only one hard-wired implicitly-represented goal: playing Tic-Tac-Toe. The ability to have multiple goals, and to achieve, detect, suspend, reactivate, and decompose them, is missing. A second problem is that the system does not learn. This may not be a fundamental problem, since connectionist systems definitely do learn, but this particular system did not learn. A third problem is that the system cannot recursively use the hierarchy for step selection and performance. One consequence of this is that, though it can perform sequences of task steps, it cannot use such sequences as lookahead searches in service of determining what steps to select.

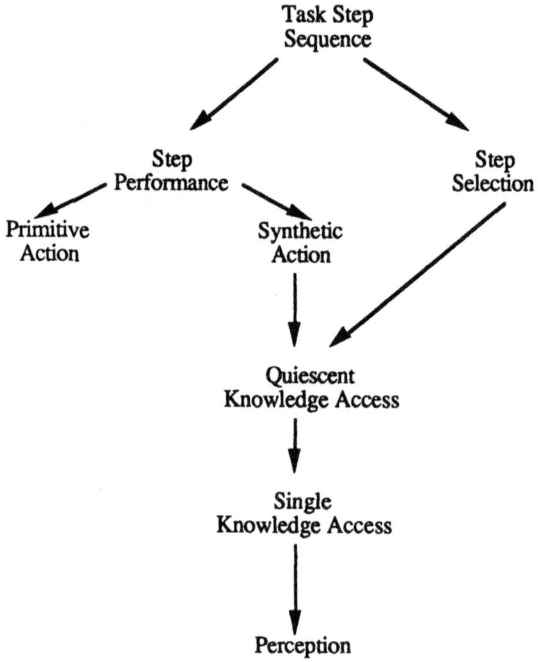

Figure 3-2: Functional capabilities provided by Tic-Tac-Toe system in Rumelhart, Smolensky, McClelland, & Hinton (1986).

Other systems provide fragments of related functionality, such as the explicit representation of the goal, and its use in hill-climbing (Kawamoto, 1986); the explicit representation of evaluation functions for states (Sutton & Barto, 1981, Anderson, 1987); traversal of hierarchical structures (Hinton, 1981, Touretzky, 1986); and the use of limited forms of lookahead search in service of step selection (Sutton & Barto, 1981). However, no connectionist system yet provides all of the requisite functionality.

4. A CONNECTIONIST SOAR

One possible approach to creating a connectionist system capable of general goal-oriented behavior is to combine Soar's well-developed capabilities for the use of goals and task step sequences, with a connectionist model of knowledge access. In addition to providing the necessary structure that is missing from connectionist systems, the creation of such a hybrid could help focus comparisons between symbolic and connectionist memories, by asking how well each supports the needs of symbolic goal-oriented behavior. This could shift the focus of the discussion from more peripheral topics, such as the binding of values to variables, to what is clearly one of the central issues in general intelligence.

Another benefit of creating such a hybrid is the promise it provides of solving some of the extant problems with Soar's current model of memory. A number of sources of evidence have recently come together to imply that Soar's existing production system memory is too powerful: the problem of expensive chunks, where learned rules severely degrade the performance of the system by requiring exponential match time (Tambe & Newell, 1988, Tambe & Rosenbloom, 1988); the difficulties in implementing Soar on highly parallel computers such as the Connection machine (Flynn, 1988); the limits on the forms of declarative knowledge that are learnable by chunking (Rosenbloom, Newell, & Laird, 1989); and work on mental models (Polk & Newell, 1988). The vector of change clearly points in the direction of more restricted models of memory. Connectionist memories, along with various forms of simpler symbolic memories, are major candidates for the new Soar memory model.

A first cut at what a connectionist Soar would look like can be obtained by combining the relevant portions of the functional mappings in Figures 2-1 and 3-1 to yield the hybrid functional mapping in Figure 4-1. When viewed from the Soar perspective, this mapping involves four substitutions of major components (Figure 4-2): production memory is replaced by a network with units and weighted links; working memory is replaced by unit activations; the chunking mechanism is replaced by a weight adjustment mechanism, such as (but not limited to) back-propagation (Rumelhart, Hinton, & Williams, 1986); and the decision procedure is replaced by functions which combine units' input activations.

Symbolic Goal-Oriented Behavior	Connectionist Soar
Goal	Determine value for context slot
Goal achievement	Determining value
Goal detection	Value determined (decision procedure)
Goal recursion	Impasse/goal/context creation
Goal suspension	Implicit (when can't make progress)
Goal reactivation	Automatic (when can make progress)
Goal decomposition	Decomposition into independent operators
Quiescent knowledge access	Activation passing until quiescence
Integration	Activation combination
Single knowledge access	One cycle of activation passing
Perception	Activation of input units
Learning	Adjustment of connection weights
Task step sequence	Operator sequence
Step performance	Operator application
Primitive action	Motor action
Synthetic action	Operator
Step selection	Operator selection
Search	Subgoal-based lookahead and reselection

Figure 4-1: Mapping of goal-oriented capabilities onto a connectionist Soar.

Symbolic Soar		Connectionist Soar
Production memory	→	Units with weighted links
Working memory	→	Unit activations
Chunking	→	Adjustment of connection weights
Decision procedure	→	Activation combination

Figure 4-2: Component substitution from symbolic to connectionist Soar.

Actually building such a hybrid is considerably more complicated than this simple set of substitutions suggests. At least six issues need to be resolved. The first issue is the expressibility of connectionist memories as associative memories; that is, what is the power of the language connectionist memories embody for describing when particular pieces of knowledge are to be accessed. Our investigations of restricted symbolic memories for Soar have revealed a number of expressibility issues that arise for various simple memory models: the representation of object cohesion, which assures that there is no confusion about which features go with which objects; the representation of undifferentiated sets of objects, which enables a rapid search over the objects in working memory during quiescent knowledge access; and the representation (and performance) of equality and inequality tests between objects in working memory. These particular issues may not be the ones that arise in using a connectionist memory, but expressibility issues are certain to arise. For each expressibility limitation that does arise, either: the memory model must be extended to overcome it; it must be possible to overcome the limitation some other way, such as by a sequence of task steps or by subgoal decomposition; or it must be shown that the additional expressibility is unnecessary.

The second issue is how to base knowledge access on an arbitrary number of cues (the knowledge in working memory), and how to access an arbitrary amount of knowledge in parallel. This is an issue that has been addressed in local connectionist systems, but not yet in a general way in completely distributed systems (Feldman, 1987).

The third issue is the adequacy of activation combination as a mechanism for decision making. Soar currently makes decisions based on a partial ordering among the alternatives (as encoded in the preferences), rather than by a total ordering (as encoded in activation levels). It needs to be determined whether a total ordering is sufficient, and if not, how a partial ordering could be implemented. One possible strategy might be to use asymmetric negative weights to implement a partial ordering: if object A is better than object B, then object A differentially inhibits object B. Another possibility is to directly store preferences in the memory and use an external decision procedure, as is currently done in Soar.

The fourth issue is how impasses are detected and classified — at least to determine whether at quiescence there are no candidates still being considered for selection, or multiple candidates. This requires that the system be able to distinguish objects that are candidates from those that are not, that it be able to detect that no unique candidate is left after quiescence is reached, and that it be able to determine whether the problem is caused by there being no candidates left or multiple candidates left. If a way is found to distinguish candidates — some structural distinction, for example — detection may be possible by determining how many candidates are above threshold at quiescence.

The fifth issue is how new problem solving contexts are created once an impasse has been detected. In the current version of Soar, the creation of a new context increases the number of slots about which decisions are to be simultaneously made. This in turn increases the amount of knowledge in working memory upon which further knowledge access is based, and may increase the amount of knowledge that will be retrieved before quiescence is reached (the second issue, above). One possible approach to this issue is to use a programmable connectionist system (McClelland, 1985). In such a system there is a single central store of knowledge, represented as a connectionist network, that controls the weights in an arbitrary number of identical programmable networks. By allocating one programmable network per subgoal, it may be possible to dynamically increase the number of slots about which decisions can be simultaneously made (at the price of some cross-talk).

The sixth issue is the relationship between Soar's learning mechanism — chunking — and connectionist learning mechanisms. Both are experiential learning mechanisms, but of different character. Chunking is an explanation-based learning mechanism that bases its generalizations on dependency analyses of single examples. Connectionist learning algorithms are more empirical, basing their generalizations on statistical regularities among sets of examples. While these differences are real, they may not be of quite the magnitude that they initially seem. The modifications made by connectionist learning algorithms — such as back-propagation — are a function of the paths by which, during performance, activation proceeded from the input units to the output units; that is, on dependency analyses of the outputs. Thus such learning algorithms may actually be performing some combination of explanation-based and empirical learning. In the field of symbolic machine learning, the combination of these two types of learning — explanation-based and empirical — is currently a major research topic (see, for instance, Flann & Dietterich, 1986).

Together, these six issues make the construction of a connectionist Soar far from the relatively trivial enterprise of just substituting the analogous connectionist mechanisms for Soar's production memory, working memory, decision procedure, and chunking mechanism. Nonetheless, there are potentially a variety of interesting payoffs from constructing such a system.

5. CONCLUSION

In this article we have presented a functional analysis of the capabilities underlying symbolic-goal oriented behavior, and mapped it onto Soar — a prototypical symbolic problem solver — and onto both basic and extended connectionist systems. From this analysis it is clear that the basic connectionist system, consisting solely of quiescent knowledge access, is missing many of the structures required to support general goal-oriented behavior. Fragments of the required structures do show up in several experimental systems, but no system yet comes close to the complete functionality that is required. Nonetheless, no fundamental roadblocks became apparent which would imply that this is impossible to do.

If the requisite structure were added to a connectionist system, the overall system is likely to resemble its symbolic cousins fairly closely, but with some interesting differences in the details. Contrasting two such systems — one connectionist and one symbolic — could provide needed focus in comparing connectionist and symbolic systems, by asking what the trade-offs are for the overall system from differences in the models of knowledge access. One concrete way of doing this is to attempt to create a connectionist Soar by replacing Soar's model of knowledge access with a connectionist model. We have provided some speculations on what such a hybrid might look like. A number of key issues make the construction of such a system far from trivial, but it does offer potential for overcoming existing problems with both Soar and connectionist systems.

ACKNOWLEDGEMENT

I would like to thank John Laird and Allen Newell for their helpful comments on an earlier draft of this article — and for a variety of useful conversations related to this material. I would also like to thank Rex Flynn and Milind Tambe for their provocative conversations on Soar's computational (that is, memory) model. Much of the inspiration, and a number of the ideas, underlying this article originated in conversations with these four people. I would also like to thank Rolf Pfeifer for prompting me to write this article.

This research was sponsored by the Defense Advanced Research Projects Agency (DOD) under contract numbered N00039-86C-0033 (via subcontract from the Knowledge Systems Laboratory, Stanford University) and by the National Aeronautics and Space Administration under cooperative agreement number NCC 2-538.

REFERENCES

Anderson, C.W. (1987). Strategy learning with multilayer connectionist representations. P. Langley (Ed.)., *Proceedings of the Fourth International Workshop on Machine Learning*. Irvine, CA, Morgan Kaufmann.

Feldman, J.A. (1987). Connectionist representation of concepts. In D. Waltz & J.A. Feldman (Eds.), *Connectionist Models and their Applications*. Ablex.

Flann, N.S. & Dietterich, T.G. (1986). Selecting appropriate representations for learning from examples. *Proceedings of AAAI-86*. Philadelphia, PA.

Flynn, R. (1988). Placing Soar on the Connection Machine 'Prepared for and distributed at the AAAI Mini-Symposium "How Can Slow Components Think So Fast'.

Hinton, G.E. (1981). Implementing semantic networks in parallel hardware. In G.E. Hinton & J.A. Anderson (Eds.), *Parallel Models of Associative Memory*. Hillsdale, NJ: Erlbaum.

Kawamoto, A.H. (1986). Solving puzzles with a connectionist network using a hillclimbing heuristic. *Proceedings of the Eighth Annual Conference of the Cognitive Science Society*. Amherst, MA.

Korf, R.E. (1987). Planning as search: A quantitative approach. *Artificial Intelligence*,**33**, 65-88.

Laird, J.E., Newell, A., & Rosenbloom, P.S. (1987). Soar: An architecture for general intelligence. *Artificial Intelligence*, **33**, 1-64.

Lenat, D.B. (1983). EURISKO: A program that learns new heuristics and domain concepts. The nature of heuristics III: program design and results.*Artificial Intelligence*, **21**, 61-98.

McClelland, J.L. (1985). Putting knowledge in its place: A scheme for programming parallel processing structures on the fly. *Cognitive Science*, **9**, 113-146.

Mitchell, T.M., Allen, J., Chalasani, P., Cheng, J., Etzioni, O., Ringuette, M., & Schlimmer, J.C. (1989). Theo: A framework for self-improving systems. In K. VanLehn (Ed.), *Architectures for Intelligence*. Hillsdale, NJ: Erlbaum. In press.

Newell, A. (1989). Unified Theories of Cognition. Cambridge, MA: Harvard University Press. In preparation.

Polk, T.A. & Newell, A (1988). Modelling human syllogistic reasoning in Soar. *Proceedings of the 10th Annual Conference of the Cognitive Science Society*, Montreal.

Rich, E. (1983). *Artificial Intelligence*. New York: McGraw-Hill.

Rosenbloom, P.S., & Laird, J.E. (1986). Mapping explanation-based generalization onto Soar. *Proceedings of AAAI-86*, Philadelphia.

Rosenbloom, P.S., Laird, J.E., & Newell, A. (1988). The chunking of skill and knowledge. In H. Bouma & B.A.G. Elsendoorn (Eds.), *Working Models of Human Perception*. London: Academic Press.

Rosenbloom, P.S., Newell, A., & Laird, J.E. (1989). Towards the knowledge level in Soar: The role of the architecture in the use of knowledge. In K. VanLehn (Ed.), *Architectures for Intelligence*. Hillsdale, NJ: Erlbaum. In preparation.

Rumelhart, D.E., Hinton, G.E., & McClelland, J.L. (1986). A general framework for parallel distributed processing. In D.E. Rumelhart, J.L. McClelland, and the PDP Research Group (Eds.), *Parallel Distributed Processing: Explorations in the Microstructure of Cognition, Volume 1: Foundations*. Cambridge, MA: Bradford Books/ MIT Press.

Rumelhart, D.E., Hinton, G.E., & Williams, R.J. (1986). Learning internal representations by error propagation. In D.E. Rumelhart, J.L. McClelland, and the PDP Research Group (Eds.), *Parallel Distributed Processing: Explorations in the Microstructure of Cognition, Volume 1: Foundations*. Cambridge, MA: Bradford Books/ MIT Press.

Rumelhart, D.E., Smolensky, P., McClelland, J.L., & Hinton, G.E. (1986). Schemata and sequential thought processes in PDP models. In J.L. McClelland, D.E. Rumelhart, and the PDP Research Group (Eds.), *Parallel Distributed Processing: Explorations in the Microstructure of Cognition, Volume 2: Psychological and Biological Models*. Cambridge, MA: Bradford Books/ MIT Press.

Sutton, R.S. & Barto, A.G. (1981). An adaptive network that constructs and uses an internal model of its world. *Cognition and Brain Theory*, **4**, 217-246.

Tambe, M. & Newell, A. (1988). Some chunks are expensive. J. Laird (Ed.), *Proceedings of the Fifth International Conference on Machine Learning*. Ann Arbor, MI.

Tambe, M. & Rosenbloom, P.S. (1989). Eliminating Expensive Chunks by Restricting Expressiveness. *Proceedings of IJCAI-89*, Detroit, MI. In press.

Touretzky, D.S. (1986). BoltzCONS: Reconciling connectionism with the recursive nature of stacks and trees. *Proceedings of the Eight Annual Conference of the Cognitive Science Society*. Amherst, MA.

Wiesmeyer, M. (1988). *Soar I/O Reference Manual, Version 2*.Department of EECS, University of Michigan.

CONNECTIONISM IN PERSPECTIVE
R. Pfeifer, Z. Schreter, F. Fogelman-Soulié, L. Steels (Eds.)

Dynamical Systems and Expert Systems

Roberto Serra
Enidata, via Aldo Moro 38 - 40127 Bologna (Italy)

Abstract—*Connectionist models are dynamical systems which aim at accomplishing Artifical Intelligence goals by exploiting the self-organizing properties of nonlinear dynamics. Several desirable features of neural networks are shared also by other dynamical systems for AI, including classifier systems and reaction-diffusion models.*

A discussion is given of the application of neural networks to tasks involving high level knowledge. In order to achieve better results it is necessary to introduce previous domain knowledge: in neural networks this is done by connections engineering, i.e. by careful wiring of the network architecture. The difficulty of connections engineering in expert tasks is stressed.

The introduction of previous knowledge in classifier systems is straightforward, since it can be done with usual knowledge engineering techniques. Moreover, classifier systems tightly couple a dynamical and an inferential subsystem, thus providing an interesting "laboratory" for the study of the interaction between the dynamical and the symbolic approach to AI. Such close coupling can lead to the automatic discovery of solutions for the task to be learnt, which mix inferencing and dynamics in an unexpected way.

The limitations of present classifier systems are briefly outlined, along with promising lines of research.

Keywords—Classifier systems, genetic algorithms, neural networks, a priori knowledge, connections engineering

1 INTRODUCTION

The dynamical systems approach to Artificial Intelligence is a very interesting alternative to the inference-based methods of classical AI (Serra and Zanarini, in press). Let us remark that the term "Artificial Intelligence" is used here in a traditional way (see e.g. the definition given Barr & Feigenbaum, 1981) while different definitions, like the one advocated by Kodratoff (1989) do not fit with the meaning used in this paper.

The basic feature of this approach is the use of truly dynamical systems, i.e. numerical variables which evolve in time according to a definite set of equations. The achievement of the "cognitive task" which is given to the system is based on the self-organizing properties of nonlinear dynamics (Haken, 1978; Nicolis & Prigogine, 1977; Serra et al., 1986), while in classical AI systems it is based on the chaining of logical inferences.

In order to deal with complex tasks, such dynamical systems need both a large number of degrees of freedom and a rich phase space, accommodating several attractors: they must therefore belong to the class of high dimensional nonlinear dynamical systems.

Learning is usually achieved by suitable modifications of the parameters' values, but it may also involve modifications in the structure of the system of equations.

Connectionist models are certainly the best known members of the class of dynamical systems for Artificial Intelligence, although they are not the only ones. Let us recall here also random boolean networks (Atlan, 1985; Kaufmann, 1970), reaction-diffusion models (Steels, 1988) and classifier systems (Holland, 1986; Holland et al., 1986).

The attractive features of connectionist models are actually based on their dynamical nature: robustness, capability of handling contradictions, generalization, fault tolerance are all consequences of "computing with dynamical attractors" (Hogg & Huberman, 1984). These properties are therefore shared by all those systems which perform cognitive tasks relying on collective properties of large dynamical systems.

Some guiding principles are necessary in order to choose among the very many possible dynamical systems. Until now, biological metaphores have provided the most widely accepted hints: connectionist models are inspired by rough models of the nervous system, random boolean networks by genetic networks, and classifier systems by genetic replication. However, other metaphores are provided by the physical world, like chemical reactions (Steels, 1987) and spin systems (Hopfield, 1982).

What is really difficult to find is a good learning algorithm for dynamical systems (actually, for any system). Learning from examples introduces a dynamics in weight space: in this case we are faced with the description of two coupled dynamical systems, one in state space and one in weight space.

The following discussion will be limited to dynamical AI systems which can learn from examples: indeed, the focus of the paper is on expert systems, a major reason for research in this direction being the hope to bypass, or to reduce the "Feigenbaum bottleneck" of knowledge engineering.

The dynamical approach to AI is endowed with several desirable features, but is also affected by some weakness. In particular, it is much less transparent than the inferential approach, and it is usually fairly difficult to explain why a network has reached a given "conclusion". Another obvious difficulty can be found in handling long chains of inferences. Moreover, if distributed representations are used, crosstalk among several patterns can give rise to confusion.

It seems therefore reasonable to view the "dynamical" and the "symbolic" approaches as complementary, rather than opposite lines of research in artificial cognitive systems. We will later review further reasons for integrating the two approaches, and indicate some promising ways to do it.

2 CONNECTIONS ENGINEERING

Connectionist models have already proven useful for low level knowledge processing, like signal analysis and recognition.

However, their usefulness in applications which require high level knowledge processing is still to be established, although some interesting examples have been presented, where connectionist models perform typical expert tasks like e.g. medical diagnosis (Bounds et al., 1988; Fogelman et al., in press), classification of personality profiles (Surkan, 1988), mortgage underwriting judgements (Collins et al., 1988) and bond rating (Dutta & Shekhar, 1988).

Serious limitations of the performance in high level cognitive tasks should be expected in all those cases where the network learns everything from examples, without any kind of previous domain knowledge. Let it suffice to consider human learning, where explicit knowledge transmission plays such a fundamental role, or to remember one of the basic results of classical AI, i.e. that domain specific knowledge is fundamental. Moreover, the time required for learning everything from examples may grow exponentially with the size of the network, at least for some tasks (Tesauro & Janssens, 1988).

Emphasizing the role of previous knowledge might seem at odds with the importance of automatic learning. However, if we want to achieve results in truly complex tasks, we really need both. We can envisage a two-step design process, where the first phase is a limited knowledge engineering phase, while the system capabilities are increased by automatic learning in the second phase.

How is it possible to introduce a priori knowledge in a neural network? This is partly done by a proper choice of the input: a clever choice of the input is a powerful technique, and it should always be given much care - not only in neural networks. However, complex problems cannot be dealt with by adding to a properly chosen set of input variables a completely general learning mechanism, at least with present day models and machines.

Further methods for introducing previous knowledge in neural networks are therefore required: they can be called "connections engineering", since they amount to a careful wiring of the connection scheme according to the problem at hand.

In tasks related to the processing of low level knowledge, like image processing or signal recognition, the design of the connection scheme is sometimes made easier by some geometrical or invariance properties of the problem.

As an example, think of an image processing task (Le Cun, 1989) , with M hidden units in the first hidden layer. It is known from the literature (previous knowledge) that a useful architecture could be based on having all the M units compute the same local property on different parts of the input (their receptive fields). In this case, each hidden unit can be connected only to a small subset of the input units, namely those belonging to its receptive field, and the same set of connections should be replicated M times. Such approach has the advantage of reducing the number of independent degrees of freedom. Similar cases can be found in analyzing time histories, where hidden units can be specialized in recognizing particular patterns at different positions in time.

However, such geometrical or symmetry properties can not be found in tasks which involve high level knowledge. Connections engineering then needs to be very specifically tailored for the problem at hand.

An interesting example is provided by a medical diagnosis system for abdominal pain, described in Fogelman et al. (in press), based on a multilayered perceptron, where the input layer describes the possible symptoms (present, absent, unknown) and the output layer the diagnoses. While the initial trials were made with complete interconnections, i.e. no a priori knowledge, the results improved significantly when a careful tailoring of the interconnection scheme was introduced, by interpreting the first hidden layer as a layer of syndromes, and allowing only the appropriate connections from symptoms and to diagnoses.

In conclusion, different recent works (LeCun, 1989; Fogelman et al., in press; Suddarth et al., 1988) all point in the same direction: introducing previous knowledge on the task domain in the network design is very important, it not only improves the performances but can also make the difference between satisfactory and unacceptable results.

The development of connection engineering techniques is a crucial step towards the development of connectionist systems for expert tasks, although the power of such techniques has not yet been established.

Connection engineering needs not be so complete as knowledge engineering does, because the former is always supplemented by an automatic learning phase. However, connections engineering is a very difficult task, probably more difficult than knowledge engineering. In a sense, the relationship between the two is reminiscent of that between electronic circuit design and microprocessor programming. In connections engineering, there are no high level languages, but one needs to precisely define the wiring scheme according to his knowledge. The problem appears more difficult in dealing with high level knowledge than in signal processing, because of the absence of general guiding principles or symmetry properties.

3 HETEROGENEOUS AND HYBRID SYSTEMS

The difficulties of connections engineering also point to the need for integrating the dynamical systems approach and the classical approach, which has already been stressed in Section 1. Although there are still very few studies focusing on the problems of such integration, the main hypotheses can be grouped according to the degree of interaction between the two approaches.

A relatively cautious proposal is that of heterogeneous systems, i.e. systems composed of two or more modules, some symbolic and the others dynamical, which are specialized for different tasks. This might be the case, e.g., of a hypothetical speech understanding system where a neural net could perform speech recognition, by proposing "recognition hypotheses" to a symbolic module for syntactic and semantic analysis.

Such solution is the less dangerous one, since the two approaches are kept separate, and they interact only through the exchange of data: the output of a given module is (a part of) the input of another module.

Tighter couplings between the two approaches are also possible: one such attempt is the proposal (Hendler, 1989) of spreading of activation between connectionist networks and semantic networks.

A different suggestion is that of using the results which can be achieved by training neural networks in order to provide hints and suggestions for the knowledge engineering phase, which is however non automatic. Some possibilities which have been suggested along this line (Fogelman et al., in press) are the interpretation in terms of high level descriptors of the structures which spontaneously develop in neural nets when trained on specific tasks, and the derivation of rules for expert systems from the analysis of the connection scheme after supervised learning.

A different approach is taken in systems which might be called "hybrid", because they integrate inferential and dynamical techniques in the same module. We will now discuss in detail this line of research, since it is particularily interesting for at least two fundamental reasons:

- it is based on a very tight coupling between the inferential and the dynamic paradigms, thus allowing a thorough investigation of the interplay between the two;
- it allows a straightforward introduction of previous knowledge, with conventional knowledge engineering techniques.

The essential idea behind this line of research is that of superimposing on a rule based system a "selectionist" (Steels, 1987) dynamics. The rules then compete and cooperate among themselves, and new rules, which are offsprings of the old ones, are generated. The knowledge base undergoes evolution and refinement in an automatic learning phase.

The introduction of previous knowledge in rule form is straightforward, since it is possible to start with an initial set of rules prepared according to knowledge engineering techniques. Moreover, some domain specific knowledge can also be introduced in the choice of the system's parameters, in a way reminiscent of connections engineering.

The interaction between the two paradigms is very tight indeed: production rules are typical inferential devices; however, a numerical variable (the "strength") is associated to each rule. The competition among the rules is based on the strengths, and also the "genetic" operators choose the "parents", from which new rules are generated, among the strongest rules.

A further reason of interest in this approach is that, while connectionist netwoks usually have a fixed structure - where only the parameter values change during learning - dynamical rule based systems undergo structure modification, thereby allowing greater plasticity and adaptability.

4 CLASSIFIER SYSTEMS AND GENETIC OPERATORS

We will now discuss the so called "classifier systems" which are an attempt at putting at work the above mentioned idea of population dynamics on a population of rules, in a complete model. We will not review here the details of classifier systems, which are described at length in Holland (1986) and Holland et al. (1986), but we will give for completeness a brief sketch of their features. Let us also remind that a domain independent package for the simulation of these systems is available (Riolo, 1987).

A classifier system is composed by a set of rules of the condition/action type, called classifiers, and by a message list (ML); it is coupled to the external environment through a set of effectors (output devices) and a set of detectors (input devices).

At each step (major cycle) the following operations are performed:

- The detectors post their messages (if they have some) on the ML, thus providing information about the present state of the environment;
- Each rule verifies whether its condition is matched by some message on the ML and, if it is, it enters a competition for firing. The competition is ruled by a numerical variable, the bid, which is a function of the classifier's strength. "Firing" also means posting a message, specified by the rule's action part. According to the so called bucket-brigade algorithm, the strength of each posting classifier is reduced by an amount determined by the bid, while the strengths are increased of those classifiers which had posted, at the previous time step, messages later matched by winning

classifiers. In this way a flow of strength is generated from a winning classifier to its "parents", i.e. those classifiers whose messages allowed it to fire. Ultimately, classifiers sending output messages are rewarded or punished by the environment. In such a way chains of classifiers leading to useful behaviours are reinforced.

- The effectors check the message list to verify whether there are output messages; the external reward, either positive or negative, is added to the strengths of those winners which posted output messages.

The evolution of the strengths of a fixed population of classifiers is ruled by the bucket-brigade algorithm, while genetic algorithms are at work in order to change the population. In order to prevent a sudden decrease in the system's performance due to randomly generated new classifiers, the genetic subsystem replaces only low strength classifiers, which have small chances to fire and should therefore have a very limited effect on the overall behaviour. Genetics thus operates on a longer time scale than that of the bucket brigade algorithm, otherwise the strength distribution might be affected by random fluctuations, rather than reflecting the "usefulness" of each classifier for the global system's performance.

Present day classifier systems have fairly poor representation scheme and matching mechanism: messages are fixed-length binary strings, while the matching mechanism is given some flexibility by adopting "don't care" and "pass through" symbols.

Also applications of classifier systems are still primitive: some examples have a "real world" flavour, but the true problems which have been tackled have been considerably simplified, as compared to typical expert system tasks. We stress however that this seems to be a consequence of the poor representation scheme, rather than an intrinsic weakness of the method.

The adoption of such simple schemes is probably due to the fact that classical genetic operators (i.e. crossover, mutation and inversion) can be introduced in a straightforward way. On the other hand, simple schemes also allow a deeper understanding of the system dynamics and, more important, of the interaction between the inferential and the dynamical subsystems.

In order to prove valuable for complex applications, dynamical rule based systems need to employ richer representations, and suitable genetic algorithms need to be defined.

In any case, also within the standard representation, the kind of genetics required for classifier systems is not identical to classical genetics. This has been already shown by preliminary experiments on limited, artificial task domains. A typical result is that a particular kind of genetic operators, which might be called also "cognitive gentics", are much more powerful than the usual "background" genetics in discovering the right classifiers.

These genetic operators (Robertson & Riolo, 1987) are the following:

- Cover detector: if there is a message from detectors which is not matched by any classifier, then this operator generates a classifier which matches that message. The rationale is that otherwise some information from the environment would not be used by the system: if no message from detectors is matched, the system can even fail to start, i.e. no classifier bids.

- Cover effector: if a mistake is detected, it generates a classifier which matches some message on the ML, with a random action.
- Triggered chaining: it helps in creating chains of rules by providing "bridging classifiers" beween a classifier active at a given time step t and another classifier active and profitable at time t+1.

Let us stress that these genetic operators are not ad hoc: they are essentially independent from the specific task domain, and are also well suited for a cognitive system, where direct feedback concerning the performance can profitably be employed.

Cognitive genetics does not possess an obvious counterpart in true genetics (i.e., that working at DNA level) but this is no major problem in the design of artificial cognitive systems, where the use of biological metaphores should provide useful hints but no rigid barriers.

5 CLASSIFIER SYSTEMS AND NEURAL NETWORKS

We will now briefly discuss the relationship between classifier systems and neural networks. Besides a theoretical interest, such comparison could provide hints about possible modifications of both classes of models. This relationship is formally investigated in another work (Compiani et al., 1988); here we will limit to sketch the major results.

Since the languages of classifiers and networks are different, in order to carry on the comparison we will try to build an "image network" which performs the same task as a classifier system. Let us associate to each possible message (recall that they are binary strings of fixed length - say N bits) a "neuron" of a huge network, which is therefore composed of 2^N nodes.

Any such neurons "fires" if it is on the message list: we are thus naturally lead to consider a boolean network. However, if a particular expression for the bid is chosen, which takes into account also the so-called 'relative support" of a classifier, then there is a continuous variable associated to each message, its "intensity": in this case the image network is a continuous one, and the output of each neuron corresponding to a message on the ML is equal to its intensity, while it vanishes for neurons representing messages which are not on the message list.

Classifiers then correspond to connections in the image network, since they propagate activation from one node to another: two nodes are coupled if there is a classifier joining them.

One is thus led to the interesting conclusion that, both in neural networks and classifier systems, learning involves modification of the connection strengths, which is achieved in the latter case by the bucket brigade algorithm.

Let us now consider the activation rules, limiting our treatment to the simpler case of a boolean image network (no relative support), and to single-condition classifiers. If message A is on the message list (its image neuron is active) at time t, then classifier A/B tends to activate message B at the following time step. The details depend upon the rule which is chosen to find the winning classifiers: one method which has been proposed, and which will be considered here, is the comparison between the classifier strength and a fixed threshold.

In this case the activation equation of neuron B is very similar to the threshold function common in neural nets, e.g. the boolean Hopfield model (Hopfield, 1982). There is however a major difference, namely that in neural networks the global input, that equals the sum of all individual excitations, is compared with the threshold, while in classifier systems, if several classifiers can excite the same node, each one is separately compared with the threshold. In the latter case the excitation mechanism is therefore much less collective and activation flows essentially between single nodes.

If we consider multiple condition classifiers, then activation of the "action" node requires that all the "condition" nodes are active: also in this case there is a difference with neural nets, where usually a subset of the input signals can excite a neuron.

Note also that the use of "don't care" symbols introduces strong correlations: different connections in the image network are bound to have the same value.

In the image network, the bucket brigade learning algorithm introduces a flow of strength among connections, while the role of genetic operators is that of generating new connections. In the beginning, a very small subset of the neurons are actually linked by existing connections. Genetics then gradually explores the power of new connections, thus allowing activation of larger subsets of the network.

6 CONCLUSIONS

Experimenting with classifier systems has already shown that the interplay between dynamics and inferencing can give rise to unusual solutions, different from the obvious solutions which a human knowledge engineer would have found, which efficiently exploit the interaction mechanisms.

These solutions can lead to the performance of a given task by a smaller number of rules than those which would be necessary for the knowledge engineer, i.e. without dynamics (Compiani et al., 1989).

We must however remark that usually these truly dynamical solutions are much less readable than the "anthropomorphic" solutions, which are based on matching and inferencing with no essential contributions from the dynamical subsystem. Dynamical solutions are also sometimes unstable, in the long run, under the action of genetic operators.

We have already stressed the limitations of present day classifier systems. However, the overall scheme of competing rules, message posting, strengths dynamics and "genetic" variations in the population of rules is a powerful one.

Experimenting with classifier systems is complicated by the presence of many possible choices and many parameters whose values must be properly chosen. On the one hand, such richness of alternatives seems important for achieving flexibility, but on the other hand the system's performance and stability are very sensitive to some of the choices. While a "good" set of parameters' settings can be found for specific tasks, the strong feedback loops which are present make it unreasonable to dream of devising a "universally good" set of parameters.

A possible solution to this problem consists in adding a control system which monitors the classifier system's behaviour and, if necessary, modifies some parameters. Such control system (another classifier system, a "classical AI" program, a neural network) would correspond to a B-brain, (Minsky, 1986) if the classifier system is regarded as the A-brain interacting with the external world.

Present day classifiers perform straightforward associations between conditions and actions. However, what is basically required from a classifier is to read and generate messages, being able to withstand a competition for posting and to undergo transformations under the action of genetic operators. This allows us to foresee a very challenging and promising line of research in building systems where simple classifiers are substituted either by more complex classifiers, with suitably defined operators for computing the action from the condition part, or by entire subsystems, which might involve other classifier systems, neural nets or symbolic programs.

The overall system would thus become a "society of mind" (Minsky, 1986) where agents which communicate through a shared message list enter the competition/cooperation dynamics imposed by a bucket brigade algorithm. Such a development of classifier systems would also allow a deeper understanding of the "society of mind" theory, which would be tested in a precise yet very flexible model.

Genetics should be deeply modified and enlarged, and genetic operators working at a suitable abstraction level need to be introduced. This seems the major problem in the development of this line of research, since its large computational requirements might be tackled only by massively parallel computers (Robertson, 1987).

Acknowledgements

The ideas presented in this paper have been deeply influenced by close cooperation with Gianni Zanarini and with some colleagues at Enidata: Mario Compiani, Daniele Montanari and Gianfranco Valastro. Very stimulating discussions with Francoise Fogelman Soulie, John Holland and Luc Steels are also gratefully acknowledged.

REFERENCES

Atlan, H. (1985). Functional self-organization and creation of meaning. In *Proceedings Cognitiva 85* (Forum, pp. 117-119). Paris: Cesta.

Barr, A. & Feigenbaum, E.A. (1981). *The handbook of artificial intelligence.* Los Altos (CA): Morgan Kaufmann

Bounds, D.G., Lloyd, P.J., Mathew, B. & Waddell, G. (1988). A multilayer perceptron for the diagnosis of low back pain. In *Proceedings of the IEEE international conference on neural networks*, San Diego (CA), (vol.II, pp. 481-490)

Collins, E., Ghosh, S. & Scofield, C.L. (1988). An application of a multiple neural network to emulation of mortgage underwriting judgements. In *Proceedings of the IEEE international conference on neural networks*, San Diego (CA), (vol.II, pp. 459-466)

Compiani, M., Montanari, D., Serra, R. & Valastro, G. (1988). Classifier systems and neural networks. To appear in E. Caianiello et al. (Eds.) *Proceedings of the workshop on neural networks and parallel architectures*, Vietri, Italy. Singapore: World Scientific.

Compiani, M., Montanari, D., Serra, R., & Simonini, P. G. (1989). *Dynamical systems in Artificial Intelligence: the case of classifier systems*. This Volume.

Dutta, S. & Shekhar, S. (1988). Bond rating: a non conservative application of neural networks. In *Proceedings of the IEEE international conference on neural networks*, San Diego (CA), (vol.II, pp. 443–450).

Fogelman-Soulie, F., Gallinari, P., LeCun, Y., Thiria, S. Network learning. To appear in Y. Kodratoff & R. Michalski (Eds.) *Machine learning*, Vol.III.

Haken, H. (1978). *Synergetics*. Heidelberg: Springer Verlag.

Hendler, J. (1989). Problem solving and reasoning: a connectionist perspective. This volume.

Hogg, T. & Huberman, B. (1984). Understanding biological computation: reliable learning and recognition. *Proceedings of the Natural Academy of Science USA*, **81**, 6871–6875.

Holland, J.H. (1986). Escaping Brittleness. In R.S. Michalski et al. (Eds.), *Machine learning. An artificial intelligence approach*, Vol.II (pp.592-623). Los Altos (CA): Morgan Kaufmann.

Holland, J.H., Holyoak, K.J., Nisbett, R.E. & Thagard, P.R. (1986). Induction. Cambridge (MA): MIT Press

Hopfield, J.J. (1982). Neural networks and physical systems with emergent collective computational abilities. *Proceedings of the Natural Academy of Science USA*, **79**, 2554–2558.

Kaufmann, S. (1970). Behaviour of randomly constructed genetic nets: binary elements nets. In C.H. Waddington (Ed.) *Towards a theoretical biology* (Vol.3, pp. 18–37). Edinburgh: Edinburgh University Press.

Kodratoff, Y. (1989). Enlarging symbols to more than numbers or Artificial Intelligence is the science of explanations. This volume.

Le Cun, Y. (1989). Generalization and network design strategies. This volume.

Minsky, M. (1986). The society of mind. New York: Simon and Schuster.

Nicolis, G. & Prigogine, I. (1977). Self-organization in non equilibrium systems. New York: John Wiley

Riolo, R. (1986). CFS-C: A package of domain independent subroutines for implementing classifier systems in arbitrary, user-defined environments. Internal report, Logic of Computers Group, University of Michigan.

Robertson, G.G. (1987). Parallel implementation of genetic algorithms in a classifier system. In L. Davies (Ed.), *Genetic algorithms and simulated annealing* (pp. 129–140). Los Altos (CA): Morgan Kaufmann.

Robertson, G.G. & Riolo, R. (1987). A tale of two classifier systems. Preprint, University of Michigan.

Serra, R., Zanarini, G., Andretta, M. & Compiani, M. (1986). Introduction to the physics of complex systems. Oxford: Pergamon Books.

Serra, R. & Zanarini, G. (in press) Complex systems and cognitive processes. Heidelberg: Springer Verlag.

Suddarth, S.C., Sutton, S.A. & Holden, A.D.C. (1988). A symbolic neural method for solving control problems. In *Proceedings of the IEEE international conference on neural networks*, San Diego (CA), (Vol.I, pp. 516–523)

Surkan, A.J. (1988). Application of neural networks to the classification of binary profiles from individual interviews. In *Proceedings of the IEEE international conference on neural networks*, San Diego (CA), (Vol.II, pp. 467–472).

Steels, L. (1988). Steps Towards common sense. In Y. Kodratoff (Ed.) *Proceedings of ECAI 88* (pp.49-54). London: Pitman Publishing.

Steels, L. (1987). Self-organization through selection. In *Proceedings of the IEEE first international conference on neural networks*, San Diego (CA), (Vol.II, pp. 55–62).

Tesauro, L. & Janssens, B. (1988). Scaling relationshpis in back-propagation learning. *Complex systems*, **2**, 39–44.

CONNECTIONISM IN PERSPECTIVE
R. Pfeifer, Z. Schreter, F. Fogelman-Soulié, L. Steels (Eds.)
Elsevier Science Publishers B.V. (North-Holland), 1989

Expert Systems and Connectionist Networks

David G. Bounds

Research Initiative in Pattern Recognition, Royal Signals and Radar Establishment
St. Andrews Rd., Malvern, Worcs. WR14 3PS, U.K.

Abstract—*This paper compares connectionist networks and expert systems for building practical working systems in expert domains. The advantages and limitations of both approaches are outlined, and an example of a connectionist network performing an expert task is described.*

Keywords—Connectionist networks, neural networks, expert systems

This paper considers the utility of connectionist networks for building practical computer programs (i.e. those with a useful level of performance) in the sorts of domains that are often approached via expert systems. The main aim is to examine the relative merits of current connectionist networks and expert systems in producing working systems that are useful in some "expert" domain. It is not concerned with philosophical considerations of the more general role of connectionism in AI, because it seems to me that both connectionist networks and all other current forms of AI are a very impoverished basis for describing all but the most primitive aspects of human cognition, which I take to be the aim of Artificial Intelligence. It seems highly unlikely that either symbolic or connectionist representations are rich enough to model human cognition, or that a single adequate framework will exist in the forseeable future. Furthermore, it can only be demonstrated that Artificial Intelligence has been achieved, even to some limited extent in a restricted domain, by producing computer programs that perform some task to a level that we would describe as expert or intelligent if a human did it. For AI the proof is in the pudding, and the production of competent functional systems is not some adjunct to theory: it is the essence of the subject. Finally, this discussion is not limited to any single neural network model; the argument is generic, although some models are more powerful than others and each has its own limitations.

What do we mean by human expertise and what is an expert task? These terms are usually used to mean quite different things. It is useful to distinguish between recognising visual patterns, speech recognition and other recognition tasks which almost all humans do and other highly specialised recognition tasks, for example medical diagnosis, which only a small number of highly trained people can perform. We call the former domain human expertise, and the latter an example of an expert task.

One of the main motivations for the current flood of work on connectionist networks is the disparity between the sorts of tasks that all of us are good at and those that digital computers can be programmed to do. A digital computer can perform arithmetical operations at 10^9 times faster than people can. However, no computer can achieve face recognition from a visual image or speech recognition except in very limited circumstances. The performance of computers for these basic human pattern recognition tasks is vastly worse than that of a small child. The difference between arithmetic and these everyday recognition tasks is that arithmetic is a man made invention. The rules are clearly defined and a computer can be programmed to carry out arithmetic operations. In contrast, we do not know how people recognise faces and so we can only guess what programs we ought to write.

Most of these basic human recognition abilities are learned by example, often in early childhood.[1] Connectionist models seek to provide architectures and algorithms that may be trained by example and might be able to do such everyday recognition tasks with a level of success approaching that of humans. So far, the success of connectionist networks has been limited (NETtalk (Sejnowski & Rosenberg, 1987) and some work in speech recognition give some reason for optimism), but the success of rule based AI in producing competent systems is also near zero despite a large amount of work over many years. Human expertise tasks will not be discussed further here.

Digital computers have been applied with rather more success to expert tasks such as medical diagnosis, bacteriological identification, chess, configuring computer systems, and a variety of applied engineering problems. The ability to do tasks like these is latent not innate; they are learned by a small number of people at a much later age than the speech and vision competencies discussed above. Often these skills are acquired only during University level education. It is tempting to think that the reason that these skills are more amenable to programming on computers is that the knowledge required is explicit: we do know what rules to program. Rule based expert systems are based on the premise that expert knowledge can be encapsulated in a set of IF ... THEN ... rules. It is certainly true that we have much more information about what human experts actually do than is the case for speech or vision. However, the problems of building successful expert systems arise because this premise is only partially true.

The difficulties of obtaining an adequate set of rules from human experts are well known. First, experts may not know, or may be unable to articulate, what knowledge they actually use in solving their problems. The Knowledge Engineer may then obtain an inappropriate set of rules, perhaps more akin to a novice than an expert. Second, the performance of expert systems at best cannot be better than the expert on which it was modelled (though it might be more consistent because computer programs don't have bad days when the car won't start, the central heating won't work, and the dog is asleep on your clean suit). Third, experts often disagree. This problem is not encountered often by Knowledge Engineers only because most expert systems are built around a single expert. This ought not to be the case. A better system could clearly be obtained in principle by pooling the knowledge of more than one expert. It would then be necessary to resolve ambiguities arising from disagreement between the experts. Fourth, in all but the simplest problems it will be necessary to introduce some numerical measures of the strengths of rules. In MYCIN (Shortliffe, 1976) for example, "confidence factors" were introduced. Experts are almost always unable to make good choices for these numerical values, on which the performance of the system critically depends. Attempts to circumvent this problem by avoiding numbers and introducing quasi-numerical measure such as "IF x THEN it is highly likely that y" succeed only in putting a rough numerical grid on the

[1]There is a large area for debate about to what extent these abilities are learned from experience of the world as opposed to innate or pre-wired. However, no-one claims that learning from experience plays no part. This is all that is necessary for the discussion above.

values that an expert can choose, and may make the problem worse.

If experts cannot articulate appropriate rules, then surely they can provide examples of their own decisions, and it might be possible to infer rules from these examples. This is the rationale for machine induction methods. A comparison of machine induction methods and connectionist network approaches to expert tasks would be very relevant to the present discussion because both depend on training by example. So far as I am aware, no direct comparison has yet been made. We are currently applying both approaches to the same problem in our laboratory.

An examination of the claims of machine induction can be found in an article by Bloomfield (1987a) and the somewhat heated subsequent correspondence (Bratko & Michie, 1987; Bloomfield, 1987b). It appears from a recent analysis of approximately seventy operational expert systems in use in industry and commerce in Britain and the USA that machine induction is not widely used in operational systems. Less than 4% of the systems studied used machine induction methods (Cullen & Bryman, 1988). This is not necessarily a poor reflection on machine induction since only 43% of the "operational" expert systems were actually being used on a working basis. "The remainder were still under development, abandoned, suspended or used for limited demonstration purposes. Of the 43% that were operational, the majority operate at a low level of sophistication, performing limited functions and routine tasks" (Cullen & Bryman, 1988). Like machine induction, neural networks seek to learn from examples a model which can mimic an experts decisions. They are best viewed as a pattern recognition approach to machine intelligence. Pattern recognition approaches to machine intelligence are not a new concept, but before describing the strengths and limitations of neural networks vis a vis other pattern recognition methods and rule-based systems, I will describe a real application in the field of medical diagnosis (Bounds et al., 1988) in order to provide a concrete example of how neural networks can be applied.

The network shown in figure 1 consists of a set of input units which correspond to various symptoms relevent to some set of diagnoses. A value of zero is sent to the next layer by an input unit if that symptom is absent in a particular patient, and one if it is present. The output layer corresponds to the diseases. Units in the hidden layer are there to capture correlations between the symptoms because diseases are characterised by combinations of more than one symptom.

Given a collection of patient medical data, this network could be trained to learn associations connecting symptoms and diagnoses. After training is complete, presentation of a new set of patient symptoms should lead to the generation of the appropriate diagnostic class.

This approach was tested for the medical problem of diagnosing low back pain (Bounds et al., 1988). Back pain is one of the commonest complaints encountered by doctors, and yet the diagnosis of the underlying cause of back pain is a difficult task since many of the symptoms found in patients who have a serious spinal problem may also be present in those with less serious problems. Furthermore, non-organic symptoms may be present which make diagnosis difficult. This is therefore a real-world task that is far from trivial. Data was available for 200 patients, each of whom was placed in one of four diagnostic classes defined by what patient management was appropriate. The network was trained on 100 examples from the patient database and tested on the remaining 100 patients. Three groups of doctors had previously been given the same information about the 100 test

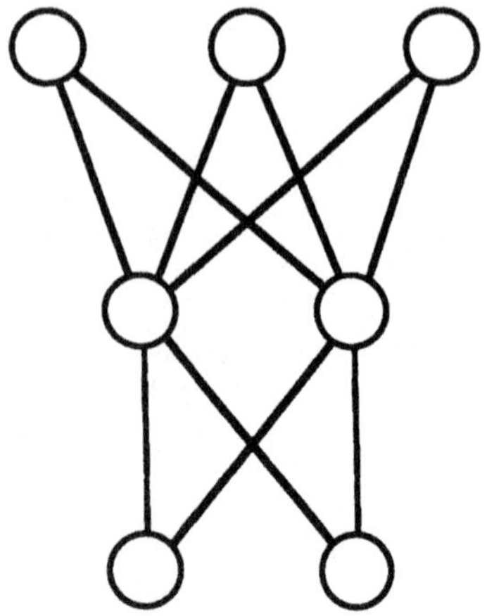

Figure 1: Schematic network for medical diagnosis

patients and asked to make a diagnosis. A correct classification is known in all 200 cases because all patients were followed up until clinical investigations were complete and a final diagnosis could be confirmed. It was therefore possible to compare the results of the network with general practitioners, orthopaedic specialists and neurosurgeons on the same set of patients.

Although clinical data on larger numbers of patients would be necessary before firm conclusions could be drawn, the initial results are promising. For the diagnostic category which it is most important to get right, because urgent surgery may be necessary, the network produces the correct classification more often than any of the three groups of doctors. The mean diagnostic accuracy over all possible diagnoses is also higher than that of the doctors. It is also interesting to look at the misclassifications. With only two exceptions, those patients misclassified by the network were also incorrectly diagnosed by the doctors—and the same wrong diagnoses were made. Some other more conventional pattern classifiers also give performances exceeding the doctors on this set of data (Bounds, 1989), but our experience over a range of pattern classification tasks suggest that better classification scores can usually be obtained from multi-layer networks.

In addition to a level of performance which often exceeds that of more commonly applied classifiers, neural networks offer several other advantages including speed in the recognition mode. While this is not important for medical diagnosis, it is vital for many industrial, commercial and military applications.

Let us turn to the disadvantages of neural networks. There is one real difficulty and also, for expert tasks, one apparent disadvantage compared with expert systems. The real problem is that a neural network is only as good as the data on which it was trained. Since networks typically minimise a sum square error over training patterns, they are really a form of non-linear regression. If the training patterns do not span the problem space adequately, then the interpolation required when new data is presented will only be useful (in the sense of producing a plausible result) by chance. The world is not full of large, representative labelled training datasets and if there is no good data training connectionist networks are not applicable.

The other problem is more controversial (judging from this conference!) and involves the representation of knowledge in neural networks. Unlike an expert system where the knowledge being applied is explicit in the form of rules, in connectionist networks knowledge is hidden as a pattern of numerical weight values. The main practical consequence of this is that it is not clear that one can query a trained network for an explanation of the basis on which a decision was made. At first sight this appears a powerful argument against connectionist networks since black boxes without any facility to give explanations are unlikely to be acceptable in most domains. However, it would not be difficult to provide explanations that are indistinguishable from those produced by an expert system. In expert systems explanations really consist of a verbal description of the rules that have fired in response to the input data. In a connectionist network system, having produced, say, a medical diagnosis, an explanation could be given couched in terms of symptoms typically observed in that disease with a check back to ensure the symptoms shown by the particular patient are consistent with the explanation, and modification of the explanation as appropriate. A front end to provide this sort of description could be constructed and it would be very difficult, perhaps impossible, to tell whether the internal decision had been made by an expert system or a connectionist network. It is not obvious therefore that the lack of explicit rules is a disadvantage in producing practical systems.

I shall end with two remarks. First, there are different kinds of expert tasks. Medical diagnosis is not the same as the problem of configuring computer systems—it deals with a natural phenomenon (organic disease) and not with a logical man-made universe. For purely logical, man-made tasks a rule based approach must be the right one. Configuring computers is not a job that should be tackled by pattern recognition. However, where the natural world provides the data and there is no strong theoretical underpinning to explain the phenomenon (unlike physics for example) pattern recognition approaches such as neural networks are very appropriate. After all, the knowledge which constitutes medicine was not carved on stone as a set of rules; it has been derived from observations of cause and effect over the centuries. Of course there is some theory of the relationship between cause and effect in some parts of medicine, derived from anatomy for example, but this knowledge is far from complete and pattern recognition has a role to play in learning correlations that are important.

Second, injudicious arguments between those who work on expert systems and those exploring connectionist networks are futile: none of these systems is sufficiently powerful that the alternative can be ignored. Most real world problems are so difficult that it is necessary to integrate knowledge from all sources, rules from experts and observations from data, in order to provide useful solutions. The problems of integrating connectionist networks and expert systems are fascinating and are likely to prove a fertile ground for research over the next few years. I have some ideas, but that is another story!

REFERENCES

Bloomfield, B.P. (1987a). Capturing expertise by rule induction. *Knowledge Engineering Review*, **2**, 55–63.

Bloomfield, B.P. (1987b). More comments on rule induction: a reply to Bratko and Michie. *Knowledge Engineering Review*, **2**, 69–70.

Bounds, D.G., Lloyd, P.J., Mathew, B., & Waddell, G. (1988). A multi-layer perceptron network for the diagnosis of low back pain. *Proc. IEEE 2nd Int. Conf. Neural Networks, San Diego, July 1988*, Vol. **2,** 481–489.

Bounds, D.G., Lloyd, P.J., & Mathew, B. (1989). A comparison of some neural network and other pattern recognition approaches to the diagnosis of low back pain. *preprint appearing shortly*.

Bratko, I., & Michie, D. (1987). Some comments on rule induction. *Knowledge Engineering Review*, **2,** 65–67.

Cullen, J., & Bryman, A. (1988). The Knowledge Acquisition bottleneck: time for re-assessment? *Expert Systems*, **5,** 216–225.

Sejnowski, T.J., & Rosenberg, C.R. (1987). Parallel networks that learn to pronounce English text. *Complex Systems*, **1,** 145–168.

Shortliffe, E.H. (1976). *Computer based medical consultations: MYCIN*. New York: Elsevier.

CONNECTIONISM IN PERSPECTIVE
R. Pfeifer, Z. Schreter, F. Fogelman-Soulié, L. Steels (Eds.)

Temporal Evolution of a Causal Network Through Conceptual Clustering*

Sanjeev B. Ahuja
Woo-Young Soh

Abstract—*In the context of* **LIBRA/Dx**, *a recently proposed competition-based parallel activation paradigm for diagnostic reasoning, this paper introduces a unique approach to the temporal evolution of a causal network through an experience-based process called "episodic learning". The proposed learning model suggests, that besides the conscious phenomenon of skills refinement that occurs through tutoring and repeated practice with "domain knowledge" among diagnosticians, there is also an unconscious aspect to learning which seeks to identify the regularities or salient characteristics that come to exist among a population of input case scenarios. This "case knowledge" is subsequently used by diagnosticians to construct and modify conceptual dependencies, so as to render more plausible diagnoses in the future. Preliminary simulation results suggest, that the proposed learning paradigm presents an intuitively plausible characterization of the transition from a novice to an expert among human diagnosticians. The underlying network architecture that evolves through this approach introduces a new dimension to connectionist modeling, by clearly delineating the domain and case knowledge, in terms of the roles that are played by each during problem solving.*

Keywords—Diagnostic reasoning, causal networks, conceptual clustering, episodic learning, expert systems, competition based parallel activation paradigm

1 INTRODUCTION

Diagnostic reasoning is a high-level cognitive task that requires the inference of an explanation for observed signs and symptoms or "manifestations", by accounting for the presence of each symptom with the hypotheses or "disorders" within the explanation. Existing symbol processing models of diagnostic reasoning do not provide adequate mechanisms to support the interactions among knowledge structures, which are necessary to capture the generative capacities of human diagnosticians in novel situations. Achieving such interactions has been one of the greatest difficulties with implementing models of diagnostic reasoning that can reason in the presence of imprecise or incomplete information, using traditional artificial intelligence (AI) representations like **scripts** (Schank, 1976), **frames** (Minsky, 1975), **schemata** (Rumelhart, Norman & Bobrow, 1976; Rumelhart, 1975), and

* Supported by: US Air Force Office of Scientific Research, Wash.D.C., UM Institute for Advanced Computer Studies, Swiss Life Insurance and Pension Company, Zurich.

production rules (Newell & Simon, 1972). The diagnostic model of **LIBRA/Dx** (Ahuja, Soh & Schwartz, 1989) makes the hypothesis that simultaneous satisfaction of multiple local constraints among domain concepts is sufficient to construct a plausible global explanation for a set of observed signs and symptoms. In this paper we additionally suggest that such local constraints are dynamic in the sense that they can adapt to a given context and further that prior episodes can be captured as "experience" by an incremental modification of these constraints. Through the formation of conceptual clusters among observed signs and symptoms, this latter phenomenon called **"episodic learning"** characterizes the transition of a human diagnostician from a **novice** to an **expert**.

The vast majority of cognitive processing lies between the highest cognitive levels of explicit logical reasoning, as with semantic networks, and the lowest levels of sensory processing as typified by neural models. As a macroscopic view of cognition, **LIBRA/Dx** has its knowledge representational basis in the symbol processing approaches of AI, and an underlying processing metaphor reflective of a neuron-like or **neurally inspired** microstructure. This approach allows knowledge structures to interact with each other and to capture the generative capacity of human reasoning in novel situations.

A diagnostician typically starts off with overlapping "descriptions" of disorders which specify sets of manifestations that are likely to be observed, in the event that any of the corresponding disorders were to occur. In general, however, the observed manifestations in a specific case indicate the simultaneous presence of multiple disorders since no single disorder can account for all of the observed manifestations, inspite of the absence of certain expected manifestations.

LIBRA/Dx provides a means by which the knowledge can be arranged in such a fashion that relevant pieces configure themselves dynamically in each context to form tailor-made explanations. A spread of activation process in this context, therefore, refers to the identification of appropriate knowledge pieces that can be assembled to form a context-sensitive explanation which is coherent and that supports inference. The combination of such a representational scheme together with the locally constrained parallel activation processing mechanism constitutes its diagnostic engine. **LIBRA/Dx** attempts to capture an existing symbol-processing approach (the Parsimonious Set Covering model) (Reggia, Nau & Wang, 1983), in a computational formalism that is plausible from the cognitive science perspective. Like the PSC model in its simplest scenario, **LIBRA/Dx** defines a diagnostic problem as the set $\{\mathbf{D}, \mathbf{M}, \mathbf{C}, \mathbf{M}^+\}$, where the first two elements characterize the scope of the problem: **D**, representing all possible elementary **hypotheses** $\mathbf{d}_i$ that can be made, and **M**, representing all possible features $\mathbf{m}_j$ that suggest the presence of each of those hypotheses. In diagnostic problem solving, hypotheses in **D** represent causative disorders (e.g., hepatitis), while features in **M** represent symptoms or manifestations (e.g. low blood count). The relation **C** captures the intuitive notion of "plausible" causation. Finally, $\mathbf{M}^+ \subseteq \mathbf{M}$ represents manifestations that are present in a specific problem. Given a diagnostic problem, an explanation **E** must *cover* $\mathbf{M}^+$, and be most *plausible*.

2 A PARALLEL ACTIVATION MODEL FOR DIAGNOSTIC REASONING

2.1 The Basic Concepts

The model is based on an underlying associative network of nodes that represent domain concepts or "knowledge atoms" (Smolensky & Riley, 1984). These nodes are connected to each other through links that represent associations (both causal and non-causal), among the knowledge atoms. The network consists of a set of hierarchically layered nodes, in which nodes within each layer connect directly only with the nodes of a layer immediately adjacent to it. There are two kinds of nodes within such a network. Nodes whose activation does not change during the course of problem-solving are called **router** or **stuck-at** nodes.

Nodes whose activation changes during the course of problem-solving are called **memory** or **accumulator** nodes. A node in the network is said to be active if it has a non-zero level of activation. Nodes with a zero activation level are said to be inactive. An active node can have a positive or a negative activation level which lies in the interval $[-1.0, +1, 0]$. The activation values can be thought of as having the following interpretations: **positive** activation signifies the *presence* of the concept which is represented by that node; **negative** activation signifies the *absence* of the concept which is represented by that node; and **zero** activation signifies *no knowledge* about the presence or absence of a concept.

A node on one layer is connected to other nodes in an adjacent layer via links. In any given network one can define a **connectivity matrix** for the nodes of two adjacent layers. Each entry in the matrix specifies the association between a pair of nodes in mutually adjacent layers if it exists, and the strength of this association. For example, if $\mathbf{n_j}$ is a node in one layer associated with a node $\mathbf{n_i}$ in a different layer, then a bi-directional link exists between the two nodes with strengths of association $\mathbf{w_{ij}}$ and $\mathbf{w_{ji}}$ respectively, from node $\mathbf{n_j}$ to $\mathbf{n_i}$ and vice versa. The pair of strengths on a link are allowed to be asymmetric (i.e., $\mathbf{w_{ij}} \neq \mathbf{w_{ji}}$ in general) and lie in the interval $[-1.0, +1.0]$, with a negative weight implying a preventive association or an **inhibitory** link and a positive weight implying a supportive association or an **excitatory** link.

The sets **D** and **M** in Figure 1 represent two adjacent layers in the parallel activation model framework. Each node $\mathbf{d_i}$ in layer **D** is connected to a set of nodes, **man**($\mathbf{d_i}$), in layer **M** through downward *causal* links. Similarly, each node $\mathbf{m_j}$ in layer **M** is connected to a set of nodes **evokes**($\mathbf{m_j}$), in layer **D** through upward *evoking* links. In each direction the associative strengths may either represent conditional probabilities or subjective causal and evoking strengths, respectively. For example, $\mathbf{w_{ij}}$ may denote the probability of node $\mathbf{n_i}$ to occur given that the node $\mathbf{n_j}$ is present, i.e., $\mathbf{p(n_i \| n_j)}$, and $\mathbf{w_{ji}}$ may denote the probability of node $\mathbf{n_j}$ to occur given that the node ni is present, i.e., $\mathbf{p(n_j \| n_i)}$. In a bipartite causal network the two conditional probabilities would be $\mathbf{p(m_j \| d_i)}$ and $\mathbf{p(d_i \| m_j)}$.

A stuck-at or router node in a causal network accommodates the idea of volunteered information, while an accumulator or memory node denotes the notion of inferred information. In the context of the parallel activation model note the following characteristics:

(a) for any active manifestation node $\mathbf{m_j}$, all plausible disorders that can account for its presence get activated initially;

(b) of the alternative disorders for a manifestation $\mathbf{m_j}$, only one disorder stays active by competitively inhibiting all the others (**single** winner-take-all). However, it may be that some of the inhibited disorders get reactivated subsequently to account for other active manifestations (**multiple** winners-take-all);

(c) each of the active manifestations are explained by at least one disorder that stays active;

- non-overlapping layers of domain concepts
- asymmetric, bidirectional inter-layer connections (only between adjacent layers)
- no intra-layer inhibitory connections
- "stuck-at" nodes denote volunteered information
- "accumulator" nodes denote inferred information
- dynamic, overlapping inhibitory concept clusters

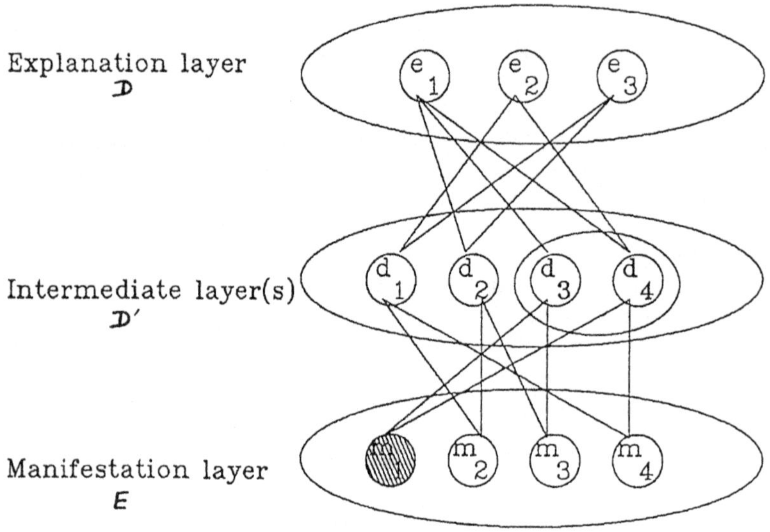

Figure 1: Architecture of **LIBRA/Dx**

(d) disorders found to be active at the end of a problem solving session, present a globally most plausible explanation.

2.2 A Spreading Activation Paradigm

In **competition-based** parallel activation models (Reggia, 1986), when a node assumes an activity level above its normal (threshold) resting level, its neighbors actively compete for the activity possessed by that node. The ability of the neighboring nodes to compete for a shared node's activity is proportional to their own respective activation levels.

The activation that each neighboring node acquires is at the expense of that which becomes available to the others and vice versa. In our approach however, we identify two separate aspects of contention between neighboring nodes, which dynamically configure themselves into an **inhibitory cluster** based on contextual information. The idea of competition is introduced by permitting the evoked disorders of manifestation $\mathbf{m_j}$ in an adjacent disorder layer, to actively compete for the total output activity of $\mathbf{m_j}$. The ability of disorder node $\mathbf{d_i}$ to compete for $\mathbf{m_j}$'s output activity $\mathbf{a_j(t)}$ is proportional to its own activation level $\mathbf{a_i(t)}$ and to $\mathbf{w_{ij}}$, the weight of its association with $\mathbf{m_j}$. Thus, the activation transferred from $\mathbf{m_j}$ in support of $\mathbf{d_i}$ at time $\mathbf{t}$, representing the contribution of node $\mathbf{m_j}$ to the belief in node $\mathbf{d_i}$, is equal to:

$$\mathbf{OUT^{+}_{ij}(t) = \frac{a_j(t) \cdot w_{ij} \cdot a_i(t)}{\sum_k a_k(t) \cdot w_{kj}}}$$

The denominator on the right hand side normalizes the flow, over all nodes in the inhibitory cluster that are competing for $\mathbf{a_j(t)}$ within an adjacent layer. The above computation enables highly activated nodes to extract a proportionately larger part of $\mathbf{m_j}$'s finite activation, leaving a successively smaller portion for competitors with lower activations.

In diagnostic reasoning, whenever supporting evidence is found for one disorder among several plausible ones that are alternatives, then not only does it contribute to a higher belief in that disorder to be present but it also takes away from the belief that one of its alternatives is present instead. In other words, each node in an inhibitory cluster actively seeks to *drain* its competitors of their respective activations. Since competing disorders influence each other via the manifestation that they all share, this drain of activation among competitors can be expressed as a correction of the original support that is received by each competing disorder di from the common manifestation node $\mathbf{m_j}$, by an amount

$$\mathbf{OUT^{-}_{ij}(t) = \left(1 - \frac{a_i(t) \bullet w_{ji}}{\sum_k a_k(t) \bullet w_{jk}}\right) \bullet a_j(t) \bullet a_i(t)}$$

We denote the flow of activation from $\mathbf{m_j}$ to $\mathbf{d_i}$ at time $\mathbf{t}$ as:

$$\mathbf{IN^{j}_{i} = OUT^{+}_{ij} - OUT^{-}_{ij}}$$

Finally, we iteratively define the measure of **belief(MB)** in a disorder node $\mathbf{d_i}$ due to each of the manifestation modes $\mathbf{m_j}$ in its $\mathbf{man(d_i)}$ set that are present at time $\mathbf{t}$ as:

$$\begin{aligned} \mathbf{MB_i(t)} &= \mathbf{MB_i(t) + \{1 - MB_i(t)\} \cdot IN^{j}_{i}(t)}, \\ & \text{for all } \textit{active } \mathbf{m_j \in man(d_i)} \text{ with } \mathbf{IN^{j}_{i}(t) > 0}. \end{aligned}$$

Similarly, we can define the measure of disbelief(MD) in a disorder node $\mathbf{d_i}$ at time $\mathbf{t}$ as:

$$\begin{aligned} \mathbf{MD_i(t)} &= \mathbf{MD_i(t) + \{1 - MD_i(t)\} \cdot \|IN^{j}_{i}(t)\|}, \\ & \text{for all } \textit{active } \mathbf{m_j \in man(d_i)} \text{ with } \mathbf{IN^{j}_{i}(t) < 0}. \end{aligned}$$

One other phenomenon that is believed to occur during diagnostic reasoning is, that the belief in the presence of a manifestation is diminished if other manifestations which share a common cause with it are not observed. This effect can be expressed as a proportionately lower belief in the presence of their common cause. We compute the active fanout $\mathbf{ACTFO_i}$: a weighted measure of the portion of the manifestations of di that are in fact found to be present. Then, $\mathbf{ACTFO_i = \sum_k w_{ki}}$, for all *active* $\mathbf{m_k \in man(d_i)}$.

Using these definitions one can compute the net flow of activity into a disorder node di at time **t** as:

$$\mathbf{F_i(t) = \{MB_i(t) \cdot ACTFO_i\} - MD_i(t)}$$

Given this competition-based parallel activation approach to satisfying local constraints among domain concepts in a causal network, a global interpretation of the effects is possible by allowing the activation levels of each accumulator node to reach a stable state. The activation of node di at time $(\mathbf{t} + \Delta\mathbf{t})$ is equal to the activation at time **t**, plus the net flow of activation $\mathbf{F_i(t)}$ into the node, minus its decay:

$$\mathbf{a_i(t + \Delta t) = a_i(t) + \beta \cdot [F_i(t) \cdot \{1 - a_i(t)\} - \delta_i \cdot \{a_i(t) - \theta_i\}]}$$

where β is a constant that is used to control the size of a time slice during numerical simulation; δ_i is the rate at which the activation of node $\mathbf{d_i}$ decays in the absence of stimulus; and θ_i is the threshold or the natural resting level of activation for node $\mathbf{d_i}$.

3 AUGMENTING DOMAIN KNOWLEDGE

Learning in neural networks is done by adjusting the association weights to produce the correct patterns of activation under "learned" situations. This approach to learning, however addresses only a tiny facet of the development of a diagnostician over time: that of acquiring cognitive skills through instruction or practice using typical case scenarios. It is generally known that there transpires a more significant period subsequently, over which a novice diagnostician gathers valuable "experience" with atypical or unexpected case scenarios and gradually transcends into the category of an "expert". We propose a strategy that attempts to capture one of these more significant developmental aspects in the evolution of an expert diagnostician.

3.1 A network Architecture for Causal Learning

What is it about the X-OR relationship that cannot be captured by a network of two layers? It is known that to realize this function, one must first be able to "detect" or recognize the co-occurrence of the two inputs and then, to suppress the output whenever this situation is detected in the input pattern. Co-occurrence of two inputs is a second-order relationship (Rumelhart & McClelland, 1986), which requires a three-layer network for realization. In general, for $(\mathbf{n})$ inputs one could potentially require $(\mathbf{n} - \mathbf{1})$ intermediate layers to faithfully realize all orders of relationships among them. In the context of diagnostic problem solving an intermediate node such as 's' is called a syndrome node, which in the case of an X-OR function denotes the simultaneous occurrence of its two inputs. Diagnosticians often utilize such knowledge to make and/or substantiate a preliminary diagnosis. Identification of such patterns or syndrome nodes, however, poses several practical problems.

First, whereas some co-occurrence patterns among the input manifestations may be known to a domain specialist, one is unlikely to know about all potential interdependencies that might exist, especially some of the higher order ones. Yet, one must also ensure that only the relevant syndrome nodes get identified while the spurious ones are either ignored or, if identified at all, gradually suppressed.

Second, in a domain model consisting of disorders, manifestations and causal associations, how is one to attribute semantics to the links which connect syndrome nodes to manifestation and disorder nodes? Are these also causal and evoking links, similar to the ones among disorders and manifestations?

Third, in some diagnostic domains at times, different types of domain knowledge may come to bear in identical situations, perhaps due to some collective characteristics of the environment or of previously encountered case scenarios. Not only do such characteristics get identified dynamically, they also contribute significantly during problem solving to the generation of an appropriate diagnosis.

3.2 Capturing co-occurence Statistics

It is not possible to determine a priori, whether a given domain model is capable of capturing the complex inter-dependencies among domain concepts that may come to exist within different environments. We need to somehow augment our domain knowledge with case-specific knowledge, without warping the existing conceptual relationships within the domain model.

We propose the creation of a complementary knowledge structure, that is not only capable of capturing the potential higher-order relationships between domain concepts, but which also automatically extracts them from input case scenarios, while simultaneously incorporating this knowledge as experience into the future decision-making process. If the disorder-manifestation (or **domain plane**) is considered to be vertical, we construct a new syndrome-manifestation (or **case plane**) orthogonal to it, which shares all the input manifestations of the vertical plane and consists of nodes that denote syndromes.

For a given set of **n** manifestations $\mathbf{M} = \{\mathbf{m}_1, \mathbf{m}_2, ..., \mathbf{m}_n\}$, there are at most ${}_{\mathbf{n}}C_2$ two-manifestation syndrome nodes in the first syndrome layer, ${}_{\mathbf{n}}C_3$ three-manifestation syndrome nodes in the second layer, and so on. Each syndrome node within a layer is connected through mandatory *causal* links to exactly '**n**' syndrome (manifestation) nodes in the adjacent layer below it, and through *evoking* links to every disorder node in the domain plane which can potentially cause it. The syndrome nodes and the links between them form the case plane, which is different from the domain plane in that it is not specified by the knowledge base author (or domain specialist) but instead, gets created dynamically by the system over a period of time.

Suppose we are given a set of disorders $\mathbf{D} = \{\mathbf{d}_1, \mathbf{d}_2, \mathbf{d}_3, \mathbf{d}_4\}$ as shown in Figure 2 and a set of manifestations $\mathbf{M} = \{\mathbf{m}_1, \mathbf{m}_2, \mathbf{m}_3, \mathbf{m}_4\}$, with the following associations between their elements: $\mathbf{man}(\mathbf{d}_1) = \{\mathbf{m}_1, \mathbf{m}_3\}, \mathbf{man}(\mathbf{d}_2) = \{\mathbf{m}_1, \mathbf{m}_2, \mathbf{m}_4\}, \mathbf{man}(\mathbf{d}_3) = \{\mathbf{m}_3, \mathbf{m}_4\}$ and $\mathbf{man}(\mathbf{d}_4) = \{\mathbf{m}_2, \mathbf{m}_3\}$. For an **M** set consisting of four manifestations, one would expect a total of ten syndrome nodes (${}_{\mathbf{n}}C_2 + {}_{\mathbf{n}}C_3$) in the syndrome plane. In the fully augmented network shown, however, note the absence of syndrome nodes $ss_1 : [\mathbf{m}_1 \cdot \mathbf{m}_2 \cdot \mathbf{m}_3]$, $ss_3 : [\mathbf{m}_1 \cdot \mathbf{m}_3 \cdot \mathbf{m}_4]$ and $ss_4 : [\mathbf{m}_2 \cdot \mathbf{m}_3 \cdot \mathbf{m}_4]$. Since the domain knowledge suggests that no single disorder can cause either one of these triplets to occur simultaneously, the corresponding syndrome nodes do not get created. If however, the domain model had suggested a possibility for say $\mathbf{m}_1$, $\mathbf{m}_3$ and $\mathbf{m}_4$ to share a common pathology, then ss_3 would have been created. Such would have been the case in fact, if some higher-level disorder $\mathbf{d}'$ could cause the two disorders, $\{\mathbf{d}_1, \mathbf{d}_3\}$.

The creation of syndrome nodes and their links therefore, is determined not only by the co-occurrence statistics within the input population but also by the other conceptual

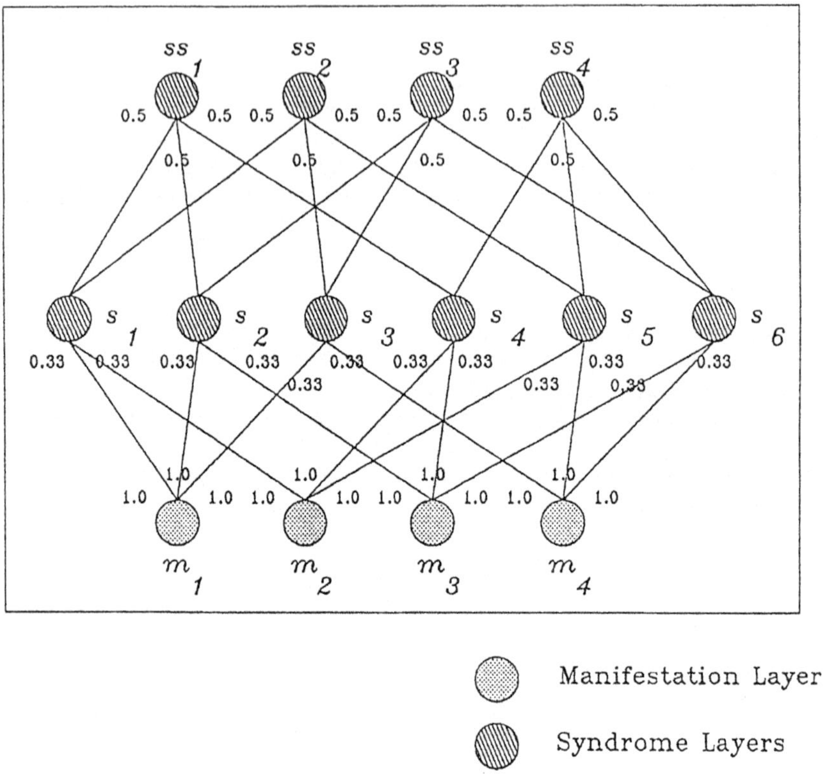

Figure 2: Capturing Co-occurence Statistics

dependencies that already exist within the domain model. It is highly unlikely that we may need to create syndrome nodes for *all* combinations of manifestations, although this could happen in application domains where disorders have significant overlaps with each other in the manifestations that they can cause, or where a large member of disorders are themselves "manifestations" of other higher-level disorders.

3.3 Proposed Learning Strategy

Within the scope of the diagnostic reasoning model described here and the proposed 3-D augmented network architecture, the flow of activation occurs along three planes: the **domain plane**, the **case plane** and the **hybrid** (diagonal) **plane**. Since the flow of activity is regulated by a different set of links in each of the three planes, learning must therefore involve the modification of each type of link. We identify the need for two separate paradigms of learning: 1) a *supervised* scheme (e.g. the generalized delta rule) within the domain plane, to instruct or tutor the system about typical case scenarios, and 2) an *unsupervised* scheme that detects the regularities among case scenarios and captures them as "experience", by modifying the internal representations within the case plane. The supervised scheme would also serve as a validation mechanism for the hybrid plane. It assimilates the knowledge captured within the representations of the case plane together with the knowledge that is tailored within the domain plane, making sure that no conceptual inconsistencies are created in the process. Whereas the former scheme addresses the **skills acquisition** aspect of learning, it is the latter (**skills refinement**) that we emphasize as a characterization of the transition from a novice to an expert with experience.

3.4 Learning within the Case Plane

The intention is to gradually modify the weights of select links in the case plane in such a way, that the regularities which are detected among the population of input stimuli, get captured within the composite representation of this plane. For a pair of manifestation nodes $\mathbf{m_j}$ and $\mathbf{m_k}$ in the input layer ($\mathbf{S^0}$), let $\mathbf{c_{ij}}$ and $\mathbf{c_{ik}}$ respectively, denote the weights on the links that connect them to the $\mathbf{i^{th}}$ syndrome node which signifies their co-occurrence, $\mathbf{s_i^1}$ in the first syndrome layer ($\mathbf{S^1}$). Then $\mathbf{c_{ij}}$ is representative of the frequency with which $\mathbf{m_j}$ is found to co-occur with $\mathbf{m_k}$, as opposed to with the other manifestations in the input layer. Similarly, $\mathbf{c_{ik}}$ is representative of the frequency with which $\mathbf{m_k}$ is found to co-occur with $\mathbf{m_j}$ as opposed to the other manifestations in the input layer.

In the reverse direction, the weight $\mathbf{c_{ji}}$ reflects the likelihood of manifestation $\mathbf{m_j}$ to be observed whenever the node $\mathbf{s_i^1}$ is activated by the presence of manifestation $\mathbf{m_k}$. Similarly, $\mathbf{c_{ki}}$ reflects the likelihood of manifestation $\mathbf{m_k}$ to be observed whenever the node $\mathbf{s_i^1}$ is activated by the presence of $\mathbf{m_j}$.

Initialization: At the time of creation of the syndrome node $\mathbf{s_i^1}$, the following weights are assigned to its links in the case plane:

$$\begin{aligned} c_{ij} &= c_{ik} = 1{\cdot}0/\|S^1\| \text{and} \\ c_{ji} &= c_{ki} = 1{\cdot}0, \end{aligned}$$

where $\|\mathbf{S^1}\|$ is the cardinality of the set of pair-syndromes ${}_n\mathbf{C_2}$. The same approach is adopted for intializing the higher layers in the case plane.

From the point of view of spreading activation through a network, no distinction is made between a syndrome node and a disorder node. Consequently, within the first syndrome layer $\mathbf{S^1}$, if $\mathbf{s_p^1}$ and $\mathbf{s_q^1}$ are two syndrome nodes that share an observed manifestation, then $\mathbf{s_p^1}$ and $\mathbf{s_q^1}$ are competitors which form an inhibitory cluster along with other syndrome nodes in the first layer that share the same manifestation. However, since syndrome nodes themselves do not form parts of an explanation, but rather help in the selection of the most plausible explanatory disorders instead, they do not compete with the disorders in seeking the activation of a share of manifestation. In this regard, syndrome nodes are thought of as "composite" manifestations and treated as such during problem solving.

Modification: On presenting a case scenario from the input population to the network and allowing the network to settle, nodes for most frequently observed syndromes which are relevant to the case will end up with the most activation in the case plane. At stabilization, the weights on links that connect these active nodes to the other nodes in the network are modified as follows: for any active node $\mathbf{s_j^{n-1}}$, connected through a weight $\mathbf{c_{ij}}$ to the $\mathbf{i^{th}}$ node $\mathbf{s_i^n}$ among the "k" nodes of the layer above, the weight $\mathbf{c_{ij}}$ gets adjusted to:

$$c_{ij} = c_{ij} - g{\cdot}(c_{ij} - \Delta c_{ij}), \text{where } \Delta c_{ij} = \frac{e_{ij}}{\sum_k e_{kj}}$$

The “error” $\mathbf{e_{kj}} = \mathbf{r_{kj}} - \mathbf{c_{kj}}$, if $\mathbf{r_{kj}} > \mathbf{c_{kj}}$, and 0.0 otherwise; for all nodes $\mathbf{s_i^n}$ to which $\mathbf{s_j^{n-1}}$ is connected above. $\mathbf{r_{ij}}$ is the ratio of the activations of the syndrome nodes $\mathbf{s_i^n}$ and $\mathbf{s_j^{n-1}}$, while the coefficient **g** is the **“Learning Rate”**. Note, that modification of the weight $\mathbf{c_{ij}}$ on the link which connects the syndrome nodes $\mathbf{s_j^{n-1}}$ and $\mathbf{s_i^{n-1}}$, is based on a redistribution from a common pool of weight. This pool is formed by proportionate contributions from each of the weights $\mathbf{c_{kj}}$ that connect the node $\mathbf{s_j^{n-1}}$ to the **k** nodes in the layer above. The coefficient “g” represents this contributing proportion and since $\sum_k \mathbf{c_{kj}} = \mathbf{1 \cdot 0}$, it is precisely the re-distribution pool after each case gets processed. The weight $\mathbf{c_{ji}}$ in the reverse direction, however, does not get modified. This latter decision is justified due to the fact that given the presence of a syndrome node $\mathbf{s_i^n}$, none of the nodes $\mathbf{s_j^{n-1}}$ whose co-occurrence it represents are expected to be absent.

4 PRELIMINARY RESULTS

4.1 Capturing Co-occurrence Characteristics

The learning paradigm for the case plane as stated above has been implemented to demonstrate its behavior. Using the high level specification language provided by **LIBRA**, a parallel activation model generator (Ahuja & Soh, 1989), this learning paradigm is encoded into **LIBRA/Dx** for the network shown in Figure 3.

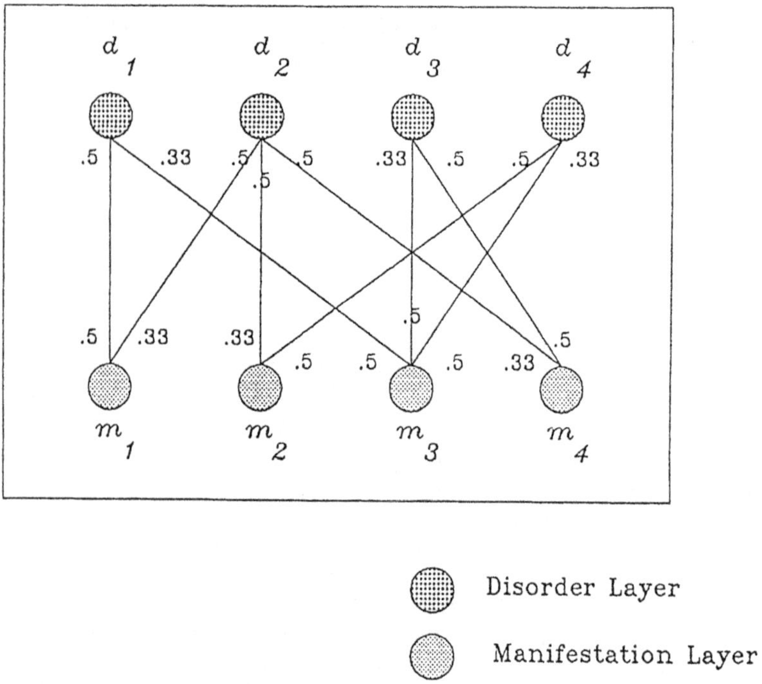

Figure 3: A Causal Network

In order to determine the impact of having augmented the basic causal network with the case and hybrid planes, it is useful to observe the diagnostic model under two different operational modes: a) the **novice** mode, or without the augmented network architecture, and b) the **expert** mode, or after the network is augmented to capture the case knowledge that is abstracted from a specific set of case scenarios using the proposed learning paradigm, as shown in Figure 4.

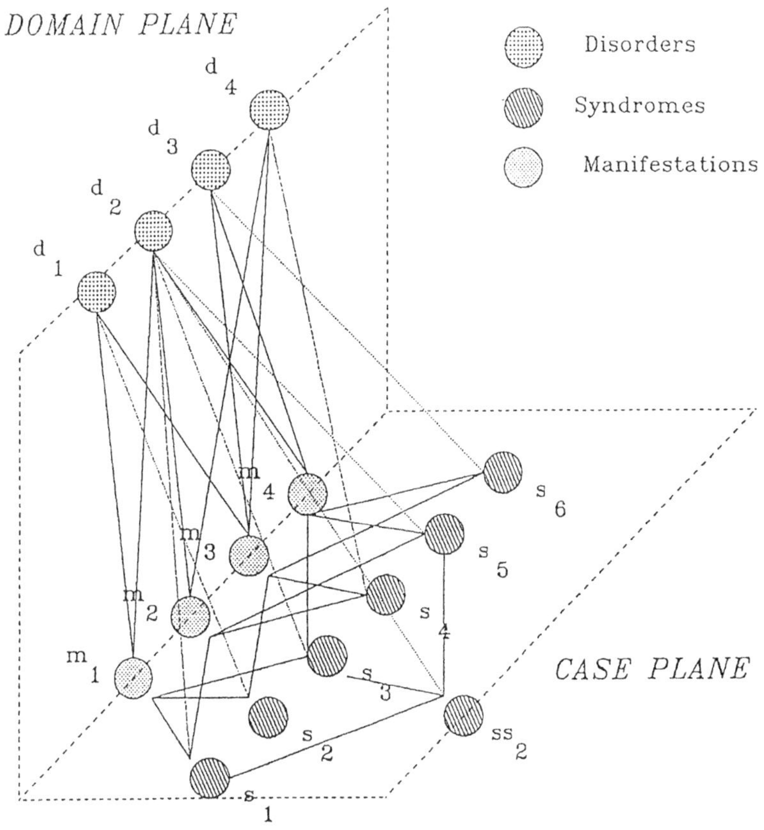

Figure 4: Augmented Network Architecture

The Novice Mode: For a case where the set $\mathbf{M}^+ = \{\mathbf{m}_1, \mathbf{m}_2, \mathbf{m}_3\}$. Using only the domain plane and the processing paradigm of **LIBRA/Dx**, the system stabilizes with the simultaneous presence of disorder nodes $\mathbf{d}_1$ *and* $\mathbf{d}_4$ as the most plausible explanation.

We presume here, that the domain plane has already been trained using the supervised learning paradigm to respond with a correct diagnosis in the learned situations. Note, however, that the network does not make use of any sort of stored case knowledge, which may have been collected while processing a prior population of input case scenarios. The diagnosis by this model, is in a sense based on "textbook" knowledge only and is therefore considered to be reflective of a novice diagnostician.

It is interesting to observe in the activation trace of Figure 5, that the presence of manifestation $\mathbf{m_1}$ immediately identifies the disorders $\mathbf{d_1}$ and $\mathbf{d_2}$ as alternatives that compete with each other to account for its presence. The ability to account for two of the three observed manifestations makes $\mathbf{d_1}$, $\mathbf{d_2}$ and $\mathbf{d_4}$ stronger candidates for the explanation as opposed to $\mathbf{d_3}$, since half of the manifestations for the latter are not observed. But the lack of knowledge about its third manifestation $\mathbf{m_4}$ makes $\mathbf{d_2}$ a weaker contender compared to $\mathbf{d_1}$ and $\mathbf{d_4}$. Consequently, both $\mathbf{d_2}$ and $\mathbf{d_3}$ are suppressed in favor of their alternatives. Even though competing with the same alternatives, $\mathbf{d_2}$ stays at a higher level of activation than $\mathbf{d_3}$. This can be explained by the fact that the alternatives $\mathbf{d_1}$ and $\mathbf{d_4}$ are collectively stronger against $\mathbf{d_3}$ (because of $\mathbf{m_3}$), than each is individually against $\mathbf{d_2}$ (through $\mathbf{m_1}$ and $\mathbf{m_2}$ respectively). During the simulation both disorders $\mathbf{d_1}$ and $\mathbf{d_4}$ maintain identical activations, as is to be expected in this case-scenario for the given causal network.

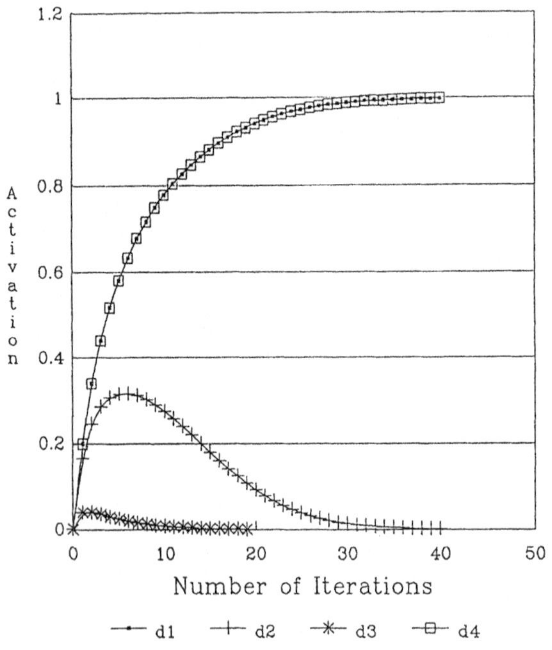

Figure 5: The Novice Mode

The Expert Mode: Let us consider a hypothetical situation, where the above model has previously processed 100 cases over ten different types of case scenarios. Each scenario and the frequency with which it is encountered is listed in the Case Data Table of Figure 6. On looking more closely at this input data, one can easily see that:

$\mathbf{m_1}$ has occurred more often with $\mathbf{m_4}$ (than with $\mathbf{m_2}$ or $\mathbf{m_3}$)
$\mathbf{m_2}$ has occurred more often with $\mathbf{m_4}$ (than with $\mathbf{m_1}$ or $\mathbf{m_3}$),

and, $\mathbf{m}_3$ has occurred more often with $\mathbf{m}_4$ (than with $\mathbf{m}_1$ or $\mathbf{m}_2$).

If during the process of diagnosing these cases, the proposed learning paradigm were to be used, it should be able to capture these co-occurrence statistics through an internal reconfiguration of link weights in the case plane.

Population of Input Patterns

Input Pattern	Frequency
$\mathbf{m}_1$ $\mathbf{m}_2$	8
$\mathbf{m}_1$ $\mathbf{m}_3$	4
$\mathbf{m}_1$ $\mathbf{m}_4$	20
$\mathbf{m}_2$ $\mathbf{m}_3$	4
$\mathbf{m}_2$ $\mathbf{m}_4$	20
$\mathbf{m}_3$ $\mathbf{m}_4$	20
$\mathbf{m}_1$ $\mathbf{m}_2$ $\mathbf{m}_3$	8
$\mathbf{m}_1$ $\mathbf{m}_2\mathbf{m}_4$	4
$\mathbf{m}_1$ $\mathbf{m}_3$ $\mathbf{m}_4$	6
$\mathbf{m}_2$ $\mathbf{m}_3$ $\mathbf{m}_4$	6

Figure 6: Case Data Table (Input Cases with Frequencies)

At the end of a simulation with the given input patterns and frequencies, it is found that the links within the case plane do in fact, get selectively changed. The learning paradigm was able to clearly emphasize the link between the node $\mathbf{m}_1$ and the syndrome node $\mathbf{s}_3$ which denotes its co-occurrence with the manifestation $\mathbf{m}_4$. Similarly, the links between the nodes $\mathbf{m}_2$ and $\mathbf{s}_5$, and between the nodes $\mathbf{m}_3$ and $\mathbf{s}_6$ also get emphasized, to capture the higher frequencies of co-occurrence of each of the respective manifestations $\mathbf{m}_2$ and $\mathbf{m}_3$ with $\mathbf{m}_4$.

Using this case plane to complement the domain model, the augmented causal network is again presented with the set $\mathbf{M}^+ = \{\mathbf{m}_1, \mathbf{m}_2, \mathbf{m}_3\}$. It is interesting to observe from Figure 7 that $\{\mathbf{d}_1, \mathbf{d}_4\}$ is no longer presented as the most plausible explanation for $\mathbf{M}^+$. Instead, the system stabilizes with the disorder nodes $\mathbf{d}_2$ *and* $\mathbf{d}_3$ in the explanation. On looking more closely at the trace for the spread of activation through the augmented network, we find that the case plane does not consider the co-occurrence of $\{\mathbf{m}_1, \mathbf{m}_2, \mathbf{m}_3\}$ as a significant triplet syndrome. Instead, nodes $\mathbf{s}_3$, $\mathbf{s}_5$ and $\mathbf{s}_6$ are the only ones that stay active: an interpretation that denotes the occurrence of $[\mathbf{m}_1 \cdot \mathbf{m}_4]$, $[\mathbf{m}_2 \cdot \mathbf{m}_4]$ and $[\mathbf{m}_3 \cdot \mathbf{m}_4]$ respectively, even though there is no knowledge about the manifestation $\mathbf{m}_4$. In doing so, the augmented network is exhibiting the two desirable properties of **categorization** and input **pattern restoration** based on past experience. It is important to note here, that the alternative explanation of $\mathbf{E} = \{\mathbf{d}_2, \mathbf{d}_3\}$ as the most plausible one does not violate the earlier conditions of providing a *cover* for the observed manifestations $\mathbf{M}^+$ and of being parsimonious: it is both non-redundant and minimal (Peng, 1986; Reggia & Peng, 1986), as described for the PSC Theory. In contrast to the novice mode, here the lack of knowledge about the manifestation $\mathbf{m}_4$ does not undermine the significance of disorders $\mathbf{d}_2$ and $\mathbf{d}_3$ as viable alternatives. By activating nodes $\mathbf{s}_3$, $\mathbf{s}_5$ and $\mathbf{s}_6$ in the case plane, the "expert" is effectively attributing some belief to the presence of $\mathbf{m}_4$ even though it could

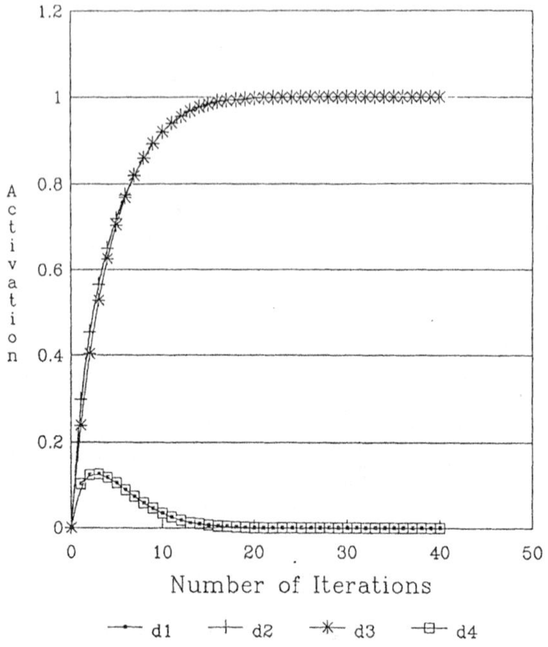

Figure 7: The Expert Mode

not be observed. This could well be the case in the real-world, if the simultaneous presence of disorders $\mathbf{d_2}$ and $\mathbf{d_3}$ were to interfere with each other in such a way that they partially eclipsed each other's manifestations. Note also, that although both $\mathbf{d_2}$ and $\mathbf{d_3}$ form a stable coalition in explaining the presence of $\mathbf{M^+}$, $\mathbf{d_3}$ lags behind its partner due to the higher significance of the unobserved manifestation $\mathbf{m_4}$ for $\mathbf{d_3}$.

Both $\mathbf{d_1}$ and $\mathbf{d_4}$ maintain identical levels of activation as before, until both are suppressed by their competitors. One other phenomenon that can be observed in comparing the two modes of operation described above, is the difference in the slopes of the activation curves of the disorders that eventually form the explanations. The slopes for disorders $\mathbf{d_1}$ and $\mathbf{d_4}$ in the **novice** mode are more gradual than to the ones for $\mathbf{d_2}$ and $\mathbf{d_3}$ in the **expert** mode, requiring twice as many time cycles (20 as opposed to 10) to become 95% active. This can be interpreted as an inability to prioritize diagnostic cues, so as to reach the final diagnosis without having to consider all the possible disorder dependencies - another novice tendency!

5 CONCLUSION

We have identified a practical approach for augmenting the **domain knowledge** within a causal network with context-sensitive **case knowledge** derived from a prior population of case scenarios. The principal motivations for doing this were, first, to enable a diagnostic system to function within the context of the collective characteristics of its environment through an experience-based process called **"episodic learning"**. Our efforts were directed specifically towards exploiting connectionist learning techniques, in order to enhance the reasoning capabilities of **LIBRA/Dx**, a connectionist processing metaphor for diagnostic problem-solving. Second, within the problem domain of diagnostic reasoning, the significant (although largely ignored) issue of whether a given connectionist network is even capable of learning, becomes extremely important. The incorporation of a case plane orthogonal to the domain plane allows the augmented causal network to represent higher-order relationships, without having to warp the original semantics that are associated with domain concepts and their mutual dependencies.

Our approach ensures that the architectural limitations of the domain model do not prevent it from learning any complex relationships that may exist among the manifestations in different contexts, as established by the prior input population of case scenarios.

In addition, the case plane successfully captures the co-occurrence statistics of frequently occurring manifestation patterns as "experience" and then, it uses this experience to render a more plausible diagnosis. This was a strong motivation by itself, since in general it is impossible to determine a priori as to what sort of complex interdependencies might come to exist between the domain concepts in the context of different populations of case scenarios. Finally, we believe that a connectionist processing mechanism lends itself more readily to the kinds of knowledge interactions that are necessary to depict the generative capacities of human diagnosticians to respond to novel situations. We suggest that this common property among human diagnosticians stems from an intrinsic ability to benefit from past experiences. Such experiences are instrumental in establishing relevant conceptual dependencies among domain concepts and effectively characterizes the transition from a novice to an expert among human diagnosticians.

REFERENCES

Ahuja, S.B., & Soh, W.Y. (1989). The LIBRA Manual, Technical Report (in preparation). Department of Computer Science, University of Maryland, Baltimore County.

Ahuja, S.B., Soh, W.Y., & Schwartz, A. (1989). A connectionist processing metaphor for diagnostic reasoning. *Int. Journal of Intelligent Systems* (in press).

Minsky, M. (1987). A framework for representing knowledge. In P.H. Winston (Ed.). *The psychology of computer vision*. New York: McGraw-Hill, 211-277.

Newell, A., & Simon, H.A. (1972). Human problem solving. Englewood Cliffs, NJ: Prentice Hall.

Norman, D., & Bobrow, D.G. (1976). On the role of active memory processes in perception and cognition. In C.N. Cofer (Ed.). *The structure of human memory*. San Francisco: Freeman, 114-132.

Peng, Y. (1986). A formalization of parsimonious covering and probabilistic reasoning in diagnostic inference. Ph.D. dissertation. College Park, MD: University of Maryland, Department of Computer Science.

Reggia, J.A. (1986). Virtual lateral inhibition in parallel activation models of associative memory. *Proceedings of the Ninth International Joint Conference on Artificial Intelligence*, 244-248.

Reggia, J.A., Nau, D., & Wang, P. (1983). Diagnostic expert systems based on a set covering model. *Int. Journal of Man-Machine Studies*, **19**, 437-460.

Reggia, J.A., & Peng, Y. (1986). Modelling diagnostic reasoning: a summary of parsimonious covering theory. *Proceedings of the Tenth Annual Symposium on Computer Applications in Medical Care (SCAMC).*

Rumelhart, D.E. (1975). Notes on a schema for stories. In D.G. Bobrow, & A. Collins (Eds.). *Representation and understanding*. New York: Academic Press, 211-236.

Rumelhart, D.E., & McClelland, J.L. (1986). Parallel distributed processing—Explorations in the microstructure of cognition. Volume 1: Foundations. Cambridge, MA: MIT Press.

Schank, R.C. (1976). The role of memory in language processing. In C.N. Cofer (Ed.). *The structure of human memory*. Freeman: San Francisco, 162-189.

Smolensky, P., & Riley, M.A. (1984). Harmony theory: problem solving, parallel cognitive models, and thermal physics. Tech. Rep. No. 8404. La Jolla, CA: University of California, San Diego, Institute for Cognitive Science.

SUBMITTED PAPERS

CONNECTIONISM IN PERSPECTIVE
R. Pfeifer, Z. Schreter, F. Fogelman-Soulié, L. Steels (Eds.)

Reference in Connectionist Language Users

Robert B. Allen[1] and Mark E. Riecken[2]
[1] Bellcore, Morristown, NJ
[2] BDM Corporation and Department of Electrical and Computer Engineering, University of New Mexico

Abstract—*Recent work has demonstrated that temporal networks can learn to answer questions about 'objects' in a microworld. These networks are termed* language users *to emphasize their use of language to describe and interact with the microworld. The research presented here extends the paradigm by considering applications to problems of reference. One set of studies shows learning of pronoun reference for objects, including demonstrations of both proximity and semantic effects. A second approach examines context in the generation of simple responses. Specifically, a network acquired rules similar to Grice's conversational maxim of Quality.*

Keywords—Anaphora, back-propagation, connectionist language users (CLUES), connectionist state machines, context, discourse, natural language processing, phrase generation, pronominal reference, temporal networks

1. INTRODUCTION

Connectionist algorithms provide a new approach to traditionally hard problems in AI and natural language processing. For instance, the back-propagation algorithm (Rumelhart, et al, 1986) has been applied to problems such as speech synthesis (Sejnowski & Rosenberg, 1987), translation (Allen, 1987), syntactic analysis (Hanson & Kegl, 1987), and disambiguation (St. John & McClelland, 1988). Beyond the usual approach to language processing, Allen (1988a, submitted a; Allen & Riecken, 1988) has suggested the development of *connectionist language users* (CLUEs) which attempt to use language rather than simply processing it. For instance, the language users might combine 'perception' of a coded microworld with 'verbal' input to answer questions. In the research reported here, this approach is applied to problems of reference, specifically to pronoun reference and context effects in response generation.

Figure 1 shows a temporal network which is one of several possible *connectionist state machines,* and is based on (Allen, 1988a; Elman, 1988; Jordan, 1986). In addition to the usual 3-layer back-propagation network, this architecture includes a layer of memory or 'state' units. Activations for the state units at time *t* are a combination of the previous values of the state units along with the activations from hidden units at *t-1*. The architecture allows for separate input fields for microworld and 'verbal' input. A number of hierarchical sequential networks may be developed with additions of channel-specific hidden layers (Allen, 1988a); for instance, a PVS network would have extra perceptual, verbal, and state hidden layers. Typically results are mixed with these more complex networks; in some cases the hidden layers may allow efficient reorganization of the inputs; however, in other cases they may weaken the error signal.

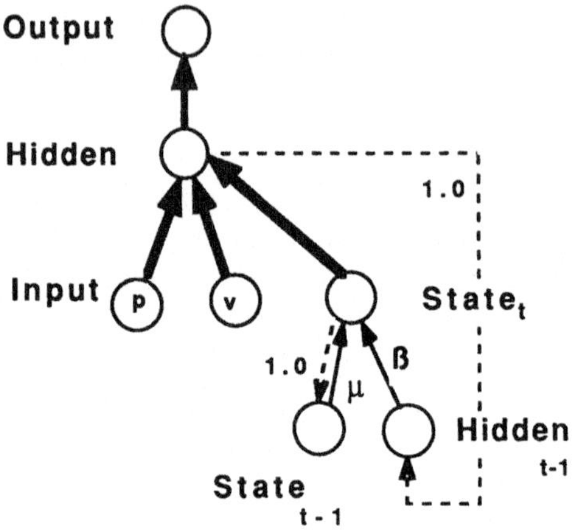

Fig. 1. Sequential network

2. PRONOUN USERS

Some research on pronominal reference has been conducted in the connectionist paradigm. Allen (1987) demonstrated that networks could identify the object of pronominal reference using full-sentence input. Indeed, this is one of the first demonstrations that networks are sensitive to semantics in language. However, the results were noisy, although some relatively complex cases were examined. Elman (1988) describes work in progress using sequential networks to identify the referent of a pronoun with sentence-like linguistic codes. The present work applies the notion of a language user to the problem of pronominal reference. In particular, networks were developed which answer questions that include pronouns, rather than simply identifying the referent of the pronoun.

2.1 A Simple Pronoun User

Networks were trained with a microworld input consisting of two slots in which objects and features associated with that object appeared. During the first cycle, a 3-word question was presented in the verbal input that identified one of the two objects. During the second cycle, a question was asked with a pronoun which referred to that object. Table 1 shows an example of that task. The questions could be interpreted as "Is the apple on the left?" and "Is it red?" To answer the question, the network had to remember which object the question was about.

cycle	microword		input	output
1	obj1/f2	obj6/f1	is obj1 left	yes
2	obj1/f2	obj6/f1	is it f2	yes

Table 1. Example of simple pronoun reference task.

2.1.1 Procedure

Templates for the questions are shown in Table 2. With these templates, combinations of the 8 objects in the two positions were generated making a total of 7976 unique patterns. 3000 of these were randomly selected as training patterns.

There were 8 objects coded with 3 bits. In addition each object possessed a 1-bit feature whose value was associated with the objects by a certain probability (see Allen, 1988a). The inclusion of a feature allowed a wider variety of questions to be asked and presumably more robust performance. Thus, each of the two slots in the microworld input consisted of 4 bits. The verbal input consisted of three word positions. There were 15 verbal input terms and these were coded with randomly assigned 5-bit -1/+1 codes. There were 4 output terms which were coded with 5-bit 0/1 codes. Table 3 shows an example of the bit encodings. 40 hidden units were used; thus the network may be described as (8/15)-40-5. Throughout this work, values of α=0.1, η=0.9, μ=0.5, and β=1.0 were employed. α and η are the learning rate and momentum of the back-propagation algorithm, while μ and β are fixed weights as shown in Figure 1.

input1	output1	input2	output2
is objX1 present	no	-	-
is objX1 present	yes	is it fX1	yes/no
is objX1 present	yes	is it objX2	no
is objX1 present	yes	is it slotX1	yes/no
is objX1 present	yes	where is it	slotX1
is objX1 fX1	yes/no	is it fX1	yes/no
is objX1 fX1	yes/no	is it fX2	no/yes
is objX1 fX1	yes/no	is it slotX1	yes/no
is objX1 fX1	yes/no	where is it	slotX1
where is objX1	slotX1	is it objX1	yes
where is fX1	slotX1	is it fX2	no
where is fX1	slotX1	is it objX1	yes
where is objX1	slotX1	is it fX1	yes/no
is objX1 slotX1	yes/no	is it fX1	yes/no
is objX1 slotX1	yes/no	is it objX2	no/yes

Table 2. Input and output templates for pronoun studies (microworld not shown).

cycle	microworld	verbal input	output
1	1 1 1 1 -1 -1 1 1	1 -1 -1 -1 -1 -1 -1 -1 1 1 -1 1 1 -1 -1	0 0 1 0 1
2	1 1 1 1 -1 -1 1 1	-1 -1 -1 1 1 -1 -1 -1 1 -1 -1 -1 -1 1 1	0 1 1 1 0

Table 3. Sample encoding of simple pronoun reference task.

2.1.2 Results

The network was trained for 400k pattern presentations. 25 sentences on which the network had not been trained were selected for a transfer test. The network completed these transfer patterns without error.

2.2 Sequential Presentation of Individual Input Terms

In the previous study the verbal input for each cycle appeared in three input slots with the sequential output. It seemed natural to attempt to present each part of the verbal input sequentially as well. Before the question was completed, no output could be trained. On these cycles, which were termed *don't care cycles* (Allen, 1988a), the error was set at zero. The network and encoding were similar to that described above, although in this network the verbal input was only 5 bits.

The same questions described in Section 2.1 were used, although they were presented sequentially. Initial testing showed somewhat weak effects; thus the word "is" which appeared in every question was dropped, resulting in two-part rather than three-part questions. A network with 30 hidden units, (8/5)-20-5, was trained for 200k cycles. On 25 transfer questions it gave incorrect answers on 18 bits (9 questions). A PVS network (see Section 1) with 8 perceptual hidden units, 5 verbal hidden units, 20 state hidden units and 20 integrating hidden units was tested. This network made errors on only 2 of the transfer questions (4 bits).

2.3 Proximity of Referent

Pronoun reference is more difficult when several referents are possible and some rule must be applied to choose the correct one. The simplest rule is to choose the noun which was presented most recently. In this study, the network was required to disambiguate those objects to which the pronoun referred. A corpus of 3-part questions was developed which asked about each of the objects in the microworld. The pronouns always referred to the object which was most recently mentioned.

A PVS network with 30 hidden units, (8/15)-30-5, was trained on 3207 questions for 600K pattern presentations. The resulting network made errors on 6 of the 25 transfer question sets (16 of 500 bits).

input1	output1	input2	output2	input3	output3
is objX1 present	yes/no	is objX2 present	yes/no	is it fX1	yes/no

Table 4. Example of pattern template for proximity studies.

2.4 Semantics, Proximity, and Pronoun Reference

While proximity effects are important in pronoun reference, they may be over-ridden by semantic effects. For instance the pronoun 'she' cannot refer to a male. To determine whether networks could use semantics along with proximity, a corpus was developed in which males and females were present in the microworld and reference to them required agreement of pronoun gender. For instance, for questions of the type shown in Table 5, the first cycle asks whether male1 is present in the microworld and the second cycle asks about female1. (To simplify the coding, the 'is' was dropped from the questions.) In the third cycle, the pronoun "he" refers to the more distant, but semantically linked male1.

Construction of an appropriate corpus required considerable care. For instance three slots were used in the microworld to guarantee that the pronoun disambiguation was not made simply because there was only one possible referent of the correct gender. In addition, many patterns which did not train discrimination between the focus and semantic effects were dropped. Moreover pilot testing demonstrated an interesting effect; depending on the state of the microworld, the answer to the first question could be 'no' but the referent still identified. For instance, in Table 5 the first question might have been "MX1 right?" Pronoun reference in these cases, in which the referent is identified in the negative, proved difficult for the network and they were also dropped from the training set. It seems likely they would be difficult for people as well.

input1	output1	input2	output2	input3	output3
MX1 left	yes	FX1 present	yes	he fX1	yes/no

Table 5. Example of pattern template for study of semantics in pronoun questions.

With the above restrictions, more than 25k patterns were able to be generated. Codes representing four males and four females in the microworld were randomly assigned. 8038 of these were randomly selected for training and 20 for transfer. A (12/10)-60-3 network was trained. Learning was slow, and the network required 1.5M presentations. However the network transferred well; 18 of 20 pronoun references were correct (errors on 3 bits out of 60).

3. CONTEXT IN RESPONSE GENERATION

While the pronoun reference study and other research have shown the sensitivity of connectionist networks to context for comprehension, context is also an important consideration in language generation. For instance, Grice (1975, p. 45) proposes a maxim of Quality for conversation: "Make your contribution as informative as is required" and "Do not make it more informative than is required ".

The task of the network is to describe the objects unambiguously. The preferred description is at the category level; however if both objects are of the same category, then the description should specify the object name. If the two objects are the same, the description should specify the distinguishing feature. While this rule for reference is simple and has exceptions in natural human language, it satisfies Grice's conversational maxim.

A network was trained to generate different descriptions about objects based on possible confusion with another object in the perceptual field. Objects could appear in one of two slots in the microworld. The objects possessed features which were explicitly coded in the input field. As shown in Table 6, the objects were randomly assigned to one of two categories. Because the category coding was arbitrary, the network had to recall category membership from previous usage. If explicit category features had been present, performance would presumably have been more robust.

category 1	category 2
obj1	obj2
obj3	obj5
obj4	obj6

Table 6. Assignment of objects to categories.

To allow for the use of feature names as modifiers (see line 3 of Table 7), sequential networks were employed. Allen (submitted a) found some instability for lengthy outputs; in any event, that should not be a factor here since the output sequences were relatively short.

3.1 Procedure

microworld		verbal input	output1	output2	output3
obj1/f1	obj2/f2	left	cat1	period	-
obj1/f1	obj4/f2	left	obj1	period	-
obj1/f1	obj1/f2	right	f2	obj1	period

Table 7. Examples of response generation tasks with responses at different levels.

Table 7 shows examples of responses at the category, object, and feature levels. For instance in the first line of the table, because obj1 and obj2 were of different categories, the category response was generated. In other respects, the coding and parameters were similar to those in the pronoun studies. The microworld and verbal input were present during each cycle of output. For instance in questions of the form shown in last row of Table 7, the feature value would be output on the first cycle, the object name on the second cycle, and the terminator on the third cycle.

There were 6 objects, each with 1 feature, which could appear in the two slots of the perceptual input. There were only two verbal inputs (left/right) and these were coded in 1 bit. In addition there were 13 output terms, which were coded in 5 bits each. The entire network was (8/1)-16-5. Because the outputs were sequential and of differing lengths, an explicit termination had to be produced for the final response. 480 patterns were generated, of which 455 were used for training and 25 were saved for transfer.

3.2 Results

The network learned this task easily and completed the transfer questions without error.

4. CONCLUSIONS

The results of Section 2 suggest that connectionist networks can readily learn simple pronoun reference to objects which appear in the microworld. The results show important properties of language. For instance, in the semantic reference pronoun task (Section 2.4) the network had to maintain a state, recalling which object had been referred to. Moreover, the ability to complete this sort of reference suggests that the networks may be capable of much more complex types of attachment.

Section 3 describes one of the first applications of temporal networks for sequential output, and further, that output is dependent not only on the objects about which the question was being asked, but also the context of those objects. This effect is similar to one of Grice's maxims of conversation; however it leaves open the question whether the maxims in natural discourse are explicitly trained or are side-effects of other training. A related effect is examined in (Allen, 1988b, submitted a) with output sequences of arbitrary feature strings. In that work, systematic patterns are introduced to output sequences depending on the input. If the context in which responses are generated is related to other people or agents which are present, rather than to objects which are present, the effects in Section 3 may also be said to demonstrate user or agent models (see also Allen, in press, submitted b).

REFERENCES

Allen, R.B. (1987). Several studies on back-propagation and natural language. In *Proceedings of the International Conference on Neural Networks*, San Diego, II/335-II/341.

Allen, R.B. (1988). Sequential connectionist networks for answering simple questions about a microworld. *Proceedings of the Cognitive Science Society*, Montreal, 489-495. (a)

Allen, R.B. (1988). Connectionist state machines. Bellcore TR-ARA88-300. (b)

Allen, R.B. (in press). User models: Theory, method, and practice. *International Journal of Man-Machine Studies*.

Allen, R.B. (submitted). Advances in connectionist language users. (a)

Allen, R.B. (submitted). Developing agent models with a neural reinforcement technique. (b)

Allen, R.B., & Riecken, M.E. (1988). Interacting and communicating connectionist agents. *Proceedings of the International Neural Network Society*, Boston, 67.

Elman, J.L. (1988). Finding structure in time. UCSD-CRL TR#8801.

Grice, H.P. (1975). Logic and conversation. In P. Cole & J.L. Morgan (Eds.) *Syntax and Semantics*, 3. New York: Academic, 41-58.

Hanson, S.J. & Kegl, J. (1987). PARSNIP: A connectionist network that learns natural language grammar from exposure to natural language sentences. *Proceedings of the Cognitive Science Society*, Seattle, 106-119.

Jordan, M.I. (Aug. 1986). Attractor dynamics and parallelism in a connectionist sequential machine. *Proceedings of the Cognitive Science Society*, Amherst, MA, 531-546.

Rumelhart, D.E., Hinton, G.E., & Williams, R.J. (1986). Learning internal representations by error propagation. In D.E. Rumelhart and J.L. McClelland (Eds.), *Parallel Distributed Processing*. (vol. 2). (pp. 318-362). Cambridge, MA: MIT Press.

Sejnowski, T.J. & Rosenberg, C.R. (1987). Parallel networks that learn to pronounce English text. *Complex Systems*, **1**, 145-168.

St. John, M.F. & McClelland, J.L. (1988). Applying contextual constraints in sentence comprehension. *Proceedings of the Cognitive Science Society*, Montreal, 26-32.

CONNECTIONISM IN PERSPECTIVE
R. Pfeifer, Z. Schreter, F. Fogelman-Soulié, L. Steels (Eds.)
Elsevier Science Publishers B.V. (North-Holland), 1989

SNARK, A Neural Optical Character Reader

Ethem Alpaydin[+] and Pierre Marchal
Microcomputer Laboratory (LAMI)
Swiss Federal Institute of Technology, Lausanne

Abstract—*Despite being comparatively easier than other applications of pattern recognition like three dimensional image recognition, or speech recognition, there exists today no man-made character reader that is as successful in this task as man. Recent developments in connectionist theory gave us the possibility to somehow imitate this capability under the name "parallel distributed processing." The work presented here concerns such an optical reader system based on a multiple layer of massively interconnected processors. The system is composed of an image preprocessor based on a set of cellular automata and a recognizer based on a neural network. It can successfully recognize any one character font completely, regardless of height. This paper also describes various networks realized during the evolution of the project.*

Keywords— Neural networks, cellular automata, pattern recognition, image processing, optical character recognition.

"The term 'writing' can have many different meanings ... However, if the definition is limited to the modern meaning, according to which it is *a technique of representing speech by a durable trace,* one can then speak of an 'invention', and attribute a historical role to it ... Through it, our species began to have at its disposal *a durable means of concretizing speech* and of holding historical knowledge back from the edge of the abyss threatening to engulf it, as collective oral memory, streched across thousands of years of transmission, could no longer suffice to do." Claude HAGEGE (Hagége, 1988) (emphasis added)

1. OPTICAL CHARACTER RECOGNITION

Pictorial pattern recognition deals with associating the pictorial data with nonpictorial information; it maps the image onto its code. In character recognition, the raw image of the document is two dimensional and is composed of two-level dots.

Characters are the simplest real life images. Considering its wide application area, character recognition is one of the most promising fields in pictorial pattern recognition.

[+] For correspondance, contact first author from EPFL-LAMI, Cour 37, 1007 Lausanne Switzerland. Email: alpaydin@elde.epfl.ch.

Computers armed with such systems will be able to capture information directly from printed or handwritten documents like books, reports, invoices, exam papers, love letters, etc. These systems will increase the speed of input operation, decrease errors because an intervening human operator will no longer be necessary. The document, once stored in a manner directly processable by a computer, can be subjected to various useful treatments; for example, it can be shared by various people, as many copies as possible can be made (all as of the same quality as the original), etc. Another advantage, from the point of view of storage, is the compaction of data. Code, when compared with image is always shorter. The image of a character defined as a 12x8 bitmap takes 12 bytes whereas its ASCII code is 7 bits, which is due to the high redundance of information processed by man, when viewed from a computer science perspective.

However, when one thinks about the hundreds of type fonts each with its own characteristics and billions of people each with his/her handwriting, curing the illiteracy of computers is still some distance away and requires still more considerable effort. As a result of this variety, automatic recognition of multi-font characters is still a problem not yet solved. Refer to (Suen, 1986) for a list of these problems. One way to bypass such problems is to impose restrictions. Special fonts have been designed and standardized to minimize ambiguities and to have character images as different from each other as possible. Two such character sets are OCRA and OCRB, by ANSI and ECMA respectively. Both sets are designed such that any character has a unique shape. Commercial machines based on these character sets achieve recognition rates as high as 99.99% with a reading speed of over 100 characters per second.

Human beings can read all printed fonts and make about 4% mistakes when reading handwriting in the absence of context. Thus, we adopted a connectionist scheme inspired by the human perception mechanism as the basis of our system.

2. NEURAL OCR SYSTEMS

Simple binary patterns are widely used as example vectors in the field of neural networks. Being the simplest real-life images, starting with Rosenblatt, character images are used as examples with neural network based pattern recognizers. Another challenge of character recognition is its being a problem not yet solved using the classical AI approaches.

Various groups are using character recognition as application in their neural systems. The groups to our knowledge follows:

- Personnaz, Guyon, and Dreyfus (1986) use restricted handwritten characters for testing projection learning rule in a Hopfield network. Their model, except the learning rule, is quite similar to the identification part of the first version of our system (cf. 3.3.4), namely by a single layer network from pixel units to letter units.

- Pan (1985) uses simplified Chinese characters to test a Hebbian rule on a Hopfield net. A quite restricted character set is used.

- Fukushima (1988) uses character recognition as application area in his multi-layer network Neocognitron with self-organization. Neocognitron, although it uses a great number of processing units, has the capability of translation invariant recognition through selective attention. In our model, translation invariance is achieved by the higher level sequentially operating character image extractor that aligns itself with the next line, word, or character (cf. 3.1).

- Graf, Jackel and Hubbard (1988) have built a neural VLSI circuit for character image normalization and feature extraction, for recognition of handwritten numerals. Their system, as ours (cf. 3.2), includes a preprocessing phase composed of size-normalization and skeletonization. As opposed to our region detectors (cf. 3.3.4), they use more sophisticated features like lines, corners, arcs, etc. Note, on the other hand, that in their model no learning phase exists.

3. SNARK, SIMULATOR OF NEURONS FOR AUTOMATIC RECOGNITION OF CHARACTERS

A useful OCR should be able to handle most of the real-life situations, that is to say, type of documents, character fonts etc. Besides, when it can not, it should be able to learn them as to increase success in a future trial.

3.1. Extraction of Character Images

There are basically two types of OCR systems; page-based or character-based depending on the type of digitizer used to input the document image. In systems, where small hand-held digitizers are used, extraction of character image is not a problem, as the user is supposed to scan the text in the correct order. In systems with page scanners, on the other hand, the system should also be able to extract the structure of the document like titles, paragraphs, lines, figures, columns and their order, etc.

Traditionally, documents are written from up to down, composed of horizontally aligned groups of characters called lines, which are separated by horizontal blank lines (interline separation). Lines are divided into words and in turn into individual characters by vertical blank lines (space), order being from left to right. Between words, the space is more than the space between characters, generally around 4 times. In page based recognition, the system should also return indications of the structure like paragraphs, end-of-line and end-of-word conditions, as they may convey an information.

3.2. Phases of Snark

The aim of the work is to have an OCR that can recognize all characters belonging to a certain family of font. For this purpose, a preprocessing phase composed of several steps for image normalization is introduced. The image is then fed to an identifier that compares this image with descriptions of the prototypes learned, and chooses the most similar.

3.3. Preprocessing

The preprocessing of the extracted character image is composed of the following passes:

(i) Noise elimination,

(ii) Skeletonization, and,

(iii) Size normalization to 16x16.

3.3.1. Noise elimination

When pictures are scanned and digitized, the image may carry a certain amount of noise which can be either due to the low quality of the scanned source or due to the low resolution of the scanner that produces smeared images. In order to eliminate unwanted noise which cause severe distortions in the image and thus poor recognition rates, a pass is incorporated to remove them. In *Snark*, this is handled by a cellular automaton that counts the "on" neighbors of each "on" pixel that decides to delete itself if the count is less than a threshold value. This process eliminates pixels with few "on" neighbors, which are also called lonely pixels. An extension that ameliores the character extraction process is to apply such a noise eliminator with a high threshold to the complete page just after scanning, as we can separate touching characters or lines due to our low resolution scanner. The circuit to implement this algorithm with a programmable threshold, is currently under development in our lab.

3.3.2. Skeletonization

The strokes that constitute the character are then thinned down to a skeleton which is composed of one pixel wide line segments. The variations in the thickness of strokes may be due to serifs, bold characters or can be due to a high resolution scanner. The algorithm used is a new one, different from the existing iterative algorithms and is based on neural networks. It is not iterative and as it is designed especially for character images, it gives better results in terms of connectivity and noise-immunity (Alpaydin, 1988a). The skeletonization pass removes the difference between the normal and **bold** versions of the same character. For this algorithm too, a circuit is under development in our lab.

3.3.3 Size normalization

To normalize the size, we enlarge the character image first to 128x128 and then reduce it to 16x16. These two steps are also implemented as cellular automatons since operations are local and can be handled synchronously over the whole matrix. This process eliminates the difference between characters of the same font with different heights.

3.3.4. Identification

When the character matrix is of uniform size and the difference due to thickness is eliminated, a structural analysis may be carried out to extract the features. Such features can be anything but it is best to extract those features that carry maximum information, which will enable the system to discriminate correctly one character from the others, while being able to generalize for different examplars of the same character.

The easiest approach named template matching, is a comparison of images on the basis of individual pixels, and choosing the most similar. In such a scheme, the value of an individual pixel is taken as a feature.

A neural network performs an association between an input vector and an output vector. In pictorial pattern recognition, the image should be somehow coded as a vector, and the code should be coded in the output vector. The easiest approach is to write the 2D binary matrix as a row-major 1D vector and feed it into the neural network. The output vector can be a unit vector where the index of the only active element gives the integer code.

Hopfield network

Our first trial was using Hebbian learning rule with a single-layer of a completely connected network of 256 binary units (Hopfield, 1982). The system however, was unable to learn even 10 numerals of 5 different fonts. This is due to the limitation of Hebbian learning which requires orthogonal vectors. When we have more than one input vector to be associated with an output vector, additional to the requirement of linear separability of 10 numerals, we also have the requirement of inseparability or closeness between 5 examplars of the same numeral, so that the system can generalize.

Interactive Activation Network

Having noticed the limitation of a single-layer network, we then decided to have a multi-layer network which would extract those features of the characters during a learning phase, and perform identification based on these features. We adopted the Interactive Activation model (McClelland, and Rumelhart, 1981) where there is a hierarchical bottom-up structure. In this network structure, cells in a layer can be connected to cells that belong to one-above and one-below layers with excitatory or inhibitory connections.

For feature extraction, we assumed some predefined regions on the 16x16 matrix. They can similarly be thought of as critical parts of the strokes which form the discriminatory parts of the strokes, for example borders, center etc. The output value of such a feature extractor depends on the number of "on" pixels in this region. The actual identification, then, can be carried out in the following layer on the basis of the values of these detector cells. The network is structured as follows:

- There are 256 binary units where the initial image is fed.
- The first layer is the feature detector layer. The units are connected to the set of units in the input layer according to the predefined region they control. The activation of a unit in this layer corresponds to the "on" pixel population in that region. As these regions may have different sizes, a function is used to map the outputs of all these cells into the range (-60..+60).
- The final layer has 10 output cells each standing for a numeral. Each numeral is defined as a particular linear combination of the region detectors, which are connected with excitatory or inhibitory links depending on the presence or absence of the region.

When P_p is the pth pixel, F_j is the jth feature, and N_i is the ith numeral, the weights from pixels to features; T_{pj}, are computed as follows:

$$P_p : (-1,+1)$$
$$T_{pj} = 1 \text{ if } P_p \text{ is an element of } R(F_j), 0 \text{ otherwise.}$$

The pixel unit is connected to a feature unit only if the pixel is an element of the set of pixels that make up the region of the jth feature; $R(F_j)$. The weights between the pixels and features therefore are fixed and predefined according to the location of feature regions. The weights between the feature detectors and the numerals, W_{ji}, in the first network were computed manually using the following formula:

F_j: (-60..+60), the value of the jth feature
N_i: (-1,+1), +1 when learning the ith numeral, -1 otherwise.

$th(F_j) = +1$ IF ($F_j > 30$), 0 otherwise.

$$W_{ji} = -\ln \frac{p(N_i = 0 \ \& \ th(F_j) = 1) \ p(N_i = 1 \ \& \ th(F_j) = 0)}{p(N_i = 1 \ \& \ th(F_j) = 1) \ p(N_i = 0 \ \& \ th(F_j) = 0)}$$

This equation is derived from a Bayesian analysis of the probability that N_i should be "on" given the effect of unit F_j filtered through a non-linear threshold function th() and vice versa. (Rumelhart, and McClelland, 1986).

Then, we removed the thresholding, and applied an extension of Hebbian learning for determination of the weights between the feature units and the numerals as follows:

$W_{ji}=N_i \ F_j$

With 18 such region detectors using 5 different fonts, around 85% success has been achieved. As the definitions of numerals in 5 fonts are quite different, we could not choose region detectors that gave similar responses for the same numeral in 5 different fonts.

Single-layer Model for One font

The final model used is a pure template checker. It can however, learn all the characters of one font only, that is to say, can accept only one examplar for each character. Due to the preceding size normalization and skeletonization, it can successfully recognize all characters of the same font family including **bold** except *italic*.

It is composed of only one layer, where there are 256 binary input cells and 256 output cells whose output can take values in the range (-256..+256) counting the similarity of the given vector with each character. The weights are determined as follows:

P_p : (-1,+1)
N_i : (-256..+256)
$c(N_i) = 1$ if we are learning the ith numeral, 0 otherwise.

$W_{pi}= P_p \ c(N_i)$

Note that in such a learning scheme, although similar to Hebbian learning, we do not have confabulation states, because learning a character involves modification of the synapses of only one output unit as they have states (0,1). Besides, the output units are not binary, so even if the pattern is similar to various prototypes, the system will choose the maximum, so the most similar one.

The system, as tested with the font family "Univers", can recognize all uppercase and lowercase letters and digits with success (Alpaydin, 1988b).

4. CONCLUSION

The *Snark* project whose evolution and current situation is described here, will continue in our lab. Actually, we have decided to move the system to hardware by building the actual circuitry, to take advantage of the synchronous parallel operation of units which property we could not exploit in software simulations.

ACKNOWLEDGEMENTS

This work is supported in part by the Fonds National Suisse de la Recherche Scientifique.

REFERENCES

Alpaydin, E. (1988a). A neural parallel algorithm for thinning digital patterns, *Internal Report* LAMI-EPFL.

Alpaydin, E. (1988b). Optical character recognition using neural networks, *Postgraduate course project report*. Department of Computer Science, EPFL.

Fukushima, K. (1988). A neural network for visual pattern recognition *IEEE Computer, March* 65-75.

Graf, H.P., Jackel, L.D., Hubbard, W.E. (1988). VLSI implementation of a neural network model *IEEE Computer, March* 41-49.

Hagége, C. (1988). Writing: the invention and the dream. In D. de Kerckhove & C.J. Lumsden (Eds.) *The alphabet and the brain* (pp.72-83). Springer-Verlag.

Hopfield, J.(1982). Neural networks and physical systems with emergent collective computational abilities *Proc. Natl. Acad. Sci.* **79**, 2554-2558.

McClelland, J., Rumelhart, D. (1981). An interactive activation model of context effects in letter perception: Part 1, an account of basic findings. *Psychological Review*, **88**, 375-407.

Pan, X.A. (1985). *Experimentation d'automates a seuil pour la reconnaissance de caracteres* PhD thesis Univ. Sci. et Med. de Grenoble.

Personnaz, L., Guyon, I., Dreyfus, G. (1986). Collective computational properties of neural networks: new learning mechanisms *American Physical Society, Phys. Rev. A* **34-5** 4217-4228.

Rumelhart, D., McClelland, J. (1986). *Parallel Distributed Processing* MIT Press.

Suen, C.Y. (1986). Character recognition by computer and applications. In T.Y. Young & K.S. Fu (Eds.), *Handbook of pattern recognition and image processing* (pp.569-586). Orlando: Academic Press.

CONNECTIONISM IN PERSPECTIVE
R. Pfeifer, Z. Schreter, F. Fogelman-Soulié, L. Steels (Eds.)

Topological Perception: A Challenge to Computational Approaches to Vision

Lin Chen
Beijing Laboratory of Cognitive Science
University of Science and Technology of China

Abstract— *The paper, on the one hand, illustrates the inadequacy of skepticism toward the human ability to perceive topological properties. On the other hand, based on the empirical data, it is further argued that, with respect to connectionism, the key point of the hypothesis of human topological perception is the EARLY perception of topological properties. Topological perception, therefore, provides a challenge to computational approaches to vision based on local geometric primitives.*

Keywords—Early vision, topological perception, connectionist models, perceptrons

Reasoning from empirical facts in visual perceptual organizations, Chen (1982) advanced the hypothesis of topological perception: A primitive and general function of the visual system may be the perception of global topological properties. The hypothesis was tested against a fairly large set of experimental data collected within a variety of approaches and paradigms in the study of perceptual organization. The results consistently support this topological hypothesis (Chen, 1983a, 1985, 1986).

It is well known that Minsky and Papert's classic result on the high complexity of topological properties in their book *Perceptrons* (Minsky & Papert, 1969) has given rise to much controversy about the capabilities and limitations of connectionist models. *Perceptrons* has been blamed for causing the next decade's dark ages of connectionism. Actually, the book's most famous and influential mathematical result is of the limitation of perceptrons for computing topological properties. That is, for perceptrons, the topological predicate is not finite order; however lower-order perceptrons can be used for computing local geometric properties. Thus the question raised by topological computation is one of the issues that lie at the core debate between traditional AI and connectionism. The hypothesis of human topological perception, therefore, has inevitably raised some interesting issues about connectionist experiments and foundations.

In one aspect, proponents of classical computational approaches to vision are skeptical of the topological hypothesis because, in their words, "The determination of topological properties is not likely to be primitive for any kind of computational system (Minsky & Papert, 1969; Ullman, 1985)" (Rubin & Kanwisher, 1985). The very nature of the symbolic processing approaches to vision makes them tend to assume that primitive elements of computation are local geometric features (e.g. Marr's "Primal Sketch").

In another aspect, with respect to the hypothesis of topological perception, two distinct arguments have been proposed by connectionists. Anderson and Rosenfeld (1988) assume the ability of perceptrons to act as psychological models. They consider this point to be what "became quite important in the resurrection of neural networks." They argued that it is true that simple perceptrons cannot compute the predicate connectedness; however, the famous experiment with the spirals (Minsky & Papert, 1969, Fig. 5.1) demonstrates that "we cannot compute connectedness either," and, "we act as if we had some of the same limitations that a perceptron does." On the other hand, it is most interesting to note that Rumelhart and McClelland (1986) apply back-propagation and Boltzmann machines to argue that Minsky and Papert's results apply only to simple one-layer perceptrons and not to the larger class of perceptron-like models, particularly multilayered perceptrons and Boltzmann machines and it is not difficult to develop networks capable of computing topological properties, such as connectedness or the inside/outside relationship. There is no doubt that connectionist models, like back-propagation and Boltzmann machines, are of great interest in providing insights into topological computation. In this light, however, can multilayered networks or Boltzmann machines really serve as a computational model for the human topological perception?

1 INADEQUACY OF SKEPTICISM TOWARD HUMAN ABILITY TO PERCEIVE TOPOLOGICAL PROPERTIES

Contrary to the skepticism toward the human ability to perceive topological properties, I addressed some commonly heard non-topological counter-examples (Chen, 1988). One more apparent counter-example from Julesz (1981) will be discussed in detail in this section.

1.1 Connectedness and Closedness Rather Than Terminators

The topological explanation for effortless texture discrimination (Chen, 1983b) has been successful to a variety of random textures that are counter-examples of Julesz's statistic theory. However, the well-known texture (Fig. 1) seems to serve as a striking exception and provide a strong challenge to the topological account (Julesz, 1981). The two figures, employed as a pair of subunits in Fig. 1, are as well known as the spirals, because they were originally used by Minsky and Papert in *Perceptrons* to prove that a diameter limited perceptron cannot compute connectedness. Since one of the two figures is connected but another is physically (spatially) separated into two parts and one of the two parts is closed, the two subunits are topologically different. However, the texture made up of them is not effortlessly discriminable.

The texture did more than served as a counter-example. It played a critical role in Julesz's local texton (the elements of texture perception) theory (Julesz, 1981). Based on the fact that both of the two subunits in Fig. 1 possess the same number (two) of terminators (i.e. end points of line segments), Julesz made a main claim in his local texton theory: in preattentive texture discrimination, only the number of terminators has perceptual significance, while the relative positions between terminators are unnoticed.

Experiment 1 For making comparison with Julesz's result, the experiment employed the textures with the same structure as this original one except that the difference in numbers

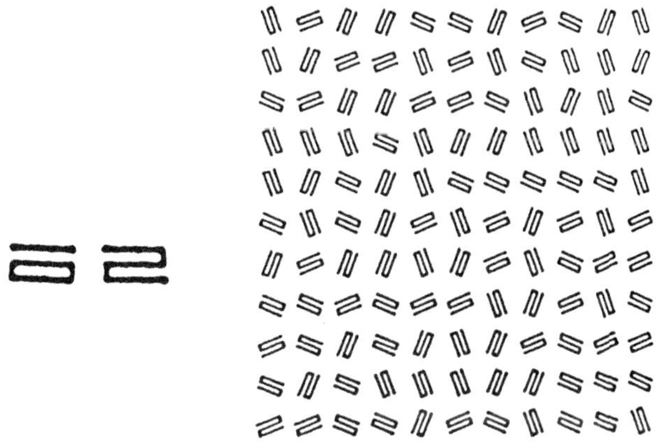

Figure 1

Figure 2a

of terminators between two subunits was systematically altered.

In turn, while the stimulus texture of Fig. 2a keeps the whole structure similar to Fig. 1, the difference in numbers of terminators between its two subunits is two vs. one; in Fig. 2b, the difference in numbers of terminators between its two subunits is two vs. three; in Fig. 2c, the difference in numbers of terminators is two vs. four. The fourth texture of Fig. 2d and fifth texture of Fig. 2e respectively reach two extreme cases: Fig. 2d represents the difference between two and six terminators, and Fig. 2e, two and zero terminators.

A standard procedure used by Julesz was also applied in the experiment. That is, each of these textures was presented to subjects for less than 160 msec. The result demonstrated that any trial of changing the terminators didn't make any remarkable difference in

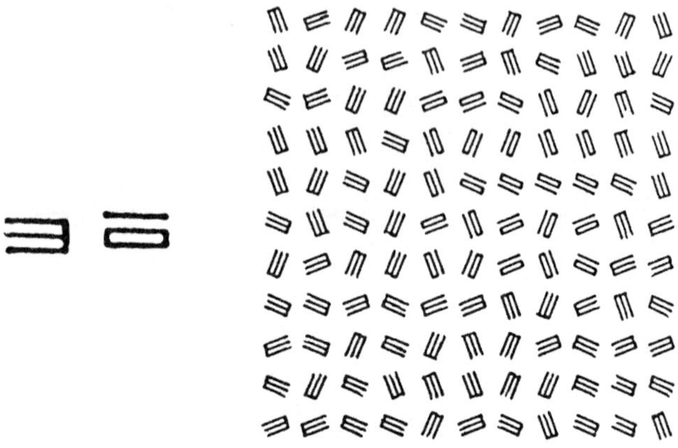

Figure 2b

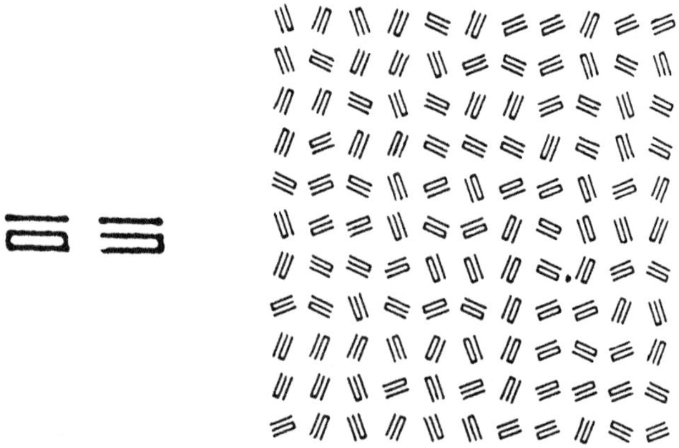

Figure 2c

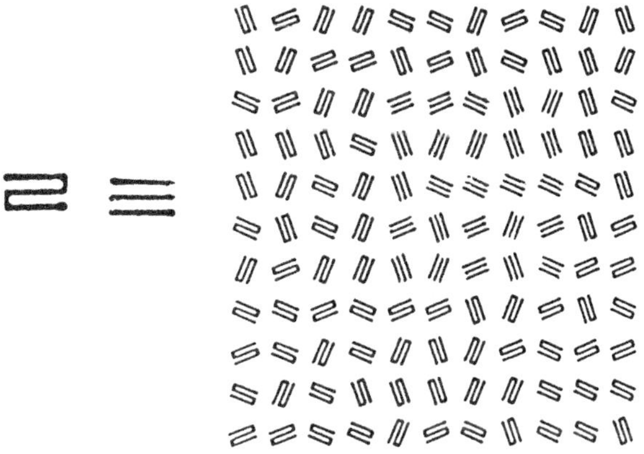

Figure 2d

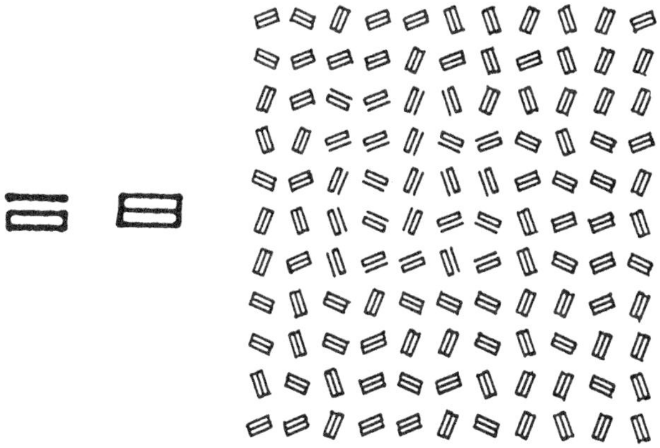

Figure 2e

discriminability of these textures despite the great extent of differences in the numbers of terminators between the two subunits.

Experiment 2 Even though the above experiments demonstrated that the terminator account does not work in general, we still face the question of why, for Fig. 1, the topological explanation seems not to work either.

The disconnected subunit in Fig. 1 is made up of two physically (spatially) separated parts, why do we accept that it represents one wholistic subunit? In addition to the physical connectedness, there are other organizational factors such as proximity and similarity at work: the three longer line-segments in the subunit are located close up to each other, parallel, with the same length, and so on. These organizational factors, which are too common to take due account of them in all cases, may make us perceive the subunit as a tolerance connected component (Chen, 1983a) and make it behave like a perceptual unit despite the fact that it is physically disconnected. Being relative to the scale of the texture made up of them, the subunits are quite small, thus these organizational factors are expected to have strong effects on perceptual organization.

A new pair of subunits in Fig. 3 was advanced to verify the above analysis. Three points were specially considered in designing the new subunits and their textures. First, to eliminate similarity effects as much as possible, the line-segments making up the subunits were all different in length and not parallel. Second, to make clearer comparison between the topological explanation and Julesz's terminator account, while the line-segments making up the subunits were deliberately arranged to reduce the similarity and proximity effect, the two new subunits must possess the same line-segments and, particularly, the same number (two) of terminators. Third, to rediscover the influence of topological factors based on physical connectedness, the two subunits were designed to correspond topologically to the two subunits of the original pair in Fig. 1: one of them is physically connected and another is physically separated into two parts, one of which is physically closed. The experiment with the new texture demonstrated that as the confounds of other organizational factors were eliminated, the rather pronounced effortless discrimination with the topologically different texture was rediscovered.

The experiments described above illustrate that, in the study of the topological structure in visual perception, certain rather prominent aspects and concepts of perceptual organization (like visibility and the other organizational factors besides physical connectedness (Chen,1988)) should be carefully considered because they make perceptual topology special for perceptual organization rather than pure mathematics.

It is observed that it is difficult to determine the physical connectedness of the spirals. It is neglected to observe, however, that there are, in addition to physical connectedness, other organizational factors such as proximity (of neighbouring curves) and similarity (of grey-level, width, curvature of the curves) in perceptual organization of the spirals. Examine and focus on the central part of the spirals. They turn out to be ambiguous figures with alternative perception of connectedness, which are produced by competing organization with the several simultaneous factors. As a focus falls on the central part of the spiral, lower visibility of its surrounding part may not provide a clearer clue about its physical connectedness. In this case, competing organization may dominate grouping in the spiral so that two alternative percepts of the spiral's connectedness occur.

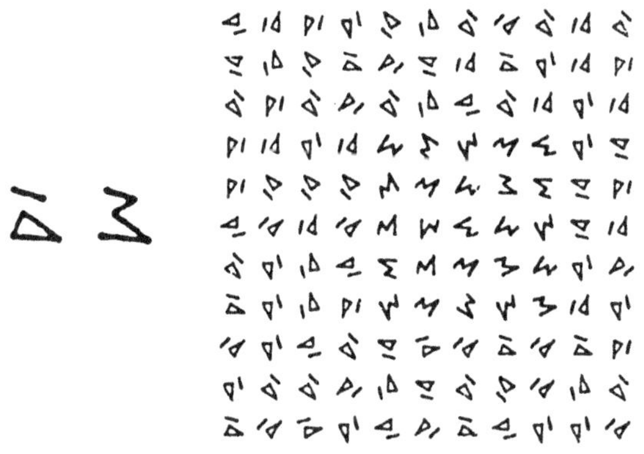

Figure 3

2 EARLY PERCEPTION OF TOPOLOGICAL PROPERTIES AND ITS IMPLICATIONS

With respect to connectionist approaches to vision, the key point of the topological hypothesis is the EARLY perception of topological properties. In the functional hierarchy of form perception (Chen, 1983a), the perception of topological properties dependent on physical connectedness occurs earlier than the perception of local geometric properties. Actually, various experiments supporting the topological perception (such as the preattentive texture discrimination described above) all also suggest the early perception of topological properties. Some of the experimental facts that are critical and straightforward to support the early perception will be further discussed in this section.

2.1 Apparent Motion (AM) and Topological Invariants

A question under a long-standing debate in the study of AM is whether motion perception precedes form perception or vice versa. To answer this question, Ullman (1979) made a claim that "the correspondence tokens are not structured form." Thus, it seems that motion perception precedes form perception. The claim may be true for structural forms such as triangles, squares and circles that represent local geometric properties. However, using "the competing motion technique", Chen (1985) found that topological perception plays a primary role in perceiving AM: subjects reported motion preference from a central figure to a figure with the same topological invariants, and, therefore, topological perception precedes motion perception. Because topological perception precedes motion perception and motion perception precedes perception of local geometric properties, topological perception precedes perception of local geometric properties. So, the topological structure in the perception of AM indicates the early perception of topological properties.

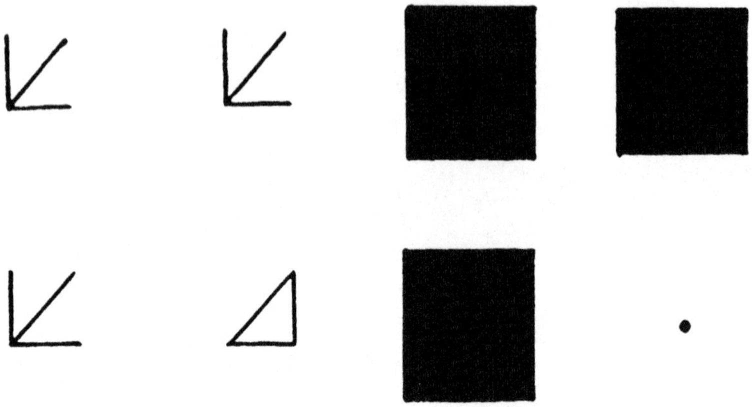

A
RT = 749 ms

B
RT = 724 ms

Figure 4

2.2 Configural Superiority Effects

Chen (1983a) measured the visual discriminability of different geometric properties by reaction times. The order of reaction times with various stimuli, representing discrimination based on a variety of geometric properties, shows a functional hierarchy similar to the gradation of geometry according to Klein's Erlangen Program. The reaction time taken to make the topological discrimination is the shortest among a variety of the stimulus displays and suggests early topological perception. For showing exactly how fast closedness is perceived, a control experiment (Pomerantz et al., 1977) is quoted here. In the stimulus display shown in Fig. 4b, the disparate quadrant contains only a very small black dot while the other three quadrants each contain a big solid square. Subjects were asked to report which quadrant was different from the rest. For the same method, we might not be able to imagine any easier discrimination task. Although the response to Fig. 4b was the fastest among their data, the RT difference between Fig. 4b and 4a, which shows discrimination based upon closedness, did not reach significance! In fact, for a brief presentation of Fig. 4b, subjects seem to make a discrimination based upon whether "there is something or nothing". Yet, the property of "there is something or nothing" is also a kind of topological property. This result, which shows no significant RT difference between these two apparently different patterns, indicates that the discriminations of both Fig. 4a and 4b share the same topological nature and occur at the early stage of vision.

A RT* 1941 MSEC | B RT* 1465 MSEC | C | D

RT* for normal people

Figure 5

Stimulus	A		B		C		D	
Visual Field	L	R	L	R	L	R	L	R
Errors (L or R)	10	7	11	6	4	2	1	1
RT ms (average of L & R)	4416		4520		2563		2951	
Errors (average of L & R)	17		17		6		2	

Table 1

2.3 Topological Perception Distinguished from Other Aspects of Form Perception: a Case of Neuropsychological Study (Zhang, 1988)

The figure discriminability of a patient who suffered from a right parieto-occipital lesion was measured in this experiment. The stimulus displays (Fig. 5) were adopted from the study of configural superiority effects described above. In turn, the task with stimulus A required discrimination of orientation of angles; the task with stimulus B, slope discrimination; the task with stimulus C, closedness discrimination; and the task with stimulus D, discrimination of whether "there is something or nothing". Stimulus D also served as a control of the base-line. A similar procedure as the previous experiment was used except that the stimulus displays were presented for the patient on either his right or left visual field.

The result is shown in Table 1, in which the capital letter L and R represent the left and right visual field, respectively. The data suggest the early perception of topological properties by not only the index of RTs (for correct responses) but also the causal sequence in form perception. These data demonstrate that the lesion indeed heavily damaged the discriminability of local geometric properties; however, in contrast, it had a much weaker effect on topological perception in the following ways. First, as the previous experiment indicates, normal people make slope discrimination with stimulus B much faster than make discrimination of the orientation of angles with stimulus A, but the brain damage completely eliminated this superiority effect; however, the performance of discrimination (of closedness) with stimulus C continued to show a strong configural superiority effect to that with stimuli A and B. Second, the great damage to the perception of stimuli A and B didn't show an influence on the topological perception also in the sense that stimuli C and D, which involved discrimination based on the same nature of topological difference, still didn't differ significantly. As mentioned before, stimulus D was used as a control of the base-line because we cannot imagine any easier discrimination task. On one hand, stimulus C is similar to stimulus B in local structure and even formed by the same line-segments as those making up stimulus A; on the other hand, it is very different from stimulus D in local structure. However, stimulus C still shares the highest discriminability with stimulus D. This fact suggests that the perception of line-segments is unlikely to be directly relevant to the topological perception of closedness. Third, the high performance error rates with stimulus A and B caused by the lesion were not transferred to stimulus D and even to stimulus C which is made up of the same line-segments as those of stimulus A. Not only the reaction time measurement but also performance error rates support the early perception of topological properties. The index of performance error rates strengthens the argument for the early topological perception from the perspective of a causal sequence, because, for line-based models, it is more difficult to explain why the significantly high error rates with perceiving the line-segments have little effect on the performance quality with perceiving the structure form made up of the exactly same line-segments. Fourth, it is also interesting to compare the results of stimuli A and B with those of stimuli C and D from the aspect of left and right visual field presentation. It is understandable that the performance with stimuli A and B at the left visual field was worse than that at the right one, because the lesion was located in the right cortex. It is a surprise, however, that, for stimuli C and D, the difference in both reaction times and errors between the left and right visual field didn't reach significance. The human ability to perceive topological properties turn out to be more robust and stable than that to perceive local geometric properties. The subject with the brain lesion offered a valuable opportunity to distinguish topological perception from other mixed factors of form perception. All these aspects of the neuropsychological data suggest the early perception of topological properties in terms of the quantity of the reaction times and the quality of the causal sequence.

Let us consider the implications of the early perception of topological properties to computational approaches, especially connectionism, starting with an example of separating figure from ground with a Boltzmann machine (Sejnowski and Hinton, 1987). Chen (1982) argued that the global properties that the distinction between figure and ground depends on, can be described mathematically as topological properties.

Sejnowski and Hinton (1987) also pointed out that separating figure from ground involves computing the inside/outside relationship, a kind of topological property. The progress of their model in overcoming the problem of being trapped in local energy minima demonstrates that the computational power of their model is significantly greater than that of early models. However, the high complexity of the inside/outside relationship is still clearly shown in the framework of the model. The model is suitable only for a quite limited case of separating figure from ground. Particularly, for the basic issue of what are the primitives of representation for visual perception, this kind of connectionist models share the same line of thinking as other computational approaches to vision, that is, assuming local geometric features to be primitive elements of computation. In the model, "the 'bottom-up' input is not the raw image itself but is a highly processed version of the image containing the location and orientation of edges" (Sejnowski and Hinton, 1987). Hence the primitives of representation for separating figure from ground are also considered as the simple parts of edges and their local geometry of location and orientation. And, in the model, the computation for separating figure from ground is subsequent upon the determination of the location and orientation of edges and is implemented as manipulations of these primitive elements. As Cowan and Sharp (1988) said, "all progress to date in the soft-wiring of nets to perform intelligent tasks rests on prior analysis by a designer of the context-dependent tasks to be performed. The intention and the meaning are supplied by the designer." The function of the model for separating figure from ground depends not only on the computational power of Boltzmann machines but also, probably more strongly, upon "the intention and meaning" about the nature of the relationship of figure and ground which were supplied by the designers. "The intention and meaning" supplied for the model adopt the same line of thinking as other computational approaches to vision based on local features. So, from what I learned from the model for computing the inside/outside relationship, there is not yet any reason to believe that for multilayered networks and Boltzmann machines, with respect to such local primitives, topological properties would not have high computational complexity. This kind of model, of course, will lead one to expect that discrimination based on local geometric properties would occur earlier than that based on topological properties—exactly the opposite of the early perception of topological properties supported by empirical facts.

How, if ever possible, to develop new computational models of human vision based on other primitives with respect to which topological properties have modest computational complexity is a challenging question. The difficulty mainly comes from two contradictory aspects. On the one hand, from the perspective of the computational analysis, the global nature of topological properties makes their computation difficult. On the other hand, the empirical data consistently support the early perception of topological properties. The order of degrees of difficulties in computing geometric invariants is puzzlingly reversed compared with the order of priority of perceiving them.

The important development of back propagation may make one doubt whether Minsky and Papert's classic result on high complexity of topological properties is broad enough to be true for multilayered networks. In my opinion, since Minsky and Papert's result is about complexity rather than computability, it is not sufficient to question its validity and generality only by developing a sample of networks capable of computing topological properties under certain limited condition. It might even be possible to construct some samples of multilayered networks someday that are capable of computing in real time some aspects of topological structure under certain limited condition. However, in comparision with other geometric properties, topological properties may still have higher complexity even for multilayered networks. Insofar as topological properties have higher complexity than local geometric properties, the difficulty for computational approaches based on local geometric features to explain the early topological perception remains. Compared with other branches of geometry, topology describes invariant properties and relationships at a more deep and stable level and is very different from metric aspects of geometric structures. This special characteristic of topology makes topological properties play a unique role in visual perception. As Cutting (1987) pointed out, topology is "the only kind of geometric information not ultimately couched as visual angles". Also, Ullman (1985) emphasized that inside/outside relations cannot be represented explicitly in the initial base representations, including the primal sketch. The mathematical proof given by Minsky and Papert is not only elegant but also simple and straightforward. After Minsky and Papert, some different measures of complexity of geometric properties and some extensions of the complexity measure given by Minsky and Papert have been advanced (Rosenfeld & Kak, 1982). However, connectedness still turns out to be highly complex. On the other hand, the practice of computer imageing processing also demonstrates that tasks related to global organization of connectedness such as segmentation and the representation of picture parts are formidably difficult. All these facts suggest that topological properties are of high complexity in some very deep sense. Minsky (1988) recently argued that multilayered networks with back propagation could compute some topological properties, but when the sample goes larger and larger, the number of hidden units needed and the time needed to learn will increase tremendously. This suggests that connectedness is still a hardbone for both classical perceptrons and perceptrons with multiple layers.

It is commonly considered that connectionist models are, in comparison to higher level cognitive processes, particularly good at lower level cognitive processes such as visual perception. However, the issues related to the topological perception, which is a primitive and general function of vision, remind me of an ancient Chinese proverb: everything is difficult at its very beginning.

Acknowledgements

This research was supported by grants from the State Commission of Science and Technology of China and the Chinese National Foundation of Sciences and by a research fellowship from the Alexander von Humboldt Foundation.

REFERENCES

Anderson, J.A. & Rosenfeld, E. (1988). *Neurocomputing*. Massachusetts: The MIT Press.

Chen, L. (1982). Topological structure in visual perception. *Science*, **218,** 699.

Chen, L. (1983a). What are the units of figure perceptual representation? *Studies in Cognitive Sciene*, No. 22, School of Social Sciences, University of California at Irvine.

Chen, L. (1983). A Topological explanation for effortless texture discrimination. *Proceedings of Fourth National Academic Conference of Biophysical Society of China*, p. 195, (in Chinese).

Chen, L. (1985). Topological structure in the perception of apparent motion. *Perception*, **14,** 197.

Chen, L. (1986). Topological perception — a possible dark cloud over computational theory. In Qian Xue (Sen Ed.), *Essays on Cognitive Sciences*, Shanghai: People's Press of Shanghai, (in Chinese).

Chen, L. (1988). Holes and wholes, submitted for publication.

Cowan, J.D. & Sharp, D.H. (1988). Neural nets and artificial intelligence. *Daedalus (Journal of the American Academy of Arts and Sciences)*, winter, 85–121.

Cutting, J.E. (1987). Perception and information. In M.R. Rosenzweig & L.W. Porter (Eds.), *Annual Review of Psychology*, **38**, California: Annual Reviews Inc.

Julesz, B. (1981). Textrons, the elements of texture perception and their interactions. *Nature*, **290**, 91.

Minsky, M. & Papert, S. (1969). *Perceptrons*, Cambridge, Mass. MIT Press.

Minsky, M. (1988). *The keynote address*, presented at the INNS, San Diego.

Pomerantz, J.R., Sager, L.C. & Stoever, R.J. (1977). Perception of wholes and their component parts: some configural effects. *Journal of Experimental Psychology: Human Perception and Performance*, **3**, 422.

Rosenfeld, A. & Kak, A. (1982). *Digital Picture Processing*, **2**, New York: Academic Press.

Rubin, J. & Kanwisher, N. (1985). Topological perception: holes in an experiment. *Perception and Psychophysics*, **37**, 179.

Rumelhart, D.E., McClelland, J.L. & The PDP Research Group (1986). *Parallel Distributed Processing*, Vol. 1. Massachusetts: The MIT Press.

Sejnowski, T.J. & Hinton, G.E. (1987). Separating figure from ground with a Boltzmann machine. In M.A. Arbib & A.R. Hanson (Eds.), *Vision, Brain and Cooperative Computation*. Massachusetts: The MIT Press.

Ullman, S. (1984). Visual Routines. In S. Pinker (Ed.), *Visual Cognition*. Massachusetts: The MIT Press.

Zhang, D.R., Chen, L. & Heng, S. (1988). Topological perception distinguished from other aspects of form perception: A case of Neuropsychological study. Paper presented at the Academic Meeting of the Center for Cognitive Science and Intelligence, Chinese Academy of Sciences, (in Chinese)

CONNECTIONISM IN PERSPECTIVE
R. Pfeifer, Z. Schreter, F. Fogelman-Soulié, L. Steels (Eds.)

Dynamical Systems in Artificial Intelligence: the Case of Classifier Systems

M. Compiani* D. Montanari* R. Serra* P. Simonini†

Abstract—*Classifier systems are dynamical systems for Artificial Intelligence like connectionist models, but they rely on production rules and are therefore closer to the classical AI paradigm based on logical inferences. They are particularly interesting because they provide a close coupling between inferencing and dynamics, and because they allow a straightforward introduction of previous domain knowledge. Given a particular task, the solutions devised by the system have either the form of static logical constructs or resort in an essential way to the possibilities of regulation which ensue from the internal dynamics. We report on our experiments on a classifier system working in a letter prediction task domain, showing that different kinds of truly dynamical solutions can be found. The stability of the solutions found by the system is discussed. Moreover, exact analytical expressions are given for the asymptotic values of the variables (the strengths of the classifiers) which are affected by the internal dynamics of the system.*

Keywords—Classifier systems, connectionist models, genetic algorithms, dynamics and prediction tasks

1 INTRODUCTION

Classifier systems are dynamical rule–based systems which are capable of learning by examples. They implement a kind of population dynamics where the rules (or *classifiers*) compete for the existing resources and to reproduce themselves. The rules which prove more useful for the overall system behaviour are rewarded on the basis of a fitness-like variable (the *strength*) while genetic algorithms meet the need for a variability mechanism which ensure partial renewal of the classifiers population and allow extensive search of the space of possible solutions. A detailed description of classifier systems may be found in (Holland, 1986a; Holland, 1986b; Riolo, 1986a).

Two learning mechanisms are operating concurrently: the so-called *bucket brigade* algorithm, which acts on a short time scale and implements a mechanism of redistribution of fitness among the existing classifiers (see section 3), and the genetic algorithms which operate with a longer time constant and change the population of classifiers, by substituting those with low fitness with the "offspring" of the fittest ones.

*ENIDATA (ENI Group) - Viale Aldo Moro 38, 40127 Bologna – ITALY
†Department of Physics, University of Bologna, Via Imerio 46, 40126 Bologna – ITALY

Although classifier systems and connectionist models differ in many respects, they share several important features. A detailed comparison of classifier systems with neural networks has been carried out in (Compiani et al., 1988), where it was shown how to build a dynamical network whose behaviour is the same as that of a given classifier system. The same problem is approached in (Davis, 1988).

Apart from formal comparisons, however, classifier systems and connectionist models are similar under a very important perspective: they both are dynamical systems for Artificial Intelligence tasks. In both cases, learning takes place through the self-organization of a dynamical system under the interaction with the external environment. In this connection the bucket brigade can be viewed as an analog of the back-propagation algorithm (Compiani et al., 1988) while the genetic algorithms further contribute to the adaptivity of classifier systems. Genetic algorithms have been used also in neural networks and their effectiveness as learning algorithms has been compared with that of the back-propagation procedure (Montana et al., 1988).

The properties of robustness and adaptivity, which make neural networks particularly attractive, are actually shared by a wider class of dynamical systems: it is therefore interesting to consider also dynamical systems which are not neurally inspired, if their computational properties are well suited for AI tasks (Steels, 1988). Classifier systems are particularly interesting because they *i)* show a very strong interaction between the dynamical and inferential features of the model and *ii)* allow a straightforward introduction of *a priori* knowledge into the system, by means of usual knowledge engineering methods, which is a difficult and important problem for neural networks (Fogelman et al., 1989). These topics are discussed in (Serra, 1989).

In this paper we report on our experiments using a classifier system designed for a specific task, namely the prediction of a sequence of letters (Riolo, 1986b). In this particular task domain, as we shall see, one can distinguish between "anthropomorphic" solutions, which appear natural to a human observer, and "non-anthropomorphic" ones. In the former case, the final solution which is devised by the system relies exclusively on the inferential mechanism, while the dynamical features play a crucial role only in the discovery phase. In the latter case the strength dynamics is very tightly coupled with inferencing and it is essential for achieving successful predictions if the task at hand requires the system to develop an internal representation of time. In Section 2 we describe the different kinds of solutions which can be found.

The stability of acquired knowledge is a crucial problem for classifier systems. Two different learning mechanisms are at work, and their combined influences can give rise to a number of instabilities. The bucket brigade dynamics is analyzed in section 3. As we shall see, the continuing action of the genetic operators after discovery of a co-adapted set of useful classifiers induces a proliferation of rules with the same phenotype, so that subpopulations of classifiers appear and grow. The dynamics and the effects of subpopulations growth are described in section 4.

2 LEARNING IN CLASSIFIER SYSTEMS

Our experiments with classifier systems have been conducted on a particular implementation of the general purpose CFS-C system developed at the University of Michigan (Riolo, 1986a; Riolo, 1986b). This program is called LETSEQ, and it is a task domain built on the

CFS-C core to simulate the task of learning ordered sequences of symbols (earlier work based on this task domain is reported in (Riolo, 1988)). In this task domain the classifier system is presented cyclically the letters of a finite length sequence; the detectors of the system read one letter per time step [1] (the "current letter"), and the system is required to learn to predict correctly which letter comes next in the sequence on the basis of the present input.

Two classes of sequences have been considered to explore the performance of the system. *Non-ambiguous* sequences, i.e. sequences where each letter is always followed by the same letter—e.g. "...abcdeabcde..."; and *ambiguous* sequences, where there is some letter with different successors, like for example the letter "a" in "...abacabac...". Similar tasks have been performed by a modified feedforward neural network in which memory of previous inputs has been forced by providing the net with "recurrent" connections from the hidden units toward the input units (Elman, 1988). Note that such connections must be hand-wired in neural networks unless they are endowed with genetic algorithms which allow the system to create new connections.

2.1 Learning non-ambiguous sequences

To fix our ideas, let us consider the sequence "...abcd...". Since it involves no ambiguity, learning such a sequence poses a hetero-associative task. This means that the system only has to discover the correlations between consecutive letters in order to associate the correct output symbol to each input symbol.

The obvious (or "anthropomorphic") solution discovered by the system[2] is shown in Figure 1.

```
C(1):  D: a, D: a / E: b
C(2):  D: b, D: b / E: c
C(3):  D: c, D: c / E: d
C(4):  D: d, D: d / E: a
```

Figure 1

Remark 1. Let us recall that classifiers always have two conditions and one action part in the CFS-C implementation. A classifier is activated when both conditions match with some messages on the message list. The classifier is then ready to produce a new message according to the information contained in its action part and in the message matching with the first condition. These messages (and the conditions) are coded as "<channel>:<letter>". For instance, "D:a" means that "a" was read by the system detectors. In LETSEQ there are four available channels:

[1] Actually, the system be configured to accept n symbols (the last n letters occurred in the sequence including the current one), but allowing the system to read more and more letters amounts to endow the system with larger and larger built-in memory of the past events. Since we decided to test the system capability of developing its own memory, we chose to let the system work under the most extreme conditions, and we restricted the width of the input window to one letter only.

[2] Suitably tuned classifier systems can learn this type of sequences with no trouble (as long as there are enough classifiers). In our experiments a set of 50 classifiers were able to learn sequences of 10 letters in an average of about 4000 steps (with a variety of different setups).

D: reserved for messages from the environment (input);
E: for internal messages which are also sent to the environment (output);
X, Y: for internal messages.

It is clear that the four rules listed above describe completely the "world" given by the cyclic sequence "abcd". The system devised this solution because the cover detector operator and the cover effector operator are "polarizing" the classifiers to have "DD/E" format. Actually, these two genetic operators are sufficient to perform an hetero-associative task of this kind. For this reason this type of solution is always the first one found by the system for this type of task, if we start with a random population of classifiers.

The four rules $C(1), \ldots, C(4)$ in Figure 1 are found almost simultaneously, compared with the typical times of the cross-over genetics. In fact the "cover" operators act quite uniformly in time, since the sub-tasks (learning one association) are independent of each other and have the same degree of complexity. The cross-over operator, on the other end, produces its effects in the longer run, when the correct classifiers have already been found, and contribute to the proliferation of $C(1), \ldots, C(4)$, which eventually develop into four distinct subpopulations of equivalent classifiers, as we shall see in section 3.

2.2 Learning ambiguous sequences

The cognitive task posed by an ambiguous sequence "...abacabac..." is obviously harder than the previous one, due to the repeated occurrence of the letter "a" followed by two different symbols and to the fact that the system is allowed to read only one letter at a time (the ambiguity disappears if we admit a two-letter input; in this case we would recover the one-to-one correspondence between input and output as in the non-ambiguous sequence).

In this case the system solves the problem using internal messages. This strategy heavily relies on a "chaining" operator which favors the creation of concatenated classifiers. A set of classifiers which disambiguate the above sequence is as follows:

Note the role of $C(3)$ and $C(6)$: they post internal messages which are used during the next step to activate $C(1)$ and $C(4)$ selectively. The internal messages play the role of a memory of the previous events: in words, they remind the system that the previous input was "b" or "c".

```
C(1):  D: a, X: c / E: b
C(2):  D: b, D: b / E: a
C(3):  D: b, D: b / X: b
C(4):  D: a, X: b / E: c
C(5):  D: c, D: c / E: a
C(6):  D: c, D: c / X: c
```

Figure 2

This is an "anthropomorphic" solution, i.e. a strategy which might typically be devised by a knowledge engineer as a solution to the problem. Alternative schemes are possible, which implement strategies using internal messages and intrinsic dynamical features (note that in the above solution the values of the strength of the classifiers are never crucial—within reasonable bounds—since only the correct rules are activated using the internal messages). We will refer to these schemes as the "dynamical" solutions. These solutions exploit the internal messages, their intensities, and the strengths of the classifiers to discriminate between classifiers which concurrently try to produce contradictory outputs during the same time step. A solution found by the system which fits into this category is shown in Figure 3.

```
C(1):  D: a, D: a / E: b
C(2):  D: b, D: b / E: a
C(3):  D: b, D: b / X: b
C(4):  D: a, X: b / E: c
C(5):  D: c, D: c / E: a
```

Figure 3

As before, $C(3)$ triggers the activation of $C(4)$ via an internal message but now a competition arises between $C(1)$ and $C(4)$ to send a message to the effectors (both are active on the same step). On this occasion the conflict resolution mechanism comes in to decide which of the two contrasting messages is to be forwarded to the effectors. The decision is taken on the basis of the relative strength of the competing classifiers and their relative supports (see Remark 3 in section 3). When the above configuration sets in as a solution, it happens that the bid of $C(4)$ is larger than that of $C(1)$ (due to the higher relative support) so that the conflict resolution[3] selects $C(4)$. When reading the "a" following "c" only $C(1)$ is activated (lacking the message "X: b" and no conflict occurs).

Variations of the above schemes have been observed experimentally, in which the effector messages were also used as internal messages. An extreme solution of this type is given in Figure 4.

```
C(1):  D: a, E: a'  / E: b
C(2):  D: b, D: b   / E: a
C(3):  D: a, E: a   / E: c
C(4):  D: c, D: c   / E: a'
```

Figure 4

where the messages posted by $C(2)$ and $C(4)$ both code for "a" although they differ in some loci of the string which are not used to code for letters or channels (they possess the same phenotype but different genotypes).

Another scheme which mixes the features of the solutions in Figures 3 and 4 is given in Figure 5.

```
C(1):  D: a,  D: a / E: a
C(2):  D: b,  D: b / E: a
C(3):  D: a, DE: a / E: b
```

Figure 5

which shows a solution for the sequence "...aabaab...". This solution is worth mentioning since here, contrary to what happens in Figure 3, no internal messages are used to activate

[3]In our experiments the conflict resolution mechanism was deterministic, based on the intensity of the messages. If this mechanism had been probabilistic, then this solution would have an unstable performance.

selectively the appropriate classifiers on the ambiguous steps. In this case, $C(1)$ and $C(3)$ always compete to post their message and the desired alternate activation is obtained in virtue of a purely dynamical mechanism. This relies on the tuning of the strengths which ensures that $C(1)$ wins the competition (having a higher bid than $C(3)$) when the system reads the first "a" and $C(3)$ wins systematically on reading the second "a". This is due to the fact that $C(3)$ turns out to have the highest bid since the classifier matches both with a detector message and the effector message posted by $C(1)$. As a final result, the bids of $C(1)$ and $C(3)$ exhibit a periodic oscillation which is exactly synchronized with the occurrence of the ambiguous letters in the sequence.

It is no surprise that the classifiers predicting the successors of the non-ambiguous letters are generated much earlier than those which solve the ambiguous part of the problem. This is due to the fact that they perform a one-step task, while the ambiguous letters can be handled only at the price of generating two classifiers and then coupling them through the chaining operator.

In this situation, if unrestricted classifier replication is allowed, chances are that the system will never solve the problem. The reason for this is that the subpopulations solving the non-ambiguous part of the sequence will replicate themselves very fast compared with the time scale of operation for the genetics that should generate the necessary couplings. This will cause an early convergence of the population, and it will also lead to the overcrowding of the message list, due to the large number of effector messages. As a consequence, there will remain no room for the internal messages which would disambiguate the sequence and the system proves capable of solving only the non-ambiguous part of the task. This is confirmed by our experiments carried out under conditions of unconstrained growth of the subpopulations.

To remedy these problems we have imposed restrictions to the spread of the subpopulations of classifiers. Limiting the maximum number of copies allowed of each genotype alleviates the competition to enter the message list though it does not solve the problem completely. In fact when the coding of information in messages and classifiers leaves some substrings unused, the creation of classifiers having the same phenotype but different genotype (e.g. the second conditions of $C(1)$ and $C(3)$ in Figure 4) makes the above restriction completely ineffective.

The solution to the ambiguous part of the sequence then comes in two stages. The first step is to develop a classifier which always answers in the same way to the ambiguous input. Such a classifier gets at least one positive reward, and will be able to stand out of the stream of useless and decaying classifiers. Eventually, the coupling operator will pick it together with one of those guessing correctly during the previous step, and it will generate the winning chain. This may be done in parallel on all the ambiguous letters of the sequence.

Sometimes, upon solving one of the ambiguities of the sequence, the bucket brigade dynamics will succeed in performing the disambiguation of the remaining part of the sequence by adjusting the strengths of the competing classifiers. In this case we will get a solution as the one in Figure 3. In the other cases the system will disambiguate the remaining parts explicitly, and the final result will be the "anthropomorphic" solution.

3 LONG TERM BEHAVIOUR

Let us now assume that the system has already discovered a set of rules that are able to react satisfactorily to any input and are able to solve the problem at issue being supported by the bucket brigade mechanism. Under these circumstances, the action of genetic operators leads to a proliferation of subpopulations of classifiers with the same phenotype, i.e. classifiers which perform essentially the same function, although they may differ in their "silent" part. It should be recalled that messages are strings of fixed length, and that only a part of the strings codes for channels and letters, while the remaining part can be regarded as composed of hidden units, which can be profitably used by the system (see e.g. Figure 4). Another possible way of creating classifiers with the same phenotype but different genotypes, in a fixed environment, is by using "don't care" symbols.

We will first consider the short term dynamics, which is rules by the bucket-brigade, ignoring the effects of genetics. The subpopulations will then remain the same, while the strengths of their members will change in time. Two essentially different types of dynamical behaviours are obtained, depending upon the message list size m, which may limit the number of classifiers allowed to post.

Let us consider a subpopulation C of classifiers which are activated periodically with period T and produce M_C messages; in the case $m > M_C$ there is no need for a competition to post, and all the bidders will post their messages.

Remark 2. Since a classifier may post more than one message, we really have to assume that m is larger than the maximum number of messages that the classifiers may post; to simplify the details of what follows, we will assume that each classifier can generate only one message per time-step.

In this case the subpopulation will reach the asymptotic values for its members without fluctuations. For each classifier these values will actually cycle, in the sense that the strength of a classifier will have, e.g., a high value corresponding to the reward received for posting a useful message, and then a sequence of decreasing values, when the classifier does nothing. This strength cycle can be computed using the formula that rules the strength update

$$s(t+1) = s(t) - Tax(t) - Bid(t) + Rew(t) \tag{1}$$

where $Tax(t)$ represents the taxes paid for various reasons by the classifier (this term usually involves a component $\alpha \cdot s(t)$ which represents a decay, and other components which represent different types of penalties for classifiers posting too many messages etc. (Riolo, 1986a)); $Bid(t)$ is the bid *paid*[4] by the classifier, which is usually equal to $k \cdot s(t) \cdot RelSupp(t)$, where $RelSupp(t)$ is the relative support; in the following discussion it will be assumed for simplicity that $RelSupp(t) = 1$. Finally, $Rew(t)$ is the sum of all the rewards received by the classifier (either from the environment or from other classifiers).

Under these conditions the asymptotic value of the strength of a classifier is determined by imposing that $s(t+T) = s(t)$. If we consider a classifier of the type D,D/E, which directly performs a guess after reading a message from the detectors, we obtain that for $t \to \infty$

$$s(t) = \frac{Rew}{1 + k \cdot (1-\alpha)^{T-1} - (1-\alpha)^{T}}. \tag{2}$$

[4]A *biased* bid is often used to select the classifiers allowed to post. This is usually equal to $Bid(t) \cdot Spec_C$, where $Spec_C$ is the specificity of the classifier.

If the reward sharing policy is active, i.e. the system reward is divided in equal parts among the classifiers that posted the selected output message, then in (2) we will have $\frac{Rew}{Mc}$ instead of Rew.

This "stroboscopic" analysis of the asymptotic dynamics of the bucket-brigade can be straightforwardly extended to classifiers which involve internal messages.

Let us now consider the longer term dynamics associated to the action of genetic operators. A very important topic regards the stability of the system knowledge, that is of the "good" rules which are used by the system to accomplish its goals. These rules may have either been discovered by the system or they may have been explicitely introduced by a knowledge engineer. It is in order to prevent the loss of useful rules that the genetic operators are allowed to replace only the weakest classifiers.

It has been experimentally observed that good rules can actually be lost by the system under the action of background (i.e., not error-triggered) genetic operators, even if reasonable parameter values are chosen. A particularly dangerous situation arises when almost all the classifiers are "good" ones, due to the growth of subpopulations of successful rules. In this case, it may happen that all the rules have essentially the same strength. The newborn classifiers are given the average strength, which is close to that of the good classifiers, so that the former have a chance to win the competition for posting. The action of error-triggered genetics can then lead to further instability.

A way to protect the useful rules may be that of prohibiting their substitution (Zhou, 1988). However, this may lead to a reduced flexibility of the system. A different approach is based on analyzing the reasons for such instabilities, and selecting parameter values which prevent them. Different kinds of instabilities, and the effects of the most important parameters, are discussed in detail in (Compiani et al, 1989a, 1989b).

4 CONCLUSIONS

Our discussion of the solutions devised by the classifier system to the problem of learning a sequence of letters allows us to draw some conclusions about the capabilities of the system. The tasks faced in this paper can be viewed as straightforward hetero-associations in those cases where the input information is rich enough. In this case, a standard feedforward neural network (McClelland & Rumelhart, 1986) can learn to perform the same task.

If this condition is not satisfied (e.g. in the case of the ambiguous sequence read letter by letter) the adaptive mechanisms of the system come into play to autonomously choose alternative tactics to compensate for the defective input and to finally discover the regularities of the external world. The anthropomorphic solution makes use of chained classifiers and internal messages to keep track of the context in which the ambiguous letters occur. Actually, the classifiers activated by the internal message and the present detector message are equivalent to a rule with two antecedents which take into account the input at two different time steps. The strategy implemented by these classifiers is very close to that used in (Elman, 1988) by means of *ad hoc* recurrent connections.

However, feeding back the output of the network to the input amounts to fixing an effective input window of fixed size, this is, it amounts to fixing the depth of the actual window which is seen by the window. It is worth noticing that classifier systems do not require this kind of previous information, since they can adapt to ambiguities of different depths (Riolo, 1986a).

In this case of the anthropomorphic solution, the sequential activation of the appropriate classifiers is achieved exclusively by selective matching with the appropriate messages, while the strengths play a limited role, in that they regulate the competition among different classifiers, ensuring that all the relevant subpopulations have access to the message list. The strength dynamics is of course fundamental for devising the asymptotic solution, but the latter can be straightforwardly read and understood without any hypothesis about the value and the dynamics of the strengths.

The dynamical solution in Figure 2 proves that the system has a great flexibility which is basically connected with the dynamical behaviour of the classifiers' strengths. Otherwise stated, the system creates a new kind of solution in which the full disambiguation is achieved by modulating the strength dynamics in order to give rise to a resonant behaviour. Under this respect, the ambiguous task can be viewed as a kind of time-learning where the system builds up an internal clock which is synchronized with the external pace specified by the ambiguous letters. The effective period can be renormalized as soon as the size of the message list becomes a limiting factor. Under such conditions the actual size of the subpopulations of classifiers predicting the same letter directly affects the asymptotic value of the strength. Another solution of interest is based on the use of hidden variables by the system, which spontaneously develops a richer coding of the input in order to disambiguate the input sequence.

Further work in progress is aimed at applying the same classifier system to more difficult tasks involving a more extensive exploitation of the dynamical properties of the system. These include learning sequences of letters with superimposed random noise and the analysis of sequences requiring longer chains of coupled classifiers.

5 THE EXPERIMENTAL SETUP

The results of our simulations with LETSEQ are shown in several pictures in this paper. The values of the crucial parameters were set as follows.
$m = 6$, *maxcfcopy* = 1, *bitpow* = 5, to study the effect of varying the cross-over rate;
cross-over rate = 0.001, *maxcfcopy* = 1, *bitpow* = 5, to study the effect of changing m;
$m = 6$, *cross-over rate* = 0.001 to analyze the performance as function of *maxcfcopy*.

The results were averaged over 20 runs with different initial random seeds for each parameter setup. Each run was considered completed when the message list was saturated with messages, and the success condition was a faultless performance for 200 steps.

All the experimental work has been carried out under some basic setup conditions which were maintained through all the runs. In particular, the startup classifier populations were randomly generated; population size was 50; the maximum number of classifier generated messages per cycle was 6; the cover detector and cover effector operators were active with activation rate 1.0; error-triggered and background genetics had activation rates of 0.01 and 0.001 respectively. The asynchronous coupling of profitable classifiers was used in the experiments on ambiguous sequences; activation rate was 0.01, minimum profit to qualify as parent was -0.5 (i.e. the classifier could have had a loss of 50% of its strength).

Acknowledgements

The authors gratefully acknowledge fruitful discussions with J. Holland and G. Zanarini. We are also indebted to R. Riolo for providing the CFS-C software.

REFERENCES

Compiani, M., Montanari, D., Serra, R., & Valastro, G. (1988). Classifier Systems and Neural Networks. *Proceedings of the 1988 Workshop on Parallel Architectures and Neural Networks*, Singapore: World Scientific Publishers.

Compiani, M., Montanari, D., Serra, R., & Simonini, P. (1989a). Asymptotic Dynamics of Classifier Systems. *Proceedings of the Third International Conference on Genetic Algorithms* (Washington DC), Los Altos, Ca: Morgan Kaufmann Publishers.

Compiani, M., Montanari, D., Serra, R., & Simonini, P. (1989b). Dynamics of Classifier Systems. *Proceedings of the 1988 Workshop on Parallel Architectures and Neural Networks*, Singapore: World Scientific Publishers.

Davis, L. (1988). Mapping Classifier Systems into Neural Networks. To appear in *Proceedings of the 1988 Conference on Neural Information Processing Systems*, Los Altos, Ca: Morgan Kaufmann.

Elman (1988). Finding Structure in Time. Center for Research in Language Technical. Report 8801.

Fogelman-Soulié, F., Gallinari, P., le Cun, Y., & Thiria S. (1989). Network Learning. To appear in Y. Kodratoff (Ed.), *Machine Learning*, Vol. III, in press.

Holland, J.H. (1986a). Escaping Brittleness. In R.S. Michalski, J.G. Carbonell & T.M. Mitchell (Eds.), *Machine Learning. An Artificial Intelligence Approach*, Volume II, pp. 592–623, Los Altos, Ca: Morgan Kaufmann Publishers.

Holland, J.H., Holyoak, K.J., Nisbett, R.E., & Thagard, P.R. (1986b). *Induction. Processes of Inference, Learning and Discovery*, Chapter 4, Cambridge, MA: MIT Press.

Montana, D.J. & Davis, L. (1988). *Training Feedforward Neural Networks Using Genetic Algorithms*, preprint.

McClelland, J.L. & Rumelhart, D.E. and the PDP Research Group (1986). *Parallel Distributed Processing*, Cambridge, MA: MIT Press.

Riolo, R.K. (1986a). *CFS-C: a package of domain independent subroutines for implementing classifier systems in arbitrary, user-defined environments*, Logic of Computers Group, University of Michigan.

Riolo, R.K. (1986). *Letseq*, Logic of Computers Group, University of Michigan.

Riolo, R.K. & Robertson, G.G. (1988). *Machine Learning* 2, 139–159.

Serra, R. (1989). Dynamical Systems and Expert Systems. this Volume.

Steels, L. (1988). Steps Towards Common Sense. *Proceedings of ECAI 1988*, 49–54, London: Pitman Publ. Co.

Zhou, H.H. (1988). A prototype of long-lived, Rule-Based Learning Systems. *Proceedings of CI 88*, ACM Italian Chapter, Milano.

CONNECTIONISM IN PERSPECTIVE
R. Pfeifer, Z. Schreter, F. Fogelman-Soulié, L. Steels (Eds.)
Elsevier Science Publishers B.V. (North-Holland), 1989

NERV — A Simulation System for Neural Nets

Alexander Genthner[1)], Reiner Hauser[1)], Heinz Horner[2)], Rupert Lange[2)], Reinhard Männer[1)]
1) Physics Institute, University of Heidelberg, 2) Institute for Theoretical Physics, University of Heidelberg

Abstract—*This paper describes the architecture of a multiprocessor system for the simulation of neural networks. Up to 320 processors 68020 are used in a single VME crate together with a Macintosh II as a host computer. This set up provides a computing power of 1600 MIPS together with a friendly graphical user interface. To support the simulation of arbitrarily interconnected networks and of asynchronous update models, the VME bus has been extended by a broadcast feature and a global max finder. It is shown that this hardware support is required for an efficient multiprocessor operation.*

Keywords—Neural networks, simulation, Hopfield model, associative memory, asynchronous update, computer architecture, multiprocessor, hardware support, broadcast, global max finding

1. INTRODUCTION

Many real-life problems of artificial intelligence cannot be handled properly by computers with traditional architectures. Typical examples are robot vision and speech recognition. Even multiprocessors of the MIMD type with 100 to 1000 microprocessors and parallel processors of the SIMD type with 1000 to 10000 processing elements (PEs) are apparently not very well suited to deal with complex and fuzzy information. It seems that the architecture of the brain fits to such types of information processing much better. In contrast to conventional computer architectures the brain consists of $\approx 10^{11}$ PEs called neurons. They are interconnected by $\approx 10^{14}$ links called synapses which have variable strength. Whereas even the low-level operation of neurons and synapses is not yet understood completely, it seems that the action of the brain is based on a massively parallel execution of a simple operation. Each neuron essentially sums up the analog signals coming in from other neurons, determines by certain criteria whether it should be activated or not, and transmits its new state to other neurons. The operation of the brain therefore depends essentially on the strengths of the synapses, which are not fixed, but adapt itself to the environment. Neural networks are therefore capable of learning and self-organization.

Artificial neural networks have been investigated for many years (Denker, 1986; Lippmann, 1988; Rumelhart, McClelland, 1986). The first mathematical models of neurons were developed by McCulloch and Pitts (McCulloch, Pitts, 1943), the first learning algorithm by Hebb (Hebb, 1949). Single layered neural networks were used in simple pattern recognition applications by Rosenblatt (Rosenblatt, 1962). Widrow and Hoff (Widrow, Hoff, 1960) applied neural networks to various problems including speech recognition and weather forecasting. A short time later, the interest in neural networks dropped rapidly after Minsky and Papert (Minsky, Papert, 1969) showed by a theoretical analysis that the principal abilities of single layered neural networks are strongly limited. Only recently, neural network architectures came into the focus of interest again for two reasons. On one hand, a small number of researchers developed learning and evaluation algorithms for multi-layered neural networks which do not have principal limits of their processing capabilities. The best known examples are the "learning logic" algorithm of Parker (Parker, 1985), the backpropagation algorithm of Rumelhart and his coworkers (Rumelhart, McClelland, 1986), and the adaptive resonance theory of Carpenter and Grossberg (Carpenter, Grossberg, 1988). On the other hand, technological advances made it possible to simulate moderately large neural networks in reasonable time and to actually set up hardware realizations of neural networks in VLSI (Hopfield, Tank, 1987; Jackel, Graf, Howard, 1987; Mead, 1987) and in optics (Farhat, Psaltis, Prata, Paek, 1985; Psaltis, Brady, Wagner, 1988; Psaltis, Park, Hong, 1988; Psaltis, Yu, Gu, Lee, 1987). Today, many network architectures have been proposed together with a high number of learning and dynamic algorithms.

Much work is currently being done on testing the various possibilities in different applications (Proc. IEEE, 1987; Proc. IEEE, 1988; Proc. Soc. Meeting, 1988). The situation is characterized by the statement that the available theories are still not powerful enough that the performance of a certain neural network architecture could be estimated for a specific application. Because it is very expensive and time consuming to set up electronic or optical neural networks, in most cases one has to rely on simulation techniques to evaluate different network architectures and algorithms, before a hardware implementation can be tackled. Such simulations, however, require a very high computing power. Many computations are therefore done on parallel computers of the MIMD type (Forrest, Roweth, Stroud, Wallace, Wilson, 1987; Garth, Pike, 1988; Kuczewski, Myers, Crawford, 1987) or the SIMD type (Hillis, 1985). Whereas such systems provide the computing power to simulate large neural networks, they are not generally available. Therefore, smaller neural networks are also simulated on mainframe computers (Feldman, Fanty, Goddard, Lynne, 1988) and on specialized coprocessors to personal computers (ANZA).

This paper describes a very flexible integrated simulation system, the NERV multiprocessor (Genthner, Horner, Lange, Männer, 1988; Hauser, Horner, Männer, 1988), with a very high computing power and a friendly user interface. Examples of other simulation systems are the Rochester connectionist simulator (Feldman, Fanty, Goddard, Lynne, 1988) and NN (Kindermann, Mühlenbein, Wolf, 1988). In the following, we outline the type of computation that has to be performed and the special requirements that ask for hardware support for an efficient implementation on a multiprocessor system. This is succeeded by a description of the NERV architecture.

2. THE SIMULATION OF NEURAL NETWORKS

A neural network consists of a high number N of interconnected neurons. In the simplest case, each neuron i is a simple PE, which can be either in the state "active" (s_i=1) or "passive" (s_i=-1). Its respective state is determined by the current state of all other neurons connected to it and the interconnections themselves. The interconnections from neuron i to neuron j (i,j=1..N) have individual strengths J_{ij}, so that the neurons influence the new state of the other neurons differently. In the most general case, the values of the interconnection strengths are not restricted. They may be positive or negative, corresponding to a stimulating or an inhibiting effect, symmetric ($J_{ij} = J_{ij}$) or asymmetric ($J_{ij} \neq J_{ij}$), and mostly or sparsely present, corresponding to a fully connected or a structured network. In the following, we proceed from the general case, a fully connected network with arbitrary interconnection strengths, because all other networks can be derived from it by properly choosing the values J_{ij}.

We first assume that the interconnection strengths J_{ij} have already been learned and are now fixed. In this case, the network is used to associate an input pattern with previously learned patterns, i.e. to find the most similar stored pattern. To do so, each neuron i computes its "local field" h_i at time t,

$$h_i(t) = \sum_{j=1}^{N} J_{ij} s_j(t).$$

The new state is computed as $s_i(t+1) = \text{sign } h_i(t)$, where a hard threshold was used to determine the activation state. Other functions like a sigmoid could also be used instead of the signum function. In the Little model (Little, Shaw, 1978) each neuron determines its new state according to this expression in parallel. After all neurons updated their states synchronously, the local fields have to be computed again. In contrast, in the Hopfield model (Hopfield, 1982) only a single neuron is selected after each iteration step at random. This neuron determines by the current value of its local field, whether its state has to be changed or not. This is called an asynchronous update. Therefore, it is not necessary here to compute the whole sum over all neurons, but only the single correction term $2J_{ij}s_j$ to this sum.

This iteration converges after roughly N steps. With a proper learning algorithm, the attractors of this iteration correspond to the stored patterns. This means that starting from an arbitrary pattern, the network always retrieves one of the learned patterns. In this way, a well defined pattern can be reconstructed from a noisy or only partly defined input pattern.

The number of patterns which can be stored is limited by the network size. In the Hopfield model, this limit is roughly $0.14 \cdot N$ patterns. If more patterns are stored, the retrieval of a pattern is not guaranteed. Instead, the network may converge to mixed states which have not been learned or it may not converge at all. To get results concerning the storage capacity of different models, simulation runs have to be done with different learning and dynamic algorithms and a varying number of learned patterns. This requires a huge simulation effort.

3. THE MULTIPROCESSOR SYSTEM

The NERV system was designed to support the simulation of large neural networks. To provide simple programmability in a high level language and high computing power, the time critical operations are done on a multiprocessor system consisting of a high number (≤320) of 32 bit microprocessors operating in parallel. The parallel processors are controlled by a master processor which is itself linked to a commercial host computer.

The multiprocessor is based on the VME bus standard. However, a few special bus lines are used for hardware support of time critical operations needed for the simulation of neural networks as described below. A single VME crate may contain up to 20 multiprocessor boards and a single master processor which provides a link to the host computer. This is a Macintosh II which offers a friendly graphical user interface. The host computer is used as a program development system for the multiprocessor, as well as for preparing and presenting input and output data during the simulation. Each multiprocessor board contains itself 16 PEs that execute the parallel learning and dynamic algorithms. A single PE simulates usually many neurons, typically 10..50. The master processor, a commercial VME board, is responsible for the communication between the host computer and the parallel processors, for synchronizing the parallel processors, for buffering often used algorithms, and for preprocessing and formatting of data. All processors in the NERV system, i.e. in the host, the master processor, and in the PEs use the 32 bit microprocessor 68020. All software, i.e. the operating system, the general simulation package, and the individual application software is written in Modula-2. By using native or cross development systems, the same programs can be run on the host for debugging purposes or on the multiprocessor for high speed execution.

A multiprocessor board of the NERV system consists of a VME motherboard with the bus interface logic. In addition, the motherboard carries subboards with autonomous PEs. They have been designed to provide only the absolute minimum of functions in order to get a high package density. 16 PEs fit onto a single motherboard. Each one consists of a 68020 CPU operating at 25 MHz, 1 MBytes of static RAM, and interface and control logic. A floating point coprocessor is not required for the computations mentioned above, neither a memory management unit.

Each PE stores its program in its local memory, as well as all data required. This includes the state of all neurons s_i and the interconnection strengths J_{ij} needed, i.e. one column of the matrix J per simulated neuron. Because each PE has a copy of the state of all neurons, state changes have to be done synchronized in all local memories. To estimate the relative overhead created be transmitting neuron state changes over the bus, we consider the following examples. During a computation of the Hopfield model, all processors have to correct the local fields of the neurons simulated by them. This takes about 3 μs per neuron. If a state change would have to be transmitted sequentially to all processor elements, this would take ≈320 μs in a 320 processor system. Because each processor element simulates typically more than 10 neurons, the time for transmitting state changes would be much higher than the computation time and the multiprocessor efficiency would be very low, e.g., below 15%. The situation gets even worse in case of the Little model. Here, much longer computation times are required, because the complete sum has to be computed for each neuron. With 320 PEs and 10 neurons simulated per PE, this takes ≈10 ms. On the other hand it is required to transmit the state of all neurons to all PEs after each iteration step. In this example, this would take ≈1020 ms and the multiprocessor efficiency would drop below 1%.

For this reason, the VME bus protocols have been extended to support broadcast transfers. Here, a write transfer into a certain part of the address space causes a simultaneous write operation to all local memories. The data transfer acknowledge signal of the VME bus cannot be used to signal a successfully terminated broadcast transfer, because the transfer has to be extended until all PEs have acknowledged. This requires a logical AND of the individual acknowledge signals. For that purpose, a free bus line was used as an broadcast acknowledge signal. It is a open collector line, whose HIGH level signals a successfully terminated broadcast write transfer. A extended version of this protocol is currently under consideration as a standard for the VME bus. The typical broadcast time is about 1 µs. With this, the communication time both for Hopfield and Little type network computations is negligible against the computation time of a PE, so that an efficiency of ≈100% is obtained. The PEs use only broadcast transfer to communicate with each other and with the master processor.

For most theoretical models it is required that all PEs are synchronized after each iteration step and that the master processor is notified of the termination of a number of iteration steps. For this, another free open collector line on the VME bus is used. This line can be set by each processor element via a register. On the VME bus, this line becomes HIGH only when all processor elements did set their register to 1. In this case, an interrupt is generated on the master processor. It can then do the required action, e.g., starting the next computation step or reading out simulation results. The usual VME bus interrupt cannot be used for this purpose, because it does not allow the required synchronization of all PEs.

Many neural network models rely on asynchronous updates of the neurons. One reason for that is that asynchronous updating together with symmetric interconnection strengths J_{ij} guarantees the convergence of the iteration. Examples for asynchronous network models are the Hopfield model, where a single neuron is selected at random which may or may not change its state, and the model, where the very neuron with the strongest local field $h_i(t)$ is selected (Horner, 1987). The computation of such models demands for selecting at each iteration step a single neuron according to a certain criterion, e.g., a random but unique number or the local field $h_i(t)$. The selection can therefore only be done, after the corresponding values of all PEs have been compared. If this would be done by software, this would take N bus transfers. In the example given above, about 5 ms are required for the compare operation, whereas the computation time for updating the neuron only requires 30..300 µs. To avoid that all processors have to wait for the global comparison most of the time, this operation has to be supported by hardware.

In the NERV system, such a global compare logic was implemented on the VME bus. Its operation is similar to the priority arbitration logic of the Futurebus system or the OR-network of the Connection Machine (Hillis, 1985). Basically, a binary coded value, e.g., a random number or the value of the local field, is asserted onto a set of open collector bus lines. Because all PEs do so in parallel, the global OR of all values is built on the bus lines. A combinatorial logic on each PE compares this global value to the local value. This is done bit sequentially, starting with the most significant bit. If a difference is found, the PE does not have the highest priority and will negate its value. With unique values, this procedure ensures that all PEs but one disconnect from the comparison bus. The remaining one is selected. In the NERV system, we use four lines for the comparison bus. A four bit value can be globally compared within ≈1 μs, but this operation can be cascaded. For the simulation of neural networks, 16 bit values will be compared, which takes ≈4 μs. This is again negligible compared to the computation time for neuron updates of 30..300 μs.

4. SOFTWARE

Even non-structured neural networks are described by a high number of parameters. Examples are different learning and dynamic algorithms and the number and type of neurons and synapses. Taking into account various network architectures, e.g. multi-layered, feed-forward and feed-back, different types of neurons etc., the possibilities to set up a special neural network are nearly unlimited. The simulation of neural networks therefore requires a very flexible and powerful system. Generally, a simulation run consists of several, well distinguished steps.

The first one is the definition of the network. The structure of the network can be considered as posing limitations to the values of the synapses. A multi-layered feed-forward network consists, e.g., of N neurons which are distributed over the individual layers. The interconnection strengths J_{ij} between neurons in the same layer are all set to 0, as well as between neurons in non-neighboring layers. Additionally, the J_{ij} are asymmetric in that all backward synapses are also set to 0. Besides defining a starting value for certain synapses in this way, this is also a restriction to the learning algorithm.

The network learning algorithm and dynamic algorithm have to be prepared before the simulation starts. For comparisons, multiple algorithms can be used. Whereas it is planned for the future to provide standard algorithms in a library, right now these algorithms have to be programmed by the user in Modula-2 or in assembler. This is done on the host computer, a MacintoshII, under MPW. Software modules can therefore be debugged to a high degree solely on the host computer within a comfortable programming environment. After this first debugging process, the modules are recompiled by the cross-development system MCDS (Hiware, 1988) and linked to other modules of the simulation package. After this, the simulation program is executable and can be loaded into the master processor.

During the essential simulation run, two tasks are executed on the host computer. One is the interactive simulation control program, which runs under a Hypercard shell. The other one is a debugger which is activated only in cases where errors are reported by the processor elements or by the master processor. The control program provides a graphic user interface that allows to start or stop the simulation, to change parameters or the network configuration, to switch between different learning or dynamic algorithms, to request intermediate or final results from the multiprocessor, to compute and display statistical information about the state of neurons and synapses etc.

On the PEs, all time critical algorithms, i.e., learning and network dynamics, are executed. Figure 1 shows the flow chart of a parallel program. This example describes the simulation of an asynchronous dynamic of the Hopfield-Greedy type. Here, a single neuron has to be selected for possible updating. If the state of this neuron is changed, this has to be broadcasted to all processors. It can be seen that the global operations to find the strongest local field, to broadcast neuron state changes, and to synchronize all PEs are used in the most inner loop of the simulation. These three operations are supported by hardware which is

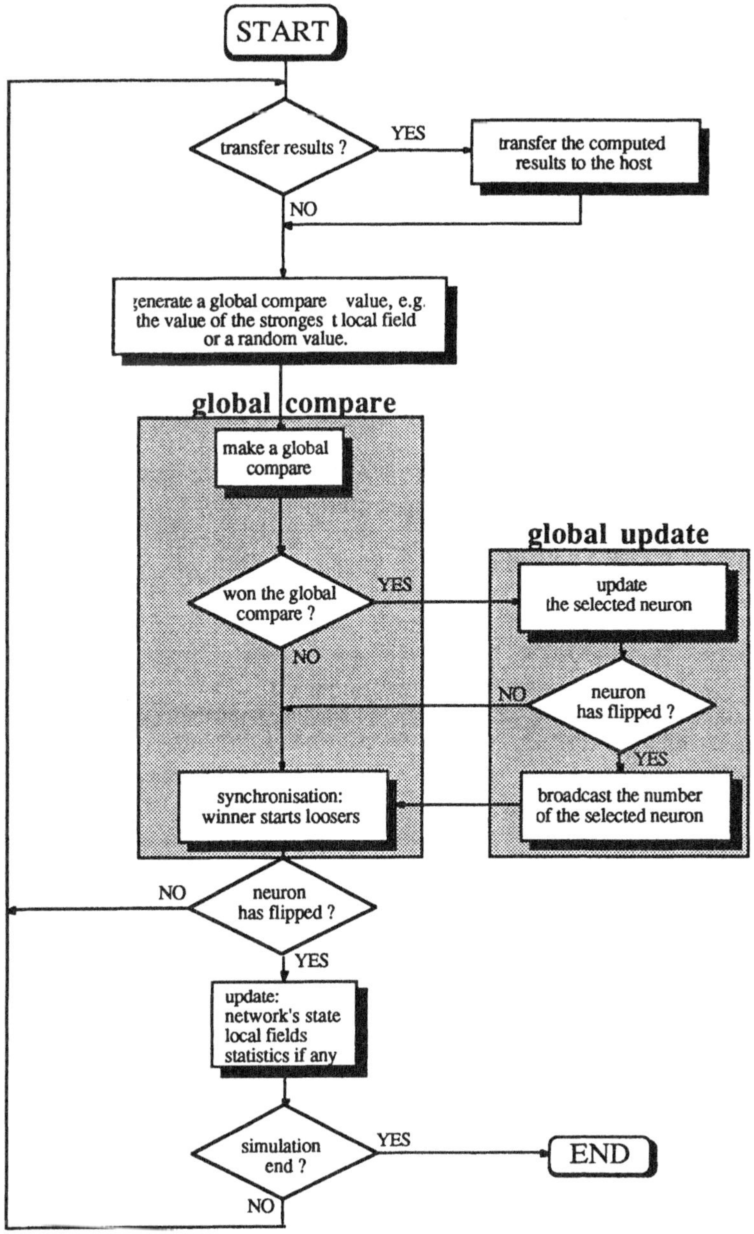

FIGURE 1. Flowchart of the dynamic program

called by a set of system routines. It is presumed that all patterns have already been learned, i.e., that all interconnection strengths are already computed.

The NERV system is operated by the user by means of the host computer. There a program package is provided which is independent of the actual simulation problem. It allows to do the network configuration, to control the execution of the simulation program, and to handle intermediate or final results computed in the parallel processor as described below. These software modules are programmed in Modula-2 and are called from the Hypercard shell.

The configuration module allows the user to specify all network parameters interactively. It is also possible to use parameter values specified in a configuration file. Because the simulation package is written to be independent of the actual parameter values, these can be chosen freely and are restricted only by the system hardware, e.g., the memory size. The most important parameters are the structure and the size of the network, the learning and dynamic algorithm, the startup values for the interconnection strengths, and the patterns to be learned. Part of the configuration is the specification which return parameters should be computed.

The execution control module is responsible for initializing and supervising the parallel processor. The initialization is done by broadcasting all routines required in the current simulation step and all necessary data, e.g. patterns. Supervision covers to start the parallel processors, to monitor the execution of the simulation, and to stop the processors after meeting a halt condition.

The evaluation module reads out intermediate or final results from the parallel processor as specified during the configuration part of the simulation. Data can be written into files for later analysis, but they may also be immediately analyzed and displayed graphically.

All time critical software of a simulation of neural networks is executed on the parallel processor itself. These modules are programmed in Modula-2 like the other ones executed on the master processor or the host computer. This allows to develop these modules on the host computer within a comfortable program development environment. Despite a few hardware specific functions that are simulated, they can be debugged and tested completely on the host. To execute them on the parallel processor simply requires them to be compiled by MCDS and linked with the runtime library supporting parallel processing. This library contains for example routines to exploit the NERV-specific hardware features like broadcast, priority compare, and processor synchronization. It also provides simple access to the global control variables which have been initialized on the host computer. Usual parallel programs are rather short. Together with all required library routines, they occupy typically 5 to 15 kBytes of local memory. This is small against the memory size required by the data which have to be stored locally, i.e., the state of all neurons and the interconnection strengths from the local neurons to all other ones.

As mentioned above, the parallel programs are written to be independent of the system size and all network parameters which can be set online in the configuration phase. The same simulation software can therefore be executed on a small system with, e.g., only a partly stuffed single VME board with six processors or on a full scale system with 320 processors. This is handled automatically by the system software, which also identifies defective processors during startup and ignores them afterwards. All processors run the same parallel program which is broadcasted by the master processor before individual simulation steps as required. The actual values of the network parameters are stored in a global memory area and are also broadcasted to all parallel processors in case of changes.

5. CURRENT STATUS AND OUTLOOK

The NERV system was developed as a prototype with a small number of PEs. Its hardware has been tested completely. The basic operating software and the essential parts of the simulation package are also tested. Currently, a compressed layout of the printed circuit board of the PE is in hand. We expect to have a VME board with 16 PEs in spring 1989. With 1 MBytes each, the total system memory will amount to 320 MBytes, so that over 15,000 fully connected neurons with over 200 Mio. synapses can be simulated.

It is important to note that the number of neurons as well as the number of synapses which can be simulated by the NERV system depend essentially on the size of the available memory. Our estimation is based on a fully interconnected network. If only sparsely interconnected networks have to be simulated, the number of neurons can be increased by up to three orders of magnitude. Similarly, if the interconnection strengths are not stored as 16 bit values, then the matrix J_{ij} requires less memory and the number of neurons can again be increased. If, as an extreme example, each neuron is interconnected only to 20 other neurons and each synapse is clipped to values of ± 1, networks with up to several hundred millions of neurons could be simulated.

If required, the system performance could be increased by another factor of 10 beyond the values given above. This could be done by interconnecting multiple VME crates via bus repeaters. The Heidelberg Polyp multiprocessor (Männer, Stucky, Ludwig, 1988) demonstrates that a system of this size is feasible. Using a comparable setup, the NERV system could use up to 3360 PEs. In this case, larger neural networks could be simulated. If the number of neurons per PE is held constant, the computation time remains the same. The NERV architecture therefore is capable to be extended to provide an extremely high computing power for the simulation of neural networks.

REFERENCES

ANZA Neurocomputing System, Hecht-Nielsen Neurocomputer Corp., San Diego, CA 92121

Carpenter G.A., Grossberg S. (1988). The ART of Adaptive Pattern Recognition by a Self-Organizing Neural Network. *IEEE Computer*, **21**, 3, 77-88

Denker J.S. (1986). Neural Network Models of Learning and Adaption. *Physica*, **22D**, 216-232

Farhat N.H., Psaltis D., Prata A., Paek E. (1985). Optical Implementation of the Hopfield Model. *Appl. Optics*, **24**, 10, 1469-1475

Feldman J.A., Fanty M.A., Goddard N.H., Lynne K.J. (1988). Computing with Structured Connectionist Networks. *Comm. ACM*, **31**, 2, 170-187

Forrest B.M., Roweth D., Stroud N., Wallace D.J., Wilson G.V. (1987). Implementing Neural Network Models on Parallel Computers. *Comp. J.*, **30**, 5, 413-419

Garth S., Pike D. (1988). An integrated system for neural network simulations. *Comp. Arch. News*, **16**, 1, 37-44

Genthner A., Horner H., Lange R., Männer R. (1988). NERV - Ein Simulationssystem für neuronale Netzwerke: Software und Benutzerinterface. Proc. gem. Workshop Sprachen, Algor. und Archit. für Parallelrechner, Fachgr. Altern. Konz. f. Sprachen u. Rechner und Parallel-Algor. und Rechnerstrukt. (PARS) of the GI, 315-329

Hauser R., Horner H., Männer R. (1988). NERV - Ein Simulationssystem für neuronale Netzwerke: Der Multiprozessor. Proc. gem. Workshop Sprachen, Algor. und Archit. für Parallelrechner, Fachgr. Altern. Konz. f. Sprachen u. Rechner und PARS of the GI, 303-313

Hebb D.O. (1949). The Organization of Behavior. New York, NY: Wiley

Hillis D.W. (1985). The Connection Machine. Cambridge, MA: MIT Press

Hiware. (1988). MCDS Modula2-Cross-Development-System User Manual, Mac-Version 1.5

Hopfield J.J. (1982). Neural Networks and Physical Systems with Emergent Collective Computational Abilities. *Proc. Natl. Acad. Sci. USA*, **79**, 2554-2558

Hopfield J.J., Tank D.W. (1987). Computing with Neural Circuits. *Science*, **233**, 625-633

Horner H.. In H. Haken (Ed.). (1987). Proc. Int'l Symp. on Synergetics, Schloß Elmau

I896 Working Group of EWICS - TC10. (1983). i896 - A Proposed Standard Backplane Bus Specification for Advanced Microcomputer Systems

Jackel L.D., Graf H.P., Howard R.E. (1987). Electronic Neural Network Chips. *Appl. Optics*, **26**, 23, 5077-5080

Kindermann J., Mühlenbein H., Wolf K. (1988). Implementierung von neuronalen Netzen. Priv. comm.

Kuczewski R.M., Myers M.H., Crawford W.J. (1987). Neurocomputer Workstations and Processors. Proc. IEEE 1st Int'l Conf'. on Neural Networks, **III**, 487-426

Lippmann R.P. (1988). An Introduction to Computing with Neural Nets. *Comp. Arch. News*, **16**., 1, 7-25

Little W.A., Shaw G.L. (1978). *Math. Biosci.,* **39**, 281

Männer R., Stucky O., Ludwig W. (1988). The Heidelberg Polyp Multiprocessor Project. to be publ. in Proc. CONPAR '88, Manchester, UK

McCulloch W.S., Pitts W. (1943). A Logical Calculus of the Ideas Imminent in Nervous Activity. *Bull. Math. Biophysics*, **5**, 115-133

Mead C. (1987). A Sensitive Electronic Photoreceptor. Proc. 1985 Chapel Hill Conf. on VLSI, 463-471

Minsky M., Papert S. (1969). Perceptrons. Cambridge, MA: MIT Press

Parker D.B. (1985). Learning-logic. Rep. TR-47, Center for Comp. Res. in Economics and Managem. Sci., MIT, Cambridge, MA

Proc. IEEE 1st Int'l Conf. on Neural Networks, San Diego, CA (1987)

Proc. IEEE 2nd Int'l Conf. on Neural Networks, San Diego, CA (1988)

Proc. 1st Ann. Int'l Neural Network Soc. Meeting, Boston, MA (1988)

Psaltis D., Brady D., Wagner K. (1988). Adaptive Optical Networks Using Photorefractive Crystals. *Appl. Optics*, **27**, 9, 1752-1759

Psaltis D., Park C., Hong J. (1988). Higher Order Associative Memories and Their Optical Implementations. *Neural Networks*, **1**, 149-163

Psaltis D., Yu J., Gu X.G., Lee H. (1987). Optical Neural Nets Implemented with Volume Holograms. Priv. comm.

Rosenblatt F. (1962). Principles of Neurodynamics. New York, NY: Spartan

Rumelhart D.E., McClelland J.L. (1986). Parallel Distributed Processing, Volumes 1 + 2. Cambridge, MA: M.I.T./Bradford Books

Widrow B., Hoff M.E. (1960). Adaptive Switching Circuits. Proc. 1960 IRE WESCON, 96-104

CONNECTIONISM IN PERSPECTIVE
R. Pfeifer, Z. Schreter, F. Fogelman-Soulié, L. Steels (Eds.)

Representation and Recognition of Spatio-Temporal Objects within a Generalized Hopfield Scheme

Andreas Herz
Sonderforschungsbereich 123 an der Universität Heidelberg
D-6900 Heidelberg, Germany.

Abstract—*We study the representation of static objects (single patterns) and temporal associations (sequences) within a generalized Hopfield scheme. Three basic ideas are combined in our approach: (a) to use a broad distribution of transmission delays, (b) to incorporate the very same delays in a single dynamical description of the network, both during the learning session and the retrieval session, and (c) to store information locally in the synapses according to the Hebb principle. As shown by theory and numerical simulations, the resulting mechanism has surprisingly fault-tolerant capabilities for the autoassociative recall of spatio-temporal objects. We illustrate this statement by some results on sequence retrieval and discuss possible applications for speech recognition problems.*

Keywords—Broad distribution of transmission delays, representation of spatio-temporal objects, Hebbian learning of temporal sequences

1. INTRODUCTION

Basic computational functions of neurobiological networks may be studied for a model introduced by Hopfield (1982), where static patterns are stored as attractors for the dynamics of the system. The analogy to spin-glass models allows the application of analytical techniques known from statistical mechanics (Amit et al. 1985, 1987; van Hemmen & Kühn 1986; van Hemmen 1987). Nevertheless, one should be aware that environmental input to a neural net always provides information *both in space and time*. It is therefore desirable to extend the original Hopfield model and to explore the possibilities for a joint representation of static patterns as well as temporal sequences in such associative networks.

Buhmann and Schulten (1987) proposed a network with symmetric excitatory connections to stabilize single patterns, additional instantaneous projections to generate transitions, and pairwise inhibition to avoid mixture states. The dynamical evolution is triggered by the influence of thermal noise which may be used as a time-dependent external parameter. Another mechanism was introduced by Peretto and Niez (1986), who use fast synaptic plasticity to induce transitions between individual patterns, which are once again stabilized by a symmetrical interaction.

A different route to the representation of dynamic objects has been proposed by Kleinfeld (1986) and Sompolinsky and Kanter (1986), who use a *single* transmission delay to construct a sequence generator. Since various signal delays are omnipresent in the brain (Miller 1987) and certainly play an important role for biological information processing (Braitenberg 1967), their integration into theoretical models seems to be rather convincing, especially if one could also deal with the distribution of the delay times involved.

As a first step, the complete temporal aspect of an external stimulus may be transformed into a spatial dimension in systems with a feedforward architecture. Within a symbolic description (Tank and Hopfield 1987), the elementary parts of a sequence, for example letters in a word, are extracted by feature detectors and delayed by time-intervals proportional to the temporal distance between the individual symbols and the end of the corresponding prototype sequences they belong to. Even if a slightly distorted sequence is offered to the system during the retrieval phase, the outputs of the delay lines will be concentrated in time and arrive rather simultaneously at indicator units, where their summed signal can be used for classification. It should be noted however, that this kind of device only uses information about the position of the elementary symbols *relative to the end of a sequence*. Temporal relationships within the sequence are not memorized so that only a minor part of the available input structure can be used during the retrieval session.

Even if the presented models seem to be plausible under certain aspects, they still lack a very important quality — the possibility to acquire knowledge through a true learning mechanism. Values for the synaptic couplings have to be calculated separately and put into the actual system by hand, which is certainly not satisfactory both from a neurobiological point of view and also for applications in artificial intelligence.

To overcome this major drawback, we interpret the Hebb principle (1949) in a careful way and show that it can be implemented in a neural network with a *broad* distribution of delays so as to handle both static patterns and temporal associations such as tunes and rhythms. That is, after the network has been taught single, stationary, patterns and temporal sequences — of course, by the *same* principle ! — it will reproduce them when triggered suitably.

2. DYNAMICS OF THE NEURONS

Throughout what follows, a neural net will be described as a collection of N formal neurons with activities $S_i(t) = \pm 1$. They are connected by modifiable synapses with efficacies $J_{ij}(\tau_{ij})$, $1 \leq i,j \leq N$, where τ_{ij} denotes the time delay for the information transport from *j* to *i*. We have studied three different models (Herz et al. 1988, 1989). In model A, there is for each pair of neurons (i,j) a *large* number of axons (possibly, interneurons) whose delays τ are independent of *i* and *j*. In both the other models only a single axon links each pair of neurons. The delay time τ_{ij} is either the sum of two parts, τ_i and τ_j, each drawn from a given distribution (B), or sampled from one distribution independent of *i* and *j* (C). In the present contribution, external stimuli are explicitly taken into account. They are fed into the system via receptor neurons with activities $\sigma_i(t)$ also taken to be ± 1. The local (dendritic) fields $h_i(t)$ will be given by

$$h_i(t) = (1-\gamma) \sum_{j\,(\neq i)} J_{ij}(\tau_{ij})\, S_j(t-\tau_{ij}) + \gamma\, \sigma_i(t)\,, \tag{1}$$

where the parameter γ measures the input sensitivity of the system. In model A an additional sum over all delay lines connecting j to i is understood.

The stochastic nature of biological processes involved in the time evolution of a single neuron may be described by a Glauber dynamics at a finite inverse temperature $\beta = T^{-1}$,

$$p[\, S_i(t+\Delta t) = \pm 1\,] = 1/2\, \{1 + \tanh[\, \pm \beta\, h_i(t)\,]\,\}, \tag{2}$$

which reduces for $T \to 0$ to the deterministic case, $S_i(t+\Delta t) = \mathrm{sgn}\,[h_i(t)]$. Updating is either performed in parallel at discrete time steps and simultaneously for *all* spins, or sequentially in that only a *single* spin may be flipped at each step Δt, which is adapted accordingly ($\Delta t \propto N^{-1}$).

3. DYNAMICS OF THE SYNAPSES DURING THE LEARNING SESSION

During the learning session the synaptic strengths may change according to the Hebb rule. In order to study the implications for a network with transmission delays, we focus our attention on a specific pair of neurons, say i and j. If neuron j has fired, a soliton-like pulse propagates via the axon to the synapse at neuron i (For more general delay types see Herz et al. 1989). Information is stored at this connection, provided neuron i's activity is concurrent with the arrival of the pulse coming from j (Kelso et al. 1986). Therefore, according to the Hebb principle, at each instant of time the efficacy $J_{ij}(\tau)$ changes by an infinitesimal amount proportional to $S_i(t)S_j(t-\tau)$. Starting with a *tabula rasa* ($J_{ij}(\tau) = 0$) we obtain

$$J_{ij}(\tau) = N^{-1}\, \varepsilon_{ij}(\tau)\, T^{-1} \int_0^T dt\, S_i(t)\, S_j(t-\tau)\,, \tag{3}$$

where N^{-1} is a scaling factor which will turn out to be useful for the theoretical analysis of a fully connected network. $\varepsilon_{ij}(\tau)$ is a weight of the synaptic efficacy $J_{ij}(\tau)$ which takes morphological characteristics of the synapse $j \to i$ with delay τ into account. We restrict ourselves to the homogeneous case, $\varepsilon_{ij}(\tau) = \varepsilon(\tau)$. For general delay types, $S_j(t-\tau)$ would be replaced by $\int_0^\infty ds\, w(s)\, S_j(t-\tau-s)$, where $w(s)$ depends on the delay *mechanism*. It is worthwhile to realize that the prescription (3) in conjunction with a broad distribution of delays τ strongly deviates from all the cycle generating mechanisms which are known at present (Willwacher 1976; Kleinfeld 1986; Sompolinsky and Kanter 1986; Amit 1987; Buhmann and Schulten 1987; Dehaene et al. 1987; Gutfreund and Mezard 1988; Riedel et al. 1988).

In the following, patterns to be memorized are specific configurations $\{\xi_i^\mu\}$ labeled by $1 \le \mu \le q$. For the sake of convenience we work with unbiased random patterns where $\xi_i^\mu = \pm 1$ with equal probability. During the learning session of duration T, we impose upon the network a *time-dependent* external stimulus $\sigma_i(t)$, $0 \le t \le T$, of the form $\sigma_i(t) = \xi_i^{\lambda(t)}$, where $1 \le \lambda(t) \le q$ is a given function of *t*. For example, $\lambda(t) = \mu \pmod q$ for $(\mu - 1)\Delta \le t \le \mu\Delta$, if we consider a cycle of q patterns, each of duration Δ.

The mathematical analysis of the Hebbian learning scheme will be greatly simplified if we consider parallel updating with $\gamma = 1$ in (1) and $T = 0$ in (2) during the learning session. This amounts to a "clamped" learning scenario, where the system evolves strictly according to the environmental inputs, $S_i(t) = \sigma_i(t - \Delta t)$. The synaptic efficacies $J_{ij}(\tau)$ may readily be calculated:

$$J_{ij}(\tau) = N^{-1} \sum_{\mu,\nu} \xi_i^{\mu}\, Q_{\mu\nu}^{(\tau)}\, \xi_j^{\nu} \equiv N^{-1} (\vec{\xi}_i, \mathbf{Q}^{(\tau)} \vec{\xi}_j), \quad \vec{\xi}_i = (\xi_i^{\mu}, 1 \le \mu \le q). \tag{4}$$

The components of the matrix $\mathbf{Q}^{(\tau)}$ are given by

$$Q_{\mu\nu}^{(\tau)} = \varepsilon(\tau)\, T^{-1} \int_0^T dt\, m_\mu(t)\, m_\nu(t-\tau)\,, \tag{5}$$

$$m_\mu(t) \equiv N^{-1} \Sigma_i \xi_i^{\mu} S_i(t) = N^{-1} \Sigma_i \xi_i^{\mu} \xi_i^{\lambda(t-\Delta t)}\,, \tag{6}$$

where the overlaps $m_\mu(t)$ measure how close the system is to state μ at time t. The $m_\mu(t)$ will also be used as macroscopic order parameters during the retrieval session. As shown by equations (3) and (5), the $J_{ij}(\tau)$ encode spatio-temporal correlations of the input stimuli. We therefore encounter a "resonance phenomenon": The $J_{ij}(\tau)$ with delays τ which match the timing of the external stimulus receive maximum strength. Note that they are also the ones that would support a stable cycle at exactly the same period (neglecting transition times) as that of the environmental input.

4. DYNAMICS OF THE NETWORK DURING A RECOGNITION SESSION

4.1. Analytical solution

The model discussed so far can be studied by numerical simulations for finite systems. Moreover, it can also be solved analytically in the thermodynamic limit ($N \to \infty$), if during the recognition session, the external stimuli are of the form $\sigma_i(t) = \xi_i^{\rho(t)}$, where $1 \le \rho(t) \le r$ is once again a given function of *t*. For the present contribution we concentrate on model A and finite cycles. Furthermore, we restrict ourselves to the case where the external stimulus always represents one of the patterns ξ_i^{μ} encountered during the learning session. Model B can be treated in a similar fashion while model C is a random-bond problem where non analytic description is known so far.

As a main idea of our approach we now show that one can group the neurons into classes with, on average, identical time evolution: For q binary random patterns $\{\xi_i^{\mu}\}$, $1 \le \mu \le q$, only 2^q different positions available are for the random vectors $\vec{\xi}_i$, namely, the 2^q corners **x** of the hypercube $[-1, 1]^q$. We may therefore introduce two notions borrowed from spin-glass theory (Grensing and Kühn 1986; van Hemmen et al. 1986, 1988), *viz.* the sublattices $I(\mathbf{x}) = \{i;\ \vec{\xi}_i = \mathbf{x}\}$ and the corresponding sublattice magnetizations

$$m(\mathbf{x}; t) = |I(\mathbf{x})|^{-1} \sum_{i \in I(\mathbf{x})} S_i(t) . \tag{7}$$

The external input $\sigma_i(t)$ can be written as

$$\sigma_i(t) = \xi_i^{\rho(t)} = \Sigma_\mu \xi_i^\mu \rho^\mu(t) \equiv (\vec{\xi}_i, \vec{\rho}(t)), \qquad \rho^\mu(t) \equiv \delta_{\mu,\rho(t)}, \tag{8}$$

and one easily verifies that the postsynaptic potential in (1) at *i* is

$$h_i(t) = (1-\gamma) \sum_y \sum_\tau (\vec{\xi}_i, Q^{(\tau)} y)\, p_N(y)\, m(y; t-\tau) + \gamma(\vec{\xi}_i, \rho(t)), \tag{9}$$

where $|I(\mathbf{x})|$ denotes the size of $I(\mathbf{x})$ and $p_N(\mathbf{y}) = N^{-1} |I(\mathbf{y})|$. As $N \to \infty$, $p_N(\mathbf{y})$ converges to $p(\mathbf{y})$ with probability one; for unbiased patterns, $p(\mathbf{y}) = 2^{-q}$. Since $\vec{\xi}_i = \mathbf{x}$ for *all* i in $I(\mathbf{x})$, the PSP depends on *i* only through the label **x** of the sublattice which *i* belongs to. In the bulk limit $h_i(t)$ therefore converges for all $i \in I(\mathbf{x})$ to

$$h(\mathbf{x}; t) = (1-\gamma) \sum_y \sum_\tau (\mathbf{x}, Q^{(\tau)} \mathbf{y})\, p(\mathbf{y})\, m(\mathbf{y}; t-\tau) + \gamma(\mathbf{x}, \vec{\rho}(t)). \tag{10}$$

Since $|I(\mathbf{x})| \sim p(\mathbf{x}) N$ as $N \to \infty$, we may use the strong law of large numbers in Eq. (7) and, if we use parallel updating, replace $|I(\mathbf{x})|^{-1} \Sigma_{i \in I(\mathbf{x})} S_i(t + \Delta t)$ by the *thermal* average of $S_i(t + \Delta t)$. It is given by $\tanh[\beta h(\mathbf{x}; t)]$ for all $i \in I(\mathbf{x})$ - see Eq. (2) - and we immediately get

$$m(\mathbf{x}; t + \Delta t) = \tanh[\beta h(\mathbf{x}; t)] . \tag{11}$$

For sequential dynamics, only a single spin, say *j*, may be flipped at time t, while $S_i(t + \Delta t) = S_i(t)$ for all neurons $i \neq j$ so that their thermal average equals $m(\mathbf{x};t)$. Neuron j belongs to $I(\mathbf{x})$ with probability $|I(\mathbf{x})|\, N^{-1}$. In a finite system the expectation value $E\{m(\mathbf{x}; t)\}$ of $m(\mathbf{x}; t)$ will then be

$$E\{m(\mathbf{x}; t + \Delta t)\} = N^{-1} (\Sigma_{i \in I(\mathbf{x}), i \neq j} S_i(t + \Delta t) + S_j(t + \Delta t)) + (1 - |I(\mathbf{x})|\, N^{-1})\, m(\mathbf{x}; t) .$$

In the limit $N \to \infty$ we rescale time as $\Delta t = N^{-1}$ and may once again use the thermal averages of S_i. Since $E\{m(\mathbf{x};t)\}$ converges to $m(\mathbf{x};t)$, we finally get a set of 2^q coupled nonlinear differential equations for the sublattice magnetizations (Riedel et al. 1988):

$$\frac{d}{dt} m(\mathbf{x}; t) = - \{ m(\mathbf{x}; t) - \tanh [\beta\, h(\mathbf{x}; t)] \} . \tag{12}$$

Explicit solutions to Eqs. (11) and (12) are not known but numerical solutions can be obtained in a rather straightforward way. The outcomes are represented most conveniently in terms of the overlaps,

$$m_\mu(t) = \sum_{\mathbf{x}} p(\mathbf{x})\; x_\mu\; m(\mathbf{x}; t) \equiv \langle x_\mu\, m(\mathbf{x}; t) \rangle . \tag{13}$$

Since $(\mathbf{x}, \mathbf{Q}^{(\tau)}\mathbf{y})$ in Eq. (10) is *bilinear* in $\mathbf{x}$ and $\mathbf{y}$, one can combine Eqs. (10), (11), and (13) to a set of q equations for the overlaps themselves,

$$m_\mu(t + \Delta t) = \langle x_\mu \tanh [\, \beta\, (1-\gamma) \sum_\tau \sum_{\nu,\sigma} x_\nu\, Q^{(\tau)}_{\nu,\sigma}\, m_\sigma(t-\tau) + \beta\, \gamma\, x_\rho(t)] \rangle . \tag{14}$$

Equation (14) describes parallel dynamics. Sequential dynamics can be treated in a similar way. Taking advantage of Eqs. (10), (12), and (13), one easily derives a set of q functional differential equations for the $m_\mu(t)$. This finishes the analysis, but some generalizations possible should be mentioned: At first, the assumption that the ξ_i^μ are ± 1 with equal probability can be dispensed with (Herz et al. 1989). Secondly, sequential updating during the learning session may be considered. Finally, one can study the case $r > q$ during the retrieval session.

4.2. Numerical results

For the present numerical study we concentrate on a specific system and analyze both the dependence upon the network architecture and the influence of the external stimulus $\sigma_i(t)$ on the dynamics.

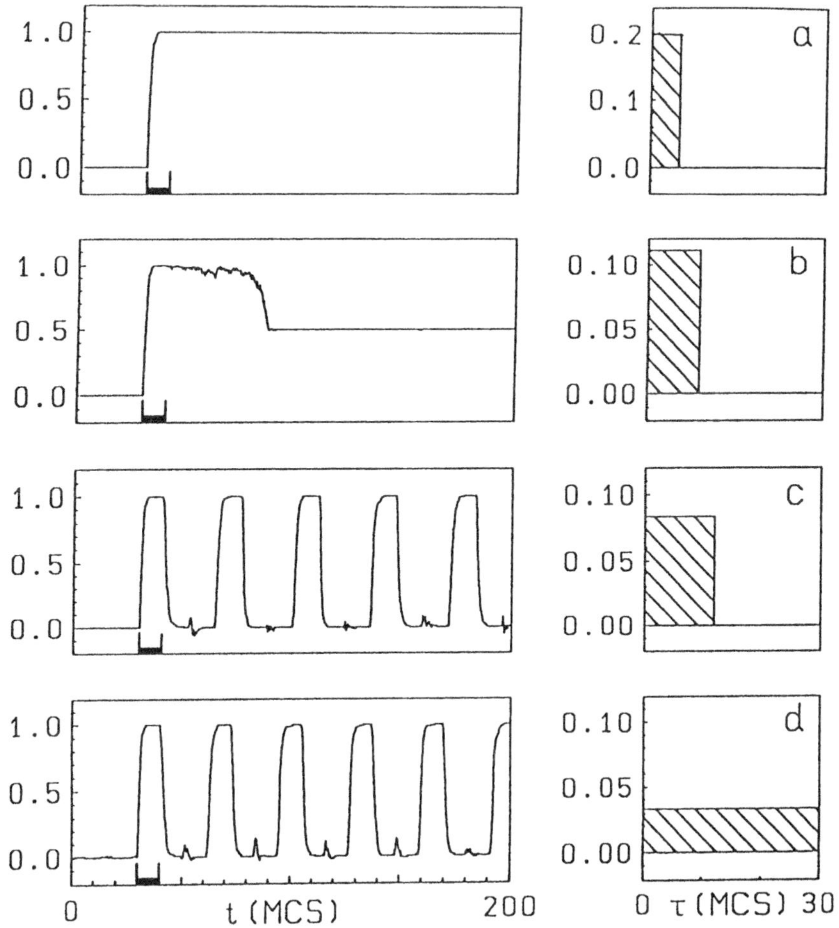

FIGURE 1. Dependence upon network architecture. Each track represents the time evolution of the overlap $m_1(t)$ with the first pattern of a cycle consisting of three for a given delay distribution, which is displayed in the corresponding box to the right of the main plot. All the distributions are discrete, with a spacing of one MCS (Monte Carlo step per spin). During the learning session, each pattern of the 3-cycle lasted for $\Delta = 10$ MCS. Besides the cycle we have taught the network 5 single patterns and we start the system in one of these attractors. Between $t = 30$ MCS and $t = 40$ MCS we stimulate the network with the first pattern of the cycle, as indicated by dark bars. In **a** there are only short delays so that the cycle as a whole is not recognized; in **b** transitions between successive patterns occur, though the cycle itself is not yet attractive; only a 3-symmetric state is reached. For $\tau_{max} > \Delta$, the cycle is recognized. Its period depends slightly on the actual delay distribution (**c** and **d**). We used sequential dynamics with $\beta = 10$, $N = 256$, and $\gamma = 0.5$.

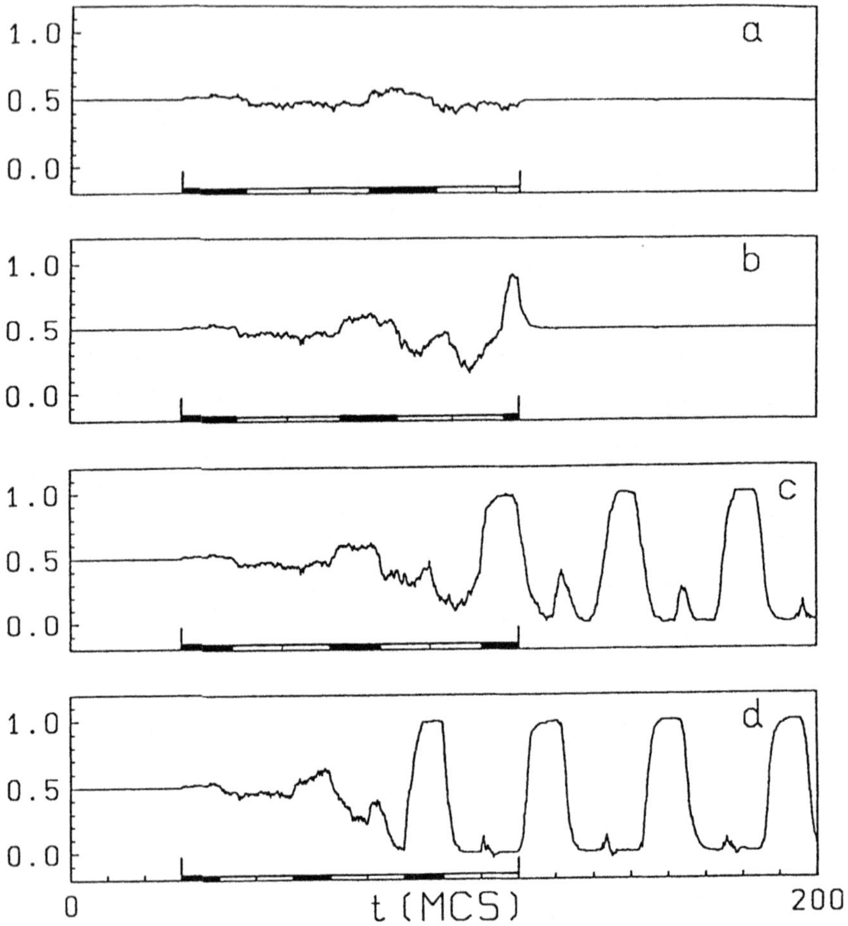

FIGURE 2. Dependence upon external stimulus. To analyze the "resonance phenomenon" mentioned in Section 3, we study transitions between states, which are attractors if no external field is coupled to the system. For the network of Figure 1d, both the 3-cycle and the 3-symmetric mixture states of its components are dynamically stable. During the retrieval period, we start the system in one of the mixture states and repeatedly present the original cycle to the system from t = 30 MCS to t =120 MCS. In order to see the resonance effects, we use a small coupling constant, $\gamma = 0.25$, and vary the frequency of the external stimulus. From top to bottom, it takes the values 0.6, 0.7, 0.75, and 1.0 relative to that of the taught sequence. Black bars once again represent the appearance of the first pattern of the cycle within the input sequence. Recognition is only achieved if the frequency of the external stimulus is between 0.75 and 1.18 (not shown here) in the units of that of the learned cycle.

5. DISCUSSION

As shown by figure 1, the retrieval quality of a generalized Hopfield network depends significantly on its architecture, described by the distribution of delays $\varepsilon(\tau)$: If the duration Δ of an individual pattern within a cycle exceeds τ_{max}, the system cannot "measure" the patterns' lifetime during the learning session. The sequence as such will not be represented in the system, and only its static components may be recalled. On the other hand, if τ_{max} is larger than Δ, the time evolution will only marginally depend on the actual delay distribution.

For a given distribution $\varepsilon(\tau)$ and noise parameter β the system will recognize a learned sequence provided that (a) it is close enough in space *and* time to one of the stored prototypes and that (b) the input sensitivity is above a certain lower bound, so that the external stimulus can sufficiently influence the internal dynamics of the network as illustrated in figure 2. If the system operates at a value of γ above but close to that of the threshold, it will have a rather narrow window for recalling spatio-temporal objects. At higher values of this parameter, the network will become more fault-tolerant, so that by choosing certain values for γ, specific recognition problems may be solved.

6. APPLICATIONS

Hebbian learning within a generalized Hopfield scheme provides an elegant mechanism for the representation of temporal sequences. And it shows two rather important qualities for applications in Artificial Intelligence: (a) Since learning is achieved by a local imprinting process rather than by some global adaptive mechanism - see Eq.(3) - the time per synapse required to memorize given sequences does not depend on the network size. (b) During the retrieval session, one can easily extract different features of learned spatio-temporal objects by a simple change of the system parameters β, γ or $\varepsilon(\tau)$.

Up to now we have used a uniform network architecture. Realistic problems, however, as for example the associative binding of acoustical data and phonetic structures in low level speech recognition, will require a distinction between external input (acoustical stimuli) and desired output (phonetic features). We propose the following approach. The speech data are preprocessed and their A/D-converted power spectrum is used as external input. The target represents individual phonetic features and consists of sequences of binary patterns. These start and end at a common pattern η_{out} and encode the temporal evolution of evidence in favor of a specific feature. During the learning session both input and desired output are fed into the network and memorized according to Eq.(3), leading to a Hebbian binding of acoustical stimuli and corresponding phonetic features. Multiple presentation of noisy inputs will create large basins of attraction around similar input sequences, a mechanism which can be interpreted as prototype formation. It facilitates the correct discrimination during the retrieval period, where the external input is coupled to the network as described by Eq.(1). η_{out} is chosen as initial configuration for the output. Recognition is accomplished by completion of sequences which represent specific input-output relations. Due to the high redundancy of the model, real-time speech processing seems to be achievable and we expect fault-tolerant capabilities similar to those encountered above for the retrieval of random sequences in networks with uniform architecture.

Despite these encouraging possibilities, I want to mention a certain restriction for Hebbian binding and demonstrate this for a special case with static patterns: The Hebb rule does not allow a represention of the XOR-problem in a Hopfield-type network of three formal neurons. We may overcome, or at least reduce this kind of limitation if we add thresholds and hidden units, a procedure similar to the introduction of hidden layers in feedforward systems. A pattern to be memorized will now consist of a specific pair of input and output data, together with a randomly chosen configuration for the hidden units. The synaptic strengths are calculated for *all* couplings according to the original local Hebb rule, so that once again there is no increase of learning time per synapse as the system size grows - in sharp contrast to back-propagation approaches. Hebbian binding with hidden units will however require a larger amount of internal nodes. The actual number depends on the complexity of the classification task which can be estimated from the bond distribution within the input-output section (publication in preparation). As for feedforward systems, there is a trade-off between exact matching and generalization, which is determined by the size of the hidden section of the network.

7. CONCLUSION

In summary, any learning scheme can only be successful, if the structure of the learning task is compatible with the network architecture and the learning algorithm. In the present context, the task is to store spatio-temporal objects, such as stationary patterns, sequences and cycles. The internal representability of these objects is guaranteed by a broad distribution of transmission delays within a highly connected feedback system. The representation itself is accomplished by the Hebb rule: Hebbian synapses $J_{ij}(\tau)$ measure and store the correlations of the external stimulus in space (ij) and time (τ). The dynamics of the neural network, operating with the very same delays, is able to extract the spatio-temporal information encoded in the $J_{ij}(\tau)$. Retrieval is therefore extremely robust.

Most of this work was done in collaboration with Bernhard Sulzer, Leo van Hemmen, and Reimer Kühn, whom I would like to thank for critically reading the manuscript. For stimulating discussions I am very grateful to the members of the neural network group at the University of Heidelberg, as well as to Michael Hart, Heidelberg and Li-Waj Tang, Munich. Finally, I would like to mention that a somewhat related study about synchronization in neural networks with delays was done by Kerszberg and Zippelius (1988).

This work has been supported by a grant of the Studienstiftung des Deutschen Volkes.

REFERENCES

Amit, D.J. (1987). Neural networks counting chimes. Racah Institute of Physics preprint. RI/87/49.

Amit, D.J., Gutfreund, H., Sompolinsky, H. (1985). Spin-glass models of neural networks. *Physical Review,* **A32**, 1007-1018.

Amit, D.J., Gutfreund, H., Sompolinsky, H. (1987). Statistical mechanics of neural networks near saturation. *Annals of Physics*, **173**, 30-67.

Braitenberg, V. (1967). Is the cerebellar cortex a biological clock in the millisecond range?

In C.A. Fox, R.S. Snider (Eds.), *The Cerebellum, Progress in Brain Research* - Vol. 25. (pp. 334-346). Amsterdam: Elsevier.

Buhmann, J., Schulten, K. (1987). Noise-driven temporal association in neural networks. *Europhysics Letters* **4**, 1205-1209.

Dehaene, S., Changeux, J.-P., Nadal, J.-P. (1987). Neural networks that learn temporal sequences by selection. *Proceedings of the National Academy of Sciences (U.S.A)*, **84**, 2727-2731.

Grensing, D., Kühn, R. (1986). Random-site spin glass models. *Journal of Physics*, **A19**, L 1153 - 1157.

Gutfreund, H., Mezard, M. (1988). Processing of temporal sequences in neural networks. *Physical Review Letters*, **61**, 235-238.

Hebb, D.O. (1949). *The organization of behavior: A neuropsycological theory.* New York: Wiley.

van Hemmen, J.L. (1987). Nonlinear neural networks near saturation. *Physical Review*, **A36**, 1959–1962.

van Hemmen, J.L., Grensing, D., Huber, A., Kühn, R. (1986). Elementary solution of classical spin glass models. *Zeitschrift für Physik*, **B65**, 53-63.

van Hemmen, J.L., Grensing, D., Huber, A., Kühn, R. (1988). Nonlinear neural networks. I. General theory; II. Information processing. *Journal of Statistical Physics*, **50**, 231-257; 259-293.

van Hemmen, J.L., Kühn, R. (1986). Nonlinear neural networks. *Physical Review Letters*, **57**, 913-916.

Herz, A., Sulzer, B., Kühn, R., van Hemmen, J.L. (1988): The Hebb rule: Storing static and dynamic objects in an associative neural network. *Europhysics Letters*, **7**, 663-669.

Herz, A., Sulzer, B., Kühn, R., van Hemmen, J.L. (1989). Hebbian learning reconsidered: Representation of static and dynamic objects in associative neural nets. *Biological Cybernetics*, **60**, 457-467.

Hopfield, J.J. (1982). Neural networks and physical systems with emergent collective computational abilities. *Proceedings of the National Academy of Sciences (U.S.A)*, **79**, 2554-2558.

Kelso, S.R., Ganong, A.H., Brown, T.H. (1986). Hebbian synapses in hippocampus. *Proceedings of the National Academy of Sciences (U.S.A)*, **83**, 5326-5330.

Kerszberg, M., Zippelius, A. (1988). Synchronization in neural assemblies. Preprint.

Kleinfeld, D. (1986). Sequential state generation by model neural networks. *Proceedings of the National Academy of Sciences (U.S.A)*, **83**, 9469-9473.

Miller, R. (1987). Representation of brief temporal patterns, Hebbian synapses, and the left-hemisphere dominance for phoneme recognition. *Psychobiology*, **15**, 241-247.

Peretto, P., Niez, J.J. (1986). Collective properties of neural networks. In E. Bienenstock, F. Fogelman-Soulié, G. Weisbuch (Eds.), Disordered systems and biological organization. (pp. 171 - 185). Berlin: Springer.

Riedel, U., Kühn, R., van Hemmen, J.L. (1988). Temporal sequences and chaos in neural nets. *Physical Review*, **A38**, 1105-1108.

Sompolinsky, H., Kanter, I. (1986). Temporal association in asymmetric neural networks. *Physical Review Letters*, **57**, 2861-2864.

Tank, D.W., Hopfield, J.J. (1987). Neural computation by concentrating information in time. *Proceedings of the National Academy of Sciences (U.S.A)*, **84**, 1896-1900.

Willwacher, G. (1976). Fähigkeiten eines assoziativen Speichersystems im Vergleich zu Gehirnfunktionen. *Biological Cybernetics*, **24**, 181-198.

CONNECTIONISM IN PERSPECTIVE
R. Pfeifer, Z. Schreter, F. Fogelman-Soulié, L. Steels (Eds.)

Logic and Reasoning with Neural Models*

Franz Kurfess†
Manfred Reich
Institut für Informatik, Technische Universität München

Abstract—*In this paper, we discuss the use of neural model methodologies in the domain of logic and reasoning. We see three promising aspects in their application to this domain: First, they can offer valuable support in the evaluation of logic programs by automatically gathering (meta-) knowledge about the evaluation process (proof) and the particular domain, thus preparing the successful application of strategies and heuristics. Second, they can provide basic building blocks (e.g. for unification) with a straightforward potential for philosophical logic extensions (non-monotonic, fuzzy, etc.). Third, self-contained inference mechanisms based on neural models could be the core of a new class of reasoning systems.*

The combination of logic and reasoning with neural models looks quite favorable due to their inherent capability of abstraction, generalization, and learning; their highly parallel scheme of operation also might provide the computational power and flexibility which still is a hindrance to the use of conventional logic-based systems. The underlying evaluation mechanism, however, has not yet been investigated thoroughly enough to allow for reliable predictions on the usability of neural models for reasoning and logic.

Keywords—Neural models, reasoning, logic, theorem proving

1 INTRODUCTION

Drawing conclusions from undisputed facts is a very essential human skill, both in everyday life and professional arguing. Whereas *reasoning* comprises the relatively informal act of drawing conclusions, (mathematical) *logic* offers a formal mechanism for the derivation of conclusions according to a validated methodology, its typical instance being first order predicate logic.

Neural Models propose a computation mechanism based on a large number of computational units with a simple internal evaluation function and a rich interconnection scheme. This alternative information processing paradigm operates in a highly parallel manner and

---

* A long version of this paper is available from the first author

† Forschungsgruppe Künstliche Intelligenz, Technische Universität München, Institut für Informatik, Augustenstr. 46 RGB, D-8000 München, WEST GERMANY. E-mail: kurfess%tumki@unido.uucp

is not based on machine instructions to be executed one after the other. In contrast, neural models feature an inherent capability of generalizing, abstracting and learning.

The goal of *reasoning*, or *natural deduction*, in contrast to formal, mathematical logic, is to achieve conclusions without a highly sophisticated, rigid logic formalism. The underlying rules of human reasoning, however, are only "more or less" generally agreed upon, and in the course of history, many a man may have suffered severely from minor differences in the ways of drawing conclusions. *Mathematical* or *formal logic*, as the result of maybe two milleniums work of logicians, offers such a framework based on exactly defined, indisputable rules for drawing conclusions. The power of logic is based on three important features: Firstly, it provides a language for the accurate *representation of knowledge*. Secondly, a framework for *processing the represented knowledge* is given in the form of a calculus defining permitted rules for drawing conclusions. Thirdly, a mechanism for *mechanical proofs* of the truth values, or equivalence, of statements can be defined. The expressiveness of these formal systems is virtually unlimited; problems, however, lie in the adequateness of the language (its coincidence with the human perception of a problem description), the efficiency of the evaluation mechanisms, and the ability to deal with inconsistencies and incomplete knowledge usually present in real-world problems.

A lot of effort in the formal logic field is aimed at the creation of an adequate representation language allowing for a natural and comprehensible description of real-world knowledge, and the construction of a "smart" evaluation mechanism. Higher efficiency in the computation can be achieved by reducing the search space via domain knowledge (appropriate strategies), experience (learning from previous work), and the use of global and local features of the proof process. Reasoning systems, incorporating "sloppy" (untidy, common-place) features, strive for applicability to less formally characterized problems of knowledge representation and information processing by probabilistic evaluation methods, non-monotonic calculi, flexible propositions or inference rules, and sloppy unification.

The central problem is to capture knowledge which cannot be described algorithmically due to incomplete specification (too much effort), an inappropriate formulation of the problem, or unrecognized features.

A potential remedy might consist in the utilization of neural models with their ability to learn from examples, extract characteristic features, process noisy (uncertain, imprecise) information, and adapt to changing situations. Their main problems lie in questions related to maturity and experience, research foundations, scalability and efficiency, and applicability. Imprudent or careless use might reveal extraparametal symptoms, untoward side-effects, or unfavourable, awkward characteristics which were not expected.

The next chapter describes some basic concepts for the direct *evaluation of logic* with neural models; chapter three concentrates on *support for logic programming systems* from neural models. In chapter four, a number of experiments combining logic and neural networks are described; the last chapter contains some tentative conclusions, and – maybe more appropriately – an outlook onto future work.

2 LOGIC PROGRAMMING SYSTEMS BASED ON NEURAL MODELS

At first glance, the combination of neural models (with their somewhat sloppy evaluation paradigm) and mathematical logic (with its strongly formal and exact aspects) seems a bit awkward. A second thought, however, might reveal that neural models exactly have their strength where formal logic has its problems: the description of "real world problems" with inconsistencies, exceptions to the rules, incomplete specifications, changes in the course of time, and similar characteristics. A lot of effort has been invested in the adaptation of formal logic towards capturing these features (e.g. modal logic, temporal logic, non-monotonic reasoning, truth-maintenance systems), but most of the approaches are still too restricted, too complicated to be dealt with efficiently on conventional computers, too unnatural for adequate specification, or all of the above.

Storage and processing of information with neural networks is more tolerant towards inconsistencies within the data items, incomplete features, and temporal changes. Their use in combination with formal logic might help to some degree in overcoming the problems mentioned above; however, some of the strong formal properties of logic (correctness and completeness) might be affected in a negative way.

2.1 Propositional Logic

The treatment of propositional logic is obviously much easier than dealing immediately with predicate logic. In this section we discuss some possibilities for the use of neural models in propositional logic. *Formula Evaluation* is a computation of the output value from given input values; the formula can be in normal form, or non-normal form, where additional treatment of the formula structure is required. The basic task here is to construct a network that corresponds to the formula under investigation; it is closely related to Boolean logic and the composition of digital circuits from basic logic gates. *Satisfiability* means to find out if there is an interpretation for the formula such that the formula is true (a model for the formula); in this case, many sets of input values (which correspond to the interpretations) have to be checked out. This problem can be solved by mapping it onto an equivalent one, which then is treated by a neural model. Two candidates for such an equivalent problem are graph coloring gradient method described later (Mayr & Reich, 1988). *Validity* of a formula expresses that the formula is true for every interpretation. Here all possible interpretations have to be checked out, either by a "brute force" or more sophisticated methods, e.g. "abstraction" of the previous models, or evaluation of the connection graph.

2.2 Predicate Logic

The treatment of predicate logic has to face some additional problems, like dealing with logical variables (and thus unification), function evaluation, and clause copies for recursive problems. These problems are quite difficult to solve with neural models, and in some cases straightforward solutions are not immediately visible (e.g. representation of variables, recursion). However, not much work has been done yet in this direction, so that there is still some hope left for satisfying answers, or at least deeper understanding. *Horn clause logic* can be tackled by reproducing the resolution calculus (Ballard, 1986), or evaluation of the connection graph (including unification). *Full first order predicate logic* may be treated using *matrix logic* (Stern, 1988), interpreting logical connectives as matrix operators acting on the two adjoint vector spaces (logic as a "macroanalogue of spin"), via "lifting" the graph coloring approach for propositional logic (graph nodes represent terms instead of simple symbols), via "lifting" the gradient method for propositional logic (higher order functions), or by an evaluation of the connection graph.

3 SUPPORTING LOGIC PROGRAMMING SYSTEMS WITH NEURAL MODELS

Maybe the most promising approach for the time being consists of using neural network methodologies for the accomplishment of tasks which cannot be treated very well with conventional (algorithmical, symbolical) techniques. It has the advantage that existing systems, together with the knowledge acquired during their construction, can be used with minor modifications and enhancements.

The evaluation of logic programs offers quite a few possibilities for integrating services to be yielded by neural models.

Choice of Strategies and Heuristics

A neural network is used to select an appropriate strategy to be used for a particular formula. *Global strategies* apply the chosen strategy once in the beginning of the proof and thus determines the overall proof process. Examples are the scope (propositional or predicate logic), the calculus (resolution, model elimination / connection method, natural deduction), the global search strategy (depth- or breadth-first), or a depth boundary (for depth-first) (Schumann, Ertel & Suttner, 1988). *Local strategies* make decisions according to the current local proof environment and are applied only during a limited period. Examples for this case are the computation strategy (execution order of the subgoals / rearrangement of the goal stack), local search strategies (choice of branches (Schumann, Ertel & Suttner, 1988), unification (appropriate algorithm: full / partial, Robinson, Martelli-Montanari, Paterson-Wegman), use of lemmata (creation and application of lemmata), and backtracking ("intelligent" backtracking, minimization of backtracking points).

The choice of a strategy heavily depends on the features taken into account. In the case of neural networks, this *feature extraction* can be provided by training examples, by previously solved tasks, or by the system designer.

Reductions

The successfull application of reductions to a formula depends on its actual structure. Some of the reduction steps are quite powerful (and may even lead to a proof or refutation of the formula), but also computationally expensive; thus it is advisable to first check out whether it is worthwhile to evoke a particular reduction step. Again in this case a neural model might be more appropriate since the task of choosing the appropriate reduction is difficult to capture algorithmically. *Global reductions* require information about the whole formula (pure literals, isolated connections). With *local reductions* it is sufficient to take into account only a part of the formula (single clauses, pairs of clauses). Examples are tautology reduction (single clause), restricted unit resolution (pair of clauses), subsumption (pair of clauses), factorization (single clause); *combinations of reductions* can lead to mutual enforcement (snowball effect), resulting in drastically smaller (in the extreme case empty) search spaces.

Matching and Unification

Matching in the simplest case consists of the comparison of two structures (patterns, graphs, terms) for identity. Unification is more complicated since variables can be involved which have to be substituted during the unification process. *Pattern matching* involves no variables; *term matching (one-way unification)* has to deal with variables on only one side at a time; *restricted unification* is constrained by annotations indicating the direction of the binding process (e.g. read-only variables); *full unification* of a pair of terms has no restrictions, and *set unification* treats a set terms in a single run. An elaborate treatment of unification with neural models can be found in (Stolcke, 1988).

4 EXAMPLES

In the following we give a brief description of some experiments done in our group, involving the combination of logic programming and neural models. For further information see the corresponding references.[1]

4.1 Logic Systems Based on Neural Models

The following three examples describe systems for the direct evaluation of logic; for obvious reasons, their scope is in these first experimentations limited to propositional logic.

Formula Evaluation (Neumayer, 1988)
The approach taken here is to construct a network from bulding blocks which correspond to basic logical primitives like and, or, implies, not. Additionally, a "syntactical unit" is integrated, allowing the direct representation of non-normal form formulae. In its construction, consideration has been paid to the integration of the representation of variables via an associative memory, and to the role of noisy data in the formalism of logic. The size of formulae to be evaluated is limited to a few symbols connected by logical primitives, mainly to implementational aspects of the simulation. The aim of the work, however, was not an efficient formula evaluator, but to show the feasibility of the approach.

Figure 1 shows a network for the evaluation of a formula consisting of two literals (ARG_1, ARG_2) connected by one of the four logical operators given on the right-hand side. The hidden layer consists of four units; one of them is activated if it is selected and the arguments have the appropriate values. Composing networks with multiple operators presents an additional problem: the formula has either to be transformed into normal form, or a syntax analysis has to be done in order to define the order of the evaluation. The second approach, of course, very soon leads to an extremely complex network.

Gradient Method (Mayr & Reich, 1988)
A propositional formula is mapped onto a (differential) equation, and the gradient of this equation is represented by the network derived from the syntactical structure of the formula in an inductive way; this network in turn is evaluated on a tool similar to the Rochester Connectionist Simulator. In principle, the equation resulting from the first transformation can be solved with numerical methods as well; it also offers a straightforward extension towards non-binary logic by using an interval (e.g. [0,1]) instead of binary values.[2]

In order to retrieve a satisfying model, a propositional logic formula is mapped onto a n-dimensional real function, evaluating the relative "validity" of the formula for its parameters, which are the mappings of the propositional variables. The range of the function and each parameter is a continuous interval, whose edges are the mapping of the boolean values true and false. As a necessary property such a function has to return true exactly if the state (i.e. the values of its parameters) corresponds to a model of the formula, and false exactly if it corresponds to one of the negated formula. Thus the *gradient* of

[1] Some of the work is only available in German at this time, but English versions are in preparation.
[2] There might also exist some relation to Stern's *matrix logic* (Stern, 1988).

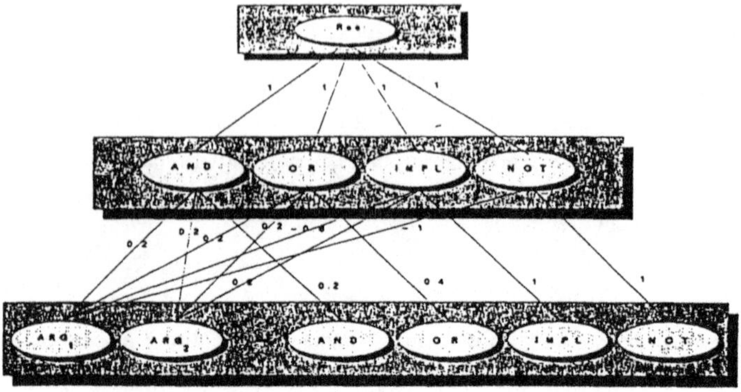

Figure 1: A network for formula evaluation

the function (i.e. the partial derivations for all variables) can be used to gain information how to reach a *goal state*, corresponding to a model, from a momentary state. This is quite similar to minimum search and related to neural networks performing an implicit energy mimimization. Finding functions as postulated above for any propositional formula is easily done by inductively defining a mapping τ on the syntactical structure of the formula:

$$\tau : \begin{cases} A & \rightarrow \quad a \\ \neg F & \rightarrow \quad 1 - f \\ F \wedge G & \rightarrow \quad f * g \\ F \vee G & \rightarrow \quad 1 - (1 - f) * (1 - g) \end{cases}$$

where A is a propositional variable, a a variable for [0,1], F and G propositional formulae with f and g as their mappings. The $\vee$-case actually can be omitted since $F \vee G = \neg(\neg F \wedge \neg G)$. Like the formula and its function, each component of the gradient has an inductive structure as well; in the above example

$$\begin{aligned} [\tau(A)]_x &= \begin{cases} 1 & \text{if } a \equiv x \\ 0 & \text{else} \end{cases} \\ [\tau(\neg F)]_x &= -[\tau(F)]_x \\ [\tau(F \wedge G)]_x &= f_x g + g_x f = \tau(F \wedge G) * (\tfrac{f_x}{f} + \tfrac{g_x}{g}). \end{aligned}$$

For efficient representation and computation of the function and its gradient a *dag*[3] can be used. With the help of the function and gradient values computed so far a step towards the goal state is made; this is the core of the gradient method in the strict sense.

Let's consider an example here: Coming from a finite form of the total differential

$$\Delta f \approx \Delta x_1 f_{x_1} + \Delta x_2 f_{x_2} + \ldots + \Delta x_n f_{x_n}$$

a correction term is proposed due to the fact that the envisaged change of the function value Δf is (true $- f$), e.g. $(1 - f)$; furthermore, the intuitive assumption that each term

[3] *directed acyclic graph*

$\Delta x_i f_{x_i}$ should contribute the same portion to Δf leads to

$$\Delta x_i := \frac{1-f}{n * f_{x_i}}.$$

To actually compute the update, the *dag* mentioned above has to be enhanced by feedback connections from the function and gradient nodes to the variables (which turns it into an ordinary graph). This graph can be implemented via a neural network, where the multi-dimensional operations are represented by nodes, and the uni-dimensional ones by links. For a visualization see figure 2.

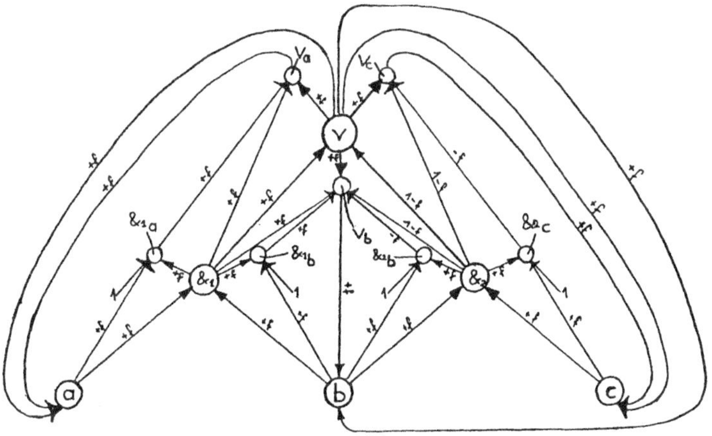

Figure 2: A network for the gradient method

Although the correctness of the computation of function and gradient implies a certain order in the evaluation of the networks' stages, experiments have shown that the method succeds in both cases — simultaneous or sequential order of computation — with only little differences in the time needed.

Like with all numerical gradient methods for minimum search, it is not guaranteed that a solution (in this case a model for the formula) is found if one exists; experiments with formulae of up to 500 literals, however, showed a success rate of more than 70%, which could be increased to more than 95% by several trials with randomized initial states.

If safety is not absolutely necessary, this method is very promising. Its static complexity is less than $O(n^2)$, where n is the number of literals; its dynamic complexity on a fine grain parallel machine can be $O(k)$, where k is a constant.

Graph Coloring (Mayr & Reich, 1988)
This method is similar to the previous one in that it tries to find a satisfying substitution for a formula by mapping this problem onto an equivalent one. The satisfiability problem for propositional logic is mapped onto the graph coloring problem; an arbitrary formula (not necessarily in normal form) can be transformed inductively via its syntactical structure

onto a graph to be colored. In the implementation on a tool similar to the Rochester Connectionist Simulator (Goddard, 1987), this graph is represented as a neural network, and the simulated annealing method is used to find a state corresponding to a satisfying substitution of the formula. The experiments show the practicability of the approach for formulae with about 100 literals. Many of the parameters greatly influence performance (representation of the graph, scaling of the weights, evaluation function, explicit or implicit modification of the temperature intervals instead of binary states), and further investigation and experimentation might lead to an increase of efficiency by choosing good parameter settings.

4.2 Proof System Support

Proof Depth Limit (Schumann, Ertel & Suttner, 1988)
In order to guarantee *completeness* for a first order predicate logic theorem prover (SETHEO: Letz, Schumann & Bayerl, 1988) with a depth-first strategy, a *depth boundary* is introduced. Thus the search tree for a given formula is completely explored to a given depth, which corresponds to proof attempts with a length equal to the explored depth. Now the optimal proof depth is the one that equals the length of the shortest proof for the formula; this number, however, is not known in advance. A good estimation of the proof depth is very important for the efficiency of the theorem prover: if it is too small, the proof cannot be found; if it is too large, the tree to be traversed can become too huge to be handled. The derivation of the optimal proof depth, or a good approximation thereof, from the formula under investigation is quite difficult; apart from trivial cases no simple strategies or algorithms are known. On the other hand, there surely is some relation between the (syntactic) structure of the formula, and the optimal proof depth. To capture this relation a neural network with backpropagation as learning procedure is combined with the theorem prover. Experimentation up to now has been restricted to propositional logic formulae with restricted size (4 clauses with 3 literals each) in order to achieve a reasonable size of the network for simulation. Such a formula is coded in a very simple way: 6 bits for each clause (three literals, which can be positive or negative), and 24 bits in total for four clauses. The clause $p \vee \neg q$, for example, is represented in the following way:

•	∘	∘	∘	•	∘
p	q	r	$\neg p$	$\neg q$	$\neg r$

where an activation of 1 (•) or 0 (∘) means that the literal is in the current clause or not.

The network consists of three layers, the input layer with 24 nodes, a hidden layer with 16 nodes, and the output layer with 5 nodes (for 5 possible proof depths). During the learning phase 5 additional target units are used, giving the optimal proof depth which has been computed for the training examples by SETHEO. Experiments have been done using the *bp* program from the PDP packet (McClelland & Rumelhart, 1988), and an implemetation of a modified backpropagation algorithm written in C (Ertel, 1988). A set of 100 training examples was generated randomly by a formula generator and evaluated by SETHEO to guarantee validity and to find the optimal proof depth. After 100 to 200 learning cycles, almost all (99 or 100) training examples were learnt correctly. The evaluation of 50 unknown examples resulted in 56% correct outputs, and in 76% of the cases a useful output (a deviation of 1 from the optima proof depth) was delivered.

The following table shows the results of the experiment described above with a varying number of training examples. The total error E_{tot} is measured (mean value over 20 runs):

$$E_{tot} = \sum_{p \in pattern} E_p$$

training examples	0	10	20	50	100
E_{tot}	71.4	51.3	60.2	55.3	43.9
correct outputs	2	4	3	19	28

Branch Choice (Schumann, Ertel & Suttner, 1988)
In contrast to the previous experiments, which deliver strategic support for the formula as a whole (global scope), the following experiments work locally and dynamically (at execution time) as well as statically on the choice of a favorable OR-branch. In the dynamic case, the network has as input momentarily relevant parts of the formula, together with some information about the current proof status. This "scope of interest" is represented by a set of features; some of these features are statical, i.e. they can be extracted before the proof starts (e.g. numbers of literals in a clause, predicate symbols, variables, constants, function symbols; connectivity, shared variables), whereas others have to be gained dynamically at run time (e.g. current proof depth, instantiated variables in the current subgoal, number of occurences of a certain predicate so far)[4]. A backpropagation network is used to derive from these features a decision about the selection of the branch to continue with. For the learning phase, optimal proofs are used which were previously generated by SETHEO, and the features in combination with the choice made represented the input for learning.

This combination of heuristics and learning not only leads to more 'intelligent' proof mechanisms, but also provides a valuable tool to investigate the relevance of features for the choice of local and global strategies.

5 CONCLUSIONS AND OUTLOOK

The main theme of this paper is to investigate and describe some efforts towards the incorporation of favorable features offered by neural models into systems for reasoning and logic programming.

One branch is aimed at the construction of simple, self-contained experimental vehicles for propositional logic, the other at evaluation support from neural models for a theorem prover, or logic programming systems in general.

The work done as of yet concentrated on aspects of *feasibility* and *gain of insight*, and not so much on appropriateness, usability, or efficiency. Present and future work (e.g. branch choice heuristics) is directed towards incorporation into existing logic systems, aiming at higher efficiency and better performance, thus leading to broader applicability.

The paper also mirrors to some degree two different positions regarding the usage of computers for the modeling of intelligent systems (Dreyfus & Dreyfus, 1988).

The first one, with *logic* as a typical instance for the underlying concepts, is traditional AI (or *GOFAI* for Good Old-Fashioned Artificial Intelligence (Haugeland, 1987)). It is based on symbolic processing, aiming at a universal symbol system to describe a formal

[4] The relevance of these features is quite difficult to judge, and an important part of the experimentation is aimed at gaining some insight herein.

theory. Reduction to logical primitives for logic and problem solving leads to the thesis that reasoning could be reduced to calculation, thus destilling an "alphabet of human thoughts" (Leibniz). Intelligence is viewed as a context-determined, goal-directed activity, where the everyday context can be reduced to a very complex system of facts together with a complex system of beliefs, thus resulting in a context-free system. The human brain and a digital computer might have – at a certain level of abstraction – a common functional description, and thus could be seen as two different instantiations of a single species of device. This viewpoint is rooted in a long, rationalist / reductionist tradition in philosophy (Socrates, Descartes, Hobbes, Leibniz, Frege, Russell, Husserl, the early work of Wittgenstein) and a shorter one in "traditional" AI (Newell, Simon, Minsky).

The second one has – after a long drought – recently gained a lot of attention in connectionism (neural networks, neural models, neuroscience). It uses computers as a medium for modeling the brain and simulates the interactions of neurons, trying to automate the procedures by which a network of neurons learns. Basic concepts are learning and statistics and a formal theory for knowledge representation seems unnecessary. It shares the more holistic view that the everyday world can not be represented by a set of context-free elements, and is related to holistic and "Gestalt" philosophy (Heidegger, the later work of Wittgenstein) with strong foundations in neuroscience (Hebb, Rosenblatt, Anderson, Kohonen, Grossberg).

Despite fascinating early results both directions could not fulfill the high expectations as of yet; a common problem lies in the combinatorial explosion apparent after the transition from toy problems to "real-world" problems. The rationalist approach of traditional AI also runs into trouble with the formalization of everyday life concepts, resulting in a seemingly insurmountable mountain of symbols and rules for capturing commonsense understanding of the everyday world. A flaw of neuroscience might be its lack of the mathematical virtues of correctness and completeness as a reasoning tool; this flaw, however, is shared with the most successfull reasoning tool in history: the human brain. But, as this paper tries to show for some very limited aspects of logic and reasoning, there is some hope that both the reductionist and the holistic views might profit from each others strengths. And in quite a few areas of both scientific and social life there are some tendencies towards a unification of the reductionist and the holistic approaches; some keywords might be *synergetics*, *self-organization*, *"eastern"* and *"western"* thinking, *environmental* issues, and – although with a lot of questionable usage – *new age*. Two instances which are somehow related to these rivaling two concepts seem to get along quite well even under severe spatial restrictions: the left and right halves of our brain.

REFERENCES

Ballard, D. (1986). Parallel Logical Inference and Energy Minimization. *TR 142*, Comp. Science Dept., University of Rochester.

Bibel, W., Kurfe, F., Aspetsberger, K., Hintenaus, P. & Schumann, J. (1987). Parallel Inference Machines. in (Treleaven & Vanneschi, 1987) 185-226.

H.L. Dreyfus & Dreyfus, S.E. (1988). Making a mind versus modeling the brain: Artificial intelligence back at a branchpoint. *Daedalus*, **117** (Winter 1988), 15–43.

Ertel, W. (1988). Backpropagation with Temperature Pattern and Random Pattern Presentation. Institut für Informatik, Technische Universität München / Nixdorf Computer AG, München.

J.A. Feldman, M.A. Fanty, N.H. Goddard, & Lynne, K.J. (1988). Computing with structured connectionist networks. *Communications of the ACM*, 31:170–187.

Goddard, N. (1987). The Rochester Connectionist Simulator. Volume 1: User Manual. Dept. of Computer Science, University of Rochester, Rochester.

Haugeland, J., ed. (1981). *Mind Design: Philosophy, Psychology, Artificial Intelligence*. MIT Press, Cambride, MA.

Haugeland, J. (1987). *Kunstliche Intelligenz – Programmierte Vernunft? (Artificial Intelligence: The Very Idea)*. McGraw-Hill, Hamburg.

Hertz, J.A. (1987). A Brief Introduction to Spinglasses and Related Complex Problems. Nordita, Copenhagen, Denmark.

Letz, R., Schumann, J., & Bayerl, S. (1988). SETHEO: A SEquential THEOremprover for first order logic. Institut für Informatik, Techn. Universität München, München.

McCarthy, J. (1988). Mathematical logic in artificial intelligence. *Daedalus*, **117** (Winter 1988), 297–311.

Minsky, M. (1988). A framework for representing knowledge. In J. Haugeland, editor, *Mind Design: Philosophy, Psychology, Artificial Intelligence*, pages 95–128. MIT Press, Cambride, MA.

Minsky, M. (1986). *The Society of Mind*. Simon & Schuster Inc., New York.

McCulloch, W. & Pitts, W. (1943). A logical calculus of the ideas immanent in nervous activity. *Bulletin of Mathematical Biophysics*,**5**, 115–133.

Mayr, K. & Reich, M. (1988). Hochparallele Algorithmen zum Erfüllbarkeitsproblem in der Aussagenlogik. Institut für Informatik, Techn. Universität München.

McClelland, J. L. & Rumelhart, D.E. (1988). *Explorations in Parallel Distributed Processing*. MIT Press, Cambridge, MA.

Manna, Z. & Waldinger, R. (1985). *The Logical Basis for Computer Programming; Vol. 1: Deductive Reasoning*. Addison-Wesley, Reading, MA.

Neumayer, G. (1988). Konnektionismus und Aussagenlogik. Institut für Informatik, Techn. Universität München.

Palm, G. (1980). On associative memory. *Biological Cybernetics*, **36**, 19–31.

Palm, G. (1987). Computing with Neural Networks. *Science*, **235**, 1227-1228.

Rumelhart D., & McClelland, J.A. (1986). *Parallel Distributed Processing*. Vol. 1&2, MIT Press, Cambridge, MA.

Robinson, I. (1986). A Prolog Processor based on a Pattern Matching Memory Device. Third Int. Conference on Logic Programming, 172-179.

Recce, M., & Treleaven, P.C. (1988). Parallel Architectures for Neural Computers. Report, University College London.

Schumann, J., Ertel, W., & Suttner, C. (1988). Learning Heuristics for a Theorem Prover using Back Propagation. OGAI-89.

Shastri, L., & Feldman, J.A. (1985). Evidential Reasoning in Semantic Networks: A Formal Theory. IJCAI 1985, 465-474.

Simpson, P.K. (1987). A Survey of Artificial Neural Systems. Report Unisys, San Diego.

Stern, A. (1988). *Matrix Logic*. North-Holland, Amsterdam.

Sternberg, R.J. (1982). Reasoning, problem solving, and intelligence. In Sternberg, R.J. ed. *Handbook of Human Intelligence*, 225-307. Cambridge University Press, Cambridge.

Stolcke, A. (1988). Generierung natürlichsprachlicher Sätze in unifikationsbasierten Grammatiken – Ein Konnektionistischer Ansatz. Institut für Informatik, Techn. Universität München.

Stanfill,C. & Waltz, D. (1986). Toward memory-based reasoning. *Comm. ACM*, **29**, 1213–1228.

Touretzky, D.S., & Hinton, G.E. (1985). Symbols Among the Neurons: Details of a Connectionist Inference Architecture. IJCAI '85.

Treleaven, P.C., & Vanneschi, M., eds. (1987). *Future Parallel Computers*. LNCS 272, Springer, Berlin.

Widrow, B. & Hoff, M.E. (1960). Adaptive switching circuits. *IRE WESCON Convention Record*, 96–104.

Zadeh, L.A. (1984). Syllogistic reasoning in fuzzy logic and its application to reasoning with dispositions. Tech. Rep., Electronics Research Laboratory, College of Engineering, Univ. of California, Berkeley, CA.

CONNECTIONISM IN PERSPECTIVE
R. Pfeifer, Z. Schreter, F. Fogelman-Soulié, L. Steels (Eds.)

A Correlative View on Backpropagation

Alexander Linden and Jörg Kindermann
al@gmdzi.uucp and joerg@gmdzi.uucp

German National Research Center for Computer Science (GMD)
Postfach 1240, D-5205 Sankt Augustin 1

Abstract—*The view of weights as correlations leads to new interpretations and extensions of backpropagation. Symmetric activation functions support the correlative interpretation of weights and activation values. Furthermore symmetric unit activations improve the performance of backpropagation.*

A new method of internal feedback is introduced which is based on backpropagation of the error signals to the input layer. It can be used to detect minimal microfeatures for input/target pairs. In addition we propose to extend backpropagation to symmetric weights which makes the network trainable on constraint satisfaction tasks. This use of backpropagation is comparable to Hopfield networks with hidden units (Boltzmann machines).

We conclude our discussion with a short overview of our research interests and the current research environment.

Keywords—Backpropagation, correlations, internal feedback, microfeatures, symmetric weights, constraint satisfaction.

1 INTRODUCTION

Information processing in neural networks is often termed "subsymbolic". This should however not lead us to view the adaptation procedures of neural networks as pure arithmetic. It is useful to interpret unit activations and link weights symbolically as correlations between concepts or features. This interpretation is of course not restricted to a localist view but also applies to distributed representations of concepts. In this paper we show some consequences of a correlative view on backpropagation.

2 WHY SYMMETRIC UNIT ACTIVATIONS ARE USEFUL

Multilayer Perceptrons such as backpropagation nets (Werbos, 1974; Rumelhart, Hinton, & Williams, 1986) raise the following questions:

- What is the meaning of a unit and its activation value?
- What is the meaning of weighted links between units?

Let us assume that units are interpreted as concepts or microfeatures. Under this assumption an activation value gives information about the absence or presence of the feature which it represents in the current environment. It seems natural that zero activation corresponds to "feature absence" and full activation to "feature presence". It therefore makes sense to interpret intermediate activation values as probabilities of the *presence* of features. Weights may be interpreted as fuzzy constraints or implications.

To be more precise, let us consider some unit i which is connected to j via some weight w_{ji}. We assume w_{ji} to be positive. Then w_{ji} is one indication[1] that greater evidence for feature i implies greater evidence for feature j. The strength of the indication depends on the absolute value of w_{ji}.

On the contrary, if w_{ji} is negative, the presence of feature i is an indication for the absence of feature j.

If the evidence for concept i (activation x_i) decreases, the evidence for the presence or absence of concept j also decreases, depending of the sign of the weight. But, if feature i is absent (i.e. $x_i = 0$), this has *no* effect on unit j, independently of the sign of w_{ji}. The following table summarizes this fact.

sign of w_{ji}	value of x_i	tendency of x_j
pos.	0	no effect
pos.	1	$\rightarrow 1$
neg.	0	no effect
neg.	1	$\rightarrow 0$

This clearly is not what we want. A small change to standard backpropagation gets rid of the asymmetry. We simply allow unit activations between −0.5 and 0.5 by using the activation function

$$f(x_i) = \frac{1}{1+e^{-x_i}} - \frac{1}{2}$$

which is symmetric with respect to the origin. Now the value −0.5 represents "concept absent" and 0.5 represents "concept present".

sign of w_{ji}	value of x_i		tendency of x_j
pos.	−0.5	$\rightarrow$	−0.5
pos.	0.5	$\rightarrow$	0.5
neg.	−0.5	$\rightarrow$	0.5
neg.	0.5	$\rightarrow$	−0.5

This symmetry provides a possibility to correlate similar concepts (positive weights) and contrary concepts (negative weights) or microfeatures with each other, using the same link. In other words, it gives more correlative power to the weights.

The modification also allows to interpret the activation value 0.0 as the neutral "don't know" value. This avoids the following dilemma of standard backpropagation where 0.5 is supposed to represent "don't know" (see e.g. (Elman, 1988)): The "don't know" value z of a network should not be changed by the activation function f, because a change to some other value would add some information to the net. Therefore one has to postulate:

$$f(z) = z$$

[1]There may be other units (indications) connected to j as well.

Furthermore z should have no effect on the net input which is the case if

$$z_i \cdot w_{ji} = 0$$

The learning rule of backpropagation also includes activation values:

$$\Delta w_{ji} = \eta \cdot \delta_j \cdot x_i$$

Therefore the "don't know" value should also have no effect on weight modification:

$$\delta_j \cdot z_i = 0$$

These three conditions can only be achieved simultaneously by an activation function which is symmetrical to the origin and the choice of 0 as "don't know" value.

In general we obtained significant improvements in convergence time and generalization behavior. This also improves the storage capacity of the network (resulting in a reduced number of hidden units needed to solve a given task). Similar results are reported by (Stornetta & Huberman, 1987) who also used a symmetric activation function, but for other reasons.

Interestingly some tasks seem simply not to be well suited for the modified algorithm. The networks had difficulties finding good minima especially for small and unstructured tasks like Xor, Parity and Symmetry. The reason is that for Xor and Parity the input is maximally uncorrelated to the output.

We hope that the acceleration method presented here might also be useful in combination with other accelerations methods for backpropagation and other neural network models, e.g. reinforcement learning and competitive learning.

3 INTERNAL FEEDBACK

3.1 The Method

Backpropagation is the technique of gradient descent for feedforward multilayer nets. It computes error signals δ_j iteratively from output units back to the bottom layer of hidden units. We write the error signal δ as

$$\delta_j = -\frac{\partial E_p}{\partial net_j}$$

with the error E_p for a given input/target pair p. All incoming weights of an arbitrary non-input unit are changed according to the following local rule:

$$\Delta w_{ji} = \eta \cdot \delta_j \cdot x_i$$

with the learning rate $\eta > 0$ and the activation value x_i of unit i which is the predecessor of unit j (including a bias unit with constant activation).

The method of internal feedback works for multilayer feedforward networks **after** the training phase. It is shortly described as a modification of the **input** vector to produce a given target vector at the output layer, i.e. it answers the question which signal should be fed into the network to produce the current output. Internal feedback computes an inverse relation of the network's feedforward mapping. The idea is simply to propagate the error signals back to the **input** layer and to **modify the input activations** instead of the weights. This results in an approximation of the desired target vector in the output layer, leaving the weights fixed.

One obvious way doing so is to determine the pseudo net input of all input units. We use the inverse of the symmetric logistic function:

$$x_i = f(net_i) = \frac{1}{1+e^{-net_i}} - \frac{1}{2}$$

$$net_i = f^{-1}(x_i) = -ln(\frac{1}{x_i + \frac{1}{2}} - 1)$$

To visualize the situation one can imagine that the input units are connected to one external unit with a constant activation. Then the pseudo net input may be seen as the "weight" on the connection from the external unit to the input unit. In practice one may only use input values from the **open** interval $(-0.5, 0.5)$ because the expressions $f^{-1}(-0.5)$ and $f^{-1}(0.5)$ are not defined. This restriction is not critical however, because it corresponds to the equivalent restriction that the global error in a backpropagation network cannot be reduced to 0.0 for target values of 0.5 and −0.5.

Thus, if we treat net_i as a "weight" coming in from a single predecessor unit h with permanent activation $x_h = +1$ we can write the change in net_i as

$$\Delta net_i = c \cdot \delta_i \cdot x_h = c \cdot \delta_i$$

where usually $c \gg 0$ because of small values for δ_i. This method actually is a gradient descent search in the **input** space instead of weight space. As with normal backpropagation, the approximation of a given target requires an iteration of this process. If c is appropriate, the process converges to a (good) local minimum.

3.2 Detection of minimal microfeatures by internal feedback.

To illustrate the discussion, consider the English discrimination network described in detail in (Kindermann & Linden, 1988). The network is trained to produce 0.5 as its output if an English word is presented. If a random string is presented, the net is trained to produce an output of −0.5. Suppose some noisy representation of an English word is given to the trained net. In a forward pass the output activation x is determined. Depending on its sign a conjecture is made whether the input is English or not. The conjecture is −0.5 for $x < 0.0$ and 0.5 otherwise. This conjecture is now used as a target pattern. The new target produces an error signal at the output unit, which can be used to adjust the input pattern via internal feedback.

At first sight one could expect that the noise in the input patterns could be reduced in this way. But it turns out that internal feedback does not do a good job on pattern completion. It affects only some input units strongly. This means that the network actually does not use the information of all input units to discriminate patterns. We developed the notion of **minimal microfeatures** to detect those input units which are really relevant to recognize a particular pattern. This technique is a combination of internal feedback with decay of the input pattern. It is described fully in (Kindermann & Linden, 1988).

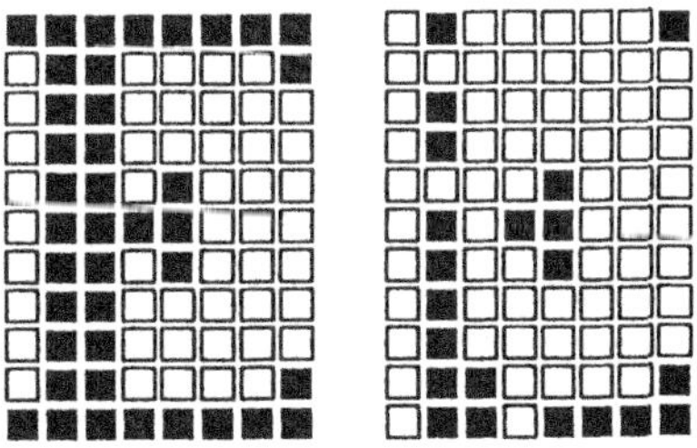

Figure 1: Minimal microfeatures of "E"

The input patterns are subjected to a slow decay towards -0.5 (which is equivalent to pushing the input "weights" net_i towards $-\infty$). Internal feedback neutralizes the decay of those units which need to have high activations (around 0.5) to produce the target pattern in the output layer. These units define the positive minimal microfeatures of the input/target pair.

Negative minimal microfeatures can be detected by a pushing the input activations towards 0.5 while iterating internal feedback. In this case one detects those units which need to have low activations (around -0.5).

Figure 1 shows an example from the domain of letter recognition. A network was trained to recognize the letters of the alphabet (26 training patterns). The figure shows the training pattern for letter "E" (left) and its positive minimal microfeatures (right). The set of microfeatures depends on the set of training patterns as well as on the random initialization of the network weights, and the learning rate. The number of minimal microfeatures for a given training set can be enlarged by the use of random noise during training. Minimal microfeatures can be used to "debug" networks and to generate self-explanations for their behaviour. A good way to see why a network comes up with a particular output for an untrained pattern is to compare this pattern to the minimal microfeatures of all the training patterns.

4 CONSTRAINT SATISFACTION WITHIN THE FRAMEWORK OF BACKPROPAGATION

The task of constraint satisfaction is to determine a complete set of data from a given partial set (which may include input data), while avoiding a violation of the underlying constraints as far as possible. There is no predefined direction of input/output-evaluation in constraint satisfaction systems.

In this context one may consider a multilayer network as a system of constraints, which are represented by the network topology and the set of weights. The discussion which follows should be taken as a motivation and a collection of ideas.

4.1 Towards constraint satisfaction with internal feedback

We assume that only subsets of the input and target activations are known. We clamp on the known input activations to the corresponding input units and leave them fixed for the whole constraint satisfaction process.

The other input units are initialized with arbitrary activation values. These initial activation values denote parts of the starting point in our search space. More specifically we perform gradient descent search in some subspace of the space of unit activations. The search space has fewer dimensions because some of the unit activations remain fixed.

To actually perform gradient descent, activate the output units, and compute the error signals from the given targets, propagate them back through the hidden units to the input units and then change the free input units according to the internal feedback rule which was given in the previous section.

One remaining problem is that only a (empty) subset of the targets is known. A heuristic may help to determine the other targets by predicting the target from the output. If an output activation x_k is positive, we conjecture a target value t_k of 0.5. Otherwise we set t_k to -0.5. A variation of this heuristic uses a positive threshold limit to make a better conjecture. Every x_k above the limit implies $t_k = 0.5$. Every x_k below the negative value of the limit implies $t_k = -0.5$. For the remaining cases we assume $t_k = 0$. Then we introduce a schedule to decrease the limit to zero. This forces the network to make careful decisions.

Anyway, these are only speculative ideas and there is reason to believe that they will show some principal difficulties. One problem arises from the minimal-microfeature property of backpropagation. The presence or absence of some features would not effect each other, while other features will have strong influence on others. These are the minimal microfeatures. Therefore it could happen that there is no information flow at all in the constraint network, although there may be clear evidence for a solution from the training set.

4.2 Towards a solution with symmetric weights

One step towards the solution of problems with minimal microfeatures is to extend the network architecture. We may allow symmetric weights (and two-way links), which is natural if weights are considered to be correlating entities. The set N of all network units is partitioned into external units E (including input **and** output units) and hidden units H. For this purpose, we have to supply each external unit with a threshold, because it now may also function as an output unit.

External units are not connected to each other to avoid feedback loops and overwriting of input information. It is questionable whether to allow recurrent hidden units. Assume for the moment that they are not recurrent. The training set consists of homogeneous patterns. No distinction is made between input and output in the training set. Nevertheless each component is associated with one external unit in the net.

One training step comprises the choice of a pattern and a set of components of that pattern vector. We clamp on this set of component values at the corresponding external units. These units define the set $I \subset E$ of current input units. The thresholds of those units have no function here. The remaining external units $O = E \setminus I$ are taken as output units. The next step is to activate[2] all units in O and modify all weights by backpropagation. The targets are the components of the pattern vector which were not chosen as input. This process has to be iterated.

[2]It might be necessary to exchange the feedforward-pass in the training- and recall-phase with a relaxation process, e.g. simulated annealing, to decrease the probability to get trapped in poor local minima.

One difficulty is obvious however: The inverse function of a backpropagation network will be a many-to one relation in general. Therefore it will not be possible to simply swap the roles of input and output units. One has to choose units from both the input and the output layer to play either role in each training cycle. We believe that the results will be optimal if the sets I and O of input and output units are selected at random for each training cycle.

After some time, we conjecture, the weights will capture the correlations between external (user coded) and internal features. There is reason to believe that this method increases the amount of information stored in each weight, and that the set of minimal microfeatures might become larger. There are also a lot of refinements possible. It might also be interesting to compare the described models with existing models (e.g. Boltzmann machine) with respect to a tradeoff between speed and accuracy. We will investigate the ideas presented in this section in near future.

5 CURRENT RESEARCH ON NEURAL NETS AT GMD/Z1

We are investigating parallel information processing systems which operate and learn in changing environments while handling inherently sequential information. Paradigmatic examples are speech/language understanding systems and the movement control of autonomous vehicles. Experimental architectures for both domains are currently under development at the GMD department Z1. These architectures involve adaptive computation by means of neural networks and genetic operators and combinations of these with non-adaptive modules in hybrid systems. Simulations of neural learning procedures like backpropagation, reinforcement learning, and competitive learning are carried out. Some results have been published in (Kindermann & Linden, 1988) and others are being prepared for publication (Mühlenbein, Kindermann, & Wolf, 1988; Kindermann & Linden, 1988). This paper focused on a theoretical aspect of our work.

Serious research on neural networks demands the development of one's own simulating environments. The construction of simulators gives valuable insights into the theory of neural nets. But even more important, new ideas make it necessary to be able to modify the simulation tools quickly.

We started development of simulation tools with the simulator NN2 which is written in Modula 2 and runs on Sun-3 workstations and on Commodore Amiga PCs. It allows for interactive construction and modification of neural networks in a most flexible way. We represent a neural net as divided up into chunks of units, each one having its special topology, parameters and learning strategies. We focus on the interaction between chunks (and different neural network types). Unlike other simulation environments, the source code of NN2 need not to be changed to alter topology or strategy of the current experiment. The user only provides a high-level specification. The speed of NN2 is comparable to specialized simulators in the same environment.

Our second development, the experimental transputer-based simulator TranSim meets the need for computing power. It runs on parallel hardware (currently on the SUPERCLUSTER computer). The minimal number of processors is four but TranSim may be reconfigured interactively for any greater number (the supercluster computer of the GMD currently has 64 transputers). Preliminary runtime measurements of network computation indicate that the performance will be in the range of supercomputers and special purpose hardware like "neural" chips. It is planned to adapt the flexibility of NN2 to TranSim.

Acknowledgements

We thank the neural net community at the University of Bonn, especially Knut Möller.

REFERENCES

Elman, J.L. (1988). *Finding Structure in Time.* Technical Report CRL Technical Report 8801, Center for Research in Language, University of California, San Diego.

Kindermann, J., & Linden, A. (1988). *Detection of Minimal Microfeatures by Internal Feedback.* Technical Report, GMD, Sankt Augustin. To appear at 5. Österreichische AI-Tagung 1989, 28.-31.March, Innsbruck.

Kindermann, J., & Linden, A. (1988). Pattern completion and classification with back-propagation. In Kindermann, J. & Lischka, C. (eds.), *Workshop Konnektionismus (Arbeitspapiere der GMD)*, GMD.

Mühlenbein, H., Kindermann, J., & Wolf, K. (1988). Implementierung neuronaler Netze. interner Bericht, GMD, Schloss Birlinghoven.

Rumelhart, D.E., Hinton, G.E., & Williams, R.J. (1986). Learning internal representations by error propagation. In Rumelhart, D. E. & McClelland, J. L. (eds.), *Parallel Distributed Processing. Vol. I + II*, MIT Press.

Stornetta, W.S., & Huberman, B.A. (1987). An improved three-layer back propagation algorithm. In *Proceedings ICNN*, SanDiego.

Werbos, P.J. (1974). Beyond regression: New tools for prediction and analysis in the behavioral sciences. PhD thesis, Harvard University.

CONNECTIONISM IN PERSPECTIVE
R. Pfeifer, Z. Schreter, F. Fogelman-Soulié, L. Steels (Eds.)

Rhythm Analysis with Backpropagation

Christiane Linster
Forschungsgruppe Expertensysteme, Institut für Angewandte Informationstechnik, GMD,
Postfach 1240, Schloß Birlinghoven
D-5205 St. Augustin

Abstract—*This paper discusses a model of analyzing musical rhythmic structures with neural networks. Some interesting applications of connectionist models have been made in speech recognition, visual perception and pattern detection. The main motivation of this work is the search for useful representations of musical knowledge in connectionist models. Research in music psychology provides theories on the perception and the analysis of music in a listener's mind. These theories have been applied to formulate the concrete problem for this project. The neural network is presented with a sequence of rhythmical events and is expected to find the hierarchical tree structure which is the most typical for this particular sequence. The backpropagation algorithm was chosen to train the network on a set of different sequences. With this learning paradigm, the system can find its own generalizations in the set of training patterns. After the training phase, the network is presented with several new rhythm sequences and the computed output is analyzed.*

Keywords—Neural networks, back-propagation, music-psychology, perception of musical knowledge, hierarchical tree structures

THE IDEA

"Musical structures articulate a time flow and are mapped into memory through concepts. The perception of music is made possible by concepts in memory that represent musical pasts that act as precedents to which some new sonic events may be matched." (Laske, 1980).

The basic processes involved when listening to music, like recognizing familiar things or making ways of recognizing new things, are important to any kind of human activity. The principal characteristic of music is that sounds stand in significant relation to another and not in isolation. The listener must start to notice relationships and identify significant groupings. At the highest level, such groupings will be very complex, corresponding to formal structures within a work. At the lowest level they will be relatively simple features of the sound pattern, characterizing small groups of notes. Music experts as well as non-musicians can make use, on a different level, of all this patterning when building up a representation of a piece of music. The difference in behavior of music experts in comparison to non-experts seems to lie in the number and complexity of the structural features which the listener is capable of representing, as well as in the degree of averseness of the structures that are used.

Experiments have shown that music which conforms to western diatonic tonal harmony is much easier to remember then music which breaks these rules (Sloboda, 1985). This shows that a composition which does not contain familiar patterns and structures cannot as easily be represented in a listener's mind. The idea to train a neural network system to do such patterning grew from all these assumptions. The system is presented with musical information and is expected to find the groupings and structures underlying this information. Since the ability to find structures in music is augmented with musical training, it seems sensible to build a system which may learn by experience and find its own generalizations. In order to facilitate the problem for the first experiments, we chose rhythm as the musical dimension to begin with.

NETWORK STRUCTURE

The goal of the backpropagation algorithm is to train a multi-layered net to form its own representations in the hidden layers. There must be at least three layers of processing elements. Connectivity between the layers is complete, but no connections exist within layers.

The information which is coming to the input layer from the outside is recoded in the hidden layer (internal representations). The output vector is computed from the internal representation vector and not directly from the input vector.

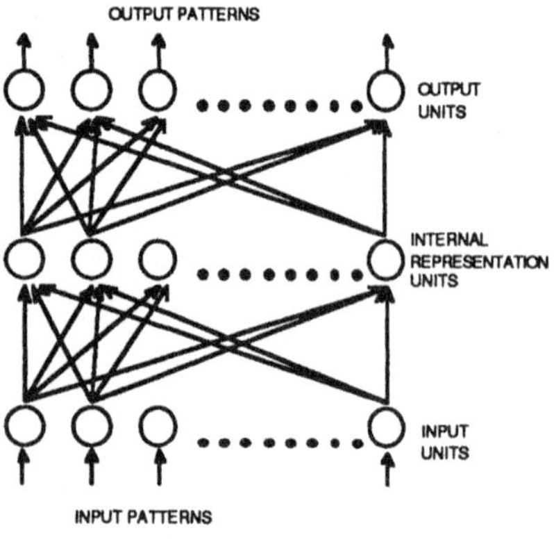

Fig 1: Three layer net

LEARNING BY ERROR-PROPAGATION

Error-propagation (Rumelhart, Hinton, & Williams, 1986) is a method of associative learning, based on the generalized delta rule. The learning procedure requires a set of pairs of input and output patterns. In a first step, the input vector is propagated through the layers, and an activation vector for the output layer is computed. The actual output vector is compared to the desired output (target-vector), and the calculated difference is used to perform weight-changes in direction of disminishing error. The algorithm decides what exactly the units in the hidden layer should represent.

RHYTHM ANALYSIS

Since music, like language is a product of the human mind, one may assume that the observed structures may tell us something about the procedures involved in producing them. Experiments have been made to show that the structure of a sequence is best represented by a constituent tree as shown in Fig 2.

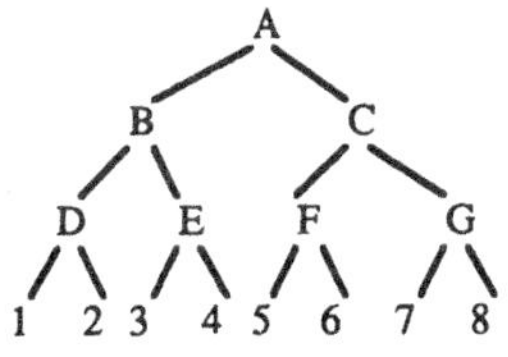

Fig 2: An idealized constituent tree structure

Sundberg and Lindblom (1976) have written a generative grammar for eight bar melodies which are all familiar to a set of swedish nursery songs written in the nineteenth century (Fig 3).

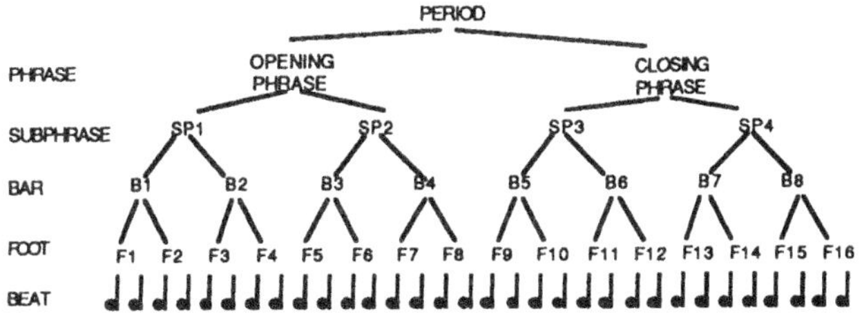

Fig 3: Constituent tree structure of tunes generated by Sundberg´s and Lindblom´s grammar (Sloboda, 1985)

The basic grammatical structure is a hierarchical tree. The structure is the same that would result by analyzing these tunes according to the rules of the classic theory of musical forms. Based on the assumption that classic western music compositions are very clearly structured and symmetrically built, their form structure can be represented in such hierarchical tree structures.

The structures and patterns that are represented in a listeners mind are composed of three musical dimensions: melody, harmony and rhythm. The form structure of a composition may be regarded as "rhythm" on a very high level. If we look only at the rhythm of a music piece, the tree structures that we will build from this reduced information (Fig 4) look very much the same as those in Fig 3. We are only looking at a different level of the music, analyzing the rhythmic events with respect to each other, instead of looking at higher level groupings.

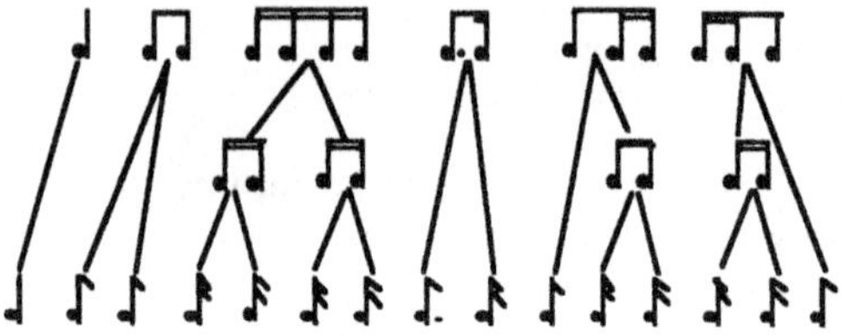

Fig 4: Hierarchical tree of rhythmical events

WHAT IS THE SYSTEM SUPPOSED TO DO?

The structure underlying the rhythm of a piece is often a metrical tree of the sort represented in Fig 2. Rosenthal (1988) describes a computer model of listening to simple rhythms. His program consists of a way of dividing the rhythm into chunks, and an organization of these chunks into a hierarchical structure. This structure represents the residue in the mind, which results from listening to a piece of music (Rosenthal, 1988).

Our system is presented with a sequence of rhythmical events. From this information, the network should compute the hierarchical tree structure which best fits the sequence. For better representation, I will use the normal notational form for rhythmic events. The grouping which is represented in the notational form by links between notes and bar lines is only a visualized form of the structures, which are normally represented by accentuations and different loudness.

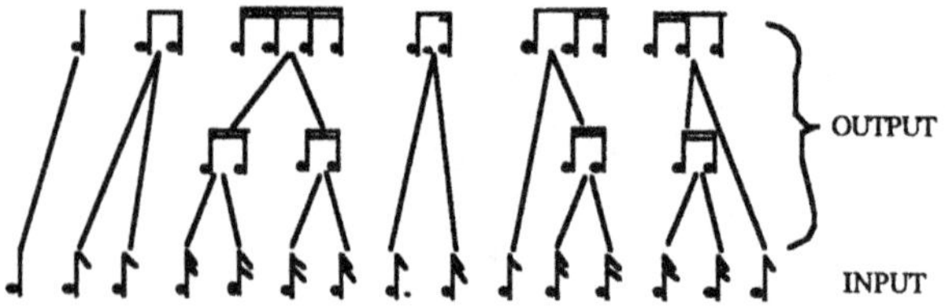

Fig 5: Net input and output

The input to the system is a sequence of rhythmic events in time, without any accentuations, i.e. there is no information on metre and measure. The output consists of the same sequence of events, to which the metrical information has been added. In the notational form explained above, the different levels of the tree correspond to the hierarchy of the events in respect to each other, which corresponds to loudness and accentuation in performance (Fig 6).

Fig 6

THE TRAINING PHASE

In order to teach the net the net to behave in the desired way, the following steps have to be taken:

1. Chose a number of training samples, each consisting of an input pattern and a target pattern.
2. Apply the backpropagation algorithm to each of the training samples.
3. Let the net find internal representations for each training sample.
4. Learn the training samples over and over until a set of weights has been found which satisfies all pairs of patterns.
5. Present the net with new input patterns, and analyze the produced output for the set of weights learned during the training phase.

This has been done for different groups of examples, including patterns from music pieces written by well known composers, as well as simple rhythm structures for different beats.

The network structure became quite large in these experiments. An average number of 90 input units, 250 hidden units and 200 output units was needed to encode the rhythm sequences in the input layer and the tree structures in the output layer. The number of units needed in the input layer results from the length of the training sequences and from time-resolution (see next paragraph). The number of the output units is dependent on the number of rhythmic events and on the depth of the output tree. For the number of units in the hidden layer, a compromise between generalization ability and simulation speed has to be found by experience.

Even with the relatively small number of training samples (50), simulation time for the training phase became very long (up to a week).

ENCODING

One of the major problems of this work has been to find a sensible representation of the rhythmic events for the units of the input layer. We have tried several ways to encode the musical information, but found only one method which lead to a satisfactory behavior.

Two general methods can be distinguished for any kind of encoding problem: using an analogue representation or some form of a code. Both ways have been tried, and have lead to different results. The analog encoding method, which will be described in detail, was the only one which lead to good generalization abilities. A more detailed description of the different behavior of the two encoding methods, and a comparison of the obtained results may be found in (Linster, 1989).

How would a listener hear a sequence of rhythmical events? The most realistic representation surely is a pitch over time representation. The articulation of an event will be heard at a certain pitch, which will slowly decrease in time. Two events are separated by a small pause. This interpretation leads to a simple representation (Fig 7):

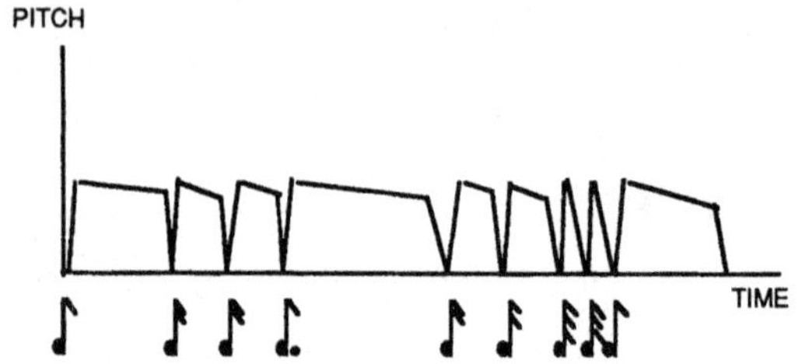

Fig 7

Since we talk about rhythmic events only, it is sensible to simplify the representation by reducing the representation to two discrete cases: pitch or no pitch (Fig 8):

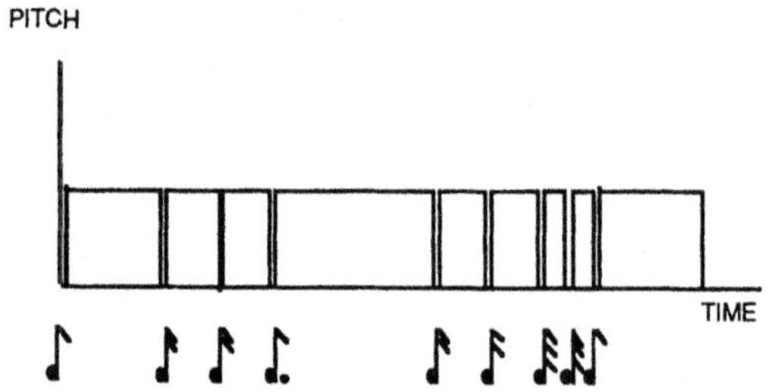

Fig 8

Experiments lead to the assumption that a listener will underlay a discrete beat onto a sequence of rhythmic events to be able to identify the relative occurrence of these. As the input layer has only a limited number of units, which, in our model, may take only two discrete states (active and inactive), I use the units as discrete time-scale, over which the rhythmic events are laid. The representation of Fig 2 would now lead to the following activation pattern in the input layer (Fig 9). (Each unit representing a beat-division of 1/32 note.)

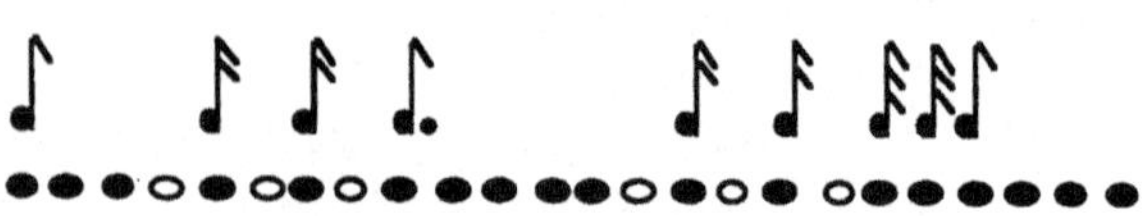

Fig 9

In rhythm analysis, only the relative placement in time of the events to one another is important for patterning, not the absolute duration. Anyway, duration and pitch level of the notes may vary according to interpretation and with the musical instrument that is used. Therefore, I chose a representation where only the starting points of events are marked by high activation level of the corresponding unit (Fig 10):

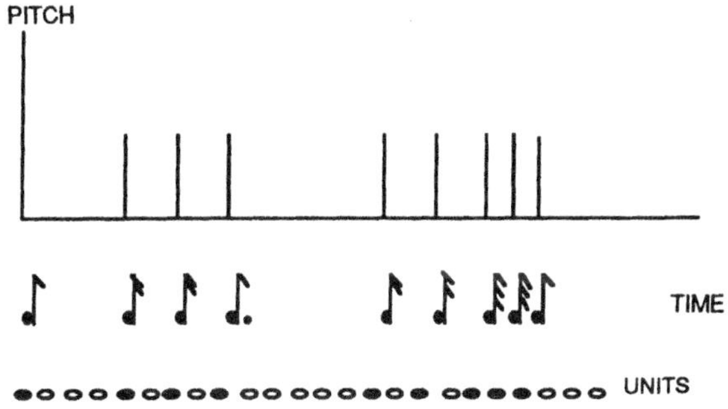

Fig 10

The encoding of the output information posed additional problems. Not only a physical information has to be encoded, but a complete tree structure which represents the hierarchy of the rhythmic events. The tree structure may easily be represented as a nested list (see Fig 14 for explanation). This representation was used to encode the information into the output units. The units in the output layer now correspond to the different levels of the tree. The time resolution used in the input layer stays the same. Activation of an output unit indicates a specific level in the hierarchy at a certain moment in time.

RESULTS

Results have been surprisingly good. A neural network was trained on fifty rhythm sequences written out of Mozart´s piano sonatas. These patterns varied in length, tempo and bar. After the training phase, the system was confronted with unknown sequences from the same compositions. Almost all computed output vectors represented the same groupings as the composer had originally written.

To demonstrate the generalization ability of the system, I will briefly explain the first experiment we made. The system was trained on 15 sequences, all containing only 1/8th and 1/16th note values. The same groups of events are presented in varying order (Fig 11).

Fig 11: The four possible groupings occurring in the experiment

The network was presented with other sequences built of the same groupings, and produced the wanted result for all of them. Additionally, I chose two patterns with note values which had never been presented before (Fig 12):

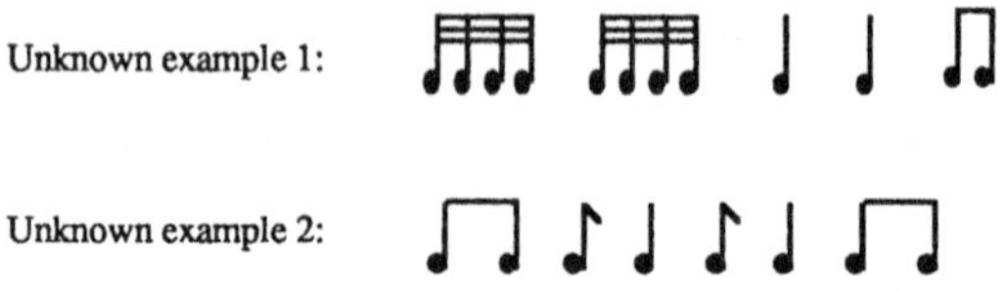

Fig 12: Two unknown examples

The result for example 1 from Fig 12 :

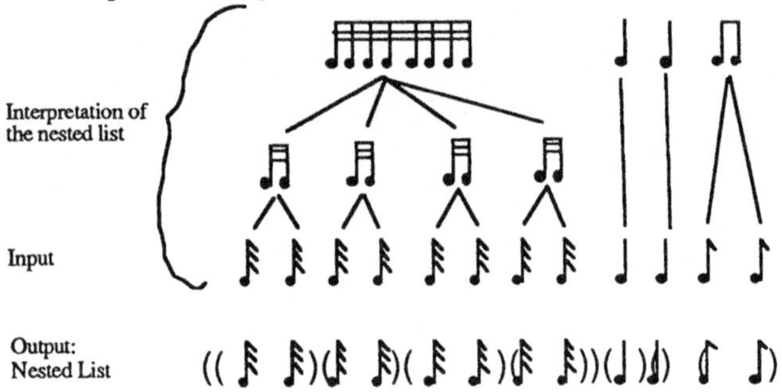

Fig 13: Interpretation of the output obtained from the first example from Fig 12

The wanted output:

Fig 14

The output is very similar to the desired target. Only the grouping of the 32/th notes differs. One should note that the same experiment did not produce any sensible results when a different form of encoding was used.

Other networks were trained on patterns from different compositions, and presented with many kinds of unknown examples. In fact, a network trained on examples from one classic composer (Mozart) could deal with almost any patterns from composers of the same style. It could not, however deal with modern composers, or Jazz patterns. For this purpose, a network had to be trained on special patterns.

In conclusion, one might say that a system can deal with any examples containing familiar structures, which must not necessarily be presented in the same order or groupings in the examples. Completely unknown structures cannot be considered.

CONCLUSION AND OUTLOOK

The problem that we formulated at the beginning of the project has been solved to our satisfaction. A neural network with a special structure has been implemented, which, after appropriate training, could build hierarchical tree structures from sequences of single rhythmic events. We think that a first step has been made in the search for ways for representation, perception and analysis of musical knowledge in connectionist models.

The system can easily be transposed to a higher level, including melody and harmony. A midi-interface for easier handling of the complex musical information is already in work.

A point of criticism is the lack of dynamics in the input information. The input to the system is always static, meaning that a sequence of events is presented parallel to the system and not a continuous flow of information. The realization of a system which will be able to handle such a temporal information flow will be the major problem we will have to work on in further projects.

REFERENCES

Laske, O.E. (1980). Toward an explicit cognitive theory of musical listening. Computer Music Journal, **4**, 73-83.

Linster, C. (1989). "Get Rhythm", A musical application for neural networks. Arbeitspapiere der GMD 365, ISSN 0732-0508.

Rosenthal, D. (1988). A model of the process of listening to simple rhythms. *Proceedings of the 14th International Computer Music Conference,* Cologne, 189-199.

Rumelhart, D.E., Hinton, G.E., & Williams, R.J. (1986). Learning internal representations by error-propagation. In: D.E. Rumelhart & J.L. McClelland (Eds.). *Parallel Distributed Processing*. Cambridge, Mass.: MIT Press.

Sloboda, J.A. (1985). The musical mind. The cognitive psychology of music. Oxford psychology series No. 5. Oxford: Clarendon Press.

Sunberg, J.and Lindlom, B. (1976). Generation Theories in language and music description. *Cognition*, **4**, 99-122

CONNECTIONISM IN PERSPECTIVE
R. Pfeifer, Z. Schreter, F. Fogelman-Soulié, L. Steels (Eds.)

Psychological Constraints upon Connectionist Models of Word Recognition

Exploring TRACE and Alternatives

G. Peeters, U. Frauenfelder, P. Wittenburg

Max-Planck-Institut fur Psycholinguistik
Nijmegen, The Netherlands

Abstract—*Psychological data are a source of information that is vital for the development of cognitive connectionist models. In this paper we evaluate the connectivity pattern and global architecture of the TRACE model of speech perception in the light of such data. Inconsistencies between simulation and psychological data as well as unrealistic assumptions in TRACE concerning the representation of time lead us to consider modifications in and alternatives to the model.*

Keywords—Speech and word recognition, local connectionist model, TRACE model, psychological constraints

1 INTRODUCTION

TRACE (McClelland & Elman, 1986) is an interactive activation model of speech perception and word recognition. It consists of units on three hierarchically structured levels of processing; the word level, the phoneme level and the distinctive feature level. Information is locally represented in TRACE with each unit standing for a hypothesis of a particular percept (e.g., word or phoneme).

TRACE has become one of the leading psychological models of word recognition because it has successfully simulated a large number of perceptual phenomena. Given the importance of constraining simulation models with psychological data, we critically evaluate TRACE in this paper in two ways; first, we relate the connectivity pattern and activation flow in the model to human performance data; second, we consider the global architecture and the representation of time in the model. This evaluation leads to some suggestions for future research directions.

2 THE CONNECTIVITY PATTERN AND ACTIVATION FLOW

In TRACE there are facilitatory connections between units on adjacent levels and inhibitory connections between units within levels (Figure 1). The excitatory or inhibitory influence of one unit upon another is proportional to the activation of the former and depends on the strength of the connection between the units. The connection strengths are weighted for each distinct type of connection and are set as parameters given as input to the model.

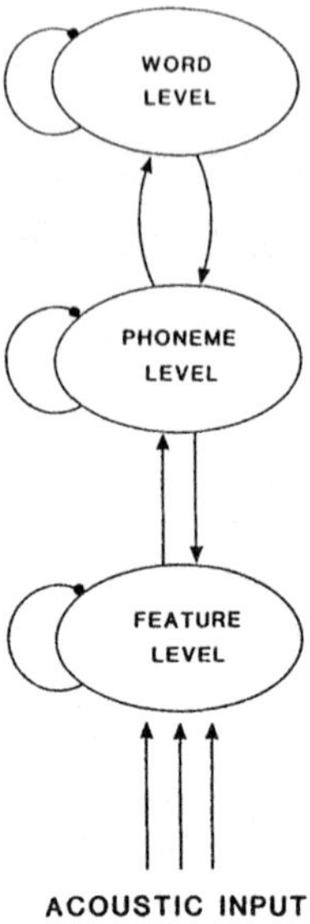

Figure 1: The connectivity pattern in TRACE: facilitatory connections in both directions between units of adjacent levels and inhibitory connections between units at the same level.

In testing the pychological reality of the activation flow assumed in TRACE, we appealed to recent experimental data from Frauenfelder, Segui & Dijkstra (1990). The confrontation between these psychological data and simulation data concerns: 1. top-down lexical feedback and 2. lexically mediated inhibition.

2.1 Top-down lexical feedback

The first psychological experiment measured the time that subjects required to detect phoneme targets located in 4 different positions within matched words and nonwords: at word or nonword onset, before the Uniqueness Point (UP) or the Nonword Point (NWP), after the UP or NWP, and at word or nonword offset, respectively. The UP refers to the point in a word at which its initial segments are shared by no other words in a phonetic dictionary and the NWP refers to the point at which the initial segments first produce a nonword in the language.

Subject reaction times were compared with the recognition times obtained in TRACE simulations for target phonemes located in comparable words and nonwords. The phoneme recognition times were computed as the number of processing cycles that were required from the moment the target phoneme was presented to the model until the moment it was recognized. A particular phoneme's recognition point was determined as the moment at which that phoneme's activation level was sufficiently higher than the activation level of its competitors, according to the Luce (1959) choice rule. The mean values for the experimental and simulation results are shown in Figure 2a and 2b, respectively.

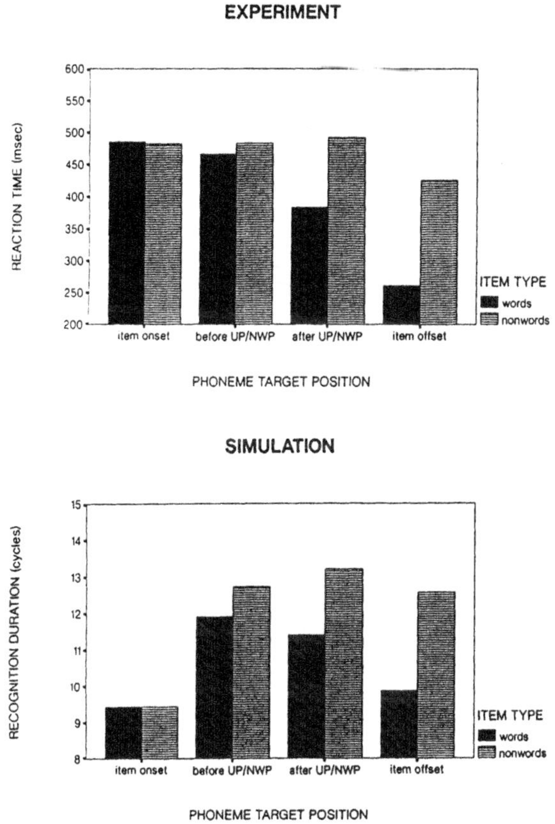

Figure 2: Mean Reaction Times (Figure 2a) and Recognition Times (Figure 2b) for phoneme targets in words and nonwords as a function of their position with respect to the UP and NWP.

The simulation results closely match the experimental data in that the amount of the top-down lexical feedback - as measured by the difference between recognition times for matched words and nonwords - increases as the target appears later in the target-bearing items. As in humans, this difference between the recognition times of phonemes within words and nonwords in TRACE is attributable to the top-down lexical feedback from the target-bearing word after the UP.

There is, however, also an important difference between the experimental and the simulation results. The phoneme recognition times for targets at the onsets of both words and nonwords are considerably shorter in the simulation than in the performance data. We attribute this decrease in recognition times to the existence in TRACE of strong lexical feedback to target phonemes in both word and nonword inputs. Both of these inputs activate a large number of words that match the initial segment(s) of the input sequence. These words provide effective feedback to the item initial phonemes which become more activated than phonemes located in any other position. This discrepancy between the human and simulation data suggests that the amount of top-down feedback from lexical units that partially match the input should be weakened or eliminated in TRACE to account for the perceptual data.

2.2 Lexically mediated inhibition

Although TRACE does not allow inhibition between units at different levels, it does predict indirect word-to-phoneme inhibition through the combined effect of facilitatory lexical feedback to the phoneme level and within-level inhibition between phoneme units. Frauenfelder et al. (1990) tested for the existence of such indirect inhibition in humans by making the lexical feedback after the UP incompatible with the bottom-up evidence for the target, like for example in the input sequence "stimupi". Subjects detected a target phoneme (/p/) that was substituted for the lexically appropriate phoneme (/l/) to produce an Inhibiting Nonword (INW) item like "stimupi". Since the original, physically absent phoneme receives excitatory feedback from the activated word unit ("stimuli") as the preceding simulation shows, this phoneme inhibits the substituted target phoneme /p/, and decreases the target's activation level. This should translate into slower detection times as compared with those for the same phoneme /p/ in a Control Nonword (CNW) item such as "skimupi" where the target phoneme submits to no inhibitory influence. In addition, the phonological distance between the original and the substituted target phoneme was varied, either large (at least 3 distinctive features) or small (1 distinctive feature). This manipulation served to determine whether the amount of inhibition was inversely related to the phonological distance.

In the simulation of the experiments recognition times for target phonemes within INW and CNW items were calculated. The mean recognition times are shown in Figure 3b along with the RTs in Figure 3a.

As we can see in Figure 3a, the psychological experiments provided no evidence for lexically mediated inhibition either for large or small phonological distances. In contrast, the results of the simulation showed strong inhibitory effects, especially in the case of small phonological distances. The failure of the simulation to replicate the behavior of human subjects is clearly problematic for TRACE.

2.3 Fitting the data

The simulation data concerning both top-down feedback and lexically mediated inhibition were inconsistent with psychological data in a number of ways. Of particular interest is determining whether TRACE can be made to fit the psychological data simply by adjusting parameter values (e.g., weight values for word-to-phoneme excitation and for lateral inhibition) or whether deeper modifications are required.

There are a rather large number of free parameters that can be altered within TRACE. We are currently exploring the effect that adjustments of various parameters as well as variations in lexicon size can have on the model's performance. Our initial findings suggest that changing a single parameter setting can have major consequences upon simulation

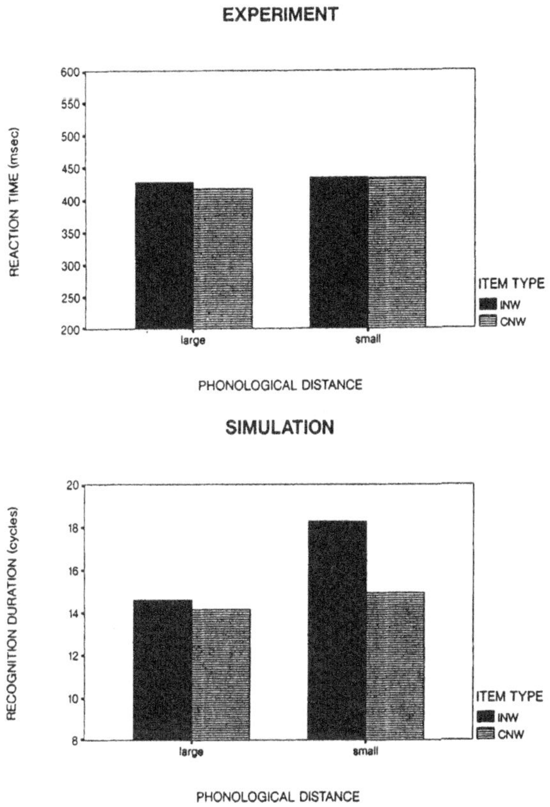

Figure 3: Mean Reaction Times (Figure 3a) and Recognition Times (Figure 3b) for phoneme targets in Inhibiting Nonwords (INW) and Control Nonwords (CNW) with either a small or large phonological distance between the target and the substituted phoneme.

results. Given the model's sensitivity to parameter adjustments, it is in principle possible to simulate a wide range of results. However, this approach is not desirable as the authors of TRACE themselves point out. In order to provide a fair test of the model it is essential to keep the parameter set as constant as possible.

Another more dramatic approach involves modifying the nature of the connectivity pattern within TRACE, for example, eliminating within-level inhibitory connections. A problem with this modification is that the activation function in the model, which is currently bounded between a minimum and maximum level, must also be altered to prevent other units from attaining the same maximum activation level as the target. In addition, parameters must be retuned (e.g., the decay level must be sufficiently high) to keep the activation levels of the different units below an upper bound (Shrager, Hogg & Huberman, 1987).

Despite these difficulties associated with adjusting parameters and modifying the model's connectivity pattern, we believe that such changes are essential. Indeed, from our perspective the psychological reality of computational models is more important than their efficiency (e.g., performance in a benchmark test). Moreover, the interaction between psychological experimentation and computer simulation can lead to the definition of new empirical research areas and to new computational models.

3 THE GLOBAL ARCHITECTURE AND THE REPRESENTATION OF TIME

The representation of time, which is straightforwardly handled in serial processing models, remains one of the major problems for connectionist models. Since speech recognition is a paradigm case of sequential processing, this problem must be confronted directly. In TRACE the problem of representing time is handled in the spatial dimension by repeating complete sets of units representing hypotheses at all levels for successive moments in time. Figure 4 shows a small part of TRACE's connectivity pattern at the word, phoneme and feature levels. The individual time-slices represent identical sub-networks at different moments in time. In each sub-network all units are repeated. In addition, there are the same connections not only within, but also across time-slices.

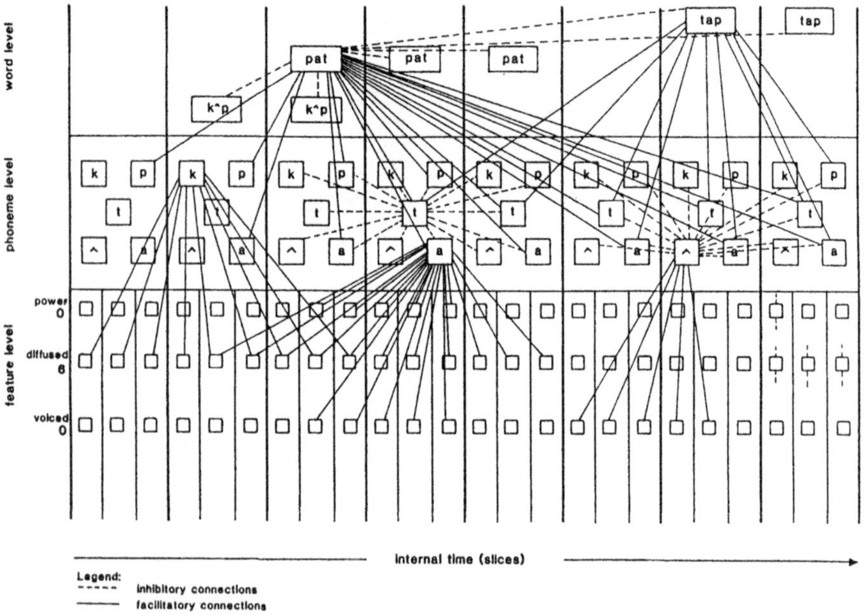

Figure 4: A selection of units and connections within multiple time-slices in TRACE. The figure illustrates the reduplication of tokens in the network for every new time-slice. Connections within and across time-slices are only exhaustively represented for some arbitrarily chosen units (e.g., "pat" on the third time-slice from the left).

As can be seen in Figure 4, the lexical unit for "pat" is reduplicated every new time-slice, and in this fashion TRACE manages to represent a word or phoneme token for every moment in time. This brute-force approach in TRACE to time is both uneconomical and psychologically unrealistic. It prevents the model from being able to learn; weights that specify the connection strength between units can be learned only locally (i.e., for one time-slice), and cannot be generalized over the entire network. As a result, learning the weights between a word token and its phonemes cannot be generalized to another token of the same word starting at a different point in the network. A final problem with TRACE's representation of time is that the model must be readjusted every time the input length surpasses its capacity, given that it must specify in advance the number of time-slices it can represent.

The suggestion to build an additional central network of units, able to tune the connections between the units "on the fly" (McClelland & Elman, 1986), only solves the problem of learning at the expense of increasing the number of required connections and units. To handle the time effectively, it is preferable to adopt distributed representations instead of local representations. Recently, alternative solutions to the representation of time in distributed networks have been proposed by Jordan (1986), Elman (1989) and Norris (1989). In these recurrent networks, the previously processed speech input is not represented in distinct units and time-slices (as in TRACE), but rather in a set of additional hidden units, called the "state units" or "context units". The output of the model is a function of both the input and the state of these units. Standard backpropagation techniques (Rumelhart, Hinton & Williams, 1986) are used to give the network learning capability. Early results suggest that this approach to representing the sequentiality of speech is promising.

4 CONCLUSIONS

The TRACE model of speech perception was submitted to a critical examination. Both the connectivity pattern and the global architecture of the model were shown to suffer from some important short-comings. First, when compared with human performance data, the model produced excessive top-down excitation to item-initial phonemes and inappropriate lexically mediated inhibition. Second, the use by TRACE of the spatial dimension to represent the temporal one raises lots of problems. We sketched some alternatives to the model that need further exploration. Efforts in this direction should provide ways of using psychological constraints to create more realistic computational models.

REFERENCES

Elman, J.L. (1989). Finding structure in time. In G. Altmann (Ed.), *Cognitive models on speech processing*. Cambridge, MA: MIT Press. In press.

Frauenfelder, U., Segui, J., & Dijkstra, T. (1990). Lexical effects in phoneme monitoring: Facilitatory or inhibitory? *Journal of Experimental Psychology: Human Perception and Performance*, in press.

Jordan, M.I. (1986). Serial order: A parallel distributed processing approach. Institute for Cognitive Science Report 8604. University of California, San Diego.

Luce, R.D. (1959). *Individual choice behavior*. New York: Wiley.

McClelland, J.L., & Elman, J.L. (1986). The TRACE model of speech perception. *Cognitive Psychology*, **18**, 1–86.

Norris, D. (1989). A dynamic net model of human speech recognition. In G. Altmann (Ed.), *Cognitive models on speech processing*. Cambridge, MA: MIT Press. In press.

Rumelhart, D.E., Hinton, G.E., & Williams, R.J. (1986). Learning internal representations by error propagation. In D.E. Rumelhart & J.L. McClelland (Eds.), *Parallel distributed processing: Explorations in the microstructure of cognition. Vol. 1. Foundations*. Cambridge, MA: MIT Press/Bradford Books.

Shrager, J., Hogg, T., & Huberman, B.A. (1987). Observation of phase transitions in spreading activation networks. *Science*, **236**, 1092–1094.

CONNECTIONISM IN PERSPECTIVE
R. Pfeifer, Z. Schreter, F. Fogelman-Soulié, L. Steels (Eds.)

Kohonen's Self-organizing Map for Modeling the Formation of the Auditory Cortex of a Bat

Thomas Martinetz, Helge Ritter and Klaus Schulten

Physik Department, Technische Universität München
D-8046 Garching, Federal Republic of Germany

Abstract—*As an example of Kohonen's self-organizing mapping algorithm we simulate the formation of a disproportionate representation of the ultrasound spectrum by the auditory cortex of a bat. We compare the results with experimental data of the cortex of the mustache bat* Pteronotus parnelli rubiginosus *and with an analytical calculation.*

Keywords—Kohonen's self-organizing maps, auditory cortex of bat, representation of ultrasound spectrum

1 INTRODUCTION

A most important task for the brain is a good representation of its sensory data. In the early stages of sensory processing, this is achieved by connecting cortical neurons to their peripheral receptors in a topology conserving fashion. In this way, neighbouring neurons in the cortex can get tuned to similar sensory inputs. The extent of cortical representations of peripheral sensory fields is greatly varying, depending on the functional importance of the sensory signals for the species behaviour. Within the cortex, the size of the population of neurons concerned with particular sensory signals depends also on the fine analysis necessary for these signals. For example, the fine analysis of visual information in higher mammals is mainly performed at the *fovea centralis*. The *fovea centralis* is a very small area near the center of the retina with a high density of sensory cells. Therefore, the resolution in this area is much higher than in the areas of the retina which are responsible for the periphery of the visual field. Although the *fovea centralis* is much smaller than the whole retina, it is represented by the largest part of the visual cortex. Similar disproportionate representations were found in the somatosensory system and the motor cortex. For instance, "hand" areas in the somatosensory and motor cortices of monkeys are of considerably larger relative size than the representation of the remainder of the body surface (Woolsey, 1958).

In the auditive cortex of mammals, however, a comparably disproportionate projection has not been found. This is probably due to the fact that the acoustic signals used by most mammals have a broad frequency range and their sound energy is commonly not concentrated at any particular frequency. The cry of a cat, for example, contains many harmonics of the principal mode, and no part of the frequency band is more important for survival than the rest. The auditive cortex of cats has been investigated very carefully, and the experiments have indicated, as expected, a nearly proportionate tonotopic representation, without any particular preference to special frequencies. Thereby high-frequency-sensitive neurons have been located on the anterior and low-frequency-sensitive neurons on the posterior part of the cortex, with neurons sensitive to intermediate frequencies lying in between. Analogous, previous investigations show a very similar structure also for the auditive cortex of dogs and monkeys (Merzenich et al., 1975).

2 THE AUDITORY CORTEX OF A BAT

A completely different case was found, when the auditory cortex of the mustache bat *Pteronotus parnelli rubiginosus* from Panama was investigated. Because of the emitted orientation signals, the frequency spectrum contains some very important parts for the mustache bat. For orientation, it has several location signals at different frequencies to measure the distances of objects in its surroundings by the time delay of the echo. In addition, the mustache bat *Pteronotus parnelli rubiginosus* uses a very intense orientation sound at 61 kHz to determine the velocity of objects by measuring the Doppler shift of the echo. A separate area of the auditory cortex is involved to analyse this Doppler shift. With this area, *Pteronotus parnelli rubiginosus* is able to determine the velocity of enemies and insects, its main food source, to a precision up to 3 cm/s (Suga & Jen, 1976).

The Doppler shift of the echo, caused by an object moving in the direction of flight of the bat, is given by (see e.g. Gerthsen et al. (1986))

$$\frac{f}{f_e} = \frac{2v_{bat}}{c} - \frac{v_{obj}}{c}. \tag{1}$$

f_e denotes the echolocation signal frequency of 61 kHz, v_{bat} the velocity of the bat, v_{obj} the velocity of the detected object and c the speed of sound. In the formula, the velocity of the bat has to be multiplied by a factor of two because of a Doppler shift during the emission of the orientation signal and an additional shift of the same amount during the reception of the echo. An additional frequency shift of v_{obj}/c is caused by the motion of the detected object. If the bat knows its own velocity, it is able to determine v_{obj} by means of the total Doppler shift f.

The excellent sonar abilities of the bat are certainly essential for its survival. But to be able to determine a frequency shift of 0.01%, which corresponds approximatly to the velocity of 3 cm/s mentioned above, a particulary high resolution of the echo near the frequency of the orientation signal is necessary. Therefore, it would not be surprising, if the interval of the frequency band around the 61 kHz of the echolocation signal is disproportionally represented at this part of the auditive cortex responsible for the analysis of the Doppler shift. Corresponding investigations at the auditive cortex of *Pteronotus parnelli rubiginosus* have been made and confirm this consideration.

Figure 1 shows the measurements of Suga & Jen (1976). In part B of Fig. 1 we see that the one-dimensional frequency band extends continuously and monotonically mainly along the anteroposterior axis. Furthermore, we can recognize the particularly highly resolved interval around the echolocation frequency of 61 kHz. To emphasize this extreme disproportionality, the shaded region of Fig. 1A is shown separately in Fig. 1C. The region of the cortex drawn shaded in Fig. 1A is associated with that part of the whole frequency band, which is relevant for the orientation of the bat. The "best frequencies" of the neurons in this region extend from their minimum of 20 kHz over the echolocation frequency to

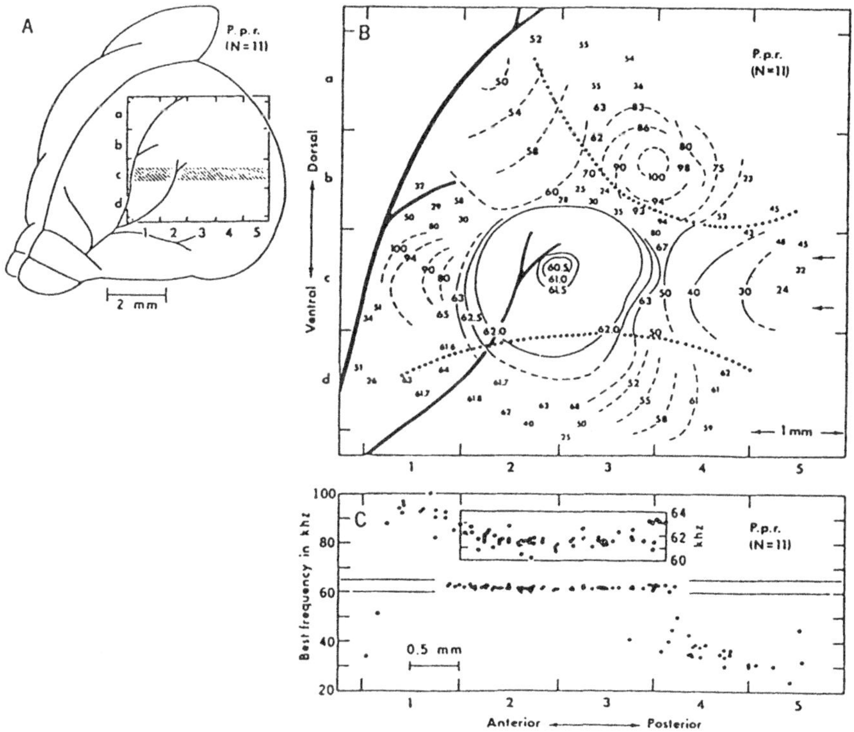

Figure 1: (A) Dorsolateral view of the cerebrum of the mustache bat *Pteronotus parnelli rubiginosus*. The auditory cortices lie inside the rectangle. (B) Distribution of best frequencies in the rectangle shown in (A). The area between the dotted lines is the primary auditory cortex (AI). The areas dorsal or ventral to AI are nonprimary auditory cortices. Orderly tonotopic representation is encountered in the areas with solid contour lines but it is more vague in the areas with dashed contour lines. In the areas where contour lines are not drawn, the tonotopic representation, if present, is obscure. Some of the best frequencies obtained in these areas are shown by small letters. (C) Distribution of the best frequencies along the anteroposterior axis in the shaded area in (A). Since the minor differences among the best frequencies in areas 2 and 3 cannot clearly be shown in (C), the distribution of the best frequencies in this area is shown by the inset with a larger frequency scale and using open circles (from Suga & Jen (1976)), (P.p.r., Pteronotus parnelli rubiginosus).

their maximum of 100 kHz (the "best frequency" of a neuron is the frequency, which causes its highest excitation). In C, these best frequencies are plotted versus their location on the anteroposterior axis. We see, that an exceptionally large fraction of all neurons is tuned to a very small interval centered around the echolocation frequency. Nearly half of this fraction of the auditory cortex is involved in the analysis of the Doppler shifted echos. This is consistent with the particularly high resolution of 0.01%, enabling the bat to orientate itself in its surroundings and to detect even the wingbeat of small insects.

3 THE MODEL

We want to model the formation of the mapping from the ultrasound spectrum, received by the mustache bat, to the auditive cortex. Several algorithms for the formation of such mappings have been suggested (Edelman, 1985; Takeuchi, 1979; Willshaw, 1976, 1979). In the following we will consider a proposal due to Kohonen (Kohonen, 1982a, 1982c, 1984). This proposal does not model biological details but captures the most essential features of such mappings. The aim is to generate a mapping of a space V of input signals onto an discrete lattice A of formal neurons. The map is generated by establishing a correspondence between inputs from V and neurons in the lattice such, that the topological (neighborhood) relationships among the inputs are reflected as faithfully as possible in the arrangement of the corresponding neurons in the lattice. The correspondence is obtained iteratively by a sequence of training steps, which can be formulated in terms of synaptic modification laws (Kohonen, 1984) for the neurons. However, for the purposes of this paper, we present the algorithm in an abstract form without explicit reference to neurons.

Each input signal is represented by a vector $\mathbf{f} \in V$. In our special case, $\mathbf{f}$ specifies the frequency of the received ultrasound signals and therefore is one-dimensional. For each training step an input $\mathbf{f} \in V$ is chosen randomly according to some probability of occurrence $P(\mathbf{f})$. Each location $\mathbf{r}$ of the lattice A carries also a vector $\mathbf{w_r} \in V$, in our application the best frequency of neuron $\mathbf{r}$. The vectors $\mathbf{w_r}$ map lattice locations $\mathbf{r}$ to points in V. In our simulation, the $\mathbf{w_r}$ are chosen randomly for the initial state of the mapping, and for each training step this mapping is adjusted by the following two steps:
1. Determine lattice location $\mathbf{s}$ for which

$$||\mathbf{w_s} - \mathbf{f}|| = \min_{\mathbf{r} \in A} ||\mathbf{w_r} - \mathbf{f}|| \tag{2}$$

where $\mathbf{f}$ is the randomly chosen input signal for the current step.
2. For all sites $\mathbf{r}$ in the neighborhood of $\mathbf{s}$ (with $\mathbf{s}$ included) adjust

$$\mathbf{w_r}^{(new)} = \mathbf{w_r}^{(old)} + \epsilon h_{\mathbf{rs}}(\mathbf{f} - \mathbf{w_r}^{(old)}), \tag{3}$$

where $0 \leq h_{\mathbf{rs}} \leq 1$ is a prespecified adjustment function of the distance $||\mathbf{r} - \mathbf{s}||$ and ϵ is a learning step size. $h_{\mathbf{rs}}$ has its maximum at $\mathbf{r} = \mathbf{s}$ and usually decays to zero, as $||\mathbf{r} - \mathbf{s}||$ increases.
By decreasing the step size ϵ and the lateral width σ of $h_{\mathbf{rs}}$ slowly with increasing number of training steps, the algorithm can be shown to gradually yield values for the vectors $\mathbf{w_r}$ which define a (discretized) neighborhood conserving mapping between lattice sites $\mathbf{r}$ and points of the input space V (Kohonen, op.cit.).

The formation of the map is driven by a random sequence of sensory input signals whose probability distribution imprints on the final map in such a way that regions of the input signal space corresponding to frequent signal occurences are mapped onto larger areas than regions corresponding to rarer input signals. In our example the input space $P(f)$ is the one-dimensional ultrasound spectrum of the bat. We model this spectrum by superimposing the spectra of white noise of a small amplitude and a gaussian distribution peaked at 61 kHz. The white noise in the frequency interval between 20 and 100 kHz describes signals of external ultrasound sources. The gaussian distribution at 61 kHz models the Doppler shifted echolocation signals and has a width of $\sigma_s = 0.5$ kHz which corresponds to an average velocity of detected objects of 2 m/s. The relative amplitudes of

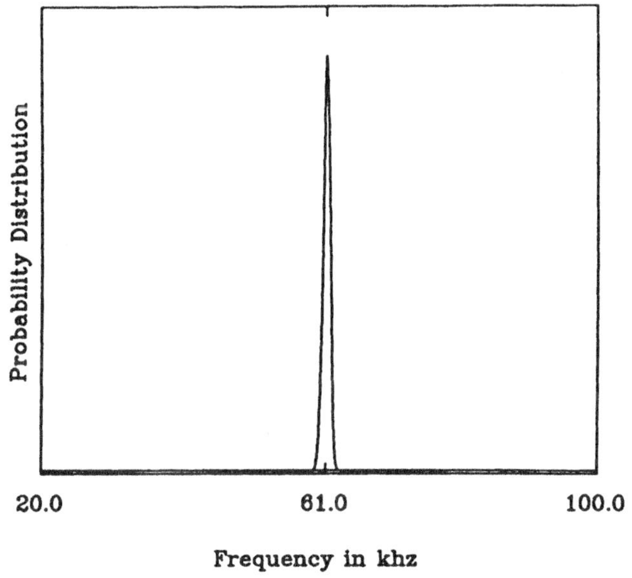

Figure 2: The probability distribution of the input signals versus the frequency of the signal, as assumed in the model. A Doppler shifted echo occures three times as frequently as a signal of external ultrasound sources.

the white noise and the gaussian distribution were chosen such that Doppler shifted echos occur three times as frequently as signals of external ultrasound sources. Figure 2 shows the resulting ultrasound spectrum.

4 THE SIMULATION

In Fig. 1B we see, that the relevant region of the auditive cortex of *Pteronotus parnelli rubiginosus* for the resolution of the echolocation signals is very narrow along the antero-posterior axis. Thus we used for our computer simulation a narrow stripe arranged as a rectangle of 5×25 neurons with the longer side running along the anteroposterior direction.

Figure 3 shows the Kohonen net during three different phases of the learning process. Each box represents a neuron and displays the value of its best frequency. Figure 3a shows the initial state. Each neuron was assigned to a frequency drawn randomly from the range between 20 and 100 kHz. In Fig. 3b, after 500 learning steps, a continous relation between the frequencies as input signals and their assigned location on the net has evolved. To build up an neighbourhood conserving topology mapping between input space and neural net is one of the main features of the Kohonen model. The final state after 5000 learning steps is shown Fig. 3c. We recognize a second main feature of the model that it represents input signals corresponding to their probability of occurrence. The extreme peak of the probability density of the input signals causes an occupation of a large part of the "auditive cortex" with best frequencies from a small interval around the

78	45	63	43	75
51	77	28	86	91
52	80	24	34	45
52	85	91	85	84
23	97	26	27	37
96	28	98	86	82
44	99	50	81	42
52	86	74	92	75
66	39	56	41	34
99	23	77	69	61
42	47	81	38	100
93	86	56	45	23
36	70	46	59	22
62	59	80	97	25
64	92	94	23	84
83	59	31	89	47
76	71	41	41	89
72	27	85	27	67
51	23	93	100	27
89	52	32	42	65
48	44	30	65	45
21	34	83	77	31
25	38	82	38	79
47	75	43	86	64
20	73	43	51	64

Fig.3a

28	28	30	32	35
28	29	31	33	36
30	31	32	35	37
33	33	35	37	39
36	37	38	39	41
40	41	41	43	44
44	44	45	46	47
48	48	49	49	50
51	52	52	52	53
54	54	55	55	55
57	57	57	57	57
58	58	58	58	58
59	59	59	59	59
60	60	60	60	60
60	60	60	60	60
60	60	60	60	60
60	60	60	60	60
60	60	60	60	60
61	61	61	61	61
62	61	61	61	61
62	62	62	62	62
63	63	63	63	62
64	64	63	63	63
64	64	64	64	63
65	64	64	64	64

Fig.3b

36	33	29	26	25
38	35	32	30	27
40	39	37	35	33
44	42	41	39	39
47	46	44	44	44
50	49	48	48	49
54	53	53	54	54
58	58	58	58	58
59	59	59	59	59
60	60	60	60	60
60	60	60	60	60
61	61	61	61	61
61	61	61	61	61
61	61	61	61	61
61	61	61	61	61
62	62	62	62	62
62	62	62	62	63
62	62	63	63	63
64	64	64	64	65
68	68	68	69	68
72	73	73	74	73
75	77	79	81	81
78	80	84	87	88
81	83	87	91	93
82	85	90	94	96

Fig.3c

Figure 3: *Fig. 3a:* The initial state of the neurons with their randomly chosen best frequencies. Each neuron is represented by a box displaying the associated best frequency. The neurons are arranged as a 5×25-lattice. *Fig. 3b:* The situation after 500 learning steps. At this stage the initial random correspondene between neurons and best frequencies has already given way to a tonotopic representation of the relevant frequency range. *Fig. 3c:* The final state of the "auditive cortex" after 5000 learning steps. As a result of the narrow peak of the probability distribution of the sensory signals at 61kHz, a very disproportionate representation of the Doppler shifted echolocation signals has emerged. The associated neurons constitute almost half of the whole cortex.

echolocation frequency of 61 kHz. For this simulation, the time dependency of the step size ϵ and the lateral width σ were chosen as follows: $\sigma(t) = \sigma_i[1 + exp(-5(t/t_{max})^2)]$ where $\sigma_i = 5$, $\epsilon(t) = exp(-5(t/t_{max})^2)$. t denotes the number of performed learning steps. The maximum number of learning steps t_{max} was $t_{max} = 5000$.

The simulation shows that it can reproduce the qualitative features of the experimental results, namely the tonotopy of the mapping along the anteroposterior axis and the disproportionally large representation of the Doppler shifted orientation signals. The latter

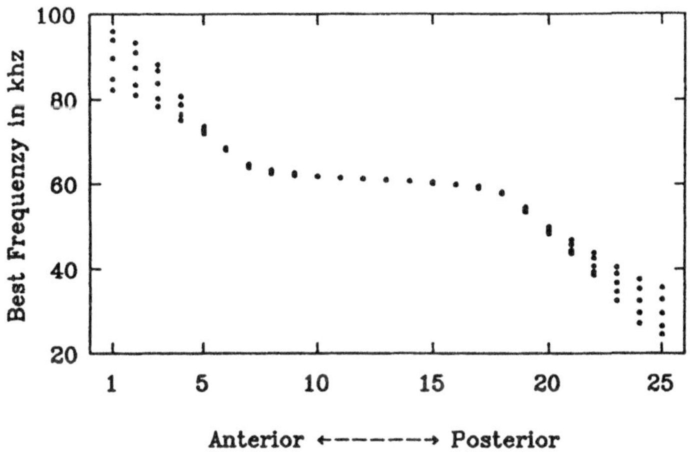

Figure 4: A representation of the results of our computer simulation analogous to the representation of the experimental data in fig. 1C. The best frequencies of all neurons are plotted versus their coordinates 1 to 25 along the anteroposterior axis of our cortex model. For each position there are five neurons, forming a row in Fig. 3.

property can be seen more easily in Fig. 4, where we chose the same representation for our theoretical data from Fig. 3 as in Fig. 1C for the measured distribution of the best frequencies. Each neuron is described by its location 1 to 25 on the anteroposterior axis of our cortex model and its best frequency. In both diagrams, Fig. 1C and Fig. 4, the plateau region indicates that nearly half of the whole cortex is devoted to the analysis of the Doppler shifted echos. The size of this plateau is only determined by the probability distribution of the input signals.

5 AN ANALYTICAL SOLUTION

With the following two assumptions the final state of Kohonen's selforganising mapping can be described mathematically.
i) We assume that for sufficiently large systems $\mathbf{w_r}$ is sufficiently slowly varying with $\mathbf{r}$ to allow replacing it by a corresponding smooth function $\mathbf{w}(\mathbf{r})$ over a continuum of $\mathbf{r}$-values. This basically assumes that the topological ordering of the final state has already occurred.
ii) We assume bijective equilibrium configurations. This also assumes that the input space is of same dimension as the used neural net.

For the equilibrium state of $\mathbf{w}(\mathbf{r})$ we get the differential equation

$$\mathbf{J} \cdot \nabla_{\mathbf{r}} \ln(P(\mathbf{w}(\mathbf{r})) \cdot J) = -\frac{1}{2}\mathbf{r}\mathbf{w}. \tag{4}$$

with the Jacobian $J_{ij} = \frac{\partial}{\partial r_j} w_i(\mathbf{r})$ and $J = Det(\mathbf{J})$ (Ritter & Schulten, 1986). In the following we are interested in the one-dimensional case, because the input space of our model, the ultrasound spectrum, is one-dimensional as well. Then, equation (4) can be written as

$$\frac{d}{dr}\ln P(w(r)) = -\frac{3}{2}\frac{d}{dr}\ln\left(\frac{dw}{dr}\right). \quad (5)$$

Since $w(r)$ represents the inverse of the mapping from the input space to the neural net, the *local magnification factor* M of the mapping is given by $M = 1/J$ with $J = dw/dr$. Now we can describe the relation between local magnification factor M and signal probability distribution $P(f)$ by the simple dependency

$$M(f) = J^{-1} = \frac{dr}{dw} \propto P(f)^{2/3}. \quad (6)$$

We solve this equation for the signal spectrum of Fig. 2. This spectrum can be written as

$$P(f) = \frac{P_0}{f_2 - f_1} + (1 - P_0)\frac{1}{\sqrt{2\pi}\sigma_s} exp\left(-\frac{(f - f_e)^2}{2\sigma_s^2}\right) \quad f_1 \le f \le f_2 \quad (7)$$

where $\sigma_s = 0.5kHz$, $f_e = 61.0kHz$, $f_1 = 20kHz$, $f_2 = 100kHz$ and $P_0 = 1/4$. P_0 is the probability for the occurence of a stimulus of the white noise. f_1 and f_2 are the band limits of the received ultrasound spectrum.

The integral over the whole distribution is not exactly equal to unity, but the error is negligible because σ_s is small against $f_2 - f_1$. Since we have chosen $P_0 = 1/4$, Doppler shifted echolocation signals occur three times as frequent as signals of the homogenous underground noise (see Fig.2). With equation (6) we get

$$\frac{dr}{dw} = C \cdot \left(\frac{P_0}{f_2 - f_1} + (1 - P_0)\frac{1}{\sqrt{2\pi}\sigma_s} exp\left(-\frac{(f - f_e)^2}{2\sigma_s^2}\right)\right)^{2/3} \quad (8)$$

with C as integration constant. Integrating yields

$$r(w) - r_1 = C \cdot \int_{w_1}^{w} \left(\frac{P_0}{f_2 - f_1} + (1 - P_0)\frac{1}{\sqrt{2\pi}\sigma_s} exp\left(-\frac{(f - f_e)^2}{2\sigma_s^2}\right)\right)^{2/3} df. \quad (9)$$

We solve this integral numerically and compare the calculated $w(r)$ with the $w(r)$ of a simulation.

For this simulation we used instead of a square lattice as "auditive cortex" a chain of 50 neurons, because our analytical calculations apply only for one-dimensional nets. In view of the narrow shape of the auditory cortex this should be a justified simplification. The simulation result and the result of the analytical calculation are compared in Fig. 5, where we used again the same display format as in Fig. 2C and Fig. 4. The data points of the simulation are fitted very well by the curve of the analytical calculation. Intuitively one would expect a local magnification factor $M(f)$ proportional to the probability density $P(f)$. This would correspond to the dashed curve in Fig. 5, which, however, significantly deviates from the simulation results.

6 CONCLUSION

We have investigated the possibility that the highly disproportionate representation of sound frequencies in the auditory cortex of the bat *Pteronotus parnelli rubiginosus* need not be

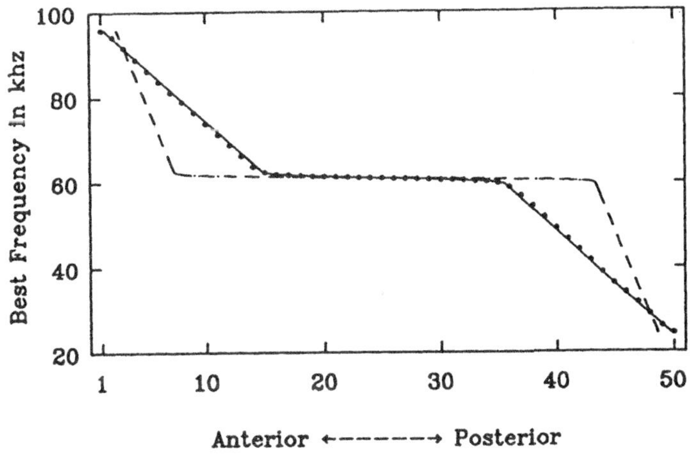

Figure 5: The solid curve represents the result of the analytical calculation. The data provided by the computer simulation are marked by points and agree very well with the theoretical curve. The dashed line shows the intuitive but incorrect expectation, namely a magnification factor proportional to the probability density of the input signals.

prewired initially but could instead result from adaptation of the neurons to repeated sensory experiences. Following a suggestion by Kohonen for a neurally plausible adaptation law (Kohonen, 1982a, 1982c, 1984), we compared the representation generated by a computer simulation and experimental data. We found good qualitative agreement, provided that the disproportionality of the frequency representation is reflected in the statistics of the sensory experiences. For the idealization of a one-dimensional cortex, the relationship between the probability distribution of the sound frequencies and the distortion of the representation resulting from the model is calculated analytically. The results support the idea that very simple adaptation laws together with suitable signal statistics can lead to the adaptive formation of interesting sensory maps.

6.0.1 Acknowledgments

This work has been supported by the German Ministry for Science and Technology (ITR-8800-G9).

REFERENCES

Edelman G.M., & Finkel, L.H. (1985). Neuronal group selection in the cerebral cortex. *1st Symposium of the Neurosciences Institute,* La Jolla, California.

Gerthsen, Kneser, & Vogel (1986). *Physik.* Springer-Verlag, Heidelberg, pp. 164–165.

Kohonen, T. (1982a) Self-organized Formation of Topologically Correct Feature Maps. *Biol. Cybern.,* **43,** 59–69.

Kohonen, T. (1982b). Analysis of a Simple Self-organizing Process. *Biol. Cybern.*, **44**, 135–140.

Kohonen, T. (1982c). Clustering, Taxonomy and Topological Maps of Patterns. *Proc. 6th Int. Conf. on Pattern Recognition*, 114–128.

Kohonen, T. (1984). *Self-Organization and Associative Memory*. Springer Series in Information Sciences 8, Heidelberg.

Merzenich, M.M., Knight, P.L., & Roth, G.L. (1975). *Journal of Neurophysiology*, **38**, 231.

Ritter, H., & Schulten, K. (1986). On the Stationary State of Kohonen's Self-Organizing Sensory Mapping. *Biol. Cybern.*, **54**, 99–106.

Suga, N., & Jen, P.H. (1976). Disproportionate Tonotopic Representation for Processing CF-FM Sonar Signals in the Mustache Bat Auditory Cortex. *Science*, **194**, 542–544.

Takeuchi, A., & Amari, S. (1979). Formation of topographic maps and columnar microstructures. *Biol. Cybern.*, **35**, 63–72.

Willshaw, D.J., & von der Malsburg, C. (1976). How patterned neural connections can be set up by self-organisation. *Proc. R. Soc. Lond. Ser. B.*, **194**, 431–445.

Willshaw, D.J., & von der Malsburg, C. (1979). A marker induction mechanism for the establishment of ordered neural mappings: its application to the retinotectal problem. *Proc. R. Soc. Lond. Ser. B.*, **287**, 203–243.

Woolsey, C.N., & Harlow, H.F. (1958). *Biological and Biochemical Basis of Behavior*. Univ. of Wisconsin Press, Madison., pp. 63-81.

A Connectionist Formulation of Motor Planning

P. Morasso*, F.A. Mussa Ivaldi†, G. Vercelli*, R. Zaccaria*
*Dept. of Computer Science, University of Genoa, Italy
†Dept. of Brain and Cognitive Sciences, M.I.T., Cambridge, U.S.A.

Abstract—*Redundancy and concurrency in motor control are basic problems for multi-joint, multi-limb humanoids. The viscous-elastic properties of muscular actuators provide an organizing factor because they define equilibrium postures that influence body movements as "postural attractors". From this it is possible to derive a planning approach which is based on the internal simulation of passive movement (what we call Passive Motion Paradigm). In this paper we show how this approach can be formulated in connectionist terms as a multiple constraints satisfaction network, driven by a potential function, similarly to a Hopfield network. We call this model "Motor Relaxation Network" (shortly, M-net).*

Keywords—Motor planning, redundancy, muscle elasticity, passive motion paradigm, motor relaxation network.

1 INTRODUCTION

In motor control theory, the basic problem is how to coordinate the degrees of freedom and the actuators of an extremely redundant system with possibly variable structure (e.g. an arm might move freely in space or constrained by a grasped object) while carrying out concurrent tasks of highly variable nature (e.g. reaching while keeping balance, carrying a water filled container without spilling, etc.). In short, the generalized coordination of movements is characterized by three main features: (i) concurrency, (ii) variability of tasks, and (iii) variability of structures. This problem includes but goes well beyond the so called "inverse kinematics"[1] which is only restricted to "open" kinematic chains for a single task: generation of assigned trajectories of the terminal element of the kinematic chain. In a previous paper (Mussa Ivaldi, Morasso, & Zaccaria, 1988), we suggest a general principle for approaching the generalised motor problem that we call Passive Motion Paradigm (PMP). According to this principle, planning the synergy of muscle activations is analogous to the "internal" simulation of passive movements, i.e. the simulation of movements that would result from the application of external disturbances, such as a force pulling the hand toward a target. The simulation exploits the viscous-elastic properties of muscles, i.e. their ability to store elastic potential energy.

[1] A kinematic chain is a cascade of joints and links. Its configuration can be characterized either in terms of the joint angles (q vector) or of the position/orientation of the terminal link (x vector). Direct kinematics is the problem of computing x from q and inverse kinematics is the opposite problem. Direct kinematics is always solvable, whereas inverse kinematics is not, particularly in the case of redundancy (x has less dimensions than q).

The importance of viscous elastic properties of muscles in motor control was first recognized by A. Feldman (1966) and was then investigated in a series of studies. To quote just a few, Bizzi, Polit & Morasso (1976) found that a passive mechanism is the main responsible of the achievement of final position in movements involving one degree of freedom; Abend, Bizzi, & Morasso (1982) studied muscle elasticity in the context of arm trajectory formation; Mussa Ivaldi, Hogan, & Bizzi (1985) formulated a precise multi-dimensional characterization of stiffness.

Muscle elasticity provides a unified treatment of posture and movement. Postures are equilibrium configurations that "attract" the different body segments as a response to mismatches due either to external disturbances or to internal disturbances, i.e. motor plans. In this sense we speak of "postural attractors". Postures are coded by the distribution of neuromuscular activity: as the distribution of this activity varies, a sequence of attractors is defined, thereby generating a movement if there are no constraints. A constraint, which might be an obstacle or a manipulated object, inhibits the planned movement and transforms it into a contact force. Therefore, movement and force planning can be causally related to the same mechanism.

According to the PMP, generation of synergies of neuromuscular activity is carried out by the internal simulation of passive motion. In this paper, we present a connectionist formulation of the PMP, that extends our previous work (Mussa Ivaldi, Morasso, & Zaccaria, 1988). We call it "motor relaxation network" (shortly, M-net).

2 M-NETS

M-nets are multiple-constraints satisfaction networks that are similar to Hopfield networks (Hopfield, 1982) because it is possible to define a global function E, which has the property of a potential function. In Hopfield nets, E is a purely abstract computational concept, although an analogy has been established with the physical behavior of a particular material (spin glasses). In M-nets, on the contrary, E is the direct consequence of a physical phenomenon of biological significance. Therefore, M-nets are a kind of analogic model in a double sense: because the computational process is a dynamic system and because there is a direct analogy between the structure of the model and the underlying physical world.

Three types of units are present in M-nets:

- skeletal segment units (s-units),
- muscle units (m-units),
- ligament units (l-units).

Let us now consider concisely their structure and function:

1. **S-units** model the different skeletal body segments, represented as rigid bodies to which complex sets of forces (muscle forces, ligament forces, external forces) are applied. These units are more complex than those usually considered in connectionist models because they deal with vector quantities (force, velocity, and rotation vectors) and perform vector operations such as vector products. The correct analogy, for an s-unit, is with a whole cortical column not with a neuron. The input is a set of force vectors $(f_1, f_2, \ldots, f_n)$ applied to a set of insertion points $(p_1, p_2, \ldots, p_n)$ distributed over the skeletal segment. The outputs are the positions of the same insertion points. The transformation operated by an s-unit is characterized by the following steps:

- compute the resultant force and torque vectors (F and N), i.e. the net vectorial input;
- compute incremental displacement and rotation vectors as sigmoidal functions of F and N, respectively;
- update the insertion points with a rigid translation/rotation.

2. **M-units** model the muscles as viscous-elastic elements characterized by a family of curves

$$f = f(l, l', \alpha)$$

indexed by the level of muscle activity α (f is the muscle force, l is the muscle length and l' is the speed of contraction). M-units are connected to two s-units in the case of single-joint muscles and to several s-units in the case of multi-joint muscles (e.g. many muscles of the hand). The inputs are the insertion points of the muscle, from which the muscle length is computed. Two kinds of output are present: one is muscle force, which is transmitted to the connected s-units, the other is muscle activation α that represents the motor output and should be transmitted to the muscles. During the simulation of passive movements, muscle lengthening/shortening is accompanied by variations of α that keep the force output approximately constant.

3. **L-units** model the joints as elastic connections with high stiffness. Complex joints can be modeled with multiple l-units, even joints distributed over several skeletal segments, such as the wrist joint. Another function of l-units is to model joint limits in a soft way, by generating increasingly stronger restoring forces as joints approach forbidden configurations. Note that joints and joint limits are not represented as hard constraints but as soft constraints. The power of this concept is that it brings geometry, kinematics, and actuator dynamics under a uniform representational scheme. From the operational point of view, l-units are simplified versions of m-units, without the mechanism of modification of α. L-units and m-units can store elastic potential energy.

M-units and l-units behave as impendances, i.e. they receive positional information and react feeding back force information. S-units, on the contrary, behave as admittances, i.e. they receive force information and react modifying positional parameters. In relation with usual connectionist models, m-units and l-units are analogous to connection weights, these weights having the meaning of stiffnesses: fixed in the case of ligaments and variable in the case of muscles.

A specialized s-unit is the "environment" (or "ground"). Gravity is represented by fictitious l-units that link to ground all the regular s-units. Environmental constraints that do not allow the movements of some skeletal segments also can be represented by means of fictitious l-units as well as motor tasks, which can be specified by means of fictitious l-units that link goal-oriented s-units (e.g. a distal phalanx in a reaching task) to the environment. Concurrent tasks are represented in a natural way by activating simultaneously multiple fictitious l-units.

Figure 1 shows the M-net of a finger. The network consists of the following units:

1. Three s-units (S1, S2, S3) correspond to the three phalanxes.

2. Another s-unit (E) identifies the environment.

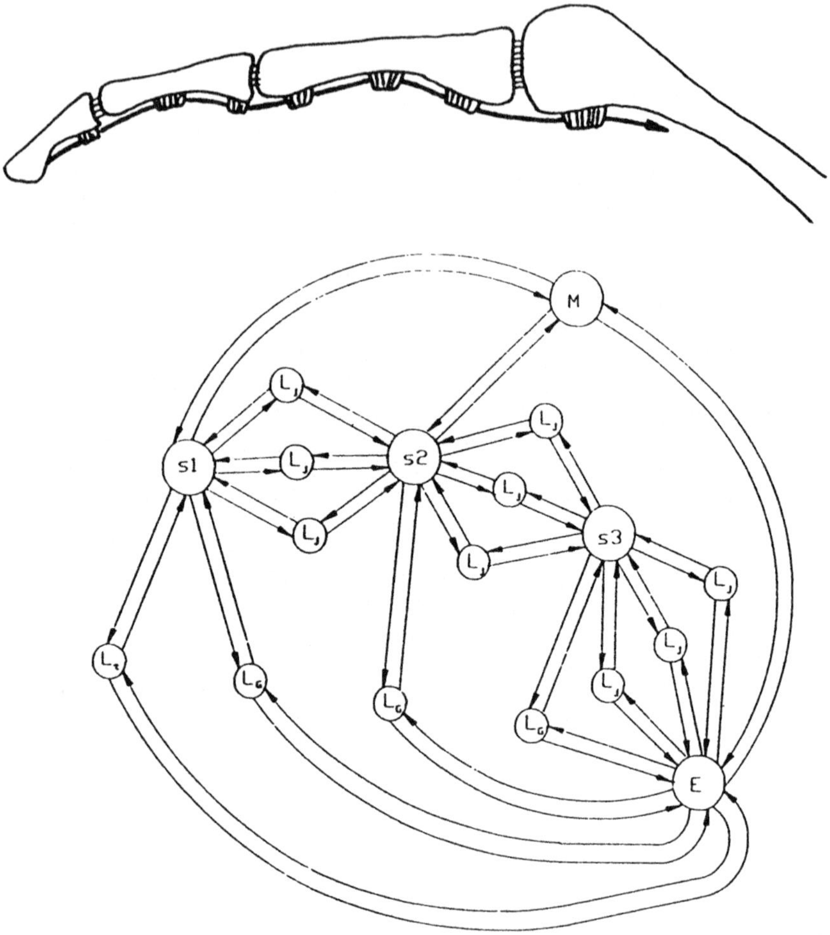

Figure 1: M-net of a finger.

3. Each one of the three joints is represented by three l-units (denoted by lj). The insertions of two of them are chosen in such a way to allow essentially a one-degree-of-freedom rotation. The insertions of the third one are defined in order to avoid too much over-extension of the joints.

4. Gravity is represented by means of l-units (lg) that connect the s-units to E.

5. For simplicity, only one m-unit is shown (it represents a multiple-joint muscle).

6. An l-unit (lt), connected to E, represents the motor goal: a trajectory of the fingertip.

The input connections to s-units carry force vectors and the output connections carry position vectors. On the opposite, input connections to m- or l-units carry position vectors and the outputs carry force vectors. Not shown in the picture is the set of α outputs from the m-units, that represent the motor commands generated by this virtual motor cortex for the muscles.

An M-net is an asynchronous network. At equilibrium, the set of forces that enter each s-unit give resultant force and torque vectors which must be null: as a consequence, the positions of the insertion points of all the muscles and ligaments remain stationary. However, even when the network is at equilibrium, muscles and ligaments may well be far from equilibrium and may in fact store considerable amounts of elastic energy.

A task node (lt in the example) pulls the network out of equilibrium. This node corresponds to a spring which connects the fingertip to a point in space (the target point). The force generated by this node breaks the equilibrium of S1 and the disturbance propagates readily to the rest of the network. A whole trajectory can be generated if the end-point of such fictitious spring is smoothly shifted toward the target.

3 SIMULATION RESULTS

A preliminary version of an M-net simulator was implemented by modifying a motor simulation and animation system - NEM - previously developed (Marino, Morasso, & Zaccaria, 1985). In the simulator, s-units are characterized by a state (the position/orientation of a geometric frame H placed at the center of gravity) and by a list of insertion points ($p_i \;\; i = 1, 2, \ldots$). The activation value of each unit is given by two vectors: the resultant force F and the resultant torque N. These vectors are computed according to standard equations:

$$F = \sum_i f_i$$

$$N = \sum_i (p_i - p_g) \times f_i$$

where p_g is the center of gravity and ($f_i \;\; i = 1, 2, \ldots$) is the set of input forces. The state of the unit is then modified by a translation vector d_1 and a rotation vector d_2 that are computed as follows:

$$d_1 = \beta F$$

$$d_2 = \gamma N$$

where β and γ are constants. H is then updated accordingly.

L-units were modeled as constant high stiffness springs with zero rest-length:

$$f = kl$$

As regards m-units, only single-joint muscles were considered, which were modeled as constant stiffness springs with variable rest-length l_0:

$$f = k'(l - l_0)$$

Joint stiffness values were chosen at least ten times bigger than muscle stiffness values.

Figure 2 shows some example of simulation results:

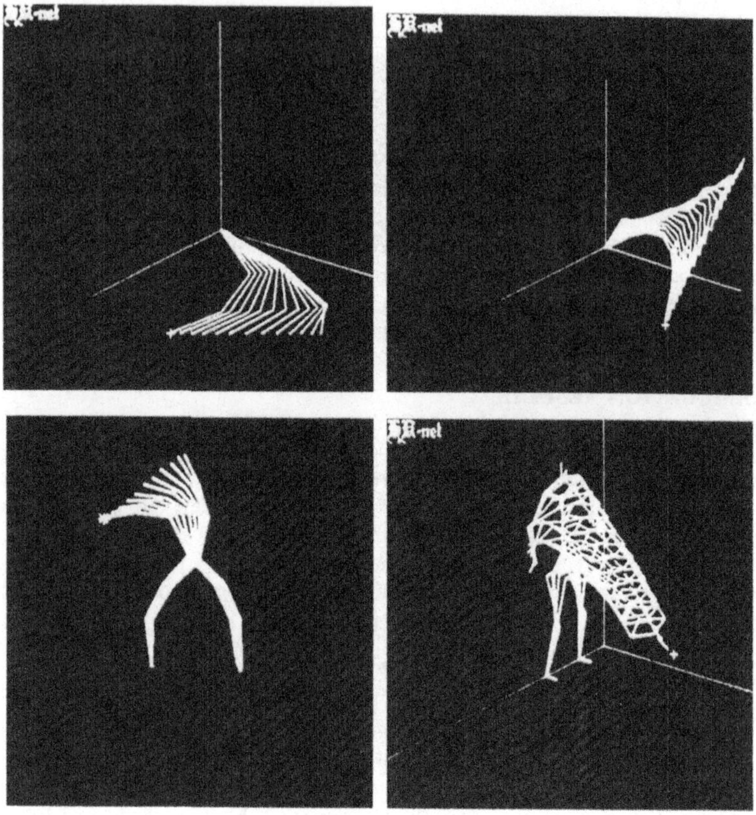

Figure 2: Simulation Results.

- 2A is a single planar kinematic chain;
- 2B is a single spatial kinematic chain;
- 2C is a multiple planar kinematic chain with closed configuration;
- 2D is a multiple spatial kinematic chain with closed configuration and double task (reaching and keeping balance).

In all the examples, there is a reaching task represented by a spring connected to the fingertip; the end-point of this spring is shifted smoothly to the target point. In the example 2D, there is an additional task component (keeping balance) which is represented by another l-unit connected to the pelvis; the end-point of this spring is moved in such a way to attract the center of gravity of the body (its projection on the support plane) towards the centroid of the support base. Note that the two task components do not need to communicate and be synchronized explicitly; they communicate indirectly through the dynamics of the network.

We are currently working on three developments of the simulation environment:

- Implementation of M-nets by using a standard connectionist simulator (the Rochester simulator);
- Implementation of M-nets on a transputer architecture;
- Development of realistic M-net formulations of some complex body parts (in particular, we are attempting to model the hand).

4 DISCUSSION

M-net is a modeling framework to express motor planning for the biological motor control system as well as for the motor control system of highly redundant robots, actuated by means of muscle-like devices.

A performing M-net provides two streams of output data:

1. a stream of "alpha activations" (nominal contraction parameters for all the muscular actuators);

2. a stream of "kinematic expectations" (the expected time course of muscle lengths, joints rotations, trajectories of the skeletal segments) that represent what von Holst called "efferent copy".

Both streams of data must interact with the incoming streams of data of the various afferent channels in order to tune and adapt the motor commands. How to model this interaction is an open question which outlines a vast and fascinating research area. In biological motor control, a sufficiently realistic M-net may prove to be an invaluable tool to formulate predictions of the structure of complex motor synergies that can be tested experimentally.

M-nets solve the inverse kinematic problem both at the joint level and at the muscle level, irrespectively of the degree of redundancy. On the contrary, most of the methods developed in robotics for dealing with redundant systems (explicit optimization and/or motions in the null-space) are only practical for simple kinematic chains and are not scalable up to the degree of complexity of the human musculo-skeletal system. Moreover, M-nets do not solve inverse kinematics only. The solution, which consists of the parallel modulation of elastic actuators, has built-in compensatory characteristics that may counteract the forces due to dynamics. At least for simple arm movements (Flash, 1987) it has been shown that this kind of dynamics compensation mechanism is sufficient to explain the experimentally recorded deviations from the straight line. In relation with other connectionist models of motor control (Bullock & Grossberg, 1988; Jordan, 1988; Kawato et al., 1987; Kuperstein, 1987) M-nets mainly differ because they explicitly use the properties of muscles, what we think is a major source of flexibility.

Acknowledgements

This paper was partly supported by Esprit projects IMU and FIRST, and by Contracts on Bioengineering and Robotics of the Ministry of Education.

REFERENCES

Abend, W., Bizzi, E., & Morasso, P. (1982). Human arm trajectory formation. *Brain*, **105**, 331–348.

Bizzi, E., Polit, A., & Morasso, P. (1976). Mechanisms underlying achievement of final head position. *Journal of Neurophysiology*, **39**, 435–444.

Bullock, D., & Grossberg, S. (1988). Neural dynamics of planned arm movements: Emergent invariants and speed-accuracy properties during trajectory formation. *Psychological Review*, **95**, 49–90.

Feldman, A.G. (1966). Functional tuning of nervous system with control of movement or maintenance of a steady posture. *Biophysics*, **11**, 137–144.

Flash, T. (1987). The control of hand equilibrium trajectories in multi-joint arm movements. *Biological Cybernetics*, **57**, 257–274.

Hopfield, J.J. (1982). Neural networks and physical systems with emergent collective computational abilities. *Proceedings National Academy of Sciences*, USA, **79**, 2554–2558.

Jordan, M. (1988). Supervised learning and systems with excess degrees of freedom. *COINS Technical Report*, 88-27.

Kawato, M., Furukawa, K., & Suzuki, R. (1987). A hierarchical neural-network model for control and learning of voluntary movement. *Biological Cybernetics*, **57**, 169–185.

Kuperstein, M. (1987). Adaptive visual-motor coordination in multi-joint robots using parallel architecture. *IEEE Conference on Robotics and Automation*, 1595–1602.

Marino, G., Morasso, P., & Zaccaria R. (1985). Motor knowledge representation. In *Proceedings of the International Joint Conference in Artificial Intelligence*, Los Angeles, California (pp. 1110–1112).

Mussa Ivaldi, F.A., Hogan, N., & Bizzi, E. (1985). Neural, mechanical, and geometric factors subserving arm posture in humans. *Journal of Neuroscience*, **5**, 2732–2743.

Mussa Ivaldi, F.A., Morasso, P., & Zaccaria, R. (1988). Kinematic networks - A distributed model for representing and regularizing motor redundancy. *Biological Cybernetics*, **60**, 1–16.

CONNECTIONISM IN PERSPECTIVE
R. Pfeifer, Z. Schreter, F. Fogelman-Soulié, L. Steels (Eds.)

Electrical Networks and a Connectionist Approach to Path-finding *

Erwin Prassler
Computer Science Department, Technical University of Munich
Arcisstr. 21, D-8000 Munich 2, Fed. Rep. of Germany
prassler@tumult.informatik.tu-muenchen.de

Abstract—*Path-finding has been an almost traditional subject for designing and investigating computer algorithms. A repertoire of classical algorithms operating on graph structures has been developed to solve path-finding problems under various aspects. We can identify two characteristic properties of these algorithms. Path-finding is typically treated as a sequential problem and the time required to solve path-finding problems is a nonlinear function of the number of nodes or a function of the number of arcs of the graph structure. In this paper we suggest an alternative approach which is based on a parallel distributed processing paradigm. While the approach, in its global convergency behavior, also depends on the number of processing elements, the number of parallel processing steps, required to find a path, linearly depends on the distance between source and destination of the desired path.*

Keywords—Spatial problem solving, path-finding, shortest path algorithms, sequential search, connectionist processing methods, gradient ascent

1 INTRODUCTION

This paper is concerned with *spatial problem solving*, especially with *path-finding*. Questions such as "Is there a path between point A and B?" or "Is there a path between point A and B that fulfills some constraint X?" characterize a class of problems solved by almost every mobile creature day by day without any mathematical analysis. In spite of that fact, the formalization of path-finding problems and the development of problem solving methods has attracted the attention of mathematicians for centuries. We have only to think of Leonhard Euler and the well-known problem of the *Konigsberger bridges*.[1]

A common way of formalizing path-finding problems is to describe the spatial environment the problem has to be solved in by means of a graph consisting of a set of *nodes* and a set of *arcs*, connecting pairs of nodes (see fig. 1). Nodes correspond to places which might be *source* or *destination* of travelling actions within a spatial environment. Arcs correspond to objects that allow traversal of the space between pairs of places or they simply express geographical adjacency between places. A path between two places in a

*This work was funded by the Deutsche Forschungsgemeinschaft (DFG) under grant Br 609/4-1.

spatial environment is described in a graph as a sequence of arcs connecting source and destination nodes via a set of intermediate nodes. Usually this sequence of arcs is also denoted as a *path*.

Based on those representations mathematicians and computer scientists have developed a repertoire of classical algorithms handling path-finding problems under various aspects. Essentially, two different kinds of approaches to path-finding problems can be found in these algorithms. One approach is to set up the adjacency matrix M of a graph G and then to compute the *transitive closure* M^* of this matrix, as it is done for example in FLOYD's algorithm (Aho et al., 1983). In M^* every path that exists in G is recorded and once M^* is computed the desired path (if it exists) can be simply looked up in this matrix.[2] However, computing M^* is very expensive. FLOYD's algorithm, for example, takes n^3 operations to compute M^*, i.e. it is of order $O(n^3)$, where n is the number of nodes in G. This kind of approach becomes inefficient when n becomes large ($n \gg 1000$).

In cases where it is not desirable to compute every existing path in a graph in advance, one might refer to another class of algorithms, searching a path only for one pair of source and destination nodes. Using some kind of search strategy, for example *depth-first search*, these algorithms successively construct sequences of arcs connecting the source node to other nodes in G, until a sequence is found that connects source node and destination node. Without any criterion that allows the search process to focus on the relevant part of a graph, i.e. on the part "between" source and destination, it might be necessary to investigate every arc in the graph. Therefore, the total amount of operations necessary to perform a the depth-first search of an entire graph, for example, is bound to $O(e)$, where e is the number of arcs in the graph.

Due to the underlying sequential and symbolic processing paradigm the above-mentioned approaches show two weaknesses. The time required to solve a path-finding problem basically depends on the extension of the underlying graph structure, i.e. on the number of nodes and arcs, and not on the length of the desired path. Therefore the application of those algorithms to larger graph structures is somewhat limited. Moreover, those approaches are not able and not supposed to cope with changes in the physical environment detected during the locomotion along an elaborated path. Changes, such as the interruption of a means of transportation, which are not detected until the real world correspondent of an elaborated path is traversed always require a reconsideration of the situation and the problem and a recomputation of the path after the graph structure has been modified properly.

Both of these properties, however, bring discredit with respect to more realistic applications such as the development of travel-plans for autonomous mobile vehicles. Growing interest in those applications as well as the upcoming of new, massively parallel processing paradigms have meanwhile led to some new approaches to path-finding problems (Miyata, 1988; Ritter, 1988; Steels, 1988).

In the remainder of this paper we describe an approach based on a parallel distributed processing scheme which is intended to overcome these shortcomings of classical algorithms. A graph is looked at as a network of simple processing elements in this approach. By means of external excitation of source and destination nodes of a path-finding task and

[1] In Konigsberg, the former capital of the German province East Prussia (now the Russian city of Kaliningrad), a park was built along the banks of the river Pregel and on two islands in the river. Within the park seven bridges connected the islands and the river banks. The problem, known as the problem of the *Konigsberger bridges*, is to find a path through the park that crosses every bridge once and only once.

[2] Those algorithms are denoted as *all pair shortest path* algorithms (Aho et al., 1983)

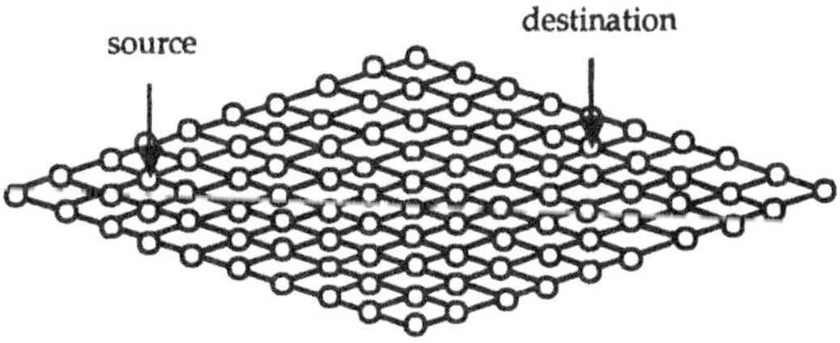

Figure 1: A path-finding problem formulated on an undirected graph consisting of 10 × 10 nodes, every node being connected to 4 neighboring nodes.

a relaxation process we provide an overall distribution of activation in the network, where the desired path is determined by maximum gradients between the activation of nodes of the network.

2 A CONNECTIONIST APPROACH TO PATH-FINDING

Let us look at an undirected graph as shown in fig. 1. How can a path between two arbitrary nodes in this graph be found without sequential search? What is needed is a local criterion that allows us to decide at every node which arc has to be traversed to approach the destination. An idea is to regard a graph not as a "flat" data structure but to introduce a kind of third dimension that yields a criterion for the relevance of an arc as part of the solution. One might think of a graph as a net thrown over a mountaineous landscape. With source and destination node of the desired path lying on the bottom and on the top of a mountain respectively, the gradient between two nodes would be a criterion to assess whether an arc belongs to the desired path or not. To find the shortest path we simply have to follow the maximum ascent. Of course, such a mountaineous landscape is required for every arbitrary pair of source and destination, i.e. this structure has to be created dynamically depending on the problem that has to be solved.

In order to dynamically create such a structure we make use of an analogy from the field of electrical networks. For a moment, we will look at a graph as a network of equal electrical resistors with arcs corresponding to resistors and nodes corresponding to their physical connections. After clamping two nodes in this network to the positive and negative terminals of a direct current source, the overall distribution of potentials arising in the network looks similar to the mountainous landscape. There is a kind of valley in terms of negative potentials around the negative terminal and a kind of mountain in terms of positive potentials around the positive terminal. At every node, except the terminal nodes, the potential approximately equals the average of potentials at neighboring nodes. We can find the shortest path between the positive and negative terminals with respect to the number of resistors by following the maximum potential gradient.

The basic idea of our approach is to simulate the behavior of such electrical networks.

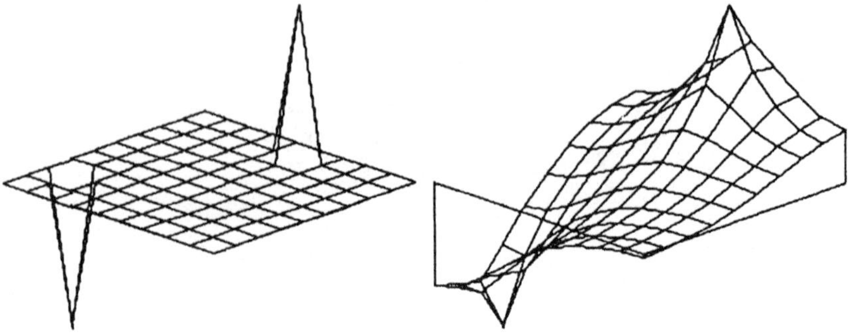

(a) (b)

Figure 2: Figure (a) shows the distribution of activation in a 10×10 network after clamping two input nodes to values -10 and +10, (b) renders the distribution of activation after 20 simulation steps when the activation gradients characterizing the shortest path, which is a sequence of 10 arcs, have emerged.

We assume that the graph is a network of simple, parallel processing units. Every node v_i is associated with an activation value $a(v_i)$, which equals 0 as long as the network is in a state of rest. To solve a path-finding task, two nodes, namely source and destination of the desired path, are clamped to activation values -10 and +10, i.e. these nodes act as input nodes receiving permanently external input. According to the electrical network metaphor the network relaxes by every node v_i striving to adjust its activation value $a(v_i)$ to the average of activation values of adjacent nodes. This adjustment operation is described by the following activation rule:

$$a(v_i) = \begin{cases} -10, & \text{if } v_i \text{ is source} \\ +10, & \text{if } v_i \text{ is destination} \\ \frac{1}{\rho_i}\sum_j r_{ji}a(v_j), & \text{otherwise,} \end{cases} \tag{1}$$

where $r_{ji} \in \{0, 1\}$ and $r_{ji} = r_{ij} = 1$, if there is an arc between v_i and v_j, and ρ_i is the *fan in* of v_i, i.e. the number of nodes v_j that are connected to v_i by an arc. To keep the network out of oscillations we let the relaxation process work asynchronously (Hopfield, 1982). This means at a given point in time every node has a fixed probability of applying its activation rule and adjusting its activation value. If this probability is equal for every node it is assured that within a certain period of time every node performs one such adjustment operation. This period is denoted as a *simulation step*.

A path-finding task is solved if this relaxation process leads to a pattern of activation which makes it possible to unambiguously determine the shortest sequence of arcs connecting source and destination. As mentioned above the information necessary to determine a path is encoded in the ascent of activation between adjacent nodes. If the desired activation pattern has emerged, a path between source and destination can simply be read off by starting at the source node and following at every node the particular arc which points to the most activated adjacent node until the destination node is reached.

In the following section we will show that the described approach indeed exhibits the desired behavior and leads to a pattern of activation which allows the determination of the desired path.

3 GLOBAL AND LOCAL BEHAVIOR

In our model, path-finding problems are formulated on the structure of an undirected graph. Connections between nodes in this structure are undirected, i.e. they are bidirectional. According to equation (1) a node v_i receives input from v_j to an amount proportional to $r'_{ji} = r_{ji}/\rho_i$ whereas v_j is activated by v_i proportionally to $r'_{ij} = r_{ij}/\rho_j$. Thus the connection between v_i and v_j is asymmetrical unless $\rho_i = \rho_j$. However, for every pair of connected nodes there are coefficients η_i and η_j such that

$$\eta_i r'_{ji} = \eta_j r'_{ij} \tag{2}$$

With this, we can use a variation of Almeida's energy function (Almeida, 1987, p. 614), suggested for recurrent networks,

$$E = -\frac{1}{2}\sum_{i \neq j}\sum a(v_i)a(v_j) + \sum_j \rho_j a(v_j)^2 \tag{3}$$

to prove that the relaxation process will get into an equilibrium state. Since for the adjustment operation of every arbitrary node v_i it holds that

$$\Delta E = -\frac{1}{2}\rho_i \Delta a(v_i)^2 < 0 \tag{4}$$

the energy E in the network decreases monotonically and the network will reach an equilibrium state. It is evident that the number c of simulation steps necessary to reach the equilibrium depends on the number n of nodes in the graph and it has shown that this number of simulation steps[3] is bound by n.

A more interesting fact is that the network does not need to settle into a global equilibrium state in order to find a shortest path. Rather, the network soon gets into a state where the flow of activation becomes very small and the activation gradients between adjacent nodes are almost stable. In 903 out of 1000 tests on a 20×20 network it took not more than $2d$ simulation steps to find a shortest path, where d is the distance between source and destination.

This seems to be quite intuitive, since the activation of the input nodes spreads out in a wavelike manner in the network and the activation value of a particular node "between"

[3]Since during a simulation step c every node performs one adjustment operation, reaching equilibrium altogether requires not more than n^2 single operations

source and destination becomes influenced by both input nodes after not more than d simulation steps. However, in our tests we also had cases where it took $10d$ and more simulation steps to find a shortest path. The activation rule in (1) therefore does not yield a linear dependency between the distance between source and destination and the number of required simulation steps, as it would be desirable.

Several interplaying reasons lead to those undesired situations where $10d$ and more simulation steps are necessary to find a shortest path. According to the activation rule in (1) a particular node v_i becomes influenced by a particular input node x after $d(v_i, x)$ simulation steps at a rate r, $|r| \geq |a(x)/\rho^{\,d(v_i,x)}|$, where ρ is the medium fan in and $d(v_i, x)$ is the distance between v_i and x. Thus the influence of an input node on a particular node v_i depends on the medium fan in and decreases exponentially with the distance of v_i. As a consequence of this the activation ascent between source and destination is not linear. There are steep ascents in the proximity of source and destination and flat ascents in some distance to source and destination. In spite of this nonlinearity the arising gradients in most cases allow it to decide unambiguously at every node which arc to traverse in order to approach the destination.

Undesired effects, however, may occur if input nodes are positioned too excentrically, i.e. close to a border of the network. In those cases some nodes, lying at a border and in the proximity of an input node, very soon become highly activated and keep their activation, whereas a large number of nodes stay in their initial state for some time because of their distance to the input units. Because of symmetry of connections in our networks an accumulation of nodes, associated with an activation value 0, itself acts as a force drawing neighboring parts of the network towards 0, where 0, however, is the initial value of a node and not a value that has arisen through correct adjustment operations. This may cause a distortion in the distribution of activation with steepest gradients leading to erroneous, i.e. not the shortest, paths. Thus 0 is not a neutral value for describing the state of rest of a node. Distortions, however, disappear as the relaxation process proceeds and the above mentioned accumulation of nodes itself gets adjusted.

So far we have tacitly assumed a quite regular structure of our networks (see fig. 1). Effects, similar to those just described, occur if the network is structured arbitrarily with every node having an arbitrary fan in. In those networks, even without source or destination being excentrically positioned, usually more than $2d$ steps were necessary to come up with a proper solution to a path-finding problem.

In order to find shortest paths without any restrictions concerning the position of source and destination node or the structure of the network but with an effort that linearly depends on the distance between source and destination we have slightly modified the activation rule in (1) to

$$a(v_i) = \begin{cases} -10, & \text{if } v_i \text{ is source} \\ +10, & \text{if } v_i \text{ is destination} \\ \frac{1}{2}(\max_j r_{ji}a(v_j) + \min_j r_{ji}a(v_j)), & \text{otherwise.} \end{cases} \tag{5}$$

Whereas in (1) a node adjusted its own activation to the medium of the activation values of all its neighbors it now computes its activation as the medium of the maximum and minimum activation values of adjacent nodes. Through this modification the rate at which a node v_i is influenced by an input node x after $d(v_i, x)$ steps is r', with

$|r'| \geq |a(x)/2^{d(v_i,x)}| > |r|$. The activation rule in (5) therefore leads to influence r' of an input node to a particular node which is not only independent of the fan in, but has also increased compared with the influence caused by (1). A second modification concerns the activation value describing the state of rest of a node. As already mentioned, problems arose in the primary approach by choosing 0 as the initial activation value of a node. Experimentally it has shown that those problems can be avoided by an initial activation value -10 which is equal to the input value to the source node.
In another series of 1000 tests this modified activation rule has in fact shown to be independent of the position of source and destination as well as of the structure of the network. Moreover, in all tests it took only d simulation steps to produce a correct solution, i.e. to find a shortest path. Thus the activation rule in (5) allows it to solve a path-finding problem with an amount of operation that linearly and solely depends on the distance between source and destination.

As described in the previous section, the rule used to determine a path by means of the activation pattern in the network is to follow at every node the particular arc pointing to the most activated neighboring node. An autonomous vehicle, for instance, following the real world correspondent of a path determined this way is guaranteed to move along the shortest path between source and destination. Breaking this rule by following arcs which do not always point to the most activated neighboring node will lead to paths which, of course, do not represent a shortest connection of source and destination.

However, it is even necessary to deviate from this rule if we want to cope with situations, where changes in spatial environment detected during the locomotion along an elaborated path, for example by an autonomous vehicle, prevent a continuation of the locomotion. If the real world correspondent of an elaborated path is interrupted unexpectedly at some point in the environment, i.e. the real world correspondent of an arc cannot be traversed, a detour within a classical approach can be worked out only by redefining the path-finding task and by elaborating a new solution. In our model, however, a detour can be found by simply considering the arc whose real world correspondent is not traversable and determining an alternative arc whose ascent is closest to the ascent of the considered arc. The only information needed for this is already encoded in the activation pattern of the network. To determine an alternative arc we simply have to compare the activation values of the neighbors of the particular node where the interruption has been detected. A detour can than be completed by again following the steepest activation ascents until the destination is reached.

Thus in our model the activation pattern that is caused by the initial path-finding task also provides information which allows it easily to deal with dynamical changes of the environment without any additional computational effort.

4 CONCLUSION

The approach suggested in this paper does not claim to replace algorithms which have proven to be powerful methods for solving path-finding tasks. It is even questionable whether it is comparable to them at all. The only reasonable measure to compare our model to a sequential algorithm would be the number of operations performed by every processing element times the number of the processing elements. But this measure, of course, neglects the appeal of a massively parallel, distributed model, based on the assumption of the availability of an in principle unlimited set of cooperating processing elements.

Altogether, the approach shows that path-finding is not a problem that can be solved by nature only sequentially; it also shows that the number of operations required to solve a path-finding task does not need to increase with the extension of the underlying spatial representation, i.e. the graph structure. Rather, we have been developing a model that is able to solve a path-finding task with an amount of operations which is proportional to the distance between source and destination and is independent of the extension of the underlying spatial representation.

REFERENCES

Aho, A., Hopcroft, J., & Ullman, J. (1983). *Data Structures and Algorithms*. Reading, MA: Addison Wesley.

Almeida, L. (1987). A learning rule for asynchronous perceptrons with feedback in a combinatorial environment. In *IEEE 1st International Conference on Neural Networks*.

Hopfield, J. (1982). Neural networks and physical systems with emergent collective computational abilities. In *Proceedings of the National Academy of Science*, **79**, pp. 2554–2558, USA.

Miyata, Y. (1988). The learning and planning of actions. ICS Report 8802, Institute for Cognitive Science, University of California, La Jolla, CA.

Ritter, H. (1988). *Selbstorganisierende neuronale Karte*. PhD thesis, Physik-Department, Technische Universitat Munchen.

Steels, L. (1988). Steps towards common sense. AI MEMO 88-3, VUB AI Lab, Brussels.

CONNECTIONISM IN PERSPECTIVE
R. Pfeifer, Z. Schreter, F. Fogelman-Soulié, L. Steels (Eds.)

The Neural Bucket Brigade

Jürgen Schmidhuber*
Institut für Informatik, Technische Universität München
Arcisstr. 21, 8000 München 2, Germany
schmidhu@tumult.informatik.tu-muenchen.de

Abstract—*Although there are straightforward methods for training neural nets to show certain types of sequential behavior, the general problem of structural and temporal credit assignment (appropriate weight changes) in networks existing in a changing environment remains unsolved. In this paper we argue that a learning mechanism for finding temporal input/output relations ought to depend solely on computations local in both space and time, and that no teacher should be required to indicate the starts and ends of relevant sequences to the network. We ask whether there are learning rules which do not depend on such external hints yet still can deal with 'hidden units' and with units whose past activations are 'hidden in time'. (Back propagation, for instance, is not even local in time.) We propose a discrete time version and a continuous time version of a simple on-line method local in space and time which is designed to deal with hidden states. The approach is inspired by Holland's idea of the bucket brigade for classifier systems, which is transformed to run on a neural network with fixed topology. The result is a recurrent 'neural' dissipative system which is consuming 'weight-substance' and permanently trying to distribute this substance onto its connections in an appropriate way. Simple experiments demonstrating the feasability of the algorithm are reported.*

Keywords—recurrent networks, credit assignment, local computations, dissipative systems, autonomous agents, internal feedback, external feedback, reinforcement learning, supervised learning, neural bucket brigade.

1 MOTIVATION

Many researchers in the field of neural network research are concerned with the study of static input/output mappings, emphasizing the parallel aspects of such networks. Standard methods for supervised learning of such mappings are Werbos' back propagation (BP)(Werbos, 1974) and Almeida's extension (Almeida, 1987) for networks with arbitrary feedback, where the activations flowing through the network have to reach a state of equilibrium. However, if we want a net to learn sequences of time-dependent outputs then an equilibrium is something we usually wish to avoid. Rumelhart, Hinton and Williams show how to correctly use BP for learning time-dependencies by utilizing Minsky and Papert's

*Research supported by a scholarship of SIEMENS AG

idea of unfolding a recurrent net into a feedforward net (Rumelhart et al., 1986). We will point out reasons why such an approach cannot give a satisfactory solution for all problems involved with time, and we want to present some constructive criticism.

A general setting for dynamic actions depending on dynamic inputs is given in the case of an autonomous agent existing in a changing environment. The agent, which shall be regarded preliminarily as a black box, is continuously receiving inputs from the environment by means of simple feature detectors. The agent is able to produce outputs (actions) by means of effectors which may influence the state of the environment. Since useful actions in general depend on previous temporal context the agent must be able to let future system states depend on the current state (i.e. short time memory storage in activations wandering around feedback loops). The agent is expected to learn succesful temporal behavior depending on time varying perceptions from the environment.

We can identify learning situations with different degrees of supervision: In a highly unsupervised situation only a global reinforcement signal may be available to the system at isolated points in time. In a highly supervised situation any part of the system is instructed by the environment at any time. In between these extremes there is a continuum of possibilities. Recurrent BP, for instance, requires teaching signals just for a subset of all units.

The system ought to find relevant structures in spatial/temporal input patterns by means of a memory that stores just the significant aspects of some particular input. Here 'relevance' and 'significance' is implicitly defined by the environment which rewards certain actions and punishes others. However, the system generally does not know in advance which spatial/temporal input patterns are relevant for fulfilling the tasks. It generally does not know how much time some particular relevant input sequence takes. It generally does not even know the beginning of such a sequence.

If the inside of the black box was a recurrent BP network the teacher would have to provide such information *a priori*: The teacher would have to tell the network when to start spreading activation, and he would have to tell it when to stop and start back-propagaton and weight changing. We identify one of the main problems of such BP networks in not being 'really' local. Although (Rumelhart et al., 1986) say that BP is a 'local' algorithm in so far as all relevant information needed to change some weight (error signal and activation signal) becomes available close to the weight (in a physical sense), BP is only what we informally call 'local in space'. It is not 'local in time', since in general the weight-changing pieces of information appear at very different, externally controlled points in time. [1]

If the inside of the black box was a network taught by an extended REINFORCE algorithm (Williams, 1988) then there would be no need of extensive book-keeping of past activations, as with BP. However, even in this case starts and ends of sequences would have to be indicated by an external teacher. Weights would not change permanently, but only after accumulation of activation information for a predefined number of time steps.

Correlation based learning rules like Hebb's rule, or e.g. Grossberg's and Kohonen's modifications, are local in both space and time and are not concerned with starts and ends of sequences. Such rules make external control of the global system behavior unnecessary. However, these methods seem to lack the ability to deal with hidden units and with unit

[1] Recently Williams and Zipser have introduced a procedure for 'supervised' learning which is local in time but not in space (Williams and Zipser, 1988).

activations hidden in time. We now ask whether there are methods local in space and time that require a minimum of external teaching information (in the sense described above) and *still* allow credit assignment to hidden units and to units whose past activations are hidden in time.

2 CLASSIFIER SYSTEMS AND THE BUCKET BRIGADE

Holland (Holland, 1985) has proposed the meanwhile well-known bucket brigade algorithm for classifier systems, which in principle incorporates the desirable properties mentioned above. In this section we shortly review the main idea of this algorithm.

Messages in form of bitstrings of size n can be placed on a global message list either by the environment or by entities called classifiers. Each classifier consists of a condition part and an action part defining a message it might send to the message list. Both parts are strings out of $\{0, 1, \_\}^n$ where the '_' serves as a 'don't care' if it appears in the condition part. (Less important for our purposes, the '_' serves as a 'pass-through' if it appears in the action part.) A non-negative real number is associated with each classifier indicating its 'strength'.

During one cycle all messages on the message list are compared with the condition parts of all classifiers of the system. Each matching classifier computes a 'bid' by multiplying its specificity (the number of non-don't cares in its condition part) with the product of its strength and a small factor. The highest bidding classifiers may place their message on the message list of the next cycle, but they have to pay with their bid which is distributed among the classifiers active during the last time step which set up the triggering conditions (this explains the name bucket brigade).

Certain messages result in an action within the environment (like moving a robot one step). Because some of these actions may be regarded as 'useful' by an external critic who can give payoff by increasing the strengths of the currently active classifiers, learning may take place. The central idea is that classifiers which are not active when the environment gives payoff but which had an important role for setting the stage for directly rewarded classifiers can earn credit by participating in 'bucket brigade chains'. The success of some active classifier recursively depends on the success of classifiers that are active at the following time ticks.

As an additional means for improving performance Holland introduces a genetic algorithm to construct new classifiers from old successful ones. This feature will not be important for our purposes.

3 THE NEURAL BUCKET BRIGADE

In this section we propose a combination of principles of the bucket brigade algorithm with principles of neural networks. Competition can be introduced naturally into neural networks by a mechanism of lateral inhibition. What we still need is a mechanism analogous to the process of bidding and paying in classifier systems. This mechanism must establish recursive dependencies 'through time'. We introduce a local method for shifting 'weight substance' (initially provided by the environment) from weights that are allowed to transport activation information at a certain time to those weights that were 'setting the stage' one time tick earlier. We assume the following scenario for the inside of the black box:

The basic structure is some rather arbitrary cyclic directed graph, where the nodes are quite familiar processing units. Some units are used for input purposes, others serve as outputs and may be coupled with effectors that may change the environment, which in turn may change the current input. Thus we have external and internal feedback.

The set of non-input units is partitioned into predefined 'competitive subsets'. All non-input units synchronously try to get activated by summing their weighted inputs at each time tick. All members of a predefined competitive subset laterally inhibit each other (by some 'winner-take-all' mechanism) thus competing for being active. All weights are randomly initialized with a positive real value, and are modifiable. Initially we will assume that there is instant decay: A unit active at time t manages to send its contributions to connected units that try to get activated at $t+1$, then the sender is switched off instantly.

All units active at time t *take away a fraction of the positive weights of their outgoing connections (if there are any) that lead to winners active at time t+1, and distribute this 'weight-substance' proportionally to the respective contributions among the incoming connections (if there are any) coming from winners (or input units) active at time t-1.* Since the weights determine the context-dependent strength of a unit, winners 'get paid' for setting the stage for their successors. Input units do not have any incoming connections that they could strengthen, they get activated by the environment thus representing holes through which the weight-substance of the system is leaking. The environment's influence is completed by sometimes rewarding (or punishing) the connections to currently active units in the case of useful output behavior. (An external critic decides what kind of behavior is useful.) The sum of all positive weights in the system remains constant, except for the weight-substance that is leaking through the input units and the new substance that is entering the system in the case of payoff. Thus we have a dissipative system which is consuming weight-substance provided by the environment.

More formally, at time t we denote the activation of the jth unit by $x_j(t)$, the weight on the directed connection between units i and j by $w_{ij}(t)$, and the contribution of some connection by $c_{ij}(t) = x_i(t-1)w_{ij}(t-1)$.

The activation rule works as follows: Unit j gets activated at time t if it is an input unit and receives a perception, or if it wins the competition between the units in the competitive subset it belongs to by having the largest positive net input $net_j(t) = \sum_i c_{ij}(t)$. We assume the simplest case: $x_j(t)$ equals 1 if unit j is active, and 0 otherwise.

If unit j is active then its weights change according to

$$\Delta w_{ij}(t) = -\lambda c_{ij}(t) + \frac{c_{ij}(t-1)}{\sum_i c_{ij}(t-1)} \sum_{k\, wins} \lambda c_{jk}(t) + Ext_{ij}(t)$$

where $0 < \lambda < 1$ determines how much of its weight some particular connection has to pay to those connections that were responsible for setting the stage at the previous time step. $Ext_{ij}(t)$ is the 'external payoff' that the environment gives to w_{ij} at time t, and may be computed like this: If the external critic does not know at time t whether useful behavior took place then $Ext_{ij}(t) = 0$. Else, if the critic notices a useful action , and if unit j was active at time t, then $Ext_{ij}(t) = \eta c_{ij}(t)$ with η being a proportionality factor. There is much room for more or less supervised strategies to determine Ext_{ij}: Every unit might get instructed at every time step, or just a few units at certain isolated time steps, etc.

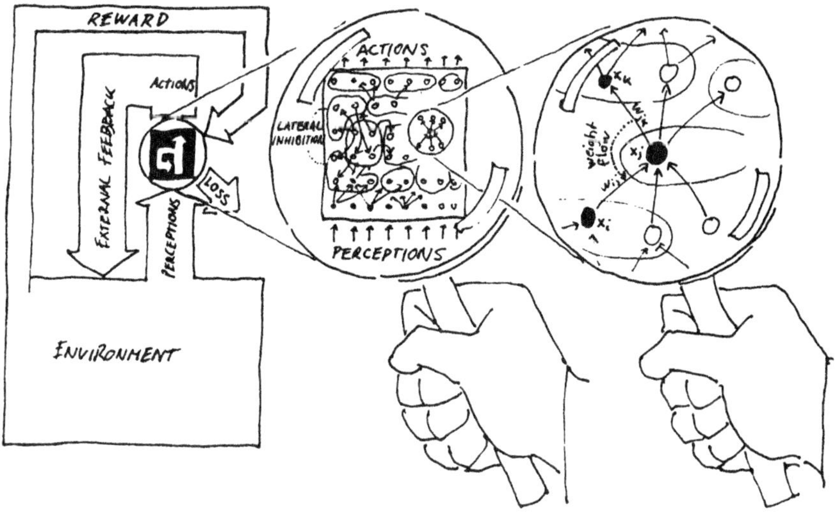

Figure 1: Weight substance given by the environment in case of successful behavior is flowing through an agent living in a changing environment. The direction of weight flow is opposite to the direction of activation flow originating from perceptions. Credit assignment (appropriate weight changes) is done by local computations only. (See text for full explanation).

The *weights* of the system (as opposed to the activations in Hopfield-networks or feedback-BP) have reached a stable state when every connection at any time is giving back as much weight-substance as it is receiving during the next time step. This means that (parallel) chains of units and connections cooperating in time have evolved.

It is important to see the local character of this method. No book-keeping of past activations is required, not even the accumulative computation of, say, a weighted sum of past activations. Each weight and each unit in principle performs the same operation at each time tick. No such things as 'epoch boundaries' are required during training.

However, the method introduced above still has elements of global control: There is the clock for synchronous updates, for instance. To come closer to asynchronous models from biology we now give up the assumption of predefined competitive subsets and of instant decay. To save the concept of winning units we explicitly introduce fixed inhibitory connections (e.g. an on-center-off-surround structure (see (Kohonen, 1988) and (Grossberg, 1976)). We assume that the output x_j of unit j and the transmission properties of the connections are governed by differential equations that say that x_j does not change significantly during the time needed to transport activation information from one unit to its successors. Then we may write down a continuous time version of the weight changes caused by the neural bucket brigade in case of net_j being greater than zero:

$$\frac{\partial w_{ij}}{\partial t} = -\lambda x_i w_{ij} x_j + \frac{x_i w_{ij}}{\sum_i x_i w_{ij}} \sum_k \lambda x_j w_{jk} x_k + Ext_{ij}$$

Only positive weights appear in this formula, the inhibitory connections have to remain fixed. Tentatively denoting $\sum_k w_{jk} x_k$ by $back_j$ we find (by letting $\frac{\partial w_{ij}}{\partial t} = 0$) that the weight-flow through a positive weight w_{ij} that does not receive external payoff has reached a dynamic equilibrium if net_j equals $back_j$ all the time.

4 SIMPLE EXPERIMENTS

Any algorithm for learning sequential tasks also should allow the learning of static pattern association, since static learning tasks can be viewed as sequential tasks where inputs and desired outputs do not change over time.

In a preliminary experiment we tested whether the NBB is capable of adjusting a network such that it solves a static non-linearily separable task. The classical example for such a task is the XOR-problem.

The network was of the feed-forward type: A layer of three input units was connected to a predefined competitive subset of three hidden units and a predefined competitive subset of two output units. The subset of hidden units also was connected to the subset of output-units.

The discrete time version of the algorithm described above was employed. 32-bit floating point arithmetic was used for the simulations. In the beginning all weights were randomly initialized between 0.999 and 1.001. At the beginning of each cycle all unit activations were reset to 0, and one of the four binary XOR input patterns was randomly chosen. During the cycle this pattern was presented to the first two input units for a period of 6 time ticks. The activation of the remaining input unit was always set to 1, in order to provide a modifiable bias for every non-input unit in the network.

The task for the network was to switch on the first output unit if the XOR of the input pattern was 1, and to switch on the second output unit otherwise. The task was formulated as a reinforcement learning task: At each time tick the environment gave a payoff (playing a role similar to the role of a reinforcement signal) $Ext_{ij}(t) = \eta c_{ij}(t)$ to w_{ij} if unit j was an output unit and if it was switched on correctly at time t. In all other cases $Ext_{ij}(t)$ was set equal to 0. (Recall that payoff can be considered as a bit of weight substance which has to be distributed in an appropriate way by the NBB algorithm.) Both η and λ were set equal to 0.005.

The network was said to correctly classify a single pattern if it switched on the corresponding output unit during the last three time ticks of a cycle, without the weight changing mechanism being employed. The network was said to have solved the problem if it correctly classified the four input patterns.

During 20 test runs the network needed an average of 619 pattern presentations to find a solution. So each of the four patterns had to be presented for about 155 times, which corresponds to the notion of 155 'epochs'. No systematic attempt has been undertaken to optimize this performance.

Most of the 20 solutions were brittle in the sense that further training did not necessarily stabilize them. For instance, after a solution had been found, another 5 training cycles could lead to worse performance, again. So we measured the number of cycles needed to achieve a stable solution.

A solution was considered to be stable if 100 additional pattern presentations did not disturb the performance of the network. During 10 test runs it was found that each pattern had to be presented for about 674 times in order to reach this criterion.

We also conducted experiments where the input patterns for successive cycles were not chosen randomly but in periodical sequential order. Here we found that the average time to find a solution increased, and that the solutions tended to be more brittle in the sense that it took much longer to achieve stable solutions. This suggests that the random element in the process of pattern selection introduces a stabilizing effect. One might suppose that similar stabilizing effects could be achieved by using stochastic activation rules. However, this has not been tested.

Where can instabilities arise from? The brittleness of the first solutions was attributed to the empirically observed fact that competing units within a competitive subset often had very similar net inputs. This in turn was attributed to a property of the NBB algorithm: Weights of connections leading to units that loose a competition remain the same. Consider a unit j that does not participate in a bucket brigade chain causing a correct classification of pattern A. This means that j's weights do not change. If the weights of j are slightly increased during the presentation of another correctly classified pattern, this modification may also lead to a winning situation for j during the next presentation of A, if the net input of the competitor of j who usually won during A's presentation was only slightly larger than j's net input. This may cause an incorrect classification of A. The interplay of these effects may lead to instabilities.

The *raisons d'être* for the NBB are non-stationary environments. One of the simplest tasks involving non-stationary environments may be to recognize different kinds of motion. We conducted a simple experiment with varying perceptions. A one dimensional 'retina' consisting of 5 input units (plus one additional unit which was always turned on) was fully connected to a competitive subset of two ouput units. This subset of output units was completely connected to itself, in order to allow recurrency. The task for the network was to switch on the first output unit after an illumination point has wandered across the retina from the left to the right (within 5 time ticks), and to switch on the first output unit after the illumination point has wandered from the right to the left.

During one cycle one of the two sequences (which had been chosen randomly) was presented to the network twice. Payoff was given as described for the stationary experiment, the same initialization and the same parameters η and λ were used. In 1 out of 10 test runs the network did not find a stable solution within 3000 cycles (according to a criterion analogue to the one used for the stationary experiment). In the remaining 9 test runs an average of 223 cycles per sequence were needed to achieve a stable solution.

The experiments described above share a rather simple nature. It remains to be seen how well the NBB can deal with more difficult problems, like the learning of motor control for autonomous agents in a changing environment. We currently do not have sufficient empirical and mathematical results to decide under which environmental circumstances solutions represent attractors, and how fast convergence could be.

5 CONCLUDING REMARKS

There is an analogy between the NBB and competitive learning (Grossberg, 1976)(Kohonen, 1988)(Rumelhart and Zipser, 1986). Competitive learning also can be interpreted as a shifting of weight substance. However, here it is the weakly contributing incoming connections to a unit that have to pay to the strongly contributing incoming connections. In contrast, the NBB causes weight shifts from outgoing to incoming connections. This is the key feature used for relating present system states to past states.

Due to the local nature of all computations, the discrete time version can easily be implemented such that the time complexity of one update cycle (activation changes and weight changes) is $O(n)$ where n is the number of weights in the system. For some particular connection all information needed at a given time is its current weight, its contribution during the current time step and its contribution during the last time step. For some particular unit all information needed at a given time is its current activation, the summed contributions it receives during the current time step, and the summed contributions it received during the last time step.

Short term memory can be identified in activations wandering around feedback loops. Such loops may even become stable: A competitive subset of units that is permanently referencing itself can lead to a local dynamic equilibrium of weight flow (and of activation flow running in the opposite direction). Such equilibria may get perturbed by new inputs from the environment or from other competitive subsets that do not participate in the loop.

One difference to Holland's bucket brigade algorithm is that there is no analogue to the creation of new classifiers at run time: The number of connections in an NBB system remains fixed. The justification for this is given by the fact that weights are modifiable, while the 'specificity' of a classifier is not. (In (Compiani et al., 1989) Compiani, Montanari, Serra and Valastro consider more relationships between classifier systems and neural networks.)

Finally we would like to address the question of biological plausibility. We certainly do not want to suggest that the brain uses a weight shifting mechanism for e.g. physically transporting transmitter substance from synapses of outgoing connections to synapses of incoming connections. However, we do not want to exclude the possibility that some kind of feedback mechanism exists whose effects on the synapses are similar to the effects caused by the NBB.

A major property of the brain seems to be that the motoric actions which it causes depend on local computations only. The major contribution of this paper is to propose at least one possibility for how completely local computations within a neural network-like system may lead to goal directed parallel/sequential behavior.

The NBB represents a general credit assignment scheme for neural network-like structures. 'General' often seems to imply 'weak'. How 'weak' is the NBB? It remains to be seen whether the NBB can be successfully applied to difficult control tasks.

REFERENCES

Almeida, L. B. (1987). A learning rule for asynchronous perceptrons with feedback in a combinatorial environment. In *IEEE 1st International Conference on Neural Networks, Vol 2*.

Compiani, M., Montanari, D., Serra, R., and Valastro, G. (1989). Classifier systems and neural networks. In Caianello, E. R., editor, *1st Workshop on Parallel Architectures and Neural Nets*.

Grossberg, S. (1976). Adaptive pattern classification and universal recoding, 1: Parallel development and coding of neural feature detectors. *Biological Cybernetics*, 23.

Holland, J. H. (1985). Properties of the bucket brigade. In *1st Conference on Genetic Algorithms*.

Kohonen, T. (1988). *Self-Organization and Associative Memory*. Springer.

Rumelhart, D. E., Hinton, G. E., and Williams, R. J. (1986). Learning internal representations by error propagation. In (Rumelhart and McClelland, 1986).

Rumelhart, D. E. and McClelland, J. L., editors (1986). *Parallel Distributed Processing*, volume 1. MIT Press.

Rumelhart, D. E. and Zipser, D. (1986). Feature discovery by competitive learning. In (Rumelhart and McClelland, 1986).

Werbos, P. J. (1974). *Beyond Regression: New Tools for Prediction and Analysis in the Behavioral Sciences*. PhD thesis, Harvard University.

Williams, R. J. (1988). Toward a theory of reinforcement-learning connectionist systems. Technical Report NU-CCS-88-3, College of Comp. Sci., Northeastern University, Boston, MA.

Williams, R. J. and Zipser, D. (1988). A learning algorithm for continually running fully recurrent networks. Technical Report ICS Report 8805, Univ. of California, San Diego, La Jolla.

CONNECTIONISM IN PERSPECTIVE
R. Pfeifer, Z. Schreter, F. Fogelman-Soulié, L. Steels (Eds.)

Accelerated Learning in Back-Propagation Nets

Jürgen Schmidhuber, Institut für Informatik
Technische Universität München
Arcisstr. 21, 8000 München 2, Germany
schmidhu@tumult.informatik.tu-muenchen.de

Abstract—*Two of the most serious problems with back-propagation (bp) (Werbos, 1974) (Parker, 1985) (Rumelhart et al., 1986) (Almeida, 1987) are insufficient speed and the danger of getting stuck in local minima. We offer an approach to cope with both of these problems: Instead of using bp to find zero-points of the gradient of the error-surface we are looking for zero-points of the error-surface itself. This can be done with less computational effort than there is in second order methods. Experimental results indicate that in cases where only a small fraction of units is active simultaneously (sparse coding), this method can be applied successfully. Furthermore it can be significantly faster than conventional bp.*

Keywords—Back-propagation, sparse coding, speed, learning rate, local minima.

1 THE METHOD

Numerous gradient descent methods for adjusting weights in neural nets are described in the literature (see e.g. articles by Parker, Dahl, and Watrous in IEEE 1st Int. Conf. on Neural Networks, Vol. 2). Common to all of these methods is that they try to find a zero-point of the gradient of the error-surface, hoping that the corresponding local minimum is 'global enough' to be acceptable. The surprising fact which is only poorly understood so far is that this works in some cases.

What we are really interested in is not so much the local minima but the zero-points of the error-function E (or points close to zero). E is the sum of all errors E_p, where E_p is the error caused by some particular pattern p. Back propagation gives us the gradient $\frac{\partial E_p}{\partial \vec{w}}$ where $\vec{w} = (w_1, .., w_n)$ is the complete weight vector of the system. In order to implement gradient descent we have to change the weights according to $\Delta\vec{w} = -\eta \frac{\partial E_p}{\partial \vec{w}}$, where η is a proportionality factor, the learning rate. What we need is a good choice for η.

Our approach will be to compute η dynamically during each pattern presentation. η will be chosen such that the changed weight vector $\hat{\vec{w}} = \vec{w} + \Delta\vec{w}$ points to the intersection of the weight hyper-plane (in $n+1$-dimensional weight-error-space) and the line defined by the current error and the current gradient. The basic assumption is that the error function can be locally approximated by its tangential hyper plane. Thus we use the gradient to do linear extrapolation, in order to gain a new weight vector whose corresponding E_p is hoped to be 0, or at least close to 0. The new weight vector is the starting point for the next iteration. (See figure 1 for an illustration of the one dimensional case.)

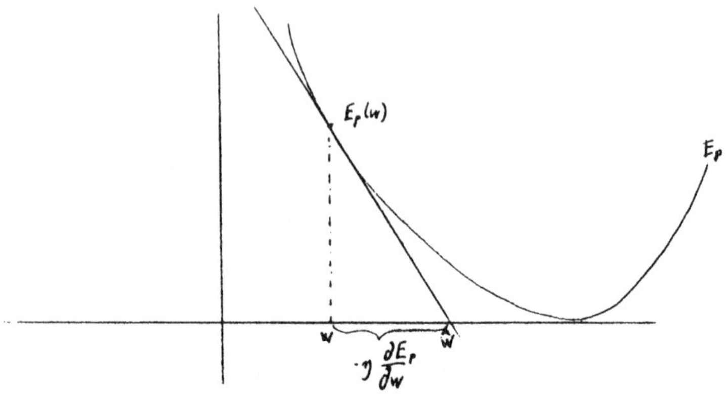

Figure 1: Illustration of a single iteration step in case of a one-dimensional weight vector.

Elementary geometry yields that in cases where the gradient is not zero η has to equal

$$\frac{E_p}{\sum_k (\frac{\partial E_p}{\partial w_k})^2}$$

where w_i is some weight, and k ranges over all weight-indices.

If the gradient vanishes then η is set equal to zero.

Since for each pattern η is set dynamically, there is no parameter tuning any more. The procedure implements a version of on-line learning, since after each pattern presentation weights are changed immediately.

The approach is reminiscent of the Newton-Raphson method of first degree (Stoer, 1976) used to find zero-points of functions that depend on only one variable (this method converges quadratically under certain assumptions). An important difference is that in general the function to be interpolated changes during two consecutive iterations.

If there exist zero-points of a non-negative E_p, they are also global minima. A system doing strict zero-point-search can not get stuck in a local minimum as long as it does not by chance hit one exactly. In fact, near the bottom of any minimum the gradient becomes close to zero, which means that η goes towards infinity, if the minimum is no zero-point at the same time. Thus the system can escape from the undesirable state by doing a large (nearly) random step. One way to have influence on the system's willingness to get stuck is to bound η. In the experiments described below the absolute value of η was bound by 20.

In cases where just a few units are turned on at a time, large jumps[1] through weight-space do not necessarily mean a catastrophe for the whole system. This is because the change of some weight is proportional to the activation of the unit it is coming from. The jumps may be large, but they are rather 'orthogonal' to most of the weights. The

[1]Large jumps can be viewed as the effect of introducing high temperature for a short time and in a controlled manner. Unlike in the case of the Boltzmann-Machine (Hinton and Sejnowski, 1986) the temperature can be viewed as being set dynamically, and locally.

probability that a new interpolation step seriously affects the result of the previous ones is lower than in cases where most units are active.

What if the error does not have any zero-points? This is the case if the output units use for instance the popular logistic function for computing their activations. In this case we can redefine the error function such that it still captures what we intuitively want, but such that it may have zero-points. A simple way to do this is to add a very small negative constant to the error.

The method does not seem to be purely local any more, due to the 'somewhat global' computation of η. However, we can achieve a similar degree of locality as in conventional bp: After having finished the error-propagation phase we introduce a second forward pass where each unit computes the sum of the squares of the error-derivatives of its incoming links. In each layer there is one unit that also is responsible for collecting the results of the previous layer. One extra layer consisting of one additional unit is needed to handle the output-layer. In a second back-pass the value of η can be distributed to all units. Thus we achieve the same order of time-complexity that distinguishes normal bp, even in a truly parallel implementation.

2 SOME EMPIRICAL RESULTS

It is difficult to compare different classes of learning algorithms, since each class shows varying performance on different classes of problems. We did evaluations of some classical tasks, however. The goal always was to associate a set of binary input patterns with a corresponding set of binary teaching patterns. In all cases, the net was of the feed forward type and consisted of three layers of units. The logistic function was used as the activation-function of each unit. The weights were initialized randomly between -.1 and +.1. With zero-point-search the absolute value of η was bound to be not greater than 20.0. The error was defined as in (Rumelhart et al., 1986), we never added a small negative constant. Both zero-point-search and bp were tested in the on-line mode: Weights were changed after each pattern presentation.

An ensemble of patterns was said to be learned if it fulfilled a criterion used by Fahlman (1988, personal communication): For each pattern each output of the system had to be less than 0.4 if the desired value was 0, and larger than 0.6 if the desired value was 1.

Some net was said to have found a local minimum if one training cycle (the presentation of all patterns belonging to some ensemble) did not cause any weight to change by more than 0.001. This is no sufficient criterion in the mathematical sense. However, additional support for believing that it is a sensible one was found empirically: The average number of cycles needed to reach this criterion used to be clearly above the average number of cycles needed to reach the success-criterion. Furthermore: If the condition above was fulfilled, the system often (not always) used to have adjusted its weights such that the activation vector of all output units was very close to some corner of the unit-hypercube of output-state-space, for all input-patterns. By the nature of bp the error-signals become very weak in such a case, and even with zero-point-search the system might get stuck, if η is bounded.

One easy way to ensure that the fraction of simultaneously active units in a 3-layered net is comparatively small is to use sparsely coded input-patterns, and not too many hidden

Problem	$\alpha = 0.9, \eta = 0.5$	runs	zero-point-search	runs
4-2-4	45	20	40	20
8-3-8	130	20	90	20
16-4-16	239	20	146	20
32-5-32	394	20	168	20
64-6-64	750	10	220	10

units.[2] A famous class of problems where these requirements are fulfilled is the n-ld$n$-n-encoding-problems (Hinton and Sejnowski, 1986).

In the first table we show results for ld$n$ from 2 to 6. The left column gives the name of the problem. In the second column we display the average number of presentations of the whole ensemble that were necessary to achieve the Fahlman-criterion for normal bp with an accelerating momentum-term where α (Rumelhart et al., 1986) was set to 0.9 and η was set to 0.5. The number of runs (with changing initial conditions) to compute the average is given next. In the fourth and fifth column we display the corresponding numbers for zero-point-search.

We were led to wonder if zero-point-search can be beneficial for more typical problems, too. Again we tested both methods, this time for random-pattern association similar to classification tasks tackled for instance in NETTALK (Sejnowski and Rosenberg, 1987). The second table can be read in a similar manner as the first one. 20 patterns of length 40 had to be associated with not more than 16 patterns of length 4, where the net consisted of an input-layer of 40 units, a hidden layer of 10 units, and an output-layer of 4 units. All patterns were chosen randomly (but there was a constraint on the bag of input-patterns: It had to be a set.) The probability P for some bit of some pattern to be one was 0.1. P measures the degree of sparseness of the input/output coding. The table shows the numbers of failures (according to the heuristic criterion for local minima) and successes obtained by running both methods on the same pattern set for a few times. If the system succeeded at least once, the average number of ensemble-cycles is given.

The example is also meant to illustrate the difficulties of getting statistically significant results. Performance depends heavily on the nature of the mapping to be learned. In general it is comparatively difficult for some net to classify two input patterns with a large Hamming-distance as belonging to output-categories with a small one. It is comparatively easy to classify two patterns with a small Hamming-distance as belonging to the same output category, since then one of the patterns can be regarded as a distorted version of the other one. This explains some 'irregularities' in the second table.

In other experiments we found that with increasing P the probability that conventional bp shows superior performance increases, too. If, for instance, P was set to 0.5, bounded zero-point-search often did not prevent the system from reaching a stuck state.

We have to mention that for some specific problem we sometimes were able to find values for α and η that were better suited. However, it is this empirical parameter tuning that we want to avoid.

[2] Currently we do not know whether bp-systems doing zero-point-search automatically develop sparse coding for their internal representations.

$\alpha = 0.9, \eta = 0.5$			zero-point-search		
Loc.min.	succ.	av.	Loc.min.	succ.	av.
1	9	122	0	10	15
9	1	262	0	10	15
0	10	52	0	10	18
8	2	350	0	10	29
0	10	69	0	10	21
0	10	77	0	10	45
8	2	302	0	10	17
3	7	133	0	10	18
0	10	24	0	10	13
0	10	60	0	10	18

2.1 How does η change over time?

We often observed during training that η had a tendency to grow until it reached its bound, then staying there for a while, then going back to low values, where it stayed if the error had 'artificial' zero-points. If the error was positive for all possible states of the system, η started growing again, although the system changed little or not at all from that time on.

We interpret this behavior: In the beginning the system makes a lot of mistakes and starts some sort of random search until it finds a promising valley in the error-surface. (From there it may escape again if the promises do not become true.) It steps down until it finds a point very close to the weight-hyperplane. Being close to zero for all patterns means that the weight-derivatives go towards zero, too. If E is positive, then due to the nature of the activation-function, η goes towards infinity but is stopped by its bound. The system remains very close to its previous state.

The values of η also had a strong tendency to be pattern-specific: The same pattern often caused similar η's during two consecutive ensemble-cycles. Again we blame the degree of orthogonality of the moves in weight-space for this behaviour.

3 CONCLUDING REMARKS

Compared with second-order-methods (e.g. Newton-method with computation of the Hessian) the amount of computation per cycle is strongly reduced. However, certain approximations to second order methods (e. g. methods using information only from the main diagonal of the Hessian) show the same order of time complexity per cycle as zero point search. Fahlman's method (Fahlman, 1988), for instance, estimates the curvature of the error surface by using first order information gained from each weight during successive time ticks. (Fahlman's method also employs a different error function to be minimized, as well as some other empirically motivated tricks.) Zero point search does not try to approximate second derivatives, it employs linear extrapolation in order to jump to points in weight space whose corresponding errors are assumed to equal zero. It remains to be seen which methods are preferable for which kind of tasks.

We want to mention that there is no formal reason why zero-point-search should not be applicable to 'feedback-propagation' (Almeida, 1987).

We want to relate this work to some results given by Palm in (Palm, 1980). Palm shows that at least for two-layer systems with binary weights the optimal capacity of the associative memory is achieved by using very sparse coding (depending on the number of patterns to be stored). Thus sparse coding is not necessarily a serious limitation, but can be something desirable.

Two questions we consider important are the following ones: In cases where the number of hidden units is high compared to the number of inputs and outputs, does a multi-layer bp-system try to develop sparse coding for its internal representations? If not, is there a way to make it do so?

The question whether there exist zero-points (or points close to zero) is another fundamental one. Currently there is no theory of e.g. 'n-layer-separable functions'. We insist that this problem does not introduce a new quality of insecurity, since bp-methods searching for local minima suffer from a similar lack of understanding.

We believe that a full explanation of the observed effects would have to focus on the dynamic behavior of the net. We did a little experiment to illustrate one reason for this belief: The error of all patterns of one ensemble was summed, and each weight summed its error-derivatives accumulated by bp during one ensemble-cycle. The weights were changed according to the rules of zero-point-search, but only after the whole ensemble had been presented (off-line learning). We might suspect that this works better because it captures more of the static essence of linear extrapolation: we want to find a zero-point of the ensemble error, which is the sum of the errors caused by the single patterns. However, this never worked well. We are led to conclude that the system can make better progress if it has the chance to concentrate on one pattern at a time. (For human beings this realization looks like a truism: We usually construct new representations of the world by building on older ones.)

We would like to hear from experimentors applying zero-point search to larger pattern-sets, e.g. to those used in NETTALK. NETTALK uses very sparse input coding (only about 3 percent of its units responsible for the (local) representation of the input can be turned on at the same time). Furthermore most of its units are input units. Therefore it might be a promising candidate for the application of zero-point search.

REFERENCES

Almeida, L. B. (1987). A learning rule for asynchronous perceptrons with feedback in a combinatorial environment. In *IEEE 1st International Conference on Neural Networks, Vol 2*.

Fahlman, S. E. (1988). An empirical study of learning speed in back-propagation networks. Technical Report CMU-CS-88-162, Carnegie Mellon Univ.

Hinton, G. E. and Sejnowski, T. E. (1986). Learning and relearning in boltzmann machines. In (Rumelhart and McClelland, 1986).

Palm, G. (1980). On associative memory. *Biological Cybernetics*, 36.

Parker, D. B. (1985). Learning-logic. Technical Report TR-47, Center for Comp. Research in Economics and Management Sci., MIT.

Rumelhart, D. E., Hinton, G. E., and Williams, R. J. (1986). Learning internal representations by error propagation. In (Rumelhart and McClelland, 1986).

Rumelhart, D. E. and McClelland, J. L., editors (1986). *Parallel Distributed Processing*, volume 1. MIT Press.

Sejnowski, T. J. and Rosenberg, C. R. (1987). Parallel networks that learn to pronounce english text. *Complex Systems*, 1.

Stoer, J. (1976). *Einführung in die numerische Mathematik, Vol. 1.* Springer.

Werbos, P. J. (1974). *Beyond Regression: New Tools for Prediction and Analysis in the Behavioral Sciences.* PhD thesis, Harvard University.

CONNECTIONISM IN PERSPECTIVE
R. Pfeifer, Z. Schreter, F. Fogelman-Soulié, L. Steels (Eds.)

Coding of Orientation by The Visual Cortex: Neural Network Modelling

Simon J. Thorpe and Alexandre Pouget
Institut des Neurosciences, Université Pierre et Marie Curie
Paris, France.

Abstract—*Neurons in the visual cortex respond selectively to oriented contours, and it is commonly believed that perceived orientation is determined by the most active of these neurons. However, recent psychophysical and neurophysiological data suggest that the most important neurons for orientation coding may not be the most active ones. We have used neural network modelling to investigate this possibility. The Delta rule was used to train a simple two-layer network, with an input layer composed of orientation selective units, and two output units to classify pairs of stimuli with different orientations. We found (i) that the network could mimic the performance of human observers on an equivalent task, and (ii) that the contribution of the most active units in the input layer was very small - the most important units were those selective for orientations offset 15° to 0° to either side of the test stimuli.*

Keywords—Orientation, visual cortex, coding, back-propagation, neural networks, psychophysics, neurophysiology.

1. INTRODUCTION

It has been known since the early 1960s that the visual cortex contains neurons which selectively respond to contours with particular orientations (See Orban, 1984; DeValois and DeValois, 1988; Howard, 1982 for reviews). However, the way in which the activity of such neurons is used to code the orientation of a stimulus remains controversial. One popular view, based on Selfridge's "Pandemonium" model (Selfridge, 1959) is to think of these orientation-selective neurons as "feature-detectors" and to suppose that perceived orientation is determined by the ones which are most active. A clear example of this "peak-activity" coding position is given in a recent review article on computational maps in the brain in which Eric Knudsen and his coworkers proposed the following formulation : "Whether the desired information is the orientation or direction of motion of a visual stimulus ...., the answer is always represented as the location of a peak of activity within a population of neurons" (Knudsen et al, 1987, page 59). However, recent psychophysical and neurophysiological data cast doubt on such a formulation, at least in the case of orientation perception. It would appear that it is perhaps not the most active neurons which determine perceived orientation, but rather the relative levels of firing in neurons tuned to orientations offset to either side of the orientation to be judged. In the present study we have used neural network modelling to try and understand how orientation selective units can be used to identify stimulus orientation. But before discussing the simulation studies, we will first briefly review the relevant psychophysical and neurophysiological evidence (see also Thorpe, in press).

Psychophysical data. If you stare at a vertical grating for a minute or two, the orientation selective neurons responding best to vertical orientations become adapted with the result that vertical gratings become harder to see. (Blakemore and Campbell, 1969). However, Regan and Beverley (1985) recently found that such adaptation does not impair the ability to detect a small change in orientation close to the vertical, although it does produce a large impairment in performance for orientations 10-15° to either side. They interpreted this as meaning that vertically-tuned units are not critical for coding the vertical, but instead are involved in coding offset orientations.

Neurophysiological data. A number of recent studies have looked at the ability of cortical neurons to signal small changes in stimulus parameters such as orientation, spatial frequency, contrast and vernier offset (Bradley et al, 1987; Parker and Hawken, 1985; Skottum et al, 1987; Tolhurst, Movshon and Dean, 1982, Swindale and Cynader, 1986). By repeatedly presenting two slightly different stimuli, one can measure the ability of a single neuron to signal the difference. Such studies indicate that the most useful neurons for signalling a change in the stimulus are not the most active ones, but rather those whose activity changes most when the stimulus changes - namely, those "selective" for offset values.

In our recent neural network modelling studies we have tried to increase our understanding of how orientation selective units can be used to code orientation by training a network with an input layer composed of such units and using the delta-rule error correction algorithm to train it to classify stimuli differing in orientation. By analyzing the "strategy" adopted by the network, our aim was to obtain independent evidence on the mechanisms of orientation coding.

2. ORIENTATION IDENTIFICATION BY NEURAL NETWORKS

The basic structure of the neural network used in this study is illustrated in Figure 1. It consists of a network with two layers (i.e. no hidden units). The input layer consists of a variable number of orientation tuned channels, with properties similar to psychophysical channels in the human visual system.

Each of the input units has a connection to both output units, labelled "A" and "B". During training, the two training orientations are presented to the network, and the back-propagation learning algorithm described by Rumelhart et al (1986) used to train the network to classify the stimuli correctly. One of the output units was trained to respond when one of the test stimuli was present, and the other trained to respond to the other. During testing, the activity of the two output units was compared and the one with the most activity determined the response of the network. Clearly, at the start of training, and with random connectivity, the network will perform at chance (i.e. 50% of the patterns will be correctly classified). However, after training, performance can reach 100%, depending on the particular situation.

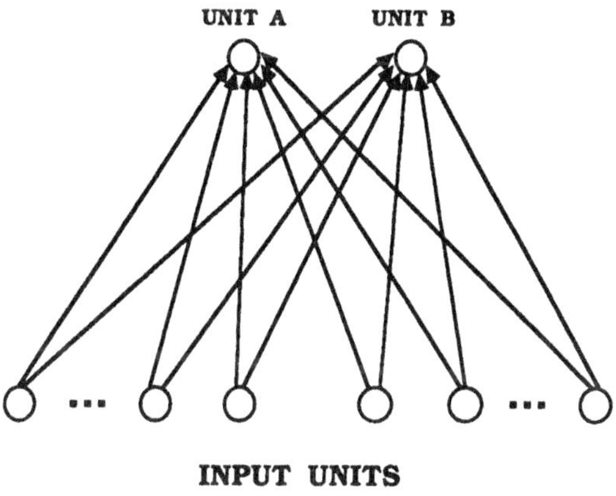

Figure 1 : Basic organization of the neural network used in this study.

There are a number of parameters which influence the performance of the network which in general were chosen to be as biologically realistic as possible.

Shape of the selectivity function for the input channels. The activity in each of the input units in response to a stimulus with a particular orientation is determined by its selectivity function. On the basis of neurophysiological and psychophysical data, (see DeValois and DeValois, 1988 for references) we opted for a Gaussian selectivity function, with a bandwidth at half height of roughly 25°. Thus the mean activity in a channel centred on orientation q_0 in response to a stimulus with orientation q is given by the formula

$$\textbf{Mean activity} = \exp((q - q_0)/(2s^2))$$

where s is the standard deviation of the tuning curve (about 10° in our simulations). Thus mean activity is equal to 1.0 when the units preferred orientation is presented, and decreases progressively with orientations further away from the preferred value.

Noise in the input units. The activity of real neurons is always influenced by noise. Neurophysiological data indicates that the variance of this noise is roughly proportional to activity (Tolhurst, Movshon and Dean, 1982). Thus in our simulations, we added gaussian noise to the activity levels of the input units. The standard deviation of this noise was given by taking the square root of the units mean response multiplied by a constant K. Tolhurst and coworkers found that in anaesthetized cats, variance was in general about 3 times the activity level. In studies in progress in our own lab (with Yves Trotter, Simona Celebrini and Michel Imbert) we have some preliminary data suggesting that variability may be less in awake primates. However, in our computer simulations we have assumed that noise in the input units has been reduced by averaging together the outputs of a number of orientation-tuned units - if the outputs of N neurons with independent noise are averaged together, the variance is reduced by a factor of N.

Separation between the input units. In the simulations described here, we used a fixed value for the separation between neighboring input units of 2 degrees. Given the 25° bandwidth of the neurons in question, this results in considerble overlap between adjacent units. However, in other studies (Thorpe and Pouget, in preparation) we have looked at the effect of systematically varying this value.

3. FIRST SIMULATION

In this simulation, there were 60 input units, covering a range from -59° to +59° (0° corresponding to the vertical) by steps of 2°. The noise level was fixed so that the variance of the units response was equal to 0.1 times its activity. This would be the level of noise that would result if between 10 and 30 individual neurons were averaged together to form each input channel.

Before the training started, the connection strengths between the input units and the output units were set at small random values. Then the two training stimuli were each presented 2000 times, with one of the test stimuli having an orientation of -1°, the other +1°. Each time a test stimulus was presented, an activity level was calculated for each of the 60 input units and target values of 0.9 and 0.1 were assigned to the two output units, depending on which test stimulus had been presented. The back-propagation algorithm was then used to modify the connection strengths between the input and output units. Once training was complete, a further 800 random test trials were presented in order to test the performance of the network.

The results are shown in Figure 2, which plots the connection strengths of the 60 input units separately for the two output units. One is immediately struck by the symmetry between the weight functions for the two units. If we consider output unit A, we can see that all the units to the left of 0° have positive weights whereas the units to the right have negative weight values. Thus the unit can be thought of as comparing the relative activity of units preferring orientations to the left of vertical with those preferring orientations to the right. A similar description applies to the right hand unit except that the values of the connection strengths have opposite signs.

One feature of the weight distribution is particularly striking. The units with the highest connection strengths are not those which were most activated by the test stimuli. Given that the test stimuli had orientations of + or - 1° relative to vertical, it is clear that the most active units would have been those centered on -1° and +1°. However, the weights of these two units are virtually zero. The units which have the most influence on the output units are those which respond best to orientations 15° to 20° to either side of the vertical.

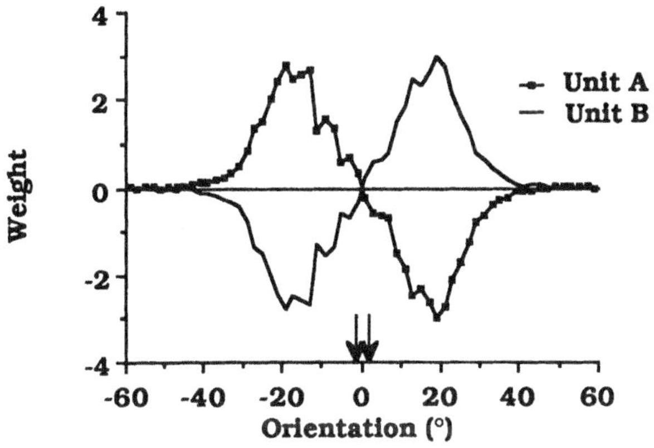

Figure 2 : Distribution of weight strengths between the 60 input units and the two output units A and B. The two test orientations (-1° and +1°) are indicated by the arrows.

Why is this so? The main reason is the Gaussian shape of the sensitivity functions for the input units. Such functions are virtually flat for orientations close to the optimal value - as a result, the activity of such neurons carries little information about a subtle change in orientation like that used in this simulation. Added to this is the fact that the neuronal activity is subject to a significant amount of noise which makes small changes in activity difficult to interpret.

In any case, the results of the simulation study tie in nicely with the psychophysical experiments of Regan and Beverley (1985). As was mentioned in an earlier section, they found that adapting the neurons most sensitive to vertical orientations produced no impairment in the subject's ability to detect a change in orientation around the vertical. By contrast, such adaptation did impair judgments 10 to 15° to either side - a value which fits well with the position of the most important units in the present simulations.

4. SECOND SIMULATION

In the second simulation, we took the same network that we used in the first experiment and investigated the effect of changing the separation between the two test orientations. In the first simulation the separation was fixed at 2° (i.e. -1° and +1°). In this series of simulations, values of 0.25°, 0.5°, 1.0°, 1.3°, 1.6°, 2.0°, 2.3°, 2.6°, 3°, 4° and 8° were used. The network was retrained separately for each test pair, before being tested without learning during 800 trials.

We were able to compare the performance of the network with the performance of human subjects on a similar task. Thorpe and Bonnardel (1986, and in preparation) used a task in which human subjects have to learn to identify two grating stimuli, differing in orientation. On each trial, the subject saw a grating which could either be tilted slightly to the left or slightly to the right of vertical, and was required to say which. Training was continued with feedback until the subject was unable to make any further progress, at which point feedback was removed and the performance of the subject during 400 trials with no feedback determined. The experimental procedure is thus essentially similar to the sort of pattern classification problems with supervised learning given to artificial networks. The only real difference between the task used with the network and that used with the human subjects is that special precautions had to be taken to prevent the humans subjects performing the task by simply comparing one stimulus with the next. These included presenting a series of random orientations as distractors in between each test presentation.

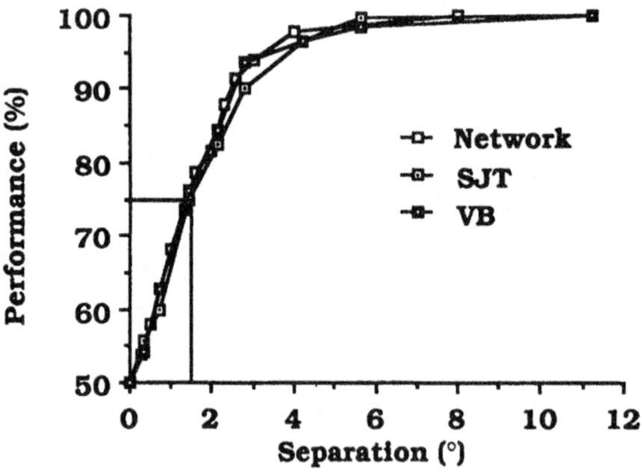

Figure 3 : Relative performance of the network and two human subjects, SJT and VB in an orientation identification task with two orientations.

As can be seen from Figure 3, the performance functions of the network and the two human subjects SJT and VB are very similar. Both network and humans start from chance levels of performance with the smallest separations, increase rapidly to reach a threshold performance of 75% correct with a separation between the two test stimuli of 1.4° and reach perfect performance with separations above about 8°. Thus we have reasonable grounds for supposing that the strategy adopted by the network may also be the one used by humans.

5. DISCUSSION

In the simulations described in this paper we have tried to combine three different types of data with the aim of achieving a better understanding of how orientation is coded by the visual system. One source of information is neurophysiological - with the aid of single-unit recording studies it is possible to specify the response properties of neurons in the visual cortex. A second source of data comes from psychophysical studies that we have carried out in human subjects. Finally, we have attempted to use neural network modelling to see if we can account for the psychophysical performance of the human subjects on the basis of the neurophysiological data. The results have been most encouraging. It would appear that we can explain the performance of human subjects using a simple two layer neural net in which the input layer is composed of an array of orientation-selective units whose properties resemble the orientation-selective neurons found in the visual cortex, and an output layer containing two units which we train to classify two different test orientations.

One of the most striking results of these simulations is that when the two orientations to be identified are situated at -1° and +1°, and the network has input neurons covering the range from -59° to +59° by 2° steps, the units which are maximally activated by the test stimuli are hardly used at all. The most important inputs are apparently those which "prefer" orientations offset by 15° to 20° to either side of the vertical. Each output unit effectively weighs the relative activity of neurons to either side of the vertical. This amounts to saying that if a subject wishes to know whether a line stimulus is tilted slightly to the left or slightly to the right of vertical, he does it not by finding the most active "feature detector" in the array of input neurons, but rather by measuring the relative activity in offset neurons. Clearly, such a suggestion is at odds with the commonly held notion, discussed in the introduction, according to which stimulus values are encoded by the location of a peak of firing in an array of tuned "feature detectors".

In fact, the method "found" by the network for identifying the orientation of an unknown stimulus is in many ways similar to the opponent-process model of colour vision proposed over 100 years ago by Hering. It is well known that the retina contains at least three kinds of cone pigments, each maximally sensitive to a different wavelength. However, it is also known that our ability to judge wavelength is not maximal at these points of maximum sensitivity, but rather in the regions of the spectrum between the cone peaks. Hering suggested that colour judgments in fact make use of the relative levels of activity in the three different cone systems - not simply the identity of the most active one. In effect, this is exactly what we see in the case of orientation. The only significant difference is that whereas the wavelength selective pigments used in the case of colour vision are found in the retina, orientation selectivity is something which only emerges at the level of the visual cortex. Nevertheless, the algorithm "chosen" by the network does essentially the same thing - namely, to calculate the relative activity in symmetrical populations of neurons.

Interestingly, Sejnowski (1988) has recently used neural network modelling to investigate the coding of stereoscopic depth. He finds that, as in the case of orientation coding, it is not the most active units which are the most critical, since high precision appears to be obtained by comparing the relative activity in groups of non-optimally activated units. It may be this sort of coding mechanism may be very widespread within neural systems, being involved not only in the coding of colour, orientation and stereoscopic depth, but many other stimulus parameters such as spatial location, spatial frequency, intensity , velocity and so on.

The approach used in the present study typifies that used in an increasing number of connectionist studies. As in the recent studies of Lehky and Sejnowski (1988) and Zipser and Anderson (1988), the aim has been to use connectionist modelling to gain insights into the way real nervous systems work, by explicitly examining how real neurons may be used. There can be little doubt that we are only just beginning to explore the potential of these new techniques, but as Sejnowski, Koch and Churchland (1988) made clear in their recent review article, the advent of increasingly powerful computing systems will make it feasible to simulate even highly complex brain functions.

6. REFERENCES

Blakemore, C. and Campbell, F.W. (1969) On the existence of neurones in the human visual system selectively sensitive to the orientation and size of retinal images. *Journal of Physiology*, **203**, 237-260.

Bradley, A., Skottum, B.C., Ozhawa, I., Sclar, G. and Freeman, R.D. (1987), Visual orientation and spatial frequency discrimination : A comparison of single units and behavior. *Journal of Neurophysiology*, **57**, 755-772.

DeValois, R. and DeValois, K.A. (1988). *Spatial vision*. Oxford University Press.

Howard, I.P. (1982). *Human Visual Orientation*. Chichester : Wiley.

Knudsen, E.I, du Lac, S. and Esterley, S.D. (1987) Computational maps in the brain. *Annual Review of Neuroscience*, **10**, 41-65.

Lehky, S.R. and Sejnowski, T. (1988), Network model of shape from shading : neural function arises from both receptive and projective fields. *Nature*, **333**, 452-454.

Orban, G.A. (1984). *Neuronal operations in the visual cortex*. Berlin : Springer-Verlag.

Parker, A. and Hawken, M. (1985), Capabilities of monkey cortical cells in spatial-resolution tasks. *Journal of the Optical Society of America*, **2**, 1101-1114.

Regan, D.M. and Beverley, K.I. (1985). Post-adaptation orientation discrimination. Journal of the Optical Society of America, **2**, 147-155.

Rumelhart, D.E., Hinton, G.E. and Williams, R.J. (1986), Learning internal representations by error-propagation. In Rumelhart and McClelland (eds.) *Parallel Distributed Processing : Explorations in the microstructure of cognition. Vol 1. (pages 318-362)*. MIT Press

Sejnowski, T.J. (1988) Modelling Stereo Hyperacuity. *Proceedings of the First European Conference on Neural Networks*, Paris, June, 1988.

Sejnowski, T.J., Koch, C. and Churchland, P.S. (1988), Computational Neuroscience. *Science*, **241**, 1299-1306.

Selfridge, O.G. (1959), Pandemonium : A paradigm for learning. In *Mechanisation of thought processes*. London : H.M.S.O.

Skottum, B.C., Bradley, A., Sclar. G., Ohzawa, I. and Freeman, R.D. (1987), The effects of contrast on visual orientation and spatial frequency discrimination : A comparison of single cells and behavior. *Journal of Neurophysiology*. **57**, 773-786.

Swindale, N.V. and Cynader, M.S. (1986),Vernier acuity of neurones in cat visual cortex. *Nature*, **319**, 591-593.

Thorpe, S.J. (1989) Coding of Simple Visual stimuli in the human visual system. In Kulikowski, J.J. (Ed.) *Seeing Contour and Colour*. Oxford : Pergamon Press.

Thorpe, S.J. and Bonnardel, V (1986), Absolute identification with two orientations. *Perception*, **15**, A23.

Tolhurst, D.J., Movshon J.A. and Dean A.D. (1982). The statistical reliability of signals in single neurons in cat and monkey visual cortex. *Vision Research*, **23**, 775-785.

Zipser, D. and Andersen, R.A. (1988), A back-propagation programmed network that simulates response properties of a subset of posterior parietal neurons. *Nature*, **331**, 679-684.

CONNECTIONISM IN PERSPECTIVE
R. Pfeifer, Z. Schreter, F. Fogelman-Soulié, L. Steels (Eds.)

Pattern Directed Real-World Interface

L.A.A. Vercauteren, R.A. Vingerhoeds, M. Lee, L. Boullart
Ghent State University, Automatic Control Laboratory, A.I. Section
Grotesteenweg Noord 2, 9710 GENT - Zwijnaarde, Belgium
e-mail: LEO@BGERUG51.BITNET

Abstract—*This paper describes our efforts to build a Pattern Recognition System that can be used as an interface between a measured process and an operator or process computer. The system has to find its own pattern recognition strategy, by means of its normal real-world input and some background information about the process. To focus attention, this is the engine of an automobile, of which the sound is measured by a simple microphone. The 'short-time' temporal sound patterns, associated to some parts of the engine, are separated by Neural Network Structure 1 (NNS1). The long-time pattern recognition, the inter-relations between the short-time patterns, and the estimation of the parameters describing the process, are managed by Neural Network Structure 2 (NNS2). A Symbolic Control System (SCS) controls and supervises NNS1 and NNS2 and also serves the interaction with the teacher and the operator or the process-computer. To demonstrate the applicability of Neural Networks, Expert Systems and massive Parallel Processing techniques for industrial use, the system will be implemented in real-world environments and real-time conditions, using a powerful transputer-based computer architecture.*

Keywords—Auditive signal processing, real-time pattern recognition, self-learning neural networks.

PROBLEM DESCRIPTON

The research is situated in the area of audio signal processing. In particular, a repetitive audio signal, such as that of an automobile engine, is examined. The here proposed pattern recognition system is a type of real-time auto mechanic automaton used in the diagnosis of the performance of an automobile engine.

The pattern recognition process comprises of two stages. In the first stage, the system is put through a learning process, where it

1) is given information about an automobile, with regards to its construction e.g. number of cylinders, a starter motor etc, and the sub-processes involved e.g. compression, firing cycles, mathematical equations describing these subprocesses, etc. and

2) is taught from examples or input signals, through the study of the converted temporal patterns, the link between the parts of the car and the individual sub-processes.

This learning is carried out for a normal operation of an automobile, as well as for some typical malfunctioning parts of the engine.

In the next stage, the system has to be capable of

1) recognising and interpreting signals from this automobile by
2) distinguishing the separate components and sub-processes. It will thus be able to diagnose the performance of the car as being either normal or abnormal. Furthermore it has to be capable of suggesting parts or processes where a defect/mal-function is likely to exist.
3) It also has to learn from measurements on a defective or mal-functioning engine to enlarge its recognizable pattern library. Therefore, the system has to ask for more background information about the malfunctioning parts to the teacher or an operator.

One of the major problems is formed by the temporal character of the auditive input signal. There are several ways to deal with this problem. One is by feeding the input signal into a shift register and recognising the temporal patterns in a static 'image' (Grossberg, 1969). An alternative is a network with recurrent connections allowing information about events occuring in the past to be retained and used in current computations. This approach is heavily investigated by a lot of researchers, while a general framework was laid out by Rumelhart, Hinton, and Williams (1986), who unfolded the recurrent network into a multilayer feedforward network that grows by one layer on each time step. When enough is known about the repetitive time structure of the sound signal, the number of layers can be limited. (see also Dehaene et al., 1987, Leman, 1988, Williams & Zipser, 1988).

Another problem is the fact that the input signal forms a 'noisy' superposition. The system receives during operation, only an input signal from one microphone. As a lot of physical parts of the engine are generating an auditive pattern, there are interferences between the various signals, reflections, deformations and irrelevant background noise. In case of a disturbance at the input, the system has to relate this to the process or to classify it as irrelevant noise. The performance of the system is measured by how far the adaptive intelligence of the system keeps producing right conclusions.

Finally, the initial learning patterns are not the result of a profound investigation by a specialised engineer. They are obtained by a simple screening of the microphone on a particular part of the engine, or by a very direction-sensitive microphone. Moreover, the car, used to obtain the learning-examples, is not placed in a special environment.

PROPOSED SOLUTION

General Description

The system has the following structure (see figure 1):

1) Process and process measuring unit.
2) Signal pre-processing unit.
3) NNS1 : Neural Network Structure 1.

4) NNS2 : Neural Network Structure 2.

5) Symbolic Control System (SCS), interacting during the initial learning with a teacher, and during the normal working with an operator or process-computer.

The noisy input signals are fed into the pre-processing unit, Where the sound signal is converted into a so called 'Basic Pattern' (BP). This is in fact a simple simulation of the ear (see Liu, 1975, Meddis, 1986).

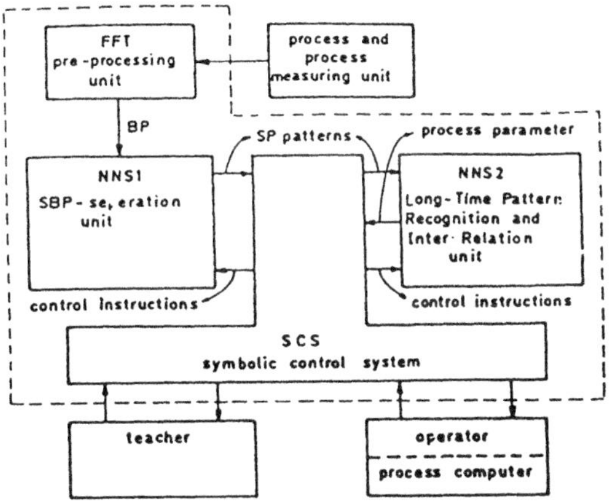

Figure 1. Schematical Layout of the complete system.

Sub Basic Pattern Separation Unit (NNS1)

The initial learning examples are related to certain parts of the engine. If the teacher judges that the engine can be divided into n sound sources, then the system will receive n initial learning BP's, namely the n SBP's (Sub Basic Patterns). The n classes of SP's (Sub Patterns) are obtained after the processing by NNS1. NNS1 is used as the SBP class separation unit and it is based on the Neocognitron, proposed by Fukushima (1987), for the short time pattern recognition.

A neocognitron (see figure 2) is a multi-layered artificial neural network with forward and backward paths or interconnections. The forward paths are used for feature extraction and thereby recognition, while the backward paths are used for selective attention, segmentation and associative recall. (See also Liu, 1975, Fukushima, 1987, Fukushima, 1987).

Figure 2 shows the mechanism of the NNS1 function. In the learning process it stores the various SBP's. During the identification or recognition process it separates the various SBP's which constitute the BP that is present at its input, into n ordered time sequences of SP-patterns. These are used for the analysis of the subprocesses. NNS1 has also the capability to recognize a SBP which has undergone even serious changes in form and/or orientation.

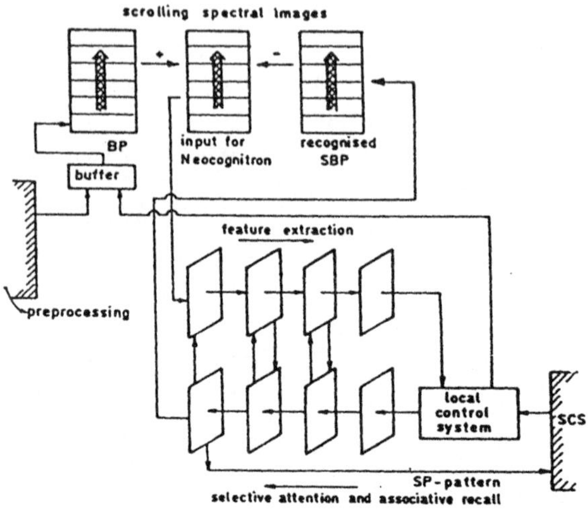

Figure 2. NNS1: Neural Network Structure 1

One of the most important features of NNS1 is that it recognizes an SBP no matter where it appears in the frequency range. Only the features of it will change. One can even consider to change the equal feature searching over the frequency range.

Suppose that the input signal is the music produced by an orchestra with several instruments. NNS1 will then separate the sounds of the different instruments.

Long-Time Pattern Recognition and Inter Relation Unit NNS2

The SP-sequences of NNS1 are fed to some topological mapping networks (see Kohonen, 1984, 1988). Each of these networks stands for a subprocess of which the parameters can be determined. This mapping reduces the dimension of the data and translates it to a for that subprocess relevant feature space. The input of the m maps can be a combination of up to n SP-sequences.

The cyclic long-time patterns have normally a much greater period then the observation time-span of NNS1. We are experimenting with a recurrent network (see figure 3) with three layers : one for the detection of an element in a sequence, one for the recognition of the normal time-delay, and one for the detection of fluctuations in these time-delays.
NNS2 has to follow or 'understand' the process. The parameters in NNS2 needed for this tracking are to be translated by SCS into the 'time' parameters describing the subprocess.

During the initial learning, the SCS has to build a suitable structure for NNS2. This structure has to learn by BP input examples, to make the connection between an input and the corresponding symbolic description of the process. A part of the SCS has to evaluate the accuracy of this structure during working and may have to adapt it if necessary. The teacher has to give the links between the SBP's and the parts of the engine, causing the SBP's. SCS and NNS2 have to be able to create new parameters, when an unknown malfunction is occuring or when a new subprocess describtion is given.

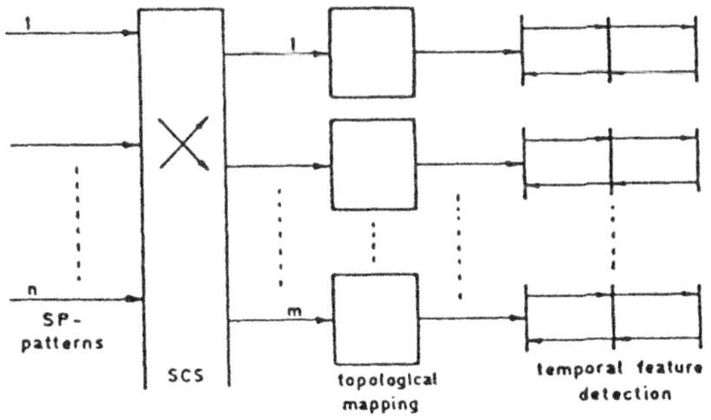

Figure 3. NNS2 : Mapping and sequential tracking

The most important concept used in NNS2 is the cyclic character of the sub-processes. After recognition of the cyclic patterns, the non-cyclic patterns need special attention. They are referring to malfunctions or to changes in the state of the process. The cyclic patterns can have a very intricated structure with regards to the presented SP-input. The parameters related to such a pattern have a certain range. A good parameter association of a cyclic pattern ensures a description of every appearing form of that pattern.

NNS2 has to perform three functions and has to generate three kinds of output.

1) A parameter estimation of the subprocesses, associated with the known cyclic patterns.
2) Detection of unknown cyclic patterns, which can be related with one or more parts of the engine, or with certain subprocesses.
3) Detection of non-cyclic patterns in the SP-input, referring to malfunctions or to changes in the state of the engine.

Symbolic Control System (SCS)

In this sub-system, several functions are grouped. It is essential that the 'variables' used in it, have a symbolic character. These symbols are better and faster manipulated by means of 'classic' expert-systems and programs.

The functions of the SCS are the following.

1) It serves as an interface between the system and an external teacher, an operator, and/or host process computer.
2) It controls and co-ordinates signal/communication flow in the system.
3) It receives the background information from the teacher, it builds a structure for NNS2, and an intelligent interpretation system of the output of NNS2. It also enables NNS1 and NNS2 to learn without dictating their weights or micro-structure.
4) It contains a strategic expert-system, that controls the selective attention capabilities of NNS1 and NNS2 and continuously monitors the state of the process and the system. This part of the SCS is very important. Once the system has determined the parameters of the cyclic processes, it can make predictions about the further BP. By this, CPU-

time for analysis can be reduced drastically. Selective attention can focus on deviations of the BP with regards to the expected BP.

5) During working, it has to supervise the self-optimisation of the system, the learning by experience and the interface to get more background information.

6) It has also to spread and co-ordinate the work over the transputer-network, to get an optimal use of the parallel processing power. So, the SCS really supervises the Pattern Recognition system.

FUTURE PROSPECTS

The individual parts of the system, except the SCS, are tested in some theoretical situations. They seem to perform quiet well. In the near future, we will link these parts and improve them in order to build a real-time, real-world interface.

REFERENCES

Dehaene, S., Changeux, J.-P., & Nadal, J.-P. (1987). Neural networks that learn temporal sequences by selection. *Biophysics,* **84**, 2727-2731.

Fukushima, K. (1983). Neocognitron: A Neural Network Model for a Mechanism of Visual Pattern Recognition. *IEEE Transactions on Systems, Man and Cybernetics,* **13** No. 5, 826-834.

Fukushima, K. (1987). Neural Network Model for selective attention in visual pattern recognition and associative recall. *Applied Optics,* **26** No. 23, 4985-4992

Fukushima, K. (1988). A Neural Network for Visual Pattern Recognition. *IEEE Computer*, March, 65-75.

Grossberg, S. (1969). Some Networks that can Learn, Remember, and Reproduce any number of complicated space - time patterns, *I. J. Math. Mechan.*, **19**, 53-91.

Kohonen, T. (1984). Self-organization and associative memory. New York: Springer.

Kohonen, T. (1988). The "Neural" Phonetic Typewriter. *IEEE Computer*, March, 11-22.

Leman, M. (1988). Sequencial (Musical) information processing with PDP-networks. *Proc. of the First Workshop on Artificial Intelligence and Music,* AAAI-88, 163-172.

Liu, B. (ed.) (1975). Digital Filters and the Fast Fourier Transform. Dowden, Hutchinson and Ross, Inc.

Meddis, R. (1986). Simulation of Mechanical to Neural Transduction in the auditory receptor. *J. Acoust. Soc. Am.*, **79**, 702-711

Rumelhart, D. E., Hinton, G. E., & Williams, R. J. (1986). Learning internal representations by error propagation. In D. E. Rumelhart, J. L. McClelland, & the PDP Research Group. Parallel distributed processing: Explorations in the microstructure of cognition. Vol. 1. Foundations. Cambridge: MIT Press/Bradford Books.

Williams, R. J., Zipser D. (1988). A learning algorithm for continually running fully recurrent neural networks (Tech. Rep. ICS-8805). La Jolla: University of California, San Diego, Institute for Cognitive Science.

ACKNOWLEDGEMENT

This paper presents research results of the Belgian National inventive program for fundamental research in Artificial Intelligence, initiated by the Belgian State - Prime Minister's Office - Science Policy Programming. The scientific responsibility is assumed by the authors.

A Connectionist System to Simulate Lexical Decisions in Information Retrieval[1]

Manfred Wettler & Reinhard Rapp

Department of Information Science
University of Constance/FRG

Abstract—*An important aspect of information retrieval is the translation of a problem description, which usually is formulated in a natural language, into an expression of the query-language. During this process the searcher must decide which words from the problem description and which additional words should be included in the query. We present a connectionist system that simulates the lexical aspects of this process. It has the form of a localist net whose units correspond to different content-words. The connective strengths between these units have been calculated on the basis of the frequencies and distributions of the words in the psychological data-bank PSYCINFO. The activation of a subset of the units leads to a process of propagation converging at specific local minima. During this process input words with low distinctiveness loose their activities and synonymes of active words become activated. These patterns of activities may be used to predict which words are to be used in the queries.*

Keywords—Connectionism, associative nets, information retrieval, query formation, lexicalization, keywords.

1. INTRODUCTION

In order to retrieve information from a data-bank, a searcher has to translate a problem description, which usually is formulated in a natural language, into an expression of the query-language. During this process the searcher must decide which words from the problem description and which additional words should be included in the query. The following example shows a problem description and the corresponding query, which has been generated by a professional searcher of a psychological information agency.

A child psychologist is interested in literature on the *effects* of the *presentation* of *aggression* in *television* upon *children*.

[1]This research is supported by the Deutsche Forschungsgemeinschaft grant No. 524/88

```
1.    188   FIND TELEVISION
2.   1277   FIND VIOLEN$ OR AGGRESS$
3.     33   FIND 1 AND 2
```

In this translation three content words of the problem description have been omitted (effects, presentation, and children), and the word "aggression" has been complemented by "violence". This paper deals with the question how such lexical decisions are accomplished.

Within the cognitive approach the generation of search-queries is described as a goal-directed process which is determined by the general aim of the searcher to fulfill the information need of the user (see e.g. Belkin & Vickery, 1985). The generation of the word "violence" in the previous example would be explained by the goal of the searcher to increase the width of the retrieved set of documents. Such cognitive descriptions of the search process are unsatisfactory because they can not explain why the searcher chose the word "violence" and not "strawberries" or "gasoline" for example.

We would like to show that such lexical decisions are controlled by automatic associative processes which can be modelled by connectionist nets: When the searcher translates a problem description into a query he relies on vague notions regarding the frequencies and the distributions of words. These notions can be described by a localist net in which each unit represents a content-word and the connective strengths between units are a function of the co-occurrences of the associated words. When the searcher deals with a problem description, the corresponding units in the lexical net become activated. The propagation of these activities through the net produces a new pattern of activation. This pattern determines which words will be included in the query.

2. GENERAL MODEL AND IMPLEMENTATION OF THE NET

A co-occurrence of two words is defined as their joint presence in one document, i.e. in its title, abstract, or list of keywords. The total number of co-occurrences of two words is equal to their intersection which may be inquired by means of the AND-operator. This permits the calculation of the connective weights through the application of formula (1), which has been used by Hinton & Sejnowski (1983) and by Rumelhart et al. (1986).

$$w_{ij} = -\ln \frac{p(x_i = 0 \;\&\; x_j = 1) * p(x_i = 1 \;\&\; x_j = 0)}{p(x_i = 1 \;\&\; x_j = 1) * p(x_i = 0 \;\&\; x_j = 0)} \qquad (1)$$

The use of this formula yields symmetric weights with positive and negative values. These weights can be computed for all possible pairs of words in different lexical samples, the structure of the connective space thus can be represented as a full crossbar. Figure 1 shows the connective strengths between seven words which have been calculated with this formula.In order to facilitate the computation of nets up to several hundred units we developed programs for the automated search in data-banks, on-line and with CD-ROM, and for the interpretation of the replies of the system. The largest net, which we have computed up to now consists of 270 words and 72630 connections. The co-occurrences of these words have been extracted from PsycLit, a psychological reference data-base which is compiled from PSYCINFO and distributed on CD-ROM. The words have been selected by chance with the only restriction concerning their minimal frequencies of occurrence.

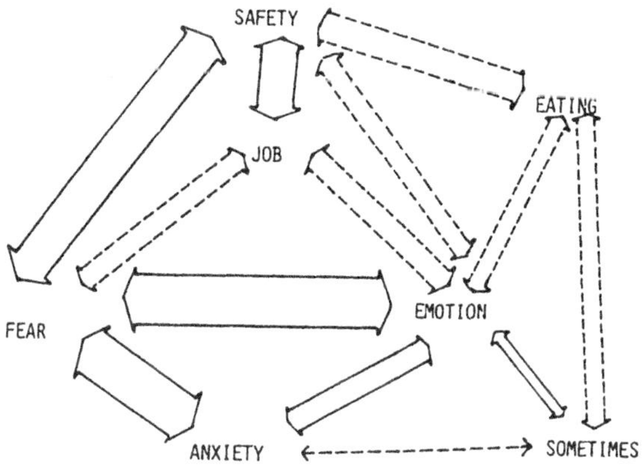

Figure 1: Connective strengths between seven words. Solid arrows represent positive and dashed arrows represent negative weights. The widths of the arrows represent the absolute strengths.

The propagation of activities proceeds in cycles. During each cycle the activities of all units are updated. At the beginning of the whole process all units have a value of zero. During the first cycle the stimulus units receive a fixed amount of activity; during the second and further cycles this activity is distributed accross the net according to the following formula:

$$a_i(t) = \text{input}_i + \frac{\sum_j a_j(t-1) * w_{ij}}{\sum_j a_j(t-1)} \quad (2)$$

where $a_u(c)$ is the activity of unit u after cycle c, and $\text{input}_u(c)$ is the activity which a heeded unit u receives during cycle c from outside; $w_{jj} = 0$.

Figure 2 shows the propagation of activities when the words "effect", "aggression", and "television" serve as stimuli, i.e. that during each cycle these words receive a constant amount of activation apart from the activation which all units receive from the other units in the net. During this process the system stabilizes and settles at a local minimum. The three units with the highest activities correspond to the words which the searcher included in the query.

3. COMPARISONS BETWEEN DIFFERENT MODELS

Within the connectionist approach different assumptions can be made with respect to the learning of the connective weights and with respect to the propagation of activities. In the following paragraphs we will analyze how these assumptions determine the patterns of activities in the lexical nets.

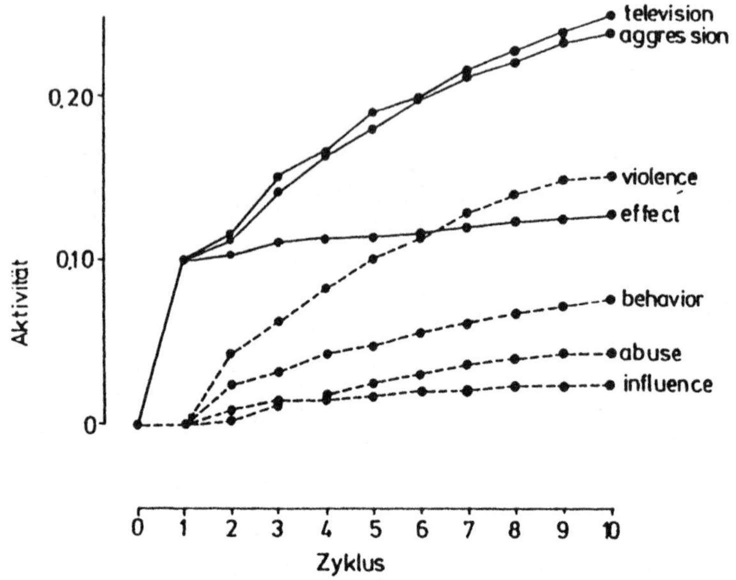

Figure 2: The propagation of activities when the words "effect", "aggression", and "television" are activated. The connective weights have been computed with formula (1).

In the examples which are shown in figures 1 and 2 the connective weights have been computed with equation (1). This formula has undefined or infinite values if one of its four terms is zero. Therefore it can not be applied whenever one of the two events is implied by the other. When we used this formula we assumed therefore that each of the four terms has a very small minimum value. This problem can be avoided if one assumes that the connective strength between two units is equal to the probability of their co-occurrence relative to their overall probabilities. Formula 3 shows this relationship:

$$w_{ij} = \frac{p(x_i = 1 \,\&\, x_j = 1)}{p(x_i = 1) * p(x_j = 1)} \qquad (3)$$

A similar formula has been used by Deese (1965) for the calculation of the associative intersection quotient. It gives weights which vary between one and zero. This contrasts with most other connectionist models which admit exhibitory as well as inhibitory connections. If one assumes that the connective weight between two units is the difference between its exitatory and its inhibitory relation then formula (3) has to be extended as follows:

$$w_{ij} = \frac{p(x_i = 1 \;\&\; x_j = 1)}{p(x_i = 1) * p(x_j = 1)} - \frac{p(x_i = 1 \;\&\; x_j = 0)}{p(x_i = 1) * p(x_j = 0)} - \frac{p(x_i = 0 \;\&\; x_j = 1)}{p(x_i = 0) * p(x_j = 1)}$$

since $p(x_i = 1 \;\&\; x_j = 0) = p(x_i = 1) - p(x_i = 1 \;\&\; x_j = 1)$

and since $p(x_i = 1) * p(x_j = 0) = p(x_i = 1) * (1 - p(x_j = 1))$

$$= p(x_i = 1) - p(x_i = 1 \;\&\; x_j = 1)$$

the above formula may be reduced to:

$$(4) \quad w_{ij} = \frac{p(x_i = 1 \;\&\; x_j = 1)}{p(x_i = 1) * p(x_j = 1)} - 2$$

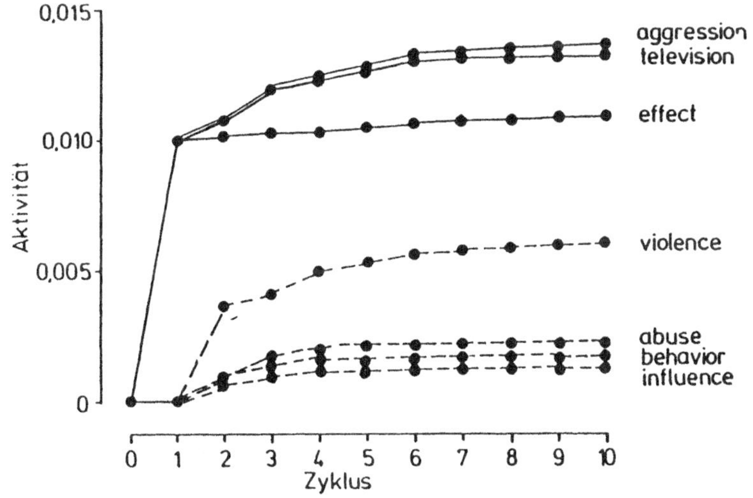

Figure 3a: The propagation of activities when the words "effect", "aggression", and "television" are activated. The connective weights have been computed with formula (3).

Figures 3a and 3b, which use the same example as figure 2, show the propagation of activities when the connective weights have been computed according to formulas (3) and (4). A comparison of fig. 3b and fig. 2 indicates that the weights computed with formula (4) and with formula (1) result in very similar pattern of activities. However, weights which are calculated with formula (3) produce a different pattern, at least in part. In all three patterns the word "aggression" receives high activity, but only in figures 2 and 3b the heeded word "effect" looses its activity. These two effects, the activation of synonymes of heeded words in all three conditions and the disactivation of heeded words with low distinctiveness in the two conditions with negative weights, have been observed with many other examples. With regard to our task-domain the calculation of the connective weights with formula (1) and with formula (4) produce similar results which are in aggreement with the behavior of the searchers.

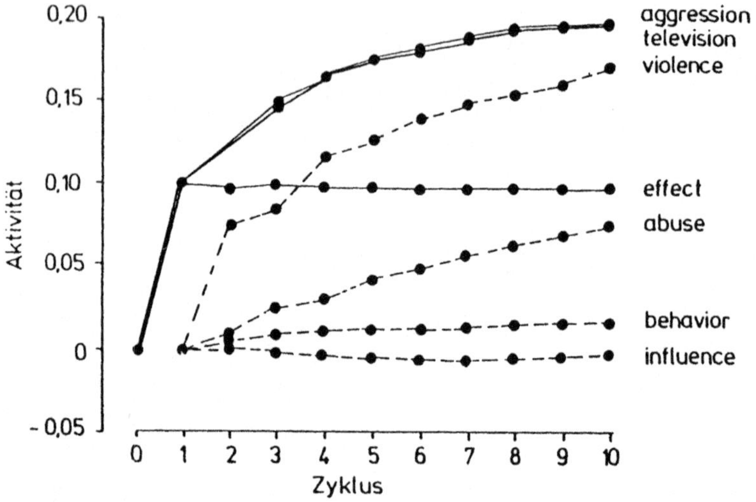

Figure 3b: The propagation of acivities when the words "effect", "aggression", and "television" are activated. The connective weights have been computed with formula (4).

Up to now the propagation of activities has been computed according to formula (2) as a linear summation. In this process units may receive activity-values below zero. The admission of negative activities however might be considered to be theoretically unsound, especially if one takes the neurological validity of connectionist models serious. In order to obviate this difficulty we introduced a cut-off mechanism which after each cycle assigns to each unit a value of either one or of zero. The model thus becomes a linear threshold model.

Figure 4 shows the activities of seven words when the previous example is run with a linear threshold model.

cycle:	0	1	2	3	4	5	6	7	8	9	10
violence		•	•	•	•	•	•	•	•	•	•
aggression			•	•	•	•	•	•	•	•	•
television		•			•	•	•	•	•	•	•
abuse				•	•	•		•		•	
behavior					•		•		•		
effect		•									
influence											

Figure 4: Activities of seven units in a linear threshold model when the words "effect", television" and "violence" are continuously activated. Black squares denote that the unit is active.

4. DISCUSSION

In paragraph 3 we have compared the patterns of activities in lexical nets whose connective weights have been computed with different equations. The results indicate that the use of negative weights is essential to produce two effects which caracterize the lexical decisions of the searchers during the query-generation: the omission of content-words with low significance (effect, relation, sometimes etc.) and the introduction of synonymes of the significant words of the problem description. The range of the units activities seems to be less important: the words which became active in the linear threshold model with activity values of one or zero are also the most active units in a linear summation model with continuous positive and negative activities of the units.

The examples which we have shown as well as many other examples not included in this paper indicate that localist lexical nets are suited for the simulation of the lexical processes which determine the generation of search-queries. We estimate that a practical application of our model in an automatic information retrieval system could be possible with a net of about 4000 words which is the number of descriptors in the thesaurus of Psycinfo. This would presuppose the availability of an adequate hardware. Up to now our programs, which are written in Pascal, were run on a personal computer.

The fact that we use a localist net with one-to-one relations between words and units prohibits to interpret it as a model of the neural processes which underly the behaviour of the searchers. However localist lexical nets seem to be an adequate level of description for the simulation of tasks where associations between words are important. The model however is not sufficient for the simulation of the whole range of processes which determine the translation of a problem description into a query. The words which become activated during the process of propagation will be submitted to rules (e.g. the rules of the query-language) which determine the syntactic position of these words in the query and introduce further constituents (publication year, publication language ect.). We suppose that these rules can best be described with a logical formalism. The elaboration of an automated query-generator is just one of many tasks where the assembly of these two kinds of formalisms is of central importance.

REFERENCES.

Belkin, N.J. & Vickery, A. (1985). Interaction in information systems: A review of research from document retrieval to knowledge-based systems. Library and Information Research Report 35.

Deese, J.J. (1965). The Structure of Association in Language and Thought. Baltimore: John Hopkins Press.

Hinton, G.E. & Sejnowski, T.J. (1983). Analyzing cooperative computation. *Proceedings of the 5th Annual Conference of the Cognitive Science Society*. Rochester, 1983.

Rumelhart, D.E., Smolensky, P., McClelland, J.L., & Hinton, G.E. (1986). Schemata and sequential thought processes in PDP models. In: D.E. Rumelhart, & J.L. McClelland, J.L. (Eds). *Parallel Distributed Processing: Explorations in the Microstructure of Cognition, vol. 2*. Cambridge, MA: Massachusetts Institute of Technology, 7-57.

TRENDS, RESEARCH PROGRAMS

CONNECTIONISM IN PERSPECTIVE
R. Pfeifer, Z. Schreter, F. Fogelman-Soulié, L. Steels (Eds.)

Neuro-Informatics Zürich

Klaus Hepp
Institute for Theoretical Physics, Swiss Federal Institute of Technology (ETH-Z),
CH-8093 Zürich, Switzerland

Neuro-informatics is the interdisciplinary field of research on massively parallel information processing in biological and technical networks of neurons and processors. Of particular interest is the connection between the physical structure and the dynamics of an information processing system and the operations, algorithms, and biological functions which it could execute efficiently.

For several years a number of scientists at the University of Zürich and the Swiss Federal Institute of Technology (ETH-Z) have pursued interdisciplinary projects in the field of neuro-informatics and have received international recognition for their work. Since the beginning of 1988 a special interest group "Neuro-Informatik Zürich" has been established, to which 18 professors belong today. They are active representatives of this field in Zürich, though most of them are not exclusively working in this domain.

This group organizes a joint "ETH-Z - University of Zürich" colloquium in neuro-informatics, a workshop on the "Biophysical and mathematical analysis of neural networks" at the Centro Franscini in Ascona (TI, Switzerland) on Oct. 8 - 14, 1989, and an international conference on "Perspectives in Neuro-Informatics" on Nov. 9 - 10, 1989, sponsored by the Goetz Foundation of the Medical Faculty of the University of Zürich. The group facilitates interdisciplinary studies and dissertations, provides an efficient sharing of knowledge and resources, and stimulates joint solutions to novel problems.

The group has submitted to the President of the ETH-Z and the Director of Education of the Canton of Zürich the proposal to create an "Institute of Neuro-Informatics" jointly between the ETH-Z and the University. The new center should pursue research and teaching in neuro-informatics and boost the competence in this important domain in Switzerland. In order to investigate efficiently biological neural networks close collaboration with the Brain Research Institute of the University is foreseen. The new center should have groups in massively parallel computation (linked to the curriculum in computer science and engineering), systems neurobiology (involved in the medical studies), and technical neurobiology (with strong ties to biotechnology):

With this goal the creation of three new joint professorships at the University and the ETH-Z have been proposed:

(a) Parallel informatics

This important field of teaching and research will also expand at the informatics departments at both the ETH-Z and the University and in electrical engineering. Therefore the research of the neuro-informatics group should have strong relevance for the understanding of biological neural networks. However, computational neurosciences should also be well integrated into the graduate studies in informatics and related curricula in Zürich.

Using exploratory simulation experiments a number of interesting heuristic results have been discovered on parallel distributed processes, which could potentially lead to the exploration of psychological processes and brain functions. It is now very important on one side to improve these sometimes rather qualitative results with the rigorous methods of informatics and numerical analysis, and on the other to strengthen their relevance for neurobiology by exploring more realistic neuron models and taking the architecture of modules in the central nervous system into consideration.

The head of the computational neurobiology group could be a computer scientist, a mathematician, physicist or engineer. Necessary is the competence in parallel informatics, established by the solution of difficult and relevant theoretical problems, experience in computer simulations and a real interest in interdisciplinary collaboration with neuroscientists.

(b) Systems neurophysiology

In this field, which is immensely relevant for medicine, the relation between brain and behavior is investigated. Many interesting aspects can be quantitatively studied by the methods of systems neurophysiology: the correlation between the discharge patterns of single neurons with sensory inputs and motor performance under controlled conditions, reversible perturbations of the system by microstimulation or chemical action on identified neuronal populations, macroscopic imaging of the electrical or metabolical activity, and the anatomical mapping of the systems up to minute details, as e.g. the 3-dimensional structure of identified neurons, whose activity has formerly been recorded in their functional information-processing context.

Of great importance is also the measurement of the normal functions of the system with the methods of psychophysics, in order to analyze the system in a natural parameter range and to relate dysfunction in patients to structural damage. The long-term goal of systems neurophysiology is to uncover explicitly the neuronal operations which are responsible for the complex sensori-motor and cognitive performance of the human central nervous system. Hypotheses on functional operations should be tested and cast into theories.

The head of the experimental systems neurophysiology group should be an eminent medical or biological scientist with a clear understanding of theoretical questions and experience with computer simulations.

(c) Technical neurobiology

The activity of this group in technical neurobiology should be considered in the context of the future development of biotechnology, molecular biology, and biomedical engineering, which are rapidly expanding both at the ETH-Z and the University. The most promising direction for the small neuro-informatics group with limited resources are biosensors for neurotransmitters. Biosensors are measuring devices consisting of cells, bacteria, immobilized enzymes and membrane receptors, which are coupled to a signal transducer system. Specific sensors for use in medicine, in laboratories, and production processes (e.g. fermentation and the monitoring of sewage) have already been tested successfully, and other applications will follow. Speed, specificity, reliability, and cost effectiveness make this technology commercially interesting. In the nervous system the information transfer from one nerve cell to the other uses the transformation of electrical activity into chemical signals of neuro-transmitters. These relatively small molecules act on post-synaptic receptors, proteins in the membrane which are coupled to transducer mechanisms and which generate postsynaptic electrical and chemical signals. Nearly all neuropharmacologically active substances interact with the mechanism of synaptic transfer, and memory traces are most probably laid down in terms of a modification of transsynaptic processes. By incorporating neuro-transmitter receptor proteins into artificial lipid membranes at the tip of a microsonde one could investigate with high resolution the "transistor-like" information processing capacities of neurons and local neuronal circuits.

The development of biosensors for neurotransmitters can use efficiently the competence in molecular biology and analytic chemistry at the ETH-Z and the University. These sensors will be used in collaboration with the groups in systems neurophysiology and parallel informatics to analyze the synaptic functions and their modulation in neural networks.

The head of this group should be a neuroscientist with high competence in molecular biology and biosensor techniques, who in addition wants to participate actively in the investigation of neural information processing.

The project has received the support of the faculties of medicine and natural sciences at the University and of computer science and engineering at the ETH-Z. There is hope that the creation of the institute and the election of creative scientists and inspiring teachers for the three chairs on neuro-informatics can be accomplished within the next years.

As a long-term goal there is the vision of a large center of theoretical, experimental and technical neurosciences, into which the present Institute for Brain Research and the future Institute for Neuro-Informatics enter, together with other affiliated groups from the University and the ETH-Z.

CONNECTIONISM IN PERSPECTIVE
R. Pfeifer, Z. Schreter, F. Fogelman-Soulié, L. Steels (Eds.)
Elsevier Science Publishers B.V. (North-Holland), 1989

Applications of Neural Networks for Industry in Europe

Andrew T. Chadwick

ANNIE Project Manager, Harwell Laboratory, U.K.

Abstract—*In the ESPRIT II project "ANNIE" ten organisations are collaborating to find the potential for applying neural network methods in industry. We are comparing these new methods with conventional approaches in 'generic' problem areas such as optimisation, using concrete examples from manufacturing applications. In an example from classification in non-destructive testing, important characteristics of neural networks are (i) ability to give a continuous measure of class membership (ii) the potential to deal with invariant recognition of patterns.*

Keywords—Neural network applications, manufacturing, pattern recognition, sensor fusion, adaptive control, optimisation, benchmarks, image, invariance, neural network equipment

1 INTRODUCTION

The Commission of the European Communities has announced funding totalling 5M ecu (net) split equally between two ESPRIT projects on neural networks over the period 1988-91. Project PYGMALION, led by Thomson CSF, will deal with network simulation and applications principally to speech and vision. This article describes project ANNIE, led by Harwell Laboratory, which will compare neural network approaches with conventional methods using a number of advanced manufacturing applications to generate case studies. It concludes with some speculations on the industrial future for neural networks.

2 ESPRIT II: PROJECT ANNIE

2.1 Objectives

The objectives of project ANNIE are to establish the industrial potential for neural network applications in Europe, and to promote the use of neural networks in industry. The theme of the work is comparison with existing conventional approaches in real industrial applications which contain difficulties such as non-linearity or a large number of variables, but are nevertheless easier than full-scale machine vision or speech recognition. We have defined four "generic problem areas" which encapsulate families of traditional methods and provide common ground within the project for collaboration between the partners on general approaches to their specific applications. These are:

(i) Pattern recognition
(ii) Sensor fusion
(iii) Adaptive control
(iv) Optimisation

The first two years of the project will be concerned mainly with benchmarking different approaches at the level of problem simulations. It is hoped then to expand the project in order to demonstrate the practical capability of neural network approaches in one or more real-time applications.

2.2 Partners

The contractors for project ANNIE are:

Harwell Laboratory (UK)
Alpha SAI (Athens)
Artificial Intelligence Ltd. (UK)
British Aerospace Sowerby Research Centre (UK)
Centre Etudes Technique Industrie Mécanique (Paris)
IBP Pietzsch (FRG)
Siemens (Kraftwerk Union) (FRG)

KPMG (Frankfurt) is acting as associate contractor to Harwell, concerned with problem analysis. Technische Hochschule Darmstadt is a subcontractor to IBP Pietsch and the National Technical University of Athens is a subcontractor to Alpha SAI.

The partners are balanced between major prodcution companies, flexible software, AI and electronics specialists, innovative research institutes and a consultancy able to carry out the transfer of technology to broader European industry.

2.3 Applications

The applications chosen to provide test cases for the ANNIE project are industrial inspection (non-destructive testing of structures and component inspection), condition monitoring (acoustic emission in industrial processes), sensing and navigation for autonomous vehicles, and control and optimisation. These cover the full range of the "generic problem areas" listed under section 2.1, "Objectives". The schematic Figure 1 indicates how we see them as a fertile proving ground for neural networks in industry, which prepare the ground for a future breakthrough in intractable areas of vision and speech technology. Our applications cover most of the automation issues in advanced manufacturing.

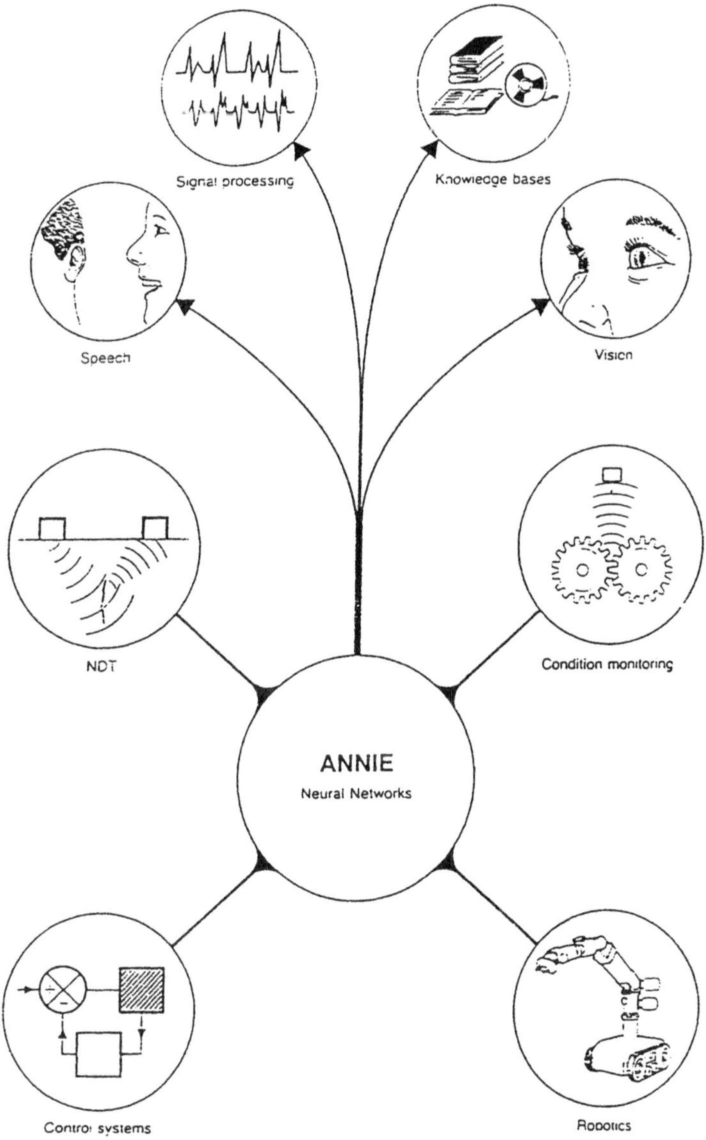

Figure 1: The ANNIE project is founded on the immediate needs of manufacturing industry and will spin off into long-term requirements within IT.

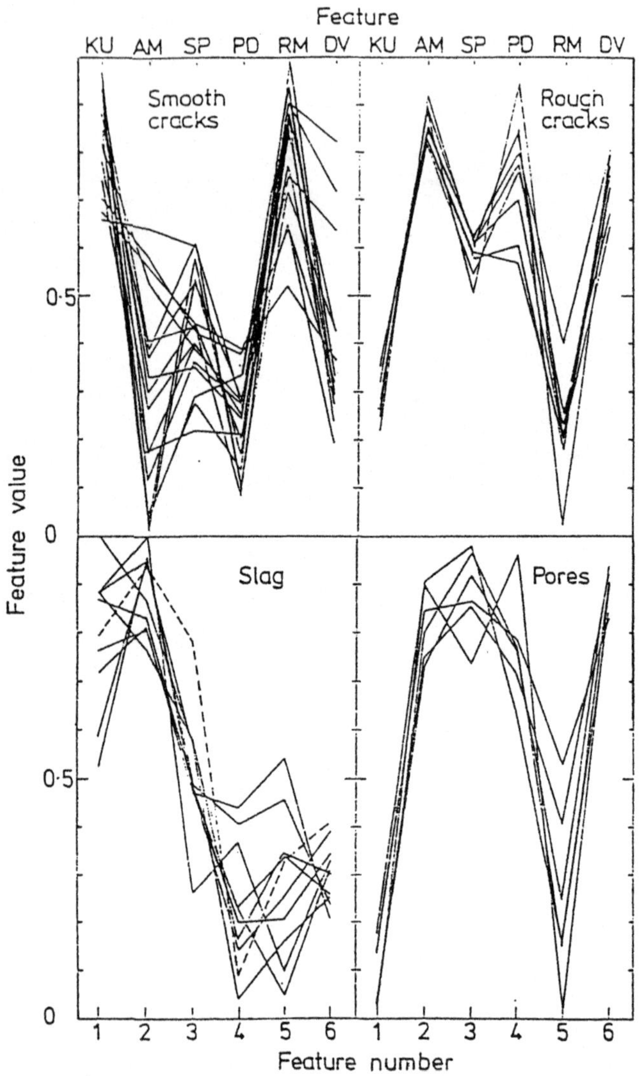

Figure 2: Feature parameters for the four classes of defects, smooth cracks, rough cracks, slag and pores. The six feature parameters are from processed ultrasonic data on test welds which included defects of known type. The parameters are plotted for a randomly chosen half of the full dataset of 83 defects. After a learning process on the other half of the dataset, the Hopfield network was able to identify all defects with occasionally a single error (shown dashed).

As an example of work done at Harwell in preparation for the ANNIE project, some results are given for neural network application in NDT.

Non-destructive testing (NDT)

The need here is to automate the detection and identification of defects in structural materials. Figure 2 shows data from ultrasonic inspection of test sections, pre-processed into six feature parameters. This shows the range of echo patterns from different types of defect. In a real pressure vessel some would be harmless, others harmful. This is therefore a classification problem. Figure 3 indicates that a neural network can give a very high percentage (>99%) correct classification in a problem of this type. It is worth noting that on an occasion when the network fails to make the correct classification, the numerical value at the network output is not close to 0 or to 1, which warns the user not to rely on the classification derived from it.

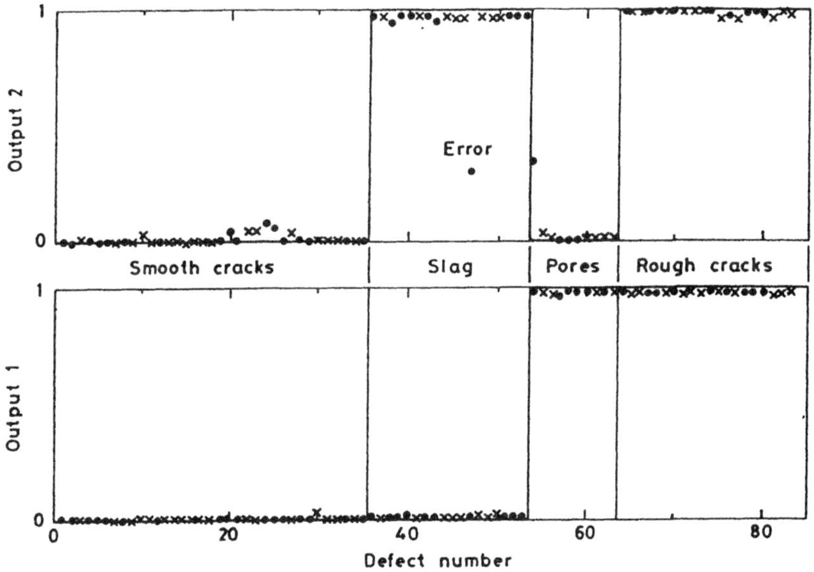

Figure 3: Classification performance of a Rumelhart network (3 hidden units) trained on 42 defects (crosses) and tested on an additional 41 defects..

The primary data in NDT can be displayed as an image (see Figure 4) and we are now testing the direct application of neural networks to bypass the manual generation of feature parameters. The resolution required for the image is around 100 x 100 and unlike many computer vision applications, there is no need for texture analysis or for methods to compensate for varying scene illumination.

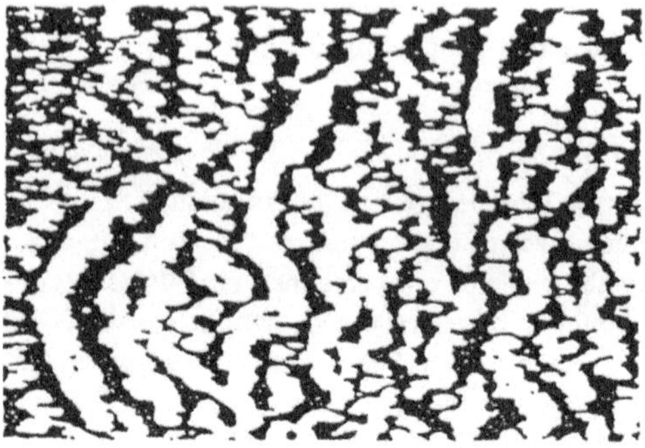

Figure 4: A problem in invariant recognition. Ultrasound echoes from three holes drilled in austenitic steel show as broad arcs agains a noisy background.

2.4 Current trends in neural networks

The early successes of neural network approaches to real problems lie in pattern recognition: by allowing curvature in the boundaries which discriminate between classes, neural network can score a few extra percent success, which may be worth a great deal in fields ranging from component inspection to credit rating. It is important that neural networks are not seen as a "magic box" but are compared with adaptive learning procedures already widely used in pattern recognition.

Truly new abilities of neural networks may come from a deeper understanding of brain structure. For example, high-order networks, which can code for neighbourhood relationships through the timing of nerve impulses, are able to carry out tasks such as graph matching which are essential in object recognition in the presence of rubber-sheet distortion. Figure 4 shows the immediate interest of such problems in on-line inspection. Harwell is taking part in the CEC's "Stimulation" BRAIN programme, in a project on invariant recognition, led by Dr. Bienenstock at the University of Paris. This ensures that project ANNIE will not take too short term a view of the potential of neural networks.

For the first two years of project ANNIE, existing digital simulations will be adequate for us to compare neural and conventional algorithms for abstracted problems. Thereafter, parallel hardware developments will probably be necessary to realise the full potential of these intrinsically highly parallel architectures for problem solving.

3 THE INDUSTRIAL FUTURE FOR NEURAL NETWORKS

The industrial future for neural networks depends on the answers to the following questions:

(1) Are they new?

There is a tendency to present the corpus of neural network methods as totally distinct from conventional information processing. This is patently incorrect. Adaptive algorithms are in widespread use in control; supervised learning procedures in pattern recognition include "linear learning machines". Once some of the modern neural network algorithms are seen as close neighbours to traditional methods, they will be taken into use much faster than would be the case for a revolutionary new method. The message should be not revolution but evolution.

(2) Are they useful?

Companies in the USA are using neural networks rather than a conventional approach, for optical on-line inspection and for mortgage underwriting. However, this does not prove that the neural network is better than the best conventional approach because the range of existing methods is already so wide. This remains to be seen and we hope that project ANNIE will add substantially to the few comprehensive comparisons that have been made across method types, using data which has clear application relevance for industry.

(3) Are they reliable?

Formula 1 cars are not seen on motorways. Neural networks are very powerful in principle and can learn complex relationships but will not be used in practice if their convergence and stability properties are in doubt. Unfortunately, these are very hard mathematical problems. Much of the literature glosses over the problems of stable learning. We intend to look at ways of incorporating statistical information about the training data in order to speed the convergence of the network. Eventually, neural networks could help to solve another type of reliability problem, as they are robust to hardware damage if implemented at a sufficiently low level of parallel hardware.

(4) Are they affordable?

Here success breeds success. The great worldwide interest in neural networks is creating a market for hardware able to simulate them efficiently. This will incidently make it economic to use conventional learning systems such as hidden Markov chains. Several authors are using "neural networks" to describe methods which have no roots in brain studies and pre-date the current fashion.

This should be seen as a positive development. Neural network conferences and the associated equipment industry are bringing together people from many fields of research — optimisation, adaptive control, multivariate statistics, signal processing, vision, speech, theoretical biology and neuroscience — who previously had little contact and in the eyes of suppliers did not constitute a viable market. Now, neural networks will be affordable because they use silicon more efficiently than serial algorithms.

4 CONCLUSIONS

We advocate a sober approach to neural network applications which recognises the established value of conventional methods. We seek to place specific neural network algorithms within the context of generic problem areas such as pattern recognition, adaptive control and optimisation, and to obtain some objective measures of performance. The industrial potential is vast when it is realised that "neural networks" are not by any means alien and difficult but are simply an effective way of thinking about problems.

5 ACKNOWLEDGEMENTS

The author would like to ackowledge the technical contributions of Colin Windsor and Steve Burch (figures 2-4) and also stimulating discussions with Ian Croall.

CONNECTIONISM IN PERSPECTIVE
R. Pfeifer, Z. Schreter, F. Fogelman-Soulié, L. Steels (Eds.)

Neural Network Applications in Artificial Intelligence

Michel de BOLLIVIER & Françoise FOGELMAN-SOULIE
Laboratoire d'Intelligence Artificielle
Ecole des Hautes Etudes en Informatique, Université de Paris 5
45 rue des Saints Pères - 75 006 PARIS

Abstract—*We present here the activities of the Team "Laboratoire d'intelligence artificielle" at EHEI. It is composed of about ten researchers, five of whom are Phd students. Its research axis include various aspects of connectionism that range from theoretical studies of connectionist models to the development of applications in different areas. It has established collaboration with industrial and university partners for those applications, and is involved in various projects (European: ESPRIT & BRAIN and National: MRES & DRET).*

Keywords—Back-propagation, data analysis, neural nets, speech processing, tomography

1 INTRODUCTION

Since 1978, the team's research interests have been in neural networks, first studying their dynamical behavior, associative memories and later their learning capabilities (including the development of the back propagation algorithm) (Fogelman Soulié et al., 1987; Le Cun, 1987). The team's present interests include the design of new learning strategies for connectionist networks, the link between connectionist and symbolic methods, and the relationships with other techniques. We have developed some applications of connectionist methods such as:

1.1 Speech processing (Bottou, 1988)

We have performed some experiments to test the validity of the Neural Nets (NN) approach for speech processing. These experiments have been realized on small sized vocabularies and multi- speaker utterances.

1.2 Processing of tomography images (Obelianne et al., 1988)

Tomography images are generated by a reconstruction algorithm similar to the filtered back-projection algorithm. This technique generates a star shaped noise (aliasing effect) that depends upon the object and the number of projections used. Multi-Layer Perceptrons, MLPs, have been taught to reduce this characteristic noise.

1.3 Signal processing (de Bollivier et al., 1988)

We have tried to automatize part of an underwater acoustic signal classification system that is presently performed by a human operator. We have built neural nets that perform a symbolic description (identical to the visual interpretation) of the sonar spectrogram lines. Those symbols and the frequency of the lines will help the identification of the signal source.

1.4 Image recognition (Keller & Fogelman-Soulié, 1988)

Matching of 2-D electrophoresis images. The task is to compare gels that are the results of an electrophoresis analysis with reference gels by using the topological maps algorithm of Kohonen (1988).

In this paper, we will first present the relationships between Data Analysis and Multi-Layer Perceptrons and then describe how to use a connectionist learning algorithm (the Gradient Back Propagation algorithm) (Le Cun, 1987; Rumelhart et al, 1986) to solve some problems such as speech processing and noise reduction in tomography images.

2 MULTI-LAYER PERCEPTRONS AND DISCRIMINANT ANALYSIS (Badran et al., 1988; Gallinari et al., 1988)

We present formal results wich allow to compare on classification tasks Multi-Layer Perceptrons with Discriminant Analysis: in the case of linear elements, these two methods can be shown to minimize the same criteria.

2.1 Discriminant Analysis

Let $x^1, \dots x^N$ be vectors in R^n. We want to classify each x^k into one of m categories C_i, wich is equivalent to associating with each x^k a desired answer y^k in R^m(hetero-association).

The aim of Discriminant Analysis is to determine an optimal subspace so that projections z^k's of the x^k's fall into well separated clusters (fig 1).

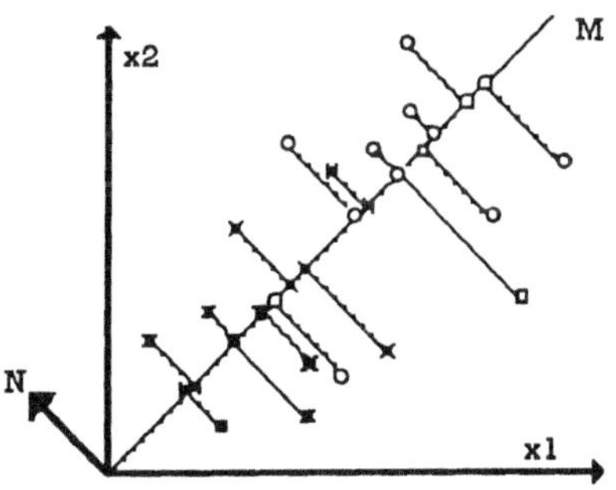

Figure 1: data x^k in R^2. Two classes: projection on M along direction N.

Let S_T, S_W and S_B be repectively the total, within-class and between-class dispersion matrices.

The projection of x^k's on a subspace with direction an nxK matrix N is given by:

- $z^k = N^t x^k$

- $$S_W = \sum_{i=1\ldots m} \sum_{x \in C_i} (x - m_i)(x - m_i)^t$$

- $$S_B = \sum_{i=1\ldots m} n_i (m_i - \underline{\underline{m}})(m_i - \underline{\underline{m}})^t$$

where $\underline{\underline{m}}$ and m_i are respectively the total average of the x^k's and the average of the x^k's within class i :

$$\underline{\underline{m}} = \frac{1}{N} \sum_i n_i m_i$$

$$m_i = \frac{1}{n_i} \sum_{x_k \in C_i} x^k$$

Obviously : $S_T = S_W + S_B$.

The dispersions matrices of the projections z^k's are respectively :

$$\underline{\underline{S}}_W = N^t . S_W . N$$
$$\underline{\underline{S}}_B = N^t . S_B . N$$

If $p = \text{rank}(S_B) = \text{rank}(S_T^{-1}. S_B)$ then $S_T^{-1}. S_B$ has p eigen vectors $w_1,\ldots,w_p$ (not necessarily orthogonal). $N = ((w_1) \ldots (w_p))$ is the *Discriminant Analysis matrix.*

We look for a matrix N such that $\underline{\underline{S}}_B$ be large and $\underline{\underline{S}}_W$ small. We use here the following cost function:

$$J(N) = \frac{| \underline{\underline{S}}_B |}{| \underline{\underline{S}}_B + \underline{\underline{S}}_W |}$$

where $|A|$ is the determinant of A .

2.2 Equivalence in the linear case

We compared Discriminant Analysis with matrix N and Multi-Layer Perceptron with one hidden layer of p linear cells ($p = \text{rank}(S_B)$). We proved that *W_1 is a Discriminant Analysis matrix* (Gallinari, 1988) i.e $J(W_1{}^t) = J(N)$.

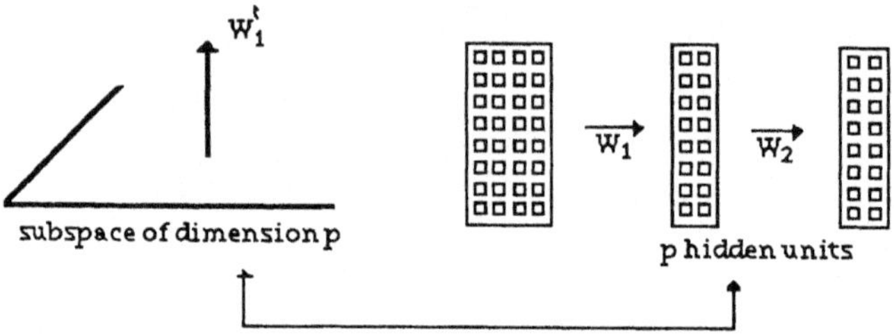

Figure 2: Discriminant Analysis (left) and MLP (right)

2.3 Experiments

We have performed several experiments, using *NON LINEAR* nets, on problems with various difficulties, that aimed at:

- comparing the performances of DA and MLPs in relation with some measure of difficulty of the problems.
- comparing qualitatively the solutions found through the two methods.
- using data analysis techniques to investigate the behavior of MLPs.

The main results are the following:

- the more non linearity in the problem, the more non linear MLPs outperform classical discriminant analysis. However there is no known measure of this increase and only heuristic measures of the difficulty of a problem can be used.
- When the problem is nearly linearly separable, the solutions found by both methods are very similar (same projection space or same set of "weights"): fig 3 to 5 .

Heuristic criteria such as J(N) computed on the different layers allow to follow the clustering of the data from layer to layer.

In the experiments, data from the different classes are increasingly well separated from layer to layer (see fig 4 & 5). MLPs progressively transform the data so as to produce a projection onto the last hidden layer which is "nearly" linearly separable. We demonstrated this behavior on the following example about the classification of three species of irises (FISHER) (Badran et al., 1988) using a network with two hidden layers of two cells each.

The results were the following:

- 98 % correct using Discriminant Analysis
- 98,8% correct using MLPs

2.4 Conclusion

Multi-Layer Perceptrons with linear elements are equivalent to performing a Discriminant Analysis on the inputs. However, it is possible to improve upon the performances of Discriminant Analysis by using non linear MLPs with more hidden units than the number of classes.

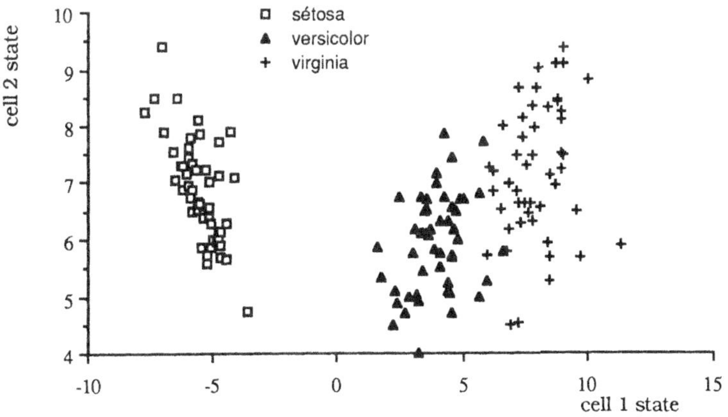

Figure 3: Classification obtained by discriminant analysis.

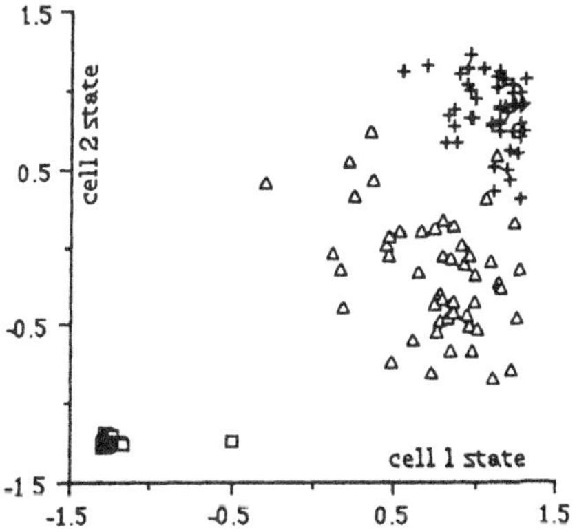

Figure 4: MLPs hidden layer 1

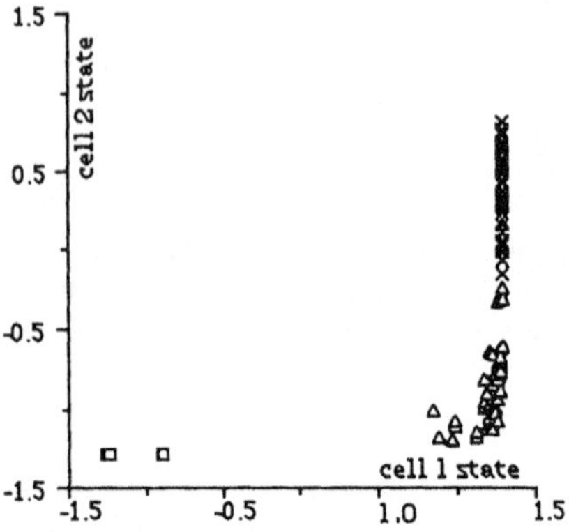

Figure 5: MLPs hidden layer 2

3 SPEECH RECOGNITION: MULTI-SPEAKER DIGIT RECOGNITION (Bottou, 1988)

3.1 Data base

The ten digits, from 0 to 9, uttered in French, have been pronounced, once each, by 26 speakers, male and female: 16 have been used for the learning-set and 10 for the test-set, each one pronouncing the ten digits. The signal is coded as a 16*65 pattern corresponding to 16 frequency levels on a Bark scale and 65*12.8ms time frames (about 800ms in total for each word). Each digit in the training set is randomly translated in 4 positions in the first 100ms of the input window to take care of the segmentation problem, giving 640 patterns for training. Similarly, performances on the test set have been measured on randomly placed utterances in the input window first 100 ms.

3.2 Network (fig 6)

We use a time delay neural net (Waibel et al, 1987). The network has 2 hidden layers:

- the first one has 31 cells implementing 8 masks 16x3
- the second one has 6 cells implementing 8 masks 8x7

3.3 Results

After 30 sweeps through the data base (1.30 h on a SUN-4), the performances are:

- 99.22 % on the learning set
- 99 % on the test set.

3.4 Conclusion

The network has acheved some speaker independence properties. We have also obtained an interesting feature extractor in the cells of layer 2 corresponding to a "phonetic" coding. Figure 7 shows for example the code obtained for sound "S" in the utterances of 6 "six" and 7 "sept" by different speakers.

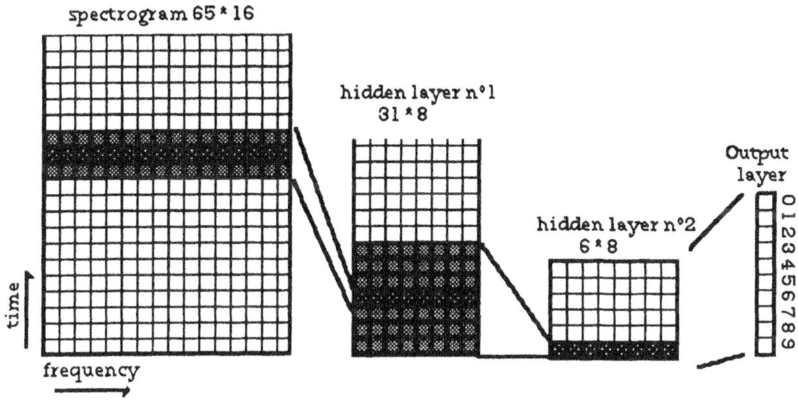

Figure 6: Network architecture with shared weights.

4 CONNECTIONIST MODELS FOR IMAGE PROCESSING (Obelianne, 1988)

4.1 Introduction

We present an example of a connectionist network which can be used in image processing for reducing noise. Tomography images of simulated "lungs", i.e. two circular regions here, are generated by a reconstruction algorithm similar to the classical filtered back projection algorithm (Rosenfeld & Kak, 1982). The reconstruction process generates a star-shaped noise, due to aliasing effects, and the signal-to-noise ratio increases with the number of projections used .

A multi-layer network is taught different examples of reconstructed "lungs" at various noise levels, i.e. with various numbers of projections. The network, used as an associative memory system, has to generate an original stored prototype, freed of noise: it has to learn prototypes and to generalize to various levels of noise.

We will show that an appropriate choice of a network architecture can lead to efficient results for increasing the signal-to-noise ratios.

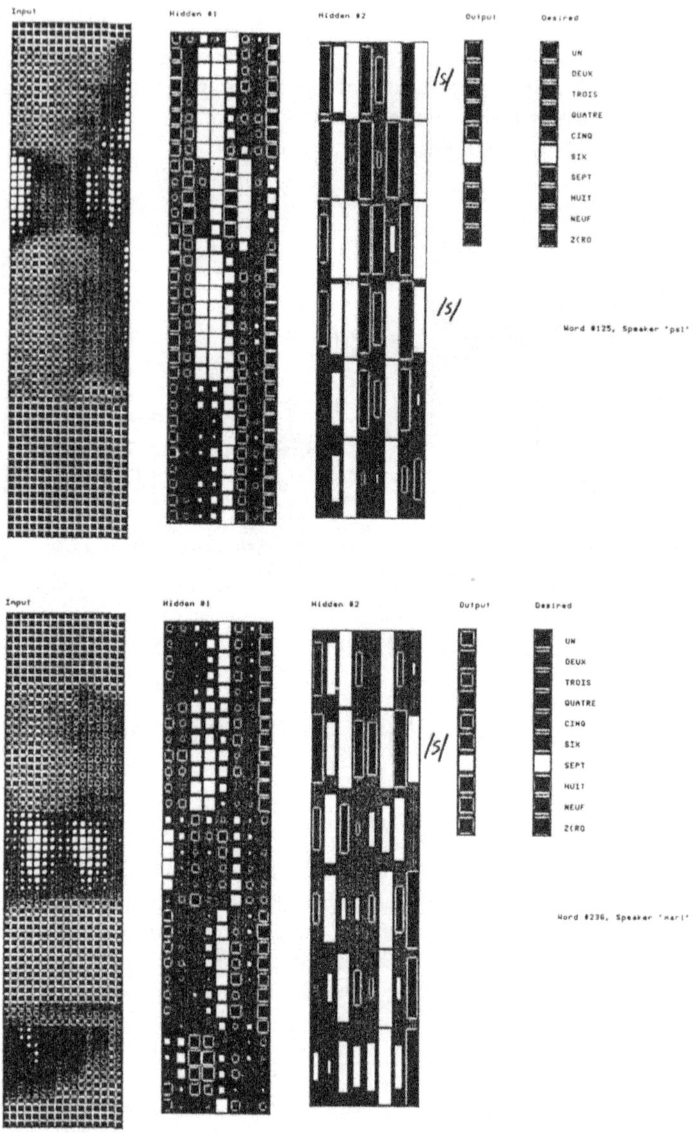

Figure 7: The figure shows the results obtained for two digits: 6 "six" and 7 "sept" pronounced by different speakers. The phoneme /s/ has been extraded by the network and coded in the last hidden layer.

4.2 Simulated Tomography

Like many techniques for medical imaging, X-ray tomography requires a two-dimensional reconstruction from multiple projection data. The general principle underlying these techniques is the following: N detectors (up to 1024), arranged either on a line or a fan-beam, measure the projection (i.e. the Radon transform of the density f) of an object along a line k (called ray k); for each position q of the machine, N measures are taken along the rays (fig.8):

$$\text{Proj}(q, \text{ray}_k) = \int_{\text{ray}_k} f(u,v)\, dv$$

There exist two main methods to reconstruct the original image f(x,y) from the set of projections Proj(q, ray_k): one is based on the computation of an inverse Fourier transform, which is long, and the other is the *back-projection* method (Rosenfeld & Kak, 1982).

In the back-projection method, each Proj(q, ray_k) is distributed equally along all the pixels intersected by ray_k (fig.9). This technique is fast, it can work in real time (in opposition to the Fourier transform), it produces relatively good results, but artifacts are systematically generated by the method, such as, for example, aliasing effects (Rosenfeld & Kak, 1982) when the ratio of number of detectors N to number of projections K does not satisfy the relationship stated by the sampling theorem for computerized tomography (Platzer, 1981).

$$K \geq (\Pi * N)/2.$$

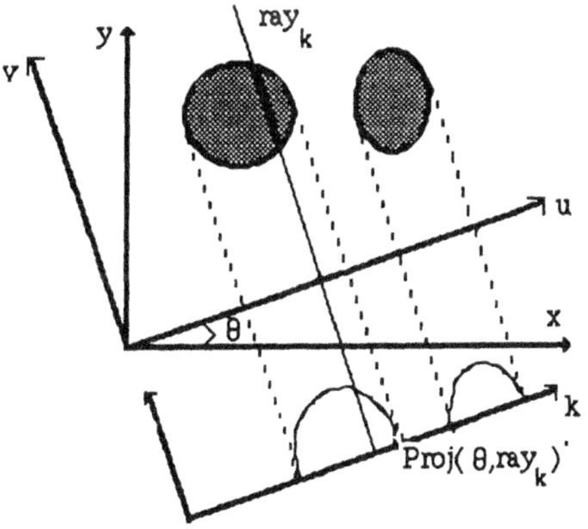

Figure 8: projection

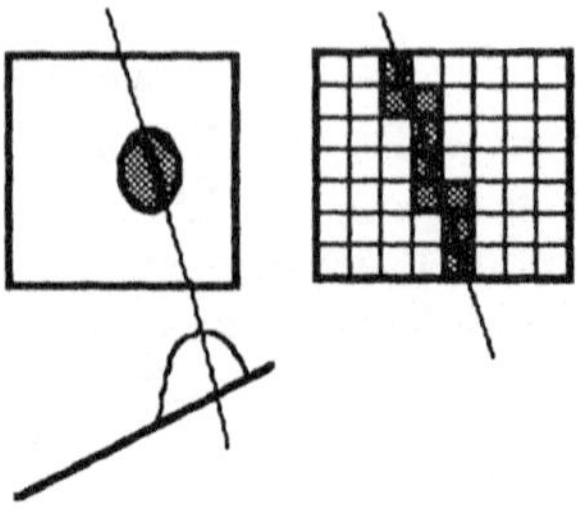

Figure 9: back-projection

We used a program developed at Thomson-LCR (Groupe Electronique Médicale) to simulate the projection and reconstruction of circular objects (Staron, & Micheron, 1986; Staron, 1988). We now present the connectionist model used.

4.3 Associative Memory

We generated 20 prototypes including two "lungs" in different positions in a 20x20 image. We then simulated the projection and reconstruction of each prototype: we generated reconstructed images for 9 values of K, the total number of projections: K = 5, 10, 12, 15, 17, 20, 25, 30, 40. Note that, from the sampling theorem, aliasing effects will automatically occur, and will be impossible to remove (unless the "lungs" lie very close to the center of the image (Waibel et al., 1987) for all values of K less than (Π*N)/2, i.e. K < 32 (since N = 20 here).

We wanted to know whether it was possible to train a network to retrieve a prototype at various levels of noise, i.e. values of K, from examples of only a few of those K values. We trained networks with various architectures on the following training set:

- the 20 original prototypes + 3 reconstructions for each of them (K= 10, 17, 30).
- The test set included the *same* prototypes reconstructed from the remaining noise levels: K = 5, 12, 15, 20, 25, 40.

We mainly compared the performances of the two following architectures:

- 3 layered network: 20 x 20 —> 80 —> 20 x 20 with total connections
- 2 layered network: 20 x 20 —> 20 x 20 with local connections (through a 5 x 5 window).

The reconstruction algorithm gives intensities in real values, but we tested our method both on real and discretized values (we then used 16 gray-levels).

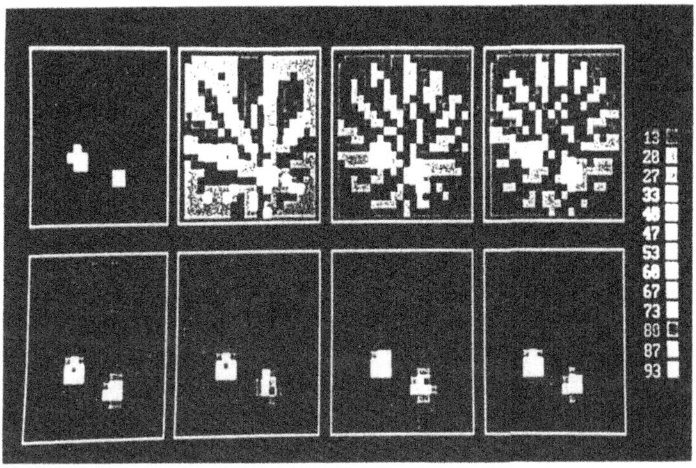

Figure 10: Simulated tomography images: prototype and reconstructed images with 5, 10, 12, 15, 17, 20, 25 projections.

Performances on the learning set always reached 100%: all prototypes were correctly memorized. Success was decided when the error rate fell below 4.10^{-3} which means that, in average, all the pixels of the output image were in the correct interval, with respect to the desired prototype.

After learning was performed, we tested generalization for different levels of noise. The best generalization performances on the test set were obtained with the 3-layered network: more than 85%, even for the 5 projections case (figs. 11 & 12).

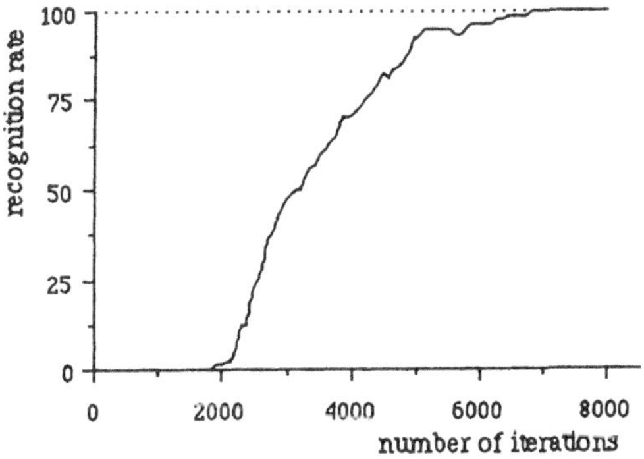

Figure 11: Recognition rate on learning set during learning.

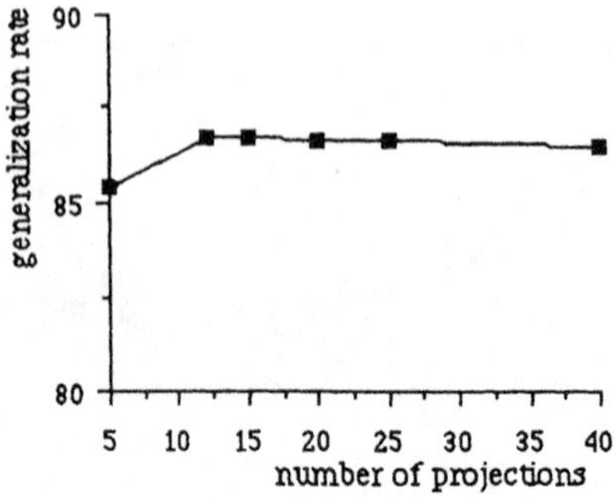

Figure 12: Recognition rate on test set, for different values of K .

4.4 Conclusion

We have presented a connectionist method which allows to significantly reduce noise in the reconstruction of (simulated) tomography images. The results show that a network can be trained to eliminate noise on stored prototypes by being shown a few examples of noise levels.

This work thus demonstrates that, in a variety of tasks in image processing, connectionist methods can be used to reduce noise: this had already been mentioned for speech processing and could also be applied in various fields of signal processing.

5 CONCLUSION

We have proved that Multi-layer Perceptrons with linear elements are equivalent to performing a Discriminant Analysis on the inputs. This work thus both provides a theoretical framework for MLPs within Data Analysis and evidence why to use Multi-Layer Perceptrons. Additional theoretical tools are actually developed to help designing the network architecture.

We have shown that neural nets can be used to solve different kinds of pattern recognition tasks such as image and speech processing. The learning algoritm can be used without a-priori knowledge of the domain. But such knowledge when available can be incorporated into the network architecture for enhanced performances.

We think that neural nets will provide efficient tools as a first step for linking data analysis and artificial intelligence symbolic processing.

ACKNOWLEDGEMENT

The research reported in this paper was partly supported by the following grants: BRAIN Project No. ST2J-0418-C, DRET Grant No. 87-808-19, GE-CGR, and PRC-IA (CNRS).

REFERENCES

Badran, F. & Thiria, S. & Fogelman-Soulié, F. (1988). Comparing data analysis and multi-layer networks . EHEI.

Bottou, L.Y (1988). Reconnaissance de la parole par reseaux multi-couches. *Neuro-Nimes 88.*

de Bollivier, M., Lemer, A., & Tanguy, J. (1988). Reconnaissance de bruits acoustiques sous-marins. *Neuro-Nimes 88.*

Fogelman Soulié, F., Gallinari, P., Le Cun ,Y. & Thiria, S. (1987). Evaluation of network architectures on test learning tasks. *1st ICNN,* San Diego.

Gallinari, P., Thiria, S., Fogelman Soulié, F. (1988). Multilayer perceptrons and data analysis, *2nd INN,* San Diego.

Keller, M. & Fogelman Soulié, F. (1988). Cartes topologiques et applications en reconnaissance d'images d'électrophorèse. Neuro-Nimes 88.

Kohonen, T. (1988). Self organization and associative memory. Springer Series in Information Sciences, vol.8. New York: Springer Verlag, 2nd Edition.

Le Cun, Y. (1987). Modèles connexionnistes de l'apprentissage, Thesis, Paris.

Obelianne, C., Fogelman Soulié, F. & Gallibourg, G. (1988). *Neuro-Nimes 88.*

Platzer H. (1981). Optical image processing. In: *Proceedings of the 2nd Scandinavian Conf. on Image Analysis,* 128-139.

Rosenfeld, A., & Kak, A.C. (1982). Digital Picture Processing, vol.1, 383-389.

Rumelhart, D.E., McClelland, J.L. (eds) (1986). Parallel and distributed processing: explorations in the microstructure of cognition. MIT Press.

Staron, A., & Micheron, F. (1986). Dispositif pour l'acquisition d'une image de contraste d'un objet placé dans un faisceau de radiations ionisantes, Thomson-CSF Patent.

Staron, A., Raymond, C., & Claudepierre C. (1988). High energy imaging using tomographic techniques: discussion and preliminary results. Med. Imaging Conf., SPIE, Los Angeles.

Waibel, A., Hanazawa, T., Hinton, G., Shikano, K. (1987). Phoneme recognition using time-delay neural networks, Tech. Report TR-I-0006, Adv. Telecom. Res. Inst., Japan.

CONNECTIONISM IN PERSPECTIVE
R. Pfeifer, Z. Schreter, F. Fogelman-Soulié, L. Steels (Eds.)

Problems and Trends in Integrated Neural Networks

L. Personnaz, A. Johannet, G. Dreyfus

Ecole Supérieure de Physique et de Chimie Industrielles de la Ville de Paris, Laboratoire d'Electronique, 10, rue Vauquelin,
75005 Paris, France

Abstract—*The paper is intended to put connectionism in perspective by comparing connectionist devices (subsequently referred to as "artificial neural networks") to classical devices, and discuss the various issues related to the silicon integration of such circuits. First the driving motivations behind the numerous attempts at integrating neural networks are outlined. The kind of artificial neurons and networks which are currently being designed, and the functions that these devices are expected to fulfill, are subsequently described. Finally, the technological issues will be outlined; we show how technologies which are used for manufacturing standard electronic devices can be used for manufacturing connectionist devices.*

Keywords—Neural network implementation, binary neurons, graded neurons, learning, feedback networks, feedforward networks, integrated circuit design, analog and digital technologies, Very Large Scale Integration, Wafer Scale Integration.

INTRODUCTION: NEURAL INTEGRATED CIRCUITS — WHY?

Integrated circuit technology is a technology whereby both the electronic components and the connections between them are manufactured on the same substrate. Manufacturing connectionist devices means a departure from the standard electronic design, since emphasis is put on the connections, not on the computing elements. Given the cost of creating a new technology, and the lack of maturity of the field of neural networks, it is clear that the designers of connectionist devices will have to use a standard electronic technology for many years: a specific technology will evolve in the future if, and only if, connectionism turns out to be very successful at solving problems. Therefore, designing and manufacturing neural networks will be a real challenge to designers for several years at least.

It is only natural to ask whether it is worthwhile to undertake such a difficult task, instead of simply performing computer simulations. Let us consider the situation as it stands now: among the various fields of applications of neural networks, pattern recognition has been the most extensively studied; as a result, there is virtually no example of a neural network performing definitely better, in terms of recognition rate, than classical methods. However, neural networks have a definite edge on other approaches as far as speed is concerned, since they are inherently parallel computing devices. Moreover, some neural networks can be shown to exhibit, to a limited extent, fault tolerance properties. Obviously, these speed and fault tolerance characteristics will be taken advantage of if artificial neural networks are actually built. Simulations are very helpful tools for making demonstrations, validating analytical predictions, or when computational speed is unimportant; in most cases, however, real-time applications will definitely require specific chips in order to reach the desired operating speed.

Therefore, it is clear that integration is an important problem for the future of connectionist models. An adverse argument which is often expressed is a matter of schedule rather than a matter of principle: given the lack of maturity of the field, it is too early to "freeze" connectionist architectures into silicon.There is indeed a lot of truth in this: there is little doubt that the integrated neural networks that are currently in the design phase will not be those used in industrial applications, if any, within a few years. However, it is very likely that the design problems that will have to be solved for future neural networks will be very similar to the problems that are being faced now during the design of today's network chips. Therefore, the development of the final circuits will take full advantage of the knowledge which is currently being accumulated during the design of nowadays' devices, however primitive they can be.

GENERAL ISSUES: WHAT KIND OF NEURONS, WHAT KIND OF NEURAL NETWORKS?

Two kinds of neurons are usually considered : the basic McCulloch-Pitts neuron, whose state is binary (with a stepwise transfer function), and a variant thereof, whose state is graded (sigmoidal transfer function). Clearly, a binary unit is easier to design, and networks of binary units are more readily amenable to mathematical analysis, than networks of neurons with a graded response. However, the computations involved in the popular backpropagation learning algorithm requires that the transfer function of the neuron be differentiable, so that neurons with a sigmoidal transfer function are used very frequently, even in cases where the problem handled by the network is purely boolean in nature and would, in principle, require binary neurons only (for instance, classification tasks with binary input and output data). Conversely, there are indeed problems in which binary units would not be suitable (for instance, statistical classification tasks for which the state of the output units are interpreted as probabilities, signal processing tasks,...). In addition, circuits which are designed so as to be really neuromimetic use neurons with graded response, which are one step closer to neurobiology than binary neurons.

The issue of the architecture of the neural network is closely related to the choice of the neurons themselves, and to the function that is to be performed by the net. Two basic architectures are usually considered:

- feedback neural networks, which have inherently dynamical properties that make them suitable for associative memory properties, for storing and recalling either static patterns (pictures), or dynamic patterns (sequences of information, time-series);
- feedforward networks, which have interesting properties for classification purposes, and which have abilities to learn classes from examples.

It can be argued that feedforward networks are just feedback neurons in which a fraction of the synaptic coefficients are forced to zero. Therefore, a fully connected network can be used, in principle, for implementing any network architecture; for this reason, most current chip designs aim at building fully connected binary neurons.

From a technical point of view, the silicon implementation of binary neurons is relatively straightforward, whereas the design of graded neurons is much more cumbersome: it requires large silicon areas if digital technology is used; analog techniques allow a much easier implementation of sigmoidal transfer functions, but they have other problems (the issue of digital vs. analog techniques will be discussed below). The difficulty of building non-binary neurons greatly hampers the design of feedforward networks. This situation will probably change soon: recent work shows that multilayer feedforward networks of binary neurons can be trained without using the backpropagation algorithm.

FUNCTIONAL ISSUES

A key element in the design of a neural network circuit is the task(s) that it will have to fulfill. The alternative is the following :

- General purpose network or *ad hoc* network?
- Integrated, on-chip learning, or off-line learning?

Most reported designs implement general-purpose networks with off-line learning. The reason for that is probably the fact that they are basically research prototypes; they are designed in order to test architecture ideas, and to get a quantitative assessment of the technological problems and limitations that arise. There are two notable exceptions to the above statement: the neuromimetic chips such as C. Mead's retina (Mead et al., 1988), which are specifically designed to mimic some definite pieces of "wetware", and the chips designed for character recognition (Graf & Hubbard, 1989).

The issue of on-line vs off-line learning will be important in the future. Since speed is one of the main assets of neural networks, it is natural to try to take advantage of this characteristics both during the training phase and during the classification or retrieval phase. Therefore, attempts are being made at designing networks which are able to modify their own synaptic coefficients; this can be done effectively inasmuch as the hardware required to implement the learning rule is basically the same as the hardware needed to implement the neurons themselves (Personnaz et al., 1989).

TECHNOLOGICAL ISSUES

In this section, we shall discuss the various options that can be taken for designing and manufacturing artificial neural networks. The first issue, which is probably the most important, is the choice between analog and digital techniques. The second issue is related to the scale of integration required for building the networks. Finally, less classical technologies will be discussed.

1) Analog *vs.* digital:

An individual neuron is an object which performs a weighted sum that is subsequently subjected to a transfer function; the latter can be either a step function or a sigmoidal function. At first sight, analog technology seems ideally suited since an operational amplifier and a couple of additional components can perform these functions in a very cost- and area-effective way. Analog devices, however, have their own drawbacks which led to a drastic decrease in the use of that technology during recent years; it is sometimes argued that, within a few years, analog technology will be used only in analog-to-digital and digital-to-analog converters, and in switched-capacitor filters. The main problem is the accuracy required for the synaptic weights in order for the network to perform efficiently. This is highly dependent on the application for which the network is built; when the network is intended to perform a classification task, this is a very crucial problem. It has been shown that neural networks used as associative memories for storing and retrieving uncorrelated prototypes require a very low accuracy, and that binary (encoded on a single bit) or ternary synapses yield satisfactory results. In the general case, the number of bits required to code for a synaptic weight is O(log2n), where n is the number of binary neurons. In analog technology, synapses are implemented as resistors or transistors, which have an inherently low accuracy and low noise immunity. For neurons with sigmoidal transfer functions, an additional problem arises, namely, the accuracy required for the computation of the sigmoid; this is a very difficult problem, which, to the best of our knowledge, has not been studied by analytical means.

To summarize, analog technology is perfectly suited to applications of neural networks which

i) do not require a high accuracy for the synaptic weights and the transfer function,
ii) are relatively immune to noise, or even require some noise, as the Boltzmann machine does (Alspector et al., 1988).

In the next section, we shall discuss two implementations using analog techniques.

Conversely, digital techniques enjoy high noise immunity, and can represent synaptic weights with an arbitrary precision; moreover, the values of the latter can be changed easily, whereas the values of resistors or the resistivity of transistor channels cannot be altered accurately in any straightforward fashion. In addition, the dynamics of the neurons can be chosen freely, whereas analog neurons cannot be clocked very easily. However, these advantages are obtained at the expense of an increase in silicon area. At the present time, the implementation of approximately one hundred neurons in standard digital technologies leads to a rather bulky chip; note, however, that the design of such a chip is not a intractable problem because it is basically cellular in nature, in contradistinction to the design of, e.g. a microprocessor or an application-specific integrated circuit, which may require a large amount of "random" logic.

2) Very Large Scale Integration (VLSI) *vs* Wafer Scale Integration (WSI)

At the present time, VLSI technology has led to the design and manufacturing of commercial circuits with a maximum area of approximately 1 cm2 and a maximum number of transistors on the order of 1 million. An alternate possibility might be the use of the whole area of the silicon wafer (with a diameter on the order of 10 cm) to build a single, huge circuit. The problems encountered in the latter technology are twofold:

i- the complexity of the design of such a circuit is extremely high, unless the circuit is cellular in nature, which is the case of neural networks;

ii- the yield problem is crucial; at the end of the fabrication process, a (possibly large) percentage of the modules present on the wafer do not operate satisfactorily. Therefore, all the circuits must be tested, and those which are operating satisfactorily must be connected together, during the so-called "reconfiguration" phase, in order to produce a working device; this technique implies obviously that the design must be highly redundant, identical replicas of the same circuit being present in several locations on the wafer, in order to be reasonably sure that at least one of them will operate properly. Therefore, the inherent fault tolerance that neural networks are claimed to exhibit make them very attractive candidates for wafer-scale integration, since the reconfiguration phase might be absent, or at least much simpler than for conventional systems. Investigations along these lines are underway.

3) Silicon technology *vs* others

All the previous sections dealt with various aspects of silicon technology, its capabilities and its limitations. However, alternate technologies might prove useful, in conjunction with silicon. Opto-electronics, for instance, is an attractive technology because it might help solving the interconnection problem. It has been used for neural network simulators, and might become attractive if it could be amenable to integration, which is not the case at the present time. The problem of interconnections could be alleviated to a considerable extent if three-dimensional connections were possible; in this respect, MOS transistors made of inorganic molecular semiconductors (doped phtalocyanines) are very attractive candidates because they are manufactured in thin film technology at room temperature, and can be stacked; this technology is far from maturity, but is definitely worth considering at the laboratory level.

REPRESENTATIVE EXAMPLES

The present section is by no means intended to give an exhaustive overview of the state of the art in neural circuit design. We shall describe circuits which are representative of the various issues discussed above.

As mentioned previously, two types of integrated circuits have been built:

i) dedicated networks, usually in analog technology,

ii) general-purpose networks, such as feedback nets, multilayer feedforward nets, or Boltzmann machines.

Typical of the first kind are the machines described in Mead et al. (1988) and Graf & Hubbard (1989). In both cases, the circuits are dedicated to a very specific task, and do not require any training. However, the generic problems that arise in the design of neural circuits are present: cellular structure, large number of interconnections, computation of weighted sums; they all exhibit a high degree of parallelism. C. Mead's retina is basically an array of operational amplifiers and of resistors, arranged in such a way as to detect the motion of objects. It is designed in a neuromimetic fashion, and indeed the response of the artificial retina is very similar to that of a natural retina, as far as motion detection is concerned.

The networks described in Graf and Hubbard (1989) are dedicated to preprocessing tasks in a handwritten character recognition device; they use binary synapses, the strengths of which are the components of the prototype vectors; an input binary vector is thus compared in parallel to all the prototype vectors, the comparison consisting either in computing the number of zeroes common to the unknown vector and each prototype vector, or the total number of common bits, depending on the specific application. Each synapse consists of MOS transistors used as resistors or programmable switches. The summations are performed by operational amplifiers. In the latest design of the authors, 46 vectors of 96 binary components each are stored, and the comparison of an unknown vector to all the stored vectors is performed in 100 ns. When such speeds are reached, input/output operations tend to become a bottleneck.

We now turn to the design of fully digital circuits. Both described devices implement fully interconnected feedback networks. The circuit described in Murray et al. (1988) is characterized by the fact that the state of each neuron can take on five values. The design of Personnaz et al. (1989) implements binary neurons with on-chip learning.

The network designed by Murray et al. (1988) is basically a rectangular grid of synapse-processors, each neuron being associated to a column of processors. The computation of the potential of the neurons being performed simultaneously through the columns, the need for long-range wiring is reduced. However, the partial sums are transmitted serially from one "synapse" to the next on several bits (16 bits if 8-bit synaptic coefficients are used). The state of each neuron is encoded on two bits plus a sign bit, thereby allowing five possibilities: 0, ±0.5, ±1.Therefore, no multiplicator is required, the operations being only a shift or a boolean operation on the sign bit. Thus, each synapse processor includes a shift register and an adder-subtractor. Once the potential of each neuron has been computed, the updated state is obtained by a thresholding operation according to the 5-state transfer function.

In the network described in Personnaz et al. (1989), an alternate approach is taken, whereby neuron-processors are used instead of synapse-processors. Each neuron is associated to a memory containing the relevant synaptic coefficients; it performs the product of the binary state of a given neuron with the corresponding coefficient (which is simply a boolean operation on the sign bits), adds it to its potential, and subsequently passes the state to the next neuron. Therefore, all n neurons perform the computation of their potential in n steps. The only information that are passed between neurons are the states, encoded on a single bit. In addition, the same architecture can be used with very little additional hardware for performing the training of the network by Widrow-Hoff's rule.

Additional references to circuit designs are: Blayo & Hurat (1989), Duranton et al. (1989), Faure & Mazaré (1989), Moopenn et al. (1988), Sivlotti et al. (1985), Tsividis & Anastassiou (1989), Verleysen et al. (1989).

CONCLUSIONS

We have attempted to give an overview of the problems and trends in the design of silicon-integrated connectionist devices. There is little doubt that this kind of research will become increasingly popular in the next years, especially if neural networks find large-scale applications in various fields. Although the experimental chips that are in existence at the present time will probably not be in commercial use, the design style that they induce, the interconnection and test problems that they generate, will certainly be beneficial to the community of chip designers. Thus, when the time of commercial applications comes, the silicon implementation of the required neural networks will be at hand.

REFERENCES

Alspector, J., Allen, R.B., Hu, V., Satyanarayana, S. (1988). Stochastic learning networks and their electronic implementation. In: D.Z. Anderson (ed). *Neural Information Processing Systems, Natural and Synthetic.* American Institute of Physics.

Blayo, F. & Hurat, P. (1989). A systolic architecture dedicated to neural networks. In: L. Personnaz & G. Dreyfus (eds). *Neural Networks from Models to Applications.* I.D.S.E.T., Paris.

Duranton, M., Gobert, J. & Mauduit, N. (1989). A digital VLSI module for neural networks. In: L. Personnaz & G. Dreyfus (eds). *Neural Networks from Models to Applications.* I.D.S.E.T., Paris.

Faure, B. & Mazaré, G. (1989). A VLSI asynchronous cellular architecture dedicated to multilayered neural networks. In: L. Personnaz & G. Dreyfus (eds). *Neural Networks from Models to Applications.* I.D.S.E.T., Paris.

Graf, H.P. & Hubbard, W. (1989).VLSI neural network for fast pattern matching. In: L. Personnaz & G. Dreyfus (eds). *Neural Networks from Models to Applications.* I.D.S.E.T., Paris.

Mead, C. & Mahowald, M.A. (1988). A silicon model of early visual processing. *Neural Networks,* **1**, 91-97.

Moopenn, A., Langenbacher, H., Thakoor, A. P. & Khanna, S. K. (1988). A programmable binary synaptic matrix chip for electronic neural networks. In: D.Z. Anderson (ed). *Neural Information Processing Systems, Natural and Synthetic.* American Institute of Physics.

Murray, A.F., Smith, V.W., & Butler, Z.F. (1988). Bit-serial neural networks. In: D.Z. Anderson (ed). *Neural Information Processing Systems, Natural and Synthetic.* American Institute of Physics.

Personnaz, L., Johannet, A., Dreyfus, G., & Weinfeld, M. (1989). Towards a neural network chip: a Performance Assessment and a Simple Example. In: L. Personnaz & G. Dreyfus (eds). *Neural Networks from Models to Applications.* I.D.S.E.T., Paris.

Sivilotti, M., Emerling, M. R., & Mead, C. (1985). A novel associative memory implemented using collective computation. In: *Proc. Chapel Hill Conf. on VLSI.*

Tsividis, Y.P., Anastassiou, D. (1987). Switched-capacitor neural network. *Electronics Letters* **23**, 958-959.

Verleysen, M., Sirletti, B., Jespers, P. (1989). A new VLSI architecture for neural associative memories. In: L. Personnaz & G. Dreyfus (eds). *Neural Networks from Models to Applications.* I.D.S.E.T., Paris.

ABSTRACTS, WORK IN PROGRESS

CONNECTIONISM IN PERSPECTIVE
R. Pfeifer, Z. Schreter, F. Fogelman-Soulié, L. Steels (Eds.)

Connectionist Approaches to the Description of Spatial Knowledge

W. Brauer, C. Freksa, and the AI/Cognition Group

Institut für Informatik, Technische Universität München, Arcisstrasse 21, D - 8000 München 21, Germany

Abstract—*The primary goal of this project is to study the applicability of connectionist approaches to the task of describing spatial knowledge in a cognitively plausible way. The particular application is a system to give directions for going from a current location to a goal location in an urban setting. Given the current state of the art in connectionist systems, we are not seeking a closed "connectionist solution" but rather exploring their usefulness for the various subtasks composing our system, like: representing spatial knowledge, finding adequate paths between a start and a goal location and generating natural language descriptions fo those paths. Extensive preliminary research has been done on the domain dependent aspects, though only recently from a connectionist viewpoint. The other subprojects are in their initial stages. Six full-time researchers and several students are currently working on this project.*

Keywords—Connectionism, spatial knowledge, path finding

CONNECTIONISM IN PERSPECTIVE
R. Pfeifer, Z. Schreter, F. Fogelman-Soulié, L. Steels (Eds.)
© Elsevier Science Publishers B.V. (North-Holland), 1989

Toward Sub-Symbolic Models of Language Understanding

Georg Dorffner

Austrian Research Institute for Artificial Intelligence
and Dept. of Medical Cybernetics and AI,
University of Vienna, Freyung 6, A-1010 Vienna, Austria

Abstract—*This paper gives some theoretical background and a series of arguments that suggest that connectionist models promise to be a more adequate model for natural language processing than classical AI systems have been. After this theoretical motivation, the goals of a project, currently being under development at the University of Vienna, and a first model are outlined. The model is designed to show the correctness of the hypotheses raised by the sub-symbolic paradigm.*

Keywords—Natural language understanding, sub-symbolic paradigm, representation, associative models

CONNECTIONISM IN PERSPECTIVE
R. Pfeifer, Z. Schreter, F. Fogelman-Soulié, L. Steels (Eds.)

Neural Networks and Research on Emotions: A Mutual Perspective

Theodor L. Gehm

University of Giessen, Department of Psychology, Otto-Behaghel-Strasse 10F6, D- 6300 Giessen, Germany

Abstract—*With reference to information processing models of emotion differentiation and to the problem of interindividual specificity of determinants within this approach, it is suggested to investigate emotion differentiation within a dynamic approach of behavior regulation. Principles of this approach (reference to clearly defined functions of information processing, complex phenomena like emotions as emergent properties of underlying idiosyncratic circuits of behavior regulation) are demonstrated. It is argued that a dynamic model based on low-level functions of information processing (pattern matching) is suitable for operationalizing emotional behavior. A simulation model (EmoGis) for this approach is presented. Interrelating the neural network approach with such a model is seen as a perspective for research on emotions (reference to physiological "hard-ware", criteria for emotion differentiation) and for cognitive sciences (integration of subjective meaning, flexibility, non-analytic reasoning).*

Keywords—Neural networks, emotion differentiation, behavior regulation, pattern matching, cognitive models of emotion differentiation, phylogenetic development, individual specificities, simulation of emotion differentiation

CONNECTIONISM IN PERSPECTIVE
R. Pfeifer, Z. Schreter, F. Fogelman-Soulié, L. Steels (Eds.)

A Principled Approach to Knowledge Representation in Connectionist Systems

Daniel Hernández

Technische Universität München, Institut für Informatik, Arcisstr. 21, D - 8000 München 2, Germany

Abstract—*Most current connectionist systems use an ad hoc form of knowledge representation. The Knowledge Representation Theory of Palmer and Furbach provides a framework for a principled development of representations based on an analysis of the relations of the task domain. We show how this methodology leads to a connectionist alternative to what has been traditionally captured in inheritance systems. Much of the confusion concerning the relationship between traditional (symbolic) and connectionist (subsymbolic) representation paradigms disappears once the latter is viewed as a way of* *realizing knowledge representation concepts and not as a way of implementing the former. Ongoing work is exploring the relationship of this methodology to other efforts directed at providing connectionist systems with well-founded semantics.*

Keywords—Knowledge representation theory, connectionist systems, concepts, coding, schemata, inheritance systems

CONNECTIONISM IN PERSPECTIVE
R. Pfeifer, Z. Schreter, F. Fogelman-Soulié, L. Steels (Eds.)

An Algebraic Model for the Interpretation of Cadastral Maps Based on Connectionist Networks

Alajos P. Krasznai

Swiss Federal Institute of Technology, Institute for Geodesy and Photogrammetry, CH- 8093 Zurich, Switzerland

Abstract—*The aim is to give a theoretical foundation for developing an automatic interpreter for cadastral maps. The interpreter must be capable (1) to extract the information from an existing map (2) thereby simulate the reasoning of a user and (3) communicate with the user. The map is embedded in a communication system and all processes of interpretation are treated algebraically. The mental and physical modelling in this system helps to create different representations of an algebraic system being composed of topologic, geometric, quantitative and attributive structures. The topologic structures treat the incidence relations. The geometric structures describe the objects of maps, based on curve theory. The quantitative structures contain information about sizes of objects. The attributes are sentences for reference systems, existenes and constraints formulated by means of semiotic AND/OR-graphs and first and/or second order logic. The isomorphism between (1) an algebraic system and a control process (2) a control process and a mental process and (3) a cadastral map and an algebraic system help to formulate algebraically the task of the interpreter. The mental processes are treated by connectionist networks. The algebraically defined characteristic variables of the objects are the parameters of control processes. Their state-variables govern the arc-values of connectionist networks.*

Keywords—Acquisition of spatial information by scanning, data structures, construction and interpretation of cadastral maps, algebraic modelling of mental processes, pattern recognition by stochastic/dynamic control processes using connectionist networks

CONNECTIONISM IN PERSPECTIVE
R. Pfeifer, Z. Schreter, F. Fogelman-Soulié, L. Steels (Eds.)

A Model for the Recurrence of Automatic Action Patterns

M. Rihs-Middel

Department of Psychology, University of Fribourg,
CH - 1701 Fribourg, Switzerland

Abstract—*The spontaneous recurrence of automatic habit patterns after a period of disuse and forgetting is a common phenomenon of many areas of psychological functioning, for example in relapse episodes after substance addiction. Recurrence of such habit patterns has been shown to emerge in ambiguous stimulus situations that lack clear-cut incentive values . To model these processes we propose a conspiracy model with partial activation of several action opportunities. The ambiguous stimulus pattern produces partial activation of a number of possible actions which conspire to produce the overlearned action that is maintained by specific feedback mechanisms.*

Keywords—Connectionism, addiction, relapse in addicts, habit patterns

CONNECTIONISM IN PERSPECTIVE
R. Pfeifer, Z. Schreter, F. Fogelman-Soulié, L. Steels (Eds.)
Elsevier Science Publishers B.V. (North-Holland), 1989

Genetic Psychology and Connectionist Networks: The Exploitation of Stable Mixture-States

Philip R. Van Loocke

State University of Ghent, Research assistant at the Belgian N.F.S.R.,
B - 9000 Ghent, Belgium

Abstract—*Genetic psychology suggests to exploit the stable mixture-states of neural networks. The stable mixtures of the Amit-network can serve as a point of departure, but the systematic use of mixtures requires some additional dynamics. This can be realized if the Amit-network interacts in a particular way with "spectral" networks. The latter induce local molecular fields in the Amit-network.*

Keywords—Amit-networks, local molecular fields, mixture states, inter-network interaction, genetic psychology

List of Contributors

Ahuja, Sanjeev B., Rentenanstalt, Swiss Life, Postfach, CH-8022 Zürich, Switzerland, Phone: (+41) 1 206 40 61/33 11 283

Allen, Robert B., 2A-367 Bellcore, Morristown, NJ 07960-1910, USA, Phone: (+1) 201 829 4315, Fax: (+1) 201 292 0067/8 E-mail: rba@bellcore.com 301

Alpaydin, Ethem, EPFL, Lab de Microinformatique, Av de Cour 37, CH-1007 Lausanne, Switzerland, Phone: (+41) 21 69 32641/2644, Fax: (+41) 21 693 39 09; E-mail: alpaydin@elde.epfl.ch 309

Ambros-Ingerson, José, Center for the Neurobiology of Learning and Memory and Computer Science Department, University of California, Irvine, CA, 92717, USA 199

de Bollivier, Michel, Ecole des Hautes Etudes en Informatique, Laboratoire LIA, Université Paris V, 45, rue des Saints Pères, F-75006 Paris, France, Phone: (+33) 1 47 03 31 27 485

Boullart, L., Ghent State University, Automatic Control Laboratory, AI Section, Grotesteenweg Noord 2, B-9710 Gent - Zwijnaarde, Belgium 455

Bounds, David, Royal Signals and Radar Establishment, St. Andrews Road, Great Malvern Worcs WR14 3PS, England, Phone: (+44) 684 892733, Fax: (+44) 684 8927 33 ext. 2540 277

Brauer, W., Technische Universität München, Inst. für Informatik, Arcisstrasse 21, D-8000 München 2, FRG 509

Bridle, John S., Royal Signals and Radar Establishment, St. Andrews Road, Great Malvern Worcs WR14 3PS, England Phone: (+44) 684 892733, Fax: (+44) 684 8927 33 ext. 2540 93

Chadwick, Andrew T., Materials Physics & Metallurgy Division, Building 521.2 Harwell Laboratory, UKAEA, Oxfordshire OX11 0RA, England, Phone: (+44) 235 24141 477

Chen, Lin , Beijing Laboratory of Cognitive Science, University of Science and Technology of China, P.O. Box 3908, Beijing, People's Republic of China. April - June 1989: c/o Prof. Jan Drösler, Psychologisches Institut, Universität Regensburg, D-8400 Regensburg, FRG 317

Compiani, M., ENIDATA, Viale Aldo Moro 36, I-40127, Bologna, Italy 331

le Cun, Yann , Department of Computer Science, University of Toronto, Toronto, Ontario, M5S 1A4, Canada. Present address: Room 4G-332, AT&T Bell Laboratories, Crawfords Corner Rd., Holmdel, NJ 07733, USA, E-mail: yann@neural.att.com 143

Dorffner, Georg, Inst. f. medizinische Kybernetik und Artificial Intelligence, Universität Wien, Freyung 6, A-1010 Wien, Austria 509

Kindermann, Jörg, GMD, Postfach 1240, D-5205 St. Augustin 1 , FRG,
Phone: (+49) 2241 142 437, E-mail: joerg@gmdzi.uucp 173, 377

Kodratoff, Yves, CNRS & Université Paris Sud, LRI, Bldg 490,
91405 Orsay, France, Phone (+33) 1 69 41 69 04, Fax: (+33) 1 69 46 19 92
and George Mason University, AI Center, Fairfax, Virginia 22030,
USA (from Jan 10th 1989) 157

Krasznai, Alajos P., ETH-Zürich, Institute for Geodesy and Photogrammetry,
CH-8093 Zurich, Switzerland, Phone: (+41) 1 377 3062 511

Kuperstein, Michael, Neurogen Laboratories Inc., 352 Harvard Street,
suite 202, Brookline, MA. 02146, USA, Phone: (+1) 617 232 82 66 49

Kurfess, Franz, Technische Universität München, Institut für Informatik,
Arcisstrasse 21, D-8000 München 2, FRG, Phone: (+49) 89 521099
E-mail: franz@lan.informatik.tu-muenchen.dbp.de 365

Lange, Rupert, Institut für Theoretische Physik der Universität Heidelberg,
Philosophenweg 12, D-6900 Heidelberg 1, FRG 341

Lee, M., Ghent State University, Automatic Control Laboratory,
AI Section, Grotesteenweg Noord 2, B-9710 Gent - Zwijnaarde, Belgium 455

Linden, Alexander, GMD, Postfach 1240, D-5205 Sankt Augustin 1, FRG,
E-mail: al@gmdzi.uucp 377

Linster, Christiane, Forschungsgruppe Expertensysteme, Inst. f. Angewandte
Informationstechnik, GMD, Postfach 1240, D-5205 Sankt Augustin 1, FRG 385

Van Loocke, Philip, State University of Ghent, Seminarie voor logica en
kennisleer, Blandijnberg 2, B-9000 Gent, Belgium 512

Lynch, Gary, Center for the Neurobiology of Learning and Memory,
University of California, Irvine, CA, 92717, USA 199

Männer, Reinhard, Physikalisches Institut der Universität Heidelberg,
Philosophenweg 12, D-6900 Heidelberg 1, FRG, Phone: (+49) 6221- 569 222 341

Marchal, Pierre, EPFL, Lab de Microinformatique, Av de Cour 37,
CH-1007 Lausanne, Switzerland,
Phone: (+41) 21 69 32641/2644, Fax: (+41) 21 693 39 09 309

Martinetz, Thomas, Physik Department, Technische Universität München,
D-8046 Garching, FRG, Phone: (+49) 89 3209-2387 403

Montanari, D., ENIDATA, Viale Aldo Moro 36, I-40127, Bologna, Italy 331

Morasso, Pietro, Università di Genova, Dipartimento di Informatica, Sistemistica e
Telematica, Via Opera Pia 11 A, I-16145 Genova, Italy, Fax (+39) 10 31 00 86 413

Mühlenbein, Heinz, GMD, Postfach 1240, D-5205 St. Augustin 1, FRG,
Phone: (+49) 2241 14-0, Fax: (+49) 2241 14 26 18 / 28 89 173

Mussa Ivaldi, F.A., Dept. of Brain and Cognitive Sciences, M.I.T., Cambridge,
Mass., USA. 413

Personnaz, L., Ecole Supérieure de Physique et de Chimie Industrielles
de la Ville de Paris, Laboratoire d'Electronique, 10, rue Vauquelin,
75005 Paris, France, Phone: (+33)1 4337 77 00 499

Peeters, Guus, Max-Planck-Institut für Psycholinguistik, PB 310, NL-6500 AH Nijmegen, The Netherlands, Phone: (+31) 80 521 911 395

Pfeifer, Rolf, Institut für Informatik der Universität Zürich, Winterthurerstr. 190, CH-8057 Zürich, Switzerland, Phone: (+41) 1 257 43 23/43 11, Fax: (+41) 1 257 40 04, E-mail: pfeifer@ifi.unizh.ch XI

Pouget, Alexandre, Institut des Neurosciences, Dept. des Neurosciences de la vision, Université Pierre et Marie Curie, 9, Quai St. Bernard, F-75005 Paris, France, Phone(+33) 1 43 36 25 25 447

Prassler, Erwin, Institut für Informatik, Technische Universität München, Arcisstrasse 21, D-8000 München 2, FRG, E-mail: prassler@tumult.informatik.tu-muenchen.de 421

Rapp, Reinhard, Universität Konstanz, Informationswissenschaft, Postfach 5560, D-7750 Konstanz 1, FRG 463

Reeke Jr., George N., The Neurosciences Institute, 1230 York Avenue, New York, N.Y. 10021, USA, Phone: (+1) 212 570-8975 E-mail: CDRNI@CUNYVM.bitnet 113

Reich, Manfred, Technische Universität München, Institut für Informatik, Arcisstrasse 21, D-8000 München 2, FRG 365

Riecken, Mark, E., BDM Corporation and Department of Computer Engineering, University of New Mexico 301

Rihs-Middel, M., Department of Psychology, University of Fribourg, Route des Fougères, CH-1701 Fribourg, Switzerland 512

Ritter, Helge, Physik Department, Technische Universität München, D-8046 Garching, FRG, Phone: (+49) 89 3209-2501 403

Rosenbloom, Paul, Information Sciences Institute, University of Southern California, 4676 Admirality Way, Suite 1001, Marina del Rey, CA 90292-6695, USA, Phone: (+1) 213 822-1511, E-mail: rosenblo@VENERA.ISI.edu 245

Rubinstein, Jorge, Neurogen Laboratories Inc., 352 Harvard Street, suite 202, Brookline, MA. 02146, USA, Phone: (+1) 617 232 82 66 49

Schmidhuber, Jürgen, Institut für Informatik, Technische Universität München, Arcisstrasse 21, D-8000 München 2, FRG, E-mail: schmidhu@tumult.informatik.tu-muenchen.de 429, 439

Schreter, Zoltan, Konfliktforschungsstelle, Psychologisches Institut der Universität Zürich, Zürichbergstrasse 43, CH-8044 Zürich, Switzerland, Phone: (+41) 1 257 45 76 XI

Schulten, Klaus, Physik Department, Technische Universität München, D-8046 Garching, FRG, Phone: (+49) 089 3209-2501 403

Serra, Roberto, Enidata, Via Aldo Moro 38, I-40127 Bologna, Italy, Phone: (+39) 51 50 56 84/85, Fax: (+39) 51 50 94 70 265, 331

Simonini, P., Dept. of Physics, University of Bologna, Via Imerio 46, I-40126 Bologna, Italy 331

Smolensky, Paul, Department of Computer Science, Campus Box 430 University of Colorado, Boulder, CO 80309-0430, USA, Phone: (+1) 303 492 0111, E-mail: pauls@BOULDER.COLORADO.edu 3

Soh, Woo-Young, Rentenanstalt, Swiss Life, Postfach, CH-8022 Zürich, Switzerland, Phone: (+41) 1 206 40 61/33 11 283

Sporns, Olaf, The Neurosciences Institute, 1230 York Avenue, New York, N.Y. 10021, USA, Phone: (+1) 212 570-8975 113

Staubli, Ursula, Center for the Neurobiology of Learning and Memory and Computer Science Department, University of California, Irvine, CA, 92717, USA 199

Steels, Luc, VUB AI Lab, Pleinlaan 2, B-1050 Brussels, Belgium Phone: (+32) 2 641 29 65 XI, 215

Thorpe, Simon J., Institut des Neurosciences, Dept. des Neurosciences de la vision, Université Pierre et Marie Curie, 9, Quai St. Bernard, F-75005 Paris, France, Phone(+33) 1 43 36 25 25 63, 447

Vercauteren, L.A.A., Ghent State University, Automatic Control Laboratory, AI Section, Grotesteenweg Noord 2, B-9710 Gent - Zwijnaarde, Belgium, E-mail: leo@bgerug51.bitnet 455

Vercelli, G., Università di Genova, Dipartimento di Informatica, Sistemistica e Telematica, Via Opera Pia 11 A, I-16145 Genova, Italy, Fax (+39) 10 31 00 86 413

Vingerhoeds, R.A., Ghent State University, Automatic Control Laboratory, AI Section, Grotesteenweg Noord 2, B-9710 Gent - Zwijnaarde, Belgium 455

Wellekens, Christian, Philips Research Lab Brussels, Av. Em. Van Becelaere 2, Box 8, B-1170 Brussels, Belgium, Phone: (+32) 2 6742275, E-mail: wlk@prlb2.uucp 103

Wettler, Manfred, Universität Konstanz, Informationswissenschaft, Postfach 5560, D-7750 Konstanz 1, FRG 463

Whitson, James W. Jr., Center for the Neurobiology of Learning and Memory and Computer Science Department, University of California, Irvine, CA, 92717, USA 199

Wittenburg, P., Max-Planck-Institut für Psycholinguistik, PB 310, NL-6500 AH Nijmegen, The Netherlands, Phone: (+31) 80 521 911 395

Zaccaria, R., Università di Genova, Dipartimento di Informatica, Sistemistica e Telematica, Via Opera Pia 11 A, I-16145 Genova, Italy, Fax (+39) 10 31 00 86 413

Printed in Dunstable, United Kingdom

91336872R00308